An Introduction to

Sustainable Transportation

Cities around the globe struggle to create better and more equitable access to important destinations and services, all the while reducing the energy consumption and environmental impacts of mobility. *An Introduction to Sustainable Transportation* illustrates a new planning paradigm for sustainable transportation through case studies from around the world with hundreds of valuable resources and references, color photos, graphics and tables.

The second edition builds and expands upon the highly acclaimed first edition, with new chapters on urban design and urban, regional and intercity public transportation, as well as expanded chapters on automobile dependence and equity issues; automobile cities and the car culture; the history of sustainable and unsustainable transportation; the inter-relatedness of technologies, infrastructure energy and functionalities; public policy and public participation; and exemplary places, people and programs around the globe. Among the many valuable additions are discussions of autonomous vehicles (AVs), electric vehicles (EVs), airport cities, urban fabrics, urban heat island effects and mobility as a service (MaaS). New case studies show global exemplars of sustainable transportation, including several from Asia, a case study of participative and deliberative public involvement, as well as one describing life in the Vauban ecologically planned community of Freiburg im Breisgau, Germany. Students in affiliated sustainability disciplines, planners, policy-makers and concerned citizens will find that the book provides many practical techniques to innovate and transform transportation.

Preston L. Schiller teaches courses in sustainable transportation for the University of Washington, Seattle, USA, and Queen's University, Kingston, Ontario, Canada. He has worked on air pollution and transportation issues at national, state and local levels with several NGOs, including the Sierra Club, as well as serving on numerous government advisory task forces and committees. His career in sustainable transportation began by walking at age one, cycling at age five, and navigating transit solo around Chicago at age 11.

Jeffrey R. Kenworthy is a Professor in Sustainable Cities at Curtin University in Perth, Western Australia, additionally holding guest positions at the Frankfurt University of Applied Sciences in Germany and the K2 Swedish Knowledge Centre for Public Transport in Lund. He has almost 40 years of experience in the transport and urban planning field, specializing in international comparisons of cities, and has published extensively on a wide range of urban topics.

'This book is a manual for how to bring about virtuous social change centred on the importance of how transport is shaping lives, cities, social justice, health and environment. It marks a watershed in sustainable transport discussions. It reveals exactly what needs to be done, why and how and links this to paradigm shift, politics and leadership. It leaves the reader in no doubt that we will abandon the jaded mobility paradigm of the last 60 years and embrace the strongly positive alternatives that are summarised so very well by the authors. We now have a choice. We can either pursue a dirty, polluted, unfair and expensive strategy (the one we now have) or the alternative of a fair, just, nurturing, people-centred, child-friendly accessibility strategy. The latter is preferable and the authors have shown we can do it.'

Professor **John Whitelegg**, *School of the Built Environment,*
Liverpool John Moores University, UK

'The second edition of *An Introduction to Sustainable Transportation* is an excellent book for instructors, students, and the general public interested in the rapidly changing world of transportation. The book reveals and explains the revolutionary changes now occurring in transportation technology, yet remains grounded in the imperative of economic, environmental, and social equity sustainability. The new edition expands on the social and cultural impacts of transportation, including extended discussions of the car culture, urban design, automated vehicles, and airport cities. The informative and humorous box stories and cartoons are a real treat!'

Professor **Andrew R. Goetz**, *Department of Geography and*
the Environment, University of Denver, USA

Praise for first edition

'This book presents the topic in a logical, coherent manner and provides an excellent and broad introduction to the key concepts behind the debate of sustainable transportation, and consequently provides a tremendously useful tool for students, academics and practitioners alike.'

Rachel Turner, *Bartlett School of Planning, UCL, UK,*
Journal of International Planning Studies

An Introduction to

Sustainable Transportation

Policy, Planning and Implementation

SECOND EDITION

*Preston L. Schiller and
Jeffrey R. Kenworthy*

Routledge
Taylor & Francis Group

LONDON AND NEW YORK

earthscan
from Routledge

Second edition published 2018
by Routledge
2 Park Square, Milton Park, Abingdon, Oxon OX14 4RN

and by Routledge
711 Third Avenue, New York, NY 10017

Routledge is an imprint of the Taylor & Francis Group, an informa business

First edition published by Earthscan 2010

British Library Cataloguing-in-Publication Data
A catalogue record for this book is available from the British Library

Library of Congress Cataloging-in-Publication Data
Names: Schiller, Preston L., author. | Kenworthy, Jeffrey R., 1955– author.
Title: An introduction to sustainable transportation : policy, planning and implementation / Preston L. Schiller and Jeffrey R. Kenworthy.
Description: Second Edition. | New York : Routledge, [2018] |
Revised edition of An introduction to sustainable transportation, 2010.
Identifiers: LCCN 2017015587| ISBN 9781138185463 (hardback) |
ISBN 9781138185487 (pbk.) | ISBN 9781138185487 (ebook)
Subjects: LCSH: Transportation—Environmental aspects. |
Sustainable development.
Classification: LCC HE147.65 .S35 2018 | DDC 388/.049—dc23
LC record available at https://lccn.loc.gov/2017015587

ISBN: 978-1-138-18546-3 (hbk)
ISBN: 978-1-138-18548-7 (pbk)
ISBN: 978-1-315-64448-6 (ebk)

Typeset in Univers and Gill
by Florence Production Ltd., Stoodleigh, Devon, UK

Visit the eResources: routledge.com/9781138185487

Contents

Note: Appendices related to this book, including descriptions and web addresses for numerous resources can be found at the Taylor & Francis website associated with this book.

Figures, tables and boxes

Figures

Tables

Boxes

Box Figures

Acknowledgements

The authors wish to express their gratitude to the editorial staff of the Routledge–Taylor & Francis Group for their support and encouragement for this second edition and to the editorial staff of Earthscan Publishing for their support and encouragement for the first edition. Special thanks to Kate Schell, Nicole Solano, Judith Newlin, Krystal LaDuc and Nicki Dennis of Taylor & Francis. The authors also wish to thank Susanne Lynette Seales for her valuable help in manuscript preparation and other contributions to the book. We thank Eric C. Bruun for his continued support and insights over many years; his valuable contribution to Chapter 4 (Modes) in the first edition is reflected in our current revision and his work on transit fortifies our Chapter 5. We especially thank those persons who have generously contributed items to either or both editions as well as the editors of publications who gave us permission to use materials. A special thanks must go to Andy Singer for the use of his fabulous car-toons.

Jeffrey R. Kenworthy would like to sincerely thank his research assistant, Ms Monika Brunetti, for her indispensable part in compiling the updated cities data that appear in this book. Yuan Gao, his PhD student, provided invaluable help in collecting the updated data on Beijing, Guangzhou and Shanghai that appear in Chapter 9. Her contribution is gratefully acknowledged, as is the assistance of Dr. Ashish Verma in providing recent data on Mumbai, and to Malcolm and Munira Mackay of Mackay Urban Design in Perth, W.A. for their permission to use materials in the urban design chapter. Students at the Frankfurt University of Applied Sciences are also gratefully acknowledged for their permission to use graphics in Chapter 6. Finally, he would also like to thank innumerable people around the world who continue to contribute to his ongoing data collection on cities and without whose help it would not be possible to create the comparative data on cities to be found in various parts of this book. These people are far too many for any to be named, but each and every one of them is owed a debt of gratitude for taking the time out of their busy days to answer emails for data. They know only too well who they are! Hopefully, in books like this and other publications that bring together some of these data, there is some value added for them by being able to see their own city in comparison to others.

Jeff dedicates his portion of this book to his three sons, Joshua, Timothy and Nathanael Kenworthy who are expected to be shining examples of the use of transit, walking and cycling! This is despite starting off in life with the great disadvantage of being constantly chauffeured by their father in automobiles to countless field hockey and other sports games in the sprawling metro region of Perth, which is simply not well-designed for other modes of transport! But in this and many other ways, he nevertheless should have done better.

Preston L. Schiller would like to thank the many encouraging individuals and supportive institutions and organizations whom he met trekking and bicycling along the path of sustainable transportation over several decades who were identified in the acknowledgments for the first edition. He would also like to thank the Master's in Sustainable Transportation Program of the University of Washington, Seattle, the Department of Geography and Planning of Queen's University, Kingston, and the Center for Canadian-American Studies, Western Washington University, and their affiliated libraries for their ongoing support and encouragement.

Preston dedicates his portion of this book's effort to his children, their children, to his aunt, the late Reva Schiller Springer, who introduced him in childhood to the joys of walking in Lincoln Park and Downtown Chicago, to his Detroit and Boston comrade-in-feet the late Clifford Craine, and to his beloved principessa, Nancy Elena van Deusen.

Acronyms and Abbreviations

AAA	Automobile Association of America
ADAS	automated driver assistance systems
AHP	analytic hierarchy process
AV	autonomous vehicle
BAU	business as usual
BCE	before the Christian Era
BRT	bus rapid transit
CAFE	corporate average fuel efficiency
CBD	central business district
CC	connected car and climate change depending on context
CEO	chief executive officer
CIA	Central Intelligence Agency (USA)
CNG	compressed natural gas
CNT	Center for Neighborhood Technology
CO_2	carbon dioxide
CSS	context-sensitive solutions
CTN	community transit network
CTR	commute trip reduction
CU	University of Colorado
CURA	Centre for Urban Research and Action
DOT	Department of Transportation
DMU	diesel multiple unit
EDF	Environmental Defense Fund
EIA	environmental impact assessment
EMU	electric multiple unit
EOQ	economic order quantity
EU	European Union
EV	electric vehicle
FHWA	Federal Highway Adminstration (USA)
FoE	Friends of the Earth
GCR	Green Car Reports
GHG	greenhouse gas
GM	General Motors
GVRD	Greater Vancouver Regional District
ha	hectare
hr	hour
HOFO	hands-off feet-off
HOT	high-occupancy toll (lane)
HOV	high-occupancy vehicle (lane)
HPV	human-powered vehicle
HVAC	Heating, Ventilation and Air Conditioning
IATA	International Air Transport Association
IBF	International Bicycle Fund
ICAO	International Civil Aviation Organization
ICC	U.S. Interstate Commerce Commission
ICE	internal combustion engine
ID	identification

IEA	International Energy Agency
ISTEA	Intermodal Surface Transportation Efficiency Act
ITDP	Institute for Transportation and Development Policy
ITS	intelligent transportation systems
km	kilometer
km/h	kilometers per hour
LAW	League of American Wheelmen
LEM	Location Efficient Mortgage (USA)
LOS	level of service
LRT	light rail transit
LUTRAQ	land use, transportation, air quality
m	meter
MaaS	mobility as a service
MagLev	magnetic levitation
MAX	Metropolitan Area (LRT) Express (Portland, Oregon)
MJ	megajoule
MM	mobility management
mph	miles per hour
MPO	Metropolitan Planning Organization
MVET	U.S. Motor Vehicle Excise Tax
NAFTA	North American Free Trade Agreement
NASCAR	National Association for Stock Car Auto-Racing
NGO	non-governmental organization
NHTSA	National Highway Traffic Safety Administration (USA)
NPR	National Public Radio
NRDC	Natural Resources Defense Council
NTS	National Travel Survey (USA)
OICA	International Organization of Motor Vehicle Manufacturers
ORV	off-road vehicle
PBS	Public Broadcasting Service
pkm	passenger kilometers
pkt	passenger kilometers traveled
pmi	passenger miles
pmt	passenger miles traveled
PMV	personal motor vehicle
PPP	public–private partnership
P&R	Park & Ride
PRT	personal rapid transit
RATP	Régie Autonome des Transports Parisiens (Autonomous Operator of Parisian Public Transportation)
RGR	regional rail
RoW	right(s) of way
RRT	rail rapid transit
RTD	regional transportation district
RV	recreational vehicle
SFMTA	San Francisco's Municipal Transportation Agency
SOV	single-occupant vehicle
SRI	Solar Reflectivity Index
ST	sustainable transportation
STOL	short take-off and landing
STOP	Sensible Transportation Options for Portland
STPP	Surface Transportation Policy Project (USA)

SUV	sports utility vehicle
TAZ	transportation analysis zone
TDM	transportation demand management
TEST	Transport & Environment Studies
teu	20 foot equivalent unit(s)
TGV	*train à grande vitesse* (high-speed train)
THE PEP	Transport, Health and Environment Pan-European Programme
TIF	tax increment financing
tkm	tonne kilometers
TMA	transportation management association
tmi	tonne miles
TND	traditional neighborhood design
TOD	transit-oriented development
TSP	transit signal priority
UGB	urban growth boundary
UHI(E)	Urban Heat Island (Effect)
U.K.	United Kingdom
UNCTAD	United Nations Conference on Trade and Development
UNDEV	United Nations Development Program
U.S.	United States
USEPA	U.S. Environmental Protection Agency
V2G	Vehicle to Grid
VAMPIRE	Vulnerability Assessment for Mortgage, Petrol and Inflation Risks and Expenses index
vkm	vehicle kilometers
vkt	vehicle kilometers traveled
vmi	vehicle miles
vmt	vehicle miles traveled
VTO	vertical take-off
WB	World Bank
WHO	World Health Organisation
WSC	World Shipping Council
WTO	World Trade Organization

Foreword

Ralph Buehler

It is a great pleasure to write the foreword for the second edition of *An Introduction to Sustainable Transportation*. Preston Schiller and Jeff Kenworthy have updated, expanded and (even) improved upon their excellent first edition of this book published in 2010. The arrival of this new edition is timely, capturing at least three major trends emerging since the publication of the first edition. First, the new edition highlights the increasing number of best practice 'exemplar' cities, regions and countries making progress moving towards a more sustainable transportation system—partly evidenced by changes in travel behavior away from single-occupancy driving. Second, changes in technology promise to revolutionize transportation, but without careful consideration of the environmental and equity aspects of sustainability these technological advances may actually result in a less sustainable transportation system with greater social inequities, fewer livable places and more car-oriented spatial development patterns. Third, as the book shows, many challenges of unsustainable transportation remain, and have the potential to get worse, such as social inequity, lack of access to destinations that serve daily needs, traffic fatalities or transportation-related CO_2 emissions.

This book provides an exhaustive, scientifically grounded, data driven and yet entertaining and accessible introduction to sustainable transportation. Initially, the authors provide a thorough grounding in past unsustainable trends in transportation. This includes the often-overlooked social dimension of 'car culture' and influences from corporations and media that have been promoting it. Subsequently, the book focuses on opportunities for positive policy change towards more sustainability.

The audience for this book includes university students, policy-makers, planners and citizens interested in policy and planning for sustainable transportation. The book comes to life through international comparisons, case studies and histories for sustainable and unsustainable transportation, and a multitude of text boxes that feature research findings from other authors, first person accounts of experiences using transportation systems, historical information, introductions to novel concepts, and case studies of sustainable transportation experiences worldwide. Examples include a discussion of 'Mobility as a Service (MaaS)' written by the originator of that concept, Sonja Heikkilä, or a text box on Urban Heat Island Effects written by distinguished architect and New Urbanist Doug Kelbaugh. Each chapter ends with thought-provoking questions for review and future development.

The authors embed their careful analysis in a deep commitment to environmental and social sustainability—in conjunction with economic progress—combining the three key dimensions of sustainability: environment, equity and economy. Similar to their easily accessible writing and inclusive approach to the audience for this book, the authors prioritize social processes and citizen involvement over technology to achieve a more sustainable transportation system. Technological innovation can help, but planning, policy and citizen input are key to guiding the development of a more sustainable transportation system. This distinguishes the authors' approach from other views of sustainable transportation that promulgate (over) reliance on technological innovation for more sustainability.

Throughout the book, the authors highlight the crucial role of land use, urban form, and built environment as key determinants of sustainable transportation. Many land-use plans and zoning ordinances are at the root of today's car-oriented communities, because they mandate spread-out, low density, single-use developments. However, zoning codes and land-use plans can also enable sustainable transportation through the mixing of land uses and greater population densities—allowing for shorter trip distances easily covered on foot or by bicycle and assuring sufficient ridership demand in catchment areas of public transportation stops. The new chapter on urban design in this updated edition is a wonderful extension of the land-use element. Poor urban design can be a significant hindrance for walking, cycling and public transportation—even in areas with mixed-land uses and higher population densities.

Overall, the book offers hope and a positive outlook on how to achieve a more sustainable transportation system. Successful case studies from around the world and a carefully crafted guide on how to achieve more sustainable transportation lead the way forward to a more sustainable future.

Ralph Buehler, PhD

Associate Professor, School of Public and International Affairs, Urban

Affairs and Planning, Virginia Tech, Alexandria, VA

Introduction and overview

This book is an effort to illuminate how to move towards sustainability in transportation. It addresses the question of how to shape transportation planning, policy-making and citizen activities in a direction of greater social and environmental benefit to society and Planet Earth. The general discussion of sustainable transportation to be found in current literature is much less developed than the general discussion of sustainability. In this second edition, we have chosen to continue to use the term 'sustainable transportation', although we recognize that the terms 'mobility' and 'accessibility' are being used by some along with 'sustainability' or are being used interchangeably with the term 'transportation'. The terms 'smart transportation' and 'smart cities' are also gaining currency worldwide, as is the influence of the increasingly sophisticated IT-based mobility management systems now covered in this book such as Mobility as a Service (MaaS). We have also updated most of the data and graphic materials presented in the first edition as well as adding much new material, including recent photos, now in color, to enhance the timeliness and attractiveness of this volume.

Transportation is one of the most basic of human activities, linked to almost all daily routines—from employment and obtaining essential services to shopping and recreation. It is intimately linked to land-use planning and critically so to urban design, to the latter of which we have now devoted an entire chapter. It allows many benefits to individuals, but aspects of it pose serious problems for the environment and society. Almost all the motorized ways or modes in which persons, goods or materials move around our cities and Planet Earth consume considerable amounts of energy and resources, most of which are not renewable. Most of these modes are highly dependent on fossil fuels and deeply implicated in the processes of greenhouse gas emissions and their atmospheric accumulation and ensuing climate change. This book explores ways in which many transportation benefits can be retained while its social and environmental burdens are reduced.

Goals of sustainable transportation (ST)

Sustainable transportation aims at promoting better and healthier ways of meeting individual and community needs while reducing the social and environmental impacts of current mobility practices. It attempts to achieve these through reducing resource inputs and waste outputs and minimizing transportation's often deleterious effects on the public realm. It is about adapting the techniques and technologies most appropriate to the type of service needed. It is about making important everyday destinations, such as shopping, employment, basic services and recreation closer and more accessible, rather than increasing mobility to

1

overcome inaccessibility. It is about healthier ways of getting around communities—ways that improve the individual's health through more activity; the few minutes walking to the transit stop or station or the pleasant bicycle trip to the store. It attempts to find ways to improve the health of communities through lowering traffic and its accompanying pollution and safety hazards.

Technical and technological factors, such as improved fuel efficiency, reduced motor emissions or systems that control traffic flow on major highways, are important but they are not the essence of sustainable transportation. Sustainable transportation involves taking many dimensions of transportation, land-use planning and urban design into account simultaneously as well as public visioning processes aimed at describing the future we desire, and then taking the steps necessary to attain that vision. It is essentially a societal, rather than strictly technical, process that depends upon planning, policy, economics and citizen involvement. It is about how technological advances such as autonomous vehicles and electric cars are deployed and the visioning process for their inclusion in the life of cities. It is not about the technologies per se.

Sustainable transportation aims at lowering financial costs to society and to the individual through lowering the dependence on automobiles as the main mode of individual mobility. At present, it appears that we are at the early stages of a significant change, or 'paradigm shift', in the ways transportation is conceived, planned, financed and implemented. The shift is away from automobile-oriented planning that emphasizes system growth—or 'bigger is better'—towards emphasizing appropriate modes, infrastructure and technologies that may tend towards 'smaller is beautiful' or 'closer is beautiful', and slowing our increasingly hypermobile societies. Sustainable transportation is tending towards greater diversity and choice in how people and goods move around, as opposed to a lopsided situation where the automobile and truck are the mode of first choice too much of the time. Several chapters explore the ways that this paradigm shift is occurring, literally and figuratively under our feet at this moment.

Why this book?

In preparation for the writing of this book, the authors reviewed numerous transportation texts. It was perceived that there was a great need for a relatively succinct and basic work that addressed the wide range of issues involved in making transportation more sustainable. The shortcomings of conventional transportation planning, policy-making and public participation needed to be subject to critique in the context of a wider view of how transportation could become more sustainable.

While there are many excellent works summarizing transportation planning, both conventional and sustainable, none available presented an accessible treatment of each by persons without advanced education in math, engineering or the physical sciences. Nor do these books provide an indication of how to effectively mobilize planning, policy-making and citizen participation in the arduous but rewarding task of moving from 'Business As Usual' (BAU) to Sustainable Transportation (ST). Hence the need for this text and its effort to create a work intended to be of use to more than one type of reader.

Students

It is hoped that students of transportation, policy and environmental issues will benefit from this book. Students are often already aware of many of the issues, but may need more background and in-depth material in their efforts to master the subject matter and apply it to their broader areas of study. Students have unique opportunities to apply their learning to practice in everyday community living, as well as bringing their life experiences and practices to bear on their studies. Through walking, bicycling or taking transit to their classes, students can model sustainable transportation. By working to attain university-wide transit-pass programs or a walking- and bicycling-friendly campus community, students can change community and institutional practices and planning in the direction of sustainability. One of the exemplary cities chosen for analysis in Chapter 9 is Boulder (Colorado, U.S.), a university and research center that has chosen to move in the direction of sustainable transportation.

Planners

Public or private sector planners and planning consultants are very well situated to help move transportation towards greater sustainability. Persons working in the transportation field, whether their background is in planning, urban design, engineering, policy or another discipline, often have a deep understanding of the ways in which planning and transportation programs work. They are well-situated to inform and educate the public and policy-makers about the range of available options and planning modalities, as well as their consequences. Many planners are already uncomfortable with BAU, but need more resources to make the transition to sustainable transportation; it is hoped that this work will be a resource for them in that effort.

Policy-makers and decision-makers

Persons who can influence public policy—how resources are invested, programs developed, laws and regulations formulated and how planning receives guidance—are well situated to help direct transportation in the direction of sustainability. In the private sector, management can influence decisions about whether facilities are located in car-dependent or transit-friendly sites, and union leadership can influence decisions about whether employees insist on free parking or accept a range of transportation benefits including transit passes or in lieu of parking rewards. Visionary and brave leaders, at the political level, within bureaucracies and in academia, have played a central role in the stories of several of the cities presented as exemplars of sustainable transportation. The authors have been inspired in their interactions with some of these bold elected officials who have taken seriously the concepts of leadership and 'politics as a vocation' in the original sense of that word: a calling, not just a job. There is also the question of whether politicians work to leave a genuine positive legacy, or are mostly in the profession for what they can get out of it.

Engaged citizens

Possibly the most important, and most neglected, resource for sustainable transportation is the citizenry. Whether as a neighborhood resident with transportation concerns, or as a user of transit, streets or paths, the citizens' point of view is often taken for granted in planning and policy processes. Often the ways in which governmental entities undertake public outreach or consultation leave much to be desired in regards to creating effective partnerships with the citizens who are the subjects of projects. Sometimes concerned citizens throw up their hands and simply reject any and all change, fearing that it will only worsen their neighborhood or their commute. But citizen input, involvement and energy are crucial to successful planning and project realization. Several of the exemplary communities and projects presented in this book have succeeded, in the main, because visionary citizens helped government to focus on problems, as well as to develop sustainable solutions.

It is hoped that interested, engaged and involved citizens, who often form the 'cement' of sustainability planning, will find this book to be useful in their efforts and we have attempted to expand on the possibilities for this here, for example through 'deliberative democracy'. The accessibility of this book should broaden the number of concerned citizens who can absorb the material and issues without the barriers of specialized jargon and advanced engineering mathematics and give renewed hope to their efforts.

Point of view: values, commitments, 'objectivity' and documentation

This work does not shy away from presenting its material from the point of view of persons committed to the values of environmental and social sustainability coupled with economic progress. The light of that commitment, which so motivates the authors' research, teaching and civic engagement, will not be hidden under an epistemologically questionable bushel of 'objectivity'. That commitment does not excuse the authors from carefully analyzing issues and documenting their assertions while presenting a broad array of references. Where making points about situations where there is demonstrated excess or disingenuousness, the text pulls no punches in its tone and outlook. This is especially the case in the 'car culture' discussion, where it is easier to demonstrate some of these excesses in a more colorful way. While there is much to criticize in current conventional planning and policy-making, examples of efforts that are moving some cities towards sustainable transportation are presented. Not all the news is bad and there is room for hope.

Much of the material presented in this book involves the integration of research results of the authors and the inclusion of some of their ongoing research results, not previously published. In addition, one of the major research problems in sustainable transportation is the lack of synthesis of a very diverse and rapidly expanding information base. This book, therefore, is also a serious research enterprise in drawing together a huge amount of technical, social, economic, environmental and cultural material into a policy-relevant synthesis, of use to all the aforementioned potential readers.

Overview of the book

While the second edition closely follows the organization, and includes a fair amount of the content of the first edition, there are some very significant changes: most of the data has been updated with more recent data to the extent of its availability; many new items, discussions and graphics have been added, which are described in the chapter summaries below; and two new chapters, one on urban design and another on transit and intercity services, have been added. Many bibliographic additions have been made throughout the book to the references and notes sections at the ends of chapters. Appendices, such as lists of relevant NGOs, informational sources, model programs and the like, have been moved to the book's website where they can be easily accessed and added to or updated as needed. Much more material about Asian cities has been included. Many of these changes are detailed in the following chapter-by-chapter description and there are several places in the book where the links between transportation and atmospheric pollution and climate change are discussed.

Chapter 1: A highly mobile planet and its challenges: automobile dependency, equity and inequity

The first chapter opens with a discussion of definitions of sustainable transportation, as well as the problems of defining such a phenomenon. It then turns to the planet's high level of mobility—'hypermobility'—of persons and freight, encouraged by an overemphasis and overdependence on automobility in many parts of the world. Automobile dependency is seen to have led to serious inequities between and within societies. A minority of the planet's populace drive and create disproportionate pollution and energy consumption, while a majority are greatly disadvantaged in their efforts to gain access to basic needs. Such inequities also affect wealthy societies. For the second edition, we have updated the data for items such as the hypermobility, environmental problems—including transportation energy use and related pollution as well as transit performance, transportation health effects, (including obesity, deaths and injuries), land use, sprawl and locational effects in a global selection of cities. We have expanded our section on equity, social justice and auto-dependence and added a boxed item about the important contribution that Robert D. Bullard has made to that issue. We have also added several new or revised charts, tables and photos.

Chapter 2: Automobile cities, the car culture and alternative possibilities

The second chapter builds upon the first and presents an analysis of the evolution of communities from walking cities to transit cities and then, for many, to automobile cities. The creation of the car culture and its bolstering in everyday popular media—such as movies, music and music videos, radio, television, literature and advertising—is explored. The value and meaning of the frequent traffic reports that permeate daily radio are questioned and tourism, the fly-drive and RV phenomena are scrutinized. A former advertising agency executive presents a critique of the ways in which 'cars are us'.

In addition to updating and expanding data, several new items have been added, such as: From Pompidou to Paris Plages and Bike-Bus Lanes; James Howard Kunstler (and the suburban 'Crapscape'); Mimi Sheller and John Urry, and the Sociology of Transportation; Pareidolia: The many faces of automobile facades; African Americans' complicated relation with Cadillacs; Car as home and your car's home away from home; cross-country 1940s non-stop Cadillac; Automobility and Safety—Ideology versus Analysis; Jeff Kenworthy, busted for walking and entering; Teen romance in the fast lane; and Jam Handy and GM—about the little-known story of how a film and publicity company shaped and promoted automobility over many decades. Several new graphics have been added including; car 'faces'; transportation scenes of Paris; Andy Singer's 'Crapscape'; a walking school bus and a traffic jam at a school; and a 1947 Cadillac that was outfitted for perpetual automobility.

Chapter 3: History of sustainable and unsustainable transportation: from walking to wheels and back to walking

The third chapter explores the rich area of transportation history. This includes land modes, water travel and aviation, telecommunications and aspects of infrastructure development, especially roads. It demonstrates the centrality of walking to human evolution and existence and how, for thousands of years, human communities were designed to maximize access to important resources and minimize travel. Several boxed items are included, presenting perspectives on topics ranging from Inca roads to Sherlock Holmes assisting a young bicyclist in distress, and how the experience of a small city with the development of the U.S. interstate highway system embodies many of the contradictory notions of what the new highways would bring. The interesting history of bicycling and its role in 'paving the way' for the automobile is explored. A table of selected historic timelines for several modes and trans-portation innovations helps the reader grasps the vast period over which these developed as well as the rapidity of the pace of change in the nineteenth and twentieth centuries and the now increasingly rapid change in the twenty-first century.

For the second edition, the historic timeline has been updated and material on nineteenth-century pedestrian contests has been added along with material about recent developments in transportation policy. Numerous bibliographic sources have also been added. Graphics additions include several about the Santiago de Compostela pilgrimage route; historic bicycles; Park Avenue (Manhattan, NYC) before and after traffic was allowed and how a recent car-free day looked; and an anti-fossil fuel demonstration in a village green that had once been slated for demolition for the construction of freeway interchange—which, fortunately, did not happen.

Chapter 4: Modes, roads and routes: technologies, infrastructure, functions and inter-relatedness

The fourth chapter brings the reader to the present and analyzes and compares the various modes by which persons move around within their communities and across longer distances. These include walking, bicycling, motorized two- and three-wheelers, personal motor vehicles (PMVs), buses, urban rail transit, intercity rail, airplanes and ships. It examines these modes in the context of their interaction with infrastructure needed or available, as well as trip purposes. It defines and describes modes beyond the physical characteristics of specific vehicles, drawing attention to how vehicles are deployed and viewed by users. It begins a discussion, continued in other chapters in the book, of the effects of different modes on the consumption of urban space and the limits to the numbers of automobiles a city can support. It examines the various factors, which are assessed by travelers, including out-of-pocket costs and the characteristics of modes chosen or preferred. It analyzes the energy efficiency of numerous modes and vehicles within modal categories and compares the discussion of vehicular energy consumption and efficiency with the discussion of the energy efficiency of cities, which is seen to vary with urban form. It also points to the huge modal 'overkill' for many transportation chores in wealthy countries, while many in poor countries still carry backbreaking loads and use pack animals.

Among the newer issues and sections added to the second edition are: considerably more material about intercity passenger rail in Europe and China—especially advances in high-speed rail (HSR) as well as the stasis of intercity passenger rail in the U.S. and Canada; the Airport City phenomenon, Aerotropolis and flying cars; electric (EVs) and autonomous vehicles (AVs), modal energy consumption and vehicle occupancy factors in global cities as well as numerous other global data; Segways versus pedestrians; Elon Musk's 'hyperloop or hyper-hype?'; electrified fast-recharging buses in Shanghai; modal integration such as bike share at a light rail station in Paris and an electric car-share recharging station in Berlin; Brisbane's passenger-only ferries; several dramatic examples of the barrier effects of large urban roads and a section on e-bikes, e-delivery vehicles, pedicabs and cargo and beer bikes. There are many photos accompanying these added materials.

Chapter 5: Urban, regional and intercity public transportation: policy, technical, land use and provider aspects

A new chapter on transit and intercity transportation public transportation has been added to this edition. This area is very important because it is one of the key building blocks of sustainable transportation. When done well, most surface public transportation modes demonstrate clear energy, pollution, social equity (mobility for all persons regardless of income or physical ability), urban design, spatial consumption and economic advantages over private modes. The majority of public transportation modes can be planned to interconnect well with other green modes and to create synergies with green urban planning. While Chapter 4 addressed many of the important aspects of modes, including transit and intercity modes and infrastructure and their interrelationship, this chapter focuses mainly on issues concerned with broader planning, policy and finance issues involving transit and intercity transportation.

Chapter 5 covers a broad range of matters including different approaches to transit planning; the 'rails versus bus' controversy; radial versus network transit systems; the relationship between polycentric urban form and transit planning; the importance of integrating transit modes, such as bus and rail, as well as the importance of integrating transit modes with intercity modes and these with other modes such as walking, cycling and car-sharing; a number of policy and planning considerations about how to help public transportation function better and attract more riders is presented; the importance of policies promoting transit and prioritizing transit over other vehicular modes is discussed; the differing situations for providing transit for special needs and rural populations is also discussed; intercity modes from coaches to trains to planes and their implications for planning and policy are discussed and compared as are the issues around private providers and the privatization of public services. The importance of features such as user-friendly information, maps, signage and schedules and a comfortable environment onboard vehicles and at public transportation facilities is also discussed.

Chapter 6: Urban design for sustainable and active transportation and healthy communities

A new chapter on the critical importance of urban design and the difference between urban planning and urban design: the latter being more about the lived experience and three-dimensional results of the interplay between architecture, public spaces, streets and roads, green spaces and the minutiae of urban design elements in cities, the kind of street furniture used, paving materials, lighting and many other factors that determine, in particular, the attractiveness and viability of walking and cycling.

The chapter revisits the concepts of the walking, transit and automobile cities and provides a detailed insight into what constitutes these three types of urban fabrics and what we have to do to ensure that walking and transit urban fabrics are recognized, respected and rejuvenated, while we minimize the creation of more automobile city fabrics and transform some of the existing ones towards the other two. Then a detailed look is given to the way urban design tools can be used to analyze different aspects such as walkability and permeability—how easy it is to walk around a place. This covers the structure of the street network and block sizes and if they are designed more for cars than pedestrians and some qualitative factors such as whether building frontages are active and interesting or blank and dangerous for people on foot. Land uses are examined in terms of increasing short-distance trips, and whether the area is legible for people on foot, with clear landmarks and differences in the urban landscape for orientation, and whether streets are safe, attractive, friendly and efficient (SAFE) for people on foot. Robustness, resilience and ability to cope with change of urban fabrics are also examined. Then the visual appropriateness of a place (legibility), its richness (sensory experience) and the level of personalization (comfort, belonging) people feel in its public spaces are examined.

Three new boxed items are included: urban heat island effects—which can be severe and even deadly—and what can be done, by distinguished architect and academic Doug Kelbaugh; free-range kids—the importance of children's independent mobility; and gated communities—what not to do in urban design.

Chapter 7: Public policy and effective citizen participation: leadership, deliberation, backcasting, scenarios, visualization and visioning

The seventh chapter addresses how policy-making and public participation can be moved away from their conventional unsatisfying and status quo maintaining forms to more rewarding change-oriented forms, where public policy truly precedes and shapes planning, takes the lead in setting a sustainability agenda and where citizens are involved in shaping policy and planning in creative and effective ways. Global and historical perspectives on transportation policy and the role of public involvement are presented. The U.S. trajectory is traced from business as usual (BAU) to the promise of change in the early 1990s reform efforts (ISTEA) and then slowly back to BAU, while identifying possible developments that may lead again to change. Examples of the key roles political leadership and energized and well-prepared citizens have played in several locales are described. The positive example of Germany's decades-long successful effort to promote bicycling at all levels of policy and planning, as well as several examples of cities, large and small, moving in the direction of sustainable transportation are presented.

Various formats and strategies, including deliberative democracy for effective public participation are described, along with several case examples of successful efforts, as well as a description of a citizen effort that headed transportation away from a more sustainable strategy. Several approaches are presented—from media messaging, town halls, citizen juries, community visioning and charrettes, to citizen science with several others in between, along with the wisdom of Dr. Seuss. A contribution from Janette Hartz-Karp, a world-recognized authority on deliberative democracy has been added. Several graphics and photos illustrate this chapter's major emphases.

Chapter 8: A new planning paradigm: from integrated planning, policy and mobility management to repair, regeneration and renewal

The eighth chapter presents a critique of conventional 'predict and provide' BAU planning and builds upon the necessity of moving towards 'deliberate and decide' sustainable planning. It proposes a new paradigm for integrating the many factors that comprise ST planning, and discusses how the types of policy-making and participation reforms presented in the previous chapter can be incorporated in it. The crucial role of 'mobility management' is present with a newly contributed item from Helsinki-based Sonja Heikkilä, pioneer of 'Mobility as a Service (MaaS)'.

Going beyond ST planning to the repair, regeneration and renewal of major transportation institutions, and society itself is presented, along with a possible ST agenda. Elements considered include car-free and car-share efforts; active transportation and designing healthy communities; addressing social inequities; harnessing the efforts of innovative NGOs; and honoring the work done by leading sustainable transportation thinkers and actors. Numerous graphics and photos illustrate this chapter including; 'before and after' the traffic calming and road diet of a busy and chaotic street in Seville's Trianna; dramatic examples of how much space devouring and how many impenetrable barriers urban highways create, while illustrating how minor barriers can protect and promote urban cycling; and how on-street parking spaces and parking lots can be converted to better use and how pavement can be painted to slow cars and celebrate community.

Chapter 9: Cities on the move: global exemplars of more sustainable transportation

Chapter 9 reviews the efforts towards sustainable transportation of nine cities of very different sizes and socio-economic and cultural frameworks: Vancouver (British Columbia), Portland (Oregon), Boulder (Colorado), Freiburg im Breisgau (Germany) and Seoul (South Korea), plus some important examination of what is happening in four cities that are considered at the forefront of motorization today in the world's largest and most rapidly industrializing countries, China and India. Significant data and trends are examined for Mumbai, Beijing, Shanghai and Guangzhou, with some surprising results that run counter to the usual portrayal of such cities.

The chapter looks at the key pillars of these cities' achievements, what sets the cities apart from other cities in special ways and how the cities have achieved their successes.

It also provides some quantitative snapshots of each city, incorporating some new research results, so that readers have a basic picture of the current state of the land use–transportation system in each place. Collectively these exemplars cover many of the issues and approaches addressed in Chapter 8, including the role of urban form, the development of superior transit systems, the integration of land uses with those systems, the provision of excellent conditions for walking and cycling, reductions in road capacity, the greening of the urban environment and the role of leadership and civil society in forging such changes in transportation and urban planning.

Chapter 10: Conclusion: growing more exemplars

The book concludes with a discussion of the most vital actions, preparations and measures that need to be taken at several levels to move from conventional, business as usual (BAU) transportation to sustainability. It attempts to draw out some common threads and themes, which can be found in many of the successful examples of sustainable transportation in this book. For example, the need for leaders who lead; citizens who participate in effective and well informed ways, often 'leading their leaders'; NGOs and transportation professionals—including academics, as well as government institutions that are transformed and move in a more sustainable direction for the 'long haul'.

Specific examples of persons and efforts in these areas are offered including: how Strasbourg (FR) has created synergy between political leadership, good planning and an exemplary NGO; how a BAU traffic engineer became transformed into an advocate for sustainable transportation; how the NGO WalkBoston has been harnessing citizen and professional energy in their effort to promote pedestrianism and pedestrian safety; how an environmental studies graduate created a career of civic engagement combined with a unique business combining pedicab service and the design and production of pedicabs and cargo bikes; perspectives on the contributions of Jane Jacobs and Jane Holtz Kay; how Vélo-Cité (City Bicycle) welcomes newcomers and teaches them how to cycle safely and competently in Bordeaux (FR); how some of the 'creative class' is rejuvenating urban areas, including ailing cities such as Baltimore and Detroit; how creativity in transit and urban planning is leading to more attractive transit-oriented developments (TODs) and public spaces, on transit or at stations or at neighborhood street corners; and, finally, life in an ecologically planned neighborhood, the Vauban in Freiburg (DE) and its 'free-range' children is described. A wealth of photos brings these and much else in the chapter to life.

Appendices and supplemental materials

An appendix is provided at the Taylor & Francis webpage associated with this book. It contains supplementary photos and information about some of the more recent efforts and developments in cities, and citizen efforts involving new technologies and planning oriented to sustainable transportation, and a Resources Toolbox, which lists and provides web addresses for numerous sources of information about data sources and organizations involved with sustainable transportation.

Endnotes are collected by chapter at the end of the text and followed by a comprehensive bibliography of the works referred to in the text. An index at the end of the book assists readers in locating specific topics in the text and a list of acronyms and abbreviations as well as a glossary with definitions of technical terms are also at the end of the book.

A highly mobile planet and its challenges: automobile dependence, equity and inequity

Sustainable transportation, accessible transportation or sustainable mobility?

This chapter presents an approach to characterizing, defining and exploring a few of the major issues associated with transportation and efforts to move it towards greater sustainability. Several differences between conventional approaches to transportation, business as usual (BAU) and sustainable transportation (ST) are delineated. A brief treatment of the expansiveness and extensiveness of freight and passenger mobility and some aspects of transportation infrastructure are presented to put some of the issues surrounding these into a broader, even global, perspective. Two major issues confronting ST, automobile dependence and (in)equity (including social justice), are discussed in depth. In recent years, the terms 'sustainable mobility' and 'accessible transportation' have come to be used interchangeably with or substituted for the term 'sustainable transportation'. This book continues the use of the longer-lived term 'sustainable transportation', while also addressing a range of accessibility and mobility issues.

What is sustainable transportation about?

ST emerged from three main sources:

1 Concerns about transportation's burdens and the counter-productivity of much conventional highway-oriented planning began to emerge around the planet from the 1970s onward as pollution increased and the destructive effects of highway expansion upon cities attracted more attention (Stringer and Wenzel 1976; Gakenheimer 1978; Newman and Kenworthy 1989, 1999a, 2015).
2 The recognition in some places that reducing traffic in cities through traffic calming (deliberately slowing personal motor vehicles, or PMVs) and pedestrianization (excluding PMVs from certain streets) had many benefits for mobility and the environment, including reductions in vehicular traffic ('traffic evaporation') and traffic-related injuries, especially those of pedestrians and bicyclists, and increases in the numbers of people walking, bicycling and using public transportation.
3 The growth of sustainability awareness, especially following the Brundtland Commission's report (WCED 1987) on sustainable development as 'development which meets the needs of current generations without compromising the ability of future generations to meet their own needs'. Many key works have emerged since, including the Millennium Development Goals from 2000,[1] the new Sustainable Development Goals as well the New Urban Agenda adopted in 2016 at the Habitat III conference

in Quito.[2] Such broad global objectives have filtered into the sustainable transport agendas worldwide.[3] There is an increasing effort globally, especially through the UN, to integrate sustainability into the mainstream of transportation policy and planning, especially as it affects climate change.[4]

4   The growth of sustainability awareness, as well as action on issues such as climate change, has been moved forward by the crucial role of citizen participation in pushing this agenda and the especially significant increase in citizen and NGO activity, particularly since 2009 (Solnit 2015; 350.org 2016).

These three strands led to a lively discussion about ST and many excellent efforts to describe, characterize or define it since the 1990s.[5] After a series of meetings and workshops in the 1990s and early 2000s, an Environmentally Sustainable Transportation working group of the Organisation for Economic Co-operation and Development (OECD) developed a brief definition:

> (A)n environmentally sustainable transport system is one where transportation does not endanger public health or ecosystems and meets needs for access consistent with (a) use of renewable resources below their rates of regeneration, and (b) use of non-renewable resources below the rates of development of renewable substitutes.[6]

While all efforts to define a field as complex as ST are fraught with difficulty, there are common threads in various efforts examining ST which emphasize that sustainability with regard to passenger transportation should:

- meet basic access and mobility needs in ways that do not degrade the environment;
- not deplete the resource base upon which it is dependent;
- serve multiple economic and environmental goals;
- maximize efficiency in overall resource utilization;
- improve or maintain access to employment, goods and services while shortening trip lengths and/or reducing the need to travel; and
- enhance the livability and human qualities of urban regions (Schiller and Kenworthy 1999, 2003; Schiller, 2004).

Differences between sustainable transportation and business as usual

Rather than attempting an objectifying definition, it might be more useful to understand sustainable transportation in contrast to that which it is opposed. The dominant transportation paradigm until now has emphasized single-mode mobility—whether automobiles, planes or huge cargo ships; 'hard path'[7] approaches relying upon facility expansion—whether roads, parking, ports or runways; as well as financing that often masks the full costs and environmental consequences of its arrangements. The paradigm of conventional transportation planning and policy may be termed BAU. The differences between BAU and ST will be visited many times throughout this book. Some of the major points of comparison are presented in Table 1.1.

Unsustainable transportation: the magnitude of the problem

The challenge facing the shift from BAU to ST is great. It touches upon almost every aspect of life: ecosystem health, livability of communities, access to jobs and services, and the costs of basic goods, including foodstuffs, to identify a few. One way of understanding the world that BAU in transportation has led to is to consider the magnitude of personal and freight mobility and the increasing length and dispersion of trips. The concept of 'hypermobility' is very useful in this regard.

TABLE 1.1 Comparison of business as usual and sustainable transportation

Business as usual (BAU)	Sustainable transportation (ST)
Emphasizes mobility and quantity (more, faster, further, noisier, dispersed)	Emphasizes accessibility and quality (closer, better, slower, smaller, more compact)
Emphasizes one mode (automobility)	Emphasizes plurality (multi-modality)
Often lacks good connections between modes	Emphasizes interconnections (inter-modality)
Accommodates and accepts trends	Seeks to interrupt and reverse harmful trends
Plans and builds based on forecasts of likely demand (predict and provide)	Works backwards from a preferred vision to planning and provision (deliberate and decide)
Expands roads to respond to travel demand	Manages transportation or mobility demand
Ignores many social and environmental costs	Incorporates full costs; planning and provision
Transportation planning often in 'silos' disconnected from environmental, social and other planning areas	Emphasizes integrated planning combining transportation with other relevant areas

Source: Preston L. Schiller (also cf. Banister 2008)

Hypermobility

The magnitude of the mobility of persons and freight and the vast trip distances generated by such mobility are presented in Box 1.1 and Table 1.2. BAU in transportation has meant that more roads have been built and expanded, which has not led to less traffic congestion. It has led to more driving, longer trips for people and freight, more sprawl, and more land and energy consumption (Newman and Kenworthy 1989, pp. 94–110; Whitelegg 1997, 2015). The magnitude of personal and freight movement has been characterized by John Adams as 'hypermobility'. Building upon the work of Ivan Illich (1973, 1976), Wolfgang Sachs (1992) and others, Adams described the serious environmental and social consequences of allowing this phenomenon to continue unchallenged:

- more dispersion of society; more sprawl and destruction of natural areas; longer distances to destinations;
- more societal polarization and inequity between the highly mobile and those denied the benefits of mobility and accessibility; more crime;
- more danger for those not in cars, especially children and other vulnerable persons; more obesity, less fitness;
- less social and cultural diversity and variety; less democratic politically; less participation (Adams 1985, 1999, 2000, 2009).

An attempt to capture a snapshot and some trends of the magnitude of this issue is presented in Box 1.1 and Table 1.2.

Ironically, much more is known about motorized movements of persons and goods across the planet than is known about non-motorized movement: people walking or bicycling—although these are the dominant trip modes on Planet Earth. Table 1.2 presents pertinent statistics about the magnitude of personal and freight mobility around our very busy planet. Wherever possible, the most recent data and data from the same year were used, but that was not always possible as data for a particular year may not be available until a few years later. Since there is no precise accounting of the total mileages and of world roads and pavements, expert estimates were used.

Complexity of the issue

Transportation has many impacts: environmental, social equity, economic, cultural, land use and urban form are but a few important ones. Currently, some of these impacts are

FIGURE 1.1
Huge freeway interchange in Dubai,
but with a metro line running across
the middle. Huge proportion of land
for transportation infrastructure and
no room for greenspace.
Source: Jeffrey R. Kenworthy

beneficial, such as when people find it easier to get to medical help in an emergency; but many are not beneficial or are even extremely harmful, such as when transportation-generated pollution threatens human health and even the survival of life on Planet Earth. Many of transportation's deleterious impacts stem from the lack of integrated planning, flawed policy-making and excluding effective public participation. The impact of transportation and what can be done about it will be examined in greater depth in subsequent chapters. For now, we will touch on some of the most common issues and dimensions in preparation for the following discussions.

The variety of issues, the many dimensions of society that are affected, the diversity of actors and interests—these all make ST an extremely interesting area of endeavor and action. Among the many important factors and dimensions that shape ST, and which vary from one society to another, are:

- culture and social organization;
- economics;
- political and social equity issues;
- environmental concerns;
- policy and planning;
- interest groups.

The problems of automobile dependence

The patterns of transportation and urban land use associated with high levels of automobile dependence present an array of environmental, economic and social problems for the sustainability of cities, as summarized in Table 1.3 (Newman and Kenworthy 1999a). Some problems are relevant to multiple categories, but for convenience are placed in only one category. For example, the problem that auto-dependence has gradually reduced many transit systems to mere shadows in the overall transportation system (e.g. in many U.S. cities, especially those in the south such as New Orleans) clearly has severe environmental, economic and social outcomes, but appears here under environmental problems. Similar comments can

> **BOX 1.1 Passenger motorization: A very mobile planet with plenty of roads**
>
> While accurate statistics on the amount of travel that is done by foot or bicycle each day on Planet Earth are sorely lacking or inadequate, there are good statistics available for motorized travel: Each day, Planet Earth's motorists drive their 1.2 billion personal motor vehicles (PMVs) a total of 55 billion kilometers (33 billion miles) and by the year's end a total of 10 trillion kilometers (6 trillion miles) and 25 trillion pkm (15 trillion pmi) of travel have been taken. In the U.S., which leads the world in personal motorized mobility, motorists daily record 13 billion vehicle kilometers traveled (vkt), or 8 billion vehicle miles traveled (vmt), adding 16 billion pkm, or 10 billion passenger miles (pmi), of travel so that by the year's end they have added 5 trillion vehicle kilometers (vkm), or 3 trillion vehicle miles (vmi), and 5.9 trillion pkm (3.7 trillion pmi) to the odometers of their fleet of 250 million PMVs. While the U.S. constitutes only 4.4 per cent of the world's population, American motorists own over one-fifth of the planet's automobiles, about five times the rate of vehicle ownership for most of the rest of the world, and account for one-quarter of the planet's travel by personal motor vehicle.
>
> Interspersed among the hundreds of millions of personal vehicles clogging the millions of miles/kilometers of the planet's streets and roads, tens of millions of trucks and lorries—ranging from small to medium to very large 18-wheelers and double and triple rigs—are busily hauling their loads. Churning across the oceans, a fleet of tens of thousands of cargo ships (mostly containerized) and tankers are hauling freight and fuel almost 53 trillion tonne kilometers annually. A larger fleet of tugs and merchant vessels transports a somewhat lesser amount of cargo along the inland waterways of the major continents.
>
> In the skies above the roads and waterways, thousands of commercial airplanes account for 37 million flights each year, hauling some 3.8 billion passengers and logging almost 3 billion pkm (1.7 billion passenger miles traveled, or pmt) each day, accumulating to over 6 trillion pkm (3.7pmi) annually. The U.S. accounts for almost 10 million annual flights (27 percent of the global total), almost one-quarter of the global commercial aviation fleet and one-sixth of the world's pkm flown, when its domestic and international flights are combined. A rapidly growing amount of freight, accounting for 188 billion tkm annually, is being carried in the holds of the commercial aviation fleet as well as by fleets of specialized air freight carriers.
>
> Bon voyage! Bonne route!
>
> *Source*: Preston L. Schiller and Jeffrey R. Kenworthy

be made about urban sprawl and many of the other dilemmas. This section provides a brief overview of this array of problems with some selected quantification where appropriate.

Environmental problems

Automobile-dependent cities have high levels of private transportation energy use, as shown in Figure 1.3, which compares per capita consumption of energy for private passenger transportation for 45 cities in the U.S., Canada, Australia, Europe and two high-income Asian cities, Singapore and Hong Kong.

Averaging these data by region, a typical American city consumes 1.5 times greater energy use for private passenger transportation than an Australian city, 1.8 times more than a Canadian city, 3.4 times more than a European city and 8.8 times more than the average for Singapore and Hong Kong (Newman and Kenworthy 2015). The change from 1995 to 2005 is mixed with U.S. cities shaving off 11% from their per capita energy use in private

TABLE 1.2 The hypermobility index (snapshots and trends; with apologies to *Harper's Magazine* and John Adams)

Transportation factor and year of most recent credible data*	Magnitude	Projection and growth	Eco-trend	Source(s)
World roads, linear km/mi; paved–unpaved (million)	64.3/38.6 (2013)	Grow; esp. China & India	Negative	CIA, IEA
U.S. roads, linear km/mi; paved–unpaved (million)	6.6/4 (2012)	1%/year	Negative	CIA
U.S. lane km/mi (includes lane mi. of multilane roads) (million)	13.9/8.7 (2013)	0.5%/year	Slowing	NTS (2016)
World automobile (PMV) fleet (billion)	1.2	4%/year	Very negative	GCR, OICA
U.S. automobile (PMV) fleet (million)	250	1.5%/year±	Negative	NTS (2016)
World human population (billion)	7.3 (2015 est.)	1.08% (2015 est.)	Negative	CIA
U.S. human population (million)	320	0.77%	Steady±	U.S.-Census
Automobiles (PMVs) per 1000 persons (world, incl. U.S.)	160	4%/yr	Very negative	GCR
Automobiles (PMVs) per 1000 persons (U.S.)	810	Plateau/slight decrease	Steady	NTS (2016)
U.S. vehicle km/mi by PMV annual (trillion)	4.8/3	Plateau or small increase	Positive	NTS (2016)
U.S. vehicle km/mi by PMV daily (billion)	13/8.2	Plateau or small increase	Positive	NTS (2016)
U.S. passenger km/mi by PMV annual (2014) trillion	5.9/3.7	Plateau or small increase	Positive	NTS (2016)
U.S. road fatalities/serious injuries (thousands/millions) 2015	35,092/ 2,400,000	Increase after declining	Negative	NHTSA
U.S. passenger km/mi daily all motor modes (air & surface) (billion)	22.1/13.8 (2014)	Plateau possibly	Steady	NTS (2016)
U.S. passenger km/mi annually all motor modes (air and surface) (trillion)	8/5 (2014)	Slow decrease	Positive	NTS (2016)
World passenger km/mi by PMV annual (trillion)	25/15 (2015)	Grow; esp. dev'ing world	Very negative	DulacIEA
World passenger km/mi by PMV daily (billion)	69/41	Grow; esp. dev'ing world	Very negative	DulacIEA
World road fatalities/serious injuries (million 2015)	1.25/20–50	Grow; esp. dev'ing world	Very negative	WHO
U.S. truck (lorry) fleet, large tractor-trailer/medium–large (million)	2.6/8.3	Slow increase	Negative	NTS (2016)
World consumption of oil; transport sector (1973) Mtoe/%	2252Mtoe/45%		Bad enough	IEA
World consumption of oil; transport sector (2013) Mtoe/%	3716Mtoe/64%	65% over 1973	Much worse	IEA

continued

TABLE 1.2 *continued*

Transportation factor and year of most recent credible data*	Magnitude	Projection and growth	Eco-trend	Source(s)
Top 20 world container cargo export 2014/2013TEU(a) (million)	127.6/122.35	Growing	Negative	WSC
U.S. freight movement by truck (lorry) tmi (trillions) 1980/2011(b)	1.3/2.6	Growing	Negative	NTS1–50
U.S. freight movement by railroads tmi (trillions) 1980/2011(b)	0.9/1.7	Growing	Positive	NTS1–50
U.S. freight movement by domestic water tmi (trillions) 1980/2011(b)	0.9/0.5	Decreasing	Negative	NTS1–50
U.S. freight movement by pipeline tmi (trillions) 1980/2011(b)	1.1/1.0	Decreasing slightly	Negative	NTS1–50
U.S. freight movement by air tmi (billions) 1980/2011(b)	4.5/12.1 (c)	Growing rapidly	Negative	NTS1–50
U.S. ton-km of freight-all modes (trillions) 1973/2014	7.1/37.2	Growing rapidly	Negative	WB
U.S. intl. marine shipping freight tkm (trillions) 2007	4.2	Growing	Negative	G&P
World freight movement by air (billion ton-km/ton-mile) 2015	188/113	1105% over 1973	Very negative	WB
World freight total (water, road, rail, air) tons (billion)	12.5	~5%/year	Negative	UNDEV
World maritime freight total ton (billion) 1970/1990/2000/2010/2014	2.6/4/6/8.4/9.8	Growing rapidly	Negative	UNCTAD
World maritime ton/km/mile (trillion) 2000/2014	49/30.8//84/52.6	Growing rapidly	Negative	UNCTAD
World number of passengers flown 1973 (million)/2015 (billion)	401.5/3.44	4–7%/yr. 1109% over 1970	Very negative	IATA, WB
U.S. passengers flown, domestic & intl. (millions) 1973/2015	163.5/800	5–15%/yr since 2004	Very negative	WB, IATA
U.S. commercial flight departures 1973/2015 (million)	5.1/9.5	Decrease (d)	Unclear	NTS
World commercial aviation flight departures 1973/2015 (million)	9.8/33	<1> to 8% growth/year	Very negative	WB, IATA
U.S. domestic and international air passenger km/mi (billion) 2005/2014	934/584//973/608	Growing	Negative	NTS
World commercial air passenger km/mi 2005//2014 (trillion)	3.9/2.3//6.1/3.7	Growing rapidly	Negative	ICAO
World commercial air passenger km/mi daily 2005//2014 (billion)	11/6.6//17/10	Growing rapidly	Negative	ICAO
U.S. commercial air passenger km/mi daily 2005//2014 (billion)	2.6/1.6//2.7/1.7	Growing slowly	Negative	NTS

continued

TABLE 1.2 *continued*

Source: Preston L. Schiller and Jeffrey R. Kenworthy

Notes: * This table is for heuristic-comparative rather than analytic purposes; figures are based on the most recent sources or authors' estimations when sources vary within a category. The frequency with which various institutions collect data varies considerably and there are often inconsistencies or disagreements among sources. Many figures are rounded for presentation purposes. Notes in Table: (a) Twenty-Foot Equivalent Unit; (b) domestic; (c) 18 billion according to Boeing; (d) larger planes, slightly smaller fleet (e) maritime freight accounts for between 80 & 90% of world freight (all modes) total. While all the links were accessible in 2016 when this table was revised, it is possible that some may become inaccessible or changed.

Abbreviations: PMV = Personal Motor Vehicle (includes automobiles and light trucks); km = kilometer; mi = mile; tkm =tonne kilometers; tmi = tonne miles

Data Sources

Boeing: www.boeing.com/resources/boeingdotcom/commercial/about-our-market/cargo-market-detail-wacf/download-report/assets/pdfs/wacf.pdf

BTS-1; www.transtats.bts.gov/Data_Elements.aspx?Data=3; www.TranStats.bts.gov/Data_Elements.aspx?Data=2; www.TranStats.bts.gov/Oneway.asp?Display_Flag=0&Per cent_Flag=0; CIA; www.cia.gov/library/publications/the-world-factbook/fields/print_2085.html (roads, etc.); www.cia.gov/library/publications/the-world-factbook/geos/xx.html

DulacIEA (2013) 'ETP 2012 transport outlook to 2050', www.iea.org/media/workshops/2013/egrdmobility/DULAC_23052013.pdf

G&P: Gilbert, R., and A. Perl (2010). *Transport revolutions: Moving people and freight without oil* (revised and updated ed., [2nd ed.]. ed.). Gabriola Island, BC: New Society (Figure 2.18 and Table 5.3).

GCR: www.greencarreports.com/news/1093560_1-2-billion-vehicles-on-worlds-roads-now-2-billion-by-2035-report

IATA: www.iata.org/pressroom/facts_figures/fact_sheets/Documents/fact-sheet-industry-facts.pdf; www.iata.org/pressroom/facts_figures/fact_sheets/Pages/index.aspx; www.iata.org/pressroom/pr/Pages/2015-11-26-01.aspx

ICAO: www.icao.int/annual-report-2014/Documents/Appendix_1_en.pdf

IEA: www.iea.org/publications/freepublications/publication/TransportInfrastructureInsights_FINAL_WEB.pdf

NATS: http://nats.sct.gob.mx/language/en/

NHTSA; https://crashstats.nhtsa.dot.gov/Api/Public/ViewPublication/812318

NTS2016: www.rita.dot.gov/bts/sites/rita.dot.gov.bts/files/NTS_Entire_16Q1.pdf

OICA: www.oica.net/category/vehicles-in-use/

Schäfer: Andreas Schäfer (2007) 'Long-Term Trends in Global Passenger Mobility', in Frontiers of Engineering: Reports on Leading-Edge Engineering from the 2006 Symposium, National Academy of Engineering, Washington, D.C., pp. 85–97, www.nap.edu/catalog/11827.html

UNCTAD: http://unctad.org/en/PublicationsLibrary/rmt2015_en.pdf

UNDEV: www.un.org/en/development/desa/policy/wesp/wesp_archive/2013chap2.pdf (esp. Box 1.1)

US-Census: http://factfinder.census.gov/faces/tableservices/jsf/pages/productview.xhtml?src=bkmk

WB (2006): http://data.worldbank.org/indicator/IS.AIR.GOOD.MT.K1?view=chart; http://data.worldbank.org/indicator/IS.AIR.PSGR; http://data.worldbank.org/indicator/IS.AIR.GOOD.MT.K1?view=chart;

WHO (2016): www.who.int/mediacentre/factsheets/fs358/en/#

WSC: www.worldshipping.org/about-the-industry/global-trade/trade-statistics

FIGURE 1.2
'Highways divide habitats'
Source: Andy Singer
(www.andysinger.com)

TABLE 1.3 Problems associated with automobile dependence

Environmental problems	Economic problems	Social problems
Oil vulnerability	Congestion costs	Loss of street life
Urban sprawl	High urban infrastructure costs for sewers, water mains, roads, etc.	Loss of community in neighborhoods
Photochemical smog	Loss of productive rural land	Loss of public safety
Acid rain	Loss of urban land to pavement	Isolation in remote suburbs with few amenities
High greenhouse gases; global warming	Poor transit cost recovery	Access problems for those without cars or access to cars and those with disabilities
Greater storm water runoff problems	Economic and human costs of transportation accident trauma and death	Road rage
Traffic problems: noise, neighborhood severance, visual intrusion, physical danger	High proportion of city wealth spent on passenger transportation	Anti-social behavior due to boredom in car-dependent suburbs
Decimated transit systems	Public health costs from air and other pollution Health costs from growing obesity due to sedentary auto-lifestyles Physical and mental health problems related to lack of physical activity in isolated suburbs	Enforced car ownership for lower-income households

Source: Jeffrey R. Kenworthy

transportation. Canadian and Asian cities also dropped 5% and 6% respectively. By contrast, Australian cities rose by 16% and European cities by 4%.

Because of high-energy use, 'automobile cities' also produce large quantities of greenhouse gases and emissions such as carbon monoxide, volatile hydrocarbons and nitrogen oxides, which contribute to the formation of photochemical smog. Figure 1.4 shows automotive smog emissions for the same groups of cities outlined above. Sulphur dioxide (from transportation and industry), when mixed with precipitation, causes acid rain and acid smog, which results in the acidification of inland waters and kills native forests across the planet. Such emissions do not respect national boundaries and therefore strengthen the need for regional and transnational agreements about abatement strategies.

It is the heavily auto-dependent cities in North America and Australia that have the highest per capita emissions. Averaging the data by region, U.S. and Canadian regions have a total of 185 kg and 165 kg per capita respectively, while Australian cities average 144 kg. On the other hand, the European cities average only 35 kg per capita and the two wealthy Asian cities average 34 kg. The good news is that this factor has improved remarkably in every region since 1995, with a 30% reduction in U.S. cities, 8% in Canadian cities, 28% in Australian cities, 57% in European cities and 23% in the Asian cities. This is due significantly to much stricter emissions controls and cleaner automotive technologies.

Automobile-dependent cities also lose large quantities of productive land or natural areas to suburban sprawl every year. With the peaking of world oil production, cities increasingly need to retain as much near-city agricultural production as possible to minimize the energy

FIGURE 1.3
Private passenger transportation
energy use per capita in 45 global
cities, 2005–6.

Source: Newman and Kenworthy (2015)

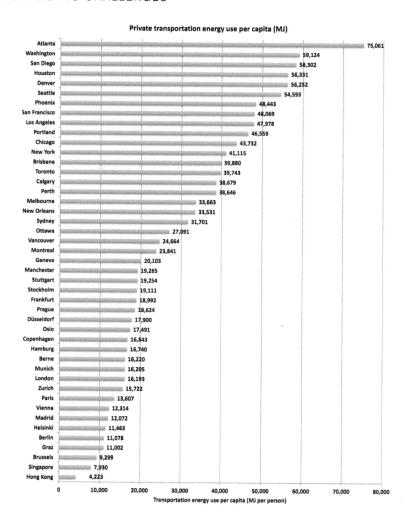

Private transportation energy use per capita (MJ)

Atlanta	75,061
Washington	59,124
San Diego	58,302
Houston	56,331
Denver	56,252
Seattle	54,593
Phoenix	48,443
San Francisco	48,069
Los Angeles	47,978
Portland	46,559
Chicago	43,732
New York	41,115
Brisbane	39,880
Toronto	39,743
Calgary	38,679
Perth	38,646
Melbourne	33,663
New Orleans	33,531
Sydney	31,701
Ottawa	27,091
Vancouver	24,664
Montreal	23,841
Geneva	20,103
Manchester	19,265
Stuttgart	19,254
Stockholm	19,111
Frankfurt	18,992
Prague	18,624
Düsseldorf	17,900
Oslo	17,491
Copenhagen	16,843
Hamburg	16,740
Berne	16,220
Munich	16,205
London	16,193
Zurich	15,722
Paris	13,607
Vienna	12,314
Madrid	12,072
Helsinki	11,463
Berlin	11,078
Graz	11,002
Brussels	9,299
Singapore	7,930
Hong Kong	4,223

Transportation energy use per capita (MJ per person)

content of food. The recent phenomenon of the '100-mile restaurant' in the U.S. and the '100-kilometer restaurant' in Canada is partly a response to this issue. Vegetated natural areas are important sinks for CO_2 and reducing the urban heat island effect.

The covering of vast areas of urban land with pavement for roads and parking and the construction of extensive low-density housing areas creates huge amounts of water runoff, which can cause flooding as well as polluted water from the oil and brake residues that build up on the pavement. Los Angeles is a prime example of this, where in some areas up to 70% of the land area is covered with roads and parking; the remainder comprises buildings, and its expansive aqueduct system is sealed in concrete to separate it from ground contamination, but is nevertheless badly polluted from pavement runoff. The problem of 'urban heat islands' is another consequence of modern cities with buildings of anti-environmental design and vast expanses of concrete and asphalt (see Chapter 6, Box 6.1 for a discussion of this and what can be done).

Traffic noise, neighborhood severance and deterioration of the public realm are a major feature of auto-dependent environments. Traffic noise pervades every aspect of life, from intrusion into dwellings and workplaces to the inability, in some cases, for conversation in public. Since the automobile began to dominate urban transport systems, neighborhoods have

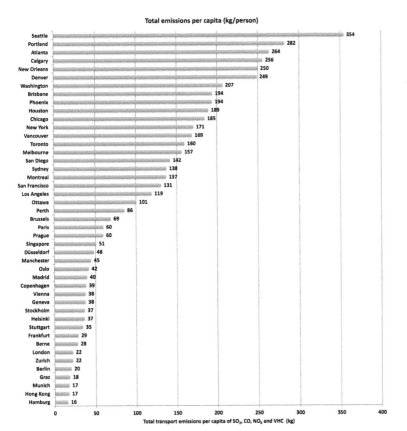

Total emissions per capita (kg/person)

Seattle	354
Portland	282
Atlanta	264
Calgary	256
New Orleans	250
Denver	249
Washington	207
Brisbane	194
Phoenix	194
Houston	189
Chicago	185
New York	171
Vancouver	169
Toronto	160
Melbourne	157
San Diego	142
Sydney	138
Montreal	137
San Francisco	131
Los Angeles	119
Ottawa	101
Perth	86
Brussels	69
Paris	60
Prague	60
Singapore	51
Düsseldorf	48
Manchester	45
Oslo	42
Madrid	40
Copenhagen	39
Vienna	38
Geneva	38
Stockholm	37
Helsinki	37
Stuttgart	35
Frankfurt	29
Berne	28
London	22
Zurich	22
Berlin	20
Graz	18
Munich	17
Hong Kong	17
Hamburg	16

Total transport emissions per capita of SO_2, CO, NO_x and VHC (kg)

FIGURE 1.4

Transportation emissions per capita from all modes in 45 global cities (NO_x, VHC, CO and SO_2), 2005–6.
Source: Newman and Kenworthy (2015)

been severed by large freeways and roads have been widened, making it impossible for neighbors to maintain contact. The U.S. Federal Highway Program, which saw thousands of miles of freeways carved into the urban fabric, destroyed hundreds of thousands of homes across the country and resulted in the fragmentation of intact well-functioning urban neighborhoods, especially working-class ones, built on easy contact among neighbors. The public realm has suffered immeasurably as streetscapes have become dominated by parking, roads and the other paraphernalia of auto-dependence, including high levels of visual intrusion from auto-scale advertising signs, or '100 km/h architecture' as Jan Gehl, the famous urban designer, calls it (Whitelegg 1993; Newman and Kenworthy 1999a; Gehl 2010).

Finally, one of the most insidious problems created by auto-dependence and its attendant land uses is the spiraling decline of transit systems. Figure 1.6 shows the annual transit service provision in vehicle kilometers provided per capita and the annual boardings per capita in 45 cities around the world. As can be seen, the U.S. and Australian cities, and, a little less so, the Canadian cities, have comparatively low levels of transit use and service. This is not because people in these cities are necessarily less willing to use transit if excellent services are provided, but rather because entire urban systems have been built around the car, resulting in the progressive marginalizing of transit systems that have become less and less able to compete in speed terms with cars—or, indeed, in most of the other factors that influence people's mode of choice, such as level of service and frequency. It is only in the European and Asian cities where transit boardings exceed 300 per capita per year that transit is competing effectively and conveniently with cars. The worst U.S. cities, Phoenix and Houston, have the equivalent of barely one transit trip per person every three weeks or so.

FIGURE 1.5 Aerial view of older grid neighbourhood with wide streets, Los Angeles

Note: LA grew as a transit city with a well-articulated street grid and one of the world's largest streetcar systems, all destroyed in the General Motors-led activity to remove streetcar systems in American cities as documented in the film Taken for a Ride (Klein and Olson, 1996).

Source: Jeffrey R. Kenworthy

Another interesting way of viewing these data is to look at the number of transit boardings for every kilometer of service provided. Figure 1.7 provides these data. In Phoenix and Houston, not even one boarding is attracted for every kilometer of service provided. On the other hand, cities such as Paris, Vienna, Zurich, Munich, Prague and even very small cities such as Graz achieve more than four boardings for every kilometer of service. New York, by the far the healthiest U.S. city in this regard, achieves 2.6 boardings per kilometer, ahead of its next closest rival, New Orleans, with 2.1. Some European cities are also less than spectacular in this regard, with Copenhagen only carrying 1.5 boardings per kilometer of service. Copenhagen also has one of the lowest densities for a European city (also see Chapter 5, Transit).

Economic problems

Automobile cities suffer many economic impacts, such as congestion costs in terms of lost time and the high costs of urban infrastructure for the extra distances that must be traversed for water, sewage and drainage systems, roads and a variety of social infrastructure such as schools, medical centers and community halls that must be duplicated as the city spreads. In the meantime, vast areas of existing urban infrastructure remain underutilized

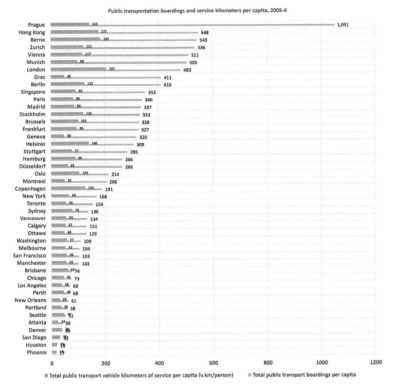

Public transportation boardings and service kilometers per capita, 2005-6

■ Total public transport vehicle kilometers of service per capita (v.km/person)　■ Total public transport boardings per capita

FIGURE 1.6

Transit system service provision and use per capita in 45 global cities, 2005–6

Note: Horizontal scale is annual boardings and vehicle kilometres per capita. Cities are ordered by boardings from highest to lowest, with corresponding service kilometers per capita.

Source: Newman and Kenworthy (2015)

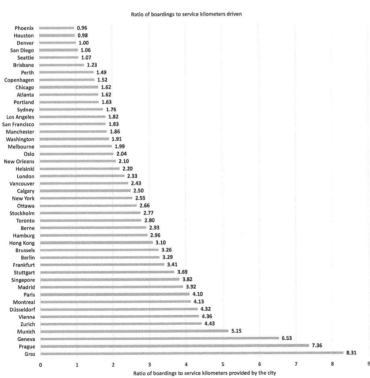

Ratio of boardings to service kilometers driven

Ratio of boardings to service kilometers provided by the city

FIGURE 1.7

Ratio of transit boardings to vehicle kilometers of service provided in 45 global cities, 2005–6

Source: Update of Millennium Cities Database (data published in another form in Newman and Kenworthy, 2015)

23

due to demographic changes and are begging for revitalization through better transit and higher densities (Newman and Kenworthy 1999a). Recent work by Trubka et al. (2012) quantifies the economic advantages, in Australian cities, of urban development in denser, more centralized forms, effectively describing urban redevelopment compared to the much more expensive fringe development. The savings in transportation and infrastructure in urban redevelopment compared to fringe development are estimated for 1,000 dwellings to be $AUD86 million up-front and $AUD250 million for the annualized transportation costs calculated over 50 years.[8]

There are also issues such as the loss of productive rural land and urban land to sprawl pavement and the conversion of corn to ethanol to feed cars rather than people. The excessive use of land in cities for the movement of cars to cater for upwards of 80% of daily trips, when other, less resource-consuming options are available, has a significant opportunity cost.

Transit systems in auto-dependent cities also tend to have lower operating cost recovery ratios—that is, the percentage of operating costs that are recovered from farebox revenues (Figure 1.8). In 2005, U.S. transit systems had the lowest recovery of all cities, at 31%, down even more from 1995 when it was 36%. By contrast, Australian cities in 2005–6 recovered 37%, Canadian cities 57%, European cities 61% and the two Asian cities of Singapore and Hong Kong achieved operating profits of 121%. Copenhagen and Manchester also operated at a profit in 2005. In contrast, Perth, Portland, Denver, Phoenix and

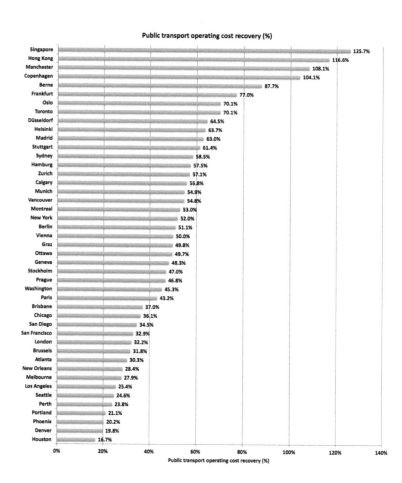

Public transport operating cost recovery (%)

Singapore	125.7%
Hong Kong	116.6%
Manchester	108.1%
Copenhagen	104.1%
Berne	87.7%
Frankfurt	77.0%
Oslo	70.1%
Toronto	70.1%
Düsseldorf	64.5%
Helsinki	63.7%
Madrid	63.0%
Stuttgart	61.4%
Sydney	58.5%
Hamburg	57.5%
Zurich	57.1%
Calgary	55.8%
Munich	54.9%
Vancouver	54.8%
Montreal	53.0%
New York	52.0%
Berlin	51.1%
Vienna	50.0%
Graz	49.8%
Ottawa	49.7%
Geneva	48.3%
Stockholm	47.0%
Prague	46.8%
Washington	45.3%
Paris	43.2%
Brisbane	37.0%
Chicago	36.1%
San Diego	34.5%
San Francisco	32.9%
London	32.2%
Brussels	31.8%
Atlanta	30.3%
New Orleans	28.4%
Melbourne	27.9%
Los Angeles	25.4%
Seattle	24.6%
Perth	23.8%
Portland	21.1%
Phoenix	20.2%
Denver	19.8%
Houston	16.7%

Public transport operating cost recovery (%)

FIGURE 1.8
Transit operating cost recovery in 45 global cities, 2005–6
Source: Newman and Kenworthy (2015)

Houston, the five lowest cities on this factor, all recovered less than 25% of their operating costs from the farebox. All these cities are low density and, although having some rail systems, are strongly bus-based systems where buses do a lot of mileage chasing passengers in scattered suburban areas (also see Chapter 5, Transit).

There are large economic costs associated with road accidents and deaths in cities. Figure 1.9 provides the number of transportation-related deaths per 100,000 people for 45 global cities as of 2005–6. It shows the vast range in this number, even in what are all relatively wealthy high-income cities. Phoenix, the highest, had 14.6 deaths per 100,000 people, while Berlin had only 2.0. The good news is that between 1995 and 2005, transportation-related deaths declined in all the regions in Figure 1.9. U.S. cities declined by 25% while Australian, Canadian, European and Asian cities went down by 31%, 4%, 39% and 28% respectively. It is unlikely that such a positive trend occurred in cities of low- and middle-income countries where motorization has clashed strongly with vulnerable non-motorized mode users.

The death toll on American roads currently stands at well over 30,000 people per year (see Table 1.2), equivalent to a full-scale war, and road crashes cost the U.S. about US$231 billion per year. Unfortunately, the improving trend for the past few years appears to be reversing itself. The global equivalent figure is about 1.25 million, of which 90% occur in low and middle income countries: around 3,300 people every day. Road accidents cost low and middle income countries about US$65billion per annum, exceeding the total amount they receive in development assistance.[9] Road accident costs worldwide are conservatively estimated to be US$518 billion.[10]

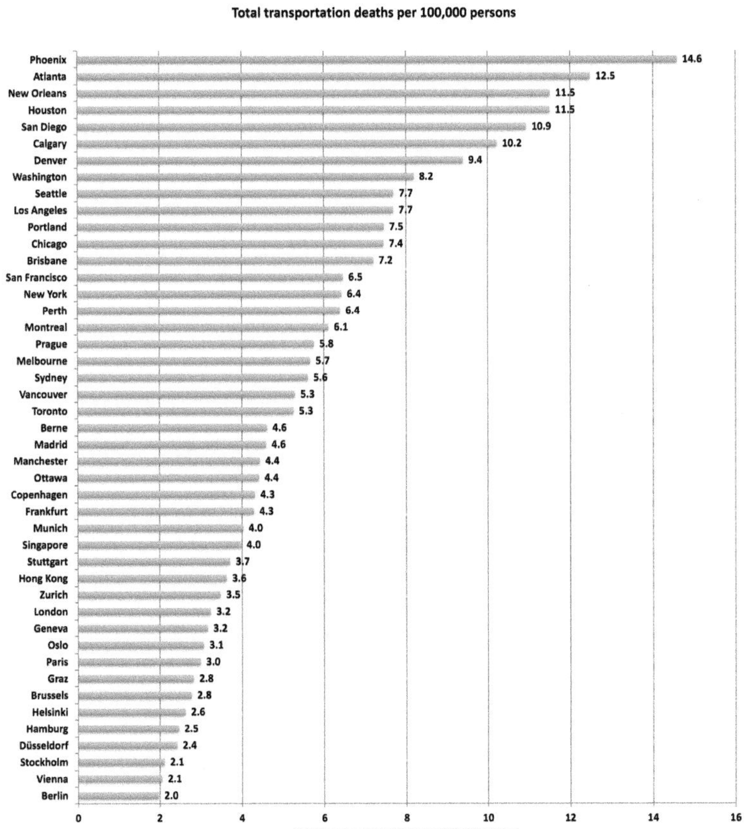

Total transportation deaths per 100,000 persons

City	Deaths
Phoenix	14.6
Atlanta	12.5
New Orleans	11.5
Houston	11.5
San Diego	10.9
Calgary	10.2
Denver	9.4
Washington	8.2
Seattle	7.7
Los Angeles	7.7
Portland	7.5
Chicago	7.4
Brisbane	7.2
San Francisco	6.5
New York	6.4
Perth	6.4
Montreal	6.1
Prague	5.8
Melbourne	5.7
Sydney	5.6
Vancouver	5.3
Toronto	5.3
Berne	4.6
Madrid	4.6
Manchester	4.4
Ottawa	4.4
Copenhagen	4.3
Frankfurt	4.3
Munich	4.0
Singapore	4.0
Stuttgart	3.7
Hong Kong	3.6
Zurich	3.5
London	3.2
Geneva	3.2
Oslo	3.1
Paris	3.0
Graz	2.8
Brussels	2.8
Helsinki	2.6
Hamburg	2.5
Düsseldorf	2.4
Stockholm	2.1
Vienna	2.1
Berlin	2.0

Total transportation deaths per 100,000 persons

FIGURE 1.9
Annual transportation deaths per 100,000 people for all modes in 45 global cities, 2005-6
Source: Newman and Kenworthy (2015)

Other, perhaps less obvious economic impacts of automobile dependence include the effects of obesity and related health problems on the health system from lack of physical activity, including walking. Studies led by Reid Ewing (2006, 2014) pursued this question and found relationships between urban form—sprawling or compact—and several deleterious health outcomes. The U.S., the world's most auto-dependent society, has approximately one-third of its adult population and 17% of its adolescents defined as officially obese, and another one-third of its adult and youth population overweight, the highest in the world (Frank et al. 2003; Levi et al. 2015; CDC 2016). In 2008, it was announced in the U.K. that there was to be a pilot program in Manchester to pay people to exercise. This was being considered because the costs to the health system for treating obesity/physical inactivity-induced health problems are so great that it would be cheaper to simply pay people to exercise to avoid such medical conditions[11] (also see the Active Transportation discussion in Chapter 6, Urban Design).

Air pollution from transportation also causes many health-related problems and even death in extreme cases, which carry an economic impact. The most obvious examples of this are the well-known 'smog events' in Los Angeles, Paris (2015) and several other cities. This is where most air pollution is created by motor vehicles leading to surface ozone levels or photochemical smog reaching dangerous levels and people being warned to stay indoors and not to exercise heavily. Photochemical smog also has other well-documented economic impacts, such as deterioration of paint on buildings, negative impacts upon car tires and the killing of leafy row vegetables and citrus crops. A current focus of attention worldwide is on the cancer-causing fine particulates (PM with a diameter of less than 10 μm (PM10) or less than 2.5 μm (PM2.5), of which diesel exhausts are a major contributor. These were behind the recent Volkswagen emissions-testing cheat scandal, which rocked the company and spread to other manufacturers where vehicles were shown not to be meeting regulatory standards.[12] This has also become a matter of concern around airports and along their flight paths in urban areas (see the discussion of Aerotropolis in Chapter 4). Cities such as Beijing are plagued with smog problems, of which particulates are a major component, and photos from the city during bad episodes have become legendary.[13]

Social problems

Perhaps less obvious than the environmental and economic issues are a host of social issues for cities linked to excessive dependence upon automobiles. Table 1.3 lists these problems, most of which can be traced back to the automobile's deleterious effect on the public realm and the nature of human interactions in auto-based societies. This is an important dimension because they relate to human capacity to respond to the demands of ST. If people lose the capacity to function in a participatory society, i.e. lose their sense of being 'citizens', then it is more difficult to enact the kind of policies and programs needed to address these problems.

Low-density auto-dependent suburbs where there are few, if any, small local shops and where little walking occurs can suffer from a lack of community feeling and a loss of street life that was common in North American and Australian suburbs only some 40 to 50 years ago. Numerous authors over many years have pointed to many problems associated with creating urban environments with a poor sense of belonging and a lack of natural surveillance. Jane Jacobs was most articulate in her defense of lively and active city streets, especially in their capacity to help form a community and enhance public safety (Jacobs 1961).

Other literature points strongly to the influence that attractive, safe and walkable environments have on the development of children, especially their capacity for independence and unassisted travel.[14] Defensive urban environments such as in gated communities and many low-density suburbs are designed for cars, not children, nor do they assist in the

FIGURE 1.10
Gated community in São Paulo, Brazil
Source: Michael Peterek

formation of friendly, interactive neighborhoods. Lasch (1991), referring to Jane Jacobs, reminds us of the important role played by the public realm in cities: that well-used public spaces, including sidewalks, teach people—especially youth—civic responsibility as opposed to cities that privatize space or restrict equitable access to public space (pp. 64–5).

We can find endless examples in cities of gated, unfriendly human environments that are the logical extension or expression of a declining public realm in cities. On the other hand, cities can give expression to cultural values associated with social interaction and shared space, which result in entirely different patterns of urban community and means of transport. For example, in central cities such as Stockholm (Sweden), Freiburg (Germany) and San Jose (U.S.), urban spaces present the kind of real public environments that encourage independence in children and convey the sense that a city is a safe and interesting place. In many Swedish urban and suburban environments, other values of community, interaction and safe streets are expressed, such as in the Skärpnack development in Stockholm, in Angered Centrum in Gothenburg and Freiburg's Vauban (the latter discussed in Chapters 9 and 10). Such environments encourage children's independence and development. The role of an attractive public realm that functions from a human perspective is paramount in delivering such urban qualities (Kenworthy 2000; Kenworthy 2010a).

The decline of the public realm in cities is well depicted in Mike Davis's (1990) book *City of Quartz*, a detailed portrayal of the decline of Los Angeles (and a metaphor for urban America, more generally), which turns primarily on the destruction of the public realm and the descent into what he calls 'Fortress LA' and the 'ecology of fear'. In an interview, Davis eloquently described Los Angeles as suffering from sprawl, social and racial polarization, brutal policing and criminalizing, fortified suburbia, irresponsible government, the movie studio creation of 'parallel urban reality' for tourists, and extreme 'malling of public space' deleterious to the social development of youth.[15]

The situation of youth, from young children through teens being hovered over and helicoptered from one structured activity to another by PMVs contrasts sharply with the situation of their counterparts in many more enlightened communities, such as the Vauban (described in Chapters 9 and 10). For a trenchant critique of 'unreal urban environments' stemming from the excessive strip-malling of U.S. urban areas see Kunstler (1996, p. 32) and Chapter 2 Box 2.2.

BOX 1.2 Size does (and doesn't) matter!

A prominent theme that crops up in discussions about urban transportation is the role of city size in understanding or even determining transportation patterns. Most commentators refer to population when dealing with this size matter, but of course the question of urban density also arises because if one combines a large population with a low density, then the physical spread of a city becomes a major issue, due to the sheer distances that must be covered for commuting and other trips. The Tri-State Metropolitan Region of New York, with some 20 million people, is developed at only twenty persons per ha and is thus very large in physical spread. This is notwithstanding the fact that New York City, a part of the region now with some 8.5 million people, has a density of around 100 persons per ha (Kenworthy and Laube 1999).

Conversely, we can have very large metropolitan regions such as Tokyo, which has a population—depending on the exact definition of the metro region—of around 34 million people (Tokyo-to metropolis plus, Kanagawa, Chiba and Saitama Prefectures), but with an urban density around 70 persons per ha (Kenworthy and Laube 1999). Thus, if we were to populate the New York region at the same density of Tokyo, we could accommodate 90 million people. Looked at another way, we could fit two-and-a-half Tokyo metro regions into the NY region.

At the other end of the spectrum, even cities with small populations can be large in physical spread, if they are developed at low densities. We, therefore, find that in the USA, for example, there are many small urbanized areas of between 150,000 and around 5–600,000 people that have urban densities lower than six persons per ha. This is less than half the density of rural Java, which in 1970 was 13 persons per ha (Penny and Singarimbun 1973). The densities are so low that all urban functions and urban life occur at a very diluted, spread out scale.

What does the question of size mean for transportation? One of the common arguments goes like this. Cities are far too big. They necessitate inordinately long travel distances that are not suited to public transportation and are most convenient by car. If we want to reduce our car dependence, cities need to be smaller.

This and other matters can be examined by referring to key data. U.S. cities have comprehensive data on many factors and provide an ideal laboratory to explore these questions. This small study by the authors uses the 128 official Urbanized Areas defined by the U.S. Census in 1990, with populations ranging from 158,553 (Utica-Rome) up to 16,044,012 (New York, North-Eastern, New Jersey) and urban densities ranging from 4.5 persons per hectare in the Chatanooga Urbanized Area to 22.4 persons per ha in the Los Angeles-Long Beach-Pomona-Ontario Urbanized Area. Assembling data from the U.S. Census, as well as the U.S. Federal Highway Administration (FHWA), it is possible to see what relationships exist between factors when mediated by population size and urban density of the urbanized areas.

Firstly, the urban density of each region was calculated from the U.S. Census data in persons per ha. The metro regions were then sorted from the highest to the lowest density (in this case 4.5 to 22.4 persons per ha). For simplicity, the 128 Urbanized Areas were divided into six groups based on urban density (sixteen cities with 0.1 to 5.9 persons per ha; thirty-six cities with a density of 6.0 to 7.9 persons per ha; thirty-one cities with 8.0 to 9.9; thirty cities with 10.0 to 12.9; ten cities with 13.0 to 16.9 and only five cities of 17.0 to 23.0 persons per ha).

For each factor, the average was calculated for each of these six groups of cities. What does this show us? Firstly, Figure 1 shows that the lowest density (and smallest) cities have the highest VKT per capita (13,300 km), while the highest density cities (and largest in both population and physical size) have the least amount of driving in private vehicles (10,100 km per capita).

We also find that the annual vehicle kilometers of travel (VKT) per capita is significantly larger in the smallest group of cities (which average only 338,000 people), while the largest urbanized areas, with an average population of 6 million people, have by far the smallest amount of VKT per capita.

These results run counter to the idea that big cities cause more travel by car due to more trips by car over longer distances. What appears to happen is that as the the city grows larger, public transportation systems become more developed and of a better standard, often involving more rail-based modes. As U.S.

continued

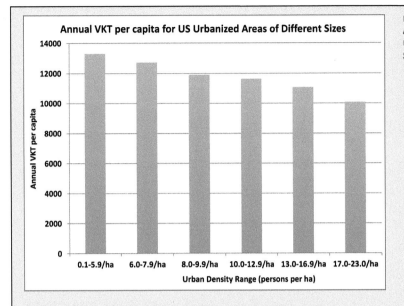

Annual VKT per capita for US Urbanized Areas of Different Sizes

BOX 1.2 FIGURE 1
Annual VKT per capita for US
urbanized areas by urban density
Source: Jeffrey R. Kenworthy

cities get bigger, the data show that they also get denser, which often means that there are significant areas where density (and mixed-land uses) grow to a level where walking, and often cycling, become more viable. The smaller cities tend to have less extensive and inferior public transit systems, mostly based only on buses.

One might also expect that in smaller cities walking and cycling would account for more travel and help to keep car use down. But this is also not the case, especially in U.S. cities, where the small urban settlements are also very low in density (and with little mixed-land use), meaning that many destinations are simply beyond a comfortable walk or bike ride. On top of that, walking and cycling infrastructure is very poor, which further discourages use of these modes due to danger and inconvenience.

In addition to the size of population and physical area of cities, it is often argued that the size of one's income also has a lot to do with how much one will choose to use private transportation modes—more income, more car use. Figure 2 shows the annual VKT per capita against the average per capita income of U.S. urbanized areas of different sizes; average income per capita grows as the cities get progressively larger and denser, while the VKT per capita declines. Apparently driving has a lot more to do with factors other than wealth.

Another way that urbanized areas differ from each other is in transportation infrastructure. For example, what is the size of the freeway system? Interestingly, we see here that as cities get bigger, their freeways get bigger in terms of lane size and the proportion of total driving that occurs within them also gets bigger. Figures 3 and 4 demonstrate these key points by showing how the average number of lanes per freeway rises from under 4.5 lanes in the smallest cities to just over 6 lanes in the largest cities. Likewise, the percentage of total driving that occurs on freeways systematically increases from over 26% in the smallest to over 37% in the largest cities.

This is notwithstanding the fact that Figure 4 shows how freeways as a proportion of total road system length remain at between only 2.8% and 3.4% and this does not vary in any systematic way across the different size urbanized areas.

Finally, however, we see a fundamental problem of private motorized transportation. That is the fact that as U.S. urbanized areas get bigger, the average freeway lane length per capita decreases, despite the other trends already explained of a growing proportion of total driving on freeways and wider freeways as cities get bigger. Figure 3 shows these data, demonstrating that the smallest cities have some 10 to 11 meters of lane length per 10 people while the biggest cities have only 6.5 meters.

continued

BOX 1.2 FIGURE 2
Per capita income and VKT
in US urbanized areas by
population size
Source: Jeffrey R. Kenworthy

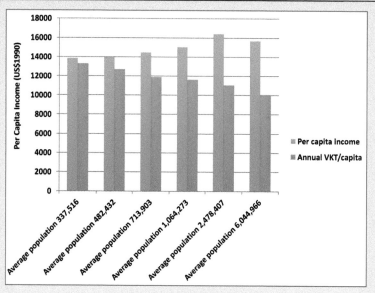

BOX 1.2 FIGURE 3
Average width of freeways
(number of lanes) and freeway
lane length per capita in US
urbanized areas by population
size
Source: Jeffrey R. Kenworthy

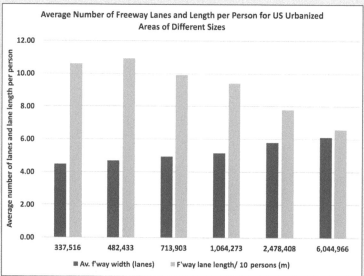

These data show that the cities with the least per capita availability of freeway capacity have the lowest amount of private motorized travel.

In short, size both matters and does not matter. It does not matter that cities are small, in the sense that smallness will not guarantee less car use due to more use of walking and cycling. On the contrary, small city size in the U.S. is associated with lower densities, high amounts of freeway availability, poor transit systems, very little walking and cycling and lots of driving.

Size does matter in terms of enabling cities to reduce the amount of driving. This is an agglomeration economies effect, with bigger cities developing higher densities, better and bigger transit systems and larger areas where densities and mixed-land use better allow for walking and cycling. Bigger cities also reach limits on how much freeway can be provided without destroying the urban fabric (Newman and Kenworthy 2015).

continued

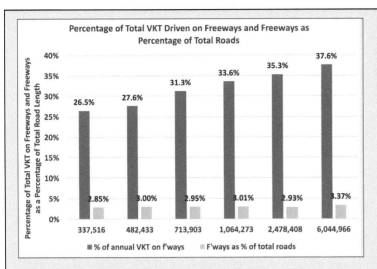

BOX 1.2 FIGURE 4
Proportion of annual VKT driven on freeways and freeways as proportion of total road length in US urbanized areas by population size
Source: Jeffrey R. Kenworthy

So, despite bigger cities having wider freeways and a higher proportion of annual travel occurring on those freeways, there is less total driving overall because there is more use of other modes. A big physical size does not generate more car travel due to longer distances.

Finally, the size of one's income also does not determine the level of private motorized travel, where in U.S. urbanized areas the wealthier cities on average have the least amount of driving per capita.

Source: Jeffrey R. Kenworthy

The public realm under the above philosophies or outlooks has become a place that is often very hostile. Such problems are not peculiar to American cities; they are also apparent in Australian cities, although perhaps in a subtler way. Social commentator Hugh Mackay (1993, 1994) offered a brilliant critique of how suburban life, especially its tendency towards the escapism of obsession with home-bound privacy and self-sufficient entertainment he terms 'caving', has seriously weakened the public realm.

While the transportation and some livability aspects of major cities, especially in North America, may seem grim, the situation of these factors in smaller cities may not be much better or even worse as the discussion in Box 1.2, 'Size does (and doesn't) matter!' indicates.

Beyond the social, economic and environmental problems associated with automobile dependence, there are serious problems of social injustice and inequity. In the following section, unequal access to transportation or urban amenities and necessities fostered or maintained by current BAU arrangements is explored.

Equity, social justice and auto-dependence

Effective access to amenities and services in cities is a key measure of the performance of the urban transportation system. A fundamental principle, then, of sound urban and transportation planning is the delivery of effective 'access for all' without discrimination as to income, ethnicity, physical ability, housing location, mode of travel or any other factor (Schaeffer and Sclar 1975). Effective and equitable access means many different things— for example, the difference between an easy and difficult commute. It may even, under certain circumstances, mean the difference between getting a job or not. It can make the difference between easy travel to schools, shops, medical services, recreational facilities and entertainment or a cumulative deprivation leading to real social problems. Access, in other words, profoundly affects the quality of urban life. It is an essential good, which depends on the effectiveness of transportation systems and, as transportation and urban theorists increasingly stress, on better urban spatial organization, which reduces the need for expensive private motorized movement.[16]

The transportation systems that help to supply access can be expensive in terms of public, environmental and other external costs. The question, then, of how transportation costs are distributed between individuals and households is very important because this distribution of costs, along with the distribution of access-related goods and services themselves, determines the equity of access which urban systems deliver (Rawls 1971). In the absence of commonly accepted standards relating to minimum household or individual entitlements—or acceptable levels of inequality—no firm judgment about equity or justice is possible (Newman et al. 1992).

In transportation, the issues that most challenge disadvantaged and discriminated-against populations and the sustainability agenda are:

- Inequitable or lack of access to transportation, especially transit, and good walking and bicycling facilities.
- Funding and planning: underrepresentation in policy-making, planning and the funding of projects that could be of benefit to them.
- Affordability: the costs of transportation, including its share of household income; poor persons pay a much larger share of their income on transportation than do wealthier persons.
- Discrimination in service and employment in the transportation industry based on socio-economic, ethnic or racialized status.
- The siting of undesirable and dangerously polluting facilities, such as major highways, airports, large freight yards in or adjacent to minority communities.
- Residential patterns that enforce uneven and unequal transportation access to employment, education, vital services and retail—including food markets for disadvantaged populations.
- Accessibility barriers—especially language and cultural barriers for recently arrived immigrants who, as a transportation disadvantaged group, can scarce afford to become car-dependent and whose assimilation and employability would be eased with quality transit.

While most societies need to grapple with some degree of inequity, the U.S. has been extremely burdened by its history of imposing the most severe of these inequities on its African-American population. Centuries of legally enforced segregation in transportation were formalized by the infamous *Plessy v. Ferguson* Supreme Court decision of 1896 in favor of the State of Louisiana's 'right' under the U.S. Constitution to segregate railway passengers in 'separate but equal' facilities—which were, in fact, separate but never equal. Such formalized segregation became commonly known as 'Jim Crow'.[17] This doctrine was extended widely to many public realms in the U.S., from residential barriers to public education until it was struck down by the Supreme Court in its 1954 *Brown v. Board of Education of Topeka* overturning of segregation laws.

Efforts at realizing transportation justice have found support in U.S. federal policy beginning with the ISTEA reforms of the 1990s[18] and in aspects of the U.S. Civil Rights Act and its amendments as well as many state and local initiatives. Prof. Robert D. Bullard has been an outstanding leader in the struggle for transportation equity and justice (see Box 1.3).

Transportation and locational disadvantage

Reduced capacity to use or afford automobiles is clearly a key factor in determining what can be termed transportation disadvantage. Land-use planning and investment in urban

BOX 1.3 Robert D. Bullard: In the forefront of the struggle for transportation justice

An important ingredient of the sustainability agenda is the realization of justice in transportation through the overcoming of barriers that maintain inequity and discriminate against and damage the socioeconomically disadvantaged and ethnic and racialized minorities. Robert D. Bullard[i] has been at the forefront of this movement for several decades, beginning with his work for decent and well-located housing opportunities for African-Americans in the 1970s and then moving into transportation planning and provision in more recent decades. In 2003, he described the range of issues involved:

> Despite the heroic efforts and the monumental social and economic gains made over the decades, transportation remains a civil rights issue. Transportation touches every aspect of where we live, work, play, and go to school, as well as the physical and natural world. Transportation also plays a pivotal role in shaping human interaction, economic mobility, and sustainability.
>
> Transportation provides access to opportunity and serves as a key component in addressing poverty, unemployment, and equal opportunity goals while ensuring access to education, health care, and other public services. Transportation equity is consistent with the goals of the larger civil rights movement and the environmental justice movement . . . as a basic right.
>
> Transportation is basic to many other quality of life indicators such as health, education, employment, economic development, access to municipal services, residential mobility, and environmental quality. The continued residential segregation of people of color away from suburban job centers (where public transit is inadequate or non-existent) may signal a new urban crisis and a new form of 'residential apartheid.' Transportation investments, enhancements, and financial resources have provided advantages for some communities, while . . . other(s) . . . have been disadvantaged by . . . decision making.
>
> (pp. 1183–4)

Bullard cites several examples of injustice and inequity and how communities have challenged these. One of the most dramatic examples was:

> . . . the kind of transit racism that killed seventeen-year-old Cynthia Wiggins of Buffalo, New York. Wiggins, an African American, was crushed by a dump truck while crossing a seven-lane highway, because Buffalo's Number Six bus, an inner-city bus used mostly by African Americans, was not allowed to stop at the suburban Walden Galleria Mall. Cynthia had not been able to find a job in Buffalo, but she did secure work at a fast-food restaurant in the suburban mall. The bus stopped about 300 yards away from the mall.
>
> (p. 1193)

In the aftermath of the killing, lawsuits won reparations for the Wiggins' family and buses were finally allowed to enter mall property. It is not uncommon in the U.S. for large shopping malls—many of them owned and managed by interests in financial centers very distant from the localities they gain income from—to either exclude transit or keep its presence at some distance from major entrances. Persons who arrive by transit, including many mall employees, are simply not seen as valued beings. The transit changes at the Walden Galleria Mall, and similar struggles elsewhere, benefit the disadvantaged considerably, but also benefit the wider public in creating a viable transit option unavailable before. But it appears that many large commercial entities are still turning a deaf ear to those seeking equitable treatment: As recent as March, 2016, a little over a mile away from the Walden Galleria Mall, a new Walmart appears to be resisting transit access (McCarthy 2016). The struggle continues.

Source: Preston L. Schiller

[i] See: drrobertbullard.com (accessed 25 March 2016). Also: Bullard 2003; Bullard and Johnson, 1997; Bullard, Johnson and Torres 2004.

infrastructure can minimize or exacerbate both the extent and the intensity of transportation disadvantage. Where those unable to use or afford automobiles live closer to employment and other essential services, or where there is access to regular and reliable transit, these vulnerabilities may not lead to serious access problems. If people find themselves in more remote fringe locations where travel distances are typically longer and transit systems are often reduced to poor demand-responsive bus systems, access problems can be great.

Economic forces over many years in many auto-oriented societies (and others, including many developing cities) have caused increasing numbers of aspiring homeowners to settle in the less well-serviced urban fringe where land is cheap. In wealthy auto-based societies, this is manifested in endless tracts of poor-quality, low-density suburban housing with few transportation options other than the automobile and few amenities (Newman et al. 1992). In developing cities, such as those in Latin America, millions of people seeking a better life in giant cities, e.g. Rio de Janeiro or São Paulo, simply inhabit slums or *favela*, or, at best, very poor makeshift housing areas, where they then flood into the employment-rich areas on informal or very low-grade formal bus systems, sometimes transferring onto metro or commuter rail systems—where those exist, and where they can afford to pay the fares (Vasconcellos 2001).

In Australian cities, where inner areas were traditionally the address for poorer working-class populations, they have now mostly become the province of the rich. There is a mixed picture in the U.S., where both poorer and wealthier households can be seen inhabiting fringe regions of metropolitan areas, and still the inner cities have many low-income neighborhoods—but this is changing with the gentrification of many older areas in U.S. cities.

Many households of low to middle income in outer areas face the choice of using poor transit or of devoting an increasing proportion of limited household income to the high costs of auto-ownership and use. Where low-density peripheral expansion or BAU continues, auto-dependence becomes increasingly built into the form and fabric of the city. Essentially, the capacity to afford and use automobiles becomes the key to the enjoyment of adequate and equitable access in the modern automobile-dependent city (Newman et al. 1992). Schaeffer and Sclar analyzed this interplay of urban form and transportation in their famous study *Access for All*, and drew attention to its ethical implications:

> The automobile has given improved mobility to the middle class, middle aged. But these owner drivers have not merely gained new mobility through the car; they have also rearranged the physical location patterns of society to suit their own private needs, and unwittingly in the process destroyed and limited the mobility and access of all others.
>
> (1975, p. 6)

In U.S. cities, these issues also have a racial dimension. Very often transportation disadvantage and inequity are centered in communities with African-American and Hispanic populations. In the early era of freeway expansion, many of the expansive roads were built in ways that concentrated minority populations within the 'walls' of surrounding expressways with most of the old connecting streets severed by the new limited-access roads. There are problems of insufficient access to transit and poor transit services, as was seen in New Orleans, where so many low-income people were unable to escape the devastation of Hurricane Katrina because there was simply no transportation to allow them to do so. Unemployment in such communities can be high, while the lower paid and unskilled jobs, which are often part-time, are frequently located in areas that demand long commutes. Automobile commuting is not economically rational relative to the amount of money being earned; where commuting on transit is not feasible, people are essentially excluded from the job markets.[19]

The sub-prime mortgage meltdown in the U.S. in 2008, with its toxic loans, was concentrated in amenity-poor, auto-based suburbs where people were already stretching budgets to make mortgage payments. The record oil prices of 2008 pushed these areas over the edge economically, with disastrous effects both for families and the global economy persisting to this time. The equity implications in an automobile-dependent city are that those who must manage without automobiles suffer not just from a lack of mobility, but also accessibility because they must travel in an urban environment that is hostile to alternative modes. Dispersed and low-density urban forms have placed important journeys beyond safe and easy walking and bicycling distance, and beyond the time reach of transit (Schaeffer and Sclar 1975). Illich (1973) was one of the first to recognize technologically driven exclusion of alternatives to the automobile as a 'radical monopoly'.

Although a substantial portion of auto-ownership costs are fixed, most transportation costs vary with distance traveled. Notwithstanding differences across income groups, all will contain some households who must travel longer distances than others. Location is critical in determining this, and those living in outer and fringe urban zones will be spending more on transportation than those living closer to urban centers. For wealthier households, who choose more remote locations for the sake of environmental amenity, this may not be a problem. But for poorer households, who may be going into debt to make ends meet, it can seriously exacerbate the difficulties and stresses of more generalized financial hardship and the relative deprivations described above (Newman et al. 1992; Morris 1981, p. 39).

Analysis of fuel consumption patterns in Sydney, Melbourne and Perth strongly confirms these observations (Newman et al. 1990). Per capita fuel use is significantly different between individual suburbs.[20] One recent study that tends to bring all this together and highlights the problems is that from Dodson and Sipe (2006, 2014), in which they produced a new index called VAMPIRE: Vulnerability Assessment for Mortgage, Petrol and Inflation Risks and Expenses. The VAMPIRE index is constructed from four indicator variables obtained from the 2001 Australian Bureau of Statistics Census, combined to provide a composite mortgage and oil vulnerability index for Australian cities. The variables are:

1   Auto-dependence: proportion of those working who undertook a journey to work by car (driver or passenger);
2   Proportion of households with two or more cars;
3   Income level: median weekly household income;
4   Mortgages: proportion of dwelling units that are being purchased (either through a mortgage or a rent/buy scheme).

The VAMPIRE map for Melbourne is available on the web, and it has been applied to other Australian cities.[21] It clearly shows the equity problem in modern cities. The amenity- and transit-rich, high-value, culturally attractive and now high-income inner areas of Australian cities have a very low vulnerability to mortgage costs, fuel prices and inflation risks. Wealthy people who have the greatest capacity to pay for accessibility and mobility now live in areas where transportation needs are at a minimum and are thus highly privileged. Lower-income households live in amenity- and transit-poor areas farthest from the core city and significant centers, where transportation needs and costs are highest, but they have the least capacity to pay. The only variant to this pattern is along the suburban rail lines, which have fingers into the far outer suburbs. Location near these lines lessens one's vulnerability.

In the U.S. and Canada, there have been several notable efforts to reverse locational disadvantage and promote location efficiency, which can be defined broadly as the encouragement of development at appropriate levels of density and mixes of uses to enable access to quality transit, walking and cycling and employment. Chicago's Center for Neighborhood Technology (CNT) has been in the forefront of this effort after the concept was first developed by the Sierra Club's John Holtzclaw and collaborators at the Natural Resources

Defense Council (NRDC) and the Surface Transportation Policy Project (STPP) as part of an effort to promote the location efficient mortgage (LEM) as a tool that could be used by federal housing authorities in the U.S. (Holtzclaw et al. 2002). The LEM would increase the amount of a mortgage loan granted for housing located close to transit. The CNT has more recently developed an excellent website called AllTransit (http://alltransit.cnt.org) accessed July 16, 2017, which reveals quantitatively the social and economic benefits of transit in communities across the USA.

Summary

This discussion of equity in relation to auto-dependence has highlighted three dimensions of transportation disadvantage and inequitable access in cities:

1   The transportation disadvantage associated with incapacities to afford or use auto-mobiles: in an urban environment in which alternative transportation modes have been effectively eliminated in many areas or are declining is perhaps the most crucial inequality. A disadvantaged group often seriously affected by automobility and locational disadvantage issues is that of recent immigrants who are sufficiently challenged by their status as 'newcomers' and can ill afford the added burden of automobile dependency.

2   The question of transportation costs borne by households and individuals: transportation, particularly private automobiles, are expensive. Lower-income households able to reach across the threshold of auto-ownership may experience greater strain and be forced to make greater sacrifices than those enjoying higher incomes.

3   The added burdens imposed by distance and poor location: notwithstanding the high fixed cost of auto-ownership, the costs of transportation vary with distances traveled. Those living closer to city centers and significant sub-centers around cities, especially those built around rail stations where access to a rich array of services is highest, are significantly better off in all income groups, whether they depend on automobiles or on centralized transit systems. Such issues in the U.S. often have an added racial dimension that urgently needs to be addressed.

Some key questions arise from all this. How close to universal auto-ownership can we realistically go, given the intractable individual human limitations of income, age, physical and mental ability and so on? Conversely, how large is the population of those unable to use automobiles likely to be in the future? In the U.S. and Australia during the early 1990s, around half the population did not have motor vehicle licenses (Zuckerman 1991), so the idea of a unitary common good, often cited in the 1950s and 1960s about the benefits of new roads and more automobiles, hardly can be justified now or then.

It is perhaps finally worth drawing attention to the fact that many households do not have access to two or more automobiles. In urban Australia, for example, less than about half of the households enjoy the luxury of two or more autos. When one adds vulnerable individuals in one-auto households to the half million or so households who have no automobile, the problems of equitable access loom much larger. Certainly, significant vulnerable populations—the young, the old, the disabled and, in some cases, significant proportions of the female population—are often very disadvantaged in automobile-dependent cities.

Importantly and, finally, even if it were possible to achieve universal auto-ownership, the other environmental, social and economic costs of auto-dependence are so great that urban systems cannot sustain endlessly expanding private mobility. Everything then points to the fundamental need for a radical rethink of the urban transportation issue and its basic tenets—a sustainability driven approach.[22]

Conclusions

This chapter has analyzed several of the key issues and challenges for ST. The sheer magnitude of travel and freight movement in everyday life, its impacts and benefits and the consequences of overdependence on automobility, with its accompanying inequities experienced under BAU transportation, mean that sustainable transportation has its work cut out for itself. The next chapter is an exploration of the 'car culture', the system of beliefs and values that maintain hypermobility, automobile dependence and inequity.

Questions for discussion

•   Discuss the strengths and limitations of the definition of sustainable transportation. How might you change it?

- Is transportation planning and provision (infrastructure, transit, etc.) in your community oriented towards business as usual (BAU) or sustainable transportation (ST)? Cite examples.

- Identify and discuss some examples of automobile dependence and hypermobility in your community and daily life.

Notes

1 See: www.unece.org/es/sustainable-development/millennium-development-goals/millennium-development-goals.html (accessed 25 March 2016).
2 See: www.unece.org/sustainable-development/sustainable-development/home.html (accessed 25 March 2016).
3 See: www.unece.org/trans/side-events/transport-for-sustainable-development.html, 2011 (accessed 25 March 2016) and https://unhabitat.org/new-urban-agenda-adopted-at-habitat-iii/ (accessed 16 July 2017).
4 See: www.unece.org/?id=9890 and www.unece.org/trans/welcome.html (accessed 25 March 2016).
5 These include Tolley (1990), Whitelegg (1993, 1997), CST (1998), Banister (2000) and Benfield and Replogle (2002).
6 See Wiederkehr et al. (2004), for this and another more detailed environmentally-oriented definition as part of their summary of the Environmentally Sustainable Transport (EST) project.
7 As opposed to 'soft path' approaches; see Lovins (1977)
8 See: www.reconnectingamerica.org/assets/Uploads/pb_cusp_urban_v_fringe_research.pdf (accessed 25 March 2016) and https://unhabitat.org/new-urban-agenda-adopted-at-habitat-iii/ (accessed 16 July 2017).
9 See: Association for Safe International Road Travel (undated) http://asirt.org/initiatives/informing-road-users/road-safety-facts/road-crash-statistics and www.who.int/mediacentre/factsheets/fs358/en/ (accessed 25 March 2016).
10 See: www.who.int/mediacentre/factsheets/fs358/en/ and http://asirt.org/initiatives/informing-road-users/road-safety-facts/road-crash-statistics (both accessed 8 October 2016).
11 See: www.telegraph.co.uk/news/uknews/1576430/Obesity-crisis-get-paid-to-lose-weight.html (accessed 25 March 2016).
12 See: Smith (2008) www.euro.who.int/__data/assets/pdf_file/0006/189051/Health-effects-of-particulate-matter-final-Eng.pdf and www.bbc.com/news/business-34324772 (both accessed 8 October, 2016).
13 See: World Air Quality (undated) aqicn.org/city/beijing/ and www.theguardian.com/cities/gallery/2015/dec/08/beijing-air-pollution-red-alert-smog-before-after-pictures (accessed 25 March 2016).
14 See Lynch (1977), van Vliet (1983), Wohlwill (1985) and Kenworthy (2000).
15 Cited in Dery 1995, pp. 43–6.
16 See Goodwin et al. (1991), Mohr (1991), Newman et al. (1992), Calthorpe (1993) and Katz (1994).
17 After a famous nineteenth-century white person in black face doing a derogatory vaudeville characterization of African-Americans; see Pilgrim, D. 2012.
18 See Box 7.2, 'ISTEA' in Chapter 7 and discussion in Chapter 5, Transit, as well as Chapter 2, Car Culture.
19 See Rothschild (2009). Also, Morgan Spurlock's television series *30 Days* dealt with this issue in the first episode of the first season, where he attempted to live on minimum wage for 30 days, using mass transit to get to several jobs from his out-of-the-way apartment.
20 For example, Fremantle and Padbury are extremes in Perth and indicate that average households spent three times as much on fuel in the low-density outer suburbs as in the compact mixed-land-use area of Fremantle.
21 See Dodson and Sipe (2006, 2014) and Infrastructure Australia citations above; for the VAMPIRE map see: Urban Research Program, Griffith University www.theage.com.au/ed_docs/Vulnerability.pdf (accessed 25 March 2016); also see Newman and Kenworthy, 2015.
22 See Whitelegg and Haq (2003), especially Chapters 1 and 25.

CHAPTER TWO

Automobile cities, the car culture and alternative possibilities

Introduction

The previous chapter provided definitions of sustainable transportation (ST) and explored two of its major challenges: automobile dependence and equity and inequity in transportation. This chapter examines how cities evolved from walking cities to automobile cities and how an elaborate and powerful 'car culture' developed around greater dependence on automobiles. The chapter also investigates several facets of the car culture: in our cognitive and affective interactions with the motor vehicle, in the media, advertising and our built environment.

Walking cities, transit cities and automobile cities[1]

Walking cities

Urban life extends back thousands of years and over this long period all cities were basically dependent upon walking for their circulation needs (Kostof 1991). Many walking cities were also walled cities and all growth had to be accommodated by increasing densities and intensifying the mixture of land uses. In Europe, the walking city was dominant up until around 1850, when walking or, at best, horse-drawn transport was the chief means of movement. These were slow forms of transport and for the city to remain accessible all destinations had to be available within about half an hour, traveling at about 5km/h. The cities, therefore, remained small and dense, with highly mixed land uses. The surrounding countryside was preserved for farming or natural open spaces such as wood lots and forests (Newman and Kenworthy 1999a). Walking cities are conceptualized in Figure 2.1.

Walking cities had many public spaces, plazas and markets, which are depicted in white in the diagram. The diagram may suggest that walking cities had little planning but in fact, ancient Chinese and Japanese cities were strongly planned around a grid-street network (e.g. Chang'an in China and the former Japanese capital, Kyoto). The Romans planned their walking settlements around two principal axes, the Cardo Maximus, the main or central north–south-oriented street, and the Decumanus Maximus, the main east–west-oriented road (Hall, 1998).

The walking city was characterized by narrow, often winding, streets and provided for an inherently egalitarian transport system. Some people had horses and carriages, but the advantages afforded by this were more related to comfort than any major accessibility benefit. No one in a walking city was locationally disadvantaged in a transport sense, which cannot be said for cities today, designed as they are around the automobile. As described in Chapter 1, in automobile cities, many people who live in the outer suburbs and urban fringe to find cheap land discover that their access needs are difficult to meet by any mode apart from the car. Such people live with enforced car ownership due to their location within the city and are especially disadvantaged with respect to walking (Newman et al. 1992; Newman et al. 2016).

Chinese cities, even in the mid-1990s, were still predominantly walking- and cycling-based (Kenworthy and Laube 2001). However, the Chinese government strongly promoted the domestic automobile industry as one of the pillars of its industrialization policy, and over two decades there has been a large increase in car ownership and car travel and a very big reduction in walking and cycling. The environment for pedestrians and cyclists has been severely disrupted throughout many Chinese cities (Kenworthy and Hu 2002; Kenworthy and Townsend 2002; Gao et al. 2015; Gao and Kenworthy 2016). Beijing reduced from 48% of daily trips by foot and bicycle in 1995 to 22% in 2012, though cities such as Shanghai, even after this period, still have some 55% of daily trips by foot and bicycle, down from 78% in 1995 (Kenworthy 2016).

Today there are many examples from around the world of walking cities that became overrun with cars during the 1950s and 1960s, but which, over time, have gradually reclaimed their walking qualities (e.g. Freiburg and Munich in Germany and Copenhagen in Denmark). In 1967, Copenhagen began to gradually remove a small per cent of central city parking spaces every year until they had transformed their city center back into its traditional walking city form (Gehl and Gemzøe 2004).

Transit cities

The transit or public transport city emerged in the industrial world around 1850 with the advent of new transport technologies—namely, the revolutionary steam train and electric tram. Preceding these modes were the horse-drawn tram operating on wooden tracks and the steam tram, pulled by chains, which were powered by a stationary steam engine. These modes facilitated faster travel (on average, a jump from about 5km/h to 15km/h) and, hence, bigger cities, although all urban development had to remain within an easy walk or bicycle trip of the tram stops or rail stations. These cities, therefore, still had quite high densities of land use and there was a well-defined 'edge' to urban settlements (nodes around rail stations and tight corridors around tramlines). A high-density, mixed-use urban form also meant that there were still a very large number of trips that could be conveniently accomplished on foot or bicycle, and the public environments of cities (their streets, squares and other places) were still very people oriented (Newman and Kenworthy 1999a). Figure 2.2 conceptualizes the urban form of the typical transit city, showing the two clear types of urban form of tram-based inner suburbs and distinct nodes or urban villages around railway stations on the steam train and later electric rail lines.

This type of city gained ascendancy in the industrial world, and during the period from about 1850 to 1940 it tended to be the dominant type of city form in industrialized countries. In other less developed parts of the world, where new technologies did not take off in the way they did in the Western world, the walking city remained dominant. These cities have had a less well-defined period of public transport development, if any. Certainly, most of them have not been shaped significantly by a period of extensive and enduring urban rail development (trains or trams), although some, such as Bangkok, did have these modes (Poboon 1997; Barter 1999). In recent years however (from about the 1970s onwards), they have tended to develop directly from pedestrian-oriented cities with some bus-based public transport systems into cities where motorcycles and cars have begun to take the upper hand. In the process, the rights of pedestrians and cyclists have been trampled on through the removal of footpaths for widened roads, the severance of neighborhoods by freeway and toll road infrastructure, and the creation of a hostile, highly dangerous public realm dominated by traffic (Kenworthy 1997).

The influence of transport technologies on the quality of public spaces in cities and the nature of social relations is clearly seen in the kinds of attractive and interactive public realms that have been created in many cities where transit systems have been given priority in city development. For example, in Zurich's Bahnhofstrasse, and in many other cities, urban space is shared between trams and pedestrians, and private space spills out into the public realm. Transit, by its nature, involves people mixing together in shared space and is an important factor in helping to shape social relations.

Interestingly, we are seeing today the creation of new transit cities as urban rail is going through a renaissance (Newman et al. 2013). Chinese cities are building metro systems at an astonishing rate and Shanghai and Beijing now have among the biggest metro systems in the world. These have virtually all developed over last two decades (Gao and Kenworthy 2016). Rather than Chinese cities becoming automobile cities, we are instead seeing the creation of what could be called 'emerging transit cities' (as opposed to mature transit cities such as New York, London or Paris), with rapidly increasing rail usage and a plateau in the growth of car use (Kenworthy 2016).

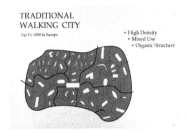

FIGURE 2.1
Conceptual diagram; walking city
Source: Peter Newman and Jeffrey R. Kenworthy

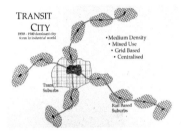

FIGURE 2.2
Conceptual diagram; transit city
Source: Peter Newman and Jeffrey R. Kenworthy

Automobile cities

Whatever one's outlook is on what the automobile has done for urban societies, it is universally agreed that it has brought enormous change. Figure 2.3 provides a conceptual diagram of the archetypal automobile city, showing the enormous expansion of developed area relative to the walking and transit cities, which its use has facilitated.

The automobile facilitated the uninhibited outward expansion of the city because people and businesses were no longer constrained to the fixed-track public transport systems or walking-scale environments of earlier times. Development became footloose and could occur anywhere that a section of black top could be laid down. The automobile's much greater speed allowed the city to get much bigger again, and densities of development dropped dramatically. Through the exercise of modern town planning principles, land uses became segregated into zones, and travel distances for all trip purposes increased dramatically. The car began to displace public transport and non-motorized modes and today achieves modal shares for all daily trips in the range of 80–95% in automobile cities in North America

FIGURE 2.3
Conceptual diagram; automobile city
Source: Peter Newman and Jeffrey R. Kenworthy

and Australia. This type of city became the dominant form in the U.S. and Australia and, to a slightly lesser extent, in Canada from the mid-1940s onward (Kenworthy and Laube 1999; Newman and Kenworthy 1999a, 2015).

Many countries in other parts of the world such as Asia, whose cities have traditionally had high-density walking-oriented urban forms, are developing their own characteristic style of automobile city forms, but only in the outer regions. This is especially true where there is little planning to control the use of cars and, indeed, little effective public planning control over urban land uses (e.g. in Bangkok and Kuala Lumpur). In the high-density, mixed-use parts of the city, where land uses would normally facilitate high levels of walking and non-motorized transport, these modes are so unattractive due to lack of facilities, noise, fumes and danger that they have been, or are being, decimated. There is also a lack of high-quality transit infrastructure, though some progress is being made with new rail systems (Newman et al. 2013). Such cities suffer particularly high levels of transport deaths, many of them of non-motorized mode users (and motorcyclists) (Barter 2000).

As a consequence of this overwhelming picture of traffic and congestion, cities such as Bangkok are sometimes labeled as automobile cities or automobile-dependent. However, they are very far from being automobile cities in their overall mobility patterns. They are, rather, 'traffic-saturated cities' and this is how they are classed in cluster analyses of global cities (Priester et al. 2013). They were never built for the car, but large numbers of cars and motorcycles have flooded their compact urban forms and rudimentary road systems, making them highly congested and dysfunctional in peak hours. The need for a better match between urban form and transportation infrastructure through ceasing large-scale road construction, extending rail systems and better integrating land use with stations in these dense cities is very clear (Dimitriou 2013). This is discussed in detail for Bangkok in APEC (2015).

Additional lessons from city types

Kenworthy's depictions of automobile dependence, equity and inequity issues in Chapter 1, and the transportation evolution of cities from walking to transit and automobile described above, provide a very helpful backdrop for a discussion of the relationship of 'car culture', to be discussed immediately below, and how urban life is organized. A few additional points may be added to his analysis:

- The walking city respected topography, and it tended to create communities within which walking was relatively easy. Fine, highly permeable grid-street patterns, as mentioned previously, were also common (e.g. Greece, Japan and China).
- Accessibility and proximity were the organizing principles of life in the walking city.
- Transit provided solutions to population growth and the need to separate residences from unhealthy industrial pollution. This separation, understandable in the context of the nineteenth and twentieth centuries, led to building codes and zoning enforcing segregated land uses long after it was necessary—as in recent decades when re-urbanization and infill are so greatly hampered by this 'weight of the past'. While transportation equity was not as great as in the walking city, most sectors of the population maintained reasonably good access to jobs and other necessities because most destinations remained within about a 10-minute walk (800 meters or half a mile) of some form of transit service (linear bands of development along tram lines and nodes of development around rail stations).
- Transit cities could expand or extend themselves along transit routes while still generally respecting their topography and the need for strong centers. This also allowed some relief from the overcrowding of pre-transit industrial cities. While transit cities generally maintained a strong urban center, they allowed for the development of sub-centers around transit nodes, also easily accessible by foot or bicycle modes. Not all trips for services and shopping needed to have the central business district (CBD) as a destination, nor did they just rely on one mode.
- The automobile allowed cities to expand without limits and without respect to topography. The automobile climbed hills that streetcars had shunned. The grid of arterial streets and expressways, rather than the lines of rail transit routes, became the defining and organizing features of mobility. Development became footloose, not needing to be anchored to a fixed transit line, but rather going anywhere that roads were built. Ironically, buses heralded this spreading city, since they had to chase diminishing transit patrons in ever-thinning development along the same road systems being built for automobiles. The earlier rail systems did the exact opposite. They attracted high-density, mixed-use development to high-quality transit lines, thus ensuring a close integration between development of the city and the availability of competitive transit. The automobile city has created great mobility opportunities for some segments of the population while generating or maintaining serious inequities in mobility and accessibility for the rest of the population.

BOX 2.1 From Pompidou to Paris Plages and bike-bus lanes

As prime minister (for Charles de Gaulle) and later as president, Georges Pompidou reshaped Paris during the 1960s and early 1970s in the name of modernization: the historic and greatly loved Les Halles market was razed and replaced by an upscale shopping area; the first and only skyscraper in the city limits, Tour Montparnasse, was built; the highly controversial design for a modern art museum, posthumously named after him, was realized; and expressways replaced the quiet pedestrian-oriented quays along the banks of the Seine River in the heart of Paris. The motorization of the banks of the Seine was justified, according to Pompidou, because 'Paris must adapt to the car'.

Adapting to the car resulted in greatly increased traffic and pollution and decreased walking. The expressways along the Seine generated traffic (see Litman 2010 for a general discussion of this matter) and replaced a great number of trips that might otherwise have been by foot or public transportation. Motor vehicles not only clogged the streets of Paris; they climbed onto and took over sidewalks and made life increasingly difficult for pedestrians in what had been previously considered to be a model 'walking city'.

In 2001, a major reversal of this trajectory began. Paris elected a socialist mayor, Bertrand Delanoë, who distinguished himself by beginning to return the banks of the Seine to persons not in motor vehicles and the sidewalks of Paris to unobstructed walking. Many streets were reconfigured with special lanes for buses, public taxicabs and bicyclists. On some major streets, bicycles share the bus lanes; on other streets, they have their own protected lanes; and numerous one-way streets have marked contraflow bicycle lanes. A highly successful bicycle-sharing service, Vélib (vélo and liberté), was introduced in 2007 (not without a few years of 'growing pains' involving theft and vandalism before these were overcome) and a car-sharing program, Autolib, was introduced at the end of 2011. All these, plus numerous traffic management efforts—including greater enforcement of traffic and parking violations—have led to a reversal of Paris's overdependence on personal motor vehicles.

Some initiatives directly challenge Pompidou's assumptions about 'adapting to the car'. Each summer since 2002, while many Parisians take long vacations, portions of the Seine riverbanks are transformed into public beaches—Paris Plages—to the delight of tourists and those residents, young and old, who stay home. Overnight, thousands of tons of sand, dozens of palm trees, hundreds of different types of beach chairs and umbrellas as well as pop-up cafés and ice-cream stands take over the riverbank roadways. Paris Plages has been extremely popular and served as the prelude to the permanent conversion of a 2.3 km (1.1 mile) stretch of riverbank roadway to the pedestrian Promenade des Berges de la Seine, which also offers gardens, cafés and restaurants afloat barges moored to the promenade.

The reconfiguring of street space to benefit buses and bicyclists, the creation of a viable bicycling network across Paris, public transportation improvements and the introduction of Vélib and Autolib have yielded positive results for sustainable transportation. Walking has reversed its decades-long slow decline and has overtaken driving as the dominant travel mode; bus performance, reliability and ridership have increased as have Paris's rail services. Bicycling, historically a very small portion of Parisian travel, has increased from a 1% share to a 4% share in just over a decade—and is increasing annually at a robust rate.

When Bertrand Delanoë decided not seek re-election in 2014, he was succeeded by fellow Socialist Anne Hidalgo, who continued and expanded upon his successful sustainable transportation accomplishments; more bicycle lanes, less parking, more emphasis on public transportation, more pedestrianization and reclamation of the banks of the Seine. She presided over Paris's first car-free day, 27 September 2015. She wanted to have all of Paris made car-free but was only able to gain police support for an automobile ban for the center of the city. Still, there was great celebration in those streets and a measurable decline in air pollution of 40% in the center briefly ensued. Mayor Hidalgo would like to see such auto-free days across all of Paris on a regular basis. The car-free days, at least in the center of Paris and along the Champs-Élysées, have now become an extremely popular monthly event and demonstrable significant decreases in air pollution in the areas made car-free have been recorded.

Despite Anne Hidalgo's valiant efforts and her continuation—even expansion—of Bertrand Delanoë's initiative, Paris is still struggling with severe air pollution. While the gains are significant they are still not enough

continued

to sufficiently reduce Paris's notorious air pollution exceedances and put an end to the emergency days limiting motor vehicles after severe smog days.[i]

Source: Preston L. Schiller

There is a wealth of material available about the recent efforts to reverse the heavy impacts of automobility in Paris, including bus and bike lanes, bike-sharing, EV sharing, further pedestrianization and car-free and automobile restriction days. Some of the most useful, including several that are well-illustrated or linked to videos, are:

www.raisethehammer.org/article/2707/bicycle-friendly_paris_refuses_to_stand_still;
www.theguardian.com/cities/2016/apr/15/paris-changed-permanently-mayor-anne-hidalgo;
www.20minutes.fr/paris/1766975-20160115-paris-2014-moins-voitures-plus-velos-capitale;
www.theguardian.com/world/2015/oct/03/pariss-first-attempt-at-car-free-day-brings-big-drop-in-air-and-noise-pollution; http://nyti.ms/TcQHIO;
www.theguardian.com/world/2012/aug/02/paris-seine-riverside-expressway-pedestrian;
http://nyti.ms/TcQHIO; http://ngm.nationalgeographic.com/print/2014/05/parisian-seine/newman-text;
http://en.visitparisregion.com/events-paris/festivals/paris-plages-2016-333852.html;
http://humantransit.org/2010/07/paris-the-street-is-ours.html;
www.takepart.com/article/2015/09/27/before-and-after-video-shows-what-happened-when-paris-banned-cars

Figures 2.4a, b and c below demonstrate the great contrasts one finds in Paris: wide boulevards with wide pedestrian-filled spaces and cafés where one can comfortably sit and people-watch; lively pedestrian zones filled with shops and bistros; and some boulevards and monumental places clogged with cars. Examples of Paris's great transit and bicycling infrastructure can be found in Chapter 4.

Paris is valiantly struggling to reverse decades of overindulgence of automobility. In this, it is aided by a great public transportation system and a willingness of many residents to support change towards restoring the health of the city. And it is making great progress.

FIGURE 2.4A
Champs-Élysées, one of the sites for periodic closures to traffic on car-free days; although pedestrians greatly outnumber motor vehicles this day, most of the space is inefficiently consumed by PMVs.
Source: Jeffrey R. Kenworthy

FIGURE 2.4B
Champs-Élysées: Space for cafés
and pedestrians
Source: Jeffrey R. Kenworthy

FIGURE 2.4C
Wagnerian traffic jam? You can
always find it at Paris' Place de
l'Opéra.
Source: Preston L. Schiller

Unfortunately, many people in North America and other overly car-dependent societies are organizing their daily lives and communities around the automobile. The phenomenon of drive-to/drive-through/drive-for-all-trips is turning almost everywhere in the U.S. and parts of Canada into a nowhere of ugly strips and malls, vast parking lots and barren roadways (Kunstler 1993, 2005). About half of the priority recommendations made by the U.S. Public Health Service's Centers for Disease Control for combating the current epidemic of obesity and inactivity address increasing physical activity: walking, bicycling, transit use and community design; another way of stating their recommendations is to urge citizens to drive less and for communities to improve their built environment to accommodate less driving and automobile-oriented design (CDC 2009; Jackson 2012; Lopez 2012).[2] And Health Canada warns that Canadians are following close behind (Starky 2005, Health Canada

FIGURE 2.5
Andy Singer's
Crapscape
Source: Andy
Singer (www.andy
singer.com)

2006, 2016). There are notable exceptions to this unhealthy trend and the beginnings of some hopeful counter-trends such as peak car use becoming evident in numerous cities, a decoupling of growth in city GDP from growth in car use, improvements in transit provision and use and some increases in metropolitan densities; however, enormous changes still need to be made (Newman and Kenworthy 2015). In short, there are many cities and urban areas where automobile dependence is being challenged with varying degrees of success. Some of these are discussed in several places in this text, especially in the exemplars chapter.

Even in automobile-dependent communities, it is possible for a combination of factors, including policy changes, to encourage the lessening of this dependence in neighborhoods, workplaces and the wider community. Chapter 9 presents several exemplary efforts to move to transportation sustainability, and Chapter 8 contains examples of how a more desirable future could be attained. New Urbanism advocate and prolific writer James Howard Kunstler discusses how automobile dependence and the false promises of suburbia dovetail in Box 2.2.

Car culture

The complex of social factors that buttress and maintain automobile dependence may be termed the 'car culture'. This term is used in the tradition of scholars of automobility, such as James Flink (1975, 1988). Car culture includes such factors as:

- self-perception, group affiliations and the centrality of the automobile to our notions of self and social valuation and reward systems (see Steg 2005);
- cultural, philosophical and institutional underpinnings—critique and criticism of the automobile's symbolism, belief systems, mediating factors and roles of institutions such as education, industry and government;

BOX 2.2 James Howard Kunstler: the war to save suburbia and the creation of the American Crapscape

James Howard Kunstler has been a trenchant critic of BAU urban and transportation planning for over twenty years in books (Kunstler 1993, 1996, 2006), blogs and his work with the Congress for the New Urbanism (CNU). In this 2005 sampling of his writing, he takes the phrase 'They Lied to Us'—this became a popular mantra criticizing U.S. President George W. Bush and his cohort of officials for misleading the American public in regards to the U.S.-led initiative known as the Iraq War, which commenced in 2003—as a point of departure for his critique of military adventurism aimed at ensuring safe supplies of oil as examples of the 'war to save suburbia':

When the American people, Democrat and Republican both, decided to build a drive-in utopia based on incessant easy motoring and massive oil dependency, who lied to them? When tens of millions of Americans bought McHouses thirty-four miles away from their jobs in Boston, Atlanta, Minneapolis, and Dallas, who lied to them? When American public officials adopted the madness of single-use zoning and turned the terrain of this land into a tragic crapscape of strip malls on six-lane highways, who lied to them? When American school officials decided to consolidate all the kids in gigantic centralized facilities serviced by fleets of yellow buses that ran an average of 150,000 miles per year per school, who lied to them? When Americans trashed their public transit and railroad system, who lied to them? When Americans let WalMart gut Main Street, who lied to them? . . .

Source: Kunstler (2005)

- role of the mainstream media—broadcast (radio, television), print, cinema and web-based—in shaping perceptions and values surrounding the automobile;
- advertising—the packaging, selling and promotion of the automobile;
- music, music videos and popular entertainment;
- literature (automobile travel as a theme);
- carchitecture—the ways in which buildings are designed to accommodate automobiles and show their most important features to passing motorists—massive advertising billboards, as well as the enshrining of automobile aesthetics;
- tourism—much of which is dependent upon motoring, especially in wealthier countries.

There are many ways in which the car culture shapes our notions of self and society. The culture of the personal motor vehicle and automobility influences our quotidian notions of self-image and self-worth—the extent to which we feel empowered (or powerless), our social status (or lack thereof) and many of the ways we wish to be rewarded or attempt to reward others. To the motorist the steel, plastic and glass entrapment of the personal vehicle can be experienced as an extra layer of skin and tissue; an insult or injury to one's vehicle is often experienced as an assault on our person, our identity. The identification of self and vehicle may help explain why some motorists become enraged by other motorists' driving behavior or violent when involved in even a minor 'fender bender' or unintentional scraping of their vehicle by another.

While Mimi Sheller and John Urry, two sociologically oriented theorists, did not invent the term 'automobility', they have written extensively about it, separately and jointly (Sheller and Urry 2000, 2004; Urry 2002, 2004, 2006, 2010). Box 2.3 features a capsule of their thinking about what it comprises.

BOX 2.3 Automobility

Automobility is:

- the quintessential manufactured object produced by the leading industrial sectors and the iconic firms within twentieth-century capitalism . . . hence, it is the industry from which key concepts such as Fordism and post-Fordism have emerged to analyse the nature of, and changes in, the trajectory of Western capitalism.
- the major item of individual consumption after housing that (1) provides status to its owner/user through the sign-values . . . (such as speed, home, safety, sexual desire, career success, freedom, family, masculinity, genetic breeding); (2) is easily anthropomorphized by being given names, having rebellious features, being seen to age and so on; and (3) generates massive amounts of crime (theft, speeding, drunk driving, dangerous driving) and disproportionately preoccupies each country's criminal justice system.
- an extraordinarily powerful machinic complex . . . including car parts and accessories, petrol refining and distribution, road-building and maintenance, hotels, roadside service areas and motels, car sales and repair workshops, suburban house building, new retailing and leisure complexes, advertising and marketing, urban design and planning.
- the predominant global form of 'quasi-private' mobility that subordinates other 'public' mobilities of walking, cycling, traveling by rail and so on; and it reorganizes how people negotiate the opportunities for, and constraints upon, work, family life, leisure and pleasure.
- the dominant culture that sustains major discourses of what constitutes the good life, what is necessary for an appropriate citizenship of mobility, and which provides potent literary and artistic images and symbols. . . .
- the single most important cause of environmental resource-use resulting from the exceptional range and scale of material, space and power used in the manufacture of cars, roads and car-only environments, and in coping with the material, air quality, medical, social, ozone, visual, noise and other consequences of pretty well global automobility . . .

Source: Sheller, M. and Urry, J. (2000)

Advertising exploits these notions as well as nurturing notions that create a persona for the vehicle as not just a material object but a creature with which we relate as with a family member or a friend, a 'buddy'. The representation of the motor vehicle as a person is widely found in the visual media, especially in movies and television especially, but not exclusively, in productions aimed at children. In a phenomenon known as pareidolia, persons, especially children, often see the fronts of vehicles as faces: the windshield as a forehead, headlights as eyes, hood ornaments as noses, the grills as mouths, some of the details as other facial parts. Sometimes the face is smiling, other times it is fearsome and frowning. Such perceptions may also be gendered and influence the direction of motor vehicle manufacturing as well as advertising as Box 2.4 indicates.

In automobile-dependent societies, a great deal of individual identity is tied to vehicle ownership; the perceived power of driving, individual status through identification with product branding and the fearful perception that life without a personal motor vehicle not only makes it extremely difficult to participate in important aspects of work and social life, but also that being stripped of one's vehicle leads to becoming an outcast. Figure 2.7 below depicts how a California government program reinforces these fears. The California law buttressing the threatening poster below allows for the seizing, for at least thirty days, of the vehicle of a motorist driving without a valid license (for recent references, search: 'California Office of Traffic Safety' + drive without a license . . . lose your car! There are many references as this is a controversial law).

Sometimes automobile advertising results from or is bolstered by the ways in which the car culture promotes automobiles as status symbols and rewards for certain attainments. In the U.S., it is not uncommon for parents to 'reward' their children with the gift of an automobile to celebrate their graduation from secondary school, or even for their sixteenth

---

BOX 2.4 Pareidolia: the many faces of automobile facades

But perhaps the most common form of pareidolia in the western world is seeing Faces in the fronts of cars, Sonja Windhager at the University of Vienna traveled to rural Ethiopia to find out whether people see the same thing. Questioning people on the roadside and in small restaurants, she was initially met with surprise. 'They thought we were a little crazy', she says. But even though the Ethiopians had not been exposed to films like Disney's Cars or the adventures of Herbie, they soon understood the purpose of the study, and rated the pictures in much the same way that Europeans do. For instance, cars with a big windscreen, round headlights and a small grill tend to be considered young and feminine: while those with flatter headlights and a bigger, squarer under-body are older and more masculine: Windhager's other studies have found that consumers tend to prefer the more dominant cars—a fact that manufacturers are already using to their advantage; in 2006, for instance, the Wall Street Journal reported that 'cuter' cars, such as the iconic Volkswagen Beetle, were experiencing falling sales—perhaps because their owners were feeling intimidated by the growing number of large SUVs. So designers decided to create cars with more dominant expressions. The Dodge Charger, for instance, was designed with thin, sloping headlights, to give it a menacing look that could outstare the other cars. 'The headlights seem to make eye contact the same way people do on the street', said Chrysler designer Ralph Gilles. 'A mean face is what we're going for'. Windhager wonders if the illusion of eye contact could impact road safety, however. For instance, we may run into danger if a car's 'face' leads us to assume the car has a mind of its own. 'Maybe children will think the car sees them coming—so they might not stop,' she says. Seeing cars with more threatening expressions might also make other drivers more anxious or aggressive, she speculates'.[i]

Source: Robson, D. (2014)

[i] More examples of "car faces" can be seen at http://imgur.com/gallery/QNrvo (accessed 12 October, 2016)

FIGURE 2.6A
Happy face car? Pareidolia; The faces of
automobile facades
Source: Preston L. Schiller

FIGURE 2.6B
Unhappy face car? Pareidolia; The faces of
automobile facades

birthday—the age when a driver's license may be obtained. Some
employers reward employees with a gift automobile for certain
achievements: the best known of these in the U.S. and Canada is the
Mary Kay Cosmetics Company's rewarding of an employee's high
sales attainment with a pink Cadillac. This program has come under
some scrutiny as some critics claim that very few employees ever
achieve this reward and most earn very little, or even lose money, as
Mary Kay representatives.[3]

FIGURE 2.7
'Lose your license, become a bicyclist', warns
the California Office of Traffic Safety
Source: Preston L. Schiller

Black Cadillacs

For African-Americans of means in the segregation era, the purchase
of the high-status Cadillac was a way to assert their achievement in

a world in which their lives were severely circumscribed by racism. As early as 1949, while many formal segregationist barriers were in place as well as many informal barriers, *Ebony Magazine*—an important publication geared to middle-class and wealthy Blacks—defended the buying of Cadillacs in a photo-editorial that featured a photo of a well-to-do African-American man posing with a Cadillac:

> Just as to white America, the Cadillac is a sign of wealth and standing so to Negro Americans the Cadillac is an indication of ability to compete successfully with whites, to maintain the very highest standard of living in this nation. . . . It is the acme of dignity and stature in the white man's world.
>
> (Johnson, J. H. 1949)

General Motors benefited considerably from Black patronage and the whole subculture that grew up around their ownership of Cadillacs, yet a complicated dance ensued between them as African-Americans bought Cadillacs in large numbers, especially in the 1950s, while GM still maintained Cadillac dealership ownership for Whites only and did not advertise in *Ebony* until after civil rights laws were formalized. In some parts of the southern U.S. states, white-owned Cadillac dealers would not even sell directly to African-Americans: this led to the quaint practice of Blacks often having to buy Cadillacs through a third party (Sugrue 2012; Betsey 2014; Brown 2004; Seiler 2009; Packer 2008).

The recent attention being paid to the 'crime' of 'DWB (driving while Black)' and the mounting numbers of African-Americans being racially profiled, continually apprehended, beaten and even killed for DWB is a sad reminder of another destructive side of the car culture in which the mobility of a racial minority is continually subjected to curtailment of its basic mobility rights.

Car as home and your car's home away from home

Another way in which advertising and the car culture combine to exploit a major emotional component of most people's lives is in the creation of an identification of the car as an extension of home or, in the case of those perpetually living a nomadic existence in a van or recreational vehicle (RV), *the* home. A recent U.S. development, with roots in the Midwest, is the darker side of well-to-do middle-aged 'empty-nesters' who downsize from their suburban faux chateaux and spacious ranch-style houses to smaller luxury accommodations closer in or in a city's center while maintaining an ex-urban large luxury storage residence for their personal motor vehicles. One car 'home away from home' some 35 miles outside of Chicago touts its 'scenic views of a 22-acre nature preserve with bike path access' and 'Convenient car-related retail plaza on site for "one-stop" shopping' (Iron Gate Motor Condos). This is an extreme segment of a U.S. movement towards 'car condos' and luxury storage units usually in ex-urban locations (Jackson, C. 2016). Box 2.5 gives us a glimpse of one example of this growing phenomenon.

Given the way that the automobile industry and its advertising extensions exploit emotionally laden areas of human existence, it is not surprising that several significant social critics have trained their sights on the car culture.

Critique and criticism of the car culture

While a fair degree of philosophical, political and cultural criticism accompanied the rise of automobility in the late nineteenth and early twentieth centuries centuries, its pace and depth grew in the decades immediately following World War II. Early criticism tended to focus on the elitist aspects of automobility, especially before Fordism made the automobile an item of mass consumption in industrially advanced nations, and then moved to criticism

---

BOX 2.5 Giving thanks for our many car blessings

Drew and Janet Richardson sold their house and bought two condominiums: One for them, and one for their cars. The empty-nesters wanted their six-car garage but not the four-bedroom house connected to it. 'We decided to downsize the house but not the garage,' he said. They moved their British sports cars to the AutoMotorPlex, a Chanhassen complex that is the only one of its kind between Chicago and Los Angeles. The deluxe garage condominiums serve as the ultimate man cave after being outfitted with the likes of 80-inch flat-screen TVs, full kitchens, plush living rooms and even basketball courts for the kids to play on while Dad tinkers with a timing belt.

Most of the owners, who paid from $39,000 to $100,000 for their spaces even before outfitting them with the extras, think of them as merely garages. Bonding is a big part of the complex's appeal—from poker games to birthday and graduation parties. Father-and-son garage owners . . . have even hosted holiday dinners in their garage. 'We moved the cars out of the way and had 40 people in here for Thanksgiving dinner last year . . . Our wives thought it was a great idea. If a kid spills gravy on a carpet, you've got a stain. Here, we just hose down the floor and get out a squeegee.

. . . Of the 135 units . . . has built so far, only two are unsold. . . . more garages in September.

. . . 'The baby boomers wanted to give up their bigger homes while keeping their toys,' said [the developer]. The 40-acre complex, complete with paved roads and a clubhouse for social gatherings, looks like a fancy mini-storage, with a Tudor twist. The cars run the gamut, from the classics to ultra-high-end sports cars. One garage holds a collection of Mustangs spanning five decades. The next is full of 1960s muscle cars and adjacent to that is one that stores a Lamborghini.

For the owners, it's all about spending time with people who share their passion for internal combustion.

Source: Strickler (2011)

---

of its effects on urban life, especially its reckless takeover of streets and the killing and harming of pedestrians. This aspect of criticism became somewhat blunted as the walking and bicycling public gradually submitted itself to traffic regulation—the early ideological cloak of automobile hegemony (Norton 2007, 2008).

The reach of automobility, in terms of ownership, driving and highway construction, expanded greatly in the late 1940s and 1950s. While welcomed at first by cities large and small, the large new expressways dumping more and more traffic into cities were experienced as destroyers of urban life. Reactions to the lack of fit between standards designed for intercity highways and city needs set in earlier in Europe than in the U.S. The Marshall Plan guiding U.S. post-World War II assistance in Europe had encouraged the construction of large expressways into and through many of the war-damaged cities that it aimed to rebuild. Its housing counterpart, the building of large Le Corbusier-style residential towers, triggered strong reactions among many advocates of a more traditional approach to transportation and land-use planning.

The 1960s were a time of massive road expansion and major protest and reaction against their destruction of the urban fabric, especially in the U.S. Jane Jacobs's *The Death and Life of Great American Cities* (1961) and Lewis Mumford's *The City in History* (1961) provided an incisive critique of the destructiveness of 1950s and 1960s business as usual (BAU) transportation, especially in its destructive impacts upon cities. Mumford's eloquent and blistering critiques of suburbia and the automobile are as relevant today as they were in 1961.

The 1970s witnessed a full flowering of critique and criticism of automobility and the car culture. Prominent among these were the critiques of Ivan Illich, whose seminal thinking on these matters was published in the incisive and pithy *Energy and Equity* (Illich 1976). Illich's thinking on this topic had already been circulating, stimulating widespread discussion and influencing parallel critiques, such as that of the French social and political philosopher André Gorz (1973). Their overlapping critiques, with Illich's much more highly developed, should be consulted in full, while a few key points are included here:

- The perceived gains derived by higher-speed, higher energy-consuming modes are illusory because the financial and time commitments demanded to support them, especially at the level of the traveler, create dependence and consume more time than lower-speed, lower-energy modes. The perceived benefits of higher speeds are offset by the amount of time people must labor to afford them, as well as the greater time commitment to travel created by greater trip distances.
- While automobility may be perceived as a mass and, therefore, 'democratic' phenomenon in industrial countries, it expands social and economic inequity.
- In industrially less developed countries the greater speed of travel achieved by elites comes at the expense of the walking and bicycling masses.

The work of Illich and Gorz attracted the attention of automobility and car culture critics and advocates for alternatives to these throughout the 1970s and subsequent decades. Among those who expanded upon their central themes were John Adams, who developed the very important notion of 'hypermobility', the excessive amount of travel fostered by destinations made more distant by urban sprawl combined with the 'mobility culture' (Adams 1999, 2000, 2009); and John Whitelegg's systematic development of the notion of 'time pollution': the ways in which excessive mobility robs people of valuable time in a variety of insidious ways (Whitelegg 1993, 1997, 2016). Kenneth Schneider's 1979 book *On the Nature of Cities: Towards Enduring and Creative Human Environments* capped off the growing 1970s disenchantment with the car, in a damning and powerful exposé of virtually every aspect of America's automobile addiction (see Box 8.9 in Chapter 8).

The reactions against automobility and highway expansion that created numerous critiques in the 1970s (see Chapter 7) were followed by several important works, some academic and some for a general audience, during the 1980s and 1990s. These were often built upon notions introduced by Illich and Gorz. Academic critique of automobility and highway expansion was aided by increasingly sophisticated analysis of traffic data that led to conclusions indicating that road expansion, often justified by traffic engineers and highway interests as the 'cure' for congestion, created more congestion than might have otherwise occurred. This well-documented phenomenon has come to be known as generated—or induced—traffic, sometimes popularly referred to as the 'field of dreams' effect after the cryptic saying from the film of that title—'if you build it, they will come' (SACTRA 1994; Noland 2001; Litman 2010).

The opposite effect, if you un-build it (or reduce road capacity), is that traffic diminishes. This has been well documented and is known as 'traffic degeneration', 'trip degeneration' or 'traffic evaporation' (Roberts 1992; Cairns et al. 1998; Newman and Kenworthy 2015). Other voices added the dimension of sensitivity to urban design and urban form to the mix. Researchers Peter Newman and Jeffrey Kenworthy analyzed the relationship between urban form, infrastructure and automobility (Newman and Kenworthy 1989, 1999a, 2015), and found that the more that cities attempted to accommodate automobility through road expansion and a variety of traffic engineering gimmicks oriented to keeping traffic flowing freely, the more congestion, sprawl, energy use and pollution they created. For wider audiences, architecture and planning critic Jane Holtz Kay (1997) and New Urbanism advocate James Howard Kunstler (1993, 1996, 2006) wrote passionately and perceptively about urban sprawl, automobile-oriented design and the culture of car-centered convenience (see Box 2.2 above). Sociologists began to develop incisive critiques of the car culture and automobility as early as the 1980s.

Sociology of transportation and the car culture

While many researchers and analysts in transportation-related fields have learned from sociologists and anthropologists, these disciplines themselves have not produced a deep and lasting commitment to the study of transportation through their disciplinary lenses. Given the pervasiveness of the automobile and automobility in shaping institutions and virtually all aspects of everyday life—especially in industrial and post-industrial societies, but also increasingly on a global scale—it is rather curious that these issues have not received more institutionalized attention from the social sciences, especially sociology and anthropology. Mimi Sheller and John Urry (Box 2.3) have long pointed out that 'the social sciences have generally ignored the motor car and its awesome consequences for social life' (2000, p. 737) and that, especially, at least three disciplines—industrial sociology, analyses of consumption and urban sociology—should be heavily engaged in such study.

In the early 1980s, Glenn Yago attempted to launch a sociology of transportation with a seminal article calling for disciplinary interest in this area, and a highly informative book comparing public transportation in the U.S. and Germany (1983, 1984). Despite these, the sociology of transportation did not grow into an identifiable sub-area within the American Sociological Association. Another notable contribution has been made by Peter Freund and George Martin (1993), who brought a sociological and environmental perspective to the problem of automobility in their work. And there have been occasional forays into the car culture on the part of anthropologists, beginning with the remarkable and widely reprinted satire 'The Sacred Rac' (Hughes 1974); however, anthropological inquiry has not been as widely institutionalized.

Automobility and safety: ideology versus analysis

Automobility and its concomitant car culture have shaped the notion of traffic safety in the direction of motorist safety almost since the automobile began to emerge as a street bully and road hog in the early years of the twentieth century.[4] Rather than posing the question 'safety for whom?', automobility reflexively equates traffic safety as motorist or passenger safety.[5]

Two main approaches dominate Business as Usual (BAU) automobility safety: engineering interventions and behavioral interventions. Engineering interventions range from product design and building safety into a motor vehicle—both in its structure and its added features such as seat belts, airbags etc—to road and street design, including traffic control devices such as signage and signals and road-widening and visual obstacle removal, supposedly to better accommodate driver sightlines at greater distances.

Behavioral interventions can involve techniques for monitoring and enforcing traffic regulations, including signboards that display a vehicle's speed as it approaches and speeder-deterring red-light cameras. They can also involve programs of driver's education and school programs, often involving police officers, teaching children to stay out of the way of motor vehicles.

BAU analysts and researchers have boasted that such interventions have greatly increased traffic safety and point to the reduction in motor vehicle crash mortality as a great accomplishment. Some analysts more oriented to public health and sustainable transportation have responded to the 'safety perspective' with some trenchant criticisms. Among these are:

- The language, metrics and orientation of BAU 'traffic safety' are inherently biased against non-motoring: one BAU safety rubric measures motor-vehicle killing and injuring of pedestrians and bicyclists in terms of motor vehicle miles or kilometers driven, i.e. such incidents, with this metric, appear to be declining, whereas the reality is that in recent decades motor vehicles are being driven more and persons have been walking and cycling less through simply not being able to due to inconvenience, or consciously limiting their exposure to dangerous traffic.[6]

- Motor vehicle incidents such as collisions with other vehicles or bicyclists and pedestrians should not be termed 'accidents'; they should be referred to for what they are: crashes. 'Accident' is something of a euphemism in that it infers that there is no blame, neglect or intentionality; 'crash' infers neglect, culpability and, possibly, intentionality.

- There is no evidence that drivers' education leads to safer driving among young motorists. In fact, the evidence seems to point in the opposite direction: that school-based drivers' education programs probably lead to higher youth casualty rates, especially when compared to programs that do not offer such courses or defer the age of driving (American Academy of Pediatrics 1999, 2006).

Furthermore, the car culture has a propensity to stigmatize public transportation, the safest form of motorized travel, just as Figure 2.6 above demonstrates how it stigmatizes walking and cycling. In recent years, the term 'loser cruiser' has been derisively applied to models of automobiles that depart from the racy or oversized and 'muscle' types glamorized in advertising, cinema and television, from smaller, practical (and fuel-efficient) cars to utilitarian family-oriented minivans (Samilton 2011). It is harmful that this term has been applied to public transportation as a term of derision in some blogospheric corners of public discussion, but it is appalling that the motor vehicle industry itself would exploit such stereotyping in self-serving publicity. No less an entity than General Motors did just such a disservice to transit when it advertised, in 2003, that transit was for 'Creeps and Weirdos'. (Nordahl 2012, p. 29) After considerable public outcry, this advertising gambit was withdrawn. In years that followed, GM began to feel threatened by the growing popularity of walking, bicycling and transit use among college students. It developed an online program pitching automobiles to that part of the demographic spectrum and advertising that implied that bicyclists and pedestrians were losers and if they would only buy GM cars they would be safe from being splashed upon by such vehicles[7] (Maus 2011).

Despite the overwhelming evidence that mobile phone usage, especially texting while driving, is extremely dangerous, neither the automobile industry nor the mobile communications industries are seriously addressing this issue. Public officials pass laws and promise better enforcement to dampen these activities, although research does not indicate much of a decline in such use. The amount of effective curtailment varies considerably from country to country. The U.K. appears to be aggressively enforcing restrictions on distracted driving due to cell phone use, while the U.S. and Canada present much less enforcement overall. In fact, aspects of internet communications encourage reckless driving, as the recent experience with 'snapchat speeding' demonstrates; drivers, mostly younger, will use the speed time feature of the snapchat.com app to see just how fast they can go while posting onto their snapchat site the speed displayed (Rogers 2016). Although less publicized, the problem of distracted walking, or even bicycling, while texting or being absorbed with one's smartphone is growing and affecting all street and sidewalk users. At airports or aboard public transportation, transit or long distance, the mobile phone is becoming a greater and greater nuisance to the extent that some rail services institute 'quiet cars' that ban their use or regularly remind users to be politer and less noisy.

The major media appear to spend a disproportional amount of effort in publicizing the relatively rare events of hazard involving public transportation, especially transit. While travel by transit has been demonstrated to be much safer than travel by private motor vehicle, a great deal of negative public perception still surrounds it, especially in the U.S. (Litman 2016).

The mainstream media and the car culture: myth overshadows reality

The media—print, broadcast and cinematic—are extremely dependent upon the revenue derived from advertising (overt or embedded) by the automobile industry and related industries and services. Consequently, they generally do not engage in criticism directed at any aspects of 'automobiledom'. Most critiques of automobility and the car culture are communicated through print such as books, periodical articles and print-related media such as websites and publications that are often associated with political and environmental organizations (see Appendix 2). Critiques sometime emerge in the mainstream broadcast media in special programs and documentaries. Some 'alternative newspapers' will publish criticism of the car culture and a few mainstream newspapers and magazines offer token critique space in their opinion sections and a rare special feature. Often, these emerge in response to an article or editorial extolling the wonders of automobility or criticizing some aspect of advocacy for improved walking, bicycling or public transportation (Engler 2009).

Some radio stations or networks offer occasional opportunities for voices that differ from BAU, although recent years have seen even the major public media in the U.S.—e.g. PBS and NPR—accepting more and more of their funding from corporate sources and accommodating their interests on boards of directors and in their programing. The corporate interests, in exchange, gain access to their broadcasts through brief announcements about their products and services, which often include fossil fuels, motor vehicles, fast food and big-box retail chains and their related interests (Kramer 2012; Guerrero 2015). No nationally broadcast alternative, such as a 'bike talk', 'transit talk' or 'walk talk' has yet emerged to challenge NPR's highly popular 'Car Talk' program, much listened to even in its re-runs phase that began in 2012.

The widely viewed documenting of the destruction of most U.S. streetcar systems and the struggle against urban freeways in *Taken for a Ride* by Jim Klein and Martha Olson (1996) was shown on the public television network (PBS) in the U.S. PBS also broadcast a documentary series on more sustainable transportation narrated by A-List actor Brad Pitt called *e2: the economies of being environmentally conscious*,[8] including episodes on London's congestion charge, Paris's bike-sharing program, food miles, aviation, Seoul's demolition of a freeway and Portland's move to sustainable transportation (the latter two described in Chapter 9). Recent years, though, have seen PBS retreating from its critique roles on environmental and urban issues as it added more conservative corporate interests (Hiltzik 2014; Mayer 2013). The series *Blueprint America* (2008–11), which had numerous episodes critically exploring a variety of environmental and urban issues, was cancelled coinciding with the rise of corporate donor influence there.

In the wake of plutocratic pressures on major public media, some smaller independent venues have emerged to offer documentary criticism of BAU transportation and urban planning and to promote sustainable alternatives. These include NGOs and public interest organizations such as streetfilms.org, among others, who often make their work widely available through youtube.com and other easily accessible websites.

Unsurprisingly, only rarely does a critique of automobility surface in cinema, commercial radio or television. Occasionally a documentary or commercial film alludes to the ways in which the automobile industry itself has stood in the way of more rapid development of electric vehicles. When criticism does emerge in the mainstream broadcast or cinematic media, it is often in the form of comedy or satire, such as Steve Martin's *L.A. Story* (1991), which includes scenes spoofing how Angelenos drive 100 feet (30m) to visit neighbors, receive guidance in life and love from traffic billboards, and engage in the sport of freeway shootouts.

The reach of automobility in the media is very broad and deep, sometimes in obvious ways and sometimes in less obvious or insidious ways. Some of it is recognizable by many

FIGURE 2.8
'Automobiles: The myth, the reality'
Source: Andy Singer (www.andysinger.com)

people as part of their everyday consciousness, although often its influence is not recognized or is deep in the psyche's unconscious. Most of it is neither healthy nor helpful to efforts to move in a more sustainable direction in transportation. The scholarly and journalistic inquiries into the influence of the automobile are extensive and a thorough treatment is beyond the scope of this book. In the following paragraphs, we will address a few of the ways in which automobility and its mythology permeates the major media.

Marketing the myth: screens, earbuds, branding, embedding and product placement

Screen danger

The automobile industry and its constellation of supporting services and products is, arguably, the largest single source of broadcast media advertising revenue. The amounts spent by the three major U.S. automobile manufacturers is enormous, and the total amounts spent by all manufacturers, dealerships and related services (including insurance companies) is staggering: the U.S. motor vehicle industry's gross output was $61 billion in 2014 (up from $45.5 billion in 2007), and automotive advertising accounted for nearly $15 billion across all media in 2012 (statista.com). In addition to the ordinary advertising of personal motor vehicles and their related accoutrements and services, automobile producers also engage in a great deal of embedded advertising and product placement where their product, or its logo, is embedded or placed into media—unusually as part of a behind-the-scenes financial arrangement (see discussion below in Product Placement). Despite many legitimate concerns around promoting automobility, the broadcast media and its advertisements—apparent as well as embedded product placements—are largely not held responsible for the health and safety consequences of such. The American Academy of Pediatrics (AAP) has found that:

> (C)urrently (1999), the average American child or adolescent spends >21 hours per week viewing television. This figure does not include time spent watching movies, listening to music or watching music videos, playing video or computer games, or surfing the internet for recreational purposes. Time spent with media often displaces involvement in creative, active, or social pursuits . . .

(M)ore than 1000 scientific studies and reviews conclude that significant exposure to media violence increases the risk of aggressive behavior in certain children and adolescents, desensitizes them to violence, and makes them believe that the world is a 'meaner and scarier' place than it is. Violence appears in various forms of media entertainment, such as movies, video games, and television news. Research has shown that news reports of bombings, natural disasters, murders, and other violent crimes have the potential to traumatize young children.

(AAP 1999)

The Academy report goes on to discuss some of this screen immersion's deleterious consequences for the exposure of youth to irresponsible sexual, tobacco and alcohol messages, and points to the documentation of the relation of screen time to obesity and decreased school performance. A later policy statement calls for much greater emphasis on physical activity as a necessary health measure (AAP 2006). Curiously, the AAP does not weigh in on the role of automobile-related violence in media, nor the relationship between pediatric health and the growing amount of time young people spend in cars, screen time in the car, or the 'helicoptering' style of (mostly) suburban child-rearing. The combination of drive-to, drive-through fast food purveyors deliberately marketing to children through TV ads and its deleterious effects on health needs more public health scrutiny (Corporations and Health 2015).

In recent decades, public health initiatives have succeeded in banning or limiting the advertising of tobacco in television and radio broadcasting. The fact-denying tobacco industry has gotten around such bans through product placement in movies and computer games and by sponsoring high-visibility televised events with billboard advertising around sports events such as NASCAR racetracks and the very prominent advertising on racing cars and driver and team uniforms. Given all the adverse effects of automobility on children and youth, ranging from death and injury in crashes to pollution-generated disease—such as the rising rate of asthma (directly correlated to air pollution and proximity to motor vehicle facilities such as expressways etc) to obesity—one has to wonder why public health and medical professions have not militated for more limitations on the ways in which automobility, and especially its extreme presentations (car-racing and motor vehicle adventure mayhem), is glorified.

Recently there has been some attention paid to the tragic involvement of American toddlers in gun-related deaths, either as victims or as playfully unwitting perpetrators (Perez-Pena 2016). Some of these tragedies have occurred in motor vehicles where handguns were available to child or toddler passengers. The reporting has called attention to the need to keep children in safety restraints and the need to secure guns or not carry such in vehicles. The issue of whether children should even be subjected to that much time in cars has not emerged.

Ownership and control of much of the mainstream media, print and broadcast in North America and many countries around the globe are highly concentrated in relatively few large corporations, which lends itself to a near monopolistic power over shaping what the public will be or will not be allowed to view or hear. A U.S. example is the multi-billion-dollar media conglomerate formerly known as Clear Channel, now rebranded as iHeartMedia, Inc.

There is a considerable need for the mainstream media, especially in automobile-oriented societies, to behave more responsibly in relation to the many problems posed by over-dependence on the personal motor vehicle. There is a great need for the commercial media, including cinema—which is a great purveyor of automobility through its many 'car movies' and product placements-embedded advertising—to develop more responsible codes of ethics in this domain. An interesting effort in this matter has been undertaken by the Province of Québec automobile insurance agency, Société de l'assurance automobile du Québec

---

BOX 2.6 Cars are us

Michael Ferro[i]

During the early twentieth century in the U.S., the consumption of consumer goods made by corporations became a new basis for defining the individual. The new art and science of advertising were chief ingredients of this development. Alfred Sloan of General Motors (GM) came up with the idea of creating new car models each year focused on functionally trivial styling and comfort features. Various car models were advertised to specific groups of buyers to maintain and increase consumption. Sloanism encouraged economic waste by defining cars as disposable objects of fashion.

Sloanism continues today in full force in the car industry as in other businesses that encourage consumption and waste. In 2006, U.S. car companies, including dealers, spent over US$18 billion in advertising, down a few per cent from the previous year. To put this in perspective, this is twice the amount of federal public transit funding for that year (FHWA 2006).

We can only be astounded at just how dominant a role the car plays in the U.S. economy. It is the industry with the highest economic output. In the 25 years from 1978 to 2002, which includes some recession years, the car industry has typically constituted about 3.5 per cent of our gross domestic product (GDP). Direct employment attributable to the car industry was 3.5 million in 1998 and was 6.6 million including all indirect economic activities. The value-added productivity for the average job in the U.S. in 2000 was US$73,000. In car manufacturing, value-added productivity during that year was US$292,000. In 2000, remuneration per employee for overall domestic industry was US$43,500. For the car industry, remuneration per employee was US$69,500.

Contradictions abound in our car-embodied selves. Love and death co-exist uncomfortably. The freedom of the road inevitably implies the entrapment of traffic and the official commands of traffic signs and signals and painted lines. We have learned to feel safe from the world as it is in these devices. Cars are made ever more comfortable and quiet, their air-conditioning units filtering what we breathe as their audio systems numb us to the realities of mechanical noise. We are also numb to the realities of cars as agents of death from crashes and other 'accidents', the waging of wars for oil, the poisoning of the environment, the epidemic of disease due to lack of exercise and the potential calamity of climate change.[ii]

[i] Michael Ferro recovered from his years in advertising in Michigan by becoming a Sierra Club and bicycling activist in Seattle. He has since returned to his origins in the San Francisco Bay area.

[ii] For more, see Rothschild (1973); Newman and Holzman (1993); McAlinder et al. (2003); FHWA (2006); Nielsen Media Research (2007); Ladd (2008); O'Hagan (2009); and Seiler (2009).

(SAAQ), in Canada to work with the automobile and advertising industries to reign in depictions of dangerous and illegal activity involving automobiles in advertising (SAAQ 2012).

Product placement: embedded and branded with the personal motor vehicle

Product placement and embedded advertising is ethically controversial in general, and is especially controversial in relation to the semi-clandestine promoting of unsafe, unhealthy and environmentally hazardous products and activities. The automobile and the world of products and services surrounding it is one of the largest sources of advertising revenue for television and radio in the U.S., and the source of a huge amount of embedded advertising and product placement in films and television—which even when unintentional still benefits the products depicted. Yet the advertising industry largely treats the motor vehicle as just another product to be promoted, embedded, surreptitiously placed, studied and reported.

Nonchalantly the advertising industry publications inform readers that the personal motor vehicle is overrepresented, perhaps even the most highly represented category, in the 'top 40 product placements of all time' (Erik 2011; Carriere 2015).

Automakers are especially keen to embed or place upscale, expensive, supersized, sporty and luxury model cars rather than the more practical, mundane and energy-efficient models. In the 1980s and 1990s the automakers, through their lobbying surrogates such as the American Highway Users Alliance, launched media campaigns against governmental efforts to promote greater fuel efficiency such as the Corporate Average Fuel Economy (CAFE) standards (Perl and Dunn 2007). While some environmental critics pointed out that greater fuel efficiency, per se, does not necessarily reduce driving due to the 'buy-back' phenomenon of fuel costs savings (which is also true of periodic lowered gasoline prices), the highway lobby obliquely criticized CAFE by pointing to supposed greater crash risks with smaller, lighter motor vehicles.

The phenomenon of 'reverse product placement' has appeared in recent years; a fictional product that attracts a great deal of attention in a movie or television program is then purchased from the media and produced and marketed in reality. Examples include the commercial production of the cereal Krusty-O's and the temporary renaming of some convenience stores by the chain (7-11) to Kwik-E-Marts, including knock-off products, after their concepts and names were originally created on The Simpsons TV program (Miller 2007).

The portion of the TV hour in the U.S. devoted to the program itself has shrunk to approximately 45 minutes, often punctuated by commercials every six minutes, while the number of commercials has increased—especially due to most being shortened from 30 to 15 seconds. A typical U.S. home has access to almost 200 channels, of which almost 20 are watched regularly (Flint 2014).[9] Lucrative embedded advertising has grown to the extent that some critics characterize the major portion of many programs as 'shill-o-vision, where commercial breaks still come and go but the commercials never end'. This is of much concern to public interest voices who see the extreme commercialization of television programming as a violation of the trust citizens place in the U.S. government's Federal Communications Commission's duty to protect the public from over-exploitation (Moore 2005).

Branding: developing a relationship between product and consumer

Most advertising aims at the creation or exploitation of a relationship: an identification, an association between product and consumer. Some advertising aims to create a feeling of satisfaction among consumers that they have been smart in their choices—even after learning that they have purchased a product that is defective, dangerous or environmentally harmful.[10]

BOX 2.7 **We just want to change your oil**

Personality interacts with the brand to influence how the customer feels about a company. The personality also determines whether a brand furthers the customer's emotional understanding of a company. For example, if the brand personality is open and friendly, it can make customers feel secure and comfortable.

Just like in person-to-person interactions, customers will respond to a brand personality that they can relate to. A brand that has a 'playful' personality attribute may appeal to customers who want to be perceived as not taking their lives too seriously. For example, a recent commercial for Jiffy Lube featured the slogan 'We don't want to change the world; we just want to change your oil'.

Source: LePla (2002)

The same company that doesn't want to change the world does not seem to want to change thinking about automobile dependence either. A flyer mailed by Jiffy Lube asks: 'Think traffic is bad? Try walking.' Evidently the acceptance of traffic at the expense of walking is aimed to make potential customers feel better about driving, especially if it is to get their oil changed.

The many themes associated with the automobile enumerated at the beginning of this section afford advertising a rich opportunity to turn fantasy and emotional valence into product sales. This has led to the phenomena of automobiles placed at the center of much covert or embedded advertising, product placement and branded entertainment. Branding, often aimed at children and teenagers—despite scathing critiques by Naomi Klein (2002) and Susan Linn (2004) and academics (Hudson et al. 2008)—continue unabated. And it appears that Bollywood is hurriedly following Hollywood down the asphalt wedding aisle of embedding automobile advertising clandestinely in films[11].

Movies and TV: the automobile as star and sponsor

Cinema has had a long love affair with the automobile, and television has enjoyed multiple serial relationships with cars. The personal motor vehicle, itself, may be the greatest and most long-lived star of cinema and TV. From the earliest days of silent cinema to the era of James Dean and *Rebel Without a Cause*, the automobile was associated with numerous themes, from emotional to utilitarian, appealing to a mass audience: pursuit, escape, rescue, endangerment, travel and leisure, power, social class distinction and competition, reward for work ethic adherence, power, domination, self-destruction, gender, sexuality, romance and eroticism. Automobile racing has been an important aspect of the car culture and cinema since the earliest days of automobility and film. The chaos of urban traffic has been mirrored in fantasy mayhems created by gangsters, motorized heists, motorcycle gangs and road warriors. For those inured to vehicular violence and for people who appreciate the dark side of the car culture, there are films such as *Death Race 2000* and *Crash*—and, lest we forget, the intergalactic hot-rodding of *Star Wars* and George Lucas's earlier paean to hot-rodding, *American Graffiti* (Hey 1983; Smith 1983; Ebiri 2015; Huffman and Magrath 2013).

More recently, the success of films such as the several *Mad Max* releases and *Cars* and *Cars 2* attests to the perennial popularity of the motor vehicle, whether depicted in 'real-life' or animation as star or lead supporting character. The technologies used in contemporary film-making blur the line between these once-separated domains as digitization effects are increasingly used in 'realistic' films and animation is sometimes based on the digitization of live actors and scenes.

Following in the tradition of talking horse or mule movies of an earlier era, cinematic and TV cars frequently talk—either to their drivers or to the audience, as in the 1960s TV sitcom *My Mother the Car* or the 1980s vigilante anti-crime series *Knight Rider* and the 2015 film spoof *Knight Rider Heroes*. It is especially interesting that the *Cars* movies animations are heavily oriented to children as well as their car-loving parents—who will likely recognize various segments and scenes depicting famous car-racing and chasing scenes paying homage to those earlier Hollywood films.

That the vehicles talk with each other and have front sections that resemble human faces (see Pareidolia section above), with large windshield eyes, front grill mouths and other parts that move as though they were limbs is an indication of how such anthropomorphization attracts juvenile attention. The *Cars* films do not feature obviously displayed brands or logos, but various of its prominent vehicle 'stars' resemble Volkswagen or Porsche models. Porsche engineers worked closely with the filmmaker to design vehicles that resembled theirs, especially for the Porsche-like character Sally Carrera, named after a classic Porsche model, chased after by *Cars* and *Cars 2* super-star Lightning McQueen. The name Lightning McQueen is a direct homage to the racing car 'Greased Lightning' in the movie *Grease*, (which name, itself, pays homage to the 1977 film of that song's name about the first African-American winner of a NASCAR race, Wendell Scott) and Hollywood racing affecianado and 'bad boy' Steve McQueen, especially in his Mustang-powered pursuits in the film *Bullitt* (Farr 2013, p. 231).

One must wonder whether the movie industry's censor rating of these films as 'G' as suitable for general audiences is irresponsible given the unending depictions of dangerous and anti-social behavior including scenes where Lightning McQueen drives through a crowd of pedestrians depicted as accomplices to villainy. One wonders whether children might be receiving such messages as 'pedestrians = villains = mayhem acceptable?' There was a generally negative reception of *Cars* and *Cars 2* by critics, especially for giving such a violent film a G rating and for its frenzied pace of short hyperactive scenes spliced together with quick cuts (*Cars 2*).

The archives and lists of films and television shows in which a personal motor vehicle with an identifiable brand is featured involve thousands of entries. One visual catalog (imcdb.org) identifies no fewer than 4,113 vehicle makes, with links to the various models of each make and further links to the various films and television shows in which they have been featured; the total is more than likely in six or seven figures, since many of the makes and models have thousands of films or TV shows in which they have appeared.

The love affair with the car has turned into one of Hollywood's longest lasting marriages in a city and industry infamous for romantic turnovers and frequent divorce. With or without formal encouragement from the auto-industry, Hollywood, on film and in its lifestyle, glamorized and romanticized the automobile. The automobile industry, especially in the U.S., quickly picked up on the power of the images projected on the silver screen and began to sponsor films advertising its wares and shaping its customer market. Present and future motorists and buyers were reached by short industry-produced films often shown as part of the screenings of feature films. Children learned about the wonderful machines and how to be good pedestrians by getting out of the way of automobiles through educational films produced and distributed by the auto-industry and its allies, such as automobile clubs and self-proclaimed safety agencies (see Box 2.11, Jam Handy and GM).

The love affair carried over into television, Hollywood's sibling—although they have become more like twins joined at the hip than the rival siblings they once were. Many of the early TV programs in the U.S. were sponsored by automobile manufacturers or allied industries such as petroleum companies, tire manufacturers and automobile servicing chains. Not only did cinema and, later, television help to popularize the automobile, but the automobile and all the related industries trailing in its comet tail have also, in turn, helped to sustain the film and TV industry through various forms of sponsorship. The huge audiences at cinemas and in front of televisions provide great opportunities for automobile advertising—overt and covert.

Radio and cars

The relation between automobiles, car culture and radio is somewhat different than that between automobiles and the visual broadcast media. Most countries that license motorists do not allow them yet to watch TV while driving—although screens are available for some models allowing backseat passengers to watch videos, and video devices are now being built into the dashboard displays of some vehicles for backwards-facing cameras as well as GIS systems. Computer-controlled or assisted automobiles that would free motorists from paying attention to traffic are becoming commercially available and may change the role of radio in motor vehicles (see Autonomous Vehicles in Chapter 4). Radio, on the other hand, was introduced into automobiles early in their history (see Chapter 3), first for emergency and police purposes and then shortly afterwards for mass consumption and entertainment while motoring. Radio requires forms of attentiveness and imagination somewhat different from the visual broadcast media. Nevertheless, radio represents a significant opportunity for automobile advertising, especially in automobile-dependent societies where most commute or spend their leisure in cars. Marketing research indicates that 9 out of 10 motoring commuters listen to traditional commercial radio stations (MarketingCharts staff 2016).

Many radio programs target specific mobile audiences, from all-night truck drivers to rush hour commuters. Traffic reports are a prominent feature on the airwaves in many North American cities during daytime hours and every few minutes during rush hours. While the efficacy of these reports is open to question, they continue to be a popular item on many commercial and even public funded stations. In Germany, if you have either a radio or a CD player operating anywhere in the country in a car, it is compulsorily and automatically interrupted for traffic reports at designated moments. One's CD player is simply overridden.

Traffic reports often emanate from media sources that are heavily involved in other forms of advertising where the automobile is prominent. One very large U.S. based global conglomerate, iHeartMedia, controls hundreds of major radio stations, transmission towers and one of the world's largest outdoor advertising corporations as well as being a major promoter of popular music. Its major radio stations also heavily promote right-wing talk (or scream?) shows, while more moderate political talk shows are relegated to its weakest stations. Motorists are treated to iHeart's radio fare as well as its large billboards as they make their way along American roadways. Airlines passengers are treated to a barrage of

---

BOX 2.8 Turn off the traffic rap

Many, perhaps most, Americans and quite a few Canadians wake to traffic reports every morning. Eggs are poached, granola munched and pre-commute nausea developed as multi-vehicle pileups, overturned trucks and stalled cars blocking freeways are reported.

Overhead in noisy helicopters or in front of traffic monitoring screens, traffic jockeys, whose main credentials derive from voice training courses, are shaping perceptions of the 'best' way to get to work. Some of the commercial traffic reporting services have names that might mislead listeners into assuming a link with a government agency. The fact that their sympathetic and concerned voices are brought to us courtesy of automobile advertising may explain why their reports center on car traffic with only an occasional transit tidbit. All the options that should be emphasized singularly or in combination in an urban area are generally ignored: mass transit, bicycling, carpooling and walking.

Radio traffic rappers may be encouraging or 'inducing' unnecessary driving when they pronounce a freeway to be 'wide open' or promote a 'good time to drive'. While promising motorists to help to keep them rolling, they maintain the myth that a solution is just around the next curve and not to worry: continue to commute in your nearly empty cars.

Traffic spinning is intruding into daily life in insidious ways. Each morning and afternoon some public radio stations devote up to 40% of local news minutes to traffic. Many commercial radio stations devote even more time to traffic. TV news provides graphic traffic reports with live coverage from hovering helicopters of police pursuing errant motorists.

Perhaps it is time to face the fact that there are no technological fixes for the automobile that will ease congestion and allow motorists to break their destructive driving patterns. Perhaps it is time to shape a viable and balanced urban system. Perhaps it is time to switch stations and turn off the traffic rap.

Source: adapted from Schiller (1992)

FIGURE 2.9
'The traffic report'
Source: Andy Singer (www.andysinger.com)

their advertising at airports and even transit users are confronted with their advertising on shelters and inside buses. Curiously iHeart is even involved with several large bicycle-sharing systems in Europe. It has also issued a widely used app in order to attract more of the digital media market (iHeartMedia, Clear Channel Outdoor, Sisario 2014; Mann 2011).

Music and the car culture

Popular music has a strong affinity for automobile themes and imagery. The relation has been fortified through powerful car radios and CD players whose audio systems seem to be designed for destroying neighborhood tranquility or, at least, the hearing of listeners. Many television and radio programs devoted to popular music ranging from the *Grand Ole Opry* to MTV have been associated with automobility. Radio and televised opera has been associated with automobility, from the 1920s to the early 1960s *Voice of Firestone* to Texaco's (later Chevron Texaco) sponsorship of radio broadcasts of the New York Metropolitan Opera from 1940 to 2004. The relationship between motoring and music has been exceptionally close in the U.S., where motorists in 1905 could sing 'In my Merry Oldsmobile', 'Get your Kicks on Route 66' in the 1940s, 'See the USA in your Chevrolet' with Dinah Shore in 1952, drive your Oldsmobile 442 to the beach to surf with the Beach Boys or chase Maybellene and her pink Cadillac with Chuck Berry in the 1960s. More socially conscious souls could join Joni Mitchell in her 'Big yellow taxi: They paved paradise and put up a parking lot' lament. The relationship between the car and rock-and-roll has been extremely close and intense, with the automobile industry recognizing this in many ways, including the Ford Motor Company's major donation to help create the Rock-and-Roll Hall of Fame Museum in Cleveland, Ohio (Belasco 1983; Berger 2001, p. 220). The relationship between the automobile and car culture, which has only strengthened through the decades, led to the rise of hip-hop, often strongly associated with automobile and limousine imagery.

Some Bruce Springsteen songs and videos show the harshness associated with urban life in the USA; the incredible dominance of the automobile in shaping life, romantic relationships and even relationships between the individual and the urban environment—especially in working class inner cities. The city is usually depicted as a kind of brutal, competitive hell from which your only escape or rescue is a car. *Born to Run, Working on the Highway,*

Thunder Road, Badlands, Darlington County and *My Hometown*, which even mentions a Buick, demonstrates that 'The Boss's' early rise to success in the late 1970s and early 1980s was partly built on extremely powerful imagery and words derived from automobile-dominated lifestyles.

While the Metropolitan Opera might still be broadcast on some radio stations, it is not likely the most listened to inside the personal motor vehicle. Beginning in the 1960s, popular music has been increasingly recorded and engineered to be listened to inside the car, and car manufacturers have been increasingly modifying their audio systems and the interiors of their vehicles to better accommodate the driver as listener. Hip-hop and rap music have been on the radio and video air waves for several decades and there are a variety of expressions within this very popular medium, ranging from social protest to 'gangsta' glorification. One of the most prominent of rap producers-performers, Los Angeles's Dr. Dre, has been credited with the creation of a style labeled "G-funk", which, he claims, was created and mixed specifically for listening in car stereo systems (Williams 2010). That gangsta rap is associated with misogyny, heroification of the pimp–drug dealer persona and ostentatious displays of many luxury items, has been the subject of much criticism (Hunter 2011).

One of the foremost commodities flaunted in gangsta videos is the luxury vehicle or limousine. This is not an artistic accident; it is a manifestation of the extent to which rap videos are platforms crowded with product placements:

> The rap video is not just a commercial for a song, but a commercial for all kinds of other products that are placed in the videos. Seventy-five per cent of songs in this (research) sample referred to products by brand name. . . . The vast majority of videos in this sample highlighted products that viewers could purchase such as Dayton Rims for cars, Nike shoes, Blackberry smartphones, many kinds of liquor (Hennesy, Alize, and Patron, for example), and dozens of cars (Cadillacs, Porsches, Lamborghinis, Magnums, Hummers, and more).
>
> (Hunter, M. 2011, p. 19)

Many teenaged drivers are saddened to discover that several automakers are now building features into their vehicles that either control the volume of the radio or other dashboard sound devices until all seat belts have been buckled. Some of these features even allow parents to pre-set maximum volume levels to help their young ones be more attentive drivers or to avoid premature hearing loss.[12]

Car culture in literature

The automobile and car culture have captured the attention of cultural critics, fiction writers and poets, ranging from Booth Tarkington, F. Scott Fitzgerald and Carl Sandburg to Jack Kerouac, Tom Wolfe, Karl Shapiro and Allen Ginsburg (Goldstein 1998). It has been the focus of many artists' work, as well as an important symbol and metaphor for the work of many others. The road trip provides the structure for many novels and poems preceding the automobile, and it has been an especially fertile literary vehicle since 1900. John Steinbeck developed several automobile motifs in *The Grapes of Wrath* (1939); some focused on the Joad family's dependence on their ancient vehicle to deliver them from the destruction of the Dust Bowl to the promised land of California, while others focused on the automobile as symbolizing class differences, as in the contrast between the wealthy landowners' fancy convertibles and the broken-down jalopies of the migrants. Late in his career Steinbeck set off with his dog in a pick-up truck and camper on a long exploration recounted in *Travels with Charley: In Search of America* (Steinbeck 1962; Berger 2001, pp. 221–6; Smoak 2007).

Not all literary treatments of motor vehicles glorify or romanticize automobility. While erotic adventure is often part of road trip literature, some authors such as J. G. Ballard, whose work *Crash* was also made into a deeply disturbing film, have used automobility as the vehicle for exploring the horrific and perverse side of the relation between automobility and sexuality (Lewis 1983, pp. 233–4; Parchesky 2006). The oddity of being a pedestrian in an automobile and TV world was a theme in many of the writings of Ray Bradbury, including *Fahrenheit 451*. The story and (later) short play *The Pedestrian* was inspired by his experience of police harassment for the 'crime' of walking around Los Angeles one evening. The story's central character, Leonard Mead, is arrested for being a pedestrian and resisting mandatory enslavement to TV by robotic police, and committed to the 'Psychiatric Center for Research on Regressive Tendencies' for rehabilitation back to TV addiction (Bradbury 1966, 2001). Box 2.9 demonstrates how, even years later and in a supposedly progressive environmentally conscious area, pedestrians are viewed with great suspicion if not alarm.

The car is featured prominently in the genre that has come to be known as 'young adult' (YA). In the automobility-expanding era of the late 1940s and 1950s, some of the most popular books for young (and some not-so-young) readers were immersed in the growing 'hot-rod' culture of the time. Many young men returned from World War II military service with considerable expertise in mechanics and other skills related to motor vehicles. Centered in Southern California, a strong subculture of colorfully customizing automobile bodies and ramping up motor performance for competition grew up. Street racing in town and drag racing on low traffic roads outside of town abounded resulting in significant youth casualties and adult calls for its control, which helped the launching of a national driver safety program led by U.S. President Dwight 'Ike' Eisenhower. Emblematic of that era was the popularity of a series of hot-rodder-themed books by Henry G. Felsen, which fed youth's (especially young men's) fascination with racing and danger while, ultimately, reinforcing the cautious and conformist morals of the parental generation (Packer 2008, esp. Chapters 1 and 7).

More recent young adult literature featuring prominent roles for motor vehicles include the Harry Potter series as well as numerous titles glorifying racing of cars and motorcycles, including dirtbike competitions. Among the top dozen titles recommended by the website of the bookseller Barnes and Noble for teens interested in car and vehicle racing fiction are an interesting array of titles and themes illustrated in Box 2.10.

Most of the racing books aimed at teens do have a more modern version of the safety moralizing discussed above but a significant difference between the 1950s hot-rod racing books and more recent ones is found in the much more active and prominent role of young women as racers rather than simply passengers or cheerleaders (as depicted in many pre-

---

BOX 2.9 Busted for walking and entering

While staying in Marin County, just north of San Francisco (CA), at some friends who weren't there but had left me the key, I was awakened on my first morning by a police officer slamming on the front door at 6.30 am, his pistol at the ready and his partner with his gun pulled covering the back door. I had been reported by neighbors for walking down the middle of the street the previous evening (there was no sidewalk) and entering the front door of the house. Evidently I was not recognized by a neighbor, who chose to call the police rather than greet me. It was walking down the middle of the quiet road that raised all the suspicions. I invited them in and showed them my passport and explained that I had needed a meal and did not have a car so had walked to a local Denny's in a big-box mall a couple of kilometers away and . . . ergghmm . . . at least 'neighborhood watch' was working . . . Welcome to California, have a nice day.

Source: Jeffrey R. Kenworthy

BOX 2.10 Teen romance in the fast lane

- *Crash into You;* 'a romance forged in the fast lane . . .';
- *Slide or Die;* '. . . Kennin is . . . anxious to start a life outside the gearhead crowd. But he can't resist the lure of all the hot, tricked-out cars in Las Vegas.'
- *Redline;* '. . . Jenessa escapes to the sanctuary of her car and the freedom of the open road. . . . But when Jenessa falls in with a group of street racers . . .';
- *Saturday Night Dirt;* 'It's a sizzling summer Saturday, and Headwaters Speedway is suddenly the place to be . . . Amber Jenkins, a strawberry blonde who has what it takes to run rings around them all. Keeping everyone on track is Melody Walters . . . a 2009 Bank Street—Best Children's Book of the Year.';
- *Checkered Flag Cheater;* 'Trace Bonham is living large as the teen driver for a pro Super Stock racing team. He's on billboards and on the road instead of stuck in school. . . .';
- *Dirtbike Daredevils;* 'Peter is a freestyle maniac who hates doing bike (motorcycle) maintenance. Jake dreams of being a motocross-race mechanic without having to race himself. They ignore warnings from their boss and his 15-year-old female ranch hand (also a motocross racer) . . .'.

Source: Barnes and Noble (2016)

---

feminism books and the films *Grease* and *American Graffiti*). Young and adult women are also showing up in the traditionally male-dominated North American recreational pastimes of professional car-racing and 'demolition derbies', where drivers compete to demolish each other's vehicles to see who one will be the last one rolling. In Bellingham, WA, a high school student made the preparing of an older pick-up truck for a demolition derby competition at the annual county fair her senior project, and there are demolition derbies where 'moms' are 'crash queens' (Millage 2008; Wright et al. 2015). A casual search of Youtube.com will reveal many videos featuring women in demolition derbies, women's only 'Powder Puff' derbies and ads for demolition derby lingerie.

'Carchitecture': reshaping architecture and urban design for automobile cities

The term 'carchitecture' is often used, sometimes derisively, to denote the ways in which the built environment has been reshaped to accommodate automobiles. It is sometimes employed to denote the ways in which automobiles are designed, although that usage will not be addressed here. Accommodating automobility and designing buildings and residences to display their most important features to passing motorists have been master trends in architecture and urban design throughout the twentieth and into the twenty-first century. The ways in which projects as different as Le Corbusier's 'Radiant City' and Frank Lloyd Wright's 'Usonian' vision for 'Broadacre City' profoundly shaped the design and redesign of cities and suburbs to accommodate or even promote automobility have been masterfully examined in Peter Hall's *Cities of Tomorrow* (1988, especially Chapters 7 and 9). At the level of residential design, modernist architects have, over many decades, blurred the distinction between living space and automobile space as garages and carports moved onto and into houses and replaced porches and formal entranceways (Kihlstedt 1983). This fundamental reshaping of urban environments around the car and how to measure, evaluate and reverse this is developed in Chapter 6 on urban design and active transportation (for the burden and distorting effects of parking on cities see Shoup 1997, 2011).

Extreme forms of this shaping, as in recent developments and proposals such the Bravern development in Bellevue, WA and Tata Gateway Towers (Mumbai) are discussed

FIGURE 2.10
Hotel garage entries across
sidewalks are typical of
'carchitecture', San Francisco
central business district
Source: Preston L. Schiller

in the modes chapter. These developments also demonstrate how the lines between home life and car life are increasingly blurred. The early proposals for Tata Gateway Towers included car elevators that would solve the problems of parking space and convenience by simply delivering car and passengers directly to their apartment. Car elevators are already in place in super-luxurious and super-expensive residential and commercial buildings from VW headquarters in Wolfsburg, DE, to former Gov. Mitt Romney's mansion in La Jolla, CA, to Manhattan, NY (Taylor 2013; High Rise Facilities 2013; O'Connell 2015; Autostadt 2016).

'Futurama': we have seen the future and it drives![13]

Over many decades, General Motors (GM) developed a vision of an automobile-centered world that went far beyond the reach of its factories and dealerships. GM's landscape, urban and rural, was to be dominated by superhighways that were, of course, never congested. In city centers, superhighways directly entered high-rise buildings. This expression reached its fullest form in the Futurama exhibit designed by Norman Bel Geddes for GM's pavilion at the New York World's Fair of 1939. In 1964, GM returned to its vision for the future of mobility that went beyond superhighways to the conquest of rainforests and outer space.[14]

Counterposed to the vision of a superhighway future was the critique and vision of urbanologist and regional planning advocate Lewis Mumford, whose life and works parallel the Bel Geddes and GM elaborations (Ellis 2005). Today, the ruins of automobile industry cities such as Detroit and Flint, Michigan, provide a sobering reminder of the dark and perhaps inevitable side of Futurama (see discussion of Flint in Chapter 8). Mumford's influence can be sensed, along with that of Jane Jacobs, in the current interest in renewing and revitalizing cities—even the badly damaged City of Detroit—and de-emphasizing automobility. Mumford's work is also drawn upon in Chapter 6 as a harbinger of the rise of urban design in the latter half of the twentieth century as a remedy for auto-fractured landscapes.

A film about Futurama was done by the Jam Handy entertainment, documentary and instructional film organization for GM in 1940 and widely distributed (Jam Handy 1940). The importance of Jam Handy for GM and many other industries is briefly discussed in Box 2.11.

BOX 2.11 Jam Handy and GM

A largely untold, or under-told, story about GM and the influence of Detroit is that of its extensive film work done through the Jam Handy organization of Detroit, MI. Henry Jamison ('Jam') Handy was a pioneer in several aspects of market research and the use of visual media, from slides to films from the early years of the twentieth century through to the late 1960s. He and his firm were innovators in the use of animation for popular films as well as films for instruction in schools and industry, public relations, product promotion and propaganda. Over many decades, they produced tens of thousands of films, including approximately 7000 that were done for the U.S. government during World War II. Fortunately, thanks to the efforts of the Prelinger Library in San Francisco, much of Jam Handy's work has been preserved and digitized (Prelinger Library). Jamison Handy was quite a fascinating character and he and the Jam Handy Organization are phenomena begging for more research. Fortunately, there is a small amount of excellent work already done that hints at the large task yet to be undertaken. Any takers?

Source: James (1998); Tohline (2009); Sandy (2002); Schreiber (2013); Woolf (2010)

Tourism: the car culture evolves into the fly-drive and recreational vehicle cultures

Tourism presents special problems and questions for sustainability and ST. There are numerous issues involving the extent to which tourism is harmful to the environment and socially harmful to many of its destinations in less wealthy nations (see Whitelegg 1997, especially Chapter 6). Tourism transportation may have several components and there are some complex issues around how tourism is defined and measured. Better data seem to exist for tourism that crosses national borders and for travel by airlines than for domestic tourism—especially that done by private motor vehicles (Page 1998; Sheller and Urry 2004; Hall 2008). Tourism is rapidly growing, and travel by the most harmful modes (aviation and personal motor vehicles, or PMVs) is similarly increasing, fueled to a certain extent by the large subsidies given to automobiles and commercial aviation, which can lead to the phenomenon of low-cost airfares with large environmental price tags. Despite the pull of drive-fly-drive culture and economy, one can find efforts, especially in Europe, at encouraging more recreational travel for individuals, groups and families to go by rail.

The largest component of international tourism is air travel between North America and Europe, although Latin American, Caribbean and Asian destinations are rapidly increasing their shares. For some long-distance tourist travel, over 90% of a vacationer's energy footprint was the air travel component (Hall 2008, pp. 204–5). The fact that U.S. residents drive much more than residents of other countries, including motoring for leisure and tourism, has led some researchers to conclude that 'most of the world's tourism takes place within the U.S.' (Gilbert and Perl 2008, pp. 90–91). The road-trip vacation has a long history in the U.S., which is intertwined with the development and rapid popularity of the station wagon (also known as an estate wagon) automobile model. While station wagon models emerged as early as the 1920s, they gained momentum after World War II, especially in the U.S., where they were promoted as *the* vehicle for the suburban housewife. From there they evolved into *the* family car, and accelerated the trend towards most vacations taking place on wheels; by 1955 85% of American vacations were by motor vehicle (Packer 2008 pp. 28–41).

A road trip vacation taken in 1983 by former corporate executive and Massachusetts Governor Mitt Romney and his family became an issue in his 2012 presidential candidacy when it surfaced that they had strapped a crated dog to the roof of their overcrowded station wagon. This created quite a ruckus in the media, especially as fodder for late-night TV programs, and among dog lovers and animal advocates (Rucker 2012). An organization,

'Dogs Against Romney', was formed (dogsagainstromney.com) to fan the flames of 'Crate-Gate'. Alas poor Mitt, if had only invested in a large recreational vehicle (RV), he would have had all the room he needed to keep the family dog Seamus in comfort inside—and it might have changed the outcome of the 2012 presidential election.

Racing is another interesting aspect of the car culture that has been discussed above in the context of the automobile and broadcast media. The relation between the early motorist associations, in the U.S. and Europe, is discussed in Chapter 3. In the U.S., millions of people drive substantial distances annually to watch hundreds of others race cars and, occasionally, motorcycles around and around a track. Many millions more watch the cars zoom and crash on TV, interrupted by frequent automobile and fast food advertising. Occasionally spectators are killed at NASCAR and other racing events when drivers lose control and crash into viewer areas or stands (Busbee 2009). National Association for Stock Car Auto Racing (NASCAR) tracks are highly profitable ventures, and they have been strategically located to draw visitors from large regional catchment areas (Mooradian 2000; ISC 2009). Racing tracks often attract fans who arrive and stay in their recreational vehicles (RVs). NASCAR is becoming a very profitable venture, overall, due to its attendees and the large revenues it derives from advertising and licensing itself as a brand (Barnes 2010).

Sales of RVs and RV travel have been growing in the U.S. and Europe. A small but growing number of US residents have taken to living year-round in RVs and are accommodated by an increasing number of special facilities termed 'RV parks', as well as in public camp-grounds, some in wilderness areas. RVs often bring along off-road vehicles (ORVs), such as small motorcycles or snow machines, to explore and further pollute natural areas. The rapid increase of ORVs (especially in North America), whose emissions are generally less controlled than those of on-road vehicles, is a growing concern of environmental agencies.

The 'walking school bus' in a suburban neighborhood, illustrated in Figure 2.12a, demonstrates that automobile dependence is not inevitable. Communities, families and

---

BOX 2.12 Louis Mattar's Perpetual motion 1947 Cadillac

Soon after purchasing his 1947 Cadillac, Louie Mattar . . . and two other men established a cross-country endurance record by driving the Cadillac from San Diego to New York and back without stopping. Their trip totaled 6,320 miles and required refueling from a moving gas truck three times!

During the trips, [they] had all the comforts of home, although space was limited. The equipment in the back seat includes an electric stove, a refrigerator, a washing machine, a chemical toilet, an ironing board, a medicine cabinet and a kitchen sink. These appliances can all be stored under the backseat cushions. Up front, in addition to the many switches and dials surrounding the dashboard, are a nationwide mobile telephone, a tape recorder, a bar, a public-address system (which has speakers in both the trailer and on the hood of the car), and a Turkish water pipe. On the right running board is a shower and at the rear taillight is a drinking fountain!

The car holds 50 gallons of water, with a reserve of 30 gallons in the trailer. The trailer also holds 230 gallons of gas and 15 gallons of oil in addition to the dining area at the end. The car automatically refills the radiator and changes the oil, and the axles are drilled, which allow the tires to be inflated while turning. Hydraulic jacks allow the wheels to be raised for changing while moving. This could be accomplished from a movable platform that attaches to the car. Clear panels in the hood allow the car to be driven while the hood is open for repairs or adjustments [of its] 1947 Cadillac engine. . . . It took . . . Mattar 5 years and $75,000 . . .

Source: San Diego Automotive Museum, 'Louis Mattar's Fabulous Car'[i]

[i]http://sdautomuseum.org/exhibit/louis-mattars-fabulous-car accessed 9 November 2016

FIGURE 2.11A
Mattar Cadillac exterior
Source: Preston L. Schiller

FIGURE 2.11B
Mattar Cadillac interior
Source: Preston L. Schiller

individuals can organize their lives to lessen their dependence upon driving. With supportive government programs aimed at improving local transit, walking and bicycling infrastructure, and improved intercity public transportation, many trips can be conveniently and enjoyably made without a personal motor vehicle.

Recent analyses demonstrate that young persons in the U.S. and Canada are delaying or avoiding obtaining driver's licenses, owning cars in shrinking numbers and driving less even when they own cars. Evidence of a big trend away from driving and even getting driver's licenses among young people can be found in Davis et al. (2012) in a revealingly titled report called *Transportation and the New Generation: Why young people are driving less and what it means for transportation policy*, which shows that young people across the USA

FIGURE 2.12A
Walking school bus in the automobile-oriented Seattle suburb of Sammamish: Lena Schiller Hanson began to walk her daughters, Sierra and Renate, to school, a mile from their home, and after a short while neighbors with their children and dogs began to join them.
Source: Preston L. Schiller

FIGURE 2.12B
Traffic jam at the school: When the walking school bus arrives at the school it must navigate its way through a traffic jam of motorized parents who don't walk with their children to school. In the background a school bus is stuck in traffic. This scene can be found at many schools in the U.S., Canada, the U.K. and Australia (and probably elsewhere).
Source: Preston L. Schiller

value their smartphones more than they do cars. In an online report based on the work of Davis et al. (2012), it states that:

> From 2001 to 2009, the average annual number of vehicle-miles travelled by young people (16 to 34 year olds) decreased from 10,300 miles to 7900 miles per capita—a drop of 23 per cent. . . . The trend toward reduced driving . . . has occurred even among young people who are employed and/or are doing well financially. . . . From 2001 to 2009, young people (16- to 34-year-olds) who lived in households with annual incomes of over $70,000 increased their use of public transit by 100 per cent, biking by 122 per cent, and walking by 37 per cent.

Similar patterns are evident in Canada, with, for example, significant drops in the rate of driver's licenses between 2004 and 2013 in Metro Vancouver in all age groups from 16–34 and significant increases in transit use among younger people (Johnson 2015).

In Australia, Raimond and Milthorpe (2010) show that in the Greater Metropolitan Area of Sydney between 1991/2 and 2008/9, the percentage of people 15–19 years of age holding a full driver's license dropped from 23% to 3% and those 20–24 years of age declined from 79% to 51% (p. 3). They conclude:

> . . . our transport modelling and transport planning needs to begin to adjust to this new paradigm of lower levels of license-holding by young people. The increasing importance of public transport access to jobs, services, and local shopping opportunities are clear, and are already reflected in the NSW State Plan priority of improving public transport access to key major centers in the metropolitan region. There is also an opportunity for cycling and walking to play a much larger role in the transport task for this age group.
>
> The changes observed in this paper should be viewed as a positive trend for road safety, for the environment, and for more livable cities. These finding also acknowledge that the transport planner's toolkit is much larger than transport infrastructure and service provision. Education policies, licensing policies and communications develop-ments are all possible contributors to this significant new trend, which may help us in our efforts to moderate the demand for car travel into the future.
>
> (p. 10)

Conclusions

This chapter has presented a present-day perspective on how most cities evolved through different transportation stages, from walking cities to transit cities and on to automobile cities. But this is not inevitable as many are attempting to move away from automobile domination and are trying to recapture favorable aspects of walking and transit cities. Recent trends are moving in an opposite direction, away from overdependence on automobiles and towards mobility based on walking, cycling and transit. Some, many in developing countries, have made a leap from walking cities to automobile and motorcycle cities without ever having developed significant transit systems. Here, too, one finds awareness of having moved in a harmful direction and efforts at moving in a better, more sustainable direction. Auto-mobile cities nurture the car culture, which can pervade almost all aspects of daily life, including recreational and vacation times. In this, one can find efforts in many places to encourage individuals, groups and families to vacation by bus and rail. The next chapter explores the history of sustainable and unsustainable transportation, how diverse modes and transportation patterns developed, and why some of its lessons need to be learned again.

Questions for discussion

- Discuss the transportation situation of your community in light of the discussion of walking cities, transit cities and automobile cities.

- Discuss whether and to what extent you or individuals close to you are experiencing 'time pollution'.

- Identify and discuss some aspects of the 'car culture' that you encounter in your community.

Additional resources

Beyond the Motor City Dir. Aaron Woolf. Blueprint America. PBS, 2010. Film. www.pbs.org/wnet/blueprintamerica. 8 February 2010

www.pbs.org/wnet/blueprintamerica/featured/beyond-the-motor-city-preview/861/
—critique of M-1; www.youtube.com/watch?v=Ld05-5OOLRg
—also search on 'Beyond the Motor City' for interesting opinions, etc. see immed. above
www.citizenkoch.com/blog/entry/we-refuse-to-be-silenced
How PBS sold its soul to a billionaire donor, Feb. 17, 2014, Michael Hiltzik, L.A. Times
www.pbs.org/ombudsman/2013/05/david_koch_and_pbs_the_odd_couple.html
www.newyorker.com/magazine/2013/05/27/a-word-from-our-sponsor
www.imcdb.org/; Internet Movie Cars Database
www.vulture.com/2015/04/29-greatest-car-movies-ever.html
www.edmunds.com/car-reviews/features/the-100-greatest-movie-and-tv-cars-of-all-time.html
https://en.wikipedia.org/wiki/List_of_films_about_automobiles (see)
http://editorial.rottentomatoes.com/article/Total-Recall-50-Most-Memorable-Movie-Cars/
Note: some sites are 'best car movies' and others are 'best movie cars'

Notes

1   The section 'Walking cities, transit cities and automobile cities' and its accompanying figures have been the effort of Jeffrey R. Kenworthy, with some material (e.g. Figures 2.1–2.3) drawn from previous joint work, such as in Newman and Kenworthy (1999a).
2   See also the active transportation discussion in Chapter 6.
3   See 'The pink pyramid scheme: *How Mary Kay cosmetics preys on desperate housewives*' by Virginia Sole-Smith, Harper's Aug. 2012, pp. 26–34; www.pinklighthouse.com/2008/04/the-mary-kay-car-program-2/; https://en.wikipedia.org/wiki/Mary_Kay; https://en.wikipedia.org/wiki/Mary_Kay#Cars; www.pinktruth.com/category/mary-kay-cars/; also, for Canada: www.princegeorgecitizen.com/news/local-news/local-sales-rep-earns-pink-cadillac-1.1038888
4   See Norton 2007, esp. chapter 7
5   A good example of such is to be found in the various treatments of safety in Berger, 2001
6   See Hillman et al. 1990.
7   For the ads themselves see: www.flickr.com/photos/rllayman/9006896; http://bikeportland.org/2011/10/11/gm-ad-urges-college-students-to-stop-pedaling-start-driving-60399; http://bikeportland.org/2011/10/11/gm-ad-urges-college-students-to-stop-pedaling-start-driving-60399
8   www.pbs.org/e2/ accessed 30 May 2016
9   Also, see http://touch.latimes.com/#section/-1/article/p2p-80166285/
10   This aspect of advertising is akin to Irving Goffman's sociological concept of 'cooling the mark out' after a 'sting'—in this case the consumer is conned through an act of questionable consumption and then 'cooled out' by feel-good advertising. See www.tau.ac.il/~algazi/mat/Goffman—Cooling.htm and the film *The Sting*.
11   Thanawala, 2007; Indiantelevision.com, 2008
12   www.autonews.com/article/20150324/OEM06/150329951/chevrolets-teen-driver-safety-feature-to-debut-on-redesigned-malibu
13   This, of course, is a play upon the famous quote attributed to Beatrice and Sidney Webb upon returning from a visit to 1930s Stalinist Russia: 'I have seen the future and it works!'
14   GMC (1940): for Part 1, see www.youtube.com/watch?v=74cO9X4NMb4; for Part 2, see www.youtube.com/watch?v=WU7dT2HId-c&feature=related; for 1964–5, see www.youtube.com/watch?v=2–5aK0H05jk&feature=related

History of sustainable and unsustainable transportation: from walking to wheels and back to walking

Transportation history: the intersection of modes, infrastructure and society

The history of transportation is a fascinating and vast field spanning millennia, from early human evolution to the exploration of space. Its purview includes walking and human evolution, early experience with marine and river travel, the use of animals for transport, the impact of the wheel and early mechanization, roads, the motor age, telecommunications, popular culture and space travel. It sheds light on issues such as the relation of mobility to the community, economic development and daily activity. Sustainable transportation has emerged as an important issue in recent decades, although aspects of sustainability are as ancient as mobility itself. This chapter will sketch the outlines of some of the important themes and issues relevant to sustainable transportation (ST) and suggest ways in which they should inform planning and policy-making. It will focus principally on land transport and major forms of transportation and infrastructure, but it will also review aspects of the history of maritime–water travel, telecommunications and aviation necessary for an understanding of subsequent chapters.

Among the major themes and issues explored are:

- Modal development, competition, succession: how modes of transport developed and competed with each other; how some modes, or varieties of the same general mode, prevailed and others did not; and how several modes reflected a desire for easier, speedier and more reliable and affordable travel but were not concerned about sustainability.
- Relations between modes, infrastructure, community form and travel: for certain modes to succeed, changes in infrastructure were needed. Modes, infrastructure, community design, and social and cultural factors interacted in complex and sometimes unpredictable ways. Transportation and land-use patterns are implicated directly on a global scale in the health and safety of people.
- How modes interact with land use, infrastructure, environment and societal and cultural factors are important considerations for planning and policy-making, especially as rapid changes occur—or need to occur. Some modal, infrastructure and urban forms are more compatible with sustainability goals than are others, and some modes work together in a sustainable manner to achieve energy efficiency, less fossil-fuel dependence, lower noise and air pollution and more compact communities than do others.

TABLE 3.1 Transportation timeline

Dates	Walking & cycling	Water	Mechanized, roads, infrastructure, cycling	Aviation	Telecom
3–7 million years ago	Bipedalism begins		Humans following animal trails and trackways		
8000–15,000 years ago	Early permanent settlements and shoes		Human trails, trackways		Fires, smoke signals, drums, horns, flags
8000–5000 BCE	Animal transport; cities	Dugouts, rafts	Sled, sleigh; wheels		
4000 BCE–400 CE	Egyptians, Greeks and Romans perfect sandals	Boats, sails, canals	Wheel spreads; Diolkos wagonway; Roman, Silk roads; wheelbarrow	Icarus-Daedalus Myth	Chinese signal lanterns (220–280 C.E.)
400–1400	Pilgrimages; tours, crusades; Dutch clogs	Vikings; crusades; sea trade routes expand	Caravan routes expand; Inca roads (1200–1500)		Mongol signal lanterns, Poland invasion (1241)
1400–1700	English Civil War (1642–1651); military footwear	Oceanic exploration; early Canada riverain beaver trade network	Intercity coaches and mail; Pascal's Paris bus (1662); Short rail-wagonways at mines/ports	da Vinci drawings (1487)	
1700–1800	European colonizers 'discover' moccasins from Canadian and American indigenous	Canals–locks; motorization (1783) Canada riverain beaver trade network expands	Watt's steam engine (1765–1769), Roads–Bridges Engineering School—France (1747)	Balloons, Paris, Versailles (1783), Air mail (1785) Reconnaissance, 1794	(Early) semaphores
1800–1860	Draisine-vélo (1817)	More canals—locks; Erie–U.S. (1825), early Welland–Canada (1829–1848) vast riverain beaver trade network across Canada	Transit in U.K., FR and U.S. (1820s); railways; U.K, CA, U.S. (1830s); Stephenson's locomotive (1829); French improve improve roads, Parisian Boulevards	First glider flight (1853); Balloon reconnaissance, Franco-Austrian War, (1859)	Telegraphs; early wireless and fax experiments (1830–40s) English Channel Cable (1851); Paris tube mail system "Pneumatique" (1866)
1860–1870	Millions of marching soldiers (U.S.); pedal vélo 'boneshaker'	Suez Canal (1869)	Railways major factor in U.S. Civil War	Balloon reconnaissance, Union Army (U.S.)	Caselli's telefax (1861); telegraph cable, U.S.–U.K. (1866)

continued

TABLE 3.1 *continued*

Dates	Walking & cycling	Water	Mechanized, roads, infrastructure, cycling	Aviation	Telecom
1870s	Many foot soldiers; Paris Communards; high-wheeler cycle;		Railways expand; early 'Good Roads' movement	Balloon reconnaissance, Franco-Prussian War	Bell's telephone (1876)
1880s	Pedestrian competitions, indoors & outdoors, U.S., CA; safety bicycle		Auto-production begins; more 'Good Roads'; Sea-to-Sea Railway done Canada (1885)	Dirigibles develop, more European use of military balloons	Hollerith's punch cards
1890–1910	Migratory labor grows; At least 500,000 hobos moving around the U.S.		Street railways; automobile mass production (Fordism)	Manned flight, Ader, Zeppelin dirigible, Wright Brothers	Tesla, Marconi wireless; early fax
1910–1920 (and WWI)	Millions of foot soldiers	Submarines, Panama Canal (1914)	Auto-production–ownership increase, trucks and tanks (WWI)	Military aviation, air mail (U.S., U.K. India) UAVs (radio drones)	
1920s	Dance marathons	Early aircraft carriers	'Car culture' spreads; tractor-trailer trucks; highway-auto-interests dominate Good Roads movement, motels, auto-camps, drive-ins	Air freight; dirigibles; rocketry; more radio-controlled aircraft and missiles	Analog computers; 2-way mobile radio (AU); wireless transoceanic fax; newspaper fax; TV (U.K.)
1930s	Poor. unemployed, hobos march, protest; recumbents banned from racing; Mochet Velocar		Great Depression; auto-migrants (U.S.); drive-thru banks, Superhighways (Germany, Italy, U.S.)	Airlines expand; DC-3 developed; anti-aircraft target drones; aerial torpedoes	Desktop calculators
1940s (and WWII)	Millions of soldiers and refugees on foot	Naval warfare; shipping and troop transport	Transit at capacity; commuters, war efforts, drive-through fast food	military aviation expands; civilians bombed; UAVs	Large mainframe digital computers; commercial TV (U.S.)
1950s	European cities embrace, then reject U.S. automobile-oriented urban design	First container ships; freight intermodalism	Suburbanization; transit services decline; auto-ownership and driving expand, cheap fuel; expansion of highways; especially U.S. and Europe	Airports, airlines expand; jets for civilian & military; Sputnik (1957); reconnaissance drones	Digitization, fibre optics, microwaves, integ. circuitry; small mainframes, mag. disk, transistors, satellite era begins; Atlantic cable

Decade					
1960s	Telstar (1962); first email (1965); early internet (1969)	Space and moon explored– militarized; Vietnam recon. drones, carpet bombing	Major increase in driving, roads, automobile ownership, suburbanization; anti-highway movements	Cargo containerizing, intermodalism expand	Peace & civil rights; March on Washington 1963, Paris 'Events of May', 'Convention in the Streets', Chicago 1968
1970s	Mobile phones; first Apple I, II computers (1976, 1977); heyday of citizen band (CB) radios	Expansion of air cargo– express services, first GPS satellite; more carpet-bombing Vietnam and Cambodia	Oil embargo; renewal of interest in energy efficiency and transit; Amtrak (U.S. 1971), ViaRail (CA 1978) founded; driving and roads increase; traffic restraint grows in Europe		Walking to school declines
1980s	Al Gore 'invents' internet; digital network; IBM-PC (1981), Macs (1984) 'Pneumatique' ends	Israel deploys military drones in Syria;	Rail double-stack containers; TGV-HSR France (1981); EU improves bicycle planning and facilities	Exxon Valdez oil spill	Euro cities begin pedestrianization, Walkathons; AIDS, charities, political
1990s	Digitality, mobility, connectivity, video-conferencing	Stealth bombers attack Iraq (1991) GPS system operational, U.S. deploys drones in Gulf Wars	ISTEA; more funding for transit, walking, cycling (U.S.)	New maritime pollution, laws especially for oil spills and mandating that oil tankers be double-hulled by 2015;	Pedestrian interest grows in U.S.; major protest against WTO, Seattle, 1999
2000-Present	Text messaging, videophones, Obama's Blackberry (2008); Uber (2009) Lyft (2012); Iphone leads mobile tech.; GPS for mobile phones and motor vehicles widespread, merging of telecom with mobility grows	Energy costs fluctuate; energy security issues; Concorde ends; jumbo jets developed; Drones spread– civilian & military; space tourism; snapchat speeding selfies and deaths; airport city phenomena identified; Aerotropolis proposed	Transit ridership-investment grows globally; EU & Asia expand passenger rail; Amtrak funds cut; road pricing interest (U.S.); congestion pricing in Europe grows; semi and autonomous vehicles and EVs progress; car and bike-sharing grows	Shippers explore sail assistance; Panama Canal and Container Ships Expand; New Coal Export Terminals defeated; U.S. exports oil again (fracking)	Lack of walking and obesity health concerns; Active transportation and healthy community emphases expand;

Source: Preston L. Schiller

For transportation to play a significant role in achieving sustainability, it is necessary to understand more of its history in order not to repeat mistakes of the past. The main transportation modalities whose history will be explored in this chapter are those related to:

- walking;
- water and maritime travel;
- sleds and related mobility devices;
- animal-assisted transport;
- wheeled apparatus;
- mechanization and motorization;
- air travel;
- communications and telecommunications.

Table 3.1 summarizes this long history, while each of the major stages are discussed in more detail below.

Walking: the original affordable, healthful and sustainable mode

While much of pre-history and paleo-history is subject to debate and speculation, it appears that the transformation of mobility from the prone positioning of tetrapedalism—using feet and arms together—to erect, feet-only bipedalism began millions of years ago. Bipedalism has been credited for evolutionary advances in physical and cognitive development and human toolmaking. Walking was mostly a slow-paced group activity. It was another long slow walk until about 500,000 years ago when *Homo sapiens* became distinguished from *Homo erectus* and began to gather in very early seasonal communities. Human development then took another long slow walk until some 20,000 years ago when our predecessors began to gather in permanent settlements. A somewhat quicker walk led to the development of early civilizations some 10,000 years ago.[1] Walking remained the primary mode even as humans developed rudimentary ways of traveling across water, used animals to lighten their loads or developed types of sleds and sleighs (Lay 1992, p. 25, *passim*). So, for most of human settlement history (until about 1850 and the appearance of current forms of transit), life proceeded at a typical speed of about 5 km/h.

From nineteenth-century pedestrian contests to 'text neck'

Even after transit began to reshape cities as well as mobility patterns and choices, walking remained a dominant mode in town and country. Walking as a means of getting around and as a competitive sport was very popular and, from about 1850 on until the bicycle boom began pedestrian, contests were quite fashionable—if not the rage. The modern Olympic sport of race-walking has its roots in the 1850s and was known as pedestrianism. Some of the historical pedestrian contests were about speed while others were about distance and endurance. Nineteenth-century pedestrian celebrities included Edward Payson Weston, among others, who first distinguished himself by responding to a wager and walked the almost 500 miles from Boston (MA) to Washington (DC) in 10 days and 10 hours in time for the inauguration and inaugural ball of President Abraham Lincoln. For decades to follow, he toured the U.S. and Europe as a professional walker. Some of the contests were outdoors and cross country, others were held in arenas filled with paying (and gambling) spectators (Duane, C. 2010). During the same time period, many women were becoming emancipated from shoes and clothing that hampered their mobility and ability to engage in athletics. Women athletes such as Ada Anderson and Exilda La Chapelle became widely acclaimed as professional 'pedestriennes' (Park 2012, also see discussion below about women and cycling). Newspapers from London (U.K.), Petersborough (ON), Canterbury (NZ) and across the U.S. regularly reported on the contests between the 1860s and 1880s.

Walking remains the dominant mode around the planet; even in the highly motorized countries, there is usually a pedestrian component to most motorized trips, whether by transit or personal motor vehicle (PMV). In many countries with high rates of PMV ownership, there is a walking renaissance; walking for health is increasing and being prescribed by health providers. Thanks to better urban planning, walking commutes and walking for non-work purposes, such as shopping and sociability, is increasing—especially in cities that have pedestrian zones or greatly improved pedestrian conditions.

Unfortunately, the near-universal prevalence of mobile communication devices has led to some less than desirable consequences, such as walking in public with a cell-phone constantly next to one's ears (and sharing one's personal conversation with neighboring pedestrians, who may be seeking peace and solitude). This has led to an increase of injuries due to 'distracted walking', which sometimes occurs when a cell-phone-engrossed pedestrian walks into traffic (Nasar and Troyer 2013), as well as a form of spinal injury known as 'text neck' (Bever 2014). Some cartoonists have even modified the well-known caricature of human evolution from crouching ape to walking erectly *Homo sapiens* by adding a final figure showing *Homo sapien cellphoneus*.[2] Figure 3.1 (below) indicates how even in health and safety-conscious Stockholm, pedestrians sometimes pay more attention to their mobile devices than to their companions and surroundings.

Early water and marine

Travel between coastal communities, along river systems and across large bodies of water resulted in increased trade, population exchanges and early forms of warfare. These developments, in turn, spurred improvements in the technology of water travel, which expanded its range, efficiency and hauling capacities. Aquatic and shoreline food sources, along with the new opportunities for trade, played a role in the development of settlements and cities. By about 5,000 years ago, several civilizations were building oar-powered complicated boats, some with sails and oars. Such ships could carry sizeable crews and cargoes and played an important role in the transport of food and the military, and the

FIGURE 3.1
From Homo Erectus to Homo Cellphoneus; Luckily these persons are in a Stockholm pedestrian zone so their "distracted walking" is not as dangerous as it can be on sidewalks or crossing streets. But even in pedestrian zones or at home humans face health risks, including "text neck" from inappropriate use of these devices.
Source: Jeffrey R. Kenworthy

political and administrative development of early states. Even as navigational skills and ship technologies improved, the uncertain conditions of weather, as well as the health difficulties of long voyages, made such forms of travel risky. Transatlantic crossings in the centuries of conquest and colonization of the Americas claimed a fair percentage of lives, and those transported as slaves had especially high rates of mortality.[3]

Animals, sleds and sleighs lighten the load

The domestication of animals and their subsequent use for carrying materials began between 5,000 and 15,000 years ago. Among the animals domesticated by humans and then used for work, mobility and war were dogs, donkeys, horses, camels, yaks, goats, llamas, alpacas and elephants. Sleds, useful for dragging loads, could be made more efficient by placing them on rollers or logs and using animals as their domestication developed. In North America, the form of sled known as the travois was first pulled by dogs, either alone or in teams, and later by horses. These were vital to indigenous peoples as they moved seasonally from village to village or from one hunting area to another. Each dog could pull a load of from 20 to 30 pounds. While the travois has all but disappeared, the dog sled remains an important winter form of transportation for many in the more northern regions.[4]

Wheels, early vehicles and travel—mostly local and for necessity

The wheel developed in Mesopotamia about 7,000 years ago and spread across many civilizations and cultures over the next few millennia, from Europe to India and China. It is thought that the wheel was first developed for milling, and only later applied to mobility when the wheelbarrow was invented in Classical Greece between the sixth and fourth centuries BCE. Civilization was not dependent upon the wheel for mobility: several societies with complex systems of mobility developed without the wheel, as in the pre-Columbian Americas. Nor was wheeled transport suited for all cultures and terrains. Much of the Middle-East, after adopting the wheel, abandoned it in favor of the camel for several centuries. The wheel opened numerous possibilities in the movement of persons and larger loads for those cultures that adopted it, although most of its use remained local and for necessity. The mechanical efficiency of the wheel also was applied to advances in milling and marine transport over time. As the wheel improved, the devices it supported became more differentiated: hand carts, animal-drawn wagons and chariots.[5]

Travel remained difficult even after the domestication of animals, wheeled transportation and boats and navigation improved. Most land travel was still on foot as animals were used more for packing loads and pulling wagons than for riding. Travel beyond the horizon was rare and reserved for special occasions and necessities. Avocational travelers were especially rare and often attached themselves to organized expeditions and caravans rather than risking solo travel. Some early explorers and geographers collected their travel observations in written or oral records that became renowned in the ancient world, shaping mythology and literature.

FIGURE 3.2
Donkey parking lot for a Berber village market, Atlas Mountains, Morocco
Source: Preston L. Schiller

Pilgrimages around the planet

Voluntary travel included the pilgrimage, which interpreted the vicissitudes of travel in religious metaphor. Shrines at Jerusalem, Bethlehem, Mecca, Spain's Santiago de Compostela and sacred sites in India and China have endured for centuries. Grueling pilgrimages, some involving forms of self-punishment, exist to this day in Latin America, the Middle East and elsewhere. Chaucer's fourteenth-century pilgrimage epic, *The Canterbury Tales*, became a pillar of English literature. More recently—between 1953, when she became alarmed by the nuclear menace of the Cold War, and 1981, when she was killed in a car crash—'Peace Pilgrim' walked 50,000 miles (80,000 km) or more across the U.S., Canada and Mexico distributing her pacifist literature and messages.[6] Box 3.1 explores an ancient and enduring pilgrimage site.

In fall 2015, modern-day pilgrims Bob Whitson—a former sustainable transportation planner with GO Boulder (see the discussion in Chapter 9) and Sue Dowgiert—hiked along the Santiago de Compostela pilgrimage route. They walked over 600 miles (1,000 km) in 55 days from St. James, France, to Santiago, Spain. Many miles were spent either lost or looking for food, drink or shelter. They encountered beautiful landscapes and well-preserved shrines, as depicted in Figures 3.3a, b and c. Interest in pilgrimage and long-distance hiking, for spiritual, mental and physical health, continues to grow and has been the subject of several recent books and media programs (ttbook.org 2016).

BOX 3.1 **Walking: the pilgrims' preferred mode**

Susanne L. Seales[i]

Most religious pilgrimages are undertaken on foot. The medieval church instructed pilgrims to shed worldly goods, wear humble garments, take up wooden staffs and walk hundreds to thousands of miles between starting points in France and the major shrines of Santiago de Compostela (a popular tourist pilgrimage in today's world) and Rome. Some travel by boat was allowed if necessary. Pious men and women, rich and poor, pursued the miraculous benefits of direct contact with relics along the routes and at their final destinations. Intended as a religious act, pilgrimages also became a conduit through which secular ideas were shared across Europe. Spreading along the routes' shrines, monasteries and cathedral schools, ideas disseminated and contributed to increased intellectual activity of the so-called twelfth-century Renaissance. Without the yearly flow of penitent walkers, the Middle Ages would truly have been dark.

Obtaining the permission of their liege lord, and presenting themselves to the local clergy as penitential sinners, poor and rich alike undertook a journey that was viewed as a metaphorical process of rebirth into a realm blessed by God and the saints. Dependent upon the charity of individuals and monastic lodges along the way, it took several months to travel the routes from France to the great shrines in Spain and Italy, and, if the sea routes were not an option, potentially years to reach the Holy Land. Wealthy pilgrims often found a way around the strict rules and rode horses. The poor walked and the disabled were given dispensation to ride donkeys.

In addition to church information, educated pilgrims consulted guidebooks, such as the twelfth-century *Codex Calixtinus*, which gave advice and detailed information about difficult terrain, dangers and the shrines en-route and at their destination. Upon arriving at the main shrines in Santiago de Compostela, Rome, Canterbury or Jerusalem, pilgrims were said to have felt great joy at the culmination of their efforts. Hymn-singing monks attended the weary and aching pilgrims at their destinations as they presented themselves for much sought-after saintly blessings, often receiving a handful of cockle shells as a memento. Then, on weary feet, they returned home across the hundreds to thousands of miles they had just crossed, most walking, a few riding, and all believing that they had for a brief instant touched the power of God.[ii]

[i] Susanne L. Seales of Bellingham, WA, has worked as a freelance editor and writer, and is currently an Instructor at Western Washington University, where she teaches history and comparative literature. She holds an MA in History from Western Washington University and a BA in Liberal Studies from Evergreen State College.

[ii] For more information on the pilgrimages of the High Middle Ages, see Sumption (1975), Davies and Davies (1982), Melczer (1993) and Shaver-Crandell et al (1995); for more on the twelfth-century Renaissance, see Haskins (1971).

FIGURE 3.3A
Ancient bridge: Scene along the
Santiago de Compostela pilgrimage
route.
Source: Bob Whitson

FIGURE 3.3B
Modern pilgrim: Scene along the
Santiago de Compostela pilgrimage
route.
Source: Bob Whitson

FIGURE 3.3C
Pilgrim's shrine: Scene along
the Santiago de Compostela
pilgrimage route.
Source: Bob Whitson

Eternal congestion: vehicles and pedestrians don't mix well

Transportation innovations did not always fit well with settlement patterns. Early traffic jams, conflict between pedestrians and noisy, wheeled conveyances on the streets of ancient Rome are frequently used anecdotes in transportation circles, reminding us that traffic congestion and noise are as enduring as the 'Eternal City' congestion caused by chariots, carriages and the luxury litters of notables that led ancient Rome to institute traffic ordinances and the banning of non-pedestrian traffic during daylight hours. Even so, walking could be quite hazardous, especially at night, when persons living above streets would dispose of feces-filled jugs by simply emptying them out of windows and into the street.[7] Animals used for transport competed for space and resources with animals quartered in cities for food. The manure from urban animals became a public health problem. Raised sidewalks were constructed for walking above the muck and manure. Most older streets were too narrow for both vehicles and pedestrians. Over time, the design of expanding cities and new settlements changed to better accommodate horse-drawn vehicles.

Mechanization and motorization transform travel and society

The history of transportation during the Early Modern and Modern eras[8] illuminates the interplay and quickened pace of technical, political and economic factors, including the Western ambition to travel further and faster. Over many centuries, wheels, wagons and carriages improved and were better able to withstand the vicissitudes of travel along the primitive roads of the Middle Ages and Early Modern Era. Travel by water followed a similar trajectory, with improvements in design, navigation and sailing techniques, which improved speed and maneuverability. The modal developments that occurred during this time, many of which continued into the Modern Era, transformed transportation and notions of travel. These included:

- increased speed of vehicles;
- increased load carrying capacity;
- travel became relatively easier, more comfortable and less uncertain compared to earlier eras.

These developments transformed the societies experiencing them in several ways:

- Perceptions of distance and travel hardship changed, and travel became less discouraging. By the end of the nineteenth century, the mentality of travel motorization—beginning with the phenomenon of railway travel and then the somewhat later experience of automobile travel—led to the perception of the 'annihilation of space and time' a widely used notion originating in the work of Karl Marx and more recently applied to the Elon Musk hyperloop proposal.[9]
- Demographics changed as populations grew, dispersed more and entered into more exchange.
- Both colonial expansion and internal migration from rural areas to growing cities became easier.
- Access to goods and services generally increased.
- Perceptions of the environment and landscape changed: geography became less of a constraint and the consumption of energy resources, from wood, peat and whale oil to fossil fuels, greatly increased. Land previously in a more natural state was increasingly converted to crops and other uses to feed growing urban populations.

From hot air to steam: Balloons, rails and early steamships

During the eighteenth century, the technology of several modes began to change. The first human-carrying hot air-balloon was launched in Paris in 1783 and instigated a series of efforts aimed at lighter-than-air travel that was widely used for military purposes, explorations and recreation for some. The interest and improvements in lighter-than-air culminated in the beginnings of aviation during the early twentieth century. Wheeled coaches were pulled by horses along tracks in the earliest form of rail transit: the 'omnibus'.[10] Primitive steam engines were developed for mining and transportation in the late seventeenth and early eighteenth centuries and improved towards the end of the eighteenth and early nineteenth centuries. Steam-driven boats slowly developed during the late eighteenth century and by the beginning of the nineteenth century were successfully used, albeit in a small way, for ships carrying passengers and freight. Steamships were used more for river and coastal routes where they could frequently stop for fuel: wood in the early days, coal later in the nineteenth century. Transoceanic steamships were slower in development due to their inefficient engines and the bulkiness of the wood or coal needed; they were not a major factor in ocean shipping until the latter part of the nineteenth century.

At the beginning of the nineteenth century, steam engines were developed to power both road and rail vehicles, with the success and refinement of rail applications spreading much faster than road applications. The success of steam rail locomotion was due in great measure to the improvements made by engineering genius George Stephenson, whose 'Rocket' locomotive won the competition for the first modern railway line that linked Liverpool and Manchester in 1829.[11] Railroads, too, made the transition from wood to coal, but not before decimating many of the forests of England, New England and wherever else early railroading spread.

Nineteenth-century motorization, along with engineering improvements to waterways[12] and roads, bridges and tunnels, made possible a major expansion of transportation's capabilities. Modern imperialism was fueled by fossils, and the global logistics of military and cargo transportation were shaped by the strategic location of coal and (later) oil depots. In many ways, transportation became less sustainable as it became more dependent upon non-renewable resources and an ever-expanding reach.

One interesting nineteenth-century invention and its infrastructure needs is instructive about the complex relation between modal innovation, competition and succession, infra-structure, transportation politics and how the culture of mobility can divert progress away from the path of sustainability.

Bicycling: the sustainable path almost taken

While the rush to motorization and fuel consumption was occurring, a highly promising mechanized—but not motorized—mode was being developed: bicycle development began early in the nineteenth century and reached most of its modern form within 100 years. Its timeline is summarized in Table 3.1.

Contrary to the popular myth of its invention by Leonardo da Vinci (see Figure 3.4), the bicycle began as a wheel-assisted walking or running machine: the 'velocipede' (Latin for 'fast foot') or 'Draisine' after its German founder, Karl (von) Drais. It was simply an in-line two-wheeled device with a crossbar for sitting and a steering bar. A forester with an inventor's streak, Drais developed this horseless conveyance after witnessing several seasons of agricultural failures, beginning in 1812, and the climate effects of the volcanic eruption of Mount Tambora, Indonesia, in 1815. Horses could not be maintained during these failures and a substitute was needed for making the rounds of fields and forests.[13]

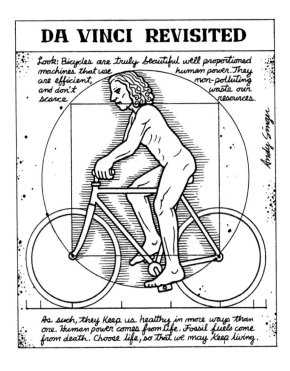

FIGURE 3.4
'da Vinci revisited'
Source: Andy Singer (www.andysinger.com)

FIGURE 3.5
Draisine display at the Karlsruhe
(DE) Transportation Museum
Source: Preston L. Schiller

The primitive wooden wheels and frame of the Draisine allowed the interaction of striding and wheels to create faster and easier mobility than walking alone did. It was less expensive than travel by horse, but it depended upon a reliable road surface to a far greater degree than did either walking or horse travel. The 'mechanical horse' stimulated a great deal of interest in its early years, but it did not lead to widespread use.

Beginning a practice that survives today, albeit sometimes in different form, the bicycle challenged its competitors: the horse and rider or the horse-drawn carriage. Along good surfaces, the Draisine acquitted itself well, occasionally surpassing or enduring better than its competition. But the Draisine did not perform well on the poor roads and streets of its day; it was an encumbrance going uphill and difficult to control downhill. Some media portrayals flattered the Draisine, but many more pilloried or satirized it. The popular term that stuck to it was 'hobbyhorse' or 'dandy-horse'. Generally seen as the domain of dandies and privileged university students, when early velocipedes took to sidewalks in search of smooth surfaces they drew the ire of the walking public and were banned. Many jurisdictions banned them from roadways because they were thought to frighten horses and interfere with traffic.

Between the 1820s and the 1850s, several mechanics (a catchall term of the period) and inventors turned their attention to improving the Draisine. Several of their three- and four-wheelers were more stable and better performing on the rutted roads and streets of the day; a few substituted a treadle-drive mechanism for striding, but all still shared with the two-wheeler the problems of having to be lugged up hills and poor downhill control. In 1821, Lewis Gompertz of Surrey, England, proposed a hand crank to power the front wheel, which would have significantly increased its speed, but was ignored. An early animal rights activist as well, Gompertz went on to invent several other transportation improvements oriented towards relieving the burdens of work animals. Drais's and Gompertz's efforts illustrate that transportation was not always viewed by inventors as a 'thing in itself', and show how inventions can spring from the desire to ameliorate a condition of human or animal difficulty or suffering. Still, the growth of bicycling was impeded in this era by a combination of poor roads and a technology that did not yet ensure easy use, safety and reliability.[14]

Cranking up the velocipede: bicycling grows and crosses social and cultural boundaries

During the 1860s, the addition of pedals and cranks to the velocipede's front wheel increased its speed, although its hard wheels and lack of suspension caused it to earn the nickname of 'boneshaker'. It attracted much interest, especially in the growing urban areas of England, North America and France where it had first been widely introduced. The familiar competitions between human-powered cycles and horses and horse-drawn carriages ensued, as did contests among cyclists.

Other 'velorutions' were associated with the new velocipede. Cycling was the first popular athletic activity open to women on a large scale, which had implications for their participation in a range of athletic activities, clothing and the feminist movement. Occasionally, women were portrayed as getting the better of male cyclist or equine competitors. Advertisements for velocipedes often featured robust, athletically attired women, symbolizing freedom or progress.[15]

During the 1860s and 1870s, velocipedes seemed to be everywhere: city streets, country roads, indoor rinks, outdoor racetracks, regular circuses, bicycle circuses on high wires and tested in distance competitions. Inventors and promoters sought wide-ranging applications for this popular invention, from the whimsical balloon-assisted mountain velocipede to police patrols.[16] Cycling clubs formed in many cities and towns and developed political agendas aimed at better treatment of cyclists and, most importantly, improved streets and roads.

A tilt towards the high wheeler: the bicycle 'improves' at the expense of widespread use

Into this milieu rode the high-wheeled bicycle.[17] The innovation of a high wheel was made possible by advances in metal wheel and frame manufacture and solid rubber tires. One crank of the pedals achieved a greater distance and velocity than the smaller-wheeled velocipede. The rubber tire afforded better traction and less bone-shaking than previous wheels, and the pedalist perched directly above the front wheel used leg power more effectively. The high wheeler's simpler and lighter frame was produced at a much lower cost. Most importantly, it was faster and allowed a greater range than its competitors. Perching upon such a contraption, navigating the still largely unimproved streets and roads required skill, learning time and courage impractical for average riders. An epidemic of broken bones and head injuries trailed close behind the high wheelers. In a theme common to much of transportation's modern history, speed and distance trumped utility, accessibility, moderation and safety. Still, an expansion of high-wheeler manufacture ensued and eclipsed the velocipede.[18]

Increased head injuries were not the only social cost of the high wheeler. The skill and time needed to master riding the high wheeler effectively limited its ridership mostly to younger men of means and the leisure sufficient to master it. The age band of riders narrowed, with few parents willing to allow youngsters to mount it and even fewer older adults willing to chance an injury. And, most tellingly, far fewer women seemed interested or willing to ride such a difficult machine. Despite these drawbacks, the high wheeler flourished for a decade or more among those inclined to master it and accept its risks.[19] High-wheeler groups on both sides of the Atlantic staged parades and processions to impress the public. In Washington, DC, the forerunners of today's bicycle couriers showed off their talents by riding their high-wheelers down the steps of the U.S. Capitol. Today, some groups on both sides of the Atlantic as well as in Australia and New Zealand keep high-wheeler, velocipede and even Draisine riding alive—although many of the riders now wear helmets (IVCA 2009).

Safety to the rescue

The poor condition of streets and roads, as well as the difficulties of mastering the high wheeler, limited its utility and adoption by a mass of the population during the 1870s. But the appetite for cycling was aroused, and by 1885 a vastly improved velocipede was introduced. It had smaller in-line wheels, took advantage of the technical improvements of the high wheeler, but added a chain-and-sprocket drive that allowed a significant mechanical advantage without a large drive wheel. The new bicycle became known as the 'safety' or 'diamond' frame because of its shape, lower height and greater ease in balance and maneuver. Many improvements followed and prices eventually stabilized between US$80 and $100 in the patent-disadvantaged US and between US$35 and $50 in England—a significant sum for the time, but far below the cost of a horse or carriage.

Women again took to the streets on two wheels, parents felt more comfortable encouraging their children to mount the safety, and several people of color became famous bicycle racers in the U.S. and Europe. Bicycle police patrols heroically chased criminals and reined in runaway horse carriages; city bicycle courier services expanded; and safety cycling youths delivered a range of goods from telegrams to groceries. Bicycle manufacturers attempted to convince the military, with little success, of the many applications of their versatile product—although a short-lived company of African-American bicycle cavalry was formed in the American West.[20] Romance was made mobile side by side, or in tandem—as expressed in the 1892 American popular song 'Daisy Bell':

> Daisy, Daisy,
> Give me your answer do!
> I'm half crazy,
> All for the love of you!
> It won't be a stylish marriage,
> I can't afford a carriage
> But you'll look sweet upon the seat
> Of a bicycle made for two.

The bicycle found a sizeable niche in Western society and soon spread to popular use in Africa and Asia. In Europe, it became well institutionalized and accepted as 'normal' for use by both sexes and all ages, in town and country. Bicycling was seen as part of the hygienic movement's healthy lifestyle and, at age 67, Leo Tolstoy took up cycling at the behest of his friends: it was believed to have eased his depression following the death of a young son.[21] Not all bicycling was seen as 'healthy'. Many poorer city dwellers resented the more well-to-do cyclists, who earned the derogatory term 'scorchers' for zooming through neighborhoods, sometimes injuring pedestrians and disrupting children at play in the street (McShane 1994, pp. 118–19; and the video by White 1992).

Beyond bloomers and bicycle faces

Among other efforts to discourage women from cycling in the late nineteenth century was the dubious medical invention of 'bicycle face', which was defined as stemming from:

> Over-exertion, the upright position on the wheel (popular term for bicycle), and the unconscious effort to maintain one's balance tend to produce a wearied and exhausted 'bicycle face' . . . usually flushed, but sometimes pale, often with lips more or less drawn, and the beginning of dark shadows under the eyes, and always with an expression of weariness . . . (and) characterized by a hard, clenched jaw and bulging eyes.
>
> (Stromberg 2015)

BOX 3.2 **Miss Smith's cycling adventure and Mrs. Bloomer's sensible fashion trends**

Susanne L. Seales[i]

Sir Arthur Conan Doyle's 'The adventure of the solitary cyclist'[ii] is the story of an independent young woman who presents Sherlock Holmes with a very interesting case. According to Dr. John Watson, Miss Violet Smith arrived at 221B Baker Street on 23 April 1895, and after a brief introduction Holmes asked what was troubling her. '"At least it cannot be your health", said he, as his keen eyes darted over her, "so ardent a bicyclist must be full of energy"' (p. 527). He had deduced this from one quick glance at her shoes 'the slight roughening of the side of the sole caused by the friction of the edge of the pedal' (p. 527). It is also possible that Holmes noticed Miss Smith's cycling skirt, with bloomers hidden underneath, sensible and popular fashions introduced by the American Mrs. Amelia Bloomer around 1851. Victorian crinolines made cycling cumbersome and dangerous, whereas Mrs. B's innovative designs presented women with garments that were liberating and safe as they peddled about town or country.

Having just arrived in London with her bicycle in tow, it is probable that Miss Smith was dressed in the late Victorian version of these garments, as were the growing number of independent young female cyclists of the time.[iii] In addition to using her bicycle to get about town, Miss Smith used it twice a week to travel between the train station and her place of employment on a rural estate. She made these trips without an escort, and would have continued without hesitation but for the recent appearance of a sinister male cyclist along a deserted stretch of the route, which caused her to seek Holmes's assistance in identifying the man. Her employer, Mr. Carruthers, had suggested switching to a horse and trap as a solution to her problem, and Holmes also hinted at safer modes when he asserted: 'It is part of the settled order of Nature that such a girl should have followers . . . but for choice not on bicycles in lonely country roads' (p. 530). However, although the plot takes an ominous turn for the cycling protagonist, in the end one is left with the impression that Conan Doyle was not criticizing Miss Smith's choice of the bicycle as her mode of transportation. He left no doubts about the risks that a young female cyclist might face in certain settings; but he also left the reader with a strong sense of the physical and mental benefits in store for a lady who chose a bicycle over a horse-driven cart.

This stance is in stark contrast to other views about female cyclists in Victorian Europe and America. 'Against bloomers and bicycles', an 1897 article in the *New York Times* (Anonymous 1897), discusses a bill introduced in the Kansas Legislature by Representative Lambert, which would 'prohibit women from wearing bloomers' or from appearing 'on a public thoroughfare riding astride a bicycle'. Citing 'eminent physicians', Lambert asserted 'that the bicycle habit destroys the health of women and unfits them for the important and sacred duties of motherhood'. Others criticized the popular cycling garments, such as in an 1895 article for *The Christian Commonwealth*, which stated that 'The "Coming Woman" is already here, and we are bound to say that we do not like her appearance. In fact, she looks more like a man than a woman'. However, many people of the late Victorian era accepted this new activity for women, including doctors who, contrary to Lambert's physicians, asserted the healthy benefits of cycling. There were also a number of articles published by feminists, such as Marguerite Merington, who in 1895 discussed a more liberated view of bloomer-clad women in *Scribner's Magazine*, stating that an 'absence of self-consciousness has characterized the woman cyclist from the outset'. Sir Arthur Conan Doyle clearly shared these views, and in the character of Miss Violet Smith he created the vision of an independent Victorian woman in sensible clothes and well-traveled shoes, taking to the city and country roads on her bicycle.[iv]

[i] For author bio, see endnote 1 of Box 3.1.

[ii] This story was first published in *The Strand* as part of the 1904–5 collection of stories *The Return of Sherlock Holmes*, which has been republished in numerous Conan Doyle anthologies, including the one used for this essay (see Conan Doyle 1903/1920).

[iii] According to Herlihy (2004, p. 266), by 1895 women made up about one-third of the bicycle market, when just a few years earlier there was a very small handful of female cyclists.

[iv] For more on women cyclists during the late nineth and early twentieth centuries, see Anonymous (1895) and Herlihy (2004); the author of this case study would also like to thank Lena C. (Schiller) Hanson for sharing her senior history paper (Western Washington University), 'The impact of the bicycle on American life from the late 19th to early 20th centuries', which provided some delightful reading and helpful insights on the subject.

Feminists fought back and Chicagoan Dr. Sarah Hackett noted the great health benefits of cycling and asserted that an anxious facial expression is only found among beginners and so-called 'bicycle face' quickly passes away (Stromberg 2015).

While the safety bicycle resolved the problem of ease and access for most, the poor conditions of streets and roads limited the use of the bicycle. In several countries, especially Britain, France and the U.S., cyclists led political movements that aimed to improve streets and roads. While the heyday of the bicycle preceded the mass introduction of the motor car, it was part of the dynamic of conquering distance by speed that launched the era of the automobile and airplane. The street and road improvement movements begun by bicyclists, especially the Good Roads movement in the U.S. and the Road Improvements Association in England, became the spearheads of efforts that paved the way for the rise of automobility.[22] Before exploring the rise of the automobile, it is necessary to examine the development of roads and streets—the infrastructural basis for walking, animal-assisted transport (wagons and carriages), bicycling and motor vehicles.[23]

Transportation infrastructure: from animal paths to 'Good Roads'

The earliest routes that bipeds trod as they stopped swinging from tree to tree and walked upright across savannas made use of animal tracks. Improving paths and trails probably began after humans formed permanent settlements and needed better connections with other settlements. Road improvements in cities and extending outwards began as early as 3,000 to 4,000 BCE in India and parts of Mesopotamia. Improving roads was more common within settlements than between settlements. Building roads between settlements increased as commerce and the use of wheeled and animal-assisted vehicles developed. Road-building began as a large-scale endeavor with the peak of the Roman Empire, roughly between 400 BCE and 400 CE. Built primarily to move large numbers of foot legions around the empire, the roads were also used for the transport of goods. Roman roads and bridges, many of which survive today, were extremely well built and stretched for 53,000 miles (85,000km). In comparison, today's vast U.S. Interstate Highway System totals less than 50,000 linear miles (80,000km).[24]

For 1,000 years after the end of the Roman Empire, road-building in Europe stagnated. Land transportation moved in the direction of connecting nearby towns and cities by the easiest routes and much of the Roman road system was abandoned. The movement of persons and goods by inland waterways, as well as by sea, continued to progress. Extensive road projects in other parts of the world included the Great Wall of China—a 5,500-mile (8,800km) network of elevated roadways for military movement to prevent invasions, keep nomadic peoples and their herds out of the protected agricultural lands and to protect the Silk Road running alongside part of it—and the vast and well-engineered Inca road network, many parts of which are in use today by pedestrians and motor vehicles.

Roads outside cities in Europe and North America from colonial days until the twentieth century were a hodgepodge of private and tolled routes, with some government-controlled routes maintained by a much resented and often ineffective system of mandatory fees and labor known as the 'corvee'. Overall, there was generally a lack of government interest in centrally directed systems of roads.[25] Some cities even had toll gates at their entries (Toronto 2009). Napoleon Bonaparte's extensive road-building program was exceptional, planned and designed for troop movements; following a French tradition, most roads were lined by trees to shade marching soldiers and horses. The early enhancement of trees had the interesting consequence of aestheticizing road travel for later users. The chaos of uneven road conditions, forced labor for maintenance and tolls over centuries made travel difficult and expensive and left travelers with an aversion to tolls and road privatization that has survived to modern times.

BOX 3.3 Silk Road to the West, Horse Road to the East

Susanne L. Seales[i]

Since the earliest settlements, travel has been linked to trade, the exchange of ideas and warfare. A dialectic between city walls, symbols of isolation and defense, and caravan routes, symbols of expansion and exchange, shaped the ancient landscape and slowly improved long-distance travel between city states and regions. Recent aerial photos of the Middle East show a vast network of caravan routes scarring the desert landscape and connecting it to regions bordering the Mediterranean and Central Asia. Some of these routes date from circa 3,000 BCE, and many were frequented by merchants and armies throughout the ancient past. Caravans were at times comprised of hundreds of individuals and pack animals, including camels, donkeys and horses that could withstand extreme desert and mountain conditions.

The Chinese also established land and sea routes for trade and warfare, and small amounts of their silk and pottery, and philosophical ideas, appeared in the West prior to the second century BCE. Around 125 BCE, however, Zhang Qian, a Han Dynasty envoy, led an expedition directly west into Central Asia in search of the fabled 'heavenly horses'. After his return, the Han emperor opened the route that Qian had taken, enabling Chinese merchants to trade their goods more frequently for horses and other Western products, including Persian metalwork, cucumbers and grapes. This route connected with others in Central Asia and became known as the Silk Road in the West, where Chinese silk was highly prized, along with pottery, jade ornaments, cinnamon and camphor. From the Chinese perspective, though, it could have been called the Horse Road for the highly prized military animals they brought back.

Over the next few centuries, these routes would link up with those connecting Central Asia to the West, eventually extending the Silk Road across the approximately 4,500 miles (7,200 km) from China to the Levant. Passing through often dangerous and difficult conditions, merchants traveled from both directions to trade in 'exotic' goods. During the fourteenth century, Marco Polo[ii] accompanied caravans going east and kept an extensive diary of his travels, which covered large sections of the Silk Road. The Muslim scholar, Ibn Battuta,[iii] also traveled these routes during his 24-year trek from Tangier to China and back. Crossing deserts and mountains, and passing through numerous lands, the Silk Road was a major conduit for the exchange of goods and ideas between the East and West from ancient times through to the nineteenth century.[iv]

[i] For author bio, see endnote 1 of Box 3.1.

[ii] There are numerous reliable translations of *The Voyages of Marco Polo* available today, including the one used for this case study, published by Orion Press (1958).

[iii] For more on the travels of Ibn Battuta, see Dunn (1989).

[iv] For more on the various routes and histories of the great Silk Road, see Wild (1992); Wilford (1993); Whitfield (1999); Wood (2002); and Manchester (2007).

During the nineteenth century, with Paris leading, many European cities began beautifying their streets: creating boulevards, widening sidewalks, adding gutters, trees, public parks and promenades—for strollers and carriages. These amenities encouraged bicycling as it emerged. Street improvement became part of a more general urban and public-health reform movement. Early forms of streetcars made their appearance: the horse-drawn omnibus at first, the cable car and electrified trams and trolleys later. The rise of urban transit played a significant role in allowing cities to expand and residents to travel without the restrictions of poor walking conditions in those parts where streets were unimproved—as was the situation in most North American cities. They also allowed all urban classes better access to parks and the natural areas at the edges of cities. In some cities, special Sunday and holiday excursion streetcars and interurban trains took riders to parks and picnics.[26] These examples demonstrate the interconnectedness of transportation, urban design and social factors.

BOX 3.4 Inca roads

While most of the Roman roads deteriorated or were abandoned, civilizations in the Americas were busily building extensive and complicated road systems even though they did not use the wheel and used animals mostly for carrying loads rather than humans. The Aztec and Inca (sometimes spelled Inka) built extensive well-engineered road systems between 500 and 800 years ago. The Spanish conquerors and explorers of the sixteenth century marveled at their accomplishments as they surpassed anything they had known in Europe. The Inca road network consisted of 23,000km (14,000 miles) extending from north-central Ecuador to central Chile through Peru and parts of Bolivia and Argentina. Its tolls and tributes were important sources of revenue for the Inca Empire and the roads were maintained by a complex system of work obligations. The older Olmec, Maya and Toltec civilizations also developed complicated communications and transportation systems, but much less is known of them than of the Incas.[i]

Source: Preston L. Schiller

[i] For its extent, see the map in Hyslop (1984, p. 4).

Bicycle boom and the Good Roads movement pave the way for early automobility

Bicycling became popular in nineteenth-century France due, in part, to their good roads. The popularity of cycling, bicycle tourism and racing brought attention to the need to improve roads further. France improved the status of road-building and civil engineering with the establishment of the École des Ponts et Chaussées (School of Bridges and Roads) in 1747. Most transportation attention and investment in England went into developing an extensive railroad system. However, roads were good enough to allow some bicycle travel and competitions between cities—thanks, in part, to the work of the British pavement innovator John McAdam, after whom the type of pavement known as macadam was named (Hindley 1971). While support for road improvements grew among bicycle advocates in France and Britain during the 1880s and 1890s, the strongest pro-roads movement developed in the rapidly growing cities of the U.S., whose streets were generally in poor condition.[27]

The 1890s Good Roads movement in the U.S. began in the 1880s as an outgrowth of the League of American Wheelmen (LAW), aided by bicycle manufacturer Alfred A. Pope. During the 1890s, its advocacy joined together urban bicyclists with the growing largely rural and small-town populist movement. Farmers exploited by monopolistic railways—while generally hostile to the 'city-slicker cyclists'—were willing to join them because good roads were needed to move goods from farm to market. The movement was further complicated with railways lending support, including railcars used to 'spread the gospel of good roads', in the expectation that better roads would extend the reach of railroads into rural areas still dependent upon rail shipment.[28] By the time the movement became influential in the early twentieth century, the automobile was fast becoming a major force in American life. By the end of World War I, most industrial nations, either at federal or state–provincial levels, had resolved to establish government funding streams to improve and expand roads. Bicycle interests were weak relative to the more powerful coalition members and their efforts for good roads led to them being driven off the road by the more powerful motor vehicle interests.

The rise of automobility

The first successful automobile was patented in 1885 by Karl Benz in Germany, produced as the 'Velo'[29] and reinvented many times across Europe and the U.S. over the next two decades. Many, perhaps most, of the automobile's early inventors and producers had roots in the bicycle industry, again illustrating an ironical connection between the bicycle and subsequent developments, such as good roads, that challenged its viability.[30] Electric automobiles were introduced in France and Great Britain in the 1880s, and in the 1890s in the U.S. Many of the electric car's earliest adapters were women—although some feminist scholars have criticized its gender-oriented marketing (Scharf 1991). It could travel 50 to 80 miles (84–134 km) on a charge. The scarcity of charging facilities between towns, the time needed to recharge and the high purchase price limited its application as a touring vehicle. The emerging automobile culture valued speed and distance over less noise and pollution. In 1912, the electronic starter was introduced and interest in electric vehicles dampened, although never disappeared, in the twentieth century.[31]

The automobile's popularity grew rapidly in the late nineteenth and early twentieth centuries, and an international 'car culture' emerged that engaged in a bitter contest with other users of streets; pedestrians, children at play and vendors (Norton 2008). Automobile clubs, the precursors of present-day automobile associations found around the globe, emerged on both sides of the Atlantic and, eventually, across the Pacific. Their original focus was organizing automobile racing and touring. Eventually, the clubs merged their efforts with those of the manufacturing and road construction interests into 'highway lobbies' that campaigned successfully for road funding, standards and regulations. Some automobile clubs developed into insurance companies, offering various services to motorists.[32]

By the eve of World War I, the development of mechanized and motorized transportation modes was well under way, with the automobile in the lead and the truck quickly replacing horse-drawn wagons.[33] Demands for improved and expanded roads increased and Fordism led to the availability of relatively affordable and useful automobiles for rural, urban, professional and working folk alike. Transit improvements, especially the streetcar, improved urban livability as well as making suburbanization possible (Jackson 1985).

After World War I, motor vehicle use and highway building rapidly increased. Consolidation and merger in the automobile sector occurred as it expanded and became a major employer in many industrial nations. The Fordist assembly line mode of production became pre-eminent and Sloanism (see endnote 30) influenced the design and marketing of automobiles. Political leadership on both sides of the Atlantic used expanding roads and increasing motorization as ways of appealing to the citizenry. The creation and standardization of road, street and traffic standards began.[34]

Motoring for the masses: depression parkways, superhighways and Hoovervilles

By 1928, the automobile was so firmly a fixture in American life that Herbert Hoover's presidential campaign was popularly depicted as promising 'A chicken in every pot. And a car in every backyard, to boot'. Just a few years later, the battered lived-in car of *The Grapes of Wrath* Joad family, driven out of Oklahoma by dust storms and overloaded with people and furniture, struggled to reach California's 'pastures of plenty'. At night, and while waiting for work, the Joads—and many families in the same circumstance—gathered in impromptu campgrounds called 'Hoovervilles' after the president who had promised them much but led them into the Great Depression.[35]

During the same period, several European nations undertook large highway and motoring projects. In 1930s Germany, Hitler accelerated the expansion of the ambitious Autobahn network, begun more democratically in the 1920s. While the Nazi regime had the military value of the Autobahn network foremost in its thinking, it simultaneously developed the 'people's car', or Volkswagen, as a way of helping the masses experience the value of the superhighways. The Italian Autostrada network of high-speed roads, begun in the more democratic time of 1921, was expanded upon by the Fascist regime in the 1930s, but never achieved the scale of the Autobahn.[36]

In the U.S., motor parkways became important expressions of the new highway culture. The early 1900s Long Island Motor Parkway—originally known as the Vanderbilt Parkway, a 45-mile (75 km) private toll road connecting Queens with wealthy Long Island suburbs— was intended to give its sponsor William K. Vanderbilt Jr. and his plutocratic neighbors a quick ride to New York City as well as a venue for their spectator-killing car-racing hobby. Later parkways, such as the 1930s federal Blue Ridge Parkway[37] or the many of Robert Moses's crafting, were designed for supposedly nobler purposes: scenic recreation, helping families get to the seashore, parks and mountains and—not to be ignored—providing commuters with the opportunity to drive to city jobs from their newly developed suburbs. In fact, many of Robert Moses's parkways were also designed to keep the poor and persons of color stuck in the cities; his parkways were designed with overpasses too low to allow buses. Parks' accesses and suburban commuting to and from city jobs or shopping was mandated to automobility (Caro 1975; Schivelbusch 2007).

Meanwhile, public transportation systems were under siege by automobility and auto-mobile interests. In the U.S., many, if not most, streetcar systems had been built by developers or utilities to promote their realty or energy source. They had promised a perpetual five-cent ride, and regulatory agencies held them to it long after it was feasible to operate a quality service at such a low fare. Quality suffered greatly as services became more crowded and less well maintained, becoming easy targets for closure or replacement by buses regardless of the General Motors-led conspiracy or that shown in *Who Framed Roger Rabbit?*[38]

During World War II, the industrial power of automobile manufacturing in several nations was retooled to produce trucks, troop carriers, tanks, cannons and even aircraft. Transit services achieved record ridership as automobile manufacture was suspended, fuel was rationed and massive numbers of newly recruited women commuted by public transportation to defense production jobs.

1945 to the present: complication, confusion, new directions, reversion, localization

The period from the end of World War II to the year 2000 presents a complex, somewhat contradictory and often confusing, array of transportation and land-use trends and counter-trends, movements and counter-movements.[39] To best understand these issues, it is helpful to divide this period into four approximate phases that vary somewhat from country to country, and continent to continent:

Phase one: rebuilding, 1945–1960

The first period is one of post-war expansion of cities; rebuilding of bombed European and Asian cities; restoration and expansion of transportation infrastructure; a rush to create more housing—which encouraged suburbanization and, in the U.S. and Canada, a lowering of urban and suburban densities and the creation of suburban mono-cultures; a weakening of transit, and the expansion of automobility; the expansion of the automobile industry to highway expansions, which also imposed highway engineering standards unnecessarily on residential streets.[40] Urban regions' transportation planning, especially in the U.S., became captive to questionable models—posing as scientific—which predicted great increases in traffic and then provided roadway capacity in the form of new roads and freeway and arterial expansions as the solution (Kenworthy 2012).

BOX 3.5 **How Interstate 5 came to Bellingham: you can't always get what you want—luckily!**

James V. Hillegas[i]

Located 60 miles (100km) south of Vancouver, British Columbia, and 100 miles north of Seattle, Washington, Bellingham's setting reflects its region's beauty: it gazes at the San Juans and Vancouver Island to the west; to the east the sun rises over Mount Baker, the region's volcanic icon. Its history since World War II reflects several important North American themes: de-industrialization and the shift from a resource-based economy to a service economy; the decline of central business districts (CBDs) and the dispersion of commercial enterprise to the urban fringe; and confusion about traffic and highway planning.

Echoing national sentiment, Bellingham planners, civic leaders and most residents saw road expansion as a way of increasing downtown property values and relieving traffic congestion while rejuvenating the central business district and industries along the city's waterfront. Perceiving this project in terms of competition with other West Coast states, in 1950 the *Bellingham Herald* asserted that the state which could build freeways more quickly and efficiently would win the race to become 'the New York of the West'.

Public sentiment welcomed state highway officials' early 1950s plan to build a limited-access highway through Bellingham. The city's civic and business leaders lobbied strenuously for a waterfront route to serve various industries, shipping terminals and the CBD. An interchange would serve the large cannery in the Fairhaven neighborhood at the waterfront's south end and another would serve the large pulp mill at the water's edge of downtown. Residents and civic leaders did not express concerns about preserving the many historic buildings in Fairhaven and the CBD. State highway officials proposed a much less expensive route circumventing the waterfront and downtown core by about one mile. After much debate the state prevailed.

While the state legislature had already purchased some rights of way, the project was greatly accelerated when President Eisenhower signed the Federal Aid Highway Act of 1956 (PL84–627). Eisenhower claimed that the interstates would be an important benefit of American citizenship while improving safety, increasing efficiency and delivering wide-ranging economic benefits. He also appealed to Cold War fears by asserting the importance of this highway system to evacuate cities during an atomic attack by the Soviet Union—although some quick calculations might have challenged this possibility. The opening of the final section of Interstate 5 through Bellingham in 1966 brought shopping and residential centers to freeway interchanges; drawing shoppers from Canada and away from Bellingham's CBD. By the mid-1990s, Bellingham's downtown, waterfront and Fairhaven areas were mere ghosts of what they had been through the 1950s.

Ironically, the large Fairhaven cannery closed the same year as the opening of Interstate 5, a victim of industry changes and dwindling salmon harvests. The massive downtown pulp mill decreased its production and workforce steadily over the decades and closed operations in December 2007; the City and Port of Bellingham and Western Washington University plan to redevelop its 137 waterfront brownfield acres. Since 2000, there has been a veritable renaissance of interest and activity in both Fairhaven and the CBD: moderate density infill development; bicycle lanes; improved sidewalks; abandoned historic buildings renovated; new multi-storey mixed-use buildings in a style consistent with historic buildings; a boardwalk and trails connect Fairhaven with the CBD; and an attractive village green hosts outdoor cinema and a farmers' market where the Fairhaven interchange had been proposed in the 1950s (Figures 3.6a, 3.6b). All along the route proposed by well-intended but short-sighted civic and business leaders for a 1950s freeway, residents are reconnecting to their waterfront and its parks, often on foot or bicycle. Lucky them.[ii]

[i] Historian James V. Hillegas holds an MA from Portland State University and a BA from Fairhaven College; he specializes in twentieth-century urban environmental history in North America and is currently writing a book on early water pollution abatement efforts along Oregon's Willamette River.

[ii] For more about the construction of Interstate 5 through Bellingham and newspaper citations, see Hillegas (2004); for the national context of interstate highway development, see Rose (1979), Lewis (1997), Gutfreund (2004) and Erlichman (2006); for the current situation, see Port of Bellingham (undated).

Phase two: expansion, 1960–1980

The second period is one of large-scale transportation infrastructure expansion: a heavy emphasis on highways in many nations and a mixture of highways, railways and public transportation emphases in others. Resistance to highway expansion, especially in cities, grew considerably and a fair amount of fresh thinking about transportation is advanced.[41] Interest in pedestrianization and traffic calming began in several cities. Some abandonment or neglect of transportation infrastructure occurred under decolonization. Increasingly severe air pollution and the 1973 energy crisis prompted government regulatory responses, mostly aimed at reducing certain 'criteria pollutants' from emissions, increasing fuel efficiency and some renewed interest in public transportation. In the U.S. and Canada, private railways withdrew from intercity passenger services and Amtrak and VIA Rail were created as federal entities in their place. Railway technology greatly improved the speed of trains as well as the ease and rapidity of laying tracks. There was wholesale abandonment of short freight rail lines in North America, and around the planet, the amount of freight transported by trucks grew significantly. In highly motorized countries, the car culture flourished and began to influence all aspects of societal life (Flink 1988).

Spared from the freeway wrecking ball, the Fairhaven Village Green nowadays hosts community celebrations as well as large demonstrations—such as the 1,200 persons, including environmental leader Bill McKibben, protesting a proposed coal export terminal for a sensitive shoreline area just north of Bellingham put forward by a combination of large shipping, mining and financial interests (Figure 3.6b). After a combination of local environmental activism and legal actions by the nearby Lummi Nation led to the 2016 defeat of that proposal, the community gathered there, again, to celebrate.

Phase three: different approaches, 1980–2000

The third is one of growing recognition of problems associated with motor vehicle dependencies and road expansion emphases as unsustainable throughout the planet. In most of western and northern Europe, there was further refinement and expansion of passenger rail and urban transit systems. Resistance to traffic expansion in cities grew, as did concern over pollution and growth in truck traffic. Several countries and many cities increased their investment in bicycle facilities, with the Netherlands, Scandinavia and Germany in the lead. Different styles of privatization and deregulation emerged; some countries engaged in increased partnerships between public and private transportation entities and refocused regulatory efforts, while others, such as the U.K., engaged in sweeping deregulation and transfer of public transportation assets to private interests. Pedestrianization and traffic calming were undertaken on a broad scale in many parts of Europe and Asia and attracted interest in North America.[42] In Latin America, the city of Curitiba began its sustainable transportation and development reforms that have led it to become a world model (Vasconcellos 2001). During the early 1990s, a short-lived effort to reform U.S. federal policy was initiated with the passage of the Intermodal Surface Transportation Efficiency Act (ISTEA) although subsequent iterations, including the most recent 'FAST Act', show that reform has been slowed or even reversed.[43]

Phase four: recent history; 2000 to the present

The fourth period is marked by a rapidly growing awareness of transportation's implication in atmospheric pollution and greenhouse gas (GHG) accumulation, as well as increasing concern about the various social and environmental problems associated with the globalization of commerce. A spirited scholarly critique of automobility also emerged (as discussed in Chapter 2). There are many cities on several continents where efforts to achieve greater sustainability are succeeding and associations of cities and mayors playing an active role in

FIGURE 3.6A
The commercial district of Fairhaven once targeted for a freeway interchange in the 1960s, now features a village green ringed by a bookstore, café, restaurants, stores, and mixed-use residential buildings—all conforming to historic district design standards: Today's event features a multigenerational Chinese–American cultural celebration of the harvest moon.
Source: Preston L. Schiller

FIGURE 3.6B Anti-coal terminal protest with Bill McKibben; the Fairhaven Village Green hosted a demonstration of over 1000 citizens organized by the NGO RE Sources on May 31, 2011 and another two years later with the Lummi Nation celebrating their success in persuading the U.S. Army Corps of Engineers to not allow the terminal to go forward.
Source: Paul Anderson (www.Paulkanderson.com)

this matter.[44] There has been an increasing contradiction between the desire of many to improve the quality of urban life with less emphasis on automobility and more emphasis on green modes and urban design that encourage accessibility and those tendencies aiming to increase automobility—and mobility in general. A few cities are removing central city freeways while other suburban areas experience ongoing expansion of roads.

Several unproven or even untested technologies magically promising to take us further faster, without environmental burden as they improve cities, daily commutes and long-distance travel have attracted mostly uncritical attention. These include the autonomous vehicle (AV) and connected car, and Elon Musk's proposed hyperloop alternative to high-speed rail—albeit existing mostly as a 'back of an envelope' concept (Schiller 2016). On the horizon, just beyond these, one can find billionaires competing to develop commercial rocketry and space tourism—or even emigration to some other part of the solar system or galaxy.

In some heavily populated countries, such as India and China, there is a conflict between wanting to develop an automobile industry and infrastructure aimed at serving a small sliver of the population while making recently viable modes, such as walking and cycling, difficult if not sometimes illegal. In many cases, there simply has not been much thought or analysis given to the spatial limitations of crowded cities that do not allow room for more motor vehicles.

From the past to the future of sustainable transportation

The future of sustainable transportation will largely be determined by whether societies learn from its history and the extent to which the greatest 'consumers' of mobility will shape their cities and travel patterns in ways that minimize the need for travel and maximize the efficiencies of the 'green modes'. This is explored in a variety ways in several chapters of this book. The ways in which the potential for several modes to reduce the size of our mobility footprints are of special importance.

Maritime and water travel

Early water and marine travel has been discussed above in this chapter. The period between the beginnings of ancient civilizations and the development of engine-powered water travel saw significant advances in navigation and maneuverability, vessel design and expansion, and provisioning for long voyages. These were part of the broader dynamic of the increasing importance of water travel for global exploration, cartography, commerce, warfare, nation- and empire-building and maintenance, colonial settlement and resource exploitation, as well as the use of water networks for travel and trade within countries.[45] The development of new routes and the exploitation of existing indigenous waterways, portages and canoe technology played a paramount role in the development of the Canadian fur trade—and the early history of Canada (Glazebrook 1964).

The development of powerful and practical engines and propulsion systems changed the dynamics of water travel. By the early nineteenth century, as steamships began using coal rather than wood, longer voyages became practical for inland waters, coasts and across oceans. From the middle to the end of the nineteenth century, the steamship was proving its value for passenger, freight and military applications. By the end of the nineteenth century, newly available oil made transoceanic transport even easier, and the completion of the Suez (1869) and Panama (1914) canals magnified the importance of intercontinental shipping. An enormous expansion of goods and passenger movement occurred because of these developments.[46] Naval ships became the principal means of projecting military might and moving troops and materials in a timely fashion around the globe. By World War I, new forms of naval warfare, including submarines and aircraft carriers, became factors in inter- rupting shipping lanes and military convoys. Oil tankers and their shipping routes became vital to keeping military and war industry running.

The preparations for World War II and its duration witnessed a vast expansion of ship- building and shipping for battle and cargo. Following World War II, the significance of traditional marine passenger travel and the importance and magnitude of maritime cargo- carrying grew as containerization, computerization and efficient intermodal transfer progressed (Gilbert and Perl 2008, pp. 99–101). Inland and coastal waters shipping have remained relatively small but important parts of maritime freight and a very small part of passenger travel. Chapters 4 and Chapter 5 discuss aspects of marine modes, especially as they are currently used.

Aviation: from the feat of flying to fly-drive excess

A long history and mythology surrounds human efforts to overcome the limitations of surface travel through flight. The most famous flight myth is that of Icarus, the son of labyrinth designer Daedalus, whose wax wings melted as he soared too close to the sun. A variety of efforts were made in antiquity and the Middle Ages and beyond to create flying mechanisms: from the floating lanterns and large kites of ancient China to Islamic Spain's experiments with gliding devices, to early rocketry. Birdwatcher Leonardo da Vinci experimented a little with gliders and designed a flying machine in 1487 that never got off the drawing board.

By the late eighteenth century, humans were floating in balloons and some were gliding back to Earth with the help of early parachutes. During the early decades of the nineteenth century, ballooning spread across Europe and made its presence felt in the U.S. Civil War. The steerable dirigible was developed by the beginning of the twentieth century, while interest in aerodynamics aided the development of gliders and early motorized unmanned flights.[47]

The first manned flights between 1900 and 1910 were the culmination of imagination: small lightweight motors, liquid fuels, aerodynamics advances and lightweight durable materials development. The airplane's significance was immediately recognized and development of flying craft quickly advanced, helped by the military of various countries. Military aircraft were used prior to World War I and extensive use of aircraft was made by both sides of that war.[48]

Between World War I and World War II, there was a steady pace of technological advance as well as rapid growth of civilian, commercial and military aviation in Europe, the U.S. and Japan. In the U.S., popular interest in aviation grew rapidly during the 1920s as former military pilots took to 'barnstorming' and 'flying circuses', flying into small towns, rural areas and county fairs to thrill crowds with aerobatics and taking passengers for short rides (Onkst, undated). Airmail took off, rudimentary passenger planes were produced and several airlines served domestic and international markets. Across the planet, public imagination was captivated by the flying machines and the heroic pilots who attempted transoceanic and around-the-world adventures. Remote regions in Canada, Africa and Latin America were made accessible by versatile bush pilots.

The 1930s witnessed further development of military and civilian aviation in Europe, Japan and the U.S. The 1937 blitzkrieg bombing of Guernica, Spain, memorialized in Picasso's monumental painting, demonstrated the great vulnerability of innocent civilian populations to this most modern form of warfare. While civilians had not been much targeted by air attacks in World War I, they have been the main casualties of aerial assault from World War II to the present.

Commercial passenger, air cargo and military aviation services and plane sizes continued to expand after World War II.[49] Aviation became firmly anchored in consciousness and travel and shipping patterns from the 1950s onward. There has been a huge growth of 'airport cities' around the globe. Aviation, airport cities and the fly-drive culture have serious environmental consequences that are discussed in Chapter 4. But there are two modes that offer alternatives to a fair amount of air travel: telecommunications and railways.

Telecommunications and transportation: from smoke signals to mobile telephones

Telecommunications is the transmission and exchange of information over distance. Early usage of the word 'transportation' often made it interchangeable with 'communications'. While some point to early elevated bonfires, crude lighthouses, smoke signals, flags, drums and a variety of horns as the origins of telecommunications, it was the development of semaphores, sometimes called 'optical telegraphs', and telegraph systems that stimulated modern telecommunications. Semaphores assisted military and national governmental communications, early train operations and shipping. The peace symbol was derived from the combination of the semaphore codes for 'N' and 'D', denoting nuclear disarmament.[50] Flag codes were used to communicate between ships as well as in land-based military operations. Rapidly growing electrical telegraph systems became the first modern form of transoceanic communications and played a major role in government, military, postal and railway operations. Telephony had significant implications for all these institutions, as well as profoundly influencing the ways in which businesses operated and people communicated.

Wireless technologies, beginning with wireless telegraphy and radio through the mobile telephone, had a strong relation to government, military, commerce, transportation and popular culture. The citizens band (CB) two-way radio, highly popular in the 1970s, is an example of a communications technology that developed a colorful culture and slang around itself since it was widely used in the 18-wheeler truck driver world to evade energy saving speed limits and their enforcement.

The relation of television to mobility is not clear. Televised educational courses and some programs may reduce some travel; but television advertising stimulates much more. One of the major sources of broadcast media advertising revenue is transportation: its largest component, the automobile and its accoutrements.[51]

The adoption of devices that provided internet connectivity occurred very rapidly beginning in the 1990s. Today connectivity, or relatively easy access to the internet, is near universal. The ubiquitous presence of the mobile telephone; in the home, at the office, in the 'privacy' of shared bathrooms or locker rooms, on sidewalks, in parks and other public spaces, was achieved with extreme rapidity, virtually within one decade after Apple introduced the first iPhone in 2007. Many less wealthy nations, lacking in traditional telecommunications infrastructure, have made rapid leaps to wireless technologies (NTIA 2014; Rainie and Poushter 2014).

The rapid rise of computers and various wireless devices for moving information speedily over long distances might substitute for some travel but likely stimulates other forms of mobility. Telecommunications speeds up many processes, especially in the world of business and commerce, and may increase travel due to making the pace of these activities more rapid. For instance, the telephone traffic between various cities may be studied by airlines marketing to assess whether new or increased services between these places is warranted.

The exact nature of the relation between telecommunications and transportation is the subject of lively debate and discussion. Some claim that telecommunications replaces travel, while others assert that it leads to increased travel. Some question whether it is even a mode of transportation. Advanced telecommunications capability is a major factor in the development of autonomous vehicle (AV) technology whose future impact is a matter of debate (see AV discussion in Chapter 4). Others point to the 'carbon footprint' of the internet as indicative of some of the often neglected issues embedded in this form.[52]

There are ways that advanced telecommunications, properly directed, could help in sustainable transportation efforts.[53] One example would be an expansion and formalization of the way that episodic conclaves, 'transit camps', of internet experts have helped agencies use available mapping resources, such as google maps and publicly available repositories of geographic information systems (GIS) data, to develop online trip planners (see Chapter 8). Government at all levels, including public transportation providers, could be encouraged to apply these widely in numerous ways from bus stop or transit center information provision to providing a range of incentives for public employees and government consultants to use these as part of a concerted effort to reduce travel and shift necessary travel, local and long distance, to green modes.

Rail and railways

The earliest efforts to harness the mechanical advantages of a fixed guideway to move heavy loads by wheeled conveyance without lateral slippage in trackways date back to Greek and Roman antiquity (Diolkos wagon way about 2,500 years ago) and can be found in European mining operations in the sixteenth and seventeenth centuries. Early trackways were generally short, often connecting a mining site with a nearby waterway. Rails were constructed of wood, later reinforced with cast-iron plates, and steel has been used since the latter half of the nineteenth century. By the early 1830s, some short railways were in operation and improvements in trackage and locomotion railways grew exponentially for the next several decades in England, Europe and the U.S.[54]

The 'growth spurt' of the railways in the mid- to late-nineteenth century in most industrially developed countries followed a variety of trajectories. Some closely resembled the trajectory of the U.K. and the U.S., some were the products of colonialism and a few were shaped by public policy to serve a wider public interest. Canadian railway development was fragmented until the arduous project of confederation led to a trans-continental railway (Berton 1972). Most railways of this period often pushed indigenous peoples off their historical lands and exploited local poor, minority and immigrant labor. Irish immigrant laborers fresh off the boat in the U.S. and Canada provided a great deal of the muscle that built railways and canals in the mid- and late-nineteenth century. The U.S. and Canadian railways of that era, especially in their western regions, imported laborers from India and China, treated them wretchedly and often did not allow them the right to bring families and settle. Throughout their history, railways played important roles in military conflicts, colonial expansion and the development of many nations. Because of their importance in colonialism and resource extraction, historians have developed the notion of 'railway imperialism' as a framework for analyzing the development of railways in former colonial countries.[55]

The present situation of railways varies considerably around the planet and historian Tony Judt (2011) eloquently emphasized the contemporary importance of the heritage left by the rail era and the need to still value this mode today, which has been under attack in the U.K. and elsewhere. In Canada and the U.S., there is much talk about railway

FIGURE 3.7A
1922: Park Avenue at 50th, New York City, before the car took over and it was quiet inside and outside of St. Bartholomew's Church (R)
Source: Jeff Prant (jeffprant.com)

improvements, including higher-speed (200 km/h) and high-speed (300 km/h) corridors—there is currently a highly ambitious, costly and controversial connection between San Francisco and Los Angeles under way without certainty of completion. In most other proposed corridors, funding or political will so far appears insufficient to realize such changes. Intercity rail barely plays a role in Mexico, where the government-controlled oil industry maintains artificially low fuel prices. Several European and Asian countries are developing high-speed systems or increments and many have improved and expanded slower but highly comprehensive networks.[56]

There is a great need to accelerate efforts aimed at promoting and restoring rail travel as an environmentally sound mode and one that could—with proper planning, funding and

FIGURE 3.7B
Park Avenue since the cars took over this avenue and most of New York's streets
Source: Jeff Prant (jeffprant.com)

FIGURE 3.7C
Park Avenue on a recent Car-Free day quiet is restored again to the street, St. Bartholomew's Church (R) and the neighborhood.
Source: Jeff Prant (jeffprant.com)

programming—become a viable alternative to driving or flying for a range of travel needs, commerce and recreation. One of the policy goals for the promotion of HSR is to substitute it for short (100–300 mi/150–500 km) and medium distance (300–600 mi/500–1,000 km) travel. Improving passenger rail links between major cities in several U.S. regions and in the Quebec–Windsor corridor in Canada could help each nation with climate change goals and reduce automobile dependence and pressures to expand regional airports.[57]

In many ways, redirecting the current and historical trajectory of overdependence on motorization, personal motor vehicles and flying-driving towards more walking, cycling and travel by public transportation—especially rail—would bring the better aspects of the past back into the present and future (Schiller, 2017).

Conclusion: lessons for sustainable transportation

This brief overview of transportation history offers a few 'lessons' related to topics addressed throughout the remainder of this book:

- Walking is a 'built-in' for humans and offers a good basis for sustainable and healthy transportation.
- Walking, bicycling and transit could be the basic building blocks of passenger mobility and offer synergies between humans and their settlements.
- Emerging modes often compete strenuously with dominant modes in ways that are shaped by cultural values and beliefs. Racing, 'conquering space and time' and 'travel as consumption' demonstrate how transportation culture interacts with innovation. Cultural values and beliefs are subject to change; recently there has been increased emphasis on co-operation and coordination among modes and the use of advanced telecommunications in recognition of the need to reduce energy-intense travel.
- The basic building blocks of freight transportation have been rail and marine shipping. These are the most energy- and space-efficient modes of freight movement, although their efficiencies are often being applied to the massive transporting of goods of questionable or controversial environmental value.
- While many innovations, in technology or planning approaches, often announce themselves as the 'solution' to certain transportation problems, when evaluated over time they often have proven to create more problems than they solved.
- Mobility for the sake of mobility—travel as a 'thing in itself'—unrelated to basic human needs, is a relatively late development in the history of transportation.

Historically, most travel, even locally, was done out of necessity, mainly for sustenance, commerce and military purposes. Communities were located and shaped to minimize travel and maximize accessibility. Today, personal travel is increasingly discretionary; a smaller percentage of trips reflect necessity and a much larger proportion involve choices of whether, where and how to travel. This offers transportation planning and policy-making many interesting challenges and opportunities that will be addressed in subsequent chapters.

Questions for discussion

- Discuss what you think our cities and countryside might look like today had personal transportation technology development stopped with the bicycle and not proceeded to the automobile and truck?
- Discuss the relationship between telecommunications and transportation. Identify ways in which telecommunications might serve sustainable transportation. Identify ways in which telecommunications works against sustainable transportation.

- At the time of the introduction of the ('free') interstate highway system in the U.S. several states were developing toll roads (turnpikes). Discuss what surface transportation might look like today in the U.S. had major intercity and suburban road systems continued to develop along the lines of toll roads and turnpikes rather than being largely supplanted by freeways.

- Will autonomous vehicles offer the advantages their proponents are claiming or will they increase automobile dependence?

- Will smartphones and other mobile devices, which provide the instant information needed for facilitating multi-modal management systems, help to reduce dependence on the automobile?

Notes

1   How many millions is also under debate: the current range is between 3 million and 7 million years ago; for more information, see www.pbs.org/wgbh/nova/sciencenow/3209/01-ask.html, www.scribd.com/doc/334778/introduction-to-paleoanthropology, Solnit (2000) and Amato (2004).
2   For a graphic of homo erectus>home cellphoneus, see www.pocketapp.co.uk/blog/2014/06/09/evolution-of-mobile-advertising
3   For more on the development of marine technology, see Derry and Williams (1993, pp. 14, 19, and Chapter 6) and Falola and Warnock (2007, pp. 277–8).
4   For more on this topic see Lay (1992, pp. 19–26), Derry and Williams (1993, pp. 191–2), and Native Languages of the Americas (2016); for how to make a traditional-style Blackfoot dog travois, see King, M. (2010).
5   For more on the development of the wheel, see Hindley (1971), Lay (1992, pp. 26–41) and Derry and Williams (1993, Chapter 6); for more information on the Inca, see Hyslop (1984); Gambino (2009) and Box 3.4, Chapter 3.
6   Between 1953 and 1964, the person identifying herself only as 'Peace Pilgrim' had logged 25,000 miles (42,000 km) and then walked across the U.S. at least seven more times (Pilgrim 1991).
7   Mumford, 1961, pp. 218–9, Quill 2011; Hughes 2011; Morris 2013; Matthews 1960.
8   The term 'Middle Ages' generally refers to 500 to 1500, 'Early Modern' to 1500 to 1800 and 'Modern' to 1800 to the present.
9   Christensen 2013; Schivelbusch, 1986, pp. 33–44; Sachs, 1992, pp. 6–12; this widely used or modified notion can be traced to the work of Karl Marx, see the Marxists Internet Archive; www.marxists.org/archive/marx/works/1857/grundrisse/ch10.htm
10 For more on the omnibus, see Lay (1992, p. 129); Derry and Williams (1993, pp. 385–8) and Bellis (undated).
11 For more on steam vehicles, see Lay (1992, pp. 137–8); Derry and Williams (1993, Chapter 6), Goddard (1996, pp. 6–7) and www.steamindex.com/people/stephen.htm
12 For more on canals and locks, see Derry and Williams (1993, pp. 436–6).
13 Economy-point.org 2006, Huttman 2006.
14 For more on the Draisine, see Gompertz (1851, pp. 42–9); Herlihy (2004, pp. 19–65) and Fletcher (2008, exhibit item 24).
15 For more details and graphics, see Herlihy (1992, 2004, pp. 138–9, 261–2).
16 Herlihy, 2004, p. 145.
17 Also known as the high wheeler, ordinary, the wheel or penny-farthing in reference to the large difference in size between its front and rear wheels.
18 According to Wilson et al. (2004, p. 19): 'The ordinary was responsible for the third two-wheeler passion, which was concentrated among the younger upper-class men of France, Britain and the United States and was fostered by military-style clubs with uniforms and even buglers.'
19 Herlihy, 2004, pp. 182–221.
20 Herlihy, 2004, pp. 259, 292–3.
21 For Tolstoy, see Troyat (2001, pp. 510–4); for a photo of Tolstoy with bicycle, see Chesterton et al. (1903, p. 6); for other general bicycle information, see Lay (1992, pp. 142–5).

22 For 'Good Roads', see Waller (1983, pp. 243–4); Hamer (1987, pp. 23–4); Goddard (2000); Gutfreund (2004) and Dobb (undated).

23 See illustrations of several early bicycles and velocipedes in Wikipedia's 'velocipede'. While there is often controversy about the accuracy of many Wikipedia entries because of the 'open' nature of their sites, the graphics are often quite useful.

24 This is the figure for the interstates' linear mileage—as opposed to 'lane mileage', which is the sum of all parallel lanes—which would equal over 200,000 miles (334,000 km) of lanes. In the year 2000, the total lane mileage of U.S. intercity highways, federal, state and local lanes was 8,239,625 (13,760,173km) (BTS and U.S. Government 2002); for more on ancient roads, see Lay (1992) and Friedman et al. (2006, p. 35).

25 France and Germany, as exceptions, each had centrally directed interests in roads, although Germany's central direction began considerably later than that of France; for more information, see Hindley (1971, pp. 74–7); Lay (1992, pp. 60, 70, 101–2, 117) and McShane (1994, pp. 103–4).

26 For more on transit and recreation, see Schaefer and Sclar (1975); Jackson (1985, p. 112) and McShane (1994, pp. 27–30).

27 For road history in France, see Hindley (1971, pp. 74–7); for roads and the popularity of bicycling in France and the Roads Improvement Association, see Flink (1988, pp. 2–4, 169–71); for England, see Hamer (1987, pp. 23–4); see also Herlihy (2004). For a different perspective, see McShane (1994), whose work emphasizes the role played by improved roads in generating interest in bicycle and automobility and conflicts between vehicles and pedestrians.

28 For more about the history, revivals and renaming of LAW to the League of American Bicyclists see LAW (undated); for more about the Good Roads movement and the 'Gospel of Good Roads', see Flink (1988), Goddard (1996, 2000) and Gutfreund (2004).

29 Also the French term for bicycle.

30 For Fordism and the GM response to it, the marketing strategy of 'Sloanism', see Rothschild (1973) and Lay (1992, pp. 160–1); for the relation between bicycles and early automobile development, see Rae (1965); Flink (1988) and Barker and Gerhold (1995, pp. 52–3).

31 For more on electric cars, see Flink (1988); Scharf (1991, pp. 35–50); Goddard (2000); Kirsch (2000); Didik (undated) and Hume (undated).

32 For early automobile clubs and how they shaped automobile culture and politics, see Rae (1965); Flink (1988); Scharf (1991); Sachs (1992); McShane (1994); Barker and Gerhold (1995, p. 55); Goddard (1996) and Gutfreund (2004).

33 For a discussion of the importance of the truck in cities as a replacement for horse-drawn wagons and the role that it played in reshaping urban transportation and road needs, see McShane (1994).

34 For more on standards, see Eno Transportation Foundation (undated); Blanchard (1919) and Rothschild (1973).

35 The quote popularly attributed to Hoover may be only partially accurate: see Safire (2008, p. 115); for the Joad's road odyssey, see Steinbeck (1939), as well as the film version. For several of Dorothea Lange's photos of Hoovervilles and migrant worker conditions in the 1930s, see http://lcweb2.loc.gov/cgi-bin/query/b?ammem/fsaall:LC-USF34–001774-C:collection=fsa

36 For the Autostrada, see Hindley (1971, p. 98); for the Autobahn and Volkswagen, see Sachs (1992) and Schivelbusch (2007).

37 Literally a linear park, 469 miles (780km) in its final form; for more on this, see Schivelbusch (2007).

38 For more, see Jackson (1985, pp. 168–71) and Klein and Olson (1996); the extent to which U.S. streetcar lines were 'killed' by conspiracy or by neglect is subject to debate; for more, see Bottles (1987), Flink (1988), McShane (1994), Goddard (1996) and Gutfreund (2004).

39 For a more detailed examination of these periods as well as their implications for policy and planning see Schiller and Kenworthy (2017), especially Chapters 3, 7 and 8.

40 For critiques of U.S. suburban development and its relation to street and road design, see ITE (2006); Kunstler (1996); Kay (1997) and Newman and Kenworthy (1999a, p. 150).

41 For a sample of critiques, reactions and rejections of highway expansion, see Jacobs (1961), Nowlan and Nowlan (1970); Plowden (1972); Schneider (1972); Rothschild (1973); Davies (1975); Schaeffer and Sclar (1975); Illich (1976) and Sachs (1983); for a sample of fresh ideas and approaches, see Stone (1971); Richards (1976); Stringer and Wenzel (1976) and Gakenheimer (1978).

42 For European transportation policy changes during this time, see Pucher (1997, 2004); Pucher and Lefevre (1996); for the spread of pedestrianization and traffic calming, see Wynne (1980); Appleyard et al. (1981); Untermann (1984); Moudon (1987); Roberts (1988); Engwicht (1989, 1993) and CNU (undated).

43 See Chapter 7 and Dilger (2015). Fixing America's Surface Transportation, P.L. 114–94.

44 See Chapters 9 and 10, Schiller and Kenworthy (forthcoming 2017).

45 Derry and Williams 1993, pp. 190–211.

46 Derry and Williams 1993, pp. 364–77.

47 Derry and Williams 1993, pp. 396–402.

48 Davidson and Sweeney 2003, pp. 128–33.

49 For discussions of the implications of the vast expansion of passenger and freight aviation in recent decades, see Gilbert and Perl (2008); for some of the popular experiences with aviation, see Davidson and Sweeney (2003, pp. 277–84).

50 For a picture of the peace symbol, see http://en.wikipedia.org/wiki/Peace_symbol.

51 See Box 2.2 in Chapter 2 of this book.

52 For the history of telephony and telegraphy, including semaphores, see Derry and Williams (1993, pp. 621–9); a good source of current information is the Telecommunications and Travel Research Program, University of California, Davis, at www.its.ucdavis.edu/telecom/; for a discussion of how telecommunications is not replacing travel, see also Mokhtarian (2003); for technical and timelines information, see Huurdeman (2003); for a discussion about relations between telecommunications and travel, see Niles (2009); for a recent view of teleconferencing as a replacement for travel, see Demerjian (2008) and FHWA and USDOT (undated).

53 See FHWA 'Teleconferencing'.

54 For more on early nineteenth-century rail systems, see Lay (1992); Derry and Williams (1993); Goddard (1996) and Morlok (2005).

55 For more, see Davis et al. (1991), especially Robinson's 'Introduction' and 'Conclusion', as well as Roman's 'Railway imperialism in Canada', Fleming's 'Profits and visions: British capital and railway construction in Argentina, 1854–86' and French's 'In the path of progress: Railroads and moral reform in Porfirian Mexico'.

56 See Chapters 5 and 7 of this book for more discussion of deregulation, privatization etc., especially for the EU and U.K.

57 With a fair amount of variance between regions, approximately 25% to 40% of commercial aviation flights are within the distances easily served by high and higher-speed rail (HSR, HrSR); see Schiller and Kenworthy 2017, especially Chapter 4.

Modes, roads and routes: technologies, infrastructure, functions, energy and inter-relatedness

Introduction

Transportation modes are ways of moving people, freight and information. Decisions about which modes to invest in and/or emphasize have long-term consequences. Previous chapters have discussed the importance of the relation of history and cultural factors to modal emphases and some of their consequences for the environment and urban life. Modes may be for passengers, freight or both, and some of their operational and infrastructure considerations are interrelated. All passenger modes have some cargo capacity or potential: personal motor vehicles (PMVs) almost always have some cargo storage; airliners carry much cargo along with baggage in their bellies; most passenger trains accommodate luggage and some carry small amounts of freight; and some ocean freighters accommodate a few passengers. Even walking and bicycling have the potential for carrying some cargo: backpacks and wheeled carts or luggage for pedestrians; panniers and trailers for bicycles, as well as bicycles built as small cargo vehicles.

This chapter focuses on passenger modes and matters related to moving transportation in the direction of greater sustainability. It explores the great variety of modes, differences between modes, and the great diversity that can exist even within a modal category. It emphasizes how modes affect or interact with many factors, including:

- infrastructure—right(s) of way (RoW), sidewalks, paths, roads, rails, ports and airports;
- land use, urban design and the built environment;
- social, economic and cultural dimensions, including equity;
- travel and trip characteristics—individual, group, purposes such as work or recreation;
- functional characteristics—for peak period, necessity or discretionary, valuation of trip;
- environmental considerations—pollution (including noise), energy and resource consumption, habitat disruption.

Any discussion of transportation modes is extremely challenging; there is a multitude of modes and combinations of modes and often there is overlap among modes. It is difficult to discuss a mode without reference to its application, utilization and impacts. Two important concepts about modes that should inform our discussion and analysis of them are:

1   *Multi-modal*: the ability to choose among several modes for a trip. One could travel by foot, bicycle, transit, PMV or any combination of these.
2   *Intermodal*: the ability to make connections between modes, such as mounting a bicycle on a bus's rack or transferring between bus and rail or between a land mode and a ferry or airport. The convenience of intermodal transfers can be of great value to persons using public modes. Intermodal is also a term that is widely used in freight to denote transfers between trucks and trains, or trucks, trains and ships.

These two approaches increase travel options or allow people to combine modes for more complicated travel thus reducing the need for automobility.

Modes involve technical and technological matters, which are discussed in this chapter; but modes are more than these and need to be understood in the context of travel situations, the system of modal technology and application, and the interrelationship of modes with the factors enumerated above. The chapter's framework will emphasize the importance of travel contexts and trip characteristics, from in-town to intercontinental.[1]

In-town modes: getting to work, school, shopping, services and recreation

Most trips taken and distances traveled generally occur in town or within an urban region. While trips to work, or commuter trips, are very important to individuals and to society—and tend to be the longest of trips taken regularly—they comprise only a small portion of the total number of trips that people make. Most travel is for shopping, services, education, recreation and family, and friendship purposes. Most trips, excluding those by commuters who live at a substantial distance from their work, are relatively short: in the range of 0.5 to 2 (or 3) miles (1 km to 5 km), easy walking and bicycling distances. But the combination of traffic and automobile-oriented urban design—segregating types of uses—have made many short trips difficult, uncomfortable or unsafe under foot power. The same conditions work against attracting riders to public transportation; if one cannot cross the street safely, one is unlikely to ride the bus. There is often a lack of good information readily available about walking, bicycling or transit. Some researchers have found that simply providing the public with personalized information about their mobility options can lead to a fair amount of selecting of previously unfamiliar choices, especially for shorter local trips (SocialData America, undated).

Many modes may serve utilitarian purposes, such as forms of transit designed principally for commuters' needs (e.g. regional rail, or RGR, vehicles), while other forms may be designed principally for a non-utilitarian purpose, such as modes that convey tourists up a steep mountain grade so that they can snap photos to send home or post on a website. The array of modes and their different uses have led analysts such as Vuchic (2007) to approach the topic through the useful concept of the 'family of modes', which combines addressing the uniqueness of some modal applications as well as the overlap and interactive phenomenon of intermodalism.[2]

The major in-town modes, in order of importance for sustainable transportation (ST), are:

1   *walking*—including walking assistance and mobility assistance devices such as wheelchairs;
2   *bicycling*—including three-wheeled variations;
3   *public transportation or transit*—including buses, rail modes, shuttle services, taxis and jitneys;
4   *PMVs*—including automobiles, two-wheelers (motorcycles, mopeds), vans and light trucks.

TABLE 4.1 Selected characteristics of transportation modes*

Mode & types of travel most applicable	Max hourly capacity (wealthy nation crowding standards)	Key functional and type of trip characteristics	Infrastructure needs, costs and cost drivers	Average speed (V) and range (R)	Environmental, health, safety impacts	Vehicle/operating costs (wealthy nation levels)
Walking: mostly local-urban; utility, recreation	Good facilities; thousands of persons/hour (pers/hr)	All trip types—if facilities are good; long trips unlikely	Paths, sidewalks; $50–500K per mile	V=2–4mph; R=I/4–4 miles	Minim. envir. impact; healthy when safe	Nothing to minimal
Bicycling: local to regional; utility & recreation	Good facilities; thousands of pers/hr	All trip types—longer with better facilities	Paths, lanes, bikeways; $100–700K per mile	V=8–20mph; R=1–15miles to 100miles/athlete	Minim. envir. impact; healthy when safe	$100–1000+ per bicycle; $0.1 per mile ± oper. cost
Bus: local transit; utility or recreation	Right of Way (RoW) C*; 3–5K pers/hr	More frequency, more riders; feeds faster modes	Minimal—shelters, signs, possible signal priority	V=6–16mph; R=entire region	Exhaust from older models; safer than PMV	$100–1100K per bus; $100–$150 per hour to operate
Streetcar or Streetrail: local to regional; utility & recreation	RoW C*; 5–10K pers/hr	More frequency, more riders; enters pedestrian zones	Modest; track, power, shelters, signal priority; $10–55mil/mile	V=6–20mph; R=entire central city	No local pollution; noise varies, good safety	$2–5mil per car; $175± per train hour of operations
Bus Rapid Transit (BRT): local to regional; utility and recreation	RoW B*; 5–10K pers/hr	Longer urban and regl. trips; more frequency, more riders	Dedicated lanes, signal priority, high cost if RoW A*; $5–60mil/mile	V=16–24mph, vary w. station spacing; R=city, suburbs	Modest noise/air pollution; safe for passengers	$500–1,500K per bus; $150± per hour operating cost
Light Rail Transit (LRT): local to regional; utility and recreation	RoW B*; 10–20K pers/hr	All types of longer urban—suburban trips; good for peak commute capacity	Dedicated lanes, stations, power, signal priority; $10–560mil/mile** (more if upgrades to RoW A)	V=16–30mph, depends on station spacing (~ BRT); R=city, suburbs	No local air pollution; safe for passengers	$3–5mil per car; $125–300 per train hour of operations
Rail Rapid Transit Metro (RRT): medium to long urban-suburban	RoW A; 15–40K pers/hr	All types; suburb to city & trans-regional; tends to all-day usage	Elevated structures-tunnels, large stations, depots, power; $200mil– 2bil/mile†	V=20–35mph, depends on station spacing; R=region	No local air pollution, noise when overhead; extremely safe	$2–3mil per car; $265 per train hour of operations

continued

TABLE 4.1 *continued*

Mode & types of travel most applicable	Max hourly capacity (wealthy nation crowding standards)	Key functional and type of trip characteristics	Infrastructure needs, costs and cost drivers	Average speed (V) and range (R)	Environmental, health, safety impacts	Vehicle/operating costs (wealthy nation levels)
Motorized 2-wheelers: local & regional	2000 persons/hr/lane in poorer countries; not issue in wealthy	All trip types where transit is poor; couriers	Dedicated lanes rare; need dedicated parking off sidewalk	V=8–70mph; R=one's endurance	Exhaust/noise extremely unsafe to users	$2–15K; $0.15–0.25 per mile
Personal Motor Vehicles: wherever allowed	1000–2000± persons/ hr/lane, depending on RoW; grade-separated, arterial or local and AVO	All trip types when alternatives lacking	Large RoWs; $2mil–3.5bil/mile† ('Big Dig')	V=11mph cong. 25–70 flow; R=as far as roads/ fuel go	Major space consumption; air, water, noise pollution; GHGs	$9000 per year ± U.S.‡
Intercity bus/ coach: usually discretionary budget travel	50–70 per bus, capacity; limited by roadway & terminal	Intercity; persons w/o PMVs; connect small towns & cities	Terminals in larger cities; many towns & cities lack terminals	V=50mph if few stops; R=up to 1K miles per day	Much pollution if old diesel; good safety some countries	$400–700K, $100 per hr±
Intercity rail: discretionary travel, recreation, some business travel	2–10K pers/hr/track; 40–80 passengers per railcar; train length depends on station platforms, etc.	Intercity; attracts choice riders, connects small and larger cities	Modest upgrades on freight track, up to $200mil per city for access improvement	V=60–120 mph; R=up to 1500 miles per day	No local air pollution if elec. minor diesel pollution rel. to load; very safe	$3mil per car, operating costs similar to RGR
High-speed rail (HSR): medium to long intercity travel; recreation, business	5–10K pers/hr/track; passengers per train depends on station platforms, etc.	Attracts persons from PMVs and airliners, esp. for trips between 200 to 600 miles	Can operate on conventional track, but needs very expensive dedicated track for high speeds	V=120–220mph, depending on stops; R=networks continually lengthening	No local air pollution; noise significant at higher speeds; extremely safe	$40mil± per train-set, oper. cost/hr higher than intercity, but lower per mile

Mode	Capacity	Use	Infrastructure	Speed/Range	Environment/Safety	Cost
Ferry and oceanic ships: ferries can be for commute or recreation, pass. only or PMVs, trucks or trains	Passenger only up to 400 and car ferries up to 2000 persons and 200+ PMVs per depart., freqs. vary; traditional oceanic pass. ships very rare	Ferry part of road system in some regions; freighters can carry the airplane averse	Large piers, loading ramps and gangways, large terminals, car storage areas	V=20–24mph for ferries and freighters, 30–36mph for pass. ships	Significant air pollution if old diesel; good safety wealthy countries	Ferries; from small ($5–25mil) large ($100mil); oceanic over $1bil; costly. ineffic. to operate
Airliners: long distance travel; business and recreation	Depends on airport capacity; 30 take-offs plus landings per hr per runway typical; 30 to 800 passengers per plane depends on size & configur	Trips of all types; lack of rail = short trips; vital to mountain and island locations	Large airports very expensive to build or expand ($bils); land acquisition very difficult	V=300–560 mph, R=100–8800 miles	Much air & noise pollution near airports; ozone-damage; pass. very safe	Wide range of costs—up to $400mil per plane largest; oper. costs range widely

Source: Eric C. Bruun, Preston L. Schiller

Note: The figures used represent estimates, averages and ranges based on N. American experience and will vary with location and local factors; All capacity figures dependent upon average vehicle occupancy (AVO), which can vary considerably. The table has been created to estimate differences between various transportation modes rather than for quantitative analysis.

*(costs in US$, velocity & distance in miles for the sake of print space; RoW A= Fully separated, B=Semi-separated, C=Mixed traffic; All figures are rough estimates or averages derived from a range of values due to varying conditions, locations, etc. see National Transit Database)

** (Huge range of capital costs due to whether an existing RoW is used or whether tunneling is done, number of stations: Latest Seattle area CBD>U. of Wash. Link LRT tunnel cost $558mil/mile)

† Huge variability of costs depending on acquisition, rural or urban, at grade, separated or in tunnel, number of lanes, interchanges/mile(km), etc.

‡ Considerable variability depending on amount driven, vehicle type etc.

Table 4.1 (above) summarizes and compares selected characteristics of modes and the types of trips for which they are most applicable, which are then discussed.

Walking

As discussed in Chapter 3, walking is the simplest and most natural form of human mobility. Walking is difficult in most urban regions, and it is especially difficult and uncomfortable in automobile-dependent cities and urban regions. With the combined efforts of policy-makers, planners, engineers and concerned citizens, it can become a safer, easier and more attractive mode.[3] Urban walking can even be joyful given the right infrastructure and circumstances (Perry et al. 2016). The exemplary cities have succeeded in improving pedestrian conditions in many parts of their communities (see Chapters 9 and 10). Some of the most important factors about walking are summarized in Table 4.1. One motorized device that has been allowed on many sidewalks, which has attracted controversy over its safety for its users and for pedestrians it might menace, is discussed below in Box 4.1.

Bicycling

Bicycling is the most energy-efficient mode of transportation, requiring less input per distance unit than walking. Along with walking, bicycling generates no emissions or noise. While

FIGURE 4.1
Wide sidewalk, downtown San Francisco leaves room for strolling friends, pets, trash cans, kiosks and there is still room for parking and a bicycle lane.
Source: Jeffrey R. Kenworthy

FIGURE 4.2
Floating pedestrian and bicycle bridge across the Danube tributary, Vienna, opens at mid-span for boat passage
Source: Eric C. Bruun

FIGURE 4.3A
Tourists on Segways take over a
sidewalk in Toulouse, France
Source: Preston L. Schiller

FIGURE 4.3B
Bicycle lanes in Vancouver's CBD
can separate and protect riders from
traffic
Source: Jeffrey R. Kenworthy

bicycling shares or overlaps many of the attractions, health and cost benefits and hazards of walking, neither is a menace for motorists; the authors know of no instances where motorists were killed as a result of colliding with pedestrians or bicyclists. Some of the most important factors regarding bicycling are summarized in Table 4.1.

Many cities have initiated bicycle rentals ('bike shares') available at strategic locations around town for small fees. Many more are planning to offer the same. While a couple of efforts experienced problems with vandalism when initiated, most seem to be working and are well used. The key to success for bike-sharing programs is to offer a large network with numerous well-placed stations for pick-up and return.

BOX 4.1 Segway rolls over legislatures and pedestrians

by Preston L. Schiller

Dean Kamen has been a prolific inventor of devices, mostly in the domain of medical apparatus and prosthetics, and a highly skilled promoter of his inventions. Kamen is a self-styled libertarian who supposedly moved his operations to New Hampshire because of their 'Live Free or Die' motto, conservative minimalist government philosophy—and no sales tax or state tax on earned income.[i] In 2001, Kamen was granted a U.S. patent for a device described as an automatically balancing vehicle that came to be called the Segway PT (Personal Transporter). The Segway was introduced to the American public in a demonstration on the ABC network's national news show 'Good Morning America' in December 2001 and was made available to the public in 2002. In the lead-up to its unveiling an aura of mystery and suspense was created by its promoters, including giving it the code name 'Ginger' after Fred Astaire's dancing partner, Ginger Rogers. Rumors abounded that it would be an invention greater than the computer or more important than the internet. It was released with a great deal of hyperbolic claim about its benefits to those with disabilities and as the solution to personal mobility, traffic congestion and air pollution. After a few years of lackluster sales, and a rising rate of injuries involving it, Segway was sold to the British entrepreneur Jimi Heselden in 2010, who literally went off the cliff on one shortly thereafter. In 2015, Segway was sold to a Beijing-based transportation robotics firm.

In 2003, Segway launched a lobbying campaign aimed at passing laws at the state level to allow it to operate on sidewalks, paths and trails where motorized devices are generally not allowed (Lawrence et al. 2005). It took advantage of all the media publicity and promotional hype it had been receiving. The campaign also aimed to win federal funding for its research as well as 'environmental' tax credits for purchasers. Within a relatively short time Segway-friendly legislation rolled through 34 state legislative bodies, despite objections from pedestrian advocates—themselves generally outgunned by wealthy high-tech and mechanized mobility interests. Because many states that passed such legislation forbade local jurisdictions from banning or regulating Segways, only a relatively small number of municipalities have succeeded in banning their use on sidewalks, shared trails or bike lanes.

At the federal level Segway achieved some interest for its possible military applications and some agency support and lowering of regulatory barriers: Kamen hired a former general counsel of the Consumer Products Safety Commission (CPSC) and, along with the support of New Hampshire Republican Rep. Charles Bass, successfully influenced that agency and the National Highway Transportation Safety Agency (NHTSA) to *not* classify the Segway as a motor vehicle—which would have prevented its classification as a 'consumer product for personal enjoyment' and barred its use on sidewalks. NHTSA and CPSC issued their favorable classification without any testing of the device. The CPSC engineer who had inspected the Segway and recommended its favorable acceptance then took a sabbatical leave to work with Segway in its efforts to gain wider governmental acceptance, especially at the state level (Armstrong and Guidera 2002). But beyond these gains Segway failed in gaining congressional support for its wish of massive federal research funding and favored tax status for purchasers. This, despite its hiring of two well-placed staff from former House Majority Leader Rep. Tom DeLay (Republican, Texas) as lobbyists and having found favor with (then) Republican Vice-President Cheney, a recipient of a Kamen-invented cardiac stent as well as the free loan of a model from Segway for moving about his DC compound (VandeHei 2003).

Although welcomed early on by some in the disability-related community, experience over a few years demonstrated that there was a good deal of injury associated with Segways, both by users and their sidewalk victims. Exact injury rates are difficult to establish because Segway injuries are not often distinguished within the category of scooters and other mechanized mobility devices. Medical and public health researchers began to document and publicize Segway injuries through emergency room records and the varnish began to peel on the Segway's image. It appears that a mobility machine that weighs around 65 pounds, can carry an adult and an additional 65 pounds of cargo and travel at 12.5 mph—three to five times the average walking pace—can do serious damage to its handler or pedestrians in crashes (Ashurst and Wagner 2015; Roider, et al. 2016). Even some vendors, such as the Edmonton (Alberta) 'All For Outdoor', appear to be compelled to warn customers about the limitations and hazards of Segways (2016).

continued

Today the Segway website boasts that '(A)s of February 2016, 45 states and the District of Columbia have enacted legislation to allow use of Segway PTs on sidewalks, bike paths, and certain roads', while cautioning that '(T)he laws differ from state to state, so it is important . . . users carefully review their state regulations . . . (and five other) states have no prohibitions against the use of powered conveyances on sidewalks and in pedestrian areas . . . local regulations may exist' (Segway 2016).

The Segway has been put to good use in warehousing and large industrial facilities, some hospitals and among some elements of security providers at airports, parking lots, parks, buildings with long corridors, some military bases or sometimes on streets (see Fig. 4.4a). In these applications personnel are probably well trained in the use of this device. But the use of the Segway as a personal mobility device has not become very widespread in the disability community or among recreational users in the U.S., or much of anywhere else. Occasionally one sees a line of guided tourists on Segways. This could be due to a combination of its high price[ii] and public awareness of its maneuverability challenges and publicity around its risk of injury.

[i] New Hampshire does, however, have one of the highest property tax rates in the U.S. Over 100,000 persons work in Massachusetts and reside over the border in New Hampshire, ostensibly to benefit from the high-income levels in one state and the low taxes in its neighbor (Dantz 2015).

[ii] Currently around $6000 for the 'true' consumer Segway—although cheaper models and imitations abound. Around $8000 for heavier duty-commercial use models.

Bicycles are very competitive with PMVs and even transit for many in-town trips. Some cities have staged commuter competitions involving various modes between major urban destinations, often separated by a few miles. The bicyclists frequently win since traffic congestion often slows motorized modes. A little help from bicycle lanes or paths helps considerably (Mapes 2009). It is also a reminder to motorists that the tortoise and hare fable applies to many of their trips. Box 4.2 compares the characteristics of the well-known diamond frame bicycle with those of the lesser-known recumbent HPV.

The characteristics of bicycles and bicycling are summarized in Table 4.1.

FIGURE 4.5
Suitcase bicycle: The late Susie Stephens, influential Seattle and U.S. bicycle advocate, tragically run over by a tour bus in downtown St. Louis, demonstrated a bicycle that folds in and out of a suitcase which can also function as a bicycle trailer.
Source: Preston L. Schiller

FIGURE 4.4
A recumbent family; Todd and Heather Elsworth and their daughter, Violet, in Bellingham, Washington
Source: Clara Elliott

BOX 4.2 **Recumbent versus diamond frame bicycles**

Michael Ferro[i]

The most familiar form of bicycle is the 'diamond frame', named after its shape. It is also referred to as the 'conventional' or 'safety' bicycle for the purposes of this discussion. Conventional upright bicycles are quite easy to learn to ride and handle. They are reasonably comfortable for most people to ride primarily because the riding posture is very close to that of a person walking. The usual bicycle seat is designed more for efficiency of movement than for comfort, and larger, more comfortable seats are sometimes the target of derision among more athletic bicyclists. Others, less athletically pure, think of the smaller seats as instruments of torture, upon which the rider's most tender, vulnerable and personal parts most surely will weigh heavily and suffer fully. In past decades, the conventional bicycle's turned-down handlebars added further postural insults to the back, neck, wrists and hands. Several handlebar options are now available allowing riders a more erect and comfortable posture.

Recumbent bicycles or tricycles allow the rider to be positioned in a reclining posture with legs pushing forward on pedals. The recumbent offers a broad resilient seat not unlike a patio lounger. Handlebars may be placed high or low, but appear not to need to bear any body weight. The recumbent's riding position looks up at the whole wide world rather than down at the surface of the road. In a short wheelbase recumbent, the bicycle's pedals are in front of the front wheel(s). The short wheelbase design is quickly responsive to turning movements. In a long wheelbase recumbent, the pedals are behind the front wheel(s). Long wheelbase recumbents are likely to be slower to respond to steering inputs and somewhat more stable. Recumbent bicycles, because of their different configuration, require a different and, for some people, more demanding set of riding skills to master (Felau 2006).

There are advantages to both designs. Recumbents offer greater rider comfort for seating, hand positioning, head and neck angles and forward visibility. They have much lower air resistance at speeds above about 15 mph and are significantly easier to pedal at higher speeds. Because of their superior speeds, they dominated bicycle racing for many years until they were made ineligible by the major bicycle racing organizations. Human-powered vehicles (HPVs) based on recumbent designs hold world speed records.

The conventional diamond frame, or 'safety' design, also has its advantages. It is easier to balance since its riding posture is similar to standing. It is easier starting up and climbing hills because the rider's weight is over the pedals. It is more suitable for turning the upper body for looking behind. Viewing of rear gear cluster is possible for checking which gear is engaged. It is more compact and lightweight, facilitating carrying and storage.

Michael Ferro of Oakland, California, has been a rider and owner of both conventional bicycles and recumbent bicycles and tricycles.

Roller luggage, handcarts, bike trailers and other auxiliary mobility assistance devices

Walkers and bicyclists can increase their carrying capacity by using trailers and other wheeled devices. In many countries, a wide array of bicycle trailers, folding bicycles and freight bicycles is now available to assist people with loads or making intermodal travel connections. Use of small-wheeled devices to assist walkers with loads, or those with mobility challenges, has increased rapidly in recent decades, including luggage with wheels and two-wheeled shopping carts that fold up compactly when not used. These assist compact mixed-use development and public modes by extending the practical walking range and increase the percentage of trips suitable for walking alone or in conjunction with other modes. Once seen primarily at airports or train stations, roller luggage or briefcases on wheels are increasingly seen around educational facilities and commercial districts.

FIGURE 4.6
Runnel stairway
in Copenhagen; the Lakes
Neighborhood; note wider runnel
for roller carts or luggage, narrower
one for bicycles.
Source: Preston L. Schiller

Public transportation or transit

This section will focus mostly on aspects of transit related to infrastructure, hardware and operational strategies. Chapter 5 will explore policy and planning issues related to transit and several other forms of public transportation. Transit can be an extremely space- and energy-efficient urban mode.[4] When done well, it can help to focus and facilitate compact development and obviate the need for private motoring for many or most urban trips. If cities are to reduce auto-usage dramatically, as well as space dedicated for their driving and storage, transit must attract a large usage. A recent innovation has been the super capacitor bus (SCB, Figure 4.7d), which has great promise for improving the way in which

FIGURE 4.7A
Electrified trolley bus, San Francisco;
energy efficient, good acceleration,
hill climbing
Source: Jeffrey R. Kenworthy

FIGURE 4.7B
E-mini-bus in Montmartre, Paris
Source: Eric C. Bruun

FIGURE 4.7C
Properly done transit mall in Portland (OR)
with lanes sufficient for boarding passengers
as well as for passing buses
Source: Preston L. Schiller

some bus services perform. According to the source for Fig. 4.7D, the information sign at one of its stations at the World Expo in Shanghai, 2010, reads:

The power system of a Super Capacity Bus (SCB) is mainly composed of super capacitors and Electric Drive Motor (EDM) Super capacitors store electricity from electrical grid, and provide power to the EDM, which drives the vehicle. A super capacity [sic, capacitor?] is characterized by high power density, long service life, a broad working temperature range, and rapid charge/discharge capability. Therefore, SCB has the advantage of zero emissions, low noise, and high-energy efficiency (at least 20% of the braking energy could be recovered).

FIGURE 4.7D
Electrified fast recharging bus Charges
at frequent station stops in Shanghai
Source: Wes Frysztacki, Weslin Consulting
Services

The all-important relationship between vehicle and the infrastructure on which it operates (right of way) is discussed next and one example is depicted in Figure 4.7c.

The performance of transit is greatly affected by its right of way (RoW) conditions. In fact, they are probably the single largest determinant. Using Vuchic's (2007) terminology, there are three basic types:

1   *RoW A*: a full separation from all other modes and all cross-traffic. The most expensive solution, it also gives the best performance.
2   *RoW B*: a lateral separation such that the mode runs in a fully separated lane, but there are still at-grade conflicts with other traffic at intersections. It is intermediate in cost and performance.
3   *RoW C*: operating in mixed traffic, it requires little investment beyond the existing roadway and is thus the least expensive. It also guarantees that transit will be slower than private automobiles.

FIGURE 4.8
Modal Integration: Bike Share at LRT station in Paris and easy to enter low floor vehicle
Source: Jeffrey R. Kenworthy

FIGURE 4.9
Private buses and taxicabs vie for passengers in RoW C, Miraflores, Lima, Peru
Source: Preston L. Schiller

The higher the standard of RoW is, in general, the higher the speed and capacity. Large cities need RoW A if they are to maintain livability. RoW B is increasingly used in medium cities, especially with the light rail transit (LRT) and bus rapid transit (BRT) modes. A range of techniques, commonly known as 'transit priority', helps to speed transit vehicles through intersections and other traffic bottlenecks, thus improving both speed and reliability of transit operating on RoW B and C. Several telecommunications techniques can provide transit riders with real-time service information and providers with ways of dynamic scheduling and flow adjustments. There is a wide variety of intelligent transportation systems (ITS) that are helping to provide more attractive and reliable services, and to help people plan their trips. This is in line with increased expectations for more information in all aspects of people's daily lives. These same ITS also generate rich data archives that facilitate further improvements in transit planning.[5] Some of the most important factors regarding public transportation are summarized in Table 4.1.

Special needs, special populations contribute to large transit subsidies

Even where ridership and farebox return are high, some aspects of transit may require public subsidy. Because of the sprawling and segregated nature of many cities, especially in the U.S., inner-city and poor residents are often at a disadvantage when commuting to jobs in distant suburbs. Sometimes special 'reverse commute' services need to be offered to help them participate in the workforce. This is one of the costs of sprawl development. In the less wealthy countries, this same inability to reach job-rich sites is an impediment to economic development, a serious financial burden to governments to provide such services, or both.

Many of the improvements needed to station and vehicle access for mobility-challenged people, such as low-floor or 'kneeling' buses, benefit the general population as well, through faster and easier boarding and alighting. But the commitment to serve mobility-challenged and transit-disadvantaged individuals sometimes unavoidably adds considerable cost to some services, vehicles and infrastructure. The accommodation of the 'mobility challenged' is mandated at the federal level in the U.S., but most of its high operational costs are met through the local transit providers' already insufficient funding. Some of the ways in which transit providers can meet the needs of special populations through innovative services that cost less than the segregated services are made available through free publications.[6]

Personal motor vehicles (PMVs)

PMVs include many types: automobiles, small town cars, vans, light trucks and sports utility vehicles (SUVs), and motorized two-wheelers (and, occasionally, three-wheelers) such as motorcycles, scooters and mopeds. Some PMVs are also used as for-hire taxis, shuttles and limousines. Motorized recreational vehicles (RVs) ranging from bus-sized to small off-road vehicles (ORVs) and snowmobiles will not be analyzed in this chapter, but are discussed in the section on 'Tourism: The car culture evolves into the fly-drive and recreational vehicle' in Chapter 2.

The large majority of PMVs in use are powered by internal combustion engines (ICEs), but an increasing number of ICE–electric hybrid and fully electric power systems are being slowly introduced for both transit vehicles and PMVs. With hybrid powered vehicles a smaller ICE motor keeps a battery storage system charged or powers the vehicle when the batteries' energy has been exhausted, or additional peak power is needed. Fully electrified PMVs are available and their range and utility are constantly improving due to technology advances and the spread of available charging stations. It is highly likely that electrified vehicles, human driven or autonomous (see discussion of EVs below) will dominate future transit and personal vehicle fleets. Some of the most important factors regarding PMVs are summarized in Table 4.1.

FIGURE 4.10
Electric carshare recharging station in Berlin
Source: Jeffrey R. Kenworthy

PMV ownership, cost-bundling or car-sharing?

Most of the costs of owning and operating a PMV are 'bundled', meaning that one pays lump sums for purchase, insurance and even storage at work or at some residential buildings regardless of the level of use of the vehicle. After assuming all the up-front bundled costs of vehicle ownership, the costs of operating a PMV are experienced as relatively cheap marginal costs. This contrasts to public transportation where there may be no up-front cost to the user but the cost of fares or passes may exceed the marginal costs of driving. One possibility for reducing the urban population of PMVs, while still offering their use as an option, is the 'car-share' organization, which allows members to pay an annual fee so that they can use a car as needed for a daily or hourly fee. Some car-share organizations, especially in major European cities, offer a bouquet of fleet vehicles, bicycles and discounted transit passes, and some are affiliated with other cities' car-share organizations so that members can use vehicles when visiting.[7] The modal characteristics of PMVs are included in Table 4.1.

Regional–metropolitan area modes: long commutes, regional services, recreation, peak demand

As previously discussed, most trips are in town and most are for relatively short distances. In large metropolitan areas, people may live at a considerable distance from their places of employment. Sometimes this is a matter of choice; sometimes the distance has been created by an employer's decision to locate or relocate in a fringe office park area where land is cheaper than in a town center. Occasionally households with two employed individuals face the complicated issue of where to live relative to either partner's place of employment.

Some regional trips are for specialized services, such as those at a medical specialty center. Other regional trips may be to a special recreational attraction, such as a sports center, zoo or museum. Facilities that either employ large numbers of people, such as regional hospitals, or attract large crowds, such as sports arenas, should be encouraged to locate in areas accessible by transit for the sake of both visitors and employees. There are several considerations relating to modes chosen or promoted for regional trips:

FIGURE 4.11A
Regional-commuter train; "Sounder", Seattle
Source: Eric C. Bruun

- *Walking*: most regional trips are not amenable to walking, although the pedestrian conditions around transit can be an important factor for choosing that mode.
- *Bicycling*: regions that have created good bicycle networks can attract small but significant percentages of travel by this mode. Where bicycles are facilitated in large numbers, such as the Copenhagen S–Tog transit system, they serve as a feeder/distributor system and their use is increased even further. Good bicycle storage or bike shares at transit facilities can also encourage cycling to and from transit trips.
- *Public transportation*: many regional trips can be attracted by transit modes when planning and provision is adequate. RRT/Metro, RGR/Regional Rail (sometimes inappropriately termed commuter rail), especially when offered throughout the week rather than just weekday peak period and peak direction, and regional bus networks (Express Bus or BRT services) and special for-hire services (buses or vans to airports and train stations) can all make significant contributions to attracting commuters and other individuals who need to travel to regional centers. In some regions, ferries play a significant role in transporting people to and from major centers. These services work best with good intermodal connections.
- *PMVs*: many auto-dependent regions have virtually no option but the PMV, except perhaps in their older, traditional parts built earlier in the twentieth century that may still have some walkability and transit. Such regions should invest in sidewalks, bicycle lanes and good transit to lessen their automobile dependence. This is becoming ever more urgent as the population ages and the numbers of transit-dependent workers' jobs relocate to such areas. Some regions have attempted to improve bus performance as well as attract more commuters to carpools or vanpools through high-occupancy vehicle (HOV) lanes on major roads. This is a questionable practice, compared to transit-only lanes and a variety of available transit priority measures as it is largely unproven and may, in fact, pull riders from true HOV transit into two person carpools, sometimes termed 'fampools'. For more on HOV see the discussion in Schiller (1998).

FIGURE 4.11B
Smaller commuter-regional train (diesel multiple unit, DMU), Portland, (OR)
Source: Preston L. Schiller

FIGURE 4.12
Brisbane's passenger-only ferries connect nodes of density in a marine region.
Source: Jeffrey R. Kenworthy

Regional roads in urban areas often face serious congestion during commuter hours and other times of great travel demand, such as sports events and holiday periods. When congestion occurs at predictable periods, usually during the morning and afternoon commuter 'rush' hours, it is referred to as peak-period congestion. The hour with the worst congestion is termed the 'peak hour'. A few years after the U.S. began its suburbanization trajectory, major congestion occurred on highways leading into and out of CBDs (or other employment areas) in the morning and late afternoon. This has been termed 'peak direction'. Today, due to some gentrification of inner urban areas, many U.S. and Canadian cities have bi-directional peak period congestion, often not as marked as unidirectional peak flows as in past decades. As more and more driving occurs for all trips, some urban regions experience peak congestion all day, into the evenings and at weekends (see Box 4.3). Road expansion as a strategy to accommodate peak PMV travel is self-defeating:

- The phenomenon of induced driving or traffic generation, where roadway expansion results in increasing levels of traffic, is well documented and explained elsewhere in the book.
- A general traffic lane for a limited-access highway can only accommodate at most 2,000 to 2,200 vehicles per hour (less for most urban arterials) before becoming unstable. It can then approach the speed at which an infant crawls, before speeding up again in phenomena called 'shock waves'.
- At peak commuter hours, PMVs generally have their lowest passenger occupancy rates, barely averaging more than one person per PMV.
- At peak hours, transit vehicles usually have their highest passenger occupancy rates.
- A roadway lane dedicated to transit only can carry the equivalent of many times the persons occupying one general-purpose lane; adding two tracks of rail transit capacity can exceed peak period roadway capacity of an entire multiple-lane freeway.
- Diverting PMV traffic to transit also reduces parking demands, an extremely important factor in the overall complexity of moving towards more sustainable transportation and land-use forms.

Rather than 'biggering' the roads, a better strategy is to manage peak period demands through improved transit, non-motorized facilities and incentives for people to work at home

---

BOX 4.3 Peak hour can last all day in some automobile cities

Bellevue, Washington, is a city that was mostly pastures and farmland before World War II. Then it became a suburb designed for the automobile, both in its exclusively zoned low-density residential neighborhoods, and in its commercial and office districts and central business district (CBD), where tall office towers and a large shopping mall are fed by ever-widening arterial roads. It has miles of strip mall-style development along many of its arterial roads. Because there is relatively little mixing of residences, offices, shops and services, and a retrograde pedestrian and bicycling environment, residents and employees drive everywhere. Often, they drive from one parking lot to another in the CBD because of the car culture, rigidly enforced restrictions in parking lots or both (Schiller 1997b). Consequently, Bellevue has become a poster child for the midday peak: employees take to their cars to run errands and find a place to meet and eat; residents take to their cars to run errands and find a place to meet and eat; and all become very frustrated by the huge traffic back-ups. The Bravern is an 'upscale' downtown mall along with expensive condominium and office towers, including fitness clubs and spas, bravely trying to outdo the existing CBD mall and adjacent high rise office and residential buildings. Some Bravern residents will not have to drive to work and all can walk to their own mall without leaving the complex unless, of course, they have a power lunch meeting elsewhere—in which case they will surely summon the valet for their car and drive. Not to be outdone by The Bravern, India's Tata Group is planning the ultimate solution to parking and car-oriented living: The proposed Tata Tower would be a vertical alternative energy-assisted parking garage with housing for 4,050 of its electric Nanos and 930 residences for its Mumbai employees. Despite skepticism from pundits such as Thomas L. Friedman about the wisdom of promoting more automobiles in an all-day traffic clogged city in great need of more and better transit and less vehicular pollution, Tata proposes this as the solution to the ever-growing traffic congestion in Mumbai, created in part by its cars (The Bravern 2016, Friedman 2007, Pathak 2010).

Source: Preston L. Schiller

---

at least part of the week and for other motorists to make discretionary trips outside of peak times.

The barrier effects of different rights of way

Virtually all forms of rights of way (RoW) for motorized modes have connectivity and barrier effects. Barrier effects that limit the ability to cross a motorized RoW can seriously affect the ways in which people travel in town, especially by walking and bicycling, and the ways in which buses are routed. Large or busy traffic roads can act as barriers to travel, commerce and sociability within neighborhoods, as well as making the areas adjacent to them unpleasant through noise and fumes. Streets where transit demand is very high and transit vehicles are so numerous as to create a 'wall of buses' should be considered as corridors for creating RoW A, either in tunnels or elevated structures. Examples of RoW barrier effects are demonstrated in Figures 13A and 13B.

Long distance: modes and types of travel

Long-distance travel can be defined as travel outside the region of one's residence and beyond the reach of local and regional public transportation. Its distance might range from 100 miles to several thousand miles. Long-distance travel occurs for several reasons: business and professional matters; family visits and emergencies; medical needs; and recreation, including international and intra-national tourism. In wealthy countries, most moderate long-distance travel is done by PMV, and very long trips involving hundreds or thousands

TABLE 4.2 Energy efficiency of land passenger modes

Mode	Average fossil or generated energy use; miles per gallon (litres/100km)	Typical passenger load		Capacity load[b] All seated = (s) Crush = (c)	
		Passengers	Miles per gallon/ passenger	Passengers	Miles per gallon/ passenger
Land					
Walking	0(0)	1	∞	2 (piggyback)	∞
Bicycle	0 (0)	1	∞	2 (s/c)	∞
e-bike (e-assisted)	1600 (0.15)	1	1600	2 (s/c)	320
e-motorcycle	350 (0.7)	1	350	2 (s)	700
Scooter (WASP)	75.0 (3.13)	1	75	2 (s)	150
Motorcycle (large/medium)	35–65 (7–3) 60 (4)	1	60	2 (s)	120
Elec. auto. (Nissan Leaf)* Hwy	101 (?)	1	101	5 (s)	505
Elec. auto. (Nissan Leaf)* City	126 (?)	1	126	5 (s)	630
Gas–electric hybrid auto—city + highway (Toyota Prius)	47.6 (4.94)	1.5	72	5 (s)	238
Very small auto—highway (Smart Car for two)	41[c] (5.73)	1.5	62	2 (s)	82
Very small auto—city (Smart Car for two)	33[c] (7.12)	1.2d	40	2 (s)	66
SUV—highway (Ford Explorer V8)	21.6[c] (10.9)	2	43	7 (s)	151
SUV—city (Ford Explorer V8)	14.1[c] (16.7)	1.2[d]	17	7 (s)	98
40-foot diesel transit bus (BC Transit—city and express average)	3.1 (76.0)	25	78	90 (c)	279
40-foot trolley bus (New Flyer low floor)	9.77 (24.06)	30	293	77 (c)	752
Light rail transit (LRT) (Siemens Combino)	13.6 (17.2)	65	887	180 (c)	2460
Rapid transit (Bombardier T-1)	8.0 (29.4)	100[a]	800[a]	315 (c)	2520
London Underground (Hybrid rapid transit/regional rail)	7.4 (31.9)	19	141	152 (c)	1125
Regional rail (GO Transit loco-powered 10 bi-level cars)	0.26 (940)	1000	260	3600 (c)	936
Intercity rail (Swedish Railways Regina EMU)	3.35 (70.3)	34	114	167 (s)	560
High-speed rail (TGV Atlantique train-set)	1.58 (149)	291	460	485 (s)	767

Notes

*The values presented in Tables 4.2 (and 4.3) are intended to be instructive for the purposes of modal comparisons rather than for purposes of technical analysis.

a = ridership varies a great deal; busy lines will average more passengers than seats over the course of a day.

b = crush load varies, typically assumed at four people per square metre in Europe and North America.

c = official U.S. Environmental Protection Agency figures, higher than seen in practice.

d = average passenger load in U.S. for PMVs during commuting hours.

Source: Strickland (2009), unless otherwise noted

FIGURE 4.13A
Bangkok Barrier effect of large urban
highway
Source: Jeffrey R. Kenworthy

FIGURE 4.13B
Los Angeles Barrier effect of large
urban highway (US)
Source: Jeffrey R. Kenworthy

of miles are usually done by airlines. Japan is one of the few exceptions to this generality, having invested wisely and heavily in a high-performance intercity rail system since the 1960s. It was then able to direct much in-country long-distance travel to this system rather than to highway or aviation expansion for such purposes.

The modes most commonly used for long-distance travel whose characteristics need to be considered are coaches (buses and jitneys), railways, airliners, ships and ferries, and PMVs. Motorcycles account for a relatively small percentage of long-distance travel, even in less wealthy countries where they are much-used for much local and regional travel. Table 4.3 summarizes and compares selected characteristics of long-distance modes, which are then discussed.

TABLE 4.3 Energy efficiency of air and water passenger modes*

Mode	Average energy usage in miles per gallon (litres per 100km)	Typical passenger load[c]		Capacity load[a]	
		Passengers	Miles per gallon/ passenger	Passengers	Miles per gallon/ passenger
Air					
Private small airplane (Cessna 172)	12.6 (18.7)	1	12.6	4	50.4
Regional turboprop (DHC 8–300)	1.19 (198)	35[c]	41.7	50	59.3
Short- to medium-range airliner (Boeing 737 'Next Generation' mixed fleet—607-mile average flight length)	0.43 (547)	96[c]	41.3	137	58.9
Medium- to long-distance airliner (Airbus 320–1358 mile average flight length)	0.447 (526)	109[c]	48.7	156	69.7
Very long-distance airliner (Boeing 777–200ER—6818-mile flight length)	0.252 (933)[b]	211[c]	53.1	301	75.8
Water					
Passenger-only double-ended ferry (Vancouver SeaBus)	0.25 (944)	140	35	400	100
Passenger + car ferry ship (BC Ferries Spirit Class)	0.0246 (9572)	1000	24.6	2100	51.7
Transoceanic luxury ship (Queen Mary 2–25 knots)	0.00753 (31,250)	2000	15.0	3090	23.2

Notes

*The values presented in this table represent a rough estimate; many factors can influence fuel economy for such craft including, for aircraft: wind, altitude and load factors; and for watercraft: currents, wind, wave conditions, loads, etc. Tables 4.2 and 4.3 are intended to be instructive for the purposes of modal comparisons rather than for purposes of technical analysis.

a = legal safe capacity of ferries is typically far exceeded in many developing countries.

b = Boeing Company, www.boeing.com/commercial/777family/pdf/777environ_1.pdf. Note: new models such as the 787 are approximately 20% more fuel efficient with a longer range.

c = 70% load factor used for typical load factor for all commercial airliners for comparison.

Source: Strickland (2009), unless otherwise notedLong-distance mode considerations

Long-distance mode considerations

- *Walking and bicycling*: very little long-distance travel is on foot or by bicycle due to time constraints and the vicissitudes of using these modes for lengthy trips. Bicycle touring is a very small but slowly growing portion of tourist travel in many countries and holds considerable promise for further growth.
- *Public transportation*: the major modes available to the public for long-distance travel are buses (coaches and jitneys), railways, ferries and ocean vessels and airliners. The role that government plays regarding these modes varies considerably from country to country. Virtually all governments regulate long-distance transportation to some extent, and international agreements and agencies play a role in international and intercontinental regulation. Some long-distance providers, including many passenger railway and ferry services and a few national airlines, are within the public sector; but

most coach services, airlines and ocean passenger vessels are not. In these cases, public transportation generally means public access, but not necessarily control.

- *PMVs*: much long-distance travel is done by PMVs, especially for trips of moderate distance that may be for business, professional or family purposes. A lot of longer-distance trips may be done by PMVs for recreational and tourism purposes, especially in countries where driving is heavily subsidized and alternatives are scarce or unappealing (see the section on Tourism and the car culture in Chapter 2).

Coaches, buses and jitneys

Coach services range from those that are incorporated and scheduled and have a substantial regional, national or international reach, to semi-formal jitney services. Some of these services are available at bus stations or intermodal facilities with good information sources; others are informal, roadside flagging-down or pick-up arrangements with little information available. Some coach and chartered services have buses of substantial size with a variety of amenities aboard – including all the old martial arts films one never wanted to see! Some provide arranged transportation and accommodation for large groups.

Coach services play an important role in countries that lack adequate passenger rail services and have low rates of PMV ownership. Their quality, reliability and comfort may range from excellent to poor. Crowding can be a serious problem in some countries, where passengers may even ride on bus roofs. They tend to be the least comfortable mode, having neither the privacy of the auto nor the space of a train, and often have less personal space than even the airliner, while the duration onboard may meet or exceed that of a very long airliner trip. Coach services could play an important role as parts of intermodal systems feeding railways in wealthy and not-so-wealthy countries. Under deregulation in North America and the U.K., this does not seem to have been the case. Coach services there enjoy some of the same subsidies associated with highway modes and often successfully compete with inadequate and often very slow passenger rail. In car-rich countries such as the U.S. and Canada, many cities, large and small, have been left with relatively few long-distance travel options, rail or coach, as railway services disappeared and profitability rather than need directs most decisions made by private coach lines.

Major cities should have a variety of long-distance travel options, but not be dependent on just PMVs and coach services. One could cite numerous examples of cities across the U.S. that lack rail or quality coach services. A recent U.S. and Canadian trend has been the proliferation of low-priced intercity coach services that often lack much, if any, infrastructure or passenger services. They provide low-cost express services between several major cities, especially undercutting the larger established coach services and Amtrak and VIA Rail. The characteristics of intercity bus and coach-type vehicles are summarized in Table 4.1.

Passenger railways

Well-planned and promoted passenger railways can be an attractive alternative to long-distance driving or flying. Japan's Shinkansen carries intercity passenger volumes similar to metropolitan regional trains elsewhere in the world. Its first line opened in 1964 with a peak speed of 200 km/h, medium speed by today's standard. Current trains run 270 to 300 km/h, with a few lines now running at 350 km/h. There are many high-speed rail (HSR) corridors and technologies across the planet, including many in Europe and Asia. China has been quickly constructing an impressive network of high-speed trains.

There are corridors in other countries where upgraded train services have also succeeded in making inroads on the airliner mode share on an increasing number of routes. This is especially true for the rapidly increasing high-speed network in Europe, where the number of origin–destination pairs for which trains can compete multiplies. High-speed trains can operate on conventional tracks as well, albeit at reduced speeds, such that more cities not on the high-speed corridor can also receive direct service.

Projects such as Europe's Railteam (2009) aim to slow or even reverse the trend of increasing reliance on the automobile for intercity and long-distance travel through integrated fares and better connections across national boundaries. Korea has its own high-speed rail system based on French *train à grande vitesse* (TGV), or high-speed train, technology, designed to attract ridership from both autos and airliners.

China introduced its first 400 km HSR line in 2003 and has expanded its rail system and HSR lines almost exponentially. By 2016, it had invested at least $300 billion in its network of approximately 7,000 km, with more in planning or construction stages, experiencing only occasional setbacks. Due to its expertise and experience, China is either currently discussing, planning or constructing railways and furnishing trains and railway technology to many other countries, especially in Asia. China's emphasis is not on the fastest of HSR trains, but rather to build an extensive network connecting many cities, regions and neighboring countries with reasonably fast trains. 'The domestic emphasis is less on attracting people from autos–since auto-ownership is still very low—instead, it aims to decrease overcrowding on existing trains, reduce the need for airport expansion and improve the economies of rural regions through better connectivity (Wang 2013; Railway Gazette 2016).

These examples, along with many others, suggest that a high or higher-speed train is probably the most dynamic intercity mode in wealthier nations, as well as some of the fast-growing nations in Asia, such as Taiwan, China and South Korea. But the very high construction cost of true high-speed rail (usually defined as greater than 250 km/h) means that compromise solutions must also play a large part. The European high-speed trains are all designed to approach stations in large or small cities on branch lines using existing tracks. By comparison, magnetic levitation (MagLev) technologies need separate infrastructure, even in highly built-up areas (see 'Futuristic modes' below for further details on MagLev).

Passenger services that run at mid-range speeds, sometimes referred to as higher-speed rail (HrSR) are also playing an increased role. They often share track with freight trains, but run at speeds faster than the automobile—up to speeds approaching the lower range of high-speed trains, with peak speeds between 140 to 250 km/h. Where they are not restricted by regulations mandating heavier machinery, as is the situation in North America for passenger trains sharing rights-of-way with freight trains, they use newer generation train designs that are lighter and more energy efficient. Some newer designed trains tilt to take curves at higher speeds. These new designs, combined with targeted additions of track at key locations, provide significant reductions in travel time and reduced operating costs for relatively modest investment. This is the approach that the Nordic countries have been taking due to challenging terrain.

The examples of Amtrak in the U.S. and ViaRail in Canada demonstrate the challenges besetting relatively slow traditional services in countries devoting lavish sums to private motoring rather than to creating modern efficient passenger railways. Both suffer from speed and capacity limitations due to decades of underfunding and conflicts with freight operations. Both were created in the 1970s to divest private railways of their historic legal obligations to provide passenger services along with their principal interest, freight hauling. While the Amtrak-owned corridor between Boston and Washington, DC, has a higher-speed service than in the rest of the continent, and gains ridership, the two national systems overall have stagnant or declining ridership levels. There are several lessons that they could learn from the European example:

- Wherever there is potential to grow ridership by linking metropolitan areas within 200 to 500 miles of each other, as in the Quebec–Windsor corridor in Canada[8] and several corridors in the U.S. including the Midwest and better linkages between the Midwest

FIGURE 4.14
Intercity high speed express trains
serve can compete effectively with
airlines for short and medium
distances purpose than mountain
tourist trains
Source: Jeffrey R. Kenworthy

FIGURE 4.14
Intercity high speed express trains serve can compete effectively with airlines for short and medium distances purpose than mountain tourist trains
Source: Jeffrey R. Kenworthy

and Northeast, the Southeast, Texas and the West Coast, a program of accelerated right-of-way acquisition and service improvement should be undertaken.

- Wherever possible there should be good intermodal connections between trains, coach services and local and regional transit services at stations.
- Passenger train cars and station platform signage should be designed for quick and convenient boarding to reduce dwell times at stations. Cars should generally have at least two good sized doors so that boarding and deboarding can be quick, rather than the one, often narrow, door per car found on most North American trains.
- Successful railway programs benefit from good marketing strategies. Information at stations and websites is generally of high quality. Pricing, fare integration and reduced-cost pass programs reflect an intention to utilize off-peak capacity fully, as well as serve goals such as competing with both automobility and flying. The French TGV is a good example, using a two-tier pricing structure, with the departures most convenient to business travelers costing more (SNCF 2009). Many European countries, with Germany in the lead, offer an abundance of regional, national and seasonal passes or discounted fares and programs to attract riders, sometimes offering group discounts that are highly attractive to families, friends and business associates traveling together. Many European countries have yet to develop a coherent railway pricing or airline taxing structure aimed at attracting motorists and airline passengers for moderate and long-distance travel. Some of the better efforts have been undermined by low-fare air services benefiting from public subsidies such as untaxed fuel and the variety of benefits that accrue to public facilities, such as airports and the highways serving them, which are operated, in good measure, to profit private interests.

Size, range and facilities for passenger rail vehicles

Services of limited frequency tend to be operated with diesel locomotive-pulled units and they are subject to regular delays due to conflicts with freight trains. Stations and terminals tend to be modest. The use of diesel multiple units (DMUs), where locomotives are replaced by individually powered cars that can be joined together for longer trains as needed, are being widely deployed in some railway corridors to serve regional needs. The attractiveness of DMUs, especially their far lower price tag compared to locomotive-pulled trains, is slowly gaining in popularity in North America. In regions where passenger rail lines are already electrified, the current trend is to replace medium-speed trains of traditional locomotive-pulled designs with electric multiple unit (EMU) designs that are substantially more energy efficient. At the opposite end are the dedicated RoW high-speed lines, where only trains of similar speed operate and reliability is very high. Stations and terminals are designed to be attractive and comfortable. In countries with advanced railway services, much thought is being given to reducing dwell times through multi-door boarding and deboarding and the incorporation of family-friendly amenities such as securely separated play areas. The general range of passenger rail is from 20–50 miles (35–80 km)—when only serving a region—to several thousands of miles for the Trans-Siberian and Trans-Canada railways. The characteristics of passenger rail vehicles and services are summarized in Table 4.1

Ferries and ocean-going ships

Before the era of long-distance aviation, ocean liners provided transoceanic and maritime coastal travel services. While ocean liners could do well from an efficiency standpoint due to passenger loads in the thousands, they had another drawback in addition to the extra days relative to an airliner (five days at least to cross the Atlantic). They had the extra expense of the hotel services to support people with food, lodging and entertainment. Ocean liners are now very limited in number and offer, essentially, luxury cruises for vacationers, although some fares competitive with air fares can be found. Ocean liners should not be confused with cruise ships. Cruise ships are very slow vessels better characterized as floating hotels (or even cities) that meander from port to port and generally would not offer the point-to-point routes that persons seeking an alternative to transoceanic flight might find attractive. A more affordable alternative to luxury transoceanic travel is an ocean freighter, many of which have a limited number of passenger compartments and might offer point-to-point travel or multiple destination cruises. People with an aversion to, or medical restriction against, flying can occupy one of the limited number of cabins on such ships. Depending

FIGURE 4.15
Cruise ship at Canada Place,
Vancouver, BC.
Source: Jeffrey R. Kenworthy

on the ports to be connected, and whether there are any intermediate stops, the fastest ocean liners and freighter routes involve at least seven to nine days each way across the Atlantic, considerably more across the Pacific.[9]

There are many ships that travel overnight, usually with sleep accommodations, or a maximum of one day that are usually defined as 'ferries', but they bear little resemblance to the ferries crossing inland waterways. They can carry walk-on passengers, private autos and motorcycles, and even passenger trains when rails are installed in the deck. Typical examples are those that operate in the Baltic and Mediterranean seas and in archipelago regions such as Indonesia and the Philippines. The characteristics of ferries and ocean-going ships are summarized in Table 4.1.

Size, range and facilities for ferry vehicles

Ferries can range from passenger-only vessels carrying a few hundred foot passengers (such as Vancouver's SeaBus or Brisbane's City Cat) to ships carrying hundreds of passengers and small numbers of motorized vehicles (such as between Indonesian islands) to ships that hold a few hundred cars, buses and trucks and over 1,000 passengers (such as ships that cross the Baltic and Mediterranean or ply the waters of Puget Sound and the Salish Sea connecting Seattle and mainland Vancouver and Vancouver Island). There are also special variants that can carry entire trains, as tracks are built into the car deck, and that have icebreaking hulls. In the case of Northern Europe, ferries may be over-water extension of the highway system where bridges are lacking. Ferries can traverse waterways ranging from relatively short distances between islands or between the mainland and a nearby island to distances of several hundred or a thousand miles as in the ferries connecting Bellingham, WA and Alaska in the U.S.

Aircraft and airliners

Direct travel by air is generally limited to travel between relatively large metropolitan destinations or as a feeder from a smaller city to a larger city with a major airport. Otherwise, connecting flights are usually required. Unlike ground modes, intermediate stops at smaller towns along the way are not possible. Commercial airports for turbofan-powered airliners require significant land and noise buffer space, and are typically very limited in number within a region.

As distances became longer, in the wealthy countries, the commercial airlines became dominant. When crossing the continent of North America, it takes five to six hours versus two to three days by ground-based modes. The crossover distance when an individual is likely to select the air mode becomes shorter when there are geographic obstacles, such as mountain ranges or bodies of water, as these further slow the competing water or ground transport relative to air travel. It becomes longer when there is a frequent train service, automobile driving conditions are favorable or the airport is in an inconvenient location. The distance of crossover from airliners to trains will also decrease in corridors where frequent and higher-speed rail is available.

Due to the paucity and poor performance of most rail services in the U.S. and Canada, the public subsidization of commercial aviation and the marketing strategies of airlines, much air travel occurs between cities less than 500 miles apart. Between 25% and 50% of a regional airport's operations may be given over to relatively short flights whose passenger loads are generally lower than longer-distance flights. This inefficiency and environmental damage could be corrected by promoting and providing better intercity rail and coach options (Schiller 2008). For transoceanic travel, the jet airliner has taken a position of extreme dominance. Its productivity and time-saving over the piston propeller airplane quickly caused the displacement of the latter.

Size, range and facilities for passenger aviation vehicles

Long-range aircraft passenger capacity ranges from 150 to 500 or more seats of mixed classes. Although some of the newest aircraft, as well as some under design, are capable of even longer non-stop flights, most routes are within the maximum range of 7,000 to 10,000 nautical miles as passengers tend not to want to endure even longer flights. Service tends to be concentrated from very large airports with major hub-and-spoke operations that feed and distribute passengers to smaller cities, although even medium-sized cities will sometimes have a few long-distance services. The new A380 is far larger than the previous largest aircraft, the 747–400, but, its popularity remains to be proven.

In terms of range of vehicles and facilities, turboprop aircraft are the most efficient for shorter distances and range up to 50 to 70 seats. A more recent trend is to go to 'regional jets' of 50 to 100 seats in size, but analogous to the trend from auto to SUV, they consume more fuel. Larger airliners range from about 100 seats to up to 250 or 300 for trunk routes between major cities. The characteristics of airliners and passenger aviation services are summarized in Table 4.1.

Airports require large amounts of land, including noise perimeters around the airport where types of development are restricted. It is perhaps fortuitous for proponents of alternative modes that suitable quantities of land are increasingly difficult to assemble and new airports are rare. But, as Box 4.4 below indicates, there are some who believe that aviation does not do much environmental harm and that we should welcome a future with more aviation and bigger airport cities.

BOX 4.4 Airport city, aerotropolis and flying cars

In the early 1930s, and through to the end of that decade, various ideas to co-locate airports and cities emerged; in 1939, the same year of General Motors' Futurama exhibit at the New York World's Fair (see discussion in Chapter 2), a *Popular Science* article presented a graphic illustration and brief discussion about this entitled 'Aerotropolis' (DeSantis 1939; Brainerd 1931). In some cases, futuristic airports proposed from the 1930s through the 1950s were simply superimposed upon the center of an existing city; in others, it was a city that was developed in tandem with a super-airport. But reality kept posing problems for such notions, especially the lack of enthusiasm and resistance of urban populations for having an airport adjacent to, in or atop their cities. Keeping these ideas up to date are more sophisticated contemporary efforts to promote airborne hypermobility and to reshape life around flying. Aerotropolitans ignore well-researched readily available information and analysis documenting the downside of the ever-quickening expansion of commercial and freight aviation and their requisite facilities (Perry 2013).

A 2011 book, *Aerotropolis: The way we'll live next*, was co-authored by sociologist turned business school professor John Kasarda and journalist Greg Lindsay. It is a 400-plus-page paean to the wonderful world of cheap labor widgets, fresh food and flowers flown thousands of miles, mostly from poorer countries to wealthier ones, to satisfy just-in-time (JIT) manufacture and market demands.[i] Throughout, it promotes the expertise of Kasarda as consultant to the wealthy and powerful considering new airports, especially in several less-than-democratic Asian and Gulf countries—where the nuisance of public involvement is nil, and planning and construction can rapidly proceed. The book had mixed reviews (Powell 2011).

When the realization of aerotropolitan plans doesn't match expectations, as in the case of New Songdo City's failure to become the corporate hub of East Asia, it is often construed as the consequence of not following, in detail, Aerotropolis's prescriptions. In fact, New Songdo City is about as much of a realization of Aerotropolis that one could find. It turns out that not very many international corporations, or their executive class, are attracted to it. Fortunately for its developers, its residential offerings have appealed to many middle-class persons priced out of the regular Inchon housing market (Williamson 2013).

continued

The book blithely romanticizes the always *Up in the Air* (movie) life of the millions of Ryan Binghams dividing their smug but sad lives between airports and their adjacent hotels; a lifestyle that most who have experienced it would not wish for their friends and loved ones (A.W. 2015, Cohen and Gössling 2015). Well-researched and analyzed negative impacts of large airports and adjacent areas include: Detrimental personal, occupational and public health problems due to excessive noise levels, increased radiation exposure from frequent flying and the under-publicized, dangerously high levels of air pollution, especially particulate matter and ultrafine particulate matter, at and around airports and along flight paths (Hudda and Fruin 2016; Hudda et al. 2014; Riley et al. 2016). The book touts the much-disputed aviation industry's low estimates of its direct GHG damages as 2% of the total, while many expert assessments place it at double or triple that amount and growing rapidly. The United States Department of Transportation in 2006 estimated that commercial aviation's contribution to GHGs was at 7% (USDOT 2006 data).

The ex-urban location, surrounding sprawl, and often-lacking public transportation and non-motorized facilities or services mean that a great many air travelers, approximately 75% at most North American airports, arrive and depart by PMV. A similar or greater percentage of airport city residents and employees also drive alone (Ruhl and Trnavskis 1998). Airport authorities continually lobby for expansions of roads serving their facilities but, especially in North America, also resist truly high-quality well-planned public transportation, local and regional, as it might cut into the revenues they derive from parking and livery vehicle fees. The book conveniently ignores the North American reality of between one-fourth and one-half of most airports arrivals and departures are for trips between 200 and 500 miles: excellent candidates for a vastly improved intercity rail network (Schiller 1997a). Research from the EU would point towards the necessity of accompanying policy and pricing measures to dampen air travel demand overall lest a 'buyback' effect from HSR services for shorter trips facilitate longer airlines trips (Dobruszkes et al. 2014). Despite evidence that quality and high-speed rail services could significantly reduce much of short- and medium-distance air travel, Kasarda and Lindsay reject it as unrealistic and probably just promoting longer-distance flying.

But, just when aerotropolitans thought that the world was becoming safe for their airport cities and ever-expanding runways, the flying car emerged. With a conceptual history predating aerotropolis, and with influential friends such as the 1960s (cartoon) Jetsons, the flying car has been on the minds of the fly-drive public for a century (Bonsor, undated; Vance and Stone 2016). Imagine flying over congested roadways on your way to work or going to your favorite drive-through fast food purveyor. Imagine living in your own perfect machine. Now, thanks to ultra-light design and regulatory largesse, you can purchase one, equipped with folding wings to fit on the road or in the garage previously occupied by your oh-so-retro surface-only vehicle, for $70,000. At present their range is a mere 531 km (330 mile) cruising at 90 knots (approximately 100 mph or 167kmh), but just wait until more work is done on the power and energy systems and soon you'll fly-drive everywhere. And you only need a backyard of about 1,000 feet (300m) for take-off and landing, and you're off. Perhaps the flying car will become a flying version of the automated vehicle (AV) or mate with the amphibi-car and then no destination on the planet will be safe from such an invention (Stenquist 2012; Vance and Stone 2016; Collie 2016).

Source: Preston L. Schiller

Sustainability considerations: fuels, pollution, electric and autonomous vehicles

There are several relevant issues and discussions around modes that tend to focus too narrowly on the technical and technological aspects that are not always well understood in media coverage or public discourse. Issues that benefit from broader analysis and discussion include: energy and environmental factors; the relation of modes to land use, urban form and urban economy; and health, safety, equity and social justice concerns.

Energy and environmental factors: tailpipe and 'fuelish' fixes

A holistic approach to the issues of transportation's environmental effects and energy consumption is needed. Discussion often focuses narrowly on end-of-the-pipe or tailpipe factors for which technological fixes are usually proposed. Transportation pollution is too often seen as a localized matter, one of reducing the levels of certain pollutants such as carbon monoxide or the oxides of nitrogen, or providing special catchment basins for road runoff, rather than a systemic problem that needs to be addressed first at the level of policy and planning, and then with technology when and where appropriate. The examples of vehicle pollution control devices and the efforts to increase motor vehicle energy efficiency, including the U.S. Corporate Average Fuel Efficiency (CAFE) standards, serve as examples of problems with tailpipe approaches. The desirability of lowered pollution and improved energy efficiency is not at question, but the sufficiency of technological approaches is open to question and reconsideration due to a broader understanding of the way in which transportation interacts with a wide array of non-technical, non-technological factors. Testimony before the U.S. Senate's Committee on Environment and Public Works by Steven Winkelman, researcher with the Center for Clean Air Policy, demonstrated that CAFE alone is insufficient to meet GHGs reduction goals; the U.S. must reduce driving (VMTs) and engage more aggressively in 'Smart Growth' (see Chapters 6 and 8) in order to achieve meaningful reductions (Winkelman 2009; also see Creutzig 2016; Vanek et al, 2014—especially Chapter 14).

Emissions controls

A variety of pollution control devices, most notable among them the catalytic converter, have been developed to reduce or eliminate certain harmful ICE emissions. Among the several issues with having pollution control devices at the center of clean air efforts are the following:

- Only a handful of pollutants are targeted and monitored for control—generally, carbon monoxide, certain oxides of nitrogen and some hydrocarbons. Carbon dioxide, the greatest global emissions threat, is not controlled by these devices and is only beginning to be subject to regulation by pollution control agencies. The great majority of pollutants emitted by motor vehicles, numbering in the hundreds, are unknown, unanalyzed or uncontrolled. The mix of tailpipe pollutants can vary with batch-specific refining and whether or not vehicle owners use fuel additives or even maintain pollution control devices properly. In many developing countries, there is the further problem of adulteration of fuel, such as the cutting of diesel fuel with kerosene.
- Some aspects of pollution control devices have undesirable impacts. Some pollution control devices reduce the fuel efficiency of vehicles, and the technologies involved might create pollution elsewhere in the vehicle's life cycle through increased mining, energy use, industrial impacts or disposal impacts.
- The technology of pollution control may be inadequate to the task at hand as the recently uncovered insufficiencies of measurement techniques based on service station or laboratory testing when compared with the generally higher values of on-road emissions, which, if done properly, can capture some of the inefficiencies of real-time driving caused by constant acceleration-deceleration etc.
- Emissions controls may be subject to manipulation and fraudulent representations by vehicle owners, service facilities or the automakers themselves, as the scandals surrounding Volkswagen, Mitsubishi and other manufacturers demonstrate (Ewing 2016; Grescoe 2016; Transport and Environment 2016a).

The risk to human health from particulate pollution, and not always well controlled in vehicle emissions control systems (as the diesel scandal cited above indicates), is well established and findings are emerging that there are great risks from even finer particulate matter than has been recognized in the past (Kaufman et al. 2016; also see Box 4.4). Particulate pollution can come from emissions as well as road dust created by motor vehicles. There are several especially toxic particulates that are generally unaddressed or insufficiently addressed in pollution control efforts. These include tire and brake particulates, which build up in road dust or end up in water systems from road runoff.

Alternative fuels and carbon sequestration

Alternative fuels and ideas about carbon sequestration, the fixing of atmospheric carbon in forms or ways that prevent its climate impacts, are much in the media and public discussion. Even if a technologically optimistic 'miracle cure', such as the controversial proposals around carbon sequestration, were to prove workable, there is still a great need for the dramatic reduction of fossil fuels—which can probably only be met with significant reductions in transportation energy consumption (McGlade and Ekins 2014). There are several issues with which ST should be concerned in terms of alternative fuels:

- The quest for lowering GHG atmospheric loadings through alternative fuels or carbon sequestration may lead nowhere. It may also divert attention away from the difficult task of reorganizing urban development and transportation systems to reduce overall levels of PMV and freight transportation.
- 'Cleaner' fuels are often not analyzed in terms of their life cycle impacts. Such is the case with ethanol, which is added to all U.S. and Canadian motor vehicle fuel stocks, ostensibly to reduce harmful exhaust emissions. Through careful analysis, ethanol has been shown to have overall negative efficiency, motor maintenance and pollution effects. But its mandate and subsidies have been maintained despite these analyses for its very lucrative effects for agricultural interests involved in its production and processing— who have had considerable political influence in the U.S. and Canada. An additional adverse effect has been the steep price rise (and lessening affordability) of corn and corn-related products, food staples in many Latin American countries. These have combined with the monopolistic practices of many of the major agribusiness corporations to make smaller-scale and locally oriented food production increasingly untenable in many of these countries.
- The production of agriculturally derived alternative fuels, even should some of these alternative fuels prove to have an environmentally positive life cycle carbon footprint, may divert needed croplands from feeding people to feeding vehicles. The equity and social justice implications of this orientation are self-evident. Increased demand for palm oil for biodiesel fuel has led to destruction of rainforests. And there is reason to believe that many of the most commonly promoted biofuels may increase carbon emissions when subject to life cycle analysis (Cappiello 2014; Transport and Environment 2016a, b).
- At present, there is much more publicity about carbon sequestration than there is evidence about the workability, practicality and long-term viability of such processes. Some proposed processes, such as the Icelandic basalt process, may also require more fossil-fueled energy to perform than the amount of carbon they permanently sequester. Others, such as the proposals and efforts to capture and store carbon in underground seams or mine shafts, are untested on a large scale and questionable in terms of their short-term viability or long-term security (Epstein et al. 2011).
- Electric vehicle technology holds great promise for energy efficiency and lessened pollution—especially in urban areas. But several caveats are in order: at present, approximately one-third of U.S. electrical generation is from coal plants, and another one-third is from natural gas; unless and until the U.S. makes a majority shift to solar, wind and, possibly, tapping the kinetic power of ocean, generated electricity is still

contributing greatly to GHGs (USEIA 2016). Additionally, there is good reason to question the viability of current levels of PMV dependency, whether the driving is electric powered and done by humans or autonomous vehicles (see the discussion of AVs below).

- Another factor related to electric (EVs) or plug-in electric hybrid vehicles (PHEVs), or the much-touted autonomous vehicle (AV), is that fleet turnovers entail many years or decades before change is effective. At the current slow rates of adoption and turnover, it will be a long time before many of the benefits promised for this technology change may be realized.

BOX 4.5 Electric vehicles

John Niles[i]

Achieving more energy efficiency in motor vehicles is good for environmental sustainability; one way to do that is through hybrid gas–electric or fully electric vehicles. Gasoline engines can be configured to turn off temporarily whenever the car pauses for a traffic signal, or to switch to a parallel, small electric motor at low speeds. These car types are called hybrids, a category in which the Toyota Prius has become a leading example worldwide since its introduction in Japan in 1997.

Electric vehicles (EVs) were dominant in early automobile and truck markets just before World War I, but languished in general consumer use for the next century after 1920 because gasoline was so convenient, cheap and plentiful (also see discussion of EVs in Chapter 3). As environmental awareness has grown and chemistry has advanced, batteries have improved continuously in the twenty-first century. A bigger battery and a charging plug were added to the Prius, and Chevrolet offered its Volt with a liquid-cooled battery to create a car that intends the gasoline motor only to be used for range extension between charging sessions. New kinds of battery-only electric cars were introduced, such as the Nissan Leaf and Tesla, which are exclusively electric, plugging into an electric socket with any standard voltage. Ranges on new EVs vary from approximately 100 to 500 kilometers, but recharging after a trip takes hours, not minutes. As of this writing, charging typically provides 15 to 30 kilometers of travel for every hour being plugged in at 240 volts. Faster charging is not out of the question, but limited as of this writing, and not likely to be as fast as a quick stop for gas.

Most commuting and other daily use of cars within urban environments is under 40 miles and would be well served by a battery-electric car, but long road trips of longer distance would be constrained until much faster charging technologies (or widespread battery swap stations) are available.

Electric-motor cars typically have acceleration that exceeds the performance of gasoline-fueled vehicles, are quieter, and have lower maintenance requirements because of fewer moving parts. While electric cars currently have a higher cost than petroleum-fueled models in capital investment not compensated by the lower fuel cost of electricity, those costs are already dropping as new battery-electric models are introduced. Technological developments are constantly improving battery-electric vehicles allowing longer range, higher reliability and lower price. Most major automotive companies state they are working to design and build electric vehicles priced for mass appeal.

The environmental impact of growing automobile use throughout the world would be reduced if a higher proportion of road vehicles were zero-emission, meaning fueled exclusively with battery-electric power instead of fossil fuels. Petroleum-powered vehicles generate both local air pollutants and greenhouse gas, and are often the biggest source of both compared to stationary sources. Worldwide, pollution from vehicles causes fatalities at the same rate as crashes.

With discharge of greenhouse gas into the atmosphere as a major threat to the viability of life on the planet, the conversion of all motorized surface transportation in cars, vans and buses to electric power is now a reasonable public policy goal, beginning with urban regions. Many national and regional governments worldwide are providing incentives for electric vehicle purchase by individuals and organizations. Norway's national government is pursuing regulations that require all new cars sold beginning 2025 to be zero-emission. Because a major shift from petroleum fuels to electric power requires growing electricity generation, there

continued

needs to be coordination with electric utility industry efforts to generate power via sustainable means, such as solar, wind and hydroelectric. The coal-powered EV is not desirable.

Electric vehicle batteries, when reaching end of life, can potentially be used in other less stressful applications, and are to be disposed of responsibly, as should be ordinary car batteries. A secondary point in favor of electric cars is lower emission of oil drippings and reduced copper droppings from brake pads, both of which reach stormwater runoff and pollute waterways. Letting the electric motor run as a generator when an EV is slowing down to stop reduces brake use and is best practice engineering.

One issue with reduced use of fossil fuels is the issue of public road financing, which is dependent in most jurisdictions on petroleum fuel taxes. The shift to electric vehicles provides new incentive to develop road user charging by the kilometer to pay for road construction and upkeep.

Electric-powered personal vehicles combined with automated braking, lane keeping and other computerized safety features present a growing challenge to the planet if these environmental and safety improvements lead to personal worldwide vehicle ownership at levels seen in advanced economies like the United States. Mitigating that threat is the fact that electrification and automation can be applied equally to commercially and government-owned multi-passenger vehicles of all sizes (including large buses), thus providing common carrier mobility as a service in urban areas as a substitute for personally-owned vehicles. Electric, automated, driverless taxi-vans and minibuses are a real possibility for the future, a big leap for what efficient public transit could mean (see Underwood, Marshall and Niles 2014).

John Niles, President of Global Telematics, is an independent researcher, trainer and change agent based in Seattle, Washington. His principal foci are telecommunications with special emphasis on transportation applications. He is a fellow of the Mineta Transportation Institute at San Jose State University (CA) and has also worked with the Center for Advanced Transportation and Energy Solutions as well as collaborated with Toronto-based Bern Grush in the End of Driving project (http://endofdriving.org/about-grush-niles-strategic/)

There is a good deal of imaginative thinking as well as hype and misrepresentation around EVs: one example is the development of a concept of a small two-passenger, folding (or even stackable) concept car under development by MIT engineers (MIT 2012, Condliffe 2012) that made is as far as an EU exhibition before a whiff of scandal as well as its likely obsolescence before production led to its demise (Frayer and Cater 2015).

ALTERNATIVE FUEL VEHICLES

FIGURE 4.16
"Alternative Fuel Vehicles"
Source: Andy Singer (andysinger.com)

Fuel and energy efficiency: vehicles, fuels or cities?

Developing and spreading the use of fuel and energy-efficient vehicles is a laudable goal. But there are several issues around the ways in which such efforts have been defined or shaped:

- Fuel efficiency may be a vehicular attribute, but the nature of the fuel itself may be inefficient when the whole production and life cycle of fuel production and distribution is considered. A major portion of transoceanic shipment is devoted to the transport of fuels and related products. Energy efficiency should be assessed in the context of life cycle analysis and the prospects of renewability. Currently, the worldwide transportation system—land, sea and air— is approximately 90% to 95% dependent upon fossil fuels, and approximately two-thirds of that dependency is for PMVs.[10]
- There is a certain irony with recent concern about fuel efficiency after decades of neglect or retrograde movement in this area. For decades, the major PMV manufacturers have been using mechanical improvements to foster performance, especially acceleration, rather than efficiency. In recent decades, the U.S. has seen highway speed limits increased and tax incentives promoting the purchase of SUVs while fuel efficiency declined overall.
- In the absence of reductions in driving and the rapidly growing motor vehicle population, tailpipe and fuel efficiency efforts may not be very effective. In most countries, there is very little in the way of formal policy or planning mechanisms to direct development into patterns that reduce driving, facilitate transit and non-motorized travel, and consequently significantly reduce the impacts of PMVs. Northern Europe and parts of Asia are the areas where the most concerted efforts are being made.

Much of the promotion of pollution control and energy-efficient vehicles unfortunately misses the point: a city could be filled up with fuel-efficient automobiles and yet be consuming energy in the extreme. As the discussions of automobile dependency (Chapter 1)

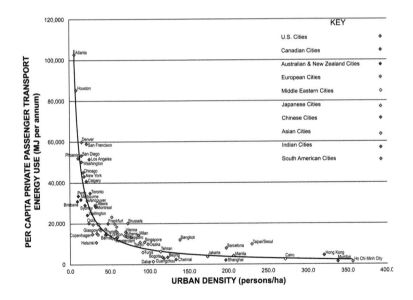

FIGURE 4.17 Total private passenger transport energy consumed decreases as the city becomes more transit-oriented due to higher density

Source: Newman and Kenworthy (2015)

and the space consumption of various vehicles[11] indicate, it is the urban pattern and the availability and promotion of quality transit, walking and bicycling provisions that shape whether a city is efficient or inefficient, extremely polluted or less polluted. The true test of reduction in energy consumption isn't on an individual vehicle basis, but on the total basis for the entire city. Figure 4.17 shows a very strong relationship between energy use per capita and density in higher-income cities. This density is only physically possible with a supportive high-capacity transit system. This not only reduces the amount of private car usage; it also enables a much higher percentage of non-motorized trips.

Modal energy consumption and occupancy factors in global cities

So far in this chapter, we have seen that the consumption of energy and vehicle occupancy factors by various modes differs significantly. Of course, it is impossible to completely generalize about such factors because they vary greatly in different circumstances. To capture a more detailed perspective on these matters in real urban situations, Table 4.4 shows the modal energy consumption per vehicle kilometer and per passenger kilometer for cars and all transit modes in 1995/6 and 2005/6 for a sample of 41 metropolitan areas around the world, averaged by region (ten American, four Australian, five Canadian, 20 European and two Asian metro areas).[12] It also shows the average annual vehicle occupancy for each mode. All data are empirical data collected in each city from relevant authorities.[13]

Energy consumption per vehicle kilometer

This factor measures the vehicular energy consumption per kilometer without any factoring in of people carried. It is a comparative measure of the technological characteristics and type of the actual vehicles, in combination with the traffic conditions that they experience in each city, as well as their fuel type, with electric modes being generally less energy-consuming than diesel, gasoline or gas-powered modes.

It is derived from the total annual energy consumed in each metro area for that mode from all energy sources (converted to megajoules—MJ) using appropriate energy conversion factors and divided by the annual vehicle kilometers of travel by that mode. Vehicle kilometers for train modes are wagon kilometers not train kilometers because train size varies significantly depending on the system.

Personal motor vehicles (PMVs or cars)

In 2005, cars varied between 3.1 megajoules per kilometer (MJ/km)[14] in European urban regions and up to 4.9 MJ/km in Canadian cities (U.S. cities 4.1 MJ/km), with an average for all the 41 cities (see endnote 12) across the globe in 2005 of 3.8 MJ/km, a decrease in energy use per kilometer of 7% over the 10-year period. The average vehicular energy consumption of cars improved in all regions in this sample except the Australian cities, where it rose by 4.5%.

Transit

On the other hand, all transit modes averaged 18.6 MJ/km in 2005, which represented a small increase in consumption over the decade of just under 3%. This higher energy use per kilometer is understandable due to the much larger size of most transit vehicles and the number of people they are expected to carry (see next section on energy use per passenger kilometer). The small increase in energy consumption rate may be due to factors such as increasing prevalence of air-conditioned transit vehicles and perhaps increasing congestion

TABLE 4.4 Average modal energy use and vehicle occupancies in various global regions, 1995/6 and 2005/6

		USA 1995	USA 2005	AUS 1996	AUS 2006	CAN 1996	CAN 2006	EUR 1995	EUR 2005	ASIA 1995	ASIA 2005	1995 All cities	2005 All cities	Per cent change
Energy consumption per VKT														
Energy use per private passenger VKT	MJ/km	4.6	4.1	4.0	4.1	5.1	4.9	3.3	3.1	5.4	4.8	4.0	3.8	-7.0%
Energy use per transit VKT	MJ/km	26.3	24.6	15.8	17.3	22.0	23.0	13.7	14.7	15.9	19.6	18.1	18.6	2.8%
* Energy use per bus VKT	MJ/km	28.8	31.3	18.0	21.9	24.1	24.9	15.7	18.8	19.2	23.5	20.3	23.1	13.8%
* Energy use per minibus VKT	MJ/km	8.5	13.2			8.1				6.9	9.5	7.9	12.9	63.2%
* Energy use per tram wagon VKT	MJ/km	19.1	19.9	10.1	11.2	12.1	14.2	12.9	14.9	5.5	5.4	12.6	14.4	14.6%
* Energy use per light rail wagon VKT	MJ/km	17.5	15.3		10.5	13.1	18.2	14.6	11.7	16.1	14.3	15.5	13.3	-14.2%
* Energy use per metro wagon VKT	MJ/km	25.3	16.1		22.6	10.6	13.5	11.0	9.3	7.8	18.7	14.4	12.7	-11.5%
* Energy use per sub. rail wagon VKT	MJ/km	51.8	50.4	12.7	11.9	48.8	43.0	14.3	15.6	8.9	14.8	23.6	23.9	1.6%
* Energy use per ferry vessel VKT	MJ/km	846.5	1073.3	144.0	140.7	290.8	283.5	151.5	141.0	601.7	641.4	327.2	358.8	9.6%
Energy consumption per PKT														
Energy use per private PKT	MJ/p.km	3.26	2.85	2.55	2.87	3.82	3.79	2.46	2.30	3.46	3.31	2.88	2.72	-5.3%
Energy use per transit PKT	MJ/p.km	2.13	2.09	0.99	0.97	1.14	1.18	0.74	0.76	0.59	0.70	1.15	1.16	0.9%
* Energy use per bus PKT	MJ/p.km	2.85	2.97	1.77	1.87	1.50	1.57	1.10	1.31	0.77	0.95	1.63	1.78	9.8%
* Energy use per minibus PKT	MJ/p.km	1.02	7.68			2.34				2.66	1.96	1.79	7.16	301.0%
* Energy use per tram PKT	MJ/p.km	0.99	1.02	0.36	0.48	0.31	0.27	0.70	0.73	0.23	0.24	0.65	0.65	-0.2%
* Energy use per light rail PKT	MJ/p.km	0.67	0.64		0.58	0.25	1.07	0.65	0.53	0.34	0.55	0.61	0.63	4.3%
* Energy use per metro PKT	MJ/p.km	1.65	0.69		0.75	0.49	0.64	0.45	0.42	0.12	0.34	0.74	0.52	-29.8%
* Energy use per sub. rail PKT	MJ/p.km	1.38	1.29	0.55	0.49	1.31	1.17	0.69	0.60	0.16	0.27	0.84	0.76	-10.4%
* Energy use per ferry PKT	MJ/p.km	5.41	6.80	2.97	2.53	3.62	1.23	4.01	4.88	3.64	4.26	4.25	4.60	8.1%
Vehicle occupancy factor														
Overall car occupancy	pers./unit	1.41	1.43	1.58	1.43	1.35	1.30	1.38	1.38	1.64	1.48	1.42	1.39	-1.9%
Overall transit vehicle occupancy	pers./unit	13.9	13.1	16.9	18.1	19.2	19.8	19.8	21.0	26.9	28.1	18.3	19.0	3.5%
* Bus vehicle occupancy	pers./unit	10.4	10.9	11.2	11.7	16.1	16.1	15.2	15.0	25.0	25.3	14.3	14.3	0.4%
* Minibus vehicle occupancy	pers./unit	8.5	2.2			3.5				2.9	4.9	5.8	2.4	-57.8%
* Tram wagon occupancy	pers./unit	19.2	19.6	27.9	23.3	38.6	51.6	23.3	22.1	24.1	22.6	24.2	26.5	9.6%
* Light rail wagon occupancy	pers./unit	25.8	24.9		18.2	51.9	28.7	26.4	27.9	47.2	28.2	29.3	24.7	-15.7%
* Metro wagon occupancy	pers./unit	19.3	22.6		30.3	22.0	21.6	27.6	26.3	65.0	56.6	28.0	27.4	-1.9%
* Sub. rail wagon occupancy	pers./unit	38.2	38.5	23.4	24.7	46.2	51.8	24.6	30.8	55.7	55.0	29.5	34.1	15.5%
* Ferry vessel occupancy	pers./unit	219.4	183.7	41.4	52.4	80.3	229.7	43.5	38.6	165.3	150.6	87.4	91.0	4.1%

Source: 1995/6 data from Kenworthy and Laube (2001); 2005/6 data derived from Kenworthy's update of Kenworthy and Laube (2001), some of which is published in Newman and Kenworthy (2015).

Notes: (1) The data above are from the same set of updated cities in each region in 1995 and 2005. (2) VKT refers to Vehicle Kilometers Traveled. (3) PKT refers to Passenger Kilometers Traveled. (4) Sub. Rail refers to suburban rail.

for modes such as buses that operate mostly in general traffic. Ferries are by far the most energy consumptive modes to run due to their often very large size and the extra energy needed to propel the vehicles through water. Ferries had an overall average of 359 MJ/km in 2005 for the systems in this sample of cities, representing an increase of almost 10% over the decade in question. U.S. urban ferry systems in this sample averaged 1,073 MJ/km.

Buses, which are very strongly dependent on diesel fuel (23.1 MJ/km), and suburban rail modes (23.9 MJ/km), where some systems are still diesel-powered—especially in North America—are the next most energy-consuming modes per kilometer of service provided.[15] The least energy-consuming modes per kilometer of service are the trams (14.4 MJ/km), LRT (13.3 MJ/km), metro (12.7 MJ/km) and minibuses (12.9 MJ/km), although the minibus energy use is quite high considering their small size. Whereas LRT and metro fell a little in their energy consumptiveness per kilometer, the others rose, with minibuses experiencing the biggest rise on average across the cities, 63%. This was mainly due to a growth in the number of minibus services in the U.S., whose average consumption rose from 8.5 MJ/km to 13.2 MJ/km.

American cities have the most energy consumptive regular buses of all cities (31.3 MJ/km in 2005, up from 28.8 MJ/km in 1995). The next highest, perhaps not surprisingly, were Canadian bus systems, but at 24.9 MJ/km in 2006, they were still a lot below the U.S. cities. Buses in European cities consume on average only 18.8 MJ/km and are the least energy consumptive buses in the sample. The American cities and, to a lesser extent, Canadian cities, distinguish themselves in having generally high energy-consuming vehicle fleets relative to other parts of the world, which may be partly a reflection of the legacy of generally lower fuel costs in North America creating less impetus for fuel efficiency in transportation.

Energy consumption per passenger kilometer and vehicle occupancy

The more meaningful way and perhaps the only legitimate way to compare energy consumption between modes in cities is to use energy use per passenger kilometer traveled, which takes account of the vehicle loadings and naturally tends to give transit generally lower energy consumption than cars due to the much higher loadings relative to cars. For example, for the global sample of cities here in 2005 (endnote 12), the average energy per vehicle kilometer for transit is 4.9 times that of cars (18.6 MJ/km versus 3.8 MJ/km), but the average occupancy of the same transit vehicles is 13.7 times more (19.0 vs 1.39 people per vehicle).

Personal Motor Vehicles (PMVs or Cars)

Cars, with their low occupancy of only 1.39[16] across the global sample (down 2% from 1995), are the most energy-consuming mode per passenger kilometer traveled. This is true of the data from this sample of cities, which shows that cars on average across all the cities consumed some 2.72 MJ/p.km (an improvement of 5.3% from 1995). This figure varied in 2005 between 3.79 MJ/p.km in the Canadian cities (U.S. cities 2.85) and a low of 2.3 MJ/p.km in the European cities. Car occupancy varies from a high in the Asian cities of 1.48 in 2005 to 1.30 in the Canadian sample (U.S. cities 1.43).

Transit

Looking at the same factor for transit across the sample, we see that it consumed in 2005 an overall average of 1.16 MJ/p.km, or 57% less than cars, and this had remained relatively stable over the 10 years (1.15 MJ/p.km in 1995). As already indicated, transit of course also averaged a much higher occupancy of 19 persons per vehicle across the global sample, up 3.5% since 1995. The relative difference between car and transit energy consumption per passenger kilometer in the groups of cities, however, varies considerably. In 2005, transit overall in U.S. cities was 27% less energy consuming per passenger kilometer than cars; Australian cities 66% less, Canadian cities 69% less, European cities 67% and the two Asian cities 79% less energy use per passenger kilometer. That the U.S. cities have the weakest difference between car and transit energy consumption per passenger kilometer is partly testament to the high-energy consumption per vehicle kilometer of U.S. transit modes, especially urban buses, compared to the other cities. In addition, the U.S. cities have generally lower occupancy levels due to so many systems operating in low-density situations and struggling to pick up passengers. The U.S. cities' transit systems achieve only 13.1 persons per vehicle—significantly below the other groups, which average between 18.1 (Australian cities) and 28.1 persons per vehicle (Asian cities). The European cities are the second best with 21 persons per vehicle.

Buses are generally the second highest energy consumers per passenger kilometer of the transit modes after ferries, though the Canadian cities' ferries average less energy use per passenger kilometer than their buses. As well, the minibuses in U.S. cities, with only 2.2 persons per vehicle, have higher energy use per passenger kilometer (7.68 MJ/p.km) than their ferries (6.80 MJ/p.km) and the U.S. ferries average 184 persons per vehicle, the best in the sample. Overall, across all the cities, minibuses (7.16 MJ/p.km) are more energy consumptive per passenger kilometer than ferries (4.60 MJ/p.km). Indeed, the minibuses and the ferries have higher energy use per passenger kilometer than do cars across the global sample, though ferries obviate the need for a lot of car travel by providing the transport connections across bodies of water that may otherwise require the construction of road traffic bridges or highly circuitous car travel to achieve the same end. Minibus services operating in low-density environments struggle to achieve good energy efficiency due to low passenger loads, but probably serve some beneficial social/equity service for the small number of people who use them.

Unfortunately, buses in U.S. cities have slightly higher energy use per passenger kilometer than cars (2.97 MJ/p.km compared to 2.85 MJ/p.km or 4% more), but all the rail modes perform much better than cars in U.S. cities (between 0.64 MJ/p.km for light rail or 77% less than cars up to 1.29 MJ/p.km for suburban rail and still 55% less than cars). This highlights the need for several important factors in U.S. cities such as:

- more fuel-efficient buses;
- higher densities of development;
- better planned and configured bus services that can achieve higher loadings, e.g. time-pulse transfer systems at various centers (such as in Edmonton, Alberta, and Austin, Texas) throughout metropolitan areas. Such configurations enable radial and circumferential travel around cities by allowing people to change directions on transit without having to travel through the CBD; and
- more protection for buses from general road congestion to improve their fuel efficiency.

It also highlights that where rail systems are provided in U.S. cities they achieve better loadings and compete strongly with the car in terms of lower energy use.

Buses in U.S. cities averaged only 11 persons per vehicle in 2005, though it did go up a little from 1995. This is the lowest bus occupancy of all groups of cities, with the Canadian cities achieving 16 people per bus, even a little better than in the European cities with 15. By contrast, rail modes in U.S. cities average between 20 and 38 people per vehicle.

Across this global sample, the least energy-consuming transit mode is the metro (0.52 MJ/p.km), followed closely by light rail and trams. The high loadings achieved by metro systems (which in turn relates strongly to dense land uses around the systems) and their low vehicular energy use per kilometer are behind this energy performance, which has in fact improved by 30% over the 10 years (down from 0.74 MJ/p.km in 1995). Globally, the different types of rail systems in this sample of cities average between 0.52 MJ/p.km and 0.76 MJ/p.km with average loadings per vehicle (wagon) of between 25 and 34 persons. The Asian cities are exceptional, with metro and suburban rail occupancies of 55 to 57 people per vehicle, although the suburban rail services provided in Canadian cities average a high 52 persons per vehicle.

Finally, despite their relatively poor energy consumption per passenger kilometer, ferries are the most heavily loaded of all the transit modes, averaging 91 persons per vessel (and up 4% since 1995). However, ferry loadings depend greatly on the size of ferries and show enormous variation around the world (the range here is 39 persons in the smaller ferries in European cities, up to 151 in the Asian cities and 184 in the ferry services in U.S. cities).

More comparisons of specific modes and energy consumption

The business as usual (BAU) discussion of modes generally avoids such considerations about urban planning factors and finds it easier to keep alive hopes that a 'green' automobile or 'clean' fuel is just around the corner. It also generally avoids discussions of modal and social inequities: the disadvantaging of certain modes and certain sectors of society through automobile dependency and limiting access to affordable alternatives either through planning and policy or pricing. But it must also be said that the current generation of individuals educated in transportation engineering, city planning and other fields related to modes and urban development are making this generalization less true every day.

Despite the above criticisms about simplistic tailpipe fixations and fuelishness in transportation energy thinking, the matter of modal energy efficiency is very important. To the extent that people will move around in motor vehicles and own some forms of PMVs, it is better that energy efficiency is considered. To the extent that people will move around cities, regions and nations, and travel between nations, it is important to consider the energy efficiencies of various modes and urban attributes and configurations. Tables 4.2 and 4.3 compare several land, air and water passenger modes. The commercial vehicle types are based on actual duty and are quite accurate. Those for private use are generally less reliable since individual driving habits, driving conditions and maintenance habits vary considerably. It is important to note that energy consumption is affected greatly by passenger loads and capacities.

BOX 4.6 **Automated and connected vehicles: Are HOFOs, ADAS, AVs and CCs high-tech hopes or hypes?**[i]

Preston L. Schiller

The autonomous vehicle (AV) appears to be very much on the minds and screens of the motoring public, if not yet in automobile dealership showrooms or on the roadways in large numbers. A great deal of funding is being made available to develop AV technologies by government and within industries associated with such technologies. The AV is also receiving unprecedented, often uncritical—if not confused—attention in the mass media around the globe. The latest technological advance, or setback, is becoming front page material in print media and receiving prominent coverage in the broadcast media.

The term 'autonomous vehicle' is commonly, and somewhat erroneously, applied to several related but somewhat distinct technologies under development for motor vehicles. First to clarify some terminology:[ii]

Hands-Off, Feet-Off' (HOFO): Human-controlled motor vehicle with very limited semi-automated functions like 'cruise control' (being rapidly surpassed by ADAS).

Automated Driver Assistance Systems technology (ADAS): Already developed and implemented HOFOs extending to an array of automated guidance (steering), braking, crash prevention and even parking

continued

technologies (driver required); more under development (Hummel et al. 2011, Trimble et al. 2014, Choi et al 2016).

Connected Car (CC): An automated vehicle dependent on its dynamic internet connection for guidance and control.

Autonomous Vehicle (AV): A vehicle which is fully automated and capable (supposedly) of guiding itself through traffic to a destination chosen for it by its owner or controller. An AV may or may not be dynamically connected to the internet

The history of AVs is long and complicated and is described in detail in Schiller (2016), much of which relates to military applications and highway interests wishing to extend and perpetuate the auto-centric transportation system.

Emerging from this history of technological development and promotion there is a culmination of grandiose claims for the advantages of AVs, many of which are encapsulated by a major global public relations player in its analysis, 'The Future of Driving: Five Ways Connected Cars Will Change Your Life':

1 *You'll be safer*: Automated driving will greatly reduce the chance of accidents – and remove the need for traffic lights!
2 *You'll have more 'me' time*: Your car will be able to drive itself and park itself. So stretch out and read a book, or chat with your friends online as you travel. Jump out the car at the restaurant and meet your friend for lunch, whilst your car goes to park itself.
3 *You'll have more money*: Your insurer will never worry about your driving history again.
4 *You'll visit the doctor less*: Your car will become the most advanced mobile device that you use, capable of becoming a 'clinic' through its healthcare apps. Get a health check-up whilst you're being driven to the office!
5 *You'll want to commute more often*: Your connected car will be part of a network that provides a commuting service for you. You'll finally be able to enjoy a stress-free, enjoyable travel experience.

(Ipsos MORI 2016, bolded in original)

Unfortunately, AVs are far from this simple. The following summarizes major issues, questions, promises and problems.

Some technical challenges facing HOFOs, ADAS, AVs and CCs

- The shortcomings of its detection systems to distinguish among things that appear similar in shape or to identify road markings, signage etc. in bad weather.
- The limitations of the algorithms that are guiding them, especially the inability to respond sufficiently as when the Google car swerved and crashed into a transit vehicle because its algorithm 'expected the bus to get out of its way'.
- The limitations of computerized mapping and GPS guidance, especially when they may not be up to date with current road conditions or infrastructure changes.
- The dilemma of whether the computer algorithm guiding the car can navigate the complex technical and ethical dilemmas inherent in vehicular mobility. The classical 'trolley problem' of ethics and philosophy, whereby an operator (in this case a computer algorithm) must choose between whose lives to save, will find its analog in AVs, especially when glitches in programs surface.

Complex public policy and governmental regulation issues

- In the U.S., and Canada to a certain extent, the federal government develops an array of policies and regulations guiding and governing safety issues and vehicle standards; but states, provinces and local governments have their own regulations and controls. And how will the integrity of the internet-based, probably multi-state, system be assured? (Nowakowski et al. 2014, Kessler 2015).

continued

Possible positive features of HOFOs, ADAS, AVs and CCs

- The greatest promises of automated vehicles can only be realized with at least a 90% market penetration, on fully grade-separated roadways and until the overwhelming majority of motorists eschew private ownership in favor of car-share arrangements (Fagnant and Kockelman 2015).
- AVs will likely be fully electric-powered, possibly with regenerative braking. This could mean significant energy use and GHGs reductions, especially on automated highways where closer packed platooning might be possible, and depending on the sources of the electricity and the time of day (or night) when charging occurs. But it is unclear how much extra energy and GHGs would be used running empty one way to or from passenger origins or destinations (deadheading) and how much generated traffic and increased demand for personal vehicular transport would be created with AVs.
- A huge reduction in parking demand is promised by AV and CC boosters. But this would likely only occur in a scenario where private ownership of vehicles is minimal and most motorists would avail themselves of AVs through car-shares or automated on-demand, ride-hailing services.
- Traffic congestion reductions: Under optimal market penetration scenarios, AVs and CCs could reduce congestion on grade-separated and controlled 'smart highways, smart infrastructure' or, possibly, on a completely separated 'smart lane'. But, without a major realistic and large-scale demonstration, it is not yet clear whether AVs and CCs would reduce vehicular congestion on most urban streets due to the great complexities of their traffic situations, especially if pedestrians and cyclists are to be appropriately accommodated (Fagnant and Kockelman 2015).
- Freight movement: automated or robotic vehicles are already used widely in carefully controlled environments in certain industrial applications, from warehousing to mining. Long distance trucking would require carefully controlled special lanes and a fair amount of 'smart infrastructure' to allow platooning and other energy and highway space saving effects. Fleets of electric automated trucks could do much to reduce some of freight movement's externalities, as well as enhancing safety. But what about the job losses? (Taso and Botha 2003; Ticoll 2015; Markoff 2016b).
- Public transit: Automated busways could probably be successfully developed in grade-separated and intersection controlled corridors, such as Los Angeles's transit system's (LACMTA) Orange Line bus rapid transit (BRT) corridor and similar BRT systems around the world. And AV minibuses in relatively uncomplicated suburban residential neighborhood traffic might be a possible 'last mile' solution to transit access and parcel delivery (Taso and Botha 2003; Heikkilä 2014; Pyle 2014; Bruun and Givoni 2015; Manjoo 2016a; Isaac 2016; Grush and Niles 2016; Richland, et al. 2016).
- It is possible that demands for increasing the capacity of major highways could be mitigated by the compression of high-speed AV/CC traffic made. What is to be done with all these extra congestion-causing motor vehicles once they leave the exit ramp.

Possible negative consequences of HOFOs, ADAS, AVs and CCs

Numerous possible or probable negative consequences could flow from wide-scale adoption of ADAS, AVs and CCs (Bruun and Givoni 2015; Wadud et al. 2016; Isaac 2016; Richland et al. 2016; Sivak and Schoettle 2016):

- Travel speeds may increase on automated highways, due to reduced crash risk, which would increase energy consumption.
- Energy consumption might rise from increased travel as the cost of drivers' time is reduced and travelers, especially commuters, can make their in-the-vehicle time more productive, which could lead to longer commutes and deadheading could also increase energy consumption.
- HOFOs and ADAs may increase distracted driving, including more sex in moving vehicles (Pedwell 2016).
- Researchers have already documented the likelihood of increased motion sickness associated with AV travel (Sivak and Schoettle 2015).
- Older persons, children and other populations traditionally excluded from the driver's wheel may increase their travel demands when AVs and CCs become widespread and readily available.

continued

- Travel demand could increase if AVs and CCs lower the marginal costs of driving through the elimination of parking fees, vehicle maintenance costs, insurance etc.
- Automating freight could reduce costs and time penalties of goods delivery, accelerating consumption (Wadud et al. 2016).
- Traffic infiltration of previously low traffic streets could increase with advanced AV/CC navigational system with disregard for neighborhood concerns or local traffic policy (e.g. see GPS.gov 2016).
- There are limits to how many personal motor vehicles, automated or not, can be crammed into urban space without rendering it unlivable and unworkable. The boosters of AVs and CCs have not done the spatial analyses necessary to test their beliefs and promises (Shin et al. 2009; Bruun and Givoni 2015; Fraade 2015).

What might the reality of automated vehicles be?

- AV and CC technologies, hardware and software—including telecommunications—might not develop as expected. There are problems in robotics that are extremely difficult to solve. Perhaps perfect driving may be beyond the reach of engineers? (Chalodhorn et al. 2010; Manjoo 2016b).
- The bugs and glitches of HOFOs, ADAS and AVs are still abundant; perfection is likely more than just a few years away (Schoettle and Sivak 2015).
- The hackability, manipulation of or control of car computers and their software by persons other than the owner and designated service personnel is a well-established problem. One can only imagine what might happen when computer savvy adolescents or mischievous experts or cyber-terrorists decide to hack AV systems to see what it would be like to race or even shut down the freeway traffic of a city (FlyerTalk Forums 2010; Hoag 2012; Perlroth 2015; Billington Cybersecurity 2016).
- Fleet turnover takes a long time: it could be many decades before appropriate market penetration could happen (Young 2015; Fagnant and Kockelman 2015).
- Infrastructure transformation needed for AV domination could be extremely expensive and may be beyond the reach of most cities or nations—especially in times of austerity budgets.

Public resistance to automated vehicles

- Inertia or resistance to major change stemming from perception, misperception, understanding or misunderstanding of the proposed or impending change often affects one's lifestyle, daily life.
- Will the public, which has been known to resist traffic signal cameras to detect and deter persons who speed and run through red lights, accept the controls instituted for AVs? (Francois 2014).
- The regulatory hurdles may be formidable and take much longer than expected (Dougherty 2015; Nowakowski, et al. 2014).
- Will vehicles and their monthly telecommunications fees be affordable for the average user?
- Can the necessary infrastructure be made foolproof or fail-safe? (McHugh 2015; Zolfagharifard 2015).
- Widespread use of AVs and CCs will not likely be possible in most developing countries (Mohan 2015; Stewart and Bertaud 2015).
- Despite efforts to 'educate' teenagers (UMTRI 2014) and adults about the attractiveness of the AV, the car culture is so powerful that much of the motoring public may be unwilling to relinquish control of their vehicles (see Chapters 1 and 2; Quain 2016).

Finally: Will the timeline for the development of a truly reliable automated vehicle be so long and far into the future that all involved will turn away from the AV hype and towards other solutions—perhaps walking or cycling or transit? (Boudette 2016).

[i] The author wishes to thank Jeffrey R. Kenworthy for his review and editing suggestions. A longer version of this article can be found at Schiller (2016).

[ii] The EU has a similar but slightly different definition; EPRS 2016, Glossary.

One thing is for certain: the AV–CC issue has taken hold of the motoring mind and its critics, from Bloomberg Philanthropies to Helsinki, and from the pages of the *New York Times* to the pages of the *New York Review of Books*, and in between and far beyond. This topic will likely be part of daily media for many years to come (Fountain 2016; Halpern 2016; Newcomb 2016).

Topographically appropriate modes: aerial and suspended trams, monorails, funiculars

There are special transportation modes that have been developed to address moving persons, often in large numbers, in topographically challenging situations. Here we review several of these.

Funiculars

Are sometimes found in cities where there is a need to offer an alternative to a steep stairway. They move slowly along a geared track or pulled along by a cable embedded under the surface. Sometimes the passenger cabins are moved through a system of counterbalancing, either involving substantial weights or by adjusting fluid levels in tanks attached to the cabins. Not very common nowadays, several of these could be found around the world in the late nineteenth century as cities began to grow and rely on various forms of transit to overcome challenging hills, often adjacent to their centers. There are quite a few funiculars around the planet, especially in Asia and Europe. Historically there were quite a few in the U.S. and Canada but only a handful are still in operation, such as the one in the old city area of Quebec City (QC) transporting persons down a steep escarpment from Château Frontenac to the pedestrianized, historically preserved Rue du Petit Champlain below and the nearby St Lawrence riverfront. Most funiculars are only a block or two in length and run alongside steep stairways as does the Montmartre funicular depicted in Figure 4.18.[17]

FIGURE 4.18 Montmartre funicular, steps and station
Source: Jeffrey R. Kenworthy

Aerial trams and gondola lifts

The aerial tram or tramway and gondolas are transport technologies that have wide application for a variety of topographical situations. They are also known as aerial ropeway transit or ART. While there are important design and construction differences between aerial trams and gondola lifts, they will be treated here under the rubric of aerial tram as they are blurred in public perceptions. These technologies have been applied to industrial purposes, as in the transport of ore cars in mountainous regions, and to passenger transport where topography required this application. Most persons associate these with tourism in mountainous, often ski resort, areas—but they also serve important transit functions in numerous locales. Aerial trams and gondola lifts consist of cabins that are suspended from cables linking two or more terminals where passengers may board and alight or where the vehicles may change direction.

Aerial trams can play interesting transportation and land use roles in cities. The Roosevelt Island Tramway spanning the East (Hudson) River between the island and Midtown Manhattan was constructed as an interim measure after a very complicated bridge connection was no longer feasible and before the subway link was in place. It became very popular and its ridership continued to grow even after the subway link was finished. With good shuttle service between the tramway, the subway and the residential portions, it has

FIGURE 4.19A Portland (OR) aerial tram at Oregon Health Sciences Center
Source: Preston L. Schiller

FIGURE 4.19B
Medellin, Colombia, aerial tram connecting low income areas with jobs and city services
Source: Julio D. Dávila

become a very popular residential location—almost car-free (as was originally planned), and very attractive for persons who don't drive or have a physical disability.

Portland (OR) developed an aerial tram connecting its medical complex on a high hill south of downtown with a streetcar extension at the base of the hill below. It is well-used by staff, students and patients and has also helped spur dense development in the neighborhood below. It also offers a magnificent view of the city and the mountains to the east. On clear days, there are great views of one of the Pacific Northwest's scenic volcanos, Mount Hood (Figure 4.19a). Aerial tramways can also help cities to connect poor and underserved parts of urban areas with centralized employment and services, thus serving social equity and transportation justice. Such has been the case with Medellín, Colombia, once notorious for its drug cartel, which changed course and turned to improving its urban mobility, both in transit and cycling, with the introduction of aerial tramways and a dramatically improved transit system and cycling situation (Figure 4.19b). According to transportation researcher Prof. Julio D. Dávila,[18] Medellín's pioneering example:

> [h]as multiplied exponentially as a solution not only in South America (La Paz has three and is building another four, Quito is building two, Medellín itself is adding two in low-income settlements, etc.) but also in European cities (e.g. France) and even Washington DC is doing something about it (also see: Brand and Dávila 2011, Dávila 2013).

Monorails

Around the world there are dozens of examples of elevated trams, which generally are suspended from or sit astride a type of beam structure that they roll along. These group transport applications are often found where topographical challenges are present or where a surface barrier, such as a road, needs to be traversed frequently—as in some large amusement parks where they usually connect parking lots with or within the park. They are frequently found as 'people movers' at airports where there are mostly constant capacity demands rather than large peak demands. They are often private services geared towards

FIGURE 4.20
The Wuppertal (DE) Suspension
Railway exits a station
Source: Preston L. Schiller

tourism rather than general urban transportation needs, such as the Seattle monorail, which became a subject of considerable debate when it was proposed as a model for significant expansion in 2005 as a major part of its public transit system (www.seattlemonorail.org). They generally do not offer the passenger capacity or higher speeds of most conventional rail transit vehicles. Their construction costs generally do not compare favorably with conventional rail transit, so they are generally not used for long distances. The size of the vehicles varies somewhat from relatively small cabins to those of similar size to a conventional streetcar (www.monorails.org). When done well a monorail can offer a comfortable ride at reasonable velocities. When not done so well, the vehicle might be swayed in strong winds or offer only a somewhat bumpy ride. The Wuppertal (DE) Suspension Railway—in operation since 1900, with modernization in 2009–10—is an instructive example: it was originally constructed over the river that ran through the heart of the historic city and connected several important destinations, including industry, the railway station, recreation and residential areas. The river provided an easy corridor for such a mode, as well as responding to some minor topographical issues; its developers had hoped to be able to replicate it in some other cities, although few developed in interest in it, preferring the use of existing streets for transit.

Futuristic, experimental or unproven modes

In addition to the autonomous vehicle (AV) discussed above in Box 4.6, there are some other modes that could be discussed as futuristic or under development: these have yet to have had either wide-scale or replicable application, or they presently have serious limitations:

- *Maglev* (magnetically levitated train): This technology is often proposed as an alternative to readily available and proven high-speed rail (HSR) forms such as the French TGV (Train à Grande Vitesse) or the Japanese Shinkansen (bullet train). There are two maglev technologies—magnetic repulsion, where the vehicle is pushed away from the track, and magnetic attraction, where the vehicle is pulled towards it. In either case, there is no physical contact between track and vehicle except at very slow speeds. Once under way, it operates on the same principle as a linear motor. Japanese and German industries have developed competing systems. The principal attractions of maglev are its lighter weight, abilities to achieve very high speeds, as much as 600 km/h (360 mph) under test conditions and 500 km/h (300 mph) in some existing operations; and to handle much steeper grades than conventional rail, which might make it very attractive in mountainous or steep, hilly terrain as it might lead to somewhat less tunneling or use of switchbacks. It appears that maglev would have substantially higher construction costs than conventional HSR but possibly lower maintenance costs—although this cannot be known until there is actual experience with a line of some magnitude. Whether maglev would be more energy efficient than HSR is the subject of some controversy. There have been a few limited applications of maglev, mostly only a few miles long, connecting airports or suburbs with city centers, such as the 30.5 km line between Shanghai and Pudong Airport. These generally operate at speeds equal to or lower than conventional HSR. A much longer line (290 km, 175 mile) is under construction between Tokyo and Nagoya and is expected to operate at a speed of 500 km/h (300 mph). Critics of maglev point to its inability to fit into existing conventional rail systems and networks—compared to several other successful HSR services; that its higher speeds tend to matter only for very long non-stop runs and matter much less when looking at realistic station spacing and that its effects on passengers, in terms of health and comfort, are unknown or little studied. The few maglev lines of greater than a few miles currently under construction will be closely scrutinized by promoters and critics alike (Vuchic and Casello 2002; Brown 2010; Steadman 2013).

- *Personal rapid transit (PRT)*: the concept is that a network of small vehicles holding two to four people operating on separated guideways will deliver individuals around the town with even more convenience than a private auto. This concept has been around since the 1960s without a large-scale or community-wide implementation.[19] It is perhaps untenable on a large scale, as it combines the high cost of grade-separated rail infrastructure with the low capacity of automobiles. It is being used successfully as a relatively small scale Podcar people-mover for Heathrow Airport and more efforts are in the works. PRT has its promoters among academics as well as its own niche developers.[20]

- *Vertical take-off (VTO) or short take-off and landing (STOL) and Pocket Jets*: an airport in every small town, backyard or, at least, neighborhood. Some have proposed variations of small or personal aircraft either for bypassing crowded highways or large airports. Frank Lloyd Wright toyed with the idea of individual aircraft and personal helicopters serving sprawled ex-urban (and automobile-dependent) developments, such as Broadacre City (Leon 2014), and James Fallows has proposed developing personal aviation options from individual lightweight aircraft to 'pocket jets' that would allow individuals or small groups in small aircraft to gain access to small airports outside urban centers, bypassing the security and runway queues common to larger airports (Fallows 2001). Variations of small VTO or STOL vehicles have been published in popular mechanical and scientific magazines. There have been a few airplane-cars and gyrocopters that one could buy. But the idea of mass use is preposterous. The safety implications would be frightening, as would the air and noise pollution impacts (also see Aerotropolis Box 4.4 above).

- *Hyperloop or hyper-hype or loopy?* In the summer of 2013, all-round high-tech whiz Elon Musk revealed his alternative to the extremely expensive and ever more costly and contentious California High-Speed Rail Project: The Hyperloop, a small passenger capsule in a low-pressure tube that could travel at speeds between 300 and 350 mph, 500–600 km/h (Musk 2013; Arrufat 2013; Pritchard 2013). It is a variant of a much-hyped but little realized application of evacuated tube technology (ETT), which some have dreamed about applying to maglev. At first there were only very rough hyper-loop sketches, then a descriptive document welcoming crowd-sourcing participation, eventually a small working model, then a larger working group of professionals with the newly formed Hyperloop One and in 2016 a prize-laden competition at Texas A&M University (Hawkins 2016). The Hyperloop has captured the imagination of the high technology-oriented from high schools and universities and throughout the cybersphere. Industry commentators, rail and transportation experts and journalists have been much less enthusiastic about the hyperloop, bringing criticism on it from technological as well as sociological perspectives (Ryan 2015; Arieff 2016). One of the most perceptive of hyperloop evaluators and critics sees it as 'vaporware' and the latest in a history of efforts to annihilate space and time by speed, criticized by perceptive observers from John Ruskin to John Muir (Christensen 2013).

A trenchant travel and rail observer, Kris De Decker (2013), writing in *Low-tech Magazine*, also took up the issue of overemphasis on speed to the detriment of acces-sibility. She documents how the emphasis on HSR and luxury, as key routes become privatized, is coming at the expense of maintaining smaller, slower, more affordable and geographically more dispersed important railway services in Europe.

- *Drones*: the main applications of drones to date have been in remote control military missions, often directed from thousands of miles away by persons probably recruited from the ranks of video game champions who seem to have difficulty discerning the differences between terrorist training camps and wedding celebrations. Smaller and less deadly versions, available for as little as $50, may be clogging the skies of neighborhoods in the future. Some are already noisily peeking over their neighbors' fences, occasionally being shot down as unwelcome (Matyszczyk 2015). Certain corporate interests, such as Amazon, have been energetically lobbying the U.S. government to develop drone-friendly regulations so that they can drop their deliveries at your doorstep more easily (Kang 2016; Manjoo 2016c). And Walmart has been testing drones for use in its warehouses (Abrams 2016). Since a great deal of parcel delivery activity is in the returning of unwanted or wrongly sized items, as in online footwear and apparel peddlers who encourage customers to try several until they find the right one and then return the rest through the same parcel services that delivered their treasures, if suc-cessful this strategy will only increase the environmental burden of online shopping (Banjo 2013; Rudolph 2016). It is also rumored that an old, and possibly mythical, Danish stork network is exploring the use of drones in its baby-delivering service. Perhaps diaper services will take note and follow.

Back to the Futuristic: e-bikes, pedicabs, cargo and beer bikes

Creative cycle developers around the planet are busily pedaling back to the future while applying developing technologies to urban needs. Several of these modes have overlapping or multiple use possibilities. A sturdy bicycle can attach a trailer that might carry cargo, children or pets around town; some three-wheelers can carry either cargo or passengers; pedicabs have been around for a long time—and in considerable use in less wealthy countries, they are now becoming a feature in wealthier cities (see Chapter 10); some cargo bikes are designed for specific purposes and are still pedal-powered while others are taking advantage of batteries for some or all their power. Still others, like 'beer bikes', are designed more for partying than passenger or cargo transport. Some cities, such as Gothenburg, Sweden, are introducing small EVs pulling trailers as well as pedal and E-cargo bikes into freight transport in their centers with a related goal of reducing traffic, GHGs and local pollution. A news-paper following this issue reports a much wider application is possible:

FIGURE 4.21A
French bicycle activist Christophe Raverdy (L), a long time official of the Nantes chapter and national Fédération nationale des Usagers de la Bicyclette (FUB; National Federation of Bicyclists) pauses in his tour of cycling facilities for a visiting researcher to discuss news with a local entrepreneur who had a pedal-powered grocery delivery (for the local organic food coop "Horizon Vert") and composting business (cannister in trailer).
Source: Preston L. Schiller (2015)

FIGURE 4.21B
German E-cargo bike; pedal power, electric and solar power
Source: Jeffrey R. Kenworthy

According to a report by the EU-funded research project CycleLogistics, an estimated 51% of goods transported in cities could be shifted to bicycles and cargo bikes, significantly reducing emissions and congestion. There are several urban delivery companies turning to cargo bikes, including Outspoken! Delivery in Cambridge which carries out sub-contracted work for major freight companies.

(Eriksen 2015)

The growing popularity of such approaches has led to numerous cargo-bike-sharing schemes in Europe (McCartney 2016).

FIGURE 4.21C Cycle Saloon beer bike loads passengers for a tour of the Fremont Neighborhood Fair in Seattle. The seated customers pedal to power the bike and a bartender steers and pours (2013).
Source: Preston L. Schiller

FIGURE 4.22
"Ghost Bike" memorial placed by anonymous advocates at an intersection adjacent to the College of Built Environments, University of Washington, Seattle, informs passers-by of the cyclist killed by a motorist there; some leave flowers on it (2013).
Source: Preston L. Schiller

Conclusions

This chapter has given an overview of the numerous considerations that must be addressed when studying transportation modes. This is a complex matter because often there are no hard and fast distinctions between or within modal categories. Issues of policy, economics and cultural preferences also enter discussions of modes. Some of the more interesting technical and planning considerations and innovations around transit are presented in the next chapter. One of the biggest modal issues to appear in the transportation space since the first edition of this book is autonomous vehicles. This chapter has provided a more holistic appreciation of the pros and cons, strengths and weaknesses of this current flavor of the month technology, which is all too often presented in simplistic technological terms and as a panacea for more transportation problems than it is realistically capable of solving.

Chapter 5 now addresses transit and other public transportation modes and services, an extremely important area of ST.

Questions for discussion

- Discuss whether one could draw accurate conclusions about the future energy efficiency of cities based primarily on the anticipated future fuel efficiency of vehicles? What are the limitations of a fuel efficiency emphasis in transportation and energy planning?

- What else gets considered in the decision to make a trip on any mode, besides the out-of-pocket costs? Of these concerns, identify and discuss those that are inexpensive and quick to accommodate compared to those which are expensive or take a long time to accommodate.

- What else is needed to define a mode besides the physical characteristics of the vehicle?

Notes

1   An excellent and thorough technically oriented work that addresses several modal, spatial, energy and environmental issues is Vanek et al. 2014—especially Units 3 and 5.
2   For a somewhat less technical introduction to the family of modes, see Grava (2003).
3   For more information about how to retrofit existing streets with non-motorized facilities in the U.S., Fruin (1971) and the National Complete Streets Coalition (2009) are good sources.
4   See discussion of transportation energy in this chapter, as well as Bruun (2007).
5   For a primer on the role of ITS in both passenger service and planning, see Bruun (2007).
6   For example, see the Transit Cooperative Research Programme.
7   For example, STATTAUTO in several German cities, and carsharing.org for other worldwide resources.
8   Schiller and his students found in 2013 that VIA's annual ridership, almost all in the Quebec–Windsor Corridor, came to a total of approximately 4mil. and had been largely stagnant in terms of growth for several years. In the same corridor, there were at least 650,000 university students, many of them within easy reach of VIA stations. While a certain percentage of VIA's ridership already consisted of students, more outreach and marketing, especially around rail passes, could easily and dramatically increase VIA's ridership. Electrification of this rail corridor would not be out of the question either, given the potential of Quebec's hydropower surplus.
9   See www.flightlesstravel.com/plan/cargo-ships/
10 See www.facethefactsusa.org/facts/93-percent-of-us-transport-remains-reliant-on-oil (accessed 1 August 2016)
11 See discussion in Bruun (2007).
12 The metropolitan areas consist of: USA: Atlanta, Chicago, Denver, Houston, Los Angeles, New York, Phoenix, San Diego, San Francisco and Washington. AUSTRALIA: Brisbane, Melbourne, Sydney and Perth. CANADA: Calgary, Montreal, Ottawa Toronto, Vancouver. EUROPE: Berlin, Bern, Brussels, Copenhagen, Düsseldorf, Frankfurt, Geneva, Graz, Hamburg, Helsinki, London, Madrid, Manchester, Munich, Oslo, Prague, Stockholm, Stuttgart, Vienna, Zurich. ASIA: Hong Kong, Singapore.
13 Energy per vehicle and passenger kilometer for cars is derived from actual annual energy consumption, vehicle kilometers and passenger kilometers traveled collected in each metropolitan area. Transit energy use per vehicle kilometer and per passenger kilometer are derived from

actual vehicle kilometers of service and passenger kilometers traveled collected from every operator in every metropolitan area. Occupancies are derived from the same data. For more information on data collection methodologies see Newman and Kenworthy (2015) and Kenworthy and Laube (1999).

14 There are many ways of expressing energy *consumption* per unit of distance or energy *efficiency* (distance traveled per unit of fuel used). For readers to do their preferred conversions, the following information can be used: there are 4.546 liters in an imperial gallon and 3.785 liters in a U.S. gallon and an average conversion factor of 34.69 MJ per liter for gasoline/petrol was used in this research (in practice it varies a little depending on the gasoline). As an example, 3.1 MJ/km has a gasoline (petrol) equivalent to 8.9 liters per 100 km, 11.2 km per liter, 31.6 miles per imperial gallon and 26.3 miles per U.S. gallon. So the average fuel consumption of cars across these global sample of cities in 2005 (3.8 MJ/km) was 10.9 liters per 100 km, 9.2 km per liter, 30.8 miles per imperial gallon, or 25.6 miles per U.S. gallon.

15 Note that the suburban rail systems with the highest energy use per wagon kilometer were in the USA and Canada, where quite a few of the suburban rail services still use more energy-intensive diesel propulsion systems (50 and 43 MJ/km in 2005, but an improvement over 1995).

16 Note that car occupancy averages over 24 hours per day, seven days a week figure and is not just a peak period figure.

17 Also see: https://en.wikipedia.org/wiki/Funicular accessed 12 November 2016

18 Personal communication with Preston L. Schiller, 27 October 2016

19 The oft-mentioned Morgantown, Virginia, system is an automated people mover using larger vehicles with few stops.

20 For a compendium of PRT related materials see Prof. Jerry Schneider's posting at faculty. washington.edu/jbs/itrans/prtquick.htm, as well as the site of the Podcar's developer www.ultra-globalprt.com/wheres-it-used/where-can-it-be-used/

Urban, regional and intercity public transportation: policy, technical, land use and provider aspects

Introduction

Public transportation generally refers to the accessibility of a transportation service more than its ownership or control. Such services, be they intercity rail or coach, and taxi or shared ride services are all usually termed 'public transportation' because it is assumed that each is open to all members of the public. For convenience, however, the shorter and simpler term 'transit' is often used interchangeably, as it has been in this book. While many major public transportation services are under public management and control, there are many transportation services that are licensed by government with the understanding that they may be accessible to the public at large. There are also many services that are owned by a public entity whose management is contracted to a private entity. Many of the technical aspects of modes associated with public transportation have been covered in Chapter 4 and the comparative usage of urban transit in cities around the world was covered in Chapter 1. This chapter will address several of the aspects of public transportation that are important to public policy and planning.

Public transportation is important because it is one of the key building blocks of sustainable transportation. One could visualize it as one of the legs of the three-legged stool of sustainable transportation (Figure 5.1)—the other two being walking and cycling. When done well, most surface public transportation modes demonstrate clear energy, pollution, social equity (mobility for all persons regardless of income or physical ability), urban design, spatial consumption and economic advantages over private modes. Most surface and underground public transportation modes can be planned to interconnect well with other green modes and to create synergies with green urban planning. While Chapter 4 addressed many of the important aspects of modes, including transit and intercity modes and infrastructure, and their interrelationship, this chapter will focus mainly on issues concerned with broader planning, policy and finance issues involving transit and intercity transportation.

Table 5.1 below summarizes the main modes of public transportation, scope, as well as policy, planning and implementation issues, most of which will be explored in the remainder of this chapter.

As Table 5.1 indicates, there is a variety of transportation modes available to the public and an array of intertwining policy and implementation issues around each. Next, we examine the very important relationship between these modes and land use and transportation planning.

Sustainable Transport/Mobility

Pedestrianism

Bicycling

Public Transport: In-City, Regional & Inter-City

FIGURE 5.1
3-Legged stool of sustainable transportation
Source: Preston L. Schiller

TABLE 5.1 Public transportation: types, modes and issues
Vertical and horizontal do not perfectly match; for modal performance specifics see Modes Chapter 4

Type	Modes	Policy issues	Planning/implementation Issues
Urban and Regional Transit	• Bus or coach • Streetrail or trams • Light rail (LRT) • Regional rail • Metro (subway, elevated, separated right-of-way) • Mode sharing (autos, bicycles) • Topo-modes: cable cars, funiculars, aerial and suspended trams	• Priority over private modes; • Appropriate funding • Public encouragement • Integrating policy and planning (not silos) • Vision and visionary • Balancing public and private dimensions • Used to overcome topographical challenges	• Designing and implementing priority measures (often controversial) • Mechanisms for synergies (codes, incentives, for TOD etc) • Designing public incentives and programs; education, passes etc. • Urban design issues around stations and stops to maintain walking and biking accessibility • May be very expensive, capacity issues?
Intercity	• Coach • Rail—conventional • Rail—high(er) speed • Aviation—commercial	• Many of the same as for urban and regional; need to work on reducing demand for and impacts of aviation	• Inter-agency and intergovernmental coordination • Effective public involvement • Designing public incentives and programs; education, passes etc.
Inter and Trans-continental	• Aviation (commercial) • Maritime • True high-speed rail to replace aviation for trans-continental	• Develop technological alternatives for inter and trans-continental, HSR, teleconferencing; encourage public to limit air travel; • Promote maritime (passengers on freight vessels, esp. for leisure)	• Reduce environmental impacts; improve intermodal connections to lessen PMV travel • Carbon and other taxes and fees
Outer Space	• Virgin Rockets	• Discourage	• More important matters on Earth
Intergalactic	• Starship Enterprise • Millennium Falcon	• Leave to books, TV, movies and fan clubs	• Best left to the imagination

Source: Preston L. Schiller

The relationship between public transportation and land use and transportation planning

Virtually all transportation modes affect and interact with land uses. Properly coordinated or integrated public transportation and land-use planning can create numerous benefits. These can include appropriate zoning and incentives to develop land adjacent to public transportation corridors and stations at densities and mix of uses supportive of such services. Such planning should encourage the use of public transportation for a variety of travel needs, not just for the commute. Station areas, especially, are great candidates for urban intensification, and the central stations, themselves, can become intermodal hubs and destinations for recreation and business purposes with restaurants, shops and meeting spaces available.

Poorly planned public transportation or land use can work against urban sustainability in several ways. Over-reliance of expressway corridors for public transportation leads to both excessive station costs and poor pedestrian, bicyclist and feeder transit accessibility—as the example of the Seattle area's over-reliance on creating transit centers around Park & Rides adjacent to freeways demonstrates (see Box 5.2 Park & Rides below). Similarly, separated or poorly integrated modal facilities may act as a detriment to easy connections between modes. Vancouver's Main Street and Pacific Central Station and Portland's Union Station each provide good North American examples of how rail and coach services can share a location and provide adequate security to ensure passenger comfort.

The following section provides a perspective on how well-planned urban transportation services and facilities can influence a city's shape and development.

Urban transport systems and their influence on urban form

Urban transport systems can exert a powerful influence on urban form. Rail-based systems, both heavy and light rail, can be powerful magnets and anchors for high-density, mixed-use development because of the fixed and highly legible nature of their routes and the generally large throughput of people through their stations. However, it is also possible to stymie this otherwise common process of consolidation around rail stations through planning provisions that are exclusionary of high-density uses, or a planning system that simply fails to actively facilitate the process through not assisting in land assembly or by failing to provide proper planning guidelines and infrastructure support.

Strategic and statutory planning in Australia has mostly turned its back on the potential of its electric rail systems to act as anchors in the suburbs for urban development, but this has changed over recent years. On the other hand, in Europe there is a long history of siting major high-density developments, both residential and mixed use, around rail stations. In Canada and, increasingly, the U.S., rail systems are being increasingly seen as primary focal points for development throughout the city. Los Angeles is doing this by detailed planning of urban village sites around both LRT and subway stations (see Chapter 10). Cities such as San Diego and Sacramento are attempting to develop an increasing number of rail station demonstration projects and to make Transit-Oriented Development (TOD) guidelines around stations a formal part of their statutory plans.

On the other hand, fixed-route bus systems are totally flexible in where they may be put and, by their very nature, tend to be given the job of following urban development wherever it proceeds. For this reason, bus systems generally do not provide the kind of facilities that actively attract and cluster urban development. With very strong planning controls that legislate precisely the kind and location of urban development, as in Ottawa and Curitiba, it is possible to develop around busways on freeways and highways, but it is comparatively rare. One reason why even buses on busways are not successful at shaping urban form is that the passenger collection process is mostly done off the busway in suburbs, so that stations are much fewer and of less intensity than with rail. Furthermore, developers perceive that a bus service can be withdrawn or changed too easily so that there is not the same security of service for their investment as that represented by rail.

Where buses are the only public transport service provided for higher-density development, pressure tends to mount rapidly for the service to be switched to rail. For example, buses have capacity and headway limits that are easily reached with the passenger demands of intense urban development, and the number of vehicles focused on confined locations creates an undesirable environment because of noise, fumes and confusion in boarding; this has happened in central Ottawa.

Bus-only public transport systems tend to be mostly an addendum to the car-based system, and generally chase their passengers, who become ever more thinly spread across the landscape and increasingly captive to cars. Service provision levels and costs rise without commensurate increase in passengers where buses merely follow urban development but can exert little influence on its form (Bly and Webster 1980). In an international

TABLE 5.2 Some implications of closing the Sydney and Melbourne rail systems

	Sydney trains	Melbourne trains	Trams
Passengers carried by rail system between 0600 and 0930	312,789	135,000	110,000
Extra number of vehicles on road assuming all these travel by car (1.2 people per car to allow for those unable to drive themselves)	260,658	112,500	91,500
Minimum extra freeway lanes (or other traffic lanes) required to move these vehicles (assuming a maximum of 2000 vehicles per hour per lane and a 2-hour peak)	65	28	23
Land for parking requirements (ha) (at an average of 30 square meters per car)	782	338	274
Football oval equivalents for parking (average of 1.5 ha per oval)	521	225	183
Equivalent floors of multi-story parking (250 cars per floor, each floor one-half a football field in size)	1042	450	366

Source: Jeffrey R. Kenworthy

comparison of cities (including Canberra), the proportion of total annual passenger travel accounted for by public transport never exceeded 5% in bus-only cities, while in cities where rail is the backbone of the system, the figure was frequently more than 25% (Newman and Kenworthy 1991). These figures exclude the more unusual Asian cities (e.g. Tokyo, Singapore and Hong Kong). The most effective role for buses is as feeders to effective rail systems.

Among urban transport options, demand-responsive bus systems, as well as van and car-pool schemes, are predicated on very low density or highly scattered urban development being inherently hard to service with anything but cars and they are generally provided to simply chase the trips that are needed by those unfortunate enough to be without direct access to a car. These services can exert no direct influence whatsoever on urban form.

Finally, the construction of freeways as the major transport facilities for new corridor development will clearly facilitate traditional urban sprawl, i.e. low-density housing and scattered office park and retail development surrounded by large amounts of parking. They will act negatively against the development of compact land-use patterns and, if planned in parallel with a rail service, will also tend to diminish the effectiveness of the rail system and the land development potential around its stations.

Densification, compact urban form and travel by green modes are facilitated by limiting the amount of surface given over to streets and parking and reducing the speed at which private motor vehicles can travel on most city streets. Some political demagogues have proposed that funding for transit be eliminated in favor of providing automobiles for all commuters. Table 5.2 presents a dramatic rebuttal of this ill-conceived proposal in Australia.

Transit as a natural monopoly

Many transportation economists treat transit as a 'natural monopoly', an essential service that offers greater efficiency and economies of scale when it permitted to dominate a substantially sized market. In exchange for its monopoly status, such services are often owned by a governmental entity or heavily regulated by government.[1] In the U.S. and Canada (to a lesser extent), most transit systems were privately owned and operated from their inception in the late nineteenth and early twentieth centuries until their demise in the second half of the twentieth century and takeover by public entities. Their demise was due to a combination of factors that sometimes varied from one city to another: over-regulation and the freezing of fares at rates too low to maintain quality by governmental regulatory agencies; loss of interest on the part of private providers; and the rise of automobility. There is a spirited debate among transportation economists and policy-makers in wealthy and developing countries as to whether, or to what extent, these services should be maintained as natural monopolies or open to privatization and/or competition (Evans 1991; Ran Kim and Horn 1999; Mees 2010).

Practical problems besetting public transportation

Overall, the trip by transit is far safer for passengers than an equivalent trip by PMV. Many transit systems have security features that can alert police when a crime, especially a violent crime, is occurring on a vehicle or at a station. While the occasional crime on transit is lamentable and in need of ever more attention, one needs to keep in perspective the amount of crime that occurs around automobility: assaults from motorists, and the dangers of parking lots and structures. Part of the problem of safety on or around transit is the lack of funding and attention paid to it in auto-centric cities and countries and often mirrors the generally shabby treatment that the poor and minorities often receive in these places.

In many countries that emphasize automobility at the expense of public transportation, there are several chronic problems; among these are perennial funding shortages, deferred maintenance and lag-times in adopting the latest ICT. In addition to these, there are often social problems that public transportation is saddled with: in many cities, major transportation facilities sometimes attract poor persons and transients who are seeking shelter as well as a convenient location for asking strangers for money. Sometimes these facilities and their surrounds also attract those seeking or selling contraband drugs or goods.

The facilities, themselves, may be inadequately staffed and unable to enforce a high degree of security for their users. Even where such facilities and their surrounds are relatively secure there may be a stigma or prejudiced view of them by a wider public—especially in the U.S. Although some researchers (Litman 2016) have cleverly demonstrated that the transit trip is many times safer than the same trip by PMV, the prejudiced viewpoint widely persists.

Because of budget cuts and other forms of governmental neglect in automobile-focused countries, some public transportation facilities are in poor repair and poorly maintained. Providers need to work extra hard to create clean, pleasant and safe-appearing facilities with good lighting, surveillance cameras and some security presence to assure the public of their safety. In response to security challenges, some facilities have even gone so far as to require those entering the facility to show a travel ticket as proof of their legitimacy and to prevent loitering on the premises. That may be a bit extreme, but it is an understandable reaction to some of the problems they have experienced and a way of assuring a safe environment for their patrons. Another safety issue, especially in the U.S. and Canada, is the private railways' (which have been highly profitable in recent years) underinvestment in safety upgrades, which would benefit their own freight services as well as the public passenger trains that pay for the use their trackage. This is evidenced by their lack of appropriate response to public concerns about making their freight cars, especially the ones carrying flammable fuels, more safe as well as several derailments due to poor maintenance or operator neglect—as the catastrophe of Lac Megantic (QC) demonstrated. The situation has been worsened by federal governments' unwillingness to invest in safety upgrading as well (Clark 2015). It is also worth noting that freight trains are much harder on the tracks themselves, in terms of wear and tear and maintenance, than are passenger trains, perhaps another reason for their separate ownership, public versus private, and management and maintenance costs.

FIGURE 5.2A
Decrepit trams, Calcutta, which
nevertheless perform an important
function.

Note: This shows the importance of
adequate investment and renewal of
inherently good quality transit systems

Source: Adam McHugh

FIGURE 5.2B
University of Queensland recent
transportation interchange which
provides good quality buses that
accommodate bikes.

Source: Jeffrey R. Kenworthy

The fast-changing mobility and accessibility landscape

In a time of rapid change, often technologically driven, it is not surprising to observe a
rapid pace of change in transportation services often pushed by technological innovation.
Among these are a variety of applications related to geographic positioning systems (GPS),
real-time transit information, online trip planners and other forms of interactivity between
riders and providers, smart cards for more efficient fare management for users and transit
operators, and internet connectivity at stations and aboard public transportation. Some
public authorities and transportation providers have responded by integrating new technologically facilitated modal options into their services and facilities, such as the German

FIGURE 5.3A
Well-appointed Berlin bus stop
Source: Jeffrey R. Kenworthy

FIGURE 5.3B
Clear paper timetables, same Berlin stop (note also clear signage on front of bus)
Source: Jeffrey R. Kenworthy

FIGURE 5.3C
Car and bike sharing station; Autolib
EV car-share and Velib bike-share
share station in Paris.
Source: Iain Cameron

railway's integration of car-sharing (Flinkster) and bicycle-sharing (hire) at many of its stations, thus making green options available when needed (DB 2016).

A promising program effort is the ICT enabled initiative 'Mobility as a Service' (MaaS) conceived by Sonja Heikkilä that involves using ICT to plan seamless multi-modal and intermodal trips taking advantage of transit, walking, cycling and shared modes (see Chapter 8, Box 8.4).

Urban public transportation: urban form and modal integration issues

The most widespread and, arguably, most important type of public transportation is that which is found in cities and urban areas. In several parts of the world, this type of public transportation is known as transit or public transit.

There are several broadly differing approaches to urban transit. One approach, as exemplified in many European and Asian cities, is to have transit as a ubiquitous feature of the city, if not the whole urbanized area. Paris or Zurich and Singapore or Tokyo are good examples—where no resident is further than a couple blocks from a metro or quality bus route and where services operate at least 18 hours each day, if not 24. In transit-ubiquitous cities, which often have land-use patterns that encourage shopping and services in virtually all neighborhoods, most citizens can live without daily need for a private vehicle. Zurich has superbly structured and time-pulsed integrated transit system that is highly coordinated across every mode: minibuses, midi-buses, standard buses, articulated buses, electric trolley buses, light rail, suburban rail and ferries as well as with intercity rail services. In Tokyo, the extensive commuter rail lines that service central Tokyo are owned by a variety of private rail companies who also own the shopping centers as the stations into which they feed their passengers.

Another approach found in many North American cities is a pattern of providing bus and occasionally regional rail service aimed at weekday commuters, especially those from outlying suburbs to city centers during 'peak hours', while attempting to maintain some level of all-day, weekend and evening transit service within the core city itself (see the discussion of this in Chapter 4). In between the two poles of ubiquitous versus commute-oriented transit are many cities that are trying to improve their service scope and offerings to attract both commute and non-commute trips.

An ongoing issue in urban transit is the efficacy of bus versus rail modes. The technical differences between these modes have been discussed in Chapter 4. Each of these has its advantages and disadvantages in terms of capacity, capital investment, user friendliness, operating costs and life cycle. Kenworthy (2008) provides a comprehensive assessment of the advantages of strong rail and weak rail cities over bus-only cities, with all the factors examined varying systematically from best in the strong rail cities, good in the weak rail and poor in the bus-only cities (e.g. lower car use, more transit service and use, less parking in the CBDs, lower emissions, fewer transportation system deaths, better economic performance of transit and more).

Another issue of interest is the way that certain modes can be used to overcome topographical challenges such as steep grades and escarpments, and whether these applications are integrated with other transit modes. These include aerial and suspended trams, cable cars and funiculars and are discussed in more detail in Chapter 4.

Other issues that transit planning and policy needs to address as services are planned and put into operation include appropriate modal conveyance; vehicular full costs, capacity and speed, and system life cycle costs; capital investment; user friendliness; planning and policy frameworks; transit and land-use integration, synergistic and urban design effects; and the accommodation of special needs populations. Many of these issues will be addressed here, as well as in other chapters (see Chapters 4, 6, 7 and 8).

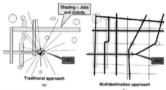

FIGURE 5.4
Comparison of traditional versus multi-destination approach
Source: Jeffrey R. Brown and Gregory L. Thompson (2008, p83)

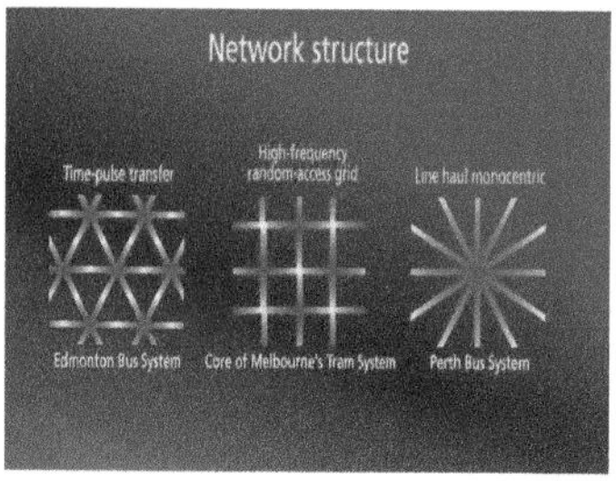

FIGURE 5.5
Three types of transit networks
Source: Felix Laube

FIGURE 5.6
Combined transit network
Source: Felix Laube

Moving away from radial planning to polycentric network planning

An extremely important aspect of modern transit planning is whether cities move away from a monocentric (CBD) orientation, often accompanied by a radial system of routes or a network almost completely focused on a region's traditional CBD, to a polycentric orientation creating a transit grid serving multiple destinations and sub-centers.

As discussed in the section on walking, transit and automobile cities (Chapter 2), the introduction of effective transit, especially the electrified streetcar, in the late nineteenth century facilitated the growth of cities and suburbs. Most of the early streetcar and commuter rail lines still converged upon the city center or CBD. This led to a radial configuration of routes linking outward suburbs and small towns with a city center. While many cities still maintain viable CBDs, for many decades there has been considerable suburban growth, often entailing the development of sub-centers or nodes of commercial, employment and residential density.

This polycentric development has often not been well-served by traditionally radial-oriented transit. Some researchers and planners propose that new light rail transit (LRT) networks would serve polycentric cities much better than traditional radial systems (Thompson and Matoff 2003). Transit researchers such as Gregory Thompson and Jeffrey Brown have proposed that cities should realign their transit networks service orientations to better accommodate this effect (see Figure 5.4 and Brown and Thompson 2008).

Figures 5.5 and 5.6 present a more complicated depiction of radial (monocentric line haul) and transit network alternatives. The time-pulse system integrates all modes and enables connections and changes of direction. When combined with the random-access grid (saturation transit services in all directions), the city becomes a transit paradise. Zurich or Bern would be good examples of the combined network.

Moving away from strictly radial transit planning focused principally on a CBD to polycentric network planning has significant implications for the interrelationship between transit planning and urban form and functioning as discussed in the next section.

Polycentrism and urban mobility

The problems of urban sprawl, characterized by vast expanses of automobile-dependent, heavily zoned land uses for housing, industry, shopping and other uses, have been known and criticized for over 50 years. Mumford (1961) in *The City in History* and Jacobs (1961) in *The Death and Life of Great American Cities* lamented the destruction of established mixed-use urban centers and neighborhoods through massive freeway construction and urban renewal and the decanting of population and jobs into vast hinterlands of low-density development accessible only by car. The radically growing levels of car ownership and car use throughout the decades following World War II (McIntosh et al. 2014) led to massive problems with traffic and congestion. This occurred even in suburban areas that were built for the car, especially as public transport systems and the ability to walk or ride a bike for urban needs dramatically diminished (Cervero 1986). The centers that once provided the density and mixed-land uses needed not only for accessibility by public transport, walking and cycling but also for a sense of place and community, disappeared, while new low-density land uses grew rapidly outwards without any real focal points except for large car-based shopping centers, office parks and industrial centers situated at the on- and off-ramps of freeways (Calthorpe 1993).

Later writers detailed the major social, economic, environmental, livability, urban design and traffic problems that multiplied as low-density cities, without a clear structure based on significant centers, spread across urban landscapes (Schneider 1979; Newman and Kenworthy 1989; Kunstler 1993). Webber's 1960s depictions of the future city based on 'the non-place urban realm' and 'community without propinquity', and premised almost entirely around unlimited car mobility, began to look problematic on many levels (Webber 1963, 1964, 1968).

Bertaud (2003) has suggested that polycentrism occurs as a kind of natural process as cities get bigger. It constitutes a move away from a monocentric urban form, which was the first model of urban spatial structure conceptualized by Alonso (1964), where cities have one unique center termed the Central Business District (CBD).

As they grow in size, the original monocentric structure of large metropolises tends with time to dissolve progressively into a polycentric structure. The CBD loses its primacy, and clusters of activities generating trips are spreading within the built-up area. Large cities are not born polycentric; they may evolve in that direction (p. 6).

Thomson (1977), in his book *Great Cities and Their Traffic*, showed how intimately urban structure, especially 'centralization' and especially the type, number and size of urban centers, is linked to the function of transport systems. He showed that even though cities may proceed from monocentric to polycentric, as suggested by Bertaud (2003), the nature of that polycentrism can be very different and the effect on traffic and mobility varies enormously. Thomson provided four archetypes of cities: (a) strong-centre strategy, (b) weak-centre strategy, (c) full motorization and (d) low-cost strategy.

Strong-centered cities have a very dominant and large central area (CBD) fed by major radial rail systems (and roads), but also with significant sub-centers located on the rail lines. The inner cities mostly have networks of underground rail lines to provide mobility within the densest parts of the region. Sometimes they have an inner ring road to funnel traffic around instead of through the center. Examples of this type of city include New York, Tokyo, London, Toronto, Hamburg and Paris. International comparative work by Kenworthy and Laube (1999 and 2001) and Newman and Kenworthy (1989, 1999a and 2015) also shows that such cities are the least car-oriented in the world (they have lower car use, more public transport use and more walking and cycling) and tend to have the lowest traffic speeds and highest public transport speeds.

Weak-center cities are those where the central city has diminished in importance and have a radial road network focused on the CBD, supplemented by radial rail lines, but with ring roads at different distances from the city. Such cities often still have a high modal split to public transport for jobs in the city center where public transport (mainly rail) provides a higher-speed service than cars. Much of the public transport service in these metro areas, however, is provided by slower bus services. The city tends to have car-oriented suburban centers clustered at the intersections of radial and ring roads, rather than major sub-centers oriented to public transport. Cars offer higher speeds than public transport for a high proportion of trips. Melbourne, Chicago, Boston, San Francisco and Copenhagen are such examples. These cities vary significantly in their levels of car use and traffic problems, but tend to fit between strong-center cities' low car dependence and the extreme car dependence of the full motorization cities described next (Newman and Kenworthy 1989, 1999a, 2015; Kenworthy and Laube 1999, 2001).

Full motorization cities are overwhelmingly car-based with a very weak central city area devoted primarily to finance (the central area is not a neighborhood like the centers of New York and Paris or even Melbourne); they have poor public transport services, which are mostly relatively slow bus-based systems (though increasingly today they are building at least some light rail systems e.g. Los Angeles now has LRT, Metro and commuter rail systems), and suburban centers dotted across the region, which are all almost totally dependent on car access and generate a lot of traffic. These cities are linked together with freeways and highways in all directions, with houses typically no more than 6 km from a freeway. Employment is very dispersed. Los Angeles, Denver, Detroit and Phoenix are examples of these kind of cities. Their car use is extreme and their public transport, walking and cycling use very low (Kenworthy and Laube 1999, 2001; Newman and Kenworthy 1989, 1999a, 2015).

Low-cost strategy cities are those that cannot afford to develop extensive transport infrastructure—either roads or public transport. They typically are very dense with a strong center and numerous high-density, highly congested, mixed-land use, linear corridors leading to the center. Walking and use of non-motorized modes can be high. Public transport is typically a very poor, very slow and unreliable bus service, often using minibuses, but usage can still be moderately high. Many cities in rapidly motorizing countries have this kind of system (e.g. in parts of Asia and Africa), though many are now developing major roads and rail systems (Newman, Kenworthy and Glazebrook 2013). For the above reasons, and of course because of lower wealth, car ownership and car use tend to be comparatively low in such cities when compared internationally (Kenworthy et al. 1995; Kenworthy 2010b).

Following from this, urban form or structure, as characterized by factors such as population and job densities and especially the number and type of centers within metropolitan areas (the CBD and sub-centers), is now widely accepted as critical to the patterns of mobility in cities. In particular, the density and internal structure of cities are paramount in determining levels of car use and transport energy use in cities (Cervero 1986, 1995, 1998; Newman and Kenworthy 1989, 1999a; Cervero and Landis 1992; Naess 1993a, b, 1995, Kenworthy and Laube 1999). As densities rise in cities, per capita car use and transport energy use decline (Newman and Kenworthy 1989, 1999a). Selectively raising urban densities, such as in centers linked to quality transit with good provision for walking and cycling (transit-oriented development, or TOD) can help to reshape cities for reduced car use and lower transport energy by improving the viability of public transport (Newman and Kenworthy 1996, 2006; Schiller, Bruun and Kenworthy 2010).

Such centers can also provide high levels of livability and walkability through sound urban design principles. This has been the hallmark of Vancouver's development of new centers throughout its metro area in the last 40 years (Punter 2003). The attractive nature of its sub-centers has contributed to Vancouver being regularly voted one of the world's most livable cities.[2]

On the other hand, Garreau (1991) describes what he calls 'edge cities'; a model of polycentrism where major suburban centers with office and commercial development are located at major highway interchanges and are almost totally car-based with little transit and very hostile public environments. These centers are generally problematic both from a traffic perspective and a human perspective (e.g. Tyson's Corner in the Washington, DC, area). For example, there are many studies that have shown how this kind of development leads to radical drops in transit use compared to central locations for work (Baillieu Knight Frank 1991, Cervero and Landis 1992), as well large increases in transport energy use and increased car trip lengths (Alexander 1980, 1981).

Newman and Kenworthy (2006) used their international comparisons of cities and detailed studies within cities to show how a minimum of 35 persons/jobs per ha (urban densities) is needed in centers to reduce automobile dependence. At densities lower than this there is an exponential increase in car use per capita because there is an insufficient concentration of activity to support a good public transport service and walking and cycling become difficult because distances are too great. The centers become car dependent and public environments are dominated by roads and parking space, which in turn reduces livability and the potential of public space to encourage community and connectedness (Gehl 1987; Gehl and Gemzøe 2004).

Newman and Kenworthy (2006) and Kenworthy (2006) suggest that if cities are to become less car-dependent, with less traffic problems, having better functioning urban transport systems and enhanced livability, polycentric urban structures or decentralized concentration will be required. Major centers should ideally be located at rail stations or significant public transport hubs such as BRT stations. For smaller centers at a neighborhood level with a pedestrian shed (ped shed) of about 1 km, a *minimum* of about 10,000 people and jobs will be required within their 300-ha area. For larger sub-centers with a catchment of about 3 km, a *minimum* of 100,000 people and jobs will be needed. Such centers can be not only more walkable within their areas because of higher densities and mixed-land uses, but they can also be fed from more distant locations and many directions by good public transport (buses or light rail services) and can have a rail line or BRT passing through them and linking the center to other parts of the region.

If cities are concentrating new development into compact sub-centers their 'ecological footprint' can be much smaller (Rees and Wackernagel 1998). The Stockholm region has been portrayed as a 'transit metropolis', with sustainable new satellite towns based around its metro system, or Tunnelbana (Cervero 1995, 1998), with generous green areas between and around its centers. Stockholm also reduced its car use per capita between 1995 and 2005 (Newman and Kenworthy 2015).

There are numerous cities worldwide now that show the benefits of polycentrism on mobility. The Frankfurt Rhein-Main Region is a polycentric region with well-defined urban settlements of various sizes and density.[3] These centers are linked together with a large public transport system (S-Bahn, regional trains, trams and buses). Frankfurt is also known as a 'green city' with large areas of city forest, other green space and agricultural land between its centers. Its car use per capita is much lower than many other developed cities, and its use of walking and cycling is high (Newman and Kenworthy 2015). Singapore has both a very strong CBD and major sub-centers at railway stations on its radial rail system. It has joined some of these more distant sub-centers together across the city using automated, driverless, high-frequency light rail services, and has virtually the lowest car ownership of any comparable developed city (100 cars per 1,000 persons) and very low car use (Newman and Kenworthy 2015). Toronto has several large sub-centers built around its subway system and could build the cross-city Sheppard subway line because it developed two major sub-centers (North York Center and Scarborough Center) on its radial metro lines dating back as far as the 1950s. The city's car use per capita is low and public transport use is high compared to other Canadian cities, as well as American and Australian cities, partly because of the legacy of transit-based sub-center structure over much of the metro area (Kenworthy 1991a; Schiller, Bruun and Kenworthy 2010).

Very many studies of the effects of polycentrism on transport focus only on commuting trips (e.g. Newman and Kenworthy 1996, 2006; Cervero and Landis 1992; Giuliano and Small 1993) that, although very important, are only a fraction of the trips taken per day in any city for a wide range of purposes. Nevertheless, in an important literature review of the effects of polycentric development on commuting patterns in metropolitan areas, Lin et al. (2012, esp. 8–9) found that polycentric urban structure has changed roadway demands away from CBDs and, with better transit networking of nodes, could achieve considerable trip efficiencies.

In a broader comparative study of accessibility for work, school, shopping and recreation travel in Riyadh and Melbourne, examining a shift from a monocentric to a polycentric structure, Alqhatini et al. (2014) found that:

> ... planned and concentrated employment and population in key activity centers may deliver significant benefits to improving the accessibility of car and sustainable modes (i.e. PT and walk) ... that combined and coordinated activity and residences redistribution into polycentric structures for Melbourne and Riyadh will bring about significant benefits and ... a more sustainable transport outcome.
>
> (p. 222)

Bus–rail integration and bus–bus integration

An extremely important aspect of transit planning in systems where there are both bus and rail services, or conventional bus and bus rapid transit (BRT) services, is the integration of these services with each other. This entails a great deal of careful planning, especially preceding the introduction of a new LRT or BRT service. Many cities, especially in the U.S. and Canada, maintain bus routes that reflect the travel patterns of an earlier era. The introduction of a new transit service such as LRT or BRT can enable planners to implement major changes in their bus system—if the stars align properly: if the planners are imaginative, if the policy-makers can be educated about this necessity, and if the public can be persuaded that the changes will, overall, be of much greater benefit to the public at large than the inconveniences to a small number of riders who may be negatively affected. Since such improvements will often entail a moving away from the 'one seat' ride prevalent in transit planning in the 1950s and 1960s, to a transfer-oriented system, one key is to create an understanding that making a transfer from one service to another will not be very painful if the services are frequent and the transfer points secure and comfortable. And if the system provides many more destinations than previously were available an overall improvement, ridership increases likely will occur.

A good example of where this has been done successfully is the 1982 redesign of Portland's (OR) bus system ahead of the introduction of the first 1986 MAX LRT line by transit planning wizard Tom Matoff.[4] Other good recent examples include the partial makeover of the Houston (TX) and the complete redesign of Baltimore's (MD) bus system currently in process assisted by innovative transit planning software.[5]

Growing transit: policy and planning issues

Since transit is an extremely important dimension of urban sustainability, it is imperative that all cities—large, medium and small—offer attractive transit options that attain and maintain significant levels of use. Here we will address several of the problems and issues common to most forms of transit. These range from affordability to effective citizen participation. Transit agencies should see their primary mission as building ridership, attracting peak and off-peak riders; commuters, shoppers and service seekers; car-owning 'choice' riders, as well as those termed insensitively as 'transit dependent';[6] the wealthy (as in many European cities) and not so wealthy; young, old and in-between.

Affordability

Maintaining the affordability and financial attractiveness of transit as a mobility option is an important factor in building its use. Most people experience transportation costs at the margins of their personal economy or in terms of their out-of-pocket expenses: most of the costs associated with automobility are bundled and sunk and do not vary much with use; car purchase and insurance payments are large costs that are paid for regardless of the level of use of the vehicle. Motorists then experience the cost of driving in terms of marginal costs, fuel and parking being the major out-of-pocket expenses. Because of this misperception, public transportation needs to present itself as a cost that is not significantly larger than these.

For the sake of attracting patronage, as well as streamlining their operations and data collection, transit agencies should provide relatively inexpensive pass programs that eliminate the necessity of riders having to purchase tickets at a station or have exact fares when boarding a bus or train. Such programs could be tailored to allow for reduced cost passes for lower-income riders and students. Vancouver's TransLink actively supported the efforts of a UBC students' referendum to charge all students a fee to attain a transit pass. According to the TransLink CEO, it was partly a strategic consideration; today's students are tomorrow's commuters and transit supporters.[7]

Transit priority: the key to reliability, speed, cost savings and passenger comfort

While transit may never be able to fully compete with the PMV in terms of convenience and creature comfort, there are several ways in which transit services can be enhanced and made into a more attractive travel option, especially for persons who have other options. An important dimension of urban transit is the establishment of its priority over general traffic. It is not so much the absolute average speed of transit services in any city; it is the ratio of the average speed of transit to the average speed of cars in different corridors in different parts of the city and at different times (Newman and Kenworthy 1999b). Such priority treatment will allow it to compete with the PMV for travel time, especially in congested traffic, and will allow it to maintain schedule reliability—an important factor for attracting ridership (Litman 2015a). This can happen in a variety of ways:

- Transit exclusive RoW (from exclusive lanes to exclusive ramp entries);
- Queue bypasses (or queue jumps; bypasses at traffic signals etc.);
- Traffic signal priority; controlling signals at intersections, especially when congested, singly or systemically to keep transit vehicles moving;
- GPS-based real-time traffic signal controls and real-time vehicle scheduling adjustments;
- Prominent signage (often lighted flashing) on buses, such as 'Yield to Bus Re-Entering Traffic' that should alert motorists to the need to yield to the bus as it pulls away from a curbside stop and shorten delays at bus pullouts.

In any area where traffic congestion might pose a problem to on-time performance transit priority measures should be undertaken. There are multiple benefits for such efforts:

- Schedule adherence significantly increases the reliability of transit and helps to attract riders.
- Saving time saves providers considerable expense; in some urban areas transit delays due to traffic congestion might add as much as 5 to 10 per cent or more to hourly operating costs (McKnight et al. 2003).
- Transit priority can keep the transit vehicle moving and more smoothly and comfortably.
- For relatively short transit trips, riders value the frequency of services more than the speed of the vehicle; they would rather just go to the stop or station without waiting longer than 5 or 10 minutes. For longer transit trips, riders prefer a speed competitive in traffic over frequency and are more willing to schedule their travel accordingly (Bruun 2013).

Planning for user friendliness and ridership growth: transparency, farebox avoidance and other ways to attract and maintain robustness

Transit providers need to strive to make their services easy to use and comprehend. An important strategy is to adopt some marketing approaches to transit. These would inform the public about several of the advantages of transit such as the ability to read, legally use mobile devices or, possibly to converse with other riders or even meet the love of one's life. A marketing approach would also strive to eliminate or ameliorate many of the issues that often deter 'choice' riders from using transit.

Some North American transit systems seem to be run for the convenience of the operator rather than for the convenience of current passengers or those who might be drawn to a more attractive system. Such systems could be characterized as 'operator-oriented', meaning that they are oriented to their own operational and service models, while systems oriented to satisfying current passengers and making it easier for potentially new riders to use the system could be characterized as 'rider-oriented'. These different orientations can manifest themselves in whether such features as timetables and fare structures are oriented towards the provider agency or being easy to grasp and convenient for riders, as Tables 5.3 and 5.4 below demonstrate. In the end, the rider-oriented models are better also for the operators because they grow transit use, increase farebox recovery ratios and build a more important role for transit within the transportation system.

While some transit agencies have incorporated many of the best features of service and social marketing in their outreach and public education efforts, many others have not. Too many transit agencies, especially in the U.S. tend to view transit as a social service, helping the transit-dependent rather than one that could and should be used by a broad swath of the public, hence they have not devoted sufficient resources and attention to these important approaches. The following are several ways in which transit systems can improve their user friendliness as well as enhancing their marketing efforts:

- *Make it simple*: Plan and develop systems that can be expressed in simple graphics; maps that are easily grasped and schedules that allow users to easily remember them. For routes that cannot be frequent, at intervals of 15 minutes or less, it is important for the schedule to adhere to 'clock face' by remaining consistent rather than changing its intervals frequently. Some bus services routinely build variation into their schedules to account for slowing due to congestion at peak periods; this is not user-friendly and such agencies should attempt to maintain consistent schedules by using transit priority measures enumerated above. Maintaining consistent schedules also allows transit agencies to display their timetables in a simple and coherent manner; a schedule can identify the starting point and direction of a route and then insert 'and every xx minutes until yy (time)' so that a rider does not have to be continually consulting transit

TABLE 5.3 Comparison of operator-oriented and rider-oriented timetables

Timetable structure

	Supply-based expansive: SERVICE approach	Demand-based retractive: COST approach	
Rider-oriented	Pulsed and regular departures	Irregular departures	Operator oriented
	No variations in the line	Many variations in the line	
	Few well-positioned high-quality lines	Many, low-quality lines	
	Demand variation largely picked up by vehicle/train size: High-frequency throughout the day	Demand variation largely picked up by number of services provided: High-frequency peak, low-frequency off-peak	

Source: Felix Laube

TABLE 5.4 Comparison of operator-oriented and rider-oriented system fare structures

Fare structure

	Line/trip based	System based	
Operator-oriented	Cheap single fares	Expensive single fares	Rider oriented
	No transfers, or expensive transfers	Free transfers (time/zone concept)	
	Periodical tickets only for same operator if any	Cheap system-wide periodical fares	
	Low proportion of pre-sold tickets	High proportion of pre-sold tickets	
	Casual users, low commitment to system	Users commit themselves to the system	

Source: Felix Laube

schedules. When schedules and systems can be easily represented in graphics and tables it is possible for some systems to incorporate maps and schedules in one document. Unfortunately, many systems, including some smaller ones, have complicated schedules and long, poorly organized rider information booklets that confuse more than edify. Whenever possible there should be relatively simple system schematic maps—such as that of the London Underground—so that riders can internalize a cognitive map of the system.

• *Make it easy to obtain and understand information*: Schedule and route information should be readily available in different formats to serve a diversity of clients: online, by telephone (either live or recorded menu/FAQs) and, where possible, satellite offices or kiosks in various public locations. Real-time information should be available online and at stations and transit centers. There should also be provision for real-time interaction, online or by telephone, with providers should riders need to address urgent situations that are not covered at websites or at other information sources.

- *Make it easy to find*: Transit signage should be prominent on streets and in stations and transit centers. Its text should be large enough to read at some distance and by those with vision challenges. Schedule boards and vehicle identifiers, at stations and on board vehicles should also be prominent and easily readable at some distance. Good wayfinding signage should also be prominent for directing riders to specific bus stops or rail platforms. Wayfinding maps can also help riders to find their way to their destinations upon exiting stations, as in the case of the Washington, DC, Metro stations. In some stations and locales, there are floor treatments that aid the visually challenged to find their way; these are also handy aids for others who may not be familiar with

FIGURE 5.7A
Attractive Tunnelbana (metro) station platform in Stockholm with high quality rolling stock in operation, large, well-lighted signage and real-time information, effort to beautify station surrounds and easy wayfinding.
Source: Jeffrey R. Kenworthy

FIGURE 5.7B
A central city Tunnelbana station in Stockholm. Many of the stations on this system provide super high quality and creative underground station environments as well as unique artwork and colour patterns which allow users easy identification of a station at a glance without searching for a station name.
Source: Jeffrey R. Kenworthy

the station's layout. Easy to remember mnemonics and icons can be incorporated into signage, maps and schedules. Portland's (OR) downtown bus mall, which stretches for a block on each of two one-way streets, incorporates simple icons identifying certain neighborhoods to guide riders to the shelter where their area's buses will stop. Similarly, neighborhood bus stops and shelters could be branded or color-coded as a wayfinding aid to riders.

- *Make it comfortable, secure and readily accessible*: That public transportation, in-city or intercity, is significantly safer than driving for comparable trips needs to be broadcast loudly and clearly as part of any transit marketing effort. When safety for transit trips and PMV trips is compared, transit travel turns out to be much safer than motorized alternatives (APTA 2016; Litman 2016; Durning 2006–10). It is especially true of longer commutes. This is true of in-vehicle safety as well as out-of-vehicle components of such travel.

  It is true that there can be some neighborhoods—cities or suburban—where there is a measure of risk in walking: to the store, to the bus stop or to a friend's house. A very small amount of crime occurs onboard or around transit stops and stations. The transit trip is still, overall, much safer than the PMV trip. The public perception is somewhat due to the uneven attention given by the media, especially the broadcast media, to the occasional crime around transit as well as the media's lack of emphasis of the relative safety of transit compared to PMV travel. First, there is a greater risk of crash with PMV trips. Second, there are few urban sites more prone to crime than PMV parking facilities (Smith 1996), so much so that there is a veritable industry in the U.S. of parking facility security services. Parking facilities are especially risky for women traveling solo. Then there is the risk of carjacking; in the U.S., there are approximately 40,000 car-jackings a year, many of which entail serious injury to car occupants and drivers, a small percentage of which entail homicides (Klaus 2004). This problem is considered of grave consequence in the U.S. and was made into a federal crime in 1992 (Wuslich 2012).

  The frequency of a transit service can also influence real and perceived rider security at stations and stops; the more frequent a service, the less the likelihood of criminal activity there. Some bus services, such as Portland's Tri-Met, allow unescorted women to alight at locations where they feel most secure, which are sometimes not regular stops, and allow only that person to alight there—thus preventing anyone from following that person.

- *Farebox avoidance onboard*: This user-friendly feature encourages ridership growth and makes transit providers more efficient. Passes, smart cards and honor systems whereby riders purchase tickets before boarding and then are subject to random ticket checks onboard or when alighting the transit vehicle are all ways which make riding easier. These also significantly decrease delay while boarding, which benefits both riders and providers. A benefit for providers is data collection when riders swipe or tap on entry. Other technological tools allow for collecting data when riders alight. Another positive feature of fare avoidance strategies is eliminating fare collection as a major source of conflict between operators and riders.

- *Easy on, easy off*: Transit providers should strive for creature comfort boarding, deboarding, on board and at the transit stop or station. This should include adequate shelter, comfortable seating and access to toilets, especially at stations. The 'kneeling bus' makes it easier to get on or off the bus. Separate doors for entering and exiting also reduce dwell time at stops, as do pre-boarding fare arrangements and easy-to-swipe card readers. Providers should bear in mind that, for many 'choice' riders, they are competing with the comforts of the PMV.

- *Make it available*: Adequate service hours throughout the week, day and evening, rather than simply daytime or peak periods, also can add to transit reliability; the rider will know that, if a work or other trip schedule changes, s/he will still be able to return home. Another service is the guaranteed ride home; if a domestic emergency occurs during the workday, the parent or caregiver is guaranteed a way to respond to it by the transit provider. While some providers might fear the abuse of such a program, in practice it turns out to be rarely used but greatly appreciated as a back-up option.

Promoting transit at all levels of government

For urban transit and regional and national public transportation to thrive requires commitment at every level—government, private sector and throughout the community. To do this effectively, such commitment must be demonstrated. Sweden has found such a way through what is called the K2 Knowledge Center for Public Transport, which sends a clear signal at every level throughout Swedish society that public transportation is valued, is a priority and will receive funding in pursuit of best practice. Its focus is on research and innovation in public transportation, not just in an academic sense, but also through linking very strongly with the operators of public transportation systems, both government and private, to ensure better implementation of ideas and funding of public transportation initiatives.[8]

Other organizations that perform similar (though not identical roles) are the UITP in Brussels (International Association of Public Transport), a global umbrella organization representing many public transportation authorities in countless cities worldwide. The ANTP in Brazil (National Association of Public Transport) is a similar umbrella organization that covers Latin America. And APTA (the American Public Transportation Association) and CUTA (Canadian Urban Transit Association) perform a similar important service. In the U.S.—despite the many challenges facing transit—there is evidence of ridership growth, especially among younger persons attracted to urban areas, another reason why there should be concerted efforts by the government to promote transit and furnish better funding (Buehler and Hamre 2016).

Overcoming stagnant and unimaginative planning

Another challenge facing public transit providers, especially in North America, is the overcoming of stagnant and unimaginative planning. Keeping in mind the widespread neglect and underfunding of transit in most of North American urban areas, which has created a 'survivalist' reaction in many agencies, there has been little motivation for innovation. Change entails risk, which many public agencies avoid by 'playing it safe' and just catering to those riders they've already captured. This is one of the reasons such agencies continue to shape their services around what they perceive to be the needs of commuters, especially to CBDs, even when data clearly point to the diminishing of that rider sector as employment becomes more regionally dispersed and discretionary travel increases. While there are planning innovations that can help providers improve their route planning and, possibly, intermodal connections,[9] it is often the risk aversion of agency personnel and policy-makers that works against the implementation of such tools.

Addressing the needs of special populations

Most public transit agencies are expected to address the needs of special populations, including the mobility challenged, the elderly, the poor, youth and others who cannot or choose not to drive. This is a noble and important service, without which many persons in these categories would have their ability to travel to work or school or for basic needs and vital services severely limited. Special transit services often entail special vehicles such as minibuses with wheelchair lifts, the modification of standard buses with low floor ramps that extend out to the curb when the bus 'kneels' or the incorporation of wheelchair lifts and special areas to secure wheelchairs. Agencies may also need to have bus stops and stations designed with access for the mobility challenged in mind.

Transit agencies are often seen as the 'provider of last resort' for persons with special mobility needs. The services, equipment and infrastructure investments are very costly. In many countries, they are mandated by federal legislative mandates, such as the Americans with Disabilities Act (ADA) in the U.S. Special paratransit services for small city bus services might consume as much as 40% of transit agencies budgets—especially in smaller cities and rural areas. Funding for such mandates is often sparse or lacking altogether.

Consequently, agencies try to meet the needs of special populations through 'mainstreaming' such riders into their regularly offered services—also supported by many advocates for special needs populations. Low-floor and kneeling buses, wheelchair lifts and related hardware adaptations have become commonplace in most transit systems and work well for many special needs persons provided that they live near or can access the service and can get to their destinations once they leave the regular conveyance. Otherwise, special paratransit vehicles may need to be dispatched to their residence.

Adequate and stable funding

Transit involves both short-term and long-term planning, strategic and operational, sometimes for matters that may occur over many years or decades. Its funding needs and commitments are complex. It needs a long-term commitment to adequate and stable funding sources and a margin of safety, either in its annual budget or in reserve funds, to address problems or emergencies that might emerge during a budget year. Transit also needs to plan for long-term capital improvements and major facility maintenance that can involve large sums, some of which may come from various levels of government, from local to national, and occasionally the private sector. Additionally, transit agencies should regularly engage in strategic planning and public involvement exercises, which may also be very costly.

Most transit vehicles are well built and have relatively long lifespans. Rail vehicles are generally very durable and long-lasting. Transit agencies also need to maintain large garages where they can service their fleets. Agencies typically replace or refurbish their vehicles on a regular basis; smaller agencies might do a fleet turnover or refurbishment every decade or less, while larger agencies may turn over a portion of their fleet every year or two.

Some transit systems with robust ridership derive a significant portion of their revenue from their fares. Many European and Asian transit systems derive a large majority of their operating funds from their fares. Many systems in automobile-oriented cities or where inefficient systems with large numbers of peak or poorly planned services prevail, especially in the U.S., find themselves subsidizing transit substantially—up to 90% in some areas. Systems with robust ridership and significant fare and pass revenues are often able to offer riders lower fares than in most U.S. cities; more ridership translates to less cost per rider.

Transit agencies generally need a variety of funding sources to maintain stable funding. Typically, individual funding sources, such as the fare or a narrowly targeted tax, can be subject to variability and economic cycle influences. Ridership may decline during an economic downturn and a variety of factors could influence the variability of a specific tax. Fortunately, most urban areas have several funding sources to choose among, many of which entail legislative processes or public votes. Policy-makers guiding the transit agency often underestimate the extent to which the public is willing to support transit, especially when major improvements or maintenance of vital services are well-thought-out and appear to represent true public value. Similarly, the public willingness to fund transit through the taxing of motor vehicles, either at purchase, licensure or the fuel pump, is often underestimated or misread by public officials.

Synergies between transit and land use

When planning and policy-making for transit and land use, especially development, are well integrated and coordinated there can be significant synergistic effects to the benefit of each. This can have important environmental benefits as energy and pollution burdens can be significantly reduced. A well-planned transit-oriented development (TOD), sited in conjunction with quality transit provision, can result in a successful outcome for the development as well as increased transit use. A variety of transit planning tools are available that can identify neighborhoods where there might be more transit demand to guide development, and a variety of land-use planning tools are available to identify areas of employment or other activity concentration that would benefit from transit improvement. These are discussed in greater depth in other sections of this chapter as well as in other chapters.[10]

Participatory planning

When transit and other public transportation agencies engage the public in meaningful ways, not just after-the-fact so-called 'consultations' (which are generally top-down take-it-or-leave-it exercises), significant benefits can be reaped. The public may have helpful information and ideas and may feel 'ownership' of the service or proposed project through the process.

All too often, public participation is done poorly—when it is done at all. There are several reasons for the poor performance of public agencies in this domain:

- Many providers shield themselves from public input or, at best, do BAU public outreach.
- Many of the governance structures of public transportation providers are flawed and often lacking in transparency of public access.
- Public outreach may be done in ways, times or places that are difficult for citizenry, especially the working public, to access.
- Often public agencies rely too heavily on input from current rather than potential riders. This is especially true of agencies that feel they have a high measure of 'captive' riders. The riders they hear from are often simply protective of existing services that work for them and are not necessarily interested in broader changes that could attract more riders and serve more goals, especially when changes to the routes they regularly use are under consideration.
- There are relatively few NGOs that advocate for improved transit, especially at the local level, and act as mediators between riders and agencies.

Fortunately, there are examples of good public involvement with transit planning. One example, Boulder's (CO) community transit network (CTN) is described in considerable detail in the Boulder case study in Chapter 9. More discussion of public participation and engagement is available in Chapters 7 and 8.

Regional and rural public transportation

Several of the issues around the modes used for regional public transportation have already been addressed in Chapter 4. This section will examine a few other issues around the provision of public transportation in urban regions, especially outside of the urbanized areas, as well as those that involve rural areas.

Types of providers and services

The types of services and their providers may vary considerably within urban regions in terms of their availability and geographic coverage, the extent to which they are coordinated with each other or other major mobility services, and whether they are provided by a public agency or a private interest. Zurich's superb transit system is operated by a plethora of private companies, but all under the control and agency of the Zurich Verkehrsverbund (ZVV), which bears the public responsibility to maintain transit excellence in every respect. Similar arrangements are found through most German-speaking countries in Europe. Often regional services are extensions of urban systems, such as the Massachusetts Bay Transportation Authority (MBTA) and public transportation services for Paris and its surrounding region, the Régie Autonome des Transports Parisiens (RATP), and the Réseau Express Régional (RER). Some regional services may be provided by a private entity, which may or may not be receiving public funding to defray some of its expenses. Sometimes there is a mix of public and private provision or partnerships for regional services. For instance, Vancouver's TransLink transportation authority tends to centralize planning and several other key functions in a public agency while contracting with private providers for the construction and operation of some of its services.

The types of regional services may range from rail systems to bus and coach lines to ferries and van and shuttle providers. Each of these modes represents different capabilities in terms of passenger capacity, costs, right-of-way issues and travel speed. Some of the services may address general mobility needs while others may target special travel needs, such as airport or regional medical facility access.

There are several issues confronting regional and rural public transportation planning and policy formulation:

- Population and activity densities in the region may influence the extent to which policy-makers believe that public transportation is a priority and whether a public agency or private entity will consider such services to be justifiable or profitable.
- The extent to which there is need for mobility services, and the type of services needed, may also influence whether public transportation is extended to regions and rural areas. Where there is significant need for travel for shopping and basic services, including medical and health services, policy-makers may be more supportive for such transportation services than if the need is for recreational access—although the need for public or public-supported transportation for recreation may be a factor when recreation is considered a local industry that benefits commerce and the region's tax base.

  An example of a special service for a recreational trip is the scheduling of regional trains or buses whose major destination is a sports venue located near transit. Even in automobile-oriented U.S. urban areas, such services are often popular with sports fans who would rather not have to worry about parking problems or fees or forgoing a drink at the event.
- The need for transportation services in low or sparse population areas may also be influenced by the demographic factors at play: the aged, low-income or otherwise disadvantaged populations may have necessitate transportation to services addressing their needs. Mobility for special needs populations may be more difficult to address in such areas than in urban areas because there may be a scarcity of public transportation providers or regularly scheduled services into which such persons could be mainstreamed.
- Users of regional and rural transportation services for recreational or long-distance travel (airport access) may be more willing or able to pay a market rate for such services, whereas lower income persons needing to travel for basic needs may not be able to afford a market rate.

When urban meets regional and rural

The relationship between urban and regional or rural transit is very important. A good interface between these differing types of service could promote ridership growth for each, while a poor interface could diminish the ridership for each. Some large urban areas are fortunate to have one agency providing or coordinating the range of transit services offered. Some regions with several transit providers are fortunate to have an agency or arrangement coordinating their services and fares. Often, regions present the public with a bewildering number of poorly or uncoordinated providers and fare arrangements.

The San Francisco Bay Area has no fewer than 24 agencies providing bus and bus and rail transit services, five ferry services and at least two dozen shuttle services, some connecting residents to the nearest rail station while others provide transportation to more specialized destinations such as hospitals, universities or commercial areas and several regional commercial coach operators. A few of these co-operate with each other in terms of scheduling and fare coordination; most do not.

Coordination and co-operation, or lack thereof, may also extend to major capital improvements as well as technology sharing (GPS, scheduling software etc). Smart card technology enables users to swipe or tap a card or mobile device at a fare collection machine allowing riders a measure of convenience over having to carry cash, especially change. London's Oyster Card, inaugurated in 2003, was one of the first large and highly successful applications of such technology. While many regions have adapted the use of this technology, some regions with multiple providers do not coordinate their fares or introduce cost-saving incentives for riders to easily transfer from one system to another; rather than being offered savings for such transfers, riders in these areas often must pay full fares for each of the services used. Such practices clearly work against goals of providing seamless and cost-effective services.

The extent to which a region can coordinate its various transit services, or even group them altogether under one regional umbrella, is largely an issue that policy-makers must address by pointing to the many positive examples of co-operation and coordination around the globe, examples that demonstrate that jobs will not be lost, riders will be gained and public revenues enhanced (Preston 2010).

Good examples of the coordination of urban and regional services can be found in several systems around the planet. Even though the station spacing for a metro system needs to be closer than the station spacing for a regional or commuter rail system, both Boston's MBTA and Paris (RATP/RER) give us many examples where transfer between the urban metro and regional rail is facilitated at several shared stations. Good examples of services that connect small towns and rural areas with intercity rail and coach stations, sometimes at a distance up to 100 miles (160kms) or more, can be found in the program of feeder buses connecting small towns and rural areas sponsored by the Oregon Department of Transportation, ODOT,[11] and some in the Thruway bus services offered by Amtrak across the U.S. in areas where passenger rail has been abandoned.[12] While lacking the capacity and some of the amenities found on trains, such services are easy to initiate and maintain and often pay for themselves.

Intercity public transportation: trains and coaches

There are limited environmentally sound options for intercity transportation, especially when that travel is for distances upwards of several hundreds of miles or a thousand km or more and the duration of travel is an important consideration. There are even fewer options available for international and intercontinental travel. Environmental considerations, especially in relation to GHG consumption, impinge upon such travel. Perhaps the most environmentally sound approach is to question whether these trips are truly important or whether there are ways of staging them to maximize use of rail and coach services or tele-video-conferencing. Sometimes taking an overnight train for long distance, where such services are available, is a possible option.

The most environmentally sound modes for intercity travel are passenger rail and coaches, as Table 4.2 indicates. Very few persons have the time, courage or stamina for long-distance travel by foot or bicycle. Noted exceptions include bicycle touring and hiking.

Intercity rail

Intercity railways, when done properly and are well patronized, offer the most environmentally sound mode of long-distance travel. Depending on their average velocity and frequencies, rail travel can be quite competitive with commercial aviation. Even at velocities averaging a little less than 100 mph (160 km/h), trains can compete favorably with PMVs and even flying for trips between 250 to 350 miles (400–550 km) for travelers for whom time is critical when the time spent for airport access and airport delays (including security screening and check-in) is considered. High- and higher-speed trains can compete favorably with commercial aviation for trips up to 1,000 miles. For persons traveling at a more leisurely pace, train travel can be a very comfortable and attractive option to driving or flying (Baker 2014). Another way in which railways can present a viable alternative to driving or flying for long distances is through the offering of reasonably priced sleeping accommodations; shared cabins (couchettes) for budget travelers (or even families or groups traveling together) or private cabins that are still competitive with hotel prices. While several expensive night train options have appeared in Europe in recent years, some of the more affordable, and less remunerative for railways, options have been cut (Mitchell 2014).

After falling slightly during the 2008–09 recession, most EU railways have been showing modest passenger growth, despite growing competition with short-distance airlines that benefit from low or no fuel taxation. While the publicly supported passenger railways in the U.S. and Canada stagnate or suffer losses in terms of ridership, Asian rail systems, especially in India and China, show robust ridership growth and, worldwide, freight railway shipments continue to grow (OECD-ITF 2013).

The availability of rail travel as an option varies considerably around the planet. Several European countries have highly developed and affordable railway systems that compete favorably with aviation or PMV options. Many others have well-developed railways that can meet a fair range of travel needs. Japan has been a world leader in modern railway services. It made a policy decision following World War II to emphasize rail rather than aviation or automobility for much of its in-country travel. China has been making significant and rapid progress in developing a national high-speed rail system linking its major urban areas. It now has the world's single largest high-speed train system, all developed within the last 20 years (Gao and Kenworthy 2016). Sadly, the U.S. and Canada have chosen to emphasize motor vehicle and aviation infrastructure and subsidies while allowing their railways to shrink and deteriorate, although they still perform a vital, and often highly enjoyable and sociable, transportation service for many who prefer not to or cannot drive or fly (Baker 2014).

Most countries with intercity rail systems maintain public ownership of these services, although aspects of these may be contracted to the private sector. Privatization of the United Kingdom's national rail system was proposed under Prime Minister Margaret Thatcher and systematically accomplished by her successor, John Major. The consequences of this are discussed below in the section on public and private relations.

Several EU countries have maintained public ownership of the railway rights-of-way (RoW) while leasing their use to competing carriers, and others have maintained public ownership of the whole passenger rail system while contracting some services, including employee training, to the private sector. One benefit of this latter arrangement is that, through special training, employees are taught how to become more customer-responsive, flexible and service-oriented rather than seeing their work merely as the completion of a list of union-approved tasks. This introduces a measure of employee initiative and individual responsibility into what had previously been akin to a military bureaucracy.

There are a few examples of small privately owned railways in the U.S.—such as the Rocky Mountain Express, which leases the use of a substantial length of tracks in western Canada–and a few smaller ones, mostly for tourist purposes rather than general public transportation; many operate only seasonally and often on narrow gauge tracks.

Intercity coach

Intercity travel by coach is usually affordable and environmentally sound compared to the alternatives of PMV or air travel. As with passenger rail provision, there is considerable variation in the quality and quantity of coach systems around the planet. Some regions and countries have well-developed coach services that offer relatively comfortable and reliable services between major cities, and between small towns and rural areas and major cities, and have good intermodal connections. Mexico has developed an array of intercity coach services across the country, some of which offer comfortable seating and passenger amenities, while others are more basic—and less expensive. Several Canadian provinces have maintained at least basic coach services linking major cities with smaller cities in outlying regions. Some are well-connected intermodally, as at Vancouver's Pacific Central Station, while others are not.

In some less wealthy countries, especially in Africa and Latin America, one often finds extensive jitney services that connect small towns and rural areas with major cities. These are important services and could benefit considerably from more co-operation among providers and more use of the relatively inexpensive internet tools currently available for online information, including real-time updates.

The situation in the deregulating U.S. is one of many areas abandoned by rail or coach services. Most Amtrak trains, outside the Northeast Corridor, operate on private freight railways' trackage, their routes largely determined by the freight railway mainlines. In recent decades, there has been wholesale abandonment of rail trackage across the U.S. and Canada, resulting in dramatically less freight and passenger rail service to communities outside of major urban areas or not located on a railway mainline. Private coach companies such as Greyhound and Trailways have found it easier to route their services on the interstate freeway system rather than secondary highways. However, there seems to be less abandonment of smaller cities in Canada than in the U.S.

The private coach services often seem to be in deliberate competition with Amtrak services in the U.S. or VIA Rail in Canada rather than striving to provide services to communities not served by railways. They have also spawned highly profitable, low-cost services such as MegaBus and Bolt Bus in many expressway corridors, which are finding significant appeal among student, lower-income and budget travelers who are finding the fares on railways to be unaffordable (Austen 2011).

The combination of railway and coach abandonment has left many small towns and rural areas without public intercity transportation. The cutting-back of commercial aviation services to smaller cities has left them further isolated.

Aviation, airports and airport cities

Here we will consider some of the ramifications of commercial aviation and 'airport cities' for the provision of transit and intercity rail (see Chapter 4 for discussion of aviation as a mode and more general material about airport cities).

Airports and airport cities

Commercial aviation facilities generally pose significant challenges for coordinating transportation and land-use planning—much to the detriment of the environment and the livability of adjacent areas. Because of noise and other pollution issues, most major city airports need to be located well outside of their city centers, often in ex-urban areas connected by expressways to the urbanized area. In the North American context, most airports consciously downplay public transportation access because they receive considerable revenues from parking and taxi concession fees. Additionally, taxi and similar interests often actively oppose convenient and quality public transportation access to protect their income. In automobile-dependent, transit-neglectful urban areas, such as the Seattle region, there is virtually one motor vehicle trip to the airport per air passenger—thus making the airport a major regional source of traffic and pollution—surface and atmospheric (Coogan et al. 2008; POS 2010). While a few authors welcome the emergence of the airport city (see the discussion of 'Aerotropolis' in Chapter 4), it is very difficult from an environmental and sustainable transportation perspective to support this phenomenon.

Many airports seem to be efficiently organized inside; signage and schedule information are generally well-displayed; internal transportation systems such as people-movers and moving sidewalks are often in evidence; toilets, food vendors and other kiosks are often conveniently located; and public phones are often available—although some airports in corporate-friendly–consumer-hostile U.S. cities such as Charlotte's Douglas International Airport (NC), one of the hubs for the southeast U.S., prides itself on having no public phones available and catering to the mobile phone industry. Quite a problem if you don't have a mobile phone or yours does not pick up the local signals.

The situation on the outside of most airports is quite a bit different. Even where there is a sprawling airport city surrounding it, the pedestrian environment is either non-existent or treacherous. A plethora of shuttles and PMVs clogs the airport's roadways, and the situation of public transportation linking the airport to the urban center it serves is often very uneven; some airports offer very good and conveniently located transit connections, others do not and do not seem to care. Where transit connections exist they are often hampered by the lack of exclusive RoW for their routes, thus making travel times somewhat unpredictable.[13] This presents a problem for the thousands or tens of thousands of airport workers, many of whom are low-income, who may be effectively forced to drive to and from work—especially in the U.S. For example, Seattle's SeaTac Airport has approximately 22,000 employees on site and there are almost another 20,000 employed in the vicinity of the airport (Coogan et al. 2008; PSRC 2005).

One of the great ironies of air travel is that the trip from origin to airport, combined with check-in and security delays at the airport, is often longer than the flight. And the trip to and from the airport by PMV may be statistically more dangerous than the flight was. PMV-dependent airports could mitigate their health and environmental impacts somewhat through improving transit access—especially by rail—for employees and travelers by having convenient connections to intercity rail and coach and organizing their shuttle and livery services more rationally to reduce their on-site numbers and offering more in the way of conference facilities and lodging for travelers.

Commercial aviation for intercity travel

Commercial aviation is the most environmentally impactful form of intercity travel and, unfortunately, the mode most often elected or seen as a necessity for long-distance travel (Whitelegg 2000; Whitelegg and Cambridge 2004). Several of the environmental burdens of airports have been discussed above in the airport cities section of this chapter. Among the environmental issues associated with commercial flight are:

- A very high GHG burden due to the more severe impact of emissions at high altitudes (Lee et al. 2009).
- Localized pollution related to emissions during take-off. Some of this pollution remains in the atmosphere, often adding to regional air pollution, while some is absorbed into water systems.
- Localized pollution, atmospheric and surface, related to the occasional dumping or jettison of fuel from either commercial or military flights while in flight.
- High levels of noise pollution, especially severe under flight patterns. Some sound-proofing of buildings can dampen this effect but only very powerful ear protectors can dampen this pollution for those wishing to spend time outdoors.
- Airports consume very large swathes of land, often adjacent or in urban areas, and generate large numbers of motor vehicle trips (PMVs and service vehicles) and adverse and undesirable land uses, including huge expanses of parking.
- The pavement associated with airports, runways and parking adds considerably to the urban heat island (see Chapter 6) and atmospheric warming.

Some of the GHG impacts could be lessened through a variety of management techniques, including restricting flights to or below an altitude of 30,000 feet or 9,144 meters (Williams and Noland 2005). There are also ways of reducing aviation's overall environmental burden through the application of various aviation traffic management technologies (Williams et al. 2007). Presently there do not seem to be aviation fuels available or under short-term development that would significantly reduce aviation's GHG burdens. Hence it is necessary to develop substitutes and incentives for using other modes or foregoing certain types of trips when possible and to resist pressures to expand airports and aviation fleets.

While there is a great deal of variability around the planet in the average flight's distance, and great variability in the availability of options for long-distance travel, there are many ways in which a significant portion of air travel can be diverted to surface modes. Between one-fourth and one-half of all flights in the U.S. are for distances of 500 miles (800 km) or less (Schiller 1997a; Tomer and Puentes 2009). In many, if not most, cases these could and should be diverted to public surface modes, especially rail and coach (also see the discussion in Chapter 4, especially Box 4.4).

Private and corporate providers and public transportation

As previously discussed above, public transportation is best defined by whether access to a mode is open to the public at large or not. Most public transportation uses publicly owned highway and rail rights-of-way (rail rights-of-way are publicly owned more so in Europe than in the U.S. and Canada) and publicly owned facilities such as train stations. But many services open to the public are private entities while some may be owned by a public entity but leased to a private entity for operational purposes. In some cases, previously owned public RoW, especially tolled roads, have been leased to private operators—in some cases for such a long time that, for all practical purposes, public ownership of these no longer exists. Below we will review some of the ways in which public transportation is provided by or benefits private ownership and the consequences of these arrangements.

Urban private transportation

While some forms of transportation are becoming more 'public' and more accessible to all, some are becoming more private and less accessible to the public at large or to significant segments of the public, especially those of a disadvantaged status. Some private taxicab companies avoid serving certain segments of the population deemed dangerous; the ride-hailing services gaining in popularity around the globe may not be accessible to those who are disabled or without smartphones; and some highly successful ICT corporations are instituting private bus services for their employees, often using public facilities to make these work. Among private providers, there is considerable variability in their accommodation of persons with disabilities—whose only travel option often is a government provider.

Taximeter cabriolets and other livery services

Even within urban areas with extensive publicly owned transit systems, one can find high levels of private provision of transportation. One of the most common forms is the taxi, taxicab, or cab; originally known in the early twentieth century as the taximeter cabriolet. This term was adapted from French words 'taximètre', meaning metered charges, and 'cabriolet', a type of horse-drawn carriage, usually covered for the passenger but open to the elements for the driver. Such services generally use automobiles and sometimes vans as their vehicles. Taxis are generally licensed by the municipality within which they operate and their drivers are generally expected to have a special operator's license. They are usually owned as fleets and then rented to individual drivers for periods of time ranging from several hours to several days. Sometimes taxicabs are owned by individual drivers who may then rent them to other drivers.

Often taxi companies are granted monopoly privileges within a municipality's boundaries, although there are commonly instances of several taxi companies being allowed to operate locally or even individual taxi drivers permitted to operate. Under most municipal licensure arrangements, taxicabs have their fares regulated, have special parking areas (taxi stands) designated for their exclusive use, and are expected to indicate with a light on or sign that they are available for hailing by clients and to not discriminate among clients along racial or ethnic lines.

Ride-hailing and ride-sharing services

Recent years have witnessed a meteoric rise of somewhat different ride-hailing services— the most well-known are Uber and Lyft. These services characterize themselves as web services that connect clients with individually contracted drivers who own their own vehicles. Clients generally hail such ride services through their mobile telephones. A great deal of controversy has been surrounding these services since they are often not licensed by the municipalities within which they operate; their drivers may or may not have the same type of driver's license that taxi drivers are required to have and their fares may vary according to the traffic and customer demand situations. Clients hailing rides at peak times often pay a much higher fare than at times of lesser demand. Taxicab drivers have protested about ride-hailing services as unfair competition and have occasionally protested them. In some localities, ride-hailing drivers have felt themselves taken advantage of by the web-services they work with and have attempted to organize their own driver unions.

Taxi and related services are generally termed 'ride-share' because a driver, when not cruising solo, is sharing a vehicle with one or more passengers—although the terminology here may confuse such services with other types of ride-sharing such as carpooling. The clients for such services range from individuals to pairs or small groups of persons who may already be acquainted and are sharing common trip origins and destinations. A variant within some ride-hailing services is a pooled ride that acts like an internet-fueled jitney, which mimics or competes with some aspects of transit (Bush 2016).

Other related ride-sharing services include limousine services where clients make reservations to be driven to a destination, often an airport, in a large stylish vehicle. Airport shuttle services, whose vehicles range in size from vans to full-sized buses, are another form of ride-share, especially when they use smaller vehicles and deliver door-to-door rides.

In many countries, there are a variety of transport services carrying patients between their residences and medical facilities. In some remote areas, there are airplane and helicopter evacuation services, such as western Canada's 'Shock Trauma Air Rescue Service (STARS)', available to deliver seriously ill or injured persons to the nearest ground ambulances or medical facilities (STARS 2016). Such services are generally supported by health insurance—mostly public, but some through private insurers—and play an important role for persons who otherwise might have face great difficulties in meeting their health and medical needs (NCSL 2015).

Mixing transit and taxis: a role for ride-hailing companies?

The town of Rimouski, Quebec (population 48,000), in 1993 inaugurated a quasi on-demand, quasi fixed-route taxi-bus service rather than a local fixed-route scheduled transit service. Evidently, the service worked well enough and demand grew so that by 2011 it had added a scheduled fixed-route minibus service and still retains its on-demand shared taxi service for areas off its fixed routes (Wyatt 2016). Evidently an on-demand system can build ridership and demand and lead to a scheduled service. At present, the ride-hailing services in most medium-to-large cities present themselves as alternatives to traditional taxi, air-porter buses and transit services (Brustein, 2016). Perhaps they could have a productive role to play in synergy with transit, especially in regards to some forms of pooled ride, late night (and other out-of-service times) and first/last mile trips? Such arrangements could lead to mutually beneficial ridership growth and present a viable alternative to universal PMV ownership in automobile-dependent cities (see OECD 2015 and the discussion of Mobility as a Service—MaaS—in Chapter 8).

Private and corporate urban jitney and bus services

Private urban bus services exist in many cities, especially in developing and less wealthy countries, where they are known as jitneys, although there are now services calling themselves 'jitneys' in wealthy countries. While providing a vital and affordable option in cities where there may be limited services offered by a public agency, there can be several problems with them:

- They generally operate in mixed traffic and usually do not have well-provided facilities such as stops, shelters, and terminals (see Figure 4.9 in Chapter 4), although they may sometimes benefit from HOV lanes in the U.S. and Canada.
- They are generally uncoordinated with other urban services and do not easily offer transfer possibilities.
- They often lack the creature comfort and security that public providers might offer.
- They may skim riders away from public services.
- They may present some risks to riders either because of faulty equipment or lack of protection for passengers.

Ironically one occasionally finds such services even in the heart of cities in wealthy nations where public transit is available although probably in need of improvement. One U.S. example is Union City, NJ, just across the Hudson River from Manhattan, which seems to want to mimic a poor country's city rather than undertake the task of improving its public transit. These services are popular with some riders but present a variety of challenges to local jurisdictions and their public transit services, from rider-skimming to creating congestion and traffic hazards for public buses and private motorists (Juri and Frassinelli 2011).

Private and corporate buses: the workday begins aboard

A recently growing form of transit in North American urban areas is the private bus. These include buses that are chartered for specific purposes, such as group travel to casinos or other recreational destinations; senior center and senior residences buses that transport elderly persons to shopping, services and recreation; the previously discussed airport shuttle; as well as buses serving corporate purposes. Some private bus services, such as Toronto's Premier Coach Company,[14] market themselves to population segments including corporations and public agencies mostly for occasional uses and specific events. In the U.S., there is a growing presence in some high-tech regions of private buses transporting urban commuters to their fairly new corporate campuses that are often located on the urban fringe and may be poorly served by transit or regional rail, such as Microsoft's headquarters in Redmond, WA and Google's 'Googleplex' headquarters in Mountain View ('Silicon Valley'), CA.

Many large corporate campuses have been developed in suburban locations because they fit with the lifestyle and assumptions of their top executives. It was fashionable in past decades to develop these sites for several reasons: one could create a sense of corporate place identity in such locations more easily than in developed urban areas; land was cheaper on the periphery so a more sprawling campus could be developed; large lawns were viewed as greenspace and vast parking lots were easier to construct. For an earlier generation of executives, access to a nearby golf course was often a decisive factor in location. Reasonable access to transit was one of the least considerations in site choice.

Microsoft, the major employer in the Seattle region, developed its corporate headquarters in the 1980s adjacent to two major highways (I-405 and SR520) along the boundary between two well-developed suburbs, Bellevue and Kirkland. It also had, and maintains, a fair amount of office space in Bellevue's CBD, a relatively short distance from the original corporate headquarters. While not as well served by transit as Seattle's CBD was, it still had reasonably good transit access and the possibility of relatively easy improvement. Its location and adjacent areas, as well as much of the SR520 corridor, was favorably zoned for on-site office expansion. After a few years, founder Bill Gates, Jr.—who had grown up in the city of Seattle—decided to create a new more remote headquarters several miles further away in an undeveloped and unincorporated area. Such a move fit with the corporate ethos of decades past whereby it was felt that a more remote, more 'park-like' environment was beneficial; it isolated employees from the distractions of easy access to their homes or adjacent neighborhoods and commercial centers. It was thought to be especially effective in establishing a distinct corporate identity and branding employees with it. It was assumed that most employees would want to buy faux chateaux in the sprawling subdivisions of Seattle's Eastside suburbs. It also had plenty of room for parking.

Microsoft was not alone in its thinking about creating a total and separately identifiable corporate identity around the campus of its headquarters. Most of the major San Francisco Bay Area high-tech corporations chose to develop sprawling campuses around the low-density peninsula communities of the Silicon Valley region. Sprawling corporate campuses strive to offer their employees a total environment; on-site eating options, gyms and other fitness and exercise options—often with spa-like features and, of course, large parking lots for PMV commuters.

Sprawl-seeking employees were the order of the day for a few years, but then a considerable shift in the high-tech workforce began to take hold; the well-paid 'techies' in Seattle, the San Francisco Bay Area's Silicon Valley (headquarters of Apple, Google, et al.) and other high-tech centers began to discover the benefits of living in urban centers. A reverse commute of center city residents commuting to suburban jobs—which had already existed among low-income minorities in inner cities—began to take shape among significant numbers of well-paid high-tech employees. These employees often eschewed PMV ownership and solo commutes and found ways of commuting by transit and, where feasible, bicycle.

Existing transit services, strongly shaped by catering to (and reinforcing) the suburb-to-city center commute of the 1950s and 1960s, were not well equipped to address this changing dynamic. Nor did the huge high-tech corporations, busy moving their huge profits to offshore banks to evade U.S. taxes, seem interested in helping improve their local transit services. Instead, some began either using or creating private bus systems that moved through the cities where the techies preferred to live, such as Seattle and San Francisco, to offer a luxury ride to work. Buses were well-furbished with Wi-Fi, of course, coffee and snacks, and very comfortable seating arrangements. The bubble of the corporate campus was thus extended to the trip to work. The workday could begin aboard the bus with less likelihood that an eavesdropping neighbor could tune into a techie conversation or glance at a nearby laptop that was busy at work.[15]

Employees at Amazon (amazon.com) are more fortunate in these regards; their corporate headquarters is located at the north end of Seattle's CBD, convenient for transit, cycling and—for some living in nearby neighborhoods—walking. Unfortunately, Seattle's housing has been becoming less and less affordable—to buy or to rent—as the city's popularity has grown for corporate offices and residence.

Special planning and policy issues around the public–private interface

There are numerous issues around the private provision of transportation services, whether they are open to the public or not, that are of interest to planning and policy-making. While there are many examples of quality services by private providers open to the public, and many examples where there have been excellent services performed by private providers under contract to public entities, there remain issues around the public–private interface and, especially, with the privatization of services previously offered by public agencies.

An important issue is whether such services are truly responsive to public needs. One issue with which city dwellers sometimes have experience is the extent to which private providers are willing to serve the public at large or whether they pick and choose their customers among the public at large. Another issue is the extent to which ride-hailing services are open to the public at large; they are only available to persons with smartphones, which may lead to the exclusion of some sectors of the populace: those in poverty, some of the aged etc.

Another problem is the fact that in many U.S. cities taxi services, as part of the 'night economy', are often targets of criminality—ranging from fare evasion to robbery, assault and even murder—much more often than other employment sectors. Consequently, taxi drivers may engage in deliberate evasion of stopping for passengers who are felt by drivers to 'look dangerous'. In practice, this often means that many persons of minority status are unable to flag down a taxi passing them on public streets, especially at times of day (or night) and in neighborhoods where transit may not be a viable option.

Taxicabs, ride-hailing and ride share services—while often expensive—offer a sometimes-needed mobility option for persons who do not own a car or are travelers to an urban area unfamiliar with its transit and cycling options, and thus perform a public service of sorts.

One problem with private services is that they may undermine support in some sectors for badly needed transit improvements. In the U.S. and Canada, these services often lobby against the expansion of transit in areas they feel to be competitive with their interests. There are many examples in the U.S. where private services have lobbied, formally and informally, against transit improvements, especially rail transit, connecting cities with their regional airports. In some cases, airport authorities have resisted, openly or behind the scenes, transit improvements because they derive revenues from parking and taxi services—or gain support from the taxi lobby for their political agendas.

Public–Private Partnerships (P3s)

Another public sector–private sector issue involves Public–Private Partnerships (P3s). A P3 may be defined as a long-term contractual relationship between a private party (or parties) involving building and/or operating a public facility or providing a service for a public entity. Supporters of P3s claim that these will lead to significant cost savings and improved performance, with the private party(ies) accepting substantial risk should these not work as well as proposed (World Bank Group 2016; PPP Canada 2016). Criticism of P3s focuses on the low public accountability and low transparency associated with these as well as questioning whether cost savings, especially around financing, occur, or even whether it is good public policy to surrender public controls and assets to the private sector. An example was the building of the Canada Line in Vancouver. It was touted as a successful example of private financing of a significant portion of the construction in line with shifting of cost risk to the private sector. But a close examination revealed that the private interest turned to two pension funds, which mostly handle public employees' retirement savings, to buy part of this investment. So, in the end, much of the risk was shifted back to the public sector (Palmer 2005; Siemiatycki 2006; Freemark 2009). A variety of P3 options are available to U.S. transit agencies for major capital facilities—although caution should be observed by the public officials guiding these, especially when they are seen by beleaguered large systems, such as the Washington (DC) Metropolitan Transit Authority (WMATA), and other systems that are considering privatizing some of their assets (T4America 2012 Cohen 2016).

Integration or segregation of public and private transit?

The elites of wealthy and not-so-wealthy countries generally do not face serious mobility problems. Their wealth enables them to escape from mundane worries about bus schedules, crowded trains, intermodal connections or even long check-in queues at airports. If their limousines are stuck in traffic they can simply busy themselves with wifi amenities, soothing libations or escape. Ride-hailing services, such as New York's 'Uber Chopper', are offering good connections with helicopters whisking patrons off to their mansions by the seashore (Atkinson 2014). For the super-rich, bored with the usual travel destinations on Planet Earth, public and private sectors may soon be expanding the number of spaceports from Virgin Galactic's Spaceport America in the New Mexico desert to equally warm Curaçao or cooler sites in Scotland. Space tourists may have to share a little of their room with communications satellites helping to defray the high costs of such launches (Airport World 2014).

But there is a more productive role that private services can play in regards to the whole traveling public. When public transportation services, intercity or urban transit, have been privatized—especially as part of a broad ideological commitment as in Prime Minister Margaret Thatcher's reign—much destructiveness and inefficiency has resulted. In cases where this has been reversed—where a public authority took back control of several privatized or abandoned services, as in the case of the London Overground—there has been a reversal of the loss of ridership and neglect of facilities that ensued under privatization (Badstuber and Smales 2013). U.K. bus deregulation had adverse impacts throughout the country, although Transport for London (TFL) was fortunately able to retain much control over transit in that city to great effect. The case of privatizing Park & Rides (P&Rs) in both the U.K. and the Netherlands led to planning and fare disconnects between various transit providers to the detriment of the riding public and the environment (Meek, Ison, and Enoch 2008; Mingardo 2013).

In contrast with the U.S., U.K. and Canadian experiences, privatization and P3-type arrangements seem to have worked well in some situations, as in Germany, when there is strong policy direction and involvement on the part of the government (Sclar 2000; Buehler and Pucher 2011a).

The effective integration of various public modes—bus-rail as well as integrating and coordinating transit services with other modes such as intercity rail, ferries and even commercial aviation—is best accomplished where there is strong public interest and policy guidance, especially when the various agencies and jurisdictions are made to see how such integration and coordination are in their own and the public's interest. An oft-heard criticism of transit and intercity rail is that it is highly inefficient due to the inherent inertia of bureaucracy and the public sector in general. Such critics often promote the wholesale privatization of public transportation services (Roth 2010). To be sure, there are many examples one could point to where bureaucracy, left to itself rather than being guided by policy, sees inertia as serving its own interest. Some transit entities fear that they will lose riders, lose revenues and, most fearfully, lose their jobs when various agencies and modes co-operate and integrate aspects of their planning and operations. But thoughtful and careful integration of transit and intercity services, which could include some public policy directed

---

BOX 5.1 Drive-to transit: Park & Ride, Kiss & Ride and the tiring of the transit planning mind

There are several issues surrounding Park & Rides (P&Rs) and other forms of drive-to transit:

- Drive-to transit access adds to emissions: it adds two more polluting cold-starts per day and, in some areas, the drive to the P&R is similar to or longer than the transit trip.
- While remote P&Rs might save a little in terms of GHGs, closer ones only increase the GHG burden of the total motor vehicle and transit trip (Truong & Marshall 2014).
- Parking lots, whether for transit or other less noble uses, have many undesirable effects associated with all forms of pavement: heat entrapment, polluted runoff, ground water recharge interference etc.
- P&Rs might pull riders off local transit (Mingardo 2013).
- A critique of Seattle-area Park & Ride investment estimated that the average P&R stall has an opportunity cost of 'in the range of US$5 to $15 per day, or more, depending on site-specific costs' (Schiller and Kenworthy 2011).
- When multiplied by the thousands of P&R stalls that might exist in an urban area, the costs and opportunity costs involved, including maintenance, operation and security, could be better applied to improving local bus services and transit centers and providing more passenger shelters and bicycle facilities along routes (Strathman and Dueker 1996).
- Even its drive-through 'cousin', the Kiss & Ride area at P&Rs or transit centers—where chauffeured riders are deposited (and perhaps kissed by the automobile driver as a reward for taking transit)—entails traffic and emissions impacts.
- Transit planners very often underestimate or discount the extent to which users are willing to walk to quality transit services (Ker and Ginn 2003).
- At the very least, motorists should pay for the privilege of using a P&R; this could either be in the form of payment per use, a monthly permit or an increment added to a transit pass. The Vancouver (BC) region's transit provider, TransLink, is moving towards fees at all P&Rs.
- P&Rs may increase a region's motor vehicle traffic overall (Parkhurst 2000).
- There is a social equity issue: these expensive investments reward those who can afford to drive at the expense of improving walking-and-waiting (bus stops) facilities for those who do not.

The P&R might be a useful facility in remote corners of a region where improving local transit and bicycling access to a major route may not be feasible. P&R should be carefully analyzed and compared to an array of alternatives including transit-oriented development (TOD), improved local transit and improved walking and cycling conditions. When done in well-developed areas or within city limits, in lieu of improved local feeder services, it can only be taken as an indication of the transit planning mind grown tired—very tired.

Source: Preston L. Schiller

at co-operation with the private sector, generally results in substantial increases in ridership and revenues for all the involved services as well as providing the public with improved services and options (Preston 2010). When pro-private sector ideology and policy dictate privatization, it often has disastrous consequences for the services, the public and the environment, as Figures 5.8a–c below demonstrate.

Park & Ride: useful or harmful?

A curious area of transit planning is the phenomenon of 'drive-to transit'. In recent decades, transit agencies have been attempting to lure riders—usually in suburbs, but sometimes in cities themselves—with free or cheap parking at a parking lot or structure serviced by one or more transit routes. Park & Ride probably grew out of the parking provided at outlying suburban and small town regional (or commuter) rail stations. Box 5.1 explores this matter.

FIGURE 5.8A
Small transit facility dwarfed by parking, South Kirkland Park & Ride lot
Source: Eric C. Bruun

FIGURE 5.8B
Mountlake Terrace P&R garage in a low-density neighborhood adjacent to a major freeway; it houses several hundred of cars at a substantial opportunity cost (see Box 5.1) but it gained a LEED energy-environmental rating because of its solar panels.
Source: Preston L. Schiller

FIGURE 5.8C $41 million "freeway flyer" express bus station attached to the Mountlake Terrace P&R garage. Would not it have been worth it to replace the adjacent P&R garage with another TOD?

Source: Preston L. Schiller

FIGURE 5.8D New TOD on the Washington DC metro system showing the architectural contrast and visual intrusion of large parking structures within station environments which should mainly prioritize pedestrian and cyclist amenity.

Source: Jeffrey R. Kenworthy

Conclusion

This chapter has covered several aspects of public transportation, including public access to privately owned or operated modes as well as challenges to public transportation from exclusively private provisions. It is evident that this is a complex and multifaceted area of research and practice, where some older technologies appear to be quite useful despite their age while some new and unproven technologies are hyped and where many new, exciting and highly useful technologies are constantly emerging. It should also be evident that public access to transportation is a vital part of any sustainable transportation agenda. The central importance of effective transit systems to urban viability, in mobility, land-use planning and urban livability, has also been explored.

Questions for discussion

- Identify examples of good and not-so-good intermodal connections in your city. What would it take to improve the not-so-good ones?

- Evaluate the claims made by some that AVs will soon replace transit as we now know it.

- What modes of public transportation are available in your city. How do they compare in terms of: (a) affordability? (b) accessibility? (c) extent of coverage? (hours, days and geographic reach)

- How is transit affecting land use/urban form in your city, if at all?

Notes

1   See: www.economicsonline.co.uk/Business_economics/Natural_monopolies.html (accessed 8 August 2016).

2   See: Mercer (2017).
3   Gesellschaft für Markt and Absatzforschung mbH, 2010.
4   See: Walker (2012).
5   See: www.remix.com
6   This is a term applied by those who cannot see very much past the windshields of their cars to those who cannot afford cars. It begs the question of whether all civilized and environmentally conscious urban dwellers should not be 'transit dependent' in some form or another?
7   Pat Jacobsen, former TransLink CEO, personal communication with P.L. Schiller, 2004.
8   www.k2centrum.se/en/news?cat=7 (accessed 8 September 2016).
9   See: getremix.com/ (accessed 25 July 2016) also see: alltransit.cnt.org/ (accessed 23 July 2017).
10 See: getremix.com, Bruun Better Public Transit Investment.
11 See: www.cascadeseasttransit.com/ and oregon-point.com/ (accessed 8 August 2016).
12 See: www.amtrak.com/accessible-thruway-bus-service and www.amtrak.com/thruway-connecting-services-multiply-your-travel-destinations (accessed 8 August 2016).
13 Boston's Silver Line (semi-BRT) regularly gets stuck in traffic between Logan Airport and the nearby CBD, disrupting the planned bus headways as they often become either clumped or have longer headways due to traffic delay and not having a continuous bus-only lane.
14 See: premiercoach.ca/ (accessed 8 August 2016).
15 See: en.wikipedia.org/wiki/Google_bus_protests; https://msshuttle.mobi; www.pugetsound anarchists.org/node/7; wstc.wa.gov/Meetings/AgendasMinutes/agendas/2010/July13/documents/ 20100713_BP8_MicrosoftConnectorCommuteFactSheet.pdf (accessed 16 August 2016).

CHAPTER SIX

Urban design for sustainable and active transportation and healthy communities

Introduction

This chapter discusses the critical importance of urban design and its focus on public environments in cities, and some historical commentaries that help to show why the profession has been propelled into greater prominence in the field of sustainable transportation and healthy communities in recent years. It explores key aspects of the urban design discipline and highlights some distinctions between it and the urban planning profession with which it is closely allied.

A new theory of urban fabrics returns to the concept of walking, transit and automobile cities, explained in Chapter 2. This theory, which is very briefly summarized from Newman et al. (2016), provides some concepts and tools for helping focus urban planning and urban design into a more refined, differentiated and coherent approach than the one-size-fits-all modernist enterprise of automobile-dominated planning in the post-World War II era. It shows how recognizing, respecting and rejuvenating these three different urban fabrics can lead to more relevant, sensitive and sustainable urban planning, transportation planning and urban design.

A detailed discussion of what can be called sustainable urban design shows the key concepts and tools that urban designers can work with to describe and analyze urban fabrics and how these might be used to help make neighborhoods and districts in cities more sustainable in their transportation and healthier in their community life. Finally, the rise of urban design in the above fields is reflected in a wider range of additional resources, tools and efforts worldwide, a sample of which is provided at the end of the chapter.

Urban planning and urban design: getting our bearings

As already discussed in various places in this book, urban land use and built form are fundamental determinants of the sustainability of urban transportation. In this regard, urban planning is critical. Through zoning, planning generally determines the nature of the land uses in any location and their density and types, whether there are mixed land uses or not, how much parking is provided for in the planning codes, how buildings are configured on the land they occupy, and whether this helps foster walkability or favors auto-access—for example through setback requirements, as opposed to active frontages along sidewalks. Due to the links between these planning factors and mobility patterns, urban planners play a fundamental role in working either for or against more sustainable transportation.

Much of this planning work is done in two dimensions, producing colored zoning maps and conceptual plans for the layout of urban territory, indicating permitted land uses and densities, the width and types of roads and highways, the location and type of greenspaces in cities and so on. Getting the urban planning right for any area is therefore essential for sustainable transportation. In particular, the urban planner largely determines whether automobile dependence is being built in from the beginning through low densities, rigid, single-use zonings and an assumption of mainly auto-access, or whether there is an emphasis on higher densities, mixed land uses, walkability and transit access.[1] However, there is a closely allied discipline, with a set of concerns and practices that are strongly related to these matters, but which deals more directly with the three-dimensional results of urban planning decisions and the relationships that exist between the many different elements of the built environment (though these three-dimensional concerns are very often expressed using maps, just like in urban planning—see later). This profession is urban design.

Urban design is intimately concerned with the actual lived results of urban planning and transportation decisions. It is critically concerned with the qualities and characteristics of the built environment through which citizens must move to fulfil their daily needs, to gain access to the amenities of the city and to develop a sense of place and community. Urban design has a major focus on the shared spaces of cities and is the key profession for ensuring the livability, convenience, conviviality and beauty of the public realm in cities. Most importantly from a sustainable transportation perspective, urban design is a major player in whether urban fabrics are developed to encourage trips by foot, bicycle and public transit, as opposed to primarily facilitating the movement of cars.

In practice though, urban design is a slightly difficult discipline to precisely pin down and describe. The architect and urbanist Peter Buchanan captures many of the key dimensions of urban design and distinguishes them from urban planning and architecture, emphasizing the critical importance of the lived results in cities and especially the public realm. Good urban design is about the physical fabric of towns and cities, mobility, placemaking and whether a notion of citizenship is imparted or strengthened (Cowan 1993; Urban Design Group).

Even a cursory consideration of the above statement will serve to highlight how the automobile, through its creation of 'no place' or 'non-places', or in the words of Kunstler (1993) 'the geography of nowhere', produces urban fabrics and qualities that are the antithesis of what good urban design tries to do.

FIGURE 6.1
Lively street scene and theatre area, Budapest, Hungary
Source: Jeffrey R. Kenworthy

The United Kingdom's Planning Policy Guidance 1 (PPG1) summarizes the urban design profession and its integral links to sustainable transportation in stating that urban design is about:

> ... the relationship between different buildings; the relationships between buildings and the streets, squares, parks, waterways and other spaces which make up the public realm; the relationship of one part of a village, town or city with other parts; patterns of movement and activity which are thereby established; in short, the complex relationship between all the elements of built and unbuilt space.
>
> (Urban Design Group)

In Chapter 1, we show that automobile-based planning and thinking has been responsible for widespread destruction of the public realm and the development of physically, socially and psychologically unhealthy places. Automobile dependence has been a major contributing factor in social isolation, the breakdown of urban community, the near-impossibility of independent mobility for children and enforced car use across all age and socio economic groups. The ability to walk, ride bikes or use transit in cities has been undermined or often eliminated through dispersed, low-density and single-use landscapes, which are the hallmarks of planning around the car. The roads and car parks that dominate the public spaces of such landscapes and fracture the urban fabric create places that are extremely hostile to people. The public life of cities is greatly diminished, and the physical and psychological health of the city's inhabitants is undermined. The streets and other public spaces that are meant to knit a city together and create the opportunity for informal contacts among people who would otherwise never meet are for the most part filled with people wrapped in the protective cocoon of their automobile, or despoiled by parked cars.

Mumford, as early as 1961, gave eloquent voice to these problems. In doing so he foreshadowed the urgent need for and the subsequent rise of the urban design profession in the late twentieth century, with its focus on more compact development, more inclusive public spaces and attention to mending the results of auto-centered urban planning, especially the car's mass destruction of the public realm:

> Under the present dispensation, we have sold our urban birthright for a sorry mess of motor cars. . . . Future generations will perhaps wonder at our willingness, indeed our eagerness, to sacrifice the education of our children, the care of the ill and aged, the development of the arts, to say nothing of ready access to nature, for the lopsided system of mono-transportation. . . . For the wider the scattering of the population, the greater the isolation of the individual household, and the more effort it takes to do privately, even with the aid of many machines and automatic devices, what used to be done in company often with conversation, song, and the enjoyment of the physical presence of others. . . . The cost of this detachment in space from other men is out of all proportion to its supposed benefits. The end product is an encapsulated life, spent more and more either in a motor car or within the cabin of darkness before a television set.
>
> (Mumford 1961, p. 512)

Urban design and sustainable transportation

Why is urban design important in sustainable transportation, building healthy and green communities and combating the urban heat island effect and climate change? Through authors and practitioners such as Bentley et al. (1985), Gehl (1987, 2010) and Gehl and Gemzøe (2000, 2004), urban design today is concerned with factors that either directly or indirectly seek to limit car-based design and planning. The main objectives in this theory and practice are to promote walkability, cycling and greater use of transit, beautify and humanize the public realm and facilitate the development of healthier communities.

The physical design and elements of urban fabrics certainly play a clear and undeniable role in fostering more sustainable urban transportation and the work of Jan Gehl and his associates in many cities around the world gives ample evidence of this (e.g. Gehl et al. 2004, 2009). Some of these changes include radical increases in residential development in central cities, widening of sidewalks, pedestrian and transit-priority streets, greening of streets, huge increases in local shopping and cafes and accompanying massive increases in pedestrian flows and public life. All these effects can be physically measured, monitored, quantified and correlated over time.

Socially and psychologically healthier communities are a little more difficult to define, characterize and measure and it is even more difficult to claim any cause and effect relationships between them and urban design or physical planning measures. One cannot assert any simple physical determinism in the creation of socially healthier urban communities. The existence of socially healthy communities, or the lack therefore, is mediated by a plethora of social and cultural norms and at least partly shaped by history, the forces and factors that have collectively helped to make a community what it is today. However, it can also be argued that these cultural norms and behaviors, which are shaped over centuries, have in turn been influenced by the types of cities people have lived in, especially the structure and quality of the public realm and whether it supports or does not support closer ties and relationships between locals and strangers alike (see later discussion of urban fabrics theory).

It is certainly possible, by conscious or unconscious design and planning, to make it very hard for a civilized, attractive and supportive public life of cities to develop and to be expressed in an obvious way in the public realm. If major parts of the public realm are alienated through motor vehicles and their air pollution, noise and danger, and their layout is fractured by huge highways and vast parking areas, then there will be little opportunity or desire for people to come together in what is left of the genuine public environments of cities, the streets, the sidewalks, the squares and the parks (Schneider 1979).

Cities then become bastions of privatism, exhibiting what has sometimes been called 'private splendor and public squalor', leading most people to simply retreat from and escape the hostility of the public realm. This escape is facilitated by the automobile and its infrastructure, the very same things that caused the decline in the first place, making the whole city 'a passage' rather than 'a place'. Such cities are often more prone to higher crime because they are lacking in any of what Oscar Newman termed 'defensible space' (Newman 1973). On the other hand, if urban spaces are made for people on foot and they fill with vibrant, colorful and attractive activities, then there is a much greater chance and desire for human community, interaction and exchange opportunities (Engwicht 1993, 2005). The city again becomes a place.

So how can we clearly distinguish the difference between the city as 'passage' and the city as 'place'? This can be encapsulated by systematically comparing the qualities of a highway, a piece of infrastructure dedicated solely to the passage of vehicles at high speed with no pretense of attempting to do anything more than that, versus those of the public realm that is multi-functional and must accommodate movement needs and social needs. Table 6.1 summarizes these differences, which strongly underpin the ideas of the late Hans Monderman, a Dutch traffic engineer who introduced the concept of 'shared space'. Under a 'shared space' treatment, urban environments are converted from being heavily regulated by a forest of signs and paraphernalia used to give precedence to private motorized traffic and purportedly to control the behavior of motorists, to places where people in vehicles must find their way amongst a range of other road users, negotiate their behavior with all these other users and live with uncertainty and surprises. Curbs, road surface markings, signs and traffic and parking regulation are simply removed. The main effect is to slow

TABLE 6.1 The difference between highways and the public realm

The highway	The public realm
Regulated	Culturally defined
Impersonal	Personal
Linear	Spatial
Single purpose	Multi-purpose
Consistent	Constantly changing
Predictable	Unpredictable
Systematic	Contextual
State-controlled	Cultural/social rules
Signs and markings	Eye contact

Source: One of two videos on the concept of 'shared space' (www.youtube.com/watch?v= RLfasxqhBNU, accessed 1 June 2016)

traffic down and change streets into calmer, more people-centered places. David Engwicht's book *Mental Speed Bumps* (Engwicht 2005) elaborates on the practical effects of Monderman's ideas in different settings and two films on shared space provide visual evidence of these results.[2] A slight caveat, however, is in order: shared space is still somewhat controversial; relatively few cities or towns have implemented shared space—or implemented it widely—and there is still a need for comprehensive study of this highly attractive concept.

Since raising densities is a critical part of more sustainable urban design, it is important to also stress that as cities become more compact with more mixed land uses, the emphasis on the public realm increases as a kind of natural compensatory mechanism. This has been the process in Vancouver, for example, discussed in the exemplars, Chapter 9 (Punter 2003). High-quality green spaces increase as a replacement for front yards and back yards, the quality of street environments becomes more important as people shift out of the protective cocoons of their vehicles and engage with public space, while walking, riding bikes and using public transit. Complete streets become more the norm, with wider footpaths, dedicated cycle-ways, bicycle parking and bike-sharing stations, trees and flowers, benches and alfresco dining (e.g. Smart Growth America 2013). This is how we create this shift from the city as 'passage', an automobile-oriented concept based on mobility instead of accessibility, to the city as 'place', a concept that sees the city's streets and circulatory systems as social space, not merely movement space.

Of course, the greening of cities described above is part of creating a better local environment, which encourages walking and cycling. But such changes are also important on another level, which affects both local livability and global sustainability—reducing urban heat islands. The accumulated heat input into the atmosphere from anthropomorphic sources such as the countless motor vehicles plying city streets and the air-conditioning and heating systems that create internal building comfort, all contribute to human outdoor discomfort in summer months and through their excessive energy use also add to the global CO_2 burden. And the big factor in all this is the very large heat absorption of asphalt and other dark exposed and unmitigated manmade surfaces, especially in the core of cities. It is therefore important to minimize these heat islands. Box 6.1 from Doug Kelbaugh summarizes this problem and offers some solutions to it.

The more pleasant environments fostered by urban design attention to streetscapes and mitigating the urban heat island, in contrast to the rather miserable places Mumford describes earlier, are ones in which people congregate in public space, intermingle comfortably with one another and develop a loose and supportive connection with each other. So, what might be some of the positive social and psychological qualities of such

BOX 6.1 **Urban cool: simultaneously fighting urban heat islands and climate change**

Doug Kelbaugh

The urban heat island or urban heat island effect (UHI or UHIE) is the term that has been developed to describe the higher air and surface temperatures in cities compared to their hinterland. The increase in local temperatures is *not* from GHGs trapping more heat in the atmosphere, but from a local increase in palpable, or *sensible*, heat, (as opposed to latent heat, which is not detectable). This heat comes from two sources: hot gases emitted from tailpipes and chimneys, and from dark surfaces—blackish rooftops, streets and parking lots—that radiate heat, because they have been heated by the sun to temperatures hotter than the surrounding air and surfaces. Both heat sources raise the average urban temperature higher than the surrounding suburbs and rural countryside, which have fewer tailpipes, chimneys and dark surfaces per acre. Figure 1 shows a heavily built-up central city section from Hong Kong displaying a built environment that helps fosters the UHIE.

The rural to urban temperature gradient can be five to seven or more degrees Fahrenheit (F) at a given time, with heat waves that may double this delta between a city's center(s) and hinterland. Land and building surface temperatures vary even more dramatically, with deltas of over 75 degrees F, which means radiant temperatures are even higher than ambient air temperatures.

UHI is both an opportunity and a burden for cities. Very importantly and very fortuitously, ways to mitigate and adapt to local UHI are complementary to ways to address global climate change (CC). And as a more manageable, local 5–10 year problem, rather than a 50–100 year global, more elusive challenge, it can more immediately and more effectively motivate people to modify their behavior. There are four ways to mitigate and adapt to the UHI to achieve urban cooling.

The first is *albedo enhancement*. Albedo is measured by the Solar Reflectivity Index (SRI), which indicates the percentage of solar radiation that is reflected back through the earth's atmosphere into outer space, before it heats up any terrestrial mass or air. Accordingly, white and light colored horizontal surfaces with a high SRI—primarily roofs and pavement—increase the urban albedo, and thereby reduce the ambient air temperature. By converting half a city's rooftops to green roofs, it is estimated that temperatures can be diminished by up to 3.5 degrees F.[i]

Obviously, the infrastructure for motorized vehicles is a fat target for albedo enhancement. The paved street and road surfaces tend to be dark colored asphalt, which absorbs the solar radiation and heats the air temperature above them. The surface area devoted to vehicles in motion is immense, as is the paved parking areas for vehicles at rest. In some cities, the combination—call it 'motorized space'—is a very high percentage

BOX 6.1 FIGURE 1
Hong Kong urban form. Air and especially surface temperatures are higher in heavily built up central city areas compared to surrounding suburban and rural areas, such as here in Hong Kong with its intense density and very high building height.
Source: Christine Finlay

continued

BOX 6.1 FIGURE 2
Excessive road space in central
Dubai. In Dubai and other UAE
cities, a high proportion of land
is devoted to roads and parking,
along with heavily built up, heat
absorbing
high-rise streetscapes.
Source: Jeffrey R. Kenworthy

of the land area. Both areas can be literally lightened up with paint, made all the more timely by recent technical and cost breakthroughs in durable pavement coatings (which could be applied by volunteer/guerilla labor in a tactical urbanist initiative). Dubai, other UAE cities and central areas anywhere that are designed around the car (e.g. in Los Angeles and Detroit) have huge areas devoted to cars, along with high car use. When added to the already intensely hot climates in some of these cities, it is easy to see the link between the UHI and transportation. Figure 2 from Dubai illustrates the problem.

The problem can be even more effectively addressed in the medium term by redeveloping many central and inner city parking areas, converting them to housing, mixed-land use and other urban activities that can include green open spaces, trees, gardens, green roofs and other green surfaces that radically reduce the heat island effect. This has the added advantage that it also provides more people with the opportunity to live a lifestyle that can rely mostly on walking, cycling and transit, thereby also generating less heat from tailpipe emissions. People living in central and inner areas have smaller energy, carbon and ecological footprints, especially from a transportation perspective (Newman and Kenworthy 2015). In both developed and developing countries, those who choose this strongly urban lifestyle typically have smaller households, which when combined with their reduced per capita energy and emissions due to location efficiency leads to much less total energy demand and carbon output. Of course, there are also synergistic benefits of redeveloping central and inner areas that relate to increased social capital through creativity, culture and the arts, for example, as well as increased productivity.

The second strategy is *sensible heat reduction*, that is, reducing the local production and release of sensible heat into the urban environment, in the form of hot air and other gases. This means decreasing the combustion of hydrocarbon fuels in both motor vehicles, power plants and industrial processes. The most significant of these anthropogenic sources of UHI is vehicle traffic. Compact, walkable, bikable, transit-oriented urbanism is an effective way to reduce tailpipe emissions of heat. Reducing tailpipe and chimney heat can be achieved by both low- and high-tech techniques, with the most effective and leanest strategy being the 'negatrip'—simply walking and biking, rather than driving—in compact, location-efficient, mixed-use, transit-served neighborhoods consistent with pre-automobile cities and New Urbanism. All the well-known arguments for greater emphasis on *accessibility* and less on *mobility* are directly germane. Cities with mixed use development on smaller blocks and a close-grained jobs–housing balance are all the more justified. And new vehicles and building HVAC systems that not only burn less fossil fuel but also emit lower temperature fumes, can play a positive role.

continued

Last, lower tech, passive cooling and dehumidification devices can reduce the voluminous hot air pumped into the urban air shed by air-conditioning systems—a fast-growing problem as the Developing World is increasingly able to afford these energy-intensive, heat-spewing mechanical systems that sometimes run 24/7 in hot, humid climates.

The third strategy is creating *cool microclimates* within the city. This cooling is achieved primarily with plants, especially shade trees, as well as by urban configurations that enhance cooling breezes that are stifled by crowded and tall buildings. Trees are the great natural multi-taskers of the environment. Trees along streets and roads and in parking lots constitute a large and particularly effective part of the urban tree canopy. The list of the environmental contributions of vegetation is long: trees provide cool shade, evapo-transpiration (evaporation from leaves) that cools and moistens the air, carbon sequestration, particulate pollution filtration, soil retention, water retention, animal habitat, nuts, fruits, flowers and fragrance, while absorbing sound, shaping/softening public space and bestowing beauty and biophilic presence.

According to the U.S. Conference of Mayors, at least 135 cities have tree inventories and planting and maintenance programs, and almost half of them have adopted tree canopy goals.[ii] For instance, Washington, DC, has incorporated a citywide 40% tree canopy goal. To achieve this goal by 2032, the city must increase its canopy cover from the existing 35% by planting 8,600 trees per year. Seattle plans to increase its tree canopy from 18% to 30% in 30 years.[iii] Many of the trees are being planted along streets, roads, sidewalks and biking/walking paths. Melbourne, Australia—where they're not just planting trees but an 'urban forest' to deal with increasing temperatures—plans to double the forest canopy from around 22% to around 40% over the next 20 years. In a city that is four to seven degrees Celsius hotter than its green suburbs, their research indicates that this will cool the city by four of those degrees.[iv]

The fourth and final strategy relates to urban morphology, or the three-dimensional configuration and spatial character of dense cities. Also called the 'urban section', it refers to the shape and height of buildings and street sections, in particular to the degree to which they trap heat in their canyons and courtyards. The city gets even hotter if there is less solar energy reflected back unimpeded from vertical building surfaces as well as all the horizontal surfaces mentioned in the first strategy. This heat retention is exacerbated when streets are narrow and buildings are tall. Like pavements, if those surfaces are dark and/or are made of heavy mass, such as stone, brick, asphalt and concrete, they act like thermal flywheels, carrying the day's higher air and radiant temperatures into the evening and night. Beijing, famously plagued with air pollution, is considering a radical strategy that is relevant to urban heat canyons: to flush its streets of dirty and hot air by removing existing high-rise buildings to encourage more natural ventilation at the urban scale. Urban design needs to reconsider both the plan and section of tight clusters of tall buildings that trap heat and stifle air movement.

The first three of these strategies are proven antidotes to global CC, on top of their urban cooling benefits. Importantly, they directly *adapt* to CC by tempering increasing global air temperatures, while quietly and indirectly helping to *mitigate* these increases. They are achievable, easily understandable strategies that lend themselves to distributed, democratic action at the local scale.

Because urban cooling emphasizes adaptation over mitigation, it appeals to the human proclivity for short-term thinking and prompt action, especially in times of crisis. Its concrete initiatives provide a proactive sense of progress during the vagaries and uncertainties of the unfurling disruption of the earth's weather and climate. Much to our good fortune, the triad of albedo enhancement, reduction in GHG emissions and cool micro-climates also frontally addresses global CC, even if those benefits take decades to manifest themselves. Last, urban cooling is essential for cities to continue to attract more residents and to keep their existing populations from migrating to their relatively cooler suburbs and countryside where their larger carbon footprints, especially from much greater automobile dependence, would aggravate CC and make *both* cities and suburbs ever hotter. It's a relatively low-tech, inexpensive and cost-effective strategy, ripe for acting on immediately.

Source: Doug Kelbaugh[v]

[i] See Brian Stone, *The City and the Coming Climate*, 2012, p. 107.
[ii] Protecting and Developing the Urban Tree Canopy, U.S. Conference of Mayors, 2008, p. 8.

continued

iii Emily Oaksford, *APA Sustaining Places*, website/blog, 18 March 2015, citing source in Sproule et al. (2014), 'Economic comparison of white, green, and black flat roofs in the United States', *Energy and Buildings*, vol 71, March, pp. 20–7.

iv See Hayley Birch, 'Where is the world's hottest city', *The Guardian*, 22 July 2015.

v Doug Kelbaugh FAIA, is Professor and former Dean of Architecture and Urban Planning, Taubman College of Architecture and Urban Planning, University of Michigan, Ann Arbor. He has had a distinguished career in architectural practice and academe, recently awarded the 2016 Topaz Medallion for Excellence in Architectural Education, North America's highest honor in the field. He is the author or editor of several books including *Repairing the American Metropolis, Common Place Revisited* (2002) and *The Pedestrian Pocket Book* (1989) and has collaborated with colleague and former partner Peter Calthorpe on many projects and publications. Doug Kelbaugh was an early leader of the New Urbanism movement. This selection is from a work in progress (2017) examining the many dimensions of the UHI and how it can be reversed.

communities? Based on the authors' practical comparative experience over decades in many different types of cities around the world, it is impossible not to notice that there are vast differences in the public face of communities, the standards of public behavior and what might even be loosely termed a kind of 'public happiness'.

Experiences in what appear to be healthier, better functioning communities around the world often include several signs. For example, people in such communities are likely to be much more accepting of difference, more likely to make eye contact with strangers and offer unsolicited greetings, outreach and friendliness, as opposed to a scowling indifference, aversion or suspicion. They are often more well-mannered and considerate of each other and perhaps slower to anger or engage in public displays of rage or selfishness in its various forms. These displays could include indiscriminate use of car horns, verbal or physical abuse in public settings, impatience or aggression in dealing with minor annoyances, jostling to board transit vehicles, queue jumping etc. The public life of such healthier communities might also be manifest and felt in several other small but cumulatively important ways, which give a community a completely different feeling to one where the opposite behaviors are on display. Such behaviors may include care in stopping for pedestrians crossing roads, giving up seats for others in transit vehicles or not occupying two seats with bags while others are standing, and perhaps a greater frequency of other random acts of kindness, care and mutual support. Small matters in the larger scheme of things, but some pointers nevertheless.

On a broader level, such communities may often manifest more public concern and involvement in local issues, more community engagement through clubs and other organizations, more volunteerism and willingness to lend a helping hand, and a generally greater feeling of trust and openness, especially towards strangers. In short, they offer up bigger and more obvious servings of the social capital that Putnam (2001) is at pains to explain has been a major casualty of the auto-based society in the United States.

Of course, there are many other more complex factors that either support or mitigate against the development of such positive qualities. However, we would argue that human-centered urban design that encourages active use of a city's public spaces by all sections of society and that promotes walking, cycling and greater use of transit has the potential to help bring people together and to foster a healthier, fairer, more equitable and inclusive community in a way that highly car-oriented cities cannot and do not do.

Indeed, some have argued that a quality public realm is democracy in action. A good public realm treats vulnerable groups such as the elderly, children and differently abled members of society with care and respect; this is critical also for the economy of a place. Barber (1995), writing in Canada's *Globe and Mail*, offered some trenchant observations about how important it was for cities to invest in their public realm.

Unlike social and psychological health, it is much easier to establish a verifiable link between a physically healthier community and urban design factors (Giles-Corti et al. 2012). Healthy communities enable their citizens to avoid obesity and other sedentary lifestyle-linked diseases by allowing them to build into their daily routines at least the 30 minutes of walking or other active transportation recommended as a minimum by physicians for cardiac health (Bassett et al. 2008, 2011; Pucher and Buehler 2010). In a wide-ranging international study embracing 14 countries, 50 U.S. states and 47 of the USA's largest cities, Pucher et al. (2010) found that at all these geographic levels there were: '. . . statistically significant negative relationships between active travel and self-reported obesity'.

In 2016, *The Lancet*, one of the top medical journals globally, published a series of three articles entitled 'Urban Design, Transport and Health' on the highly detrimental effects of planning around cars. Anne Moudon, one of the co-authors explained that: 'City planning policies supporting urban individual car travel directly and indirectly influence such risk exposures as traffic, air pollution, noise, physical inactivity, unhealthy diet, personal safety and social isolation' (quoted in Kelley 2016).

Urban design and physically healthy communities are therefore intimately connected with the quality of the public realm, the spaces and linkages that bind together the private and semi-private spaces of the city and the way in which this permits or prohibits active transportation. This design is particularly important because mobility by foot, bike and public transit also must be practical and convenient enough to fit within the daily travel time budget or Marchetti Constant of one hour per person per day, or in practice 65 to 70 minutes (Marchetti 1994). Residents of cities that are designed around the automobile find that their entire daily travel time budget is eaten up by driving because origins and destinations are so spread out and distant that the car is essential. There is simply no time and no possibility for active modes.

In the U.S., a battle rages around the extent to which parents should hover over and 'helicopter' their children through their lives or enable and encourage them to be independent and 'free ranging' within the limits of safety. The differences between the 'hovering helicoptering' approach and a free-range approach are also presented in the discussions of the exemplary city Freiburg (Chapter 9) and the Vauban (Chapter 10). The value of a free-range approach to child-rearing and the need to create environments amenable to it is demonstrated in the case of a long-time colleague of Jeff Kenworthy's: Felix Laube, brought

FIGURE 6.2
A Critical Mass bike ride in Vancouver, British Columbia, campaigning for more bicycle-friendly and health-supportive physical environments
Source: Jeffrey R. Kenworthy

BOX 6.2 Felix the free-range kid who became a transit whiz

Jeffrey R. Kenworthy and Felix Laube[i]

Over the course of our very long association, Dr Felix Laube proved himself time and time again to have uncanny and exceptional abilities in navigation and orientation, mapping, sense of place and a deep personal appreciation for what it means to have a decent public transit system and cities that allow children to be an active and independent part of public life. He has worked tirelessly over his career, in technical and policy capacities, to try to ensure that the benefits of first-class transit systems (especially rail systems) and a quality public realm are available to others.

Felix traveled on Switzerland's rail system—independently and alone—beginning at age seven, and he demonstrated to me on more than one occasion that he had the entire and very complex (yet also simple in many ways) Swiss rail system with all its interchanges and service details substantially hard-wired in his head. These excursions into different parts of Switzerland at such a young age probably also did no harm to the development of his exceptional language skills—given the prevalence of German, French and Italian (and English) in different parts of the country. Without Dr Laube, the Millennium Cities Database for Sustainable Transport—which is featured early in this book—would never have been possible: He worked not only in the four languages already mentioned, but also many others of which he had a working understanding.

He states about his own childhood:

Growing up as a rather independent-minded child, being blessed with a parental abode right next to a well-served train station was my ticket to freedom. I had quickly figured out how to use the trains and my parents could trust me to travel wherever I chose and to return home safe at the humble age of seven. I put all my pennies left after investing in ice cream to purchasing day train passes that let me explore my country. I often set out on the first train in the morning and would not return before the last, blindly relying on the system to never leave me stranded. These escapes into independence helped me to develop a view of the world which was independent of that of any of my custodians, be it parents or teachers. I am far from an antisocial rebel as a character, but these may have been the seeds to make me the person I am today, who is always prepared to challenge an authoritative and accepted view based on facts I can observe myself and independently.

[i] Dr Felix Laube, Process Management Design in the new Danish Traffic Management System, Emch+Berger Gruppe, Switzerland (www.emchberger.ch)

---

up in Zurich, is an example, par excellence, of the benefits that can be gained by allowing and enabling children to be free-range. His brief cameo in Box 6.2 and Jeff Kenworthy's introduction to it, show the positive benefits that can be derived from this powerful combination of parental guidance and faith in the abilities of one's own offspring and the planning excellence and support needed to create the environments where parents feel it is safe to give children this right to independent mobility.

The planning and urban design challenge then becomes to create urban environments where this is not the case, where daily travel needs can be met by modes that are usually slower than the car, namely walking, cycling and transit. This means developing denser, more mixed-land uses, a city of shorter distances. Newman and Kenworthy (2006) explore what this means in terms of creating centers in cities that have a minimum density of 35 persons per ha.

Urban fabrics theory

The above ideas form a starting point from which a more comprehensive urban design theory and praxis can be developed, one which supports sustainable transportation and better communities. The basis of this is understanding more deeply the three basic city types

TABLE 6.2 Fabric elements of walking, transit and automobile city fabrics

	Walking city	Transit city	Automobile city
Fabric areas	0–2 km 1–2 km (less intensive)	2–8 km 8–20 km (less intensive)	8–20 km 20–40 km (less intensive)
Fabric elements			
Street widths	Narrow	Wide enough for transit	Wide enough for cars/trucks
Squares and public spaces	Frequent as very little private open space	Less frequent as more private open space	Infrequent as much greater private open space
Street furniture	High level for pedestrian activity	High level for transit activity (bus stops, shelters)	High level for car activity (signs, traffic lights)
Street networks	Permeable for easy access, enables high level of service for pedestrians	Permeable for pedestrians, networks to reach transit stops, corridors enable high levels of transit service	Permeability less important, enables high levels of service for cars on freeways, arterials and local roads
Block scale	Short blocks	Medium blocks	Large blocks
Building typologies	High density Minimum usually 100/ha	Medium density minimum usually 35/ha	Low density <35/ha
Building set backs	Zero set backs	Setbacks minimal, for transit noise	Setbacks large for car noise
Building parking	Zero for cars, seats for pedestrians and often racks for bikes	Minimal for cars, seats for pedestrians and transit users and often racks for bikes	Full parking for cars in each functional area
Level of service for transport mode	Pedestrian services allow large flows of pedestrians	Transit services allow large flows of transit users	Car capacity allows large flows of car users

Source: Slightly modified from Newman and Kenworthy (2015)

FIGURE 6.3B
Transit city urban fabric
(Paris, France)
Source: Jeffrey R. Kenworthy

FIGURE 6.3C
Automobile city urban fabric
(Perth, Western Australia)
Source: Jeffrey R. Kenworthy

introduced in Chapter 2: the walking, transit and automobile cities and how they exist in different proportions in all cities today. Newman and Kenworthy (2015) and Newman et al. (2016) have presented this as a new theory of urban fabrics in which the key to future urban planning and urban design is to first recognize where these different fabrics exist in every city, respect the inherent qualities of each fabric and attempt to rejuvenate them in ways that support less automobile dependence. The following sections and graphics build upon what Newman et al. proposed in their 2016 publication. The elements, functions and lifestyles and qualities of walking, transit and auto-city fabrics are set out in Tables 6.2 to 6.4.

The key to better urban planning and urban design in cities becomes how to recognize and protect existing walking and transit city fabrics, rehabilitate them where they have been

TABLE 6.3 Fabric functions and lifestyles of walking, transit and automobile city fabrics

	Walking city	Transit city	Automobile city
Fabric areas	0–2 km 1–2 km (less intensive)	2–8 km 8–20 km (less intensive)	8–20 km 20–40 km (less intensive)
Fabric functions and lifestyles			
1. Movement/accessibility functions	High by walking Medium by transit Low by car	Medium by walking High by transit Medium by car	Low by walking Medium by transit High by car
2. Consumer services – Shopping – Personal services	High local – especially niche services	High in corridors – especially sub-centers	High everywhere – especially shopping centers
3. Large-scale consumer services – Hypermarkets – Warehouse sales – Car yards	Low	Medium	High
4. Process Industry functions	Small – more white collar	Medium – more labour intensive e.g. hospitals, education	Large – more blue collar
5. Face-to-face functions (knowledge economy) – Financial + administration – Creative decision-making (aka Richard Florida) – Knowledge exchange –The arts	High	Medium	Low
6. Car-less functions	High	Medium	Low
7. Lifestyles Walking city lifestyle Transit city lifestyle Automobile city lifestyle	Major Possible Possible	Possible Major Possible	Not possible Difficult Major

Source: Slightly modified from Newman and Kenworthy (2015)

negatively impacted by auto-city design, and extend them selectively into existing automobile city fabrics. The corollary to this is to then minimize the creation of more automobile city fabric in new areas, while recognizing that some parts of cities will remain auto-oriented, but that the excesses and impacts of this orientation can be minimized. Table 6.5 provides some design and statutory guidelines about how to reduce automobile dependence and support more sustainable mobility patterns in each of the three areas.

It is obvious from the above that changing urban fabrics in favour of sustainable modes of transportation needs to be a key focus of urban planning, transportation planning and urban design. Urban design especially needs to deal with the minutiae of design elements in the public realm of cities and attempt to make them more favourable to transit patrons, pedestrians and cyclists. However, there is one overriding and clear factor that needs to be addressed to make workable the prescriptions of the urban fabrics theory just outlined: the

TABLE 6.4 Fabric qualities of walking, transit and automobile city fabrics

	Walking city	Transit city	Automobile city
Fabric areas	0–2 km 1–2 km (less intensive)	2–8 km 8–20 km (less intensive)	8–20 km 20–40 km (less intensive)
Fabric qualities			
1. Urban form qualities			
– Density	High	Medium	Low
– Mix	High	Medium	Low
2. Transport qualities			
– Car ownership	Low	Medium	High
– Level of Service (LOS)	High pedestrian LOS	High transit LOS	High car LOS
– Transport activity	High pedestrian activity	High transit activity	High car activity
3. Economic qualities			
– Development infrastructure costs per capita	Low-medium	Medium-low	High
– GRP per capita	High	Medium	Low
– Labour intensity	High	Medium	Low
4. Social qualities			
– Difference between rich and poor	Low	Medium	High
– Ability to help car-less	High	Medium	Low
– Health due to walking	High	Medium	Low
– Social capital	High	Medium	Low
– Safety	Variable	Variable	Variable
5. Environmental qualities			
– GHG per capita	Low	Medium	High
– Oil per capita	Low	Medium	High
– Footprint per capita	Low	Medium	High

Source: Slightly modified from Newman and Kenworthy (2015)

space allocation for different transportation modes. Gössling et al. (2016) make this factor patently clear by developing a new methodology for identifying and quantifying existing modal space allocation and assessing how fair it is in relation to existing patterns of transportation usage and in allowing modes other than private motorized transportation to compete.

Their case study city is Freiburg, one of the exemplars examined in detail in Chapter 9 as well as in Chapter 10, Box 10.7, which by global standards is already very good in its modal split, its transit system and its general environmental quality for pedestrians and cyclists. However, even here the overwhelming transportation space allocation is in favour of private motorized modes:

> . . . in three of the city quarters studied, 58–59% of all urban transport space is allocated to motorized individual transport, in the form of roads and parking. Only in one recently planned quarter, Vauban, this share is considerably lower at 40%, also because of planning for sustainable transportation that offers opportunities to conveniently use public transport (tram line) and to participate in car-sharing programs.

TABLE 6.5 Design and statutory guidelines to reduce automobile dependence in the three city fabrics

Walking fabric	Transit fabric	Automobile fabric
• Provide walking infrastructure that can cope with pedestrian flows that are the highest priority of the transport system in the area; • Don't widen streets, or insist on setbacks; • Respect the squares, parks and other public spaces of the area and find out their value and potentials; • Ensure sufficient walking space and traffic signals have large times for pedestrian flows; • Enable laneways to be connected and active; • Apply housing policies and planning that maintain a good level of housing with high density and mixed use; • Keep parking to an absolute minimum and preferably underground; • Remove automobile city functions that are harmful to walking and cycling such as through traffic and fast traffic of one-way streets with green light waves and street-based parking in narrow streets; • Remove automobile city elements such as sections of freeway that are harmful to pedestrians or renew them to fit the walking urban fabric.	• Provide quality transit as the major transport system in each corridor of transit-related development; • Ensure corridors are well serviced with transit otherwise the lifeblood of the fabric will shift to automobiles; • Apply housing policies and planning that maintain a good level of housing conditions with at least medium density; • Maintain and create good qualities of the street scale environment to enable local service units to stay and service the local residents within proper walking distances; • Remove automobile elements that are harmful or renew them to fit the transit urban fabric, e.g. maintain roads wide enough for buses and trams, but not high-capacity car use; • Provide as far as is feasible, reserved rights-of-way for transit operations to ensure on-time running and speed-competitiveness with cars; • Optimise transit infrastructure to ensure a high quality of service (e.g. passenger information systems, shelters, system maps); • Build up corridors and centres along historical and new tram and train lines; • Keep parking to a minimum through maximum allowable parking instead of minimum parking requirements.	• Separate functions into clear residential, industrial, retail and other uses, but where it is reasonable, mix the functions that need to be mixed; • Provide large set backs on buildings that need vehicle space but avoid inefficiency where feasible; • Don't increase densities and mixed use without subsequent transit systems to support such densification; • Provide high-capacity roads where needed especially for freight but not for people-orientated economic activity; • Provide sufficient car parking but avoid the large asphalt expanses associated with twentieth-century shopping malls and office parks.

Source: Newman et al. (2016, p. 452)

In comparison, bicyclists were found to be the most disadvantaged in all quarters studied, with transport space allocations of 1.3–4.1% for bicycle lanes. Given that almost every third trip in Freiburg is made by bicycle, findings suggest that bicyclists are at a considerable disadvantage in terms of transport area allocation ...

(p. 674)

Sustainable urban design

In practical terms, how do urban designers assess and compare the multifaceted and complex aspects of different urban fabrics, thereby highlighting where deficiencies exist and where and what kind of interventions might be made to improve those fabrics? Kevin Lynch's seminal 1960 book *The Image of the City* began to systematize in design terms

---

BOX 6.3 Gated communities

Jeffrey R. Kenworthy

A counterpoint to the inclusive, permeable and attractive public environments described next in this chapter is the gated community. Sometimes confused with 'urban villages' (which they are not; see, for example, Sucher 2003), a gated community is the antithesis of everything represented in this chapter on urban design.[i] Gated communities are driven primarily by fear of what is perceived as a dangerous city inhabited by people who are a threat (Blakely and Snyder 1999). As urban development becomes more and more fragmented and the basic services that used to be the province of government become more and more privatized and corporatized, there is a real tendency for people to wall themselves off in private enclaves where amenities, safety and public security are ensured on a private basis (Saul 1999; Graham and Marvin 2001).

These tendencies can be found everywhere from the USA to Brazil, from China to the Middle East (Pow 2009; Bagaeen and Uduku 2012). Gated communities are completely closed either by walls or fences and often guarded. In some parts of the U.S., there are even signs with a silhouette of a person pointing a gun and warning of an 'armed response'. There is no general entry and one must have some type of electronic pass key to open the gates. Only those living there can walk around the streets, but even here the tendency is to drive as gated communities are also based on private transportation where public buses are unable to circulate and metro or suburban train systems do not enter.

Some effort is generally made to at least present a cosmetic face of beauty and amenity within the developments, but fundamentally, gated communities are not predicated on the idea that the vibrancy of public spaces is important or that interaction and mutual support is edifying or even necessarily or especially needed, at least not among 'strangers'. The qualities that are reinforced are exclusivity and a shared, perhaps semi-conscious, awareness that those living all around within the walled estate are driven by the same fears of violation and need for protection and come from the same more privileged class as oneself.

[i] Kenworthy 1991b; Newman and Kenworthy 1992.

---

an understanding of the way cities are laid out and to identify critical elements in city structure—a way of evaluating city form, achieving orientation and legibility of the built environment and thereby a method of making the city more vivid, logical, useable and memorable for residents and visitors alike. He added a new phrase to the designer and planner's lexicon: the 'imageability' of the city. His main elements were *paths*, the main connections along which people travel; *edges*, natural and manmade barriers, both real and perceived; *districts*, significant slices of the city, which are unified in character or qualities or function; *nodes*, major focal points; and *landmarks*, identifiable structures that enable orientation and legibility of an environment (Lynch 1960).

Fast-forward 25 years and we have the publication of another seminal, though perhaps less well-known, work called *Responsive Environments: A Manual for Designers* (Bentley et al. 1985). Bentley and his colleagues foreshadowed the importance of urban design in achieving urban sustainability, especially sustainable transportation and healthier communities. They set out a series of key urban design principles, many of which are quantifiable in various ways and able to be mapped to produce visual representations of what they mean for any slice of urban fabric. These elements provide a systematic way of both comparing the strengths and weaknesses of different places and obtaining the analyses and information needed for thoughtful and focused interventions to improve a place.

The key elements of urban design in this framework, which build on and extend the work of Lynch, are outlined below. In working with these key elements, a series of tools has been developed to portray these elements in their various dimensions and perspectives.[3] This section presents these ideas and tools and shows their relevance to sustainable urban transportation and healthier communities.

(1) District structuring of an area

This is to understand how a place works or does not work, in terms of efficient movement and exchange of goods and services. How can people go about their daily activities? Where are the various centers in a district? Where and of what type is the transit, and how accessible is it? Where are the amenities of a district or region and the workplaces and how are they distributed, and how do these relate to the centers?

Key tool:

Urban structure map

This is done through a mapping exercise and can be used to assess on a regional or district scale where the strengths and weaknesses are in the overall urban design of a place and its interconnectedness. All major and neighborhood centers are respectively marked with 800-meter and 400-meter pedestrian sheds or 'ped-sheds', (see next section) and the major roads and public transport links are highlighted.

(2) Permeability

Good urban fabric, which encourages more sustainable transportation, should have an interconnected network of streets to give a choice of routes and directness between uses for people on foot or bike, and enable easy access to transit as well as allowing transit to easily penetrate and service an area. Permeability, along with the other urban design qualities that follow, make the car simply unnecessary for a high proportion of trips.

Some key tools:

(a) Ped-shed mapping

This involves working out how much of the urban fabric is genuinely accessible by foot, using the limitations of the available street network within a five-minute (400-meter radius) and 10-minute (800-meter radius) walk of a location, typically a center of some sort or perhaps a railway station. Figure 6.4 shows two centers in Perth, Western Australia, a car-based suburban shopping center surrounded by typical suburban houses laid out on curvilinear roads and culs-de sac with a 400-meter and 800-meter circle drawn around their geographic centers. The pink colored areas are the 400-meter pedsheds and the blue are the 800-meter pedsheds.

When the lots that are reachable within a genuine 400-meter and 800-meter walk are expressed as a percentage of the total land area of each circle, we find that for the 400-meter circle surrounding the suburban center, only 10% of the area can be reached on foot and for the 800-meter walk, only 15%. The structure of the road system and the possibilities to walk simply do not permit people on foot to reach more places, due to the circuitous nature of travel.

By contrast, the traditional small center in the inner city of Perth, based on a 'main street' center, and surrounded by residential development on a grid-street network, has 72% of its 400-meter area accessible by foot and 61% of the 800-meter or 10-minute walking radius. The differences are striking and show how it is possible to build-in walkability or, contrariwise, create an urban layout that ensures no one can walk much for any purpose. Both centers fulfilled the urban planning regulations of their day, but the suburban center by its design did not allow for any effective walking access (or cycling and transit). It hard-wired into its design the assumption of a car for nearly all access needs.

(b) Street network/block size and type mapping

Another way of visualizing and quantitatively assessing the ease with which pedestrians (and cyclists) can move around any piece of urban fabric is by measuring the block sizes. A block is defined by any completely connected set of streets (e.g. the four streets that create a traditional perimeter block or the curvilinear roads that form huge blocks of a deformed shape). Culs-de-sac do not form 'blocks' as they terminate and are not interconnected. Block sizes determine how far people must walk to access things, especially how far they need to go before they can change direction. For a reasonably permeable and accessible street layout, blocks should generally be less than 10,000 square meters—that is, no more than 100 meters by 100 meters.

Figure 6.5 demonstrates how typical car-based suburban development creates what are sometimes called 'superblocks' that are impossible for a pedestrian to penetrate. It shows that the major (only) block in the middle is formed by a curvilinear road, which has the

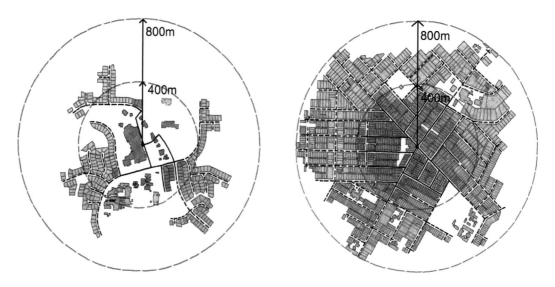

FIGURE 6.4
Ped-sheds of a typical car-based suburban shopping center (left) and more traditional center (right) in Perth, Western Australia
Source: Malcolm and Munira McKay, McKay Urban Design, Perth, Australia

FIGURE 6.5
Huge, impermeable block sizes in car-based suburban layouts
Source: Drawn by Jeff Kenworthy using Google Maps background map at https://www.google.de/maps/@-37.6645664,145.0651309,17z?hl=en (accessed March 14, 2017)

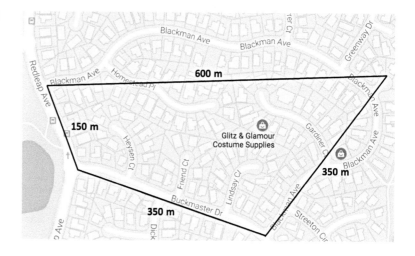

FIGURE 6.6
Large, impermeable, auto-based
superblocks, using road hierarchies,
curvilinear roads and culs-de-sac,
Perth, Western Australia
Source: Jeffrey R. Kenworthy

rough dimensions of 150 m × 600 m × 350 m × 350 m. It means that for pedestrians to get from the lot in the cul-de-sac head in the middle of the southern side of the block to the property in the middle of the northern side, they would need to walk a minimum of 650 meters, whereas the direct route, if there was one, would be less than 200 meters. A more traditional square block of about 100 m × 100 m allowing for short walks and easy changes in direction, would not present such a problem. Figure 6.6 demonstrates the problem in Perth's northern suburbs.

Figure 6.7 shows an actual block size mapping exercise for the 800-meter radius around two town centers in the Frankfurt region, Germany. It shows that, even without many culs-de-sac, parts of the urban fabric can still be not very permeable or pedestrian friendly—such as in significant parts on the east and south of the Neu-Isenburg town center, with a large area of this center having block sizes well over the notional ideal of 10,000 m² or

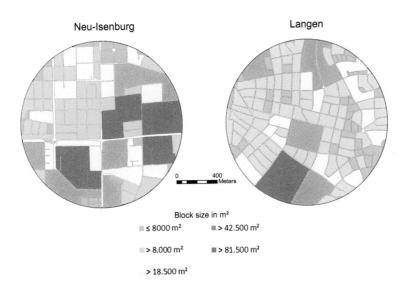

Neu-Isenburg   Langen

Block size in m²

■ ≤ 8000 m²   ■ > 42.500 m²

■ > 8.000 m²   ■ > 81.500 m²

  > 18.500 m²

FIGURE 6.7
Block size mapping in two similar
sub-centers in the Frankfurt region,
Germany
Source: Allam et al. (2016)

less. Langen town center, it can be seen, presents a more permeable environment for pedestrians over a high proportion of its area.

(c) Street connectivity mapping

Another way of measuring permeability is through an analysis of intersections. The number and the kind of intersections determines choice of movement and affects the legibility of the street network for everyone, not only pedestrians. Four-way intersections provide directness of movement to destinations, both visually and physically. T-intersections reduce the choice of movement and force people to change direction. For someone on foot making a local trip (e.g. home to a shop) and wanting to do it quickly and conveniently, the number of turns should be minimized, ideally less than three. In general, a high proportion of four-way intersections and few culs-de-sac afford good connectivity and permeability within urban fabrics, especially for pedestrians and cyclists and they also allow for better circulation by transit vehicles.

Figure 6.8 shows the location, number and type of intersections within a slice of pedestrian-impermeable, auto-based suburbia around a major shopping center and an older, traditional, pedestrian-friendly neighborhood center, both in Perth. Four-way intersections are shown in red, T-intersections in blue and culs-de-sac in yellow. By using a scoring system (e.g. allocating two points for a four-way intersection, one point for a T-intersection and –1 point for a cul-de-sac), it is possible to derive a weighted score for any area in terms of intersections per km² to highlight and compare the level of street connectivity. The location on the left has the equivalent of only eight intersections per km², whereas the one on the right has 100 per km².

(d) Blind frontage mapping

In practice, the permeability of an area for pedestrians is not just determined by block sizes and the structure of the street network. It also depends on more subjective factors such as how personally secure people feel in moving around an area. This can be influenced by how active and safe the street frontages feel. People feel safer when there is a high level of

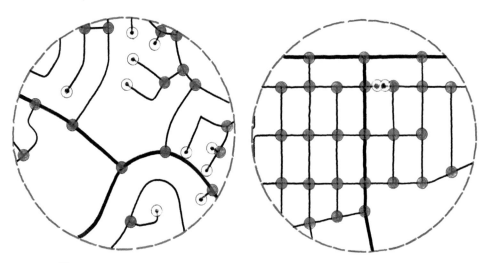

FIGURE 6.8 Street connectivity differences in an auto-based suburban area (left) and an older traditional neighbourhood center with a grid street pattern (right), Perth, Western Australia
Source: Malcolm and Munira McKay, McKay Urban Design, Perth, Australia

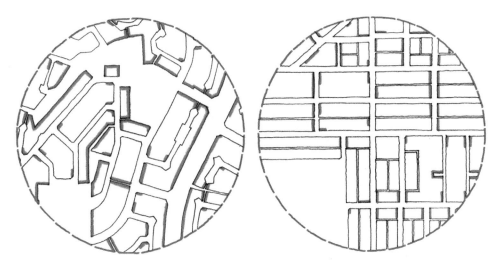

FIGURE 6.9 Blind frontages in red for a suburb (left) and traditional neighborhood (right) in Perth, Western Australia
Source: Malcolm and Munira McKay, McKay Urban Design, Perth, Australia

casual surveillance through windows and doors facing directly onto the street. People feel less safe in an environment where there are blank walls such as high garden fences or the sterile perimeters of large buildings such as banks, supermarkets, many office buildings and parking garages. Highlighting how urban fabrics perform on this factor of blind frontages can be achieved by simply drawing a red line along any sides of a street where properties present a blank face. Figure 6.9 shows this again for two contrasting areas, one a traditional inner city neighborhood and the other a suburban area, both in Perth. The suburban area on the left has 28% blind frontage and the traditional area on the right has 15%, another factor that mitigates against the walkability of auto-city fabrics. Figures 6.10a and b show this issue with a positive and negative example from Copenhagen.

(3) Variety

Variety is a key factor in promoting more sustainable transportation through urban design. The most obvious need for variety is in land uses, i.e. compatible mixed uses, combined with reasonable density are fundamental to encouraging walking, cycling and transit and minimizing car use by shortening travel distances. There is a need to maximize exchange possibilities while minimizing the distance needed to achieve this (e.g. a 200-meter walk to a corner shop, instead of a 5 km drive to a big-box shopping center). For a place to function in a more socially and psychologically healthy way, variety is also needed in the kind of people who inhabit a place, which in turn depends somewhat on the lot sizes that are available for different types of development and the type and range of dwellings that get built for different household types. Variety is also needed in the types of community facilities available, the provision of parkland/greenspaces of different kinds for different types of use and a variety of workplaces.

Some key tools:

(a) Land-use mapping

A major factor in variety is in land uses. Land-use mapping, together with subsequent quantitative analyses, reveal a lot about potential mobility options in an area and the

FIGURE 6.10A A blind street
frontage in Copenhagen, Denmark
Source: Jeffrey R. Kenworthy

FIGURE 6.10B An active street
frontage in the old harbor,
Copenhagen, Denmark
Source: Jeffrey R. Kenworthy

likelihood or otherwise that the area will be a lively and healthy place socially. Figures 6.11 and 6.12 show the land uses in the same two town centers in the Frankfurt region discussed previously. In addition to each map, Figure 6.13 provides pie charts showing the percentage of each different type of land use.

A visual inspection of the maps shows the mixing of land uses to be much greater in Neu-Isenburg and Figure 6.13 shows this quantitatively. Langen has 54% of its area with pure residential uses and 26% of its land area taken up by roads, whereas Neu-Isenburg has 38% residential uses and only 17% of land for roads. In Neu-Isenburg there is a generally better spread of land uses, though both areas have main street style mixed use development on the major roads running north–south (Neu-Isenburg) and east–west (Langen).

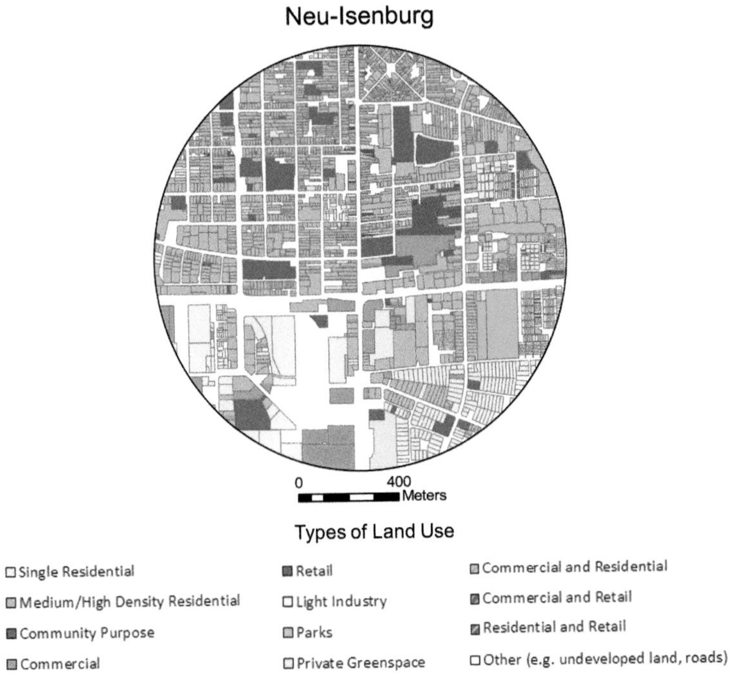

Neu-Isenburg

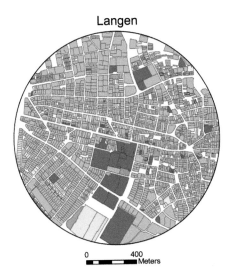

0   400
▬▬▬▬ Meters

Types of Land Use

☐ Single Residential   ▣ Retail   ▣ Commercial and Residential
▣ Medium/High Density Residential   ☐ Light Industry   ▣ Commercial and Retail
▣ Community Purpose   ▣ Parks   ▧ Residential and Retail
▣ Commercial   ☐ Private Greenspace   ☐ Other (e.g. undeveloped land, roads)

FIGURE 6.11
Land use variety map of Neu-
Isenburg town centre, Frankfurt,
Germany
Source: Allam et al. (2016)

Langen

0   400
▬▬▬▬ Meters

Types of Land Use

☐ Single Residential   ▣ Retail   ▣ Commercial and Residential
▣ Medium/High Density Residential   ☐ Light Industry   ▣ Commercial and Retail
▣ Community Purpose   ▣ Parks   ▧ Residential and Retail
▣ Commercial   ☐ Private Greenspace   ☐ Other (e.g. undeveloped land, roads)

FIGURE 6.12
Land use variety map of Langen
town centre, Frankfurt, Germany
Source: Allam et al. (2016)

FIGURE 6.13
Distribution of different types of
land use in two sub-centers in the
Frankfurt Region.
Source: Allam et al. (2016)

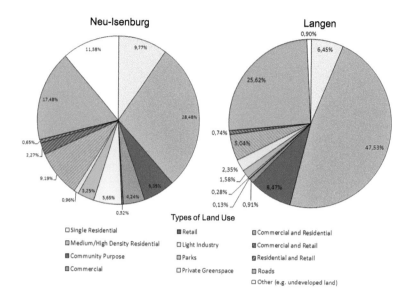

FIGURE 6.13
Distribution of different types of
land use in two sub-centers in the
Frankfurt Region.
Source: Allam et al. (2016)

(b) Lot size mapping

To have a good mix of land uses, lots sizes need to be varied because different land uses simply require different sizes of lots, including a variety of residential lot sizes to allow for many styles of dwellings and densities. This in turn then supports a variety of household types who might occupy those dwellings and thereby creates a more mixed community.

Figures 6.14a and b provide maps and pie charts demonstrating the great uniformity in low-density suburban lot sizes in typical auto-city type of fabric (leading to monocultural types of households and mobility patterns based on cars). This contrasts to typical inner areas with walking and transit city fabrics and a great variety in lots sizes, a good mix of different kinds of households and diverse mobility options based on all modes of transportation.

The pie charts reveal how virtually 50% of the lots in the auto-city fabric are between 500–750 m^2, designed for standard suburban houses, whereas in the walking-transit city fabric there is a strong variety in lots sizes, reflecting both different land uses and different types of housing as well. Of course, this exercise can be repeated for residential lot sizes only, as this is particularly instructive in specifically assessing housing diversity.

(c) Other variety features

In highlighting variety in any community there are a range of other maps that can be produced based on, for example, dwelling types, workplaces, community facilities, parklands and other features. These serve to highlight the strengths and weaknesses of a area and possible opportunities for improvement, especially to diversify mobility choices and to minimize trip distances.

(4) Legibility

In the same way that people read books, it is possible to read urban environments, or not. Imagine being parachuted blindfolded from an aircraft, not knowing at all where one is. You land in the middle of New York City (or the inner part of a city such as Paris, London, Amsterdam, San Francisco, Zurich, Munich or many others). Within moments you know where you are or, if not, there are plenty of ways to work it out. Why? Because there are so

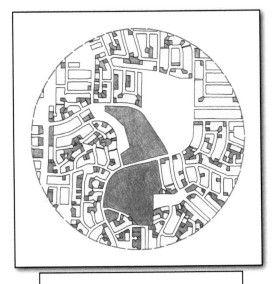

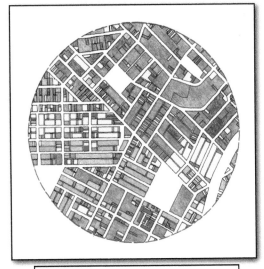

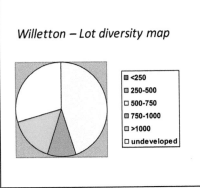

Willetton – Lot diversity map

Mount Lawley – Lot diversity map

Legend:
- <250
- 250-500
- 500-750
- 750-1000
- >1000
- undeveloped

FIGURE 6.14A
Lot size variety in auto city fabric, Perth, Western Australia
Source: Malcolm and Munira McKay, McKay Urban Design, Perth, Australia

FIGURE 6.14B
Lot size variety in walking/transit city fabric, Perth, Western Australia
Source: Malcolm and Munira McKay, McKay Urban Design, Perth, Australia

many visual cues and signs, so many landmarks and features and other things such as odors and noises that can help to identify the place and distinguish it from other cities. The city by its very nature has enabled you to read it. For the same reasons, in a short time, one would quickly figure out where one is standing within the city and thereby how to navigate to some other place. Every corner one turns there is likely to be something different that distinguishes it from the next vista, thus providing a sense of orientation, of being able to go somewhere on foot or by some form of transit that is likely to be nearby (e.g. entry to a named metro station). One is drawn along by the visual interest and diversity of the streets and buildings and a feeling that the urban environment is navigable and understandable.

Then imagine being parachuted blindfolded into some vast suburban area in any city with literally nothing but suburban houses for as far as the eye can see. The houses all look the same, the streets go around in circles, there's nothing over one story high, all the houses are the same age and of similar design, there are no mixed land uses, no signs on any buildings. The urban landscape simply repeats itself with nothing distinctive or unusual to provide a landmark or guidepost. It would be very difficult for anyone to pick what city they had been cast into and almost impossible to navigate to anywhere else, certainly not on foot and probably not by transit either. Possibly the only real visual cues as to your location would be the number plates or stickers on the cars and a car would be the only way out of the maze. Legibility is therefore about how easy is it to understand an urban environment and to orient oneself within it, particularly on foot. Can we read the urban fabric? What kind of a sense of place does it exude? What characteristics within a place make it unique and enable people to distinguish it from other places? Automobile city fabrics mostly fail abysmally on this, whereas walking and transit city fabrics, with their density and variety and more permeable and logical street patterns, perform much better.

Some key tools:

(a) Legibility analysis mapping

This tool is drawn straight from Lynch (1960) and maps the key elements of a district, neighborhood and street, including buildings and public places. It follows Lynch's analysis of paths, nodes, landmarks, edges and districts, marking each on a map with identifiable colors. It is akin to the district structuring exercise, though with more detail.

(b) SAFE Walk Assessment mapping

This map refers to how *Safe*, *Attractive*, *Friendly* and *Efficient* is each street in a district or neighborhood. It is aimed at assessing the pedestrian amenity and quality of a street and highlighting that streets need attention for improvement and in what respects. Each street is scored based on fieldwork using a method that ranks each street as poor, medium or good, and color-codes them as such on a map to show a quick visual impression of the distribution of such streets in an area (the method is described in detail in an online figure for Chapter 6 on the Taylor & Francis website). The method is subjective by nature and is best done with pairs of assessors so that some joint decision is made on the street's performance. Both sides of each street are assessed. Figure 6.15 shows a map of the two previous town centers in the Frankfurt region that were assessed in this way.

The results indicate that generally pedestrian amenity in both these centers is either good or very good, with only two streets being considered poor.

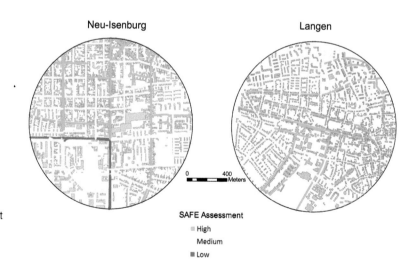

Neu-Isenburg   Langen

0   400
Meters

SAFE Assessment
■ High
   Medium
■ Low

FIGURE 6.15
Results of a SAFE street assessment
of pedestrian amenity in two
Frankfurt town centers.
Source: Allam et al. (2016)

(5) Robustness

Robustness is the flexibility and ability of a place to change or reinvent itself over time. This includes the block and street layout, buildings and public spaces. The walking and transit city fabrics in cities worldwide have shown remarkable robustness, though many have also been destroyed by auto-city design and planning such as huge freeways barreling through neighborhoods and other factors such as war or 1960s-style 'urban renewal'. The core areas of countless European cities today contain buildings and street layouts that date back to mediaeval times. The city of Bern, for example, contains many hundreds of occupied stone buildings that today sell clothes, mobile phones, food, furniture and a myriad of other modern wares etc., but that many centuries ago may have been occupied by blacksmiths, tanneries and other uses typical of that period (see online photo in Chapter 6).

In attempting to assess this item in any area and to look for ways in particular of rejuvenating urban fabrics for reduced automobile dependence, greater sustainability and better communities, urban designers often look for particular features in the built environment, to map them and then explore how they might be exploited to improve an area.

Some key tools:

(a) Robust lot and building mapping

Here urban designers look for possibilities for redevelopment. For example, corner lots offer good potential because they have two street frontages that might permit mixed use development compatible with the different types of streets. Some larger lots can be subdivided into smaller ones to allow more dwellings to be constructed or redeveloped for multi-family housing. They also look for older buildings with the potential to be changed to another more suitable or relevant use, or mixed uses, through vertical or horizontal subdivision.

(b) Solar orientation mapping

Urban designers also look towards maximizing the number of lots that are oriented for passive solar design and energy efficiency (e.g. maximizing solar gain in the winter period, basically on a north–south or east–west axis). Typically, car-based suburbs using curvilinear roads have many lots that are arranged in a haphazard fashion with no thought for solar orientation, whereas urban fabrics employing a grid-street system generally have a high proportion of better oriented lots.

(c) Building edge mapping

The walkability of an area also depends on the qualities of the way buildings interact with the street (see also previous discussion of blind frontage mapping—Figure 6.9). Generally, walkability is improved where privatized or ambiguous space is minimized and publicly accessible buildings are maximized. This creates a greater sense of security and interest for pedestrians. Ground floor building edges, such as blank walls or those facing hostile land uses such as car parks, can exude a sterile atmosphere and appear unfriendly, unsafe and cold for people passing by. On the other hand, buildings can have windows that allow an inside view or attractive activities outside them which provide a sense of surveillance both from residential and non-residential buildings. The latters supports a richer public life and more sustainable mobility.

(6) Visual appropriateness

Visual appropriateness is one of three remaining characteristics of sustainable urban design that have a degree more subjectivity than the previous ones. Visual appropriateness is about how buildings read and whether it is easy to interpret the uses that occur inside. It can be argued that this quality relates strongly to public buildings, such that a town hall should look like a town hall and its design should reflect its civic function and be recognized as such by people wishing to access it.

Visual appropriateness helps people to recognize the things they are looking for and therefore to get there faster. For example, it is common in some areas for residential buildings to be converted to law suites and doctors' or dentists' surgeries or perhaps office uses. This enhances mixed use and supports shorter trips, but it can also be difficult to locate these facilities when the building is reading as a house or apartment.

It can also be argued that in pedestrian-based environments, where people are moving at 3 or 4 km/h, buildings should have aesthetic qualities and details that can only be appreciated at that speed and that enhance the beauty and enjoyment of walking, as opposed to structures designed to be 'read' at automobile speeds of 60 km/h or more (Gehl 2010).

Key tool:

Visual appropriateness photography

This is done by photographing key publicly relevant buildings in an area and assessing whether they work in terms of their function and if not how they might be improved to assist the navigability of an urban enviornment.

(7) Richness

This is another urban design quality that influences both the walkability of a community and its sociability and attraction for people. It is about color, vibrancy and the sensory experience of a place, not just with the eyes, but also sound, odor and movement. Urban environments should provide a variety of sensory experiences for people throughout the day. Sergio Porta, professor of urban design at Strathclyde University, talks about 'olfactory cones' in a city, which basically involves producing maps of streets according to the dominant scents that occur in different places such as coffee or flowers (personal communication 2001).

Some key tools:

(a) Day/night use mapping

For town and neighborhood centers it can be important to keep the area active in some form throughout most of the day. This means it needs uses that attract people for different purposes throughout the day and night. It is important for walkability to maintain a sense of public safety and having some critical mass of activity and natural surveillance during the night assists this. The adequacy of this factor can be explored and opportunities for improvement suggested through day/night mapping, which involves identifying and marking on a map in different colors those publicly relevant buildings that are occupied only during the day (post office, libraries, many shops etc), those that are only active in the night (night clubs) and those that are operating day and night (cinemas, drug stores, gyms etc).

(b) Visual interest photography and mapping of public buildings and places

This can be used to characterize the richness of urban fabrics or the lack of it. Older town centres are often composed of publicly relevant buildings (theatres, pubs, shops) that are beautiful in their design and architecture. In modern manifestations of the same kind of centers, buildings have frequently become monotonous and unattractive with bulky concrete forms, blank walls and unimaginative facades. Distinguishing features in the urban environment which are critical for people's mental maps of an area are rare and poor street layouts combine to make places harder to find. Mapping and photographing the publicly relevant buildings and assessing their visual interest can help to find ways of enhancing the buildings to improve the richness of an area and improve walkability.

(8) Personalization

Personalization is about whether people of any age, background, religion, gender or ethnic origin feel a sense of ownership and comfort in their public environments or at least some parts of it. This, in turn, can significantly affect whether they want to negotiate an area on foot or bike. It also affects the length of time they are likely to spend in a public environment and therefore whether they will develop any sense of community and connection with others and the strength of that bond. A public realm that, for example, caters for activities such as chess or other games, table tennis etc. in an attractive setting will encourage people to spend more time there. This increases people's familiarity with a place and also their desire to arrive by foot or bike. Such places are not those that one drives to because they are not in settings that are car-oriented. Also, it has been shown that the longer people spend in the public spaces of a city, the more money they are likely to spend, so it tends to also be good for the local economy (Monheim 1988).

Key tool:

Sense of place photography and mapping of shopping places

This is aimed at capturing the human qualities, people-friendliness and sense of shared ownership that public spaces exude, and identifying the places where this is not working and how that might be improved. Mapping the different kinds of shopping places— essentially the three major types of main street, big box or mixed pedestrian/bike/transit/car shopping areas—can help to identify how this major local activity can be made less car-dependent and attractive as a human experience and where interventions might be made to improve these two aspects. The three photos from Frankfurt, Budapest and Lisbon in Figures 6.16a, b and c show this feeling of 'personalization' in public spaces.

FIGURE 6.16A
People of all ages need to feel at home in cities, Frankfurt, Germany
Source: Jeffrey R. Kenworthy

FIGURE 6.16B
A mother and child feel comfortable
enough in a city square to
spontaneously sit down and enjoy it,
Budapest, Hungary
Source: Jeffrey R. Kenworthy

FIGURE 6.16C
Groups of men gather and linger in
public spaces, Lisbon, Portugal
Source: Jeffrey R. Kenworthy

Conclusion

This chapter has reviewed the importance of urban design as a force in cities for helping to create excellent public environments that knit together urban fabrics. The linkages to sustainable transportation are clear and compelling. Fractured and ugly automobile-dominated landscapes make walking and cycling almost impossible because of the distances involved and the hostility of the public realm for people. Similarly, transit can't work properly in places designed around and for the automobile. On the contrary, beautiful and functional public environments, streets, squares and parks designed for the enjoyment and comfort of people rather than the convenience of the car help bring communities together and facilitate non-automobile access. The discussion has introduced a theory of urban fabrics built around the concept of the walking, transit and automobile cities (Chapter 2) and how urban and transportation planners might change their practices based on an understanding of these different types of urban fabrics. The chapter has also briefly explained a key set of tools that urban designers use to assess urban environments and to formulate proposals for the betterment of places so that they might appeal much more to people on foot and bicycle and those who use transit.

Questions for discussion

- Why is urban design so critical in shaping cities towards more sustainable transportation?
- What are the key pillars of urban design that work in favour of reducing automobile dependence?
- What tools are available for assessing the urban design qualities of cities and proposing improvements to urban places?
- Choose a piece of urban fabric in your own community and assess it for its urban design quality and formulate proposals to address any shortcomings found. What would be needed to implement such changes?

Additional resources

Good urban design and planning for walkability and healthier communities are receiving increasing recognition around the world. Below are some resources that link urban design, sustainable transportation and healthy communities. They represent a small sample of some of the tools, implementation strategies and new directions that are specifically aimed at enhancing walkability, active transportation and healthy communities and that embrace or expand upon the key principles described above (all accessed 23 May 2016):

- Walkability Index from UBC: health-design.spph.ubc.ca/tools/walkability-index/ (includes published articles: e.g. Frank et al. (2010) The development of a walkability index: application to the 'Neighborhood quality of life study', *British Journal of Sports Medicine*, vol 44, no 13, pp. 924–33).
- Walk Score: www.walkscore.com/walkable-neighborhoods.shtml (provides a rating of whole cities and a walkability score for every address in the USA, Canada and Australia).
- Walkable Communities: www.walkable.org
- Walkable City: Jeff Speck, summarized in: www.citylab.com/cityfixer/2012/12/10-techniques-making-cities-more-walkable/4047/ (Speck 2012).
- Walkable America: www.walkableamerica.org/checklist-walkability.pdf (detailed micro-scale walkability checklist).
- Smart Growth America: Complete Streets: www.smartgrowthamerica.org/complete-streets and www.smartgrowthamerica.org/complete-streets/complete-streets-fundamentals/complete-streets-faq
- Urban Land Institute: Retrofitting Suburbia, uli.org/wp-content/uploads/2009/10/Sustainable-Suburbs-Retrofitting-Suburbia.pdf (also see: Dunham-Jones and Williamson 2011).
- Safe, Healthy and Active Transportation. Toolkit—www.safestates.org/?TranspToolkit2.
- *Mexico City's new office of urban design or Public Space Authority*—citiscope.org/story/2016/what-mexico-city-learned-devoting-office-designing-public-spaces?utm_source=Citiscope&utm_campaign=a7dbbe3fba-Mailchimp_2016_03_31&utm_medium=email&utm_term=0_ce992dbfef-a7dbbe3fba-71030809

- *www.urb-i.com* Provides before and after photographs of worldwide examples of public space transformations (accessed January 1, 2017).

Notes

1   See Levine 2006 for a discussion of how much U.S. metropolitan planning and zoning work against TOD and densification and promotes sprawl development patterns.

2   See: www.youtube.com/watch?v=RLfasxqhBNU and www.youtube.com/watch?v=wuxMuMr XUJk (accessed 3 June 2016).

3   These tools were collected together into a *Sustainable Urban Design: Practical Fieldwork Project* booklet (Department for Planning and Infrastructure 2002a) by urban designers (Malcolm and Munira McKay) in the then Department for Planning and Infrastructure in Western Australia, and utilized for a course on Sustainable Urban Design. This section utilizes information in this booklet.

Public policy and effective citizen participation for more sustainable transportation: methods and examples

The public, policy and participation

This chapter examines the areas of transportation policy and public participation with a view towards how each of these areas can interact with and help sustainable transportation (ST) efforts. Policy-making, planning and participation can be viewed as intimately entwined processes. Defining what makes for good policy-making and effective public participation is neither an easy matter nor one about which there is much consensus. Both may be viewed as areas of 'wicked problems', areas that do not lend themselves to simple and 'scientific' solutions (Rittel and Webber 1973), as well as of 'contested definitions', matters about which there is often little agreement as to how an issue or problem is defined (Day 1997; Roberts 2004). The variety of approaches to policy-making and the general study of policy, as opposed to closely linking policy and political behavior, are complicated fields that are attracting more attention (John 2012). It is important to understand much of transportation policy-making and participation in the context of process rather than product because of their complex and multifaceted nature. Policy-making and participation for ST emphasize processes informed by a vision for a preferred future. Because they are so closely interrelated, they are treated together here rather than in separate chapters.

Who is the 'public', what is 'public'?

The 'public' generally refers to a large body of individuals, the 'people', sharing or united in some broad common characteristic such as citizenship in the same nation. That which is 'public' (open to use or access by citizens) is often best understood in contrast to its opposite, 'private'—that which is owned by individuals or corporations and not subject to access or use by a people at large. But these meanings often become blurred when one considers real-life situations. Most streets and roads are 'public', open to the people at large and usually built at public expense. But most vehicles are privately owned, serving private purposes. Many other facilities, such as shipping ports, terminals and airports, are financed by public funds but operated for the benefit of private entities such as shipping lines and airlines. The public may have access to such facilities but the facilities benefit private interests.

Participation in planning and arriving at the best solutions to problems relies also on notions of what constitutes the public interest. In previous decades, the automobile lobby was very effective at creating the illusion that the interstate highway system in the U.S. constituted a kind of 'unitary public interest' where everybody in society, without exception, would be unequivocally benefited by the new freeway network. This is crudely—and today laughably— presented in a film, *Highway Hearing*, whose opening credits state: '*As A Public Service, The Dow Chemical Company Presents . . .*' and proceeds in a manipulative way to show that any opposition to the Interstate system at the time was simply misguided. Various misguided individuals from farmers to primary school teachers, are depicted throughout the film as gradually, and sometimes reluctantly, coming around to the idea of its 'undeniable benefits for everyone, especially children, of big new roads everywhere across the country and through all the cities'.[1]

The question of what is the 'public interest' in any planning exercise is a complex and difficult topic and it is beyond the scope of this book to give adequate voice to it.[2] There are many 'public interests' in every setting and for every problem in planning and transportation, so that there is no unitary public interest. The problem (and opportunity) this presents in sustainable transportation is summarized by Townsend (2003):

> From the point of view of those who see motorisation as good, it is the free choices of individuals which lead to changes, and rent seekers or special interests which prevent solutions and the accommodation of motorisation, leading to sub-optimal outcomes. From the point of view of those who view too much motorisation as destructive, it is through the actions of automotive interests and lobby groups that transport choices are reduced.
>
> (pp. 306–7)

Public policy

Public policy as a field developed as part of the movement towards improved planning, rationalization of governmental processes, and greater accountability and transparency to the public and its officials. While there are many excellent and competing attempts at defining public policy by scholars (Gerston 1997; Cochran and Malone 1999; Anderson, 2000; Birkland 2005; John 2012), public policy can be defined for the purposes of this chapter as the creation and institutionalization of government plans of action, the definition of terms and concepts involved in such policies, and the body of discussion and discourse that surrounds and emerges from policy formulation and deliberation. Dimensions and differentiations within public policy include:

- the locus of policy-making, as well as its geographical target and locus of implementation—local, regional, state, provincial, national or international;
- types of policy that include 'substantive' (addressing what government wants to do), 'procedural' (addressing how government should accomplish its goals and objectives), 'promoting' change, control/regulation, or distributing/redistributing certain goods or services;[3]
- policy scope, which refers to whether policy is intended to be narrow or far reaching, long enduring or of a delimited timeframe.

Scholars of public policy also categorize policy as to whether it is administrative, within a legislative framework, or whether it is action-oriented, such as a mandate to create many new jobs within a short time to resolve an economic crisis. They also pay close attention to the cast of 'actors' in policy 'dramas', as well as how a policy agenda is developed and executed.

Transportation policy: from mobility promotion to mobility management and sustainability

Transportation policy is a domain of public policy, and ST policy is a recent area that has developed out of dissatisfaction with business as usual (BAU). It is a challenging area because it involves the environment, the economy, the spatial form of cities and personal behavior and values. At present, while BAU still dominates much policy, there are many efforts under way to develop and promote ST policy. These range from broad policy studies to localized efforts to reduce the domination of private motor vehicles. Some governments are actively developing ST policies, while some of those that are lagging are being prodded by non-governmental organizations (NGOs) to develop better policies.[4]

Prior to the twentieth century, most transportation planning and policy-making was formulated in response to technological developments and innovations, such as the newly emerging railroad, steamship, bicycle or automobile and improved road surfaces and engineering. Strategic developments involving decades or centuries of comprehensive planning and resource commitments, such as the Roman ports and roads networks and Inca roads system, were exceptions. Much policy was ad hoc, developing around specific projects. Some policy-making in the nineteenth and early twentieth centuries was oriented towards 'grand visions', such as the Erie Canal, linking the Hudson River with the Great Lakes in North America, or France's vision of an improved road network linking Paris with the most far-flung of provinces. With France and Germany as exceptions, most policy was oriented towards a lesser scale—a small canal, a few miles of turnpike or an improved port facility. Rarely were these linked to a national plan or policy, systematized or even seen as in need of broad-ranging intervention.[5]

The complexity of transportation issues

The locus of transportation policy-making ranges from local and regional to national and international. From the point of view of ST, some of the most interesting and exciting initiatives are occurring at the local and regional levels. This section surveys this range broadly, with more detail about exemplary efforts included in the case studies. Part of the complexity that policy-makers face is trying to sort through and address the many issues posed to them, including:

- Whose trips are most valuable and to whom: individual citizens, freight interests, tourists?
- Which trips are most valuable and for whom: commute to work, local goods distribution, long-distance freight, farm to market, leisure or service-seeking?
- How can one manage the conflicts among these competing interests, levels of society and broader issues, such as economy and the environment?
- Which services and investments should be supported from public funding and which should be left to individuals and private-sector interests?

These questions are often in the minds of policy-makers and policy-shapers at all levels of transportation decision-making.

Transportation policy in the twentieth century: a global perspective

A survey of the greatly varied terrain of transportation policy around the globe captures the great differences between what occurs in the wealthier nations and cities and the situation of the poorer nations and cities. Many wealthy countries seem to have an oversupply of roads, while many less wealthy countries seem to suffer from an undersupply of good roads and few mobility options in town or countryside. Many nations are giving much attention to the facilitation of global freight movement, which is seen by some as contradicting efforts to address climate change and greenhouse gas production (Curtis, undated). The national and international emphasis on freight mobility contrasts with 'stage centre' concerns about personal or passenger transportation in most cities and urban regions, wealthy or impoverished. The great variation in response to urban transportation issues across the spectrum of wealth and poverty is striking. Some cities, rich or poor, are investing significantly in transit, walking and bicycling, while many, rich or poor, are investing in roads and private vehicle expansions. Many nations are directing policy efforts towards deregulation, liberalization and expansion of transportation to facilitate global trade, while some cities within these same nations are struggling to better manage personal mobility and promote localization. Interest in significant changes in policy formulation, especially around integrating the various 'silos' of transportation decision-making, has been growing in recent years, especially in Europe (Givoni and Banister 2010) but, except at the level of some progressive cities, the U.S. and Canada seem to be moving along the BAU trajectory. Hence, any generalizations must be taken with caution since so much variability is involved.

After World War II, large-scale development of transportation policy began to occur.[6] The post-war period may be viewed as three somewhat different periods: 1945 to 1970, 1970 to 1990 and 1990 to the present.

1945–1970: reconstruction and expansion American style and its discontents

Some of the important elements of transportation history in the post-World War II period have been summarized in Chapter 3. In general, the most important policy issues of the period from 1945 to 1970 centered on developing policies, plans and resources for rebuilding or expanding transportation infrastructure, and refurbishing, replacing and modernizing transportation material such as buses, trains, shipping and aviation fleets that were damaged, destroyed or simply worn out in the war years.

There were wide-ranging differences as well as some convergences in policy and investment emphases among nations and regions during this period. At one end of the spectrum was the U.S. policy and investment emphasis on highway expansion that culminated in the 45,000 linear miles (72,000 km) of an interstate highway system. At the other end was Japan, which began planning for major rail improvements in the 1950s and opened its first high-speed rail line, the Shinkansen, connecting Tokyo and Osaka, on 1 October 1964, in time for the Tokyo Olympics. Most other industrial countries were in between, contenting themselves with modest improvements to existing railways, or allowing railways to shrink, while some highway expansion was undertaken.

Decolonization began in several developing parts of the planet. There was a fair amount of variability as to whether the colonial transportation systems, roads and railways, designed for resource extraction and military and administrative movements, were maintained, abandoned or, in a few cases, improved. Some countries, such as Senegal and Zimbabwe, have maintained the good road systems that have been one of their few useful legacies from the colonial era. Others, such as Cameroon, have not maintained their roads well.[7] Commercial aviation services, generally affordable only by business and government officials, replaced some of the former colonial surface transportation services leading to the deterioration of some surface networks and services. This period also saw the beginnings of trade liberalization, deregulation and privatization that were to significantly affect several aspects of national and international policy and practice, especially in freight and air services over the next several decades.[8]

1970–1990: rethinking cities and highways; beginnings of global 'liberalization'

The period from 1970 to 1990 saw many public and political reactions against the policy emphasis on roadway expansion in many places, especially in cities, as well as their continued expansion in other places. In some countries, including the U.S., Canada and the U.K., both occurred.[9] Some reactions against pro-highway policy led to innovations aimed at improving the overall quality of urban life. The movement towards traffic calming in cities began in the 1970s and 1980s, spreading in the 1990s across the globe from Europe to Australia, Japan and, eventually, the U.S. and Canada.[10] A few Latin American cities re-examined their planning policies. The city of Curitiba, Brazil, led the way in planning for future growth and environmental and transportation needs, and influenced changes for transit, walking and bicycling that have taken place in Bogotá, Colombia, in recent years.

At the national and international levels, a few countries began railway improvements, but most policy energy was directed towards liberalization, deregulation and privatization.[11] Such efforts resulted in the lowering of barriers to long-distance transportation services—whether on land, sea or air—as well as significant movement in the direction of promoting competitiveness among providers. Privatization of services previously in the public sector and deregulation took several forms and varied considerably from country to country. In some cases, private-sector expertise in management and personnel preparation assisted in the modernization of public services. In other cases, such as that of Thatcher's England, the way privatization and deregulation occurred served to weaken and undermine many public services (Pucher and Lefevre 1996; Bruun 2014).

FIGURE 7.1
Traffic calming antique cannon and cannonball bollards protect pedestrians in Old Havana, Cuba, and are authenticated by Latin America Colonial historian Nancy Elena van Deusen.
Source: Preston L. Schiller

BOX 7.1 **Curitiba and Bogotá: political leadership makes a big difference**

Curitiba, Brazil, and Bogotá, Colombia, exemplify how political leadership can influence urban planning and investment in a sustainable direction. Theirs are two very different stories. Curitiba planned a concentration of population along developing corridors to be served by a busway. Bogotá made planning and investment changes within the context of an already built environment to improve equity through bicycle and pedestrian amenities. Both opted for the lower-cost bus rapid transit (BRT). But as ridership grows, the limits of BRT become evident, and when politics changes—as it has in Bogotá—some of the recent accomplishments are at risk.

Curitiba has attracted much global attention to its accomplishments. During the 1960s, this Brazilian city—with approximately 1.9 million residents (metro area 3.4 million)—began to transform its planning: environmental,

continued

land use, social and transportation. Architect, planner and later Mayor Jaime Lerner was in the forefront of this transformation. The result has been linear dense development served well by a BRT system of about 60 km that has brought many innovations to that transit form. Daily transit ridership is approximately 2 million.

In the mid- to late1990s and early 2000s, under the political leadership of Mayors Enrique Peñalosa (1995 to 2001, re-elected in 2015) and Antanas Mockus (2001 to 2003), Bogotá (city population 7.9 million and a metro area of about 10 million) moved in a more progressive transportation direction. It created a *ciclovía* bicycle–pedestrian way, expanded parks, reclaimed some street space from cars for larger pedestrian and public spaces, cleared some slums to create public spaces, improved housing in other areas for its poor, and introduced the TransMillenio BRT, whose daily ridership currently is approximately 2.2 million over a 12-line network of 88 km, providing a much needed efficient and affordable transportation option for all citizens. The city became safer and municipal government became more honest and transparent. Some of that progress was lost due to political change after Peñalosa's departure when some of the progressive changes in parking controls and pedestrianization were weakened or reversed—a demonstration of the fragility of some urban transportation reform efforts. Peñalosa returned as mayor of Bogotá in 2015 and immediately resumed his important work there, which included hosting the 2016 World Summit of Local and Regional Leaders of the United Cities and Local Governments (UCLG).[i]

[i] For more information see Margolis (1992), Hyatt (2005) and Pardo (2008); for more information on the role of Gil (Guillermo) Peñalosa, whose important work on walking, bicycling, parks and other public spaces preceded his brother Enrique's mayorship, see Parasram (2003), Peñalosa (2005), McManus (2006), Cohen (2008) and www.walkandbikeforlife.org; for more recent accounts of Peñalosa see www.pps.org/reference/epenalosa-2/; http://citiscope.org/story/2016/bogota-mayor-enrique-peñalosa-making-better-cities and www.bogota2016.uclg.org/en

Source: Preston L. Schiller

1990s to present: transportation policy moves in various directions at different levels

At the international level, the Kyoto Climate Change Protocol, commonly referred to as the 'Kyoto Accords', spurred an interest in moving transportation in a more sustainable direction. The extent to which the goals of Kyoto have been met is controversial since progress in meeting these goals can be confounded by the effects of global recession. Despite the Kyoto efforts, transportation-related greenhouse gas emissions (GHGs) continue to rise.[12] International efforts, such as COP-21 in Paris in 2016 and its successors,[13] continue to address climate change but do so without the sense of urgency and mandate that many environmentalists believe is necessary at this time.

More than a few countries have developed policy and planning discussions that show some promise in terms of ST, including pricing reforms, carbon taxes and other measures that might lead to reduced transportation emissions, although the thrust of investment has not always been matched by results. Many countries in Europe and Asia have expanded and improved performance of railways, with better intermodal integration for freight and passengers, and a few have begun programs aimed at moving some freight off rubber wheels and onto steel wheels.

China, after an aggressive period of automobile promotion and freeway construction, has also developed a nationwide high-speed train network of over 11,000 km (which is half the world total) with a planned total of 22,481 km as of September 2014. Since 2011, it has also begun to show signs in its cities of a plateau and reversal in car use growth. China is also building metro systems in some 82 cities, with Shanghai and Beijing having among the longest systems in the world, developed essentially in about a 20-year period.

The exemplars chapter provides more detail about Chinese urban transportation in Beijing, Shanghai and Guangzhou (Gao and Kenworthy 2016).

A few nations are promoting bicycling at city and intercity levels. However, as in the 1970s and 1980s, much national and international effort has gone into the transportation side of trade liberalization, deregulation and other factors facilitating globalization and the '3000 mile Caesar salad'.[14,15] There are several promising ongoing discussions, but little in the way of enactment outside of progressive cities and a few countries (see Box 7.3 below).

More progress towards ST has been achieved at the level of cities and urban regions than at state, national or international levels. Many cities in Europe and several in Asia have been working for greater traffic restraint, more pedestrianized commercial streets and public spaces, and improved transit and cycling networks (for several examples see Chapters 9 and 10). A few national and international alliances of cities have formed around the goals put forward in the Kyoto Accords. In the European Union, the CIVITAS Initiative promotes ST projects among its many members, from Ploesti to Preston and Toulouse to Tallinn. The Partnership on Sustainable Low Carbon Transport (SLoCaT), which is described in the 'growing more exemplars' chapter, is a 'multi-stakeholder partnership of

---

BOX 7.2 The unfulfilled promise of the U.S. Intermodal Surface Transportation Efficiency Act (ISTEA) reform

Although the U.S. did not join in the Kyoto Accords, it did open the door to a new policy direction with its passage of the Intermodal Surface Transportation Efficiency Act (ISTEA) in 1991 when Congress decided that the old way of building highways, without regard to the negative consequences for communities, had to change. The federal government provides a large amount of transportation funding to state and local government, and its funding and guidelines influence and leverage a great deal of planning and projects construction at those levels. The 1991 bill had several remarkable departures from previous BAU bills: it improved funding for walking, bicycling and transit, and attempted to shift a good deal of decision-making from the State Departments of Transportation (SDOTs) to the regional Metropolitan Planning Organizations (MPOs), but was unable to comprehensively change the overall direction of transportation policy and investment. Highway investments and planning continued to dominate, and highway interests weakened the next several iterations of 'Transportation Equity Act for the 21st Century' (TEA–21 1998), which preserved most of ISTEA's important policy features but began several compromises in which SDOTs regained more authority;[i] the 'Safe, Accountable, Flexible, and Efficient Transportation Equity Act of 2005: A Legacy for Users' (SAFETEA–LU 2005), which continued the attempt to address funding equity issues among states while adding a few new programs and not significantly changing the policy provisions of TEA-21; the 'Moving Ahead for Progress in the 21st Century' (MAP-21 2012) legislation reflects the inability of co-operation between the Executive and Congressional branches in the years leading up to the Transportation Act's reauthorization, their inability to agree upon long-term policy and funding fixes, generally gave SDOTs more power at the expense of MPOs, consolidated the several pedestrian and bicycle programs into one program and cut its funding. The next act, 'Fixing America's Surface Transportation Act' (FAST 2015), continues the trajectory of devolving federal transportation authority to the SDOT; it has a couple of good policy measures, such as including rail transportation in the general transportation bill, and a few interesting program innovations, but did not fix the impending bankruptcy of the major funding source (the Highway Trust Fund) but simply started dipping deeply into general federal revenues (T4A 2011, 2015; Dilger 2015).

[i] For more information about acts, see Schiller and DeLille (1997), Schiller (2002a, pp. 11–12) and Gifford (2003). More information is also available at www.tpl.org/tier3_cd.cfm?content_item_id=10863& folder_id=188 and ntl.bts.gov/DOCS/424MTP.html (accessed 24 August 2016), and Slater and Linton (2003).

Source: Preston L. Schiller

BOX 7.3 Germany: Bicycle policy transformation at federal, state and city levels

Over several decades, a policy transformation that promotes bicycling has been occurring at national, state and city levels in Germany. The transformation is the result of interactions and synergy between these levels of society and government. Some of the transformation is due to policy changes in road transportation thinking, such as reduction of speed limits in cities and the promotion of traffic calming, while some policy change has been specifically targeted at bicycle promotion. Two prominent researchers see the improvements in bicycling conditions and gains in riding as the result of an overall transformation of German transportation policy that coordinates efforts between local, regional, state and national levels. According to Pucher and Buehler (2009, p. 17):

> There are five categories of government policies that have been particularly important for transport sustainability in Germany. First, taxes and restrictions on car use help to limit car use and mitigate its harmful impacts. Second, the provision of high-quality, attractively priced, well-coordinated public transport services offer a viable alternative to the car for many trips, especially in large cities. Third, infrastructure for non-motorized travel has been vastly improved to increase the safety and convenience of walking and cycling. Fourth, urban development policies and land-use planning have encouraged compact mixed-use development, discouraged low-density suburban sprawl, and thus kept many trips short enough to make by walking or cycling. Fifth, these policies have been fully coordinated to ensure their mutually reinforcing impact.

Buehler and his colleagues (Buehler et al. 2016) have reviewed progress in reducing car dependence, not only in German cities (Munich, Berlin, Hamburg), but also in Vienna and Zurich. They summarize their work by saying (p. 1):

> The key to their success has been a coordinated package of mutually reinforcing transport and land-use policies that have made car use slower, less convenient and more expensive, while increasing the safety, convenience and feasibility of walking, cycling and public transport. The mix of policies implemented in each city has been somewhat different. The German cities have done far more to promote cycling, while Zurich and Vienna offer more public transport service per capita at lower fares. All five of the cities have implemented roughly the same policies to promote walking, foster compact mixed use development and discourage car use. Of the car-restrictive policies, parking management has been by far the most important. The five case study cities demonstrate that it is possible to reduce car dependence even in affluent societies with high levels of car ownership and high expectations for quality of travel.

At the national level, the promotion of traffic calming and pedestrian zones began as early as 1961 and became widespread, including bicycle promotion, by the 1970s and 1980s. During the same period, the federal government began to modify its motor vehicle-oriented road standards in the direction of allowing more flexibility at the local level, which has facilitated walking, bicycling and neighborhood safety through the lowering of urban speed limits. It began providing research, analysis and encouragement, including some funding, for bicycle improvements. Several states actively supported this transformation, with North Rhein–Westphalia (Nordrhein–Westfalen) in the lead. This has resulted in regional bicycling programs from paths to planning and information provision that have encouraged cycling between towns and for tourism.

The transformation has been most dramatic at the level of cities, small to large. Münster (population circa 280,000) has won wide acclaim for its bicycling achievements. Heavily bombed in 1944, it rejected the automobile–suburban orientation common to many rebuilding plans and chose to restore itself along traditional lines, but with greater building heights and densities, on average, than before. Bicycling grew and became an important mode, achieving a 35% modal share. By the 1980s a combination of bicycle-promoting policies, including counter-flow bicycle lanes on one-way streets, street redesign, provision of facilities (from bicycle paths and promenades to parking), and bicycle priority in traffic, had made Münster an international leader. Freiburg, one of the cities featured in Chapters 9 and 10, focuses on improving all 'green modes', as well as creating highly effective synergies between land use, transportation and other key planning and policy areas.

continued

More recently, several Chinese cities have been going in the opposite direction to this, allowing cars to take over sidewalks or even formally painting car bays on the sidewalks (see Figure 7.2 in Dalian).

Klinger et al. (2013) examined in detail the issue of 'mobility cultures' in 44 German cities using a wide range of 23 quantitative variables. They arrived at a set of six clusters into which all cities were grouped. They found that eight of the 44 cities could be classed as 'Cycling Cities', one of which was Münster. The others were Bremen, Hamm, Leverkusen, Lübeck, Oldenburg, Osnabrück and Neuss. They demonstrated that even within the same country, unified by an overall similar, political and national context, the variation in transportation orientation was large, due significantly to the different policy and local cultural influences at work in each city. The other groups of cities were: four Transit metropolises, Köln, Düsseldorf, Hamburg and Munich; eight 'Transit cities with multi-modal potential' such as Karlsruhe, Nürnberg and Heidelberg; seven 'Walking cities with multi-modal potential' such as Frankfurt am Main, Bonn and Stuttgart; and seven 'Transit cities' such as Potsdam, Leipzig and Dresden. The most populated city cluster was, however, the 10 more 'Auto-oriented cities', which included Duisburg, Essen and Wiesbaden (this is 'auto-oriented' in a German context and cannot be compared to the auto-orientation of for example U.S. cities, which is far more extreme).

Source: Preston L. Schiller and Jeffrey R. Kenworthy

TABLE 7.1 Cities moving towards sustainable transportation: A selection

City (Country)	Selected accomplishments
Bogotá (Colombia)	Ciclovía bicycle–pedestrian–greenway and bus rapid transit (BRT); quality transportation options to poor neighbourhoods, car-free celebrations
Boulder (Colorado, USA)*	Integrated planning, community transit network—ecopasses, bicycle emphasis, pedestrianization of central business district (CBD), university–city co-operation
Copenhagen (Denmark)	Early leader in pedestrianization, public spaces, emphasis on bicycling
Curitiba (Brazil)	Integrated planning—ecological emphasis, BRT and urban intensification—emphasis on lower-income housing
Freiburg (Germany)*	Integrated planning—ecological emphasis, integration of all transportation modes, pedestrianization, traffic calming
Groningen (The Netherlands)	Early leader in greening of transportation policy and planning, motor vehicle restraint, pedestrianization and bicycling emphasis
Lund (Sweden)	Leader in moving from vision to implementation, outreach to households, first LRT (2017–18)
Münster (Germany)	Early leader in greening of transportation policy and planning, extremely successful bicycling–bicycle streets emphasis
Paris (France)	Ubiquitous transit–intermodal leader, reclaiming automobile space for transit, bicycling and pedestrians and creation of circle line of light rail transit (LRT) to complement the metro
Portland (Oregon, USA)*	Transportation policy public participation, successful light rail transit (LRT) and transit-oriented development (TOD) integration, public space in CBD, new bicycling emphasis
Seoul (South Korea)*	Elimination of major highway; major transit improvements
Stockholm (Sweden)	Early leader in rethinking pedestrianization and pedestrian safety, passenger intermodalism, development along rail lines and new LRT to complement its Tunnelbana (Metro) system
Vancouver (British Columbia, Canada)*	Transit–walkability-oriented development; passenger intermodalism, significant rail development
Zurich (Switzerland)	Passenger intermodal integration, maximizing existing streets for transit

Note: * Cities featured and explored in greater depth in Chapter 9.
Source: Preston L. Schiller and Jeffrey R. Kenworthy

over 90 organizations (representing UN organizations, multilateral and bilateral development organizations, NGOs and foundations, academe and the Business Sector)'[16].

The U.S. Conference of Mayors sponsors the Mayors Climate Protection Center to administer and track a Mayor's Kyoto Accords agreement, as well as to promote energy efficiency and more sustainable transportation at the urban level. The growth in pedestrianized zones in many cities, especially in Europe, coupled with a transportation policy emphasis on walking, bicycling and transit as the modes of choice, has encouraged a small but influential movement towards car-free cities.[17] A few of the many cities making significant progress towards sustainable transportation through reorientations of policy are listed in Table 7.1.

Policy conclusions

There is quite a bit of variation between and within nations and regions in the extent to which transportation policy is moving in the direction of sustainability or remaining stuck in BAU. While much transportation policy remains oriented towards preserving the status quo, there are promising signs that some countries and cities are moving in the direction of sustainability. Programs such as the Transport, Health and Environment Pan-European Program (THE PEP) and similar programs of integrated policy are examples of current ST efforts (Schwedler 2007; Givoni and Banister 2010). Table 7.2 summarizes some major differences between BAU and ST.

The next section considers the crucial role of public participation in transportation planning and policy-making and its implications for sustainability.

The public and participation: from Arnstein to Aarhus and the Rio Declaration

The issue of public participation is an important and complex one for democratic societies. Participation, when and where it occurs, is generally in institutions and processes defined as public or governmental: elections, planning, projects, schools and neighborhood issues. There are few ways in which the average citizen can participate in private-sector decision-making. The public is rarely invited to participate in the governance of corporations or in the planning of privately controlled projects unless they affect the public realm—and even then, public participation or scrutiny is often at the end of private processes. Because of this exclusion, a great deal of public energy is exercised in influencing the public side of the public–private relationship.

One problem in discussing public participation is defining who the 'public' is, what 'public participation' is and what is 'successful'. One of the original leaders in this field, Sherry Arnstein, stated that 'the idea of citizen participation is a little like eating spinach; no one is against it in principle because it is good for you'. Arnstein also included a highly useful 'Ladder of Citizen Participation' that graphically illustrated the range of public participation, with 'Nonparticipation's manipulation' as the bottom rung and its ascendance through 'Tokenism' to 'Citizen Power', with 'Citizen Control' as its highest rung (1969, pp. 216–20). Whether it is analogous to eating spinach or not, there is a consensus that citizens should participate in one form or another in the governance of a democratic society.

Until recent decades, most governments practiced top-down (or 'one to many') 'consultation' with the public about major programs or projects, mainly through carefully controlled informational meetings or public hearings.[18] A new emphasis on bottom-up participation began to emerge by the 1960s. In the U.S., a 'War on Poverty' invited 'maximum feasible participation'. Growing awareness of the consequences of pollution—industrial and vehicular—led to the creation of environmental legislation and regulatory agencies in many countries during the 1960s and 1970s with a concomitant increase of

TABLE 7.2 Policy characteristics: Business as usual (BAU) versus sustainable transportation (ST)

Dimension	Business as usual (BAU)	Sustainable transportation (ST)
Process	Predict (forecast) and provide	Build scenarios, backcast, deliberate, decide
Data analysis	Accepts current trends, forecasts	Uses analysis to interrupt harmful trends
Funding–investing	Supports current situation and trends	Reflects and shapes desired outcomes
Feedback–evaluation	Not generally built into planning	Ongoing feedback and evaluation: all phases
Benchmarking	Not always included or heeded	Serious part of planning, feedback, evaluation
Planning	Usually in separated 'silos'	Maximizes integration of planning and policy

Source: Preston L. Schiller

FIGURE 7.2
Dalian, China; vehicles blocking pedestrians or encroaching upon pedestrian space signify a failure of policy, planning and law enforcement.
Source: Jeffrey R. Kenworthy

public participation in their processes. A large-scale US study has attempted to sort through the various levels and venues of public participation, especially in environmental review processes where some form of public participation is mandated. The study includes many useful observations and recommendations and concluded that: 'When done well, public participation improves the quality and legitimacy of a decision and builds the capacity of all involved to engage in the policy process. It also can enhance trust and understanding among parties' (Dietz and Stern 2008, pp. 1–5). The insufficiencies of conventional public participation have also been noted in discussions of the preparation of Canadian planners (Hodge and Gordon 2014, Chapters 14 and 15).

Discussions about public participation have been the subject of many efforts focused on sustainable development issues. The United Nations 1992 Rio Declaration on Environment and Development, Principle 10, calls for: public access to information; public participation in decision-making processes; and public access to judicial and administrative redress—often termed 'access to justice' (Bruch 2002, p. 2). It recommends that the public be involved early in the decision-making process, 'when options are still open'.[19] The work of the Rio Declaration was built upon through the work of the United Nations Aarhus Convention (UN Aarhus Convention on Access to Information 1998). Public participation in transportation will now be examined to assess what might be needed to advance the goals of ST.

Public participation in transportation: ways to get everyone involved—including trees

Much early citizen participation was in opposition to major projects, technologies or developments felt to be injurious to their interests. Beyond the occasional protest or political campaign, there was little organized citizen effort to participate and relatively little welcoming of the public before the era following World War II. As citizens, government and private interests interacted more around transportation issues, a multifaceted 'transportation public' emerged in many countries, which includes:

- individuals directly affected by a project or proposal or new policy or plan or need;
- users, consumers, employees, providers and employers;
- interested citizen(s), sometimes as community members, sometimes as taxpayers;
- commercial interests, businesses, professionals;
- stakeholders and interest groups; professional/business/labor associations, lobbies, environmental and other NGOs.[20]

Despite the comprehensive nature of the transportation public, there are many groups and interests often left out of participation and policy-making in transportation because they are insufficiently organized, socially marginal or without voice unless championed by an interest group. These include:

- children (rarely allowed to represent themselves; have mobility and safety concerns);
- guest workers and recent immigrants (legal or illegal);
- socially marginal individuals (homeless, discriminated-against sectors);
- wildlife often at risk of becoming 'road kill' or endangered by highway construction or new development and, some might assert, nature itself!

In case studies of three cities in South-east Asia (Bangkok, Singapore and Malaysia), Townsend (2003) provided an in-depth and very revealing account of how decision-making concerning transportation infrastructure involved no public participation, but was rather determined by coalitions of interest in each city and their complexion in each place. The powerful and narrow interests used the notion of public interest to gain outcomes they

---

BOX 7.4 Dr Seuss on "biggering" the roads

In 1971 Theodore Geisel, a.k.a. 'Dr. Seuss', published another of his fabulous childrens' tales, *The Lorax* (Geisel 1971). This powerful fable is about the simple-living environmentalist Lorax, who protects and speaks for the trees, and finds himself pitted in struggle against the greedy forest consuming Once-ler. The book has become a perennial favorite among people of all ages and is often memorized by young readers. The book was the basis of a 1972 animated TV special as well a 2012 3-D animated full-length film.

The voraciously consuming Once-ler chops down all the 'Truffula' trees in sight for the sake of producing more and more 'Thneeds'—products of dubious value. This is all part of his corporate plan to 'bigger' his business. In order to bigger his business and factory (and money) he had to bigger his roads. Alas, the clear-cut forest system collapses and all the creatures that dwelled within vanish. The roads lead to nowhere.

Yet, there is hope. Years later, an old and repentant Once-ler confers the last Truffula tree seed upon a youngster who has ventured into this bleak landscape. Will the trees, the forest-dwelling creatures and even the Lorax return? . . . Stay tuned. . . .

Source: Preston L. Schiller

desired and subvert the multiple broader, but less powerful public interests. Through his findings in these cities, he reveals the more general importance of genuine public participation and civil society action in achieving fairer and more sustainable transportation outcomes, as well as a warning about the limitations of public policy and planning in certain circumstances.[21]

Despite the difficulties facing public participation, interest and activity in this vital part of transportation have been growing around the globe, from the North Sea to the South Seas (Gil, Calado and Bentz 2011; Laing et al. 2012; Hairulsyah 2013).

How the transportation public participates

Since the 1960s, many countries have made some form of public participation mandatory for major transportation projects and policies.[22] Forms of public participation and their effectiveness vary from one level of government to another and within civil society. This section describes many public participation types, techniques, venues and effects and attempts to evaluate them in terms of their relevance for achieving changes in policy in the direction of ST.

There are many forms, venues and degrees of structure and organization of public participation:

- *Media communications*: include information from transportation agencies; citizens' responses include letters to editors and comments on articles and blog-postings, letters or petitions, calling in to talk shows, televising of public meetings, web blogs, web social media postings and networking.
- *Town meetings*: public forums, if open to all citizens and done fairly—rather than manipulated by public officials—where pressing issues can be debated and deliberated.
- *Public consultations* and *public hearings*: examples of top-down formats; informational conveyances usually organized by government. These venues typically present developed plans and record reactions; there is little depth discussion of the plan or alternatives. Improvements could include having alternative viewpoints as part of a roundtable discussion and small group discussions.
- *Committees and commissions*: governments at various levels, including transit providers, may create special committees or commissions for advice or even assistance in developing policies and plans.
- *Citizens juries*: This is a technique influenced by jurisprudence processes, wherein a panel of citizen jurors is convened to deliberate a controversial issue over a period ranging from one to several days and then reach a 'verdict' of recommendations. The ways in which this technique is structured and the extent of its post-deliberation influence can vary. The Minneapolis-based Jefferson Center has done much work in this area and offers much useful information.[23] The credibility and meaning of such an approach can be greatly enhanced by the decision maker(s) agreeing to abide by the decision of the jury and implement the findings, even if it goes against the preferred direction of the decision maker. A former state government minister in Western Australia made such a commitment and abided by it in a difficult road decision (Gollagher and Hartz-Karp 2013; see also Box 7.9). In cases where this form of deliberative democracy has considerable influence with public officials, its findings may gain considerable media coverage and encourage its participants as well as other citizens that participation can be meaningful.
- *Study circles*: formed by people with an interest in an area or issue that they hope to influence or shape. It is a 'bottom-up' approach to learning and preparation for effective participation.[24]

- *Social movements*: citizens' concerns about a transportation-related matter may be addressed through an existing social movement, as when environmental movements include transportation matters in their agenda or when parent associations include safe walking routes to school or 'walking school buses' as a major concern.
- *Politically oriented participation*: includes 'watch-dogging', coalitions, lobbying, litigation and political contest. Citizen 'watchdogs' might closely follow an issue or inspire media investigations. Some NGOs undertake lobbying or litigation. Electing or un-electing officials is the most widespread form of public participation in government. While it makes clear who is accountable for government decisions, participation rates vary and major reform may be slow. In some countries or regions within countries, the law permits citizens to launch initiatives or referenda or recall elected officials.
- *Citizen science*: began as a critique of the ways in which the scientific establishment marginalized or even mocked public participation in policy deliberations around scientific and technological issues—even when citizens directly involved or impacted by an issue or a project attempted to voice concerns (Irwin 1995). It has since developed into a broad movement, sometimes termed crowd science, stressing collaboration between scientists, technologists and the concerned public. Citizen scientists often formally collaborate with scientists in data gathering and other necessary processes as well as the shaping of projects and their reporting and public discussion (Scientific American 2016; Citizen Science Alliance 2016).

Box 7.5 illustrates some ways in which citizens and policy-makers can work together to change the direction of ST at the neighborhood and city levels.

BOX 7.5 City–community collaboration: Seattle neighborhood traffic circles

Many cities around the world suffer from speeding motorists and too much traffic. When urban traffic grows without control, it spills over from major thoroughfares into and through residential neighborhoods or around school districts. Speeding or 'rat-running' (sometimes termed 'maze-running') motorists become a problem.

One way to slow local traffic down and increase street safety is the neighborhood traffic circle (or roundabout), usually constructed at an intersection or at mid-block. This device is very popular in Seattle (Washington), Portland (Oregon) and many other U.S. cities. The traffic circle needs to be of sufficient radius so that motor vehicles slow considerably as they maneuver around it, but allow width sufficient for delivery trucks and emergency vehicles. A well-done traffic circle is landscaped to add aesthetic value to the neighborhood and has a sign explaining how to maneuver around it. To be effective, traffic circles need to be installed at multiple intersections in a neighborhood, especially along those streets that are subject to rat-running motorists. If successful, traffic circles slow and inconvenience through motorists sufficiently so that they remain on major thoroughfares.

The City of Seattle has a highly effective program. Neighborhood residents are invited to analyze their street problems and then submit a proposal to the Seattle Department of Transportation. If neighborhood residents volunteer to maintain the traffic circle as a garden spot, the city will provide soil and plantings; otherwise asphalt will cover it. The City also collaborates with neighborhoods with the creation of small greenspaces, rain gardens and walkways along streets lacking in sidewalks and boulevard strips. More recently a collaboration between citizens and the Seattle Department of Transportation has led to a rapidly growing program of bicycle boulevards known as neighborhood greenways.[i]

[i] For more information on traffic circles, see Johnson (2008) and the following websites: www.seattle. gov/transportation/trafficcircles.htm and www.trafficlogix.com/traffic-calming-history.asp. For the neighborhood greenways collaboration see www.seattle.gov/transportation/greenways.htm and http://seattlegreenways.org/.

Source: Preston L. Schiller

FIGURE 7.3
Attractive N.E. Seattle traffic circle slows motor vehicles, makes the intersection safer and is maintained by the neighborhood; the flag indicates that traffic calming can be patriotic and the maple leaves embossed in the cement curbing connote the neighborhood's identity; Maple Leaf.
Source: City of Seattle Transportation Department

Techniques and processes of participation for sustainable transport

Several techniques, processes and venues can be used to enhance citizen participation in transportation. Some are visually oriented or incorporate visualizations. Among these are the following:

- *Analytic hierarchy process (AHP)*: a planning technique that attempts to incorporate a variety of evaluation techniques and information sources within a coherent framework for analysis and decision-making. It may incorporate information from essentially qualitative sources (preference surveys, expert panels, visualizations etc.) and information from quantitative sources (project costs, returns on investments, modeling etc.) into a framework whereby scaled values representing weights of importance for aspects of the project or proposal under analysis may be applied and used to arrive at rankings. It weights the importance of goals and the effectiveness of each proposed project alternative towards meeting that goal. Similarly, it weights the importance of negative impacts or costs and the severity of each proposed project alternative with respect to that impact or cost. The result is a set of benefit-to-cost ratios more realistic and inclusive than the traditional net present value analysis based primarily on monetary or monetized values. It also lends itself to further sub-analyses and reiterations of the decision-making process.[25]
- *Charrette (or charette)*: a technique often used in planning and urban design where small groups are involved in an intensive process with the goal of arriving at consensus about a plan, policy or project design. Typically, one or more specialists present information, including graphics about the issue under review, some of which may be spontaneously developed. The group may consist of other planners or designers, government officials, people who represent special interests related to the matter under review—sometimes known as 'stakeholders'—members of the public or a combination of these (Schommer 2003).
- *Visualizations and simulations*: computerized techniques allow comparisons of alternatives and multiple perspectives and simulations to test ideas about traffic and transit. These may be combined with other techniques described in this section (Batty et al. 2000; Levy 2006).

- *Visioning*: a process through which a community or a government agency, or both, may develop a consensus of a preferred future and then begin to shape policies and plans to attain it (Okubo 2000; also, see the item below on 'Scenarios and backcasting').
- *Visual preference survey*: a technique that records citizen, planner and developer reactions to a variety of street, building and community design possibilities. Participants record their reaction, usually along a positive-to-negative numeric scale.[26]
- *Scenarios and backcasting*: when forecasting and trends indicate an undesirable outcome, possible outcome scenarios could be constructed and the most desirable and least harmful chosen. The group could then turn its attention to 'How do we get there from here?' It could engage in a backcasting exercise and identify planning and policy measures necessary to attain the desired future.[27]
- *Hybrid and comprehensive approaches*: agencies, developers and citizens' groups may incorporate several of the techniques described above. An excellent source describing several successful TOD and context-sensitive solutions (CSS) efforts using multiple participation techniques, including visualizations, simulations and a variety of types of community outreach, concluded that: 'One of the most compelling findings in these cases is how in each project, those involved challenged conventional approaches to transportation planning and design' (Schively 2007, p. 2).[28]

The potential for public participation

A study of several European cities indicates that citizen activity played a major role in redirecting policies, planning and investments towards sustainable transportation. Table 7.3 illustrates how—by the 1990s, through great and prolonged effort commencing in the 1960s and 1970s—the five cities studied slowed or reversed the growth of automobile transportation and enhance and increase travel by transit and non-motorized modes. Later data obtained for these cities are also shown. It reveals that the positive trend was very strongly continued in Basel and Freiburg (which are very close to each other and tend to follow each other in their transport policies), while in the other cities there were both positive and negative trends. For example, in Zurich walking and cycling increased from 35% to 41% of all daily trips but transit declined from 37% to 29%, with an overall result of a small increase in car use by 2005 (28% to 30%, a modal split for cars that most cities would want on the front page of every newspaper).

To put the accomplishments of these cities in perspective, most U.S. cities would have an automobile share between 80% and 90% (or more), a transit share between 1% and 5% and a walk–bicycle share between 1% and 5%.[29] Canadian cities, on average, do better than their U.S. counterparts, with a few approaching European transit mode levels. Vancouver (British Columbia), Portland (Oregon) and Boulder (Colorado) have been making policy and citizen-led efforts to change their modal splits over the past 30 years; their experiences are presented in Chapter 9 of this volume.

Public participation can also be misguided

A cautionary note is in order: while greater participation is generally a welcome phenomenon, and many citizen initiatives lead to outcomes in the direction of ST, some move away from a sustainable outcome. Such was the case of a 1999 citizen initiative in Washington State (see Box 7.6). Such problems are also discussed in Chapter 10 on growing more exemplars.

The Initiative 695 case study illustrates the confusion surrounding some issues. Motorist resentment, weak public understanding of the issues and policy-maker lack of fortitude combined to deal public transportation a major setback. Subsequent voter support for local transit tax increases indicates that the I-695 vote was not anti-transit *per se*. In the absence of effective public participation and deliberation, policy-makers might misperceive public intent.

TABLE 7.3 Modal split in percentages (for all residents' trips) in six European cities with strong citizen activity in transportation, 1990* and post-2000

City (Country)	Automobile	Transit	Walk–bicycle
Zurich (Switzerland)	28	37	35
Zurich (2005)	30	29	41
Basle (Switzerland)	38	30	32
Basle (2010)	21	28	49
Amsterdam (The Netherlands)	31	23	46
Amsterdam (2008)	38	20	42
Groningen (The Netherlands)	36	6	65
Groningen (2008)	44	10	46
Freiburg (Germany)**	42	18	40
Freiburg (2001)	30	18	52

Notes: * Or latest available year prior to 1999; figures are percentages of total trips.
** Freiburg is explored in-depth as an exemplary city in Chapter 9 and a little more in Chapter 10.
Source: adapted from Bratzel (1999, p. 183) and latest data from www.epomm.eu/tems/cities.phtml (European Platform on Mobility Management)

Citizens' initiatives can often play a positive environmental role, even in defeat. In Washington State, a growth management initiative organized and campaigned for by the environmental community was defeated in a 1990 vote. Heeding the words of martyred Swedish-American labor activist Joe Hill (1879–1915), quipped at his firing squad execution in Utah after years of organizing unions and strikes in the Pacific Northwest region of the U.S.—'Don't mourn—organize!'—the environmentalists went to work and succeeded in moving the state legislature to pass a Growth Management Act in 1991.

A comprehensive critique of public participation in transportation found that important factors inhibiting progress include the tendency for many government officials to underestimate the extent of public support for ST solutions. As a response to such inhibiting factors, the author called for engaging citizens in significant roles in deliberative decision-making as continuously and inclusively as possible.[30] Box 7.7 discusses some of the lessons the author learned in his study, life and planning practice.

Boxes 7.8 and 7.9 provide successful examples of broad public participation efforts that used several visioning and deliberative techniques and effectively influenced policy-makers in Perth, Western Australia.

From business as usual (BAU) to sustainability in transportation

Because transportation is a very complex field, touching many aspects of everyday life and activity, it offers many challenges to policy-makers, planners and citizens wishing to move it away from BAU. However, there are many fine examples of how transportation policy is breaking out of the confinements of conventionality and giving us glimpses of how sustainability can be attained in this domain. Public participation, too, is a difficult and complicated area, but there are many examples of how it can be an effective ingredient of planning and policy-making.

Equally, there are unfortunately many cases, especially in less-developed countries, where governance is very inadequate and effective civil society and citizen participation is absent, very weak or too scared to express itself for fear of retribution. In these situations, powerful coalitions of interest, political, economic or both, wield their unchecked influence in planning and transportation in their own self-interest, which is often to the detriment of many people whose needs are not met and whose voices are simply not heard.

BOX 7.6 Initiative 695: A citizen participation and policy-maker failure

In 1995, self-styled Seattle pro-automobility populist Tim Eyman began a lucrative and controversial career of soliciting donations and organizing citizen initiatives in Washington State—one of several U.S. states that allows citizens to initiate legislation (initiative), nullify an existing law (referendum, which also allows the legislature to refer measures to citizens for a vote) or even recall elected officials (recall). Some of these options exist in several other U.S. states, parts of Canada and a few other countries such as Switzerland. Annually, Eyman and his organization, Permanent Offense, challenge transportation and property taxes, affirmative action laws, high-occupancy vehicle (HOV) lanes and public projects that they dislike. They win some, they lose some.

In 1999, the Eyman-organized Initiative 695 (I-695), repealing the Motor Vehicle Excise Tax (MVET), passed by a margin of 56% to 44%. MVET was a tax levied on the value of a motor vehicle. It imposed an annual fee ranging from very little for older cars to hundreds of dollars or more for newer, more expensive models. While most transportation taxes are unpopular with motorists, MVET was especially unpopular since it assessed a vehicle's tax value somewhat higher than standard estimates. Washington's state constitution dedicates all revenues from fuel taxes to highway purposes. MVET was not encumbered in this way. Its revenues were applied to public transportation and a variety of social and educational programs. Washington State is considered by many experts to be somewhat backwards and regressive in its tax policies; it has no state income tax and relies heavily on sales tax and MVET was one of its few progressive taxes.

Opponents of I-695 waged a weak battle against it. The legislature chose not to reform MVET. When I-695 passed, it was immediately challenged in court. While the case was being litigated, Governor Gary Locke called the legislature into a special session to lower the MVET to a fixed US$30 per year fee—in effect, ratifying Eyman's victory. When, a few months later, the state Supreme Court found I-695 to be unconstitutional, neither the governor nor the legislature reversed their hasty action.

Many transit agencies could recoup some of their funding losses through local voter-approved tax increases. But most of these measures took years to pass and some agencies have not been able to regain the level of funding that they had before 1999. The state's rail program is now several years behind in its efforts to improve passenger rail, despite increased popularity.[i]

Recent years have seen Eyman losing more than winning. He and his allies have been winning some local initiatives against traffic signal cameras that take photos and issue citations to motorists not stopping for red lights. Permanent Offense's recent state initiative measures have mostly been defeated or invalidated by judicial review. Although occasionally investigated for possible criminal and election fraud offenses he has, nevertheless, attracted the attention of a right-wing billionaire supporter—so Permanent Offense remains as an example of not-so-enlightened public participation (Westneat 2016).

[i] For Eyman's financial improprieties, see www.permanent-offense.org/; see also Washington State Attorney General's 2002 press release, *State Reaches Settlement with Eyman and Permanent Offense*, www.atg.wa.gov/pressrelease.aspx?&id=5798 and www.seattlepi.com/local/65900_eyman10.shtml; for information on Washington State Supreme Court decision, see *I-695 Declared Unconstitutional by State Supreme Court*, www.mrsc.org/subjects/finance/695/i-695.aspx; and additional information on Eyman, see www.mrsc.org/mc/courts/supreme/142wn2d/142wn2d0183.htm and portfolio.washington.edu/tarabl/495/25293.html (all accessed 24 August 2016).

Source: Preston L. Schiller

BOX 7.7 **Participative democracy: deliberative decision-making and social learning**

Eric Manners[i]

My master's study concluded that more direct, deliberative, discursive and participative forms of decision-making were needed for better citizen involvement and better planning and policy outcomes (Manners 2002). Participation also gives citizens an opportunity for 'social learning'—hearing the views of other citizens, talking through the range of possible solutions and comparing the impacts of various alternatives in terms of their own and others' short-term and long-term interests. My research was informed by numerous studies and critiques[ii] and I concluded that to be successful in moving towards sustainability, deliberative planning processes should be:

- broad scale;
- consensual/collaborative;
- discursive/dialogical;
- empowered/independent;
- local;
- multi-scale; and
- ongoing/continuous.

I learned that the Brazilian city of Porto Alegre involves thousands of its citizens in setting annual local 'participatory budgets', with local representatives contributing towards regional budgets.[iii] Elected 'neighborhood councils' in Mexico and Norway provide citizens with more direct influence over local decisions.[iv] The Vision 2020 process in Hamilton–Wentworth, Ontario, Canada, allowed 1000 citizens to help set out a community vision for sustainability over which they then felt a greater sense of ownership.[v] And the TravelSmart travel demand management and dialogue marketing program in Perth, Western Australia, although a more top-down approach, was a broad-scale process bringing information to every household in the city on how they could change their travel behavior (Transport W.A. 1999), and could be expanded to include a two-way dialogue on transport improvements and policy.

The main challenge in my experience, working in local government, has been finding the necessary time and funding to run meaningful, ongoing engagement processes. While the dominant voice is still the motorist, implementation of ST policy will be challenging, but it may be our best chance to beat the climate change clock.

[i] Transport Policy and Planning, London Borough of Islington.

[ii] Barber (1984); Dryzek (1990); Forester (1989); Innes (1995); Gunderson (1995); Arnstein (1969); Fischer (1990); Irwin (1995); Dewey (1920, 1950); Mumford (1938); Milbrath (1989); Lee (1993).

[iii] Abers (1998, 2000); Sandercock (1998).

[iv] For Mexico see Flores (2002); for Norway see Aarsæther et al. (2002).

[v] UNESCO (undated); Hamilton–Wentworth Regional Municipality (1997).

BOX 7.8 Visioning, dialogue and deliberation in Perth, Western Australia

Jeffrey R. Kenworthy[i]

Faced with a huge increase in urban sprawl and car dependence, the state government decided to involve the community on an unprecedented scale to develop a future vision for Perth for 2030. The process involved a community survey of over 1,700 households and a one-day forum involving 1,000 participants. A critical part of the forum was a game that each group of ten people played to plan for the expected increase in population. Each decision taken had a flow-on effect, which was either positive or negative. People were thus forced to confront the dilemmas of urban planning, trading-off personal lifestyle preferences with systems effects, such as loss of bushland, traffic congestion and other implications.[ii]

An action plan called The Network City, superseded by Directions 2031and Beyond[iii] proposed that around 60% of new dwelling construction within existing built-up areas to reduce car dependence and sprawl forced participants to consider the social, economic and environmental considerations wrapped up in all urban planning (see Box 7.9 for more detail).

Source: Kenworthy (2006)

[i] Jeffrey R. Kenworthy is Professor of Sustainable Cities at the Curtin University Sustainability Policy Institute (CUSP) at Curtin University in Perth, Western Australia.
[ii] All results were recorded and a final report can be found at www.dpi.wa.gov.au/dialogue/finalproc.pdf.
[iii] See: www.planning.wa.gov.au/publications/826.asp (accessed 24 August 2016); the process is described in more detail in Marinova et al. (2004).

BOX 7.9 Deliberative democracy Down Under

Janette Hartz-Karp[i]

In Australia, competent land use and transport plans often gather dust, never to be implemented. Prepared by experts and decided by technocrats and elected members, with the public involved too little too late in the process, they only come to attention if they raise public ire or gross apathy, both tending to lead to non-action. Governments have reversed this trend when they have been willing to 'share power' with citizens. Participants, descriptively representative of the broad population, have been given opportunities for inclusive, empowered deliberation on issues of importance—collaboratively framing and problem-solving dilemmas, then co-designing and co-deciding plans. This is called 'deliberative democracy' or 'discursive politics'.

'Dialogue with the City' was a classic example, with over 1,000 diverse participants deliberating for a day to co-design and co-decide the broad features to be included in land use and transport plans for the Perth metropolis. Aided by online deliberation with networked computers and a mapping game, priority objectives and basic design elements were determined. One hundred of the participants later worked together with experts to develop the detailed plans, which were presented to the State Cabinet and accepted. When a looming election threatened to overturn this plan, it was the public that stood up for it and ensured it was retained (as well as the government supporting it). Over a decade later, this plan still drives Perth metropolis land use and transport planning.

In another example of more implementable decision-making, a citizens jury resolved a contentious issue of the routing of a highway extension exit. Neither suburb involved wanted it, with local lobbyists effectively preventing its resolution. The Minister for Planning and Infrastructure made a commitment to the Citizens' Jury to implement their consensus decision, providing it didn't cost more than $100,000 more than already planned. The citizens jury participants, a random sample of 12 residents (6 from one suburb, 6 from the other) resolved the issue after half a day's deliberation. Although their finding was the same as that proposed by the Department of Main Roads, the Department had misunderstood the reasons for the dispute, thinking it

continued

was yet another case of NIMBYism (Not in My Back Yard). However, the impasse was the safety of a school and playground given increased traffic, not NIMBYism. After reaching their unanimous decision, the citizens jury spent the remaining time 'spending' the $100,000 they figured was still available, on a solution to protect the children's safety. Their solution was implemented after a trial, and the dispute was resolved.

Collaborative planning and co-deciding 'with' the people instead of 'for' the people has been repeated in cities across Australia to positive effect. While social media plays an important role, its task is to gather public 'opinion', which has some limited value in terms of determining what the 'common good' might be. Deliberative democracy aims to move past opinion towards 'public judgment' and 'public wisdom', by creating opportunities for diverse voices to carefully consider alternative viewpoints, including the science, weigh the options according to agreed criteria and arrive at a coherent, reasoned voice, a way forward. Diverse voices are often achieved by 'lottery', random sampling of the population to reflect the demographics of the people. Careful consideration is achieved by learning about different perspectives, and deliberation in small groups, in an egalitarian environment. An agreed way forward is achieved by those involved deciding how they will decide. Research across the globe has shown that the public is more trusting of such outcomes than they are of political decisions. Indeed, by applying 'power with' the people rather than 'power over' them, governments have succeeded in bolstering both public trust and legitimacy.

[i] Professor Janette Hartz-Karp, Curtin University Sustainability Policy (CUSP) Institute, Western Australia, is a renowned practitioner, teacher and researcher in deliberative democracy. She worked with the Western Australian Planning and Infrastructure Minister to find innovative ways to institute deliberative democracy in transport and planning. Hartz-Karp co-designed and co-facilitated Australia's first Citizens' Parliament, and has worked with cities in Canada, USA, India, Israel, Egypt and Denmark to implement deliberative democracy. The four-year Australian Research Council initiative to create a deliberative community and collaborative governance in the City of Greater Geraldton, WA, which she led, has won national and international awards.

In the next chapter, the ways in which a new paradigm of planning can build upon policy leadership and effective citizen participation will be explored.

Questions for discussion

- Identify and discuss some of the ways in which the forms of policy-making and public participation in your community are supporting business as usual (BAU) or sustainable transportation (ST).

- Discuss and evaluate whether and to what extent technology is changing the ways in which public participation occurs. What are some positive aspects of this? What are some negative aspects of this?

- Discuss Arnstein's Ladder of Citizen Participation and the various public participation and deliberation–decision-making techniques described in this chapter to their applicability in planning, policy-making and public participation processes in your community.

- Where and how might deliberative democracy fit in your life? Work? Studies? Neighborhood? City?

Notes

1 Dow Chemical Company (undated).
2 See: Alexander (2002), esp. p. 226
3 Cochran and Malone (1999, pp. 12–14); Anderson (2000, pp. 7–18); Birkland (2005, pp. 139–49)

4 The Scandinavian countries, the Netherlands and Germany are among the leaders in developing ST policies; the U.S., the U.K. and Canada are examples of countries lagging behind. For an international sampling see Whitelegg and Haq (2003).

5 Akaha (1990); Stevens (2004); also see Chapter 3 above in this volume.

6 Gifford (2003); Stevens (2004); pp. 15–16 T4A 2011.

7 For more information on the road systems in these countries, consult http://travel.state.gov/travel/cis_pa_tw/cis/cis_1013.html, www.1uptravel.com/travelwarnings/zimbabwe.html or http://travel.state.gov/travel/cis_pa_tw/cis/cis_1081.html

8 Pucher and Lefevre (1996); Stevens (2004); Button and Hensher (2005).

9 For more on the history of these issues, see Chapter 3 of this volume.

10 See the pioneering work of the late John Roberts (1989) and his organization, Transport and Environment Studies (TEST), especially *Quality Streets*.

11 Consult the Glossary for definitions of these terms; see also Button and Hensher (2005).

12 For more information about the Kyoto goals, see Doyle (2007), Kanter (2009) and Pincas Jawetz's 2009 post on SustainabiliTank; also Boisson de Chazournes (undated).

13 www.cop21.gouv.fr/en/

14 Including China, Spain, Germany and France, among many others.

15 For more on the future of these transportation goals, see Brown (2008, especially Chapter 2) and Jim Kunstler's report *Clusterfuck Nation: A Glimpse into the Future* at www.kunstler.com/mags_ure.htm.

16 See: www.slocat.net/slocatpartnership (accessed 24 August 2016).

17 CIVITAS stands for CIty–VITAlity–Sustainability; see www.civitas-initiative.org/main.phtml?lan=en; for U.S. mayors' efforts and critiques, see www.seattle.gov/mayor/climate/default.htm#what and www.eukn.org/netherlands/news/2007/01/climate-change-uscities_1015.html; for car-free cities, see www.worldcarfree.net/. See also Low and Gleeson (2003) and Koppenjan (undated).

18 Campbell and Marshall (2000).

19 For more, see Bruch (2002, pp. 9–12), although, curiously, transportation issues are not included in this very valuable discussion. See also Transportation Research Board (2002).

20 Hook 2005, Chapter 4.

21 Townsend (2003; esp. pp. 311, 313, 314, 315, 317).

22 See discussion of ISTEA and Arnstein's Ladder in this chapter; there were other early FHWA/NEPA-inspired studies and handbooks from the 1960s and 1970s with contributions from Arnstein, Julie Hoover and Alan Altshuler (Arnstein and Metcalf 1976). See also Warburton et al. (undated) and Wassenhoven (2008).

23 An NGO that specializes in citizens juries is the Jefferson Center, www.jefferson-center.org/citizen-juries/. For a discussion of the merits of including this form of deliberative democracy, see Smith and Wales (2000).

24 Sometimes called Swedish study circles after their country of origin; for more information, see Haines (2006) and Warner (undated).

25 See Bruun (2007, pp. 269–76).

26 Since the 1990s, the originator Anton Nelessen has been working to refine this technique and others have developed their own variations; see also www.lgc.org/freepub

27 The term 'backcasting', as used here, refers to the process that follows scenario-building and is directed towards achieving visioned goals; see Gilbert and Wiederkehr (2002), especially Chapter 1. Another form of backcasting, not used here, assesses the effects of projects after their construction or implementation and compares these with their intended effects.

28 See Schively (2007, p. 3) and her sources for excellent graphic examples and general references on public participation techniques; another good source is the International Association for Public Participation (IAP2), www.iap2.org/, especially the 'Public Participation Toolbox'.

29 New York City has the highest transit share of 27%, with a handful of cities between 10% and 15%; a few cities have a slightly higher rate than 1% to 5% for non-motorized.

30 Manners (2002, pp. 9–11, 32–35, 45–69); also see Box 7.8.

A new planning paradigm: from integrated planning, policy and mobility management to repair, regeneration and renewal

Lessons learned from preceding chapters

This chapter builds upon current ideas based on conclusions reached in preceding chapters to develop a model incorporating their findings within planning and implementing sustainable transportation (ST). We call this approach the 'new paradigm' because it offers a clear distinction from the old paradigm of business as usual (BAU – see Box 8.1). The new paradigm is based upon the interaction of:

- integrated policy and planning, and mobility management (or transportation demand management: TDM);
- several important 'background' factors that need to inform policy and planning;
- the development of appropriate infrastructure, techniques and technology.

Interest in developing a new paradigm in transportation is not necessarily new. Many researchers and analysts have been pointing to the shortcomings of the BAU paradigm and the need for its replacement for many years. Significant names in previous work to create a new paradigm for transportation include John Adams, David Banister, Terence Bendixson, Eric Britton, Werner Brög, Eric Bruun, Ralph Buehler, Robert Cervero, Jan Gehl, Phil Goodwin, Carmen Hass-Klau, Mayer Hillman, Felix Laube, Rolf Monheim, Peter Newman, Anthony Perl, Stephen Plowden, John Pucher, Richard Register, John Roberts, Kenneth Schneider, Eduardo Vasconcellos, Vukan Vuchic and John Whitelegg. Such a list can never be exhaustive and there are many more, but all those cited above have in one way or another attempted to draw attention to the need to rein in the dominance of the private automobile in the setting of transportation and urban planning policy and, especially, the future sustainability of cities. The need for a new paradigm incorporating the advances possible with improved intermodalism in both freight and passenger transportation has also been articulated by Joseph S. Szyliowicz (2003) and others.

The new paradigm understands ST not as an end state or static product, but as a dynamic ongoing process (see also Litman 2003; Banister 2010; Whitelegg 2016). It builds on feedback, reiteration, revisiting of original visions and a long-term perspective. It is constantly adjusting and is informed by new information.

The recognition of the need for a new paradigm: the Buchanan Report and its critics

As early as the 1960s, some in the profession of traffic engineering[1] and planning were beginning to question BAU. Stephen Plowden (1972) offered a prescient critique of conventional transportation planning in *Towns against Traffic*, his response to the influential British government report *Traffic in Towns* (Buchanan 1963), also popularly known as the Buchanan Report after its principal author, Colin Buchanan. The Buchanan Report has shaped much of U.K. transportation planning between towns, in towns, around towns and through towns since that time. For the most part, the Buchanan Report reflected conventional traffic planning with a slightly greater emphasis on protecting town centers and neighborhoods from the excesses of traffic, through rigorous traffic separation schemes that divided local from through traffic, than was the standard practice of the 1940s and 1950s.

Plowden's (1972) critique begins with a rejection of the traffic engineer's tenet that 'all traffic demands should be met' (pp. 14–15), and proceeds to the understanding that increasing road supply simply increased demand for driving: 'Very broadly speaking, the amount of traffic is governed by what is regarded as a tolerable level of congestion' (p. 15). Early in his critique, Plowden cited a prominent American traffic engineer's observation that travel demand and traffic congestion were directly related to road supply:

> As traffic engineering measures and new streets and highways have added capacity to road systems, more motor vehicles have been put into use almost immediately. New roads and more motor vehicle miles of travel have gone hand in hand in the United States.
>
> (Plowden 1972, p. 16)[2]

Plowden then brought attention to the fact that while traffic congestion was rampant in most cities, it never reached the level of 'gridlock' predicted in many forecasts. He then linked road expansion to urban sprawl: 'New roads will also encourage people to live further from their work or other places of activity' (p. 18). Plowden was one of the earliest, if not

FIGURE 8.1A
Busy, clogged and chaotic San Jacinto Street in the Trianna district of Seville, Spain, before traffic calming; note that the person encircled by cars is directing parking for tips from motorists; if this picture had sound it would be loud horns, car alarms, much traffic noise (2009).
Source: Preston L. Schiller

FIGURE 8.1B
San Jacinto Street after traffic
calming and street redesign; one
traffic lane, defined parallel parking
for cars and motorcycles, sidewalk
widened, bicycle lanes added.
Patients in the hospital (right) can
now enjoy more quiet and much less
traffic noise and pedestrians can
safely cross the street (2015)
Source: Preston L. Schiller

FIGURE 8.1C
San Jacinto Street pedestrianized as
it approaches the now road-dieted
and pedestrian and cyclist improved
Trianna Bridge (2015)
Source: Preston L. Schiller

the first, to characterize conventional transportation planning and traffic engineering as a 'predict and provide' (p. 19) enterprise.

Plowden's critique of 'predict and provide' has been echoed in years since by a series of prominent scholars and analysts.[3] This has helped to establish the basis for a new paradigm for ST.

Figures 8.1a, b and c graphically depict how a major commercial and residential street in a neighborhood in Seville, Spain has made a transition from a business as usual (BAU) traffic and transportation orientation towards sustainable transportation (ST) in just a matter of a few years.

BOX 8.1 Problems and shortcomings of the business as usual paradigm

The business as usual (BAU) paradigm:

- largely ignores environmental and social equity impacts that are associated with capacity-oriented transportation planning, or, at best, attempts to mitigate its damages after the fact or far from where the capacity expansion occurred;
- is largely oblivious to the ways in which it promotes longer-distance urban area travel and facilitates low-density sprawled development;
- allows pricing distortions that promote motoring at the expense of walking, bicycling and public transportation;
- lends itself to a 'build its way out of congestion' approach rather than managing demand;
- highlights the fact that the main economic benefits of a congestion mitigation strategy are purported time savings, which are illusory because new roads just allow people to travel further, not to save time;
- tends to almost always favor one mode (motoring) and one technology (the private vehicle) over a balanced menu of modes and technologies;
- is usually resistant to effective public participation;
- often develops standards for urban roads that are fit only for intercity expressways;
- defines 'safety' very narrowly, usually as motorist safety.

Source: Preston L. Schiller

Overview of the new paradigm: integrated policy-making, planning and mobility management

Integrated policy-making

Integrated policy-making is a key factor in the creation of a new paradigm. Currently, many policy efforts in the domains of transportation, environment, health and general social well-being pursue parallel but usually uncoordinated trajectories. An important effort to integrate these separate policy 'silos' is under way with the Transport, Health and Environment Pan-European Programme (THE PEP) and a valuable definition is offered:

> Policy integration concerns management of cross-cutting issues in policy-making that transcend the boundaries of established policy fields. It also includes management of policy responsibility within a single organization or sector. Integrated policy-making refers both to horizontal integration between policy sectors (different departments and/or professions in public authorities) and vertical intergovernmental integration in policy-making (between different tiers of government), or combinations of both.[4]

Towards better management of existing transportation features

A key ingredient of a new paradigm is better management and maximization of the benefits of current transportation programs, services and infrastructure. The critique of conventional transportation planning by Plowden (1972) and others from the 1970s and 1980s to the present call for managing transportation systems better, rather than embarking on reflex road and highway expansions. This approach is known as transportation demand management (TDM), as well as 'mobility management'.[5] Mobility management refers to a range of policies, programs and planning strategies intended to make existing transportation resources function more efficiently, as well as directing users of those resources towards more efficient use of them (see Table 8.1).

During recent years, a combination of trends has increased the importance of mobility management and positioned it as a more valued solution to a variety of problems, including road and parking congestion, increasing facility costs, excessive consumer costs, high accident rates, energy dependency, inadequate mobility for non-drivers, inefficient land-use development and inadequate public fitness and health. Until recently, most traffic safety experts assumed that the total amount and type of mobility are unchangeable, their efforts focused on reducing crash rates per vehicle kilometer. New research indicates that mobility management can significantly reduce per capita crash rates and therefore can be considered as a traffic safety strategy. Similarly, mobility management is now recognized as an important component of congestion reduction, energy conservation, emissions reduction, public health and community redevelopment programs. As more of these objectives are recognized, the justification for integrated mobility management increases.

Types and strategies of mobility management

Mobility management includes a variety of specific strategies that tend to fall into five major categories:

1   improving and expanding travel options;
2   priorities for transit and efficient modes as incentives for use;
3   land-use solutions to transportation problems: smart growth multi-modal development;
4   programmed implementation;
5   new ways of integrating approaches and options; 'Mobility as a Service' (MaaS Box 8.4).

Improving and expanding travel options

Mobility management often involves improvements, including performance, security, information and user comfort, for public transportation, as well as improved connections between modes (intermodalism). It promotes the expansion of mobility options, such as walking, bicycling, ride-sharing, car-sharing and taxi services, many of which are specifically helpful in solving 'the last (or first) mile' problem in using transit. It also supports trip reduction strategies, such as telework (use of telecommunications to substitute for physical travel), teleconferencing and video-conferencing and delivery services. Outreach programs, where participants are provided with details about transit systems in their area and are given free tickets to try it, have been shown to change behavior (Socialdata.org; Brög and Erl 2003).

New options appearing in mobility management schemes include a wide range of innovative schemes to help people avoid the need to use or own their own car. These include car-sharing and bike-sharing schemes, which may be 'stand alone' programs or ancillary to a transportation provider such as a railway. Anecdotal evidence in Germany is showing that such schemes can result in households selling a car or deciding not to buy one. Payment is time-based and smartphone apps allow users to locate the nearest available car (see Box 8.4 below).

Priorities for transit and efficient modes and congestion offsets as incentives for use

Incentives to encourage use of efficient modes include bus lanes and transit priority, and various types of pricing and financial incentives and disincentives. It is important to stress that quality transit means a comprehensive system—not just peak or weekday services, but must include comprehensive regional and weekday-weekend-evening coverages. Depending upon the roadway and the volume of bus service, some bus lanes can be shared

FIGURE 8.2A
Against the flow: Some cities are facilitating bicycling with counter-flow bicycle lanes on one-way streets, as in this Copenhagen, Denmark, example.

Source: Preston L. Schiller

FIGURE 8.2B
Bicycle rentals strategic locations around town, such as the BIXI bike share in Montreal are proving popular in many cities and reintroducing many residents to this pleasant form of mobility. Bike share facility outside an entrance to the Montreal metro.

Source: Jeffrey R. Kenworthy

with ride-share vehicles and taxis, and in some situations buses can co-exist with bicycles. On freeways and major arterials, and in transit-rich CBD areas, transit should be afforded bus-only lanes and transit priority measures that create greater speed and reliability than driving on congested roadways.[6] Urban highway traffic congestion tends to maintain equilibrium—traffic volumes increase until congestion delays discourage additional growth. Public transit service quality can affect the point of equilibrium: if transit is relatively fast, reliable and comfortable, potential motorists will be more willing to shift, reducing the congestion delay experienced by people who continue to drive; but if transit service is poor, motorists will be reluctant to change modes even if congestion is severe, increasing delay to all users.

Bradley and Kenworthy (2012) have developed an idea for a citywide system of congestion control that would allow buses, the only mid-level load travel option available in cities, to compete fairly with the car. Box 8.2 summarizes, in very simple terms, the ideas behind this 'congestion offsets system'.

TABLE 8.1 Summary of transportation demand management (TDM) strategies and tools[i]

General strategy	Tools or components
Improve options	Better, faster, more reliable, frequent and prioritized transit; better walking and bicycling facilities and priorities; ride-/car-share, car-on-demand, taxis; better travel information and trip planner websites. Now there are also many smartphone apps that enable people to make more informed on the minute decisions about the best way to get from A to B through a combination of modes, rather than just defaulting to the car.
Trip avoidance	Flextime, telework, teleconferencing, video conferencing.
Incentives/disincentives	Road pricing; congestion and distance-based fees; commuter benefits; transit passes, worksite amenities; parking; pricing, regulation and 'cash-out'; fuel and vehicle de-subsidization, 'pay-as-you-drive' insurance; driving and vehicle restrictions.
Land-use management, smart growth	Transit-oriented (and location-efficient) development (TOD); parking management; traffic calming; car-free planning; reducing parking requirements; mixed-use development and retrofit; more residential options near major employment centres.
Implementation and management programs	Commute trip reduction (CTR); school/campus transportation programs; mobility management and individualized marketing; tourist transportation management; freight transport management; Integrated Mobility Management Systems using smartphone apps to access multi-modal, seamless information about all travel options for any trip.

Source: derived from various sources at www.vtpi.org

[i] For more detailed information about some of these, see the excellent resources available at Victoria Transport Policy Institute (2009c), www.vtpi.org/tdm/index.php#incentives.

BOX 8.2 **Congestion offsets: controlling congestion citywide and allowing buses to compete**

Jeffrey R. Kenworthy and Matthew Bradley

Bus-only lanes are an ostensibly easy and not technically difficult way to improve bus services throughout a region. The difficult part in dedicating bus lanes is political, but the reality is that cars already take much more than their fair share of road space, and buses and bus patrons are the ones who suffer most from this inequitable situation through significantly increased journey times, despite taking up a fraction of the road space per person that is used by single-occupancy or even multiple-occupancy cars. Dedicated bus lanes can help relieve some of this inequality.

Citywide congestion controls, such as congestion offsets that penalize private cars for overusing public roads, can also enhance the competitiveness of bus services. For years now, cities worldwide have been talking about policies such as road pricing (electronic and otherwise), carbon taxes and so on to reduce car use, especially in peak periods. They have proven to be unpopular with politicians and the general population. A handful of cities, such as London, charge a fee for driving a car into the central city during peak times—not something that will address the broader congestion problem that afflicts most cities.

In Bradley and Kenworthy (2012), we suggest one possibility for such rethinking. The paper needs to be read because the technical justification of the approach and how to

continued

implement it are too much to explain in such a short summary. There is a longer summary of the thinking in Newman and Kenworthy (2015, pp. 196–99). Here is the simple version:

We should think more about congestion as a regulatory problem for which we construct a system of fines, the same way we do with parking and other roadway transgressions. This approach contrasts to the road pricing approach which tackles congestion by treating road space as a commodity to be sold at a price. The problem with road pricing is that roadways are a 'commons', owned by the public, and people don't like to pay for something they already own. We are suggesting that roads should be considered a part of 'the commons', and usage of the commons is regulated in just about every other sphere of life. We protect the commons because it is something that must function properly for everyone.

The penalties charged to motorists who contravene regulations about controlling congestion in peak periods would be termed 'congestion offsets'. Money so raised would be used to provide bus passengers, who are only using a tiny share of available road space compared to car occupants, with sharply reduced bus fares and better bus services. The under use of roadways by bus passengers would offset overuse by car occupants, with bus passengers being rewarded for their roadway under use and car occupants being penalized for their roadway over use. In this way, congestion could be cleared.

We could also go as far as suggesting that the present system of road usage and its attendant congestion in cities is a kind of 'perverse' socialism. We queue to obtain access to a scarce commodity, peak period road space, instead of recognizing that we are never going to be able to provide enough to meet demand, so we must control, in some way, the usage of the road space we do have. Some form of citywide congestion control is needed in just about every city in the world. So far, virtually no city has had the courage to introduce genuine citywide controls on car use in peak periods. Singapore is the only city to have comprehensively tried to keep its roads as free as possible from excessive car use through a variety of mechanisms. By discouraging overuse of cars in peak periods, congestion offsets would relieve traffic in our cities and allow buses to operate more efficiently and effectively.

FIGURE 8.3
The few congesting the many: One of many injustices inflicted on bus passengers in cities around the world. Innumerable public buses stuck in perpetual traffic jams along one of Sao Paulo's major downtown arteries. Crossing the street to get to the buses is very difficult and once in the bus, it moves at about the equivalent of walking pace. Note: Buses in Sao Paulo annually contribute 50 billion passenger kilometers and drive only 1.6 billion vehicle kilometers to do it. Cars contribute 80 billion passenger kilometers but have to drive 56 billion vehicle kilometers to achieve that, hence the traffic jams and the injustice of a biased transportation system (Newman and Kenworthy, 2015, p.93/4).
Source: Jeffrey R. Kenworthy

Pricing disincentives can include PMV ownership reduction strategies, such as those in Singapore and Shanghai and now Beijing and some other Chinese cities (Zhao et al. 2014; Gao et al. 2015; Newman and Kenworthy 2015), which have been or are beginning to be quite effective at suppressing the growth of PMV ownership and use. Through certificates of entitlement, would-be car owners must bid at an auction to purchase the right to own a car, which can amount to many thousands of dollars. They must then pay for the actual car. The schemes are designed to try to keep the incoming rate of new cars roughly equal to the attrition rate to achieve a relatively flat growth in car ownership, but they do not address the issue of road user equity that congestion offsets could (Box 8.2). It should be noted that pricing incentives and disincentives are among the most potent of the measures available to mobility management (Komanoff 1994). (See Table 8.1, p. 255.)

Land-use solutions to transportation problems

Since land-use patterns and urban form affect transportation, policies and programs that help to create more accessible and multi-modal communities are an important part of mobility management. Often the solution to a transportation problem is found in land use. David Nowlan and Greg Stewart (1991) found that adding residential units in Toronto's core significantly reduced automobile trips. Adding 100 residential units to a central area reduced the number of peak period trips to the center by 120. Toronto has had an aggressive increase in downtown housing, with many thousands of added dwellings facilitating easier trips to work for many residents. If a city wants less PMV traffic, it needs to add housing close to employment centers, shopping and services. Forms of development that foster traffic reduction may be called 'smart growth', 'new urbanism', 'transit-oriented development (TOD)', 'walkable communities' or 'location-efficient development'. These all include the features listed in Box 8.3, which are intended to improve accessibility and reduce per capita automobile travel.

In addition to the above approaches, another increasingly popular land-use response in Europe is car-free housing developments, or developments, such as Vauban in Freiburg (see Chapters 9 and 10), that require that people owning a car park it in a separate multilevel parking garage at the edge of the community to keep most of the public space within the community traffic-free. Many places are now also introducing the idea of decoupling the purchase or rental of a dwelling from a car parking place. Purchasers can choose to buy a dwelling without a car park, thus saving tens of thousands of dollars on the purchase price, or they can save a significant sum in monthly rent by renting without a car park. If this is also backed up with strict on-street residential parking regulations, it can be a big disincentive to car ownership and use. In Tokyo, where there is simply no room for cars in the densely built-up parts of the city, it is not possible to purchase a car unless you can provide certification that you have an off-street bay to park the car. This severely limits car ownership while keeping streets much freer of parked cars. In the context of the excellent transit systems in Japanese cities, and the very good walking and cycling conditions, such an approach seems fair and equitable.

Some cities are also reversing the traditional planning practice of 'maximum allowed density and minimum parking requirements' to 'minimum density, maximum parking' to ensure that in critical areas there is appropriate higher densities and reduced parking in recognition of good transit services and walking and cycling possibilities (see Lewyn and Rosenman 2015).

Implementation programs including Mobility as a Service (MaaS)

Mobility management programs may be found in, or organized by, local governments, large employers, campuses, business associations, transportation agencies and NGOs, such as transportation management associations (TMAs). Public transit both supports and is

---

BOX 8.3 New urbanism neighborhood design features

- Development is compact and mixed, with residential density averaging at least six units per acre (15 units per ha), a variety of building types, including small-lot single-family, multi-family, residential over retail, and various commercial and institutional structures close together.
- The community has a discernible activity center with a transit station. This is often a plaza, square or green, and sometimes a busy or memorable intersection.
- Most dwellings are within a five-minute walk from the center. Streets are designed for walking and cycling, with sidewalks on both sides, bike lanes where needed, good crossings, traffic calming features used to control motor vehicle traffic speeds, and other features to encourage non-motorized travel.
- Special attention is paid to protecting the public realm and creating quality public spaces, including sidewalks and paths, parks, streetscapes and public buildings.
- Buildings at the center are placed close to the sidewalk and to each other, creating an urban sense of spatial definition. Buildings towards the edges are placed further away and further apart from each other, creating a more rural environment.
- There are shops and services sufficient to meet common household needs, such as convenience stores, a post office, a bank machine and a gym.
- There should be an elementary school close enough so that most children can walk from their dwellings. This distance should not be more than one mile (1.6 km).
- There are parks, trails and playgrounds not more than one-eighth of a mile (200 m) from each dwelling.
- Thoroughfares are relatively narrow and shaded by rows of trees that slow traffic and create an appropriate environment for pedestrians and bicyclists.
- Networks of highly connected roads and paths provide multiple routes between destinations, increasing accessibility and reducing problems if one route is closed.
- Parking supply is minimized and managed for maximum efficiency.

Source: Swift (undated)

---

supported by mobility management. Consequently, transit planning, funding and program development are often the basis for comprehensive mobility management program development. TDM programs require a combination of resources and professional skills, including planning and evaluation, program management, appreciation of facility and community-design principles, understanding of transit planning and marketing skills.

Mobility management planning can produce a variety of benefits for individuals and society. Specific strategies have specifiable effects linked to specific benefits. A car-share program or co-operative (or car-on-demand scheme) could lead to lower per capita vehicle ownership, which relieves parking demands, as well as encouraging car-share co-op members to consider walking, bicycling or taking transit before driving. In European cities, people wishing to join a car-sharing scheme who can show that they also have an annual transit pass receive the cars for a significantly lower rate than non-committed transit users. Similarly, some smart growth strategies encourage more walking and bicycling and, therefore, are more health promoting than strategies that encourage driving.

Implementation of mobility management options is increasingly moving towards smartphone applications, which can also involve an integrated payment system for all modes (Box 8.4).[7]

Integrated planning

Integrated planning can improve the quality of public involvement as well as the planning processes and products (Givoni and Banister 2010). It may also improve policy-making,

BOX 8.4 Mobility as a Service (MaaS): a user-friendly way to optimize modal options

Sonja Heikkilä[i]

MaaS is a novel way of utilizing the already existing physical transport network by bringing new digital interfaces to make better use of the existing vehicles and resources already on streets, underground and on water as a way of optimizing the whole transport network with all its modes.

To do this, MaaS crowdsources the needs of individual persons to travel from point A to point B. For example, a person sends an inquiry to the MaaS operator, and all the modes of transport that interface digitally send their offers for the ride – bus, tram, metro, car-sharing, city bike, Uber or a shared ride, or anything in between. The system then mathematizes the available transport options for the ride, takes into consideration the personal preferences of the customer and offers the most suitable solution. Preferences can include anything, ranging from the user's budget and values (e.g. environmental friendliness, fastness, only direct routes, nice views etc.) to constraints (age, cases to carry, permanent or temporary incapacities etc.) Preferences can also be subject to time, specific trip or even weather. MaaS operators could interface with a user's calendar and suggest a mobility solution that is sufficient for the time available. The system could see if a person is late for a meeting or must make a confidential call on the way to the meeting. The intelligent MaaS operator system could also get accurate weather information from sensors on the windscreens of connected cars and perceive that it is raining and suggest those modes of transport that offer most shelter.

Figure 1 depicts the operational model of this approach. MaaS operators do not own any assets, neither cars nor drivers, but simply operate on the digital layer offering a marketplace for physical mobility services operated by the transport service providers. The mobility marketplace could be operated by a few competing 'MaaS operators' with similar—yet differentiated—mobility service offerings, including monthly subscription models. Users would then get to decide which one to use. MaaS introduces a huge leap, from either owning a car with all the hassle of it or adapting to the specific routes and timetables of public transit, to customers choosing their desired level of service (LOS) from the mobility solutions pool. LOSs could be priced differently. MaaS outsources all the planning and scheduling of one's personal mobility.

MaaS as 'mobility on demand' understands the real-time mobility needs of customers, and respectively, the availability of options in real-time. It collects the offerings of all modes of transport to the same 'fleet of mobility options', as it collects the needs of customers into the same 'pool of mobility inquiries'. With a highly

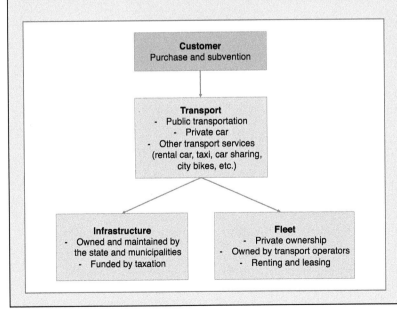

BOX 8.4 FIGURE 1
Present value chain in transportation
Source: Sonja Heikkilä

continued

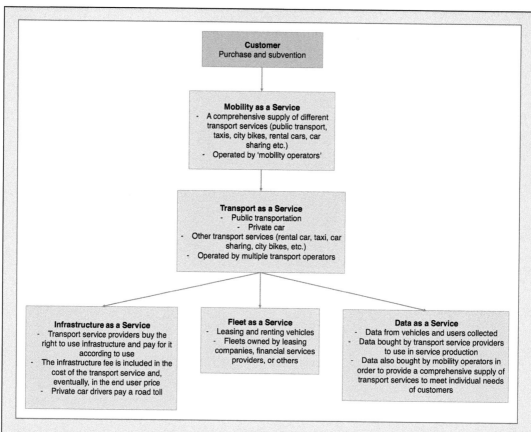

BOX 8.4 FIGURE 2 Reorganized value chain in transportation, according to the Mobility as a Service model.
Source: Sonja Heikkilä

intelligent system, the mobility operator organizes those options and inquiries to meet each other—in a matter of seconds. The result is the best possible offer for the customer and the most efficient use of the transport system. MaaS is a concept that can be applied under all local conditions; it always builds on top of the existing transport network. It also creates a fruitful ecosystem for bringing new services into itself, since small mobility service providers can reach a wide customer base through MaaS operators at once.

By organizing transportation in this way, MaaS enables us to greatly elevate the user experience, and it can be achieved with the resources that we already have. Private persons, companies, cities and states have already invested in so many vehicles—and possibly over-invested in private cars. The utilization rates of these, depending on location, could generally be higher. This particularly applies to private cars that are an unexploited resource, active generally for no more than an hour a day and simply depreciating in value. Cars can be utilized in many ways as shared cars or on-demand ride services, but the key is to seamlessly integrate these services to the rest of the transport network, especially public transit. Private cars or shared rides will almost always be needed to extend the reach of the public transit network, to perform the 'last mile' solutions at the ends of the transit system. Transit systems will likely not be built in places with few people. The future is not about owning things but about developing and utilizing services that are suited to each case in question. By utilizing and crowd-sourcing the whole transport network, MaaS will provide the same level of service, if not better than, private cars.

The concept of Mobility as a Service came to the knowledge of a wider audience in 2014, when my master's thesis at Aalto University in Finland was published.[ii] The thesis was preceded by working on a modern transport

continued

policy guided by the government. That work involved several companies and public organizations. The new transport policy wanted to respond to challenges in transportation, the possibilities offered by new technologies, and the ambitions of future users—the younger generations that drive digital and sharing economies. Challenges include the negative environmental effects of transport and lack of space in cities for cars and parking. We see much potential in new technologies and digitalization that could be applied in transportation, including physical infrastructure and vehicles. As Finns happen to be rather tech savvy and early adopters regarding new technologies, it is natural for us to see benefit from it in all fields of business. We feel that technology can bring places closer to each other and make physical resources serve as many people as possible. Finland is a country with only five million people and with great distances in between cities and towns.

Societal and economic changes, digitalization and new technologies, even autonomous cars, will radically change how we move in the future. But I believe that the need for moving will remain. Despite remote work possibilities, virtual reality and any other new technologies, people will want to move out of the house, see others, feel the air and real physical environments, enjoy random incidents. On the other hand, I think that people will evolve as customers to begin to demand more. I think this is a general trend, strengthened by the global exchange of information, that will not bypass transportation. Transportation might, in the end, require physical items operated locally; nevertheless, many aspects of the services can and will be revised globally. User experiences, price models and business models are shared worldwide. I would argue that transportation will face more demanding customers in the coming years, represented especially by the younger generations. These demanding customers are not satisfied with a nicer car, but they expect a greater level of service by the transport system. This trend of praising the good user experience can already be seen in the great popularity of Uber.

Mobility as a Service was born as a vision that needs to come down to concreteness. As described earlier, MaaS is an ecosystem that brings together all travel modes and mobility options. This is the reason why it requires a lot of work to be done by several parties. Mobility as a Service has become the backbone of the Finnish transport policy, as it is the backbone of many companies' strategies to enter the era of new mobility. We also see new companies, either startups or from different business sectors, entering the mobility field.

One of them is OP Financial Group, my current employer, the largest financial-sector player in Finland, with businesses including banking, wealth management and insurances. Surprisingly, OP sees mobility as a highly interesting area of new business development. The same goes with TeliaSonera Finland, a large

BOX 8.4 FIGURE 3
Sonja Heikkilä ready to board the bus at the Kamppi Multi-use/Multi-modal facility in Helsinki's center. Note the line of brass pieces inserted into the floor to help guide the vision challenged to the loading gate.
Source: Sonja Heikkilä

continued

telecommunications provider in the Nordic and Baltic countries. In addition to these bigger players, there are startups—such as Tuup, MaaS Global and PayiQ—that develop MaaS businesses around Finland, just to mention a few. It is an asset to have so many companies with differing know-how and business goals to work together in this fiel and, moreover, supported by the public sector. Optimally, Mobility as a Service would operate on open interfaces to the timetables, real-time location information and payment systems of different transport modes, so that MaaS operators could truly seamlessly integrate the whole service offering to their customers in an optimal way. I think Finland serves well as a test bed for MaaS, since Finland is a country of open data and open interfaces, especially on the public side.

[i] Sonja Heikkilä works at OP Financial Group, where she heads OP's strategy in mobility. She has a Master of Science in Engineering from Aalto University. As mobility is an expanding area for OP, Sonja works on new business development heading several initiatives on new mobility. Heikkilä has strong know-how in future mobility solutions and digital mobility services. Sonja is one of the pioneers of Mobility as a Service, and she has received widespread recognition for visioning and studying the future of mobility. See www.youtube.com/results?search_query=Sonja+Heikkilä+ for several videos about MaaS in which she is featured.

[ii] (*Mobility as a Service – A Proposal for Action for the Public Administration, Case Helsinki*, https://aaltodoc.aalto.fi/handle/123456789/13133)

especially through its research and implementation–evaluative/feedback dimensions. The logic of computer-based BAU transportation modelling that has prescribed more roads as a solution to congestion is a classic case of reductionist planning. It failed to examine the rebound and feedback effects between transportation and land use, and the holistic implications for the whole city of building more and more roads.[8] An integrated approach, described in the next section, will be able to better address several important ST planning issues.

Description of the new paradigm of integrated planning

The new paradigm of ST can be understood as the intersection of three major domains (Figure 8.4):

1. Planning and policy factors;
2. Background factors;
3. Technical and infrastructure factors.

Each of these domains is made up of numerous factors representing issues or questions that policy-makers, citizens and planners should address. Each of these is listed and then briefly described, drawing on material in the preceding chapters.

Circle 1: Planning and policy factors

Critical event

A critical event is often triggered by a serious problem or threat that creates great concern or crisis, which can be directed into a positive and creative solution. A road expansion plan, 'Route 20', for the inner-western suburbs of Brisbane was the critical event that triggered a citizens' reaction, leading to an exemplary traffic calming proposal for the whole community (Engwicht 1989, 1993). Some other critical events in cities are described in

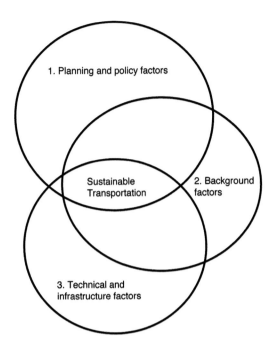

FIGURE 8.4
Sustainable transportation as the
intersection of three major domains
Source: Preston L. Schiller

The new paradigm of integrated planning can be graphically understood as a Venn diagram depicting the intersection of three circles: background factors; planning and policy factors; and technical and infrastructure factors.

Circle 1: Planning and policy factors

- Critical event
- Policy-makers, integrated policy making, policy adequacy
- Citizens and community leaders
- Careful analysis, economic evaluation, impacts
- Scenario building, evaluation of all options
- Vision of a preferred future, backcasting to inform planning
- Appropriate planning structure, motivated staff
- Deliberative planning
- Good data, evaluation
- Soft path / mobility management orientation
- Effective communications

Circle 2: Background factors

- History, heritage, culture and values
- Geography–topology
- Accountable governance systems
- Social organization
- Existing transportation and land use systems

Circle 3: Technical and infrastructure factors

- Appropriate infrastructure and energy sources
- Availability of appropriate hardware
- Appropriate standards and measurements
- Orientation and skill sets of technical personnel
- Existing built environment
- Technical aspects of environmental impacts assessment

Chapter 9, such as the City of Vancouver's banning of freeway development, Freiburg's decision to drop plans for nuclear energy, Portland's opposition to a freeway expansion and decision to build light rail and Seoul's demolition of a major freeway. One of Curitiba's most celebrated events is the 'over the weekend' conversion of one of its main streets in the central city to a pedestrian mall. Such events can change the entire course of a city because of their symbolic and practical value. Other critical events can be hallmark experiences, such as hosting of the Olympic Games, which may promote new transit investments.

Policy-makers, integrated policy-making and policy adequacy

Are policy-makers informed of the issues? Are they engaged in and supportive of a sustainable solution? Does the existing policy-making framework sufficiently integrate the relevant policy domains? Are policies about promoting walking, bicycling and walk-to transit in synchrony with investment priorities favoring sidewalks, bicycling and local transit improvements? Is current policy adequate for planning needs (Peñalosa 2003)? The crucial leadership of many mayors is addressed in several places throughout this book.

Citizens and community leaders

Are community leaders and citizens well informed about and engaged in the issue at hand? Are they supportive of a sustainable solution? Are there effective channels of communication between citizens, policy-makers and planners? Are leaders prepared to lead and take bold courses of action?

Careful analysis of problems, economic evaluation and impacts

Has the problem or issue been properly analyzed and subject to research, including economic evaluation? Have the social and environmental impacts been assessed? Is the economic analysis a broad enough one to incorporate the economic, social, environmental and cultural dimensions of sustainability for the issue being studied? Is transit evaluated for its widespread community benefits and benefits to non-users, or is it limited to the traditional balance sheets of the operators?

Scenario-building and evaluation of all options

Have analysis and research informed the development of possible future scenarios? Have all reasonable options been considered and by whom?

Vision of a preferred future: Backcasting to inform planning

Has a visioning process been undertaken, incorporating research and analysis findings within scenario-building? Has backcasting been used to inform planning for that future? Have visualization and simulation techniques been used? Has citizen science been made good use of in the process?

Appropriate planning structure

Are current decision-making bodies, procedures and codes adequate to the tasks of responding to policy changes and planning ST? Are the statutory planning frameworks and the machinery of planning geared towards producing paradigm change or BAU? It is one thing to change policy and quite another to make changes to statutory and regulatory mechanisms needed to implement and enforce policy. Are staff allowed to effectively participate and explore innovative solutions, or is the planning structure sclerotic, rigidly hierarchical and geared towards pattern maintenance? Are consultants merely brought in to rubber-stamp BAU planning or are they allowed to truly and effectively explore alternatives and engage the public in their process? If staff cannot effectively deliberate, how could they possibly engage their citizenry in deliberative processes?

Deliberative planning

There are several issues around deliberative planning that should be considered (see also Box 9.9). Do planning processes involve effective interaction with policy-makers, stakeholders and involved citizens? Is it 'deliberate and decide' (or 'debate and decide') rather than 'predict and provide'? Is there trust and confidence in the planning system and political decision-making processes that, once engaged in deliberative democracy processes, the results will be honored? Are citizens empowered to participate in deliberative democracy processes? Involvement has costs, such as child care, and needs direct support for the individuals who want to be involved. Involvement of citizens may also entail evening or weekend meetings and finding locations more convenient than city office buildings. It is important that young persons, even children, should be engaged in these processes as well.

Good data and effective evaluation

There are several issues involving good data and evaluation that should be considered. Have data sufficiently accurate for the planning process been gathered? Is there an effective and ongoing evaluation process in place to provide feedback to the policy and planning processes? Is there a reliable set of regularly monitored and reported sustainability indicators by which to determine if things are getting better or worse? For example, which way is per capita car and transit use headed? Are urban densities increasing? What is happening to walking and cycling rates? The results of such quantification help to determine the effectiveness of policy and implementation strategies.

Soft path and mobility management orientation

Are soft path and mobility management approaches favored when feasible in plan and program development?

Effective communications

Are there good forms of multidirectional communication and information-sharing in place around policy and planning processes, including web-based capacities, media and social media outreach?

Circle 2: Background factors

History, heritage, culture and values

Are these factors, both in their general and local expressions, acknowledged and taken into consideration and built upon in efforts to move towards ST? Culture and history and values can cut both ways. They can be exploited constructively to help forge change and they can be used as a reason for not changing in certain directions.

Geography, topology and climate

Are the natural physical characteristics of the locality taken into consideration and accommodated in ST efforts? The accounting of these factors needs to be positive in the direction of change. They can equally be used as an excuse for not changing. For example, it is sometimes said that people in cold climates in North America will not use transit, walk or cycle, without accounting for widespread exceptions to that rule (e.g. the whole of Scandinavia). Similarly, it is sometimes said that only cold places are ever densely populated, whereas in warm climates people want space and open lifestyles to enjoy the sun. This assertion ignores hundreds of very dense cities in hot climates and tropical zones and countless low-density cities in cold climates. In Switzerland, where topographical and climate factors often work strongly against non-motorized transport, the rate of use of these modes is still high. New technologies can also help overcome physical constraints, such as the proliferation of pedelecs in Europe, which provide electric power assistance for bike riders to negotiate hilly terrain and greatly extend the range of potential bike trips.

Legal and political systems

Are local or societal notions of polity, privilege and justice considered in ST efforts? Are systems of governance reliable and accountable, or are they supportive of the vested interests and nepotism?

Social organization

Is the organization of family, work, neighborhood and friendship networks considered and built upon in ST efforts? Is the built environment, through its treatment of the public realm, supportive of the development of loose social networks, or does it make it very hard by eliminating possibilities of 'accidental interactions'?

Existing transportation and land-use systems

Are existing systems scrutinized for improvement, including changes to make them more amenable to ST efforts, before costly changes or expansions are proposed?

Circle 3: Technical and infrastructure factors

Appropriate infrastructure and energy sources

Sustainable transportation depends upon the provision of walking, bicycling and public transportation infrastructure. Good telecommunications resources also help. Attention should also be paid to energy efficiency, as well as the generation of 'green energy'. In many parts of the world, it might be possible to directly link a source, such as local wind power or another renewable energy form, to a transit project, such as an electrified trolley or tram, as a demonstration project. In 2001, a decision was made to run Calgary's LRT system on wind energy. The program is called Ride the Wind.[9]

Availability of appropriate hardware

A diverse range of sturdy bicycles for different purposes (e.g. bikes transporting children and shopping loads, pedelecs), plenty of buses in good repair and attractive trains are the building blocks of ST. This largely depends upon funding for sustainable modes of transportation and, in particular, the relative funding treatment of infrastructure for private transportation relative to the 'green modes'.

Appropriate standards and measurements

Attention should be given to applying the appropriate standards and measurements. For example, it makes no sense to measure traffic mortality and morbidity (especially pedestrian and bicyclist deaths/injuries) in terms of miles/kilometers driven by motor vehicles, as is the practice in some automobile-dependent countries. In the U.K., claims were made that road 'improvements' (i.e. usually expansions) led to reduced traffic crash and death rates per kilometer, especially for pedestrians. Examination of this claim by Hillman et al. (1990) determined that lower crash and death rates were caused by people, especially children, walking and cycling less and thus reducing their exposure to the road system and the dangerous conditions for walking and bicycling.

Orientation and skill sets of technical personnel

It is important that staff be interested in and enthusiastic about ST. Their skills sets should be broad and multifaceted and include the ability to gather and analyze data well. Staff morale, especially within transit agencies, is dramatically affected by how much importance is placed on transit as a valued service, whether funds are being made available to expand the system and how many new major projects are being undertaken.

Existing built environment

Wherever possible, the existing built environment should be adapted and maximized to benefit ST, further the goals of compact development and reduce environmental harms. This applies to neighborhoods as well as streets. For example, are there programs to change the nature of streets to 'livable' or 'complete' streets through support for the development of social space and not just movement space? Is increasing density accompanied by parallel and complementary improvements to the public realm?

Technical aspects of environmental impact assessments

The role of the environmental impact assessment (EIA) can be crucial to whether a project is understood or well presented to the public. Some of the issues that need to be considered involve the quality of its preparations and dissemination. Has the EIA been properly done? Is it adequately understood by all those involved? Do the media understand the EIA?

New paradigm factors summary

The above sections provide an overview of several of the many ingredients involved in creating sustainable transportation. The process of introducing ST may vary depending upon the locality, population and problems addressed; there is not a set recipe. Taking advantage of critical events when they occur and ensuring that policy-making is incorporated and informed by effective citizen participation will help to set the stage for deliberative planning.

Appraisal of preliminary processes

From integrated policy-making, effective citizen participation and the various dimensions of visioning, the new paradigm approach moves to integrated planning and begins with an appraisal of:

- better management or maximization of existing resources (mobility management or TDM);
- an assessment of pertinent background factors, such as local history, the legal system, existing facilities, geography or culture that might affect the plan or its implementation;
- specifying and developing a plan around what has been learned from visioning, back-casting and other co-operative efforts between policy-makers, planners and citizen interests that have led to a vision of a desirable outcome or future.

Appropriate infrastructure and environmental assessments

The planning process then moves on to assess whether or when the limits of mobility management would indicate that new technology or infrastructure is needed to attain the goals developed in the visioning and backcasting processes. This part of the planning process necessitates consideration of:

- evaluation of all options;
- economic evaluation;
- environmental impact assessments;
- social and cultural impacts.

Evaluation of all options

Modes, technologies, routes and other factors should be evaluated for appropriateness of the plan or project under consideration at present, as well as for its future appropriateness. Assessment of technologies should ensure that it is sensitive to human aspects. For example, people have shown preferences for electrically powered transit modes over diesel ones, sometimes termed the 'sparks effect',[10] and easy to navigate and understand fixed-track systems over flexible bus systems, whose organization is sometimes opaque to the user (Hass-Klau et al. 2003).

Economic evaluation

Proposal costs and benefits, investment strategies, financing and pricing should all be carefully reviewed and analyzed. In times of governmental austerity, the possibility of tapping into new sources of funds for sustainable transportation through the private sector (such as for transit projects) should be thoroughly considered.[11]

Environmental impact assessments

In some cases, ST projects, if done well, can have environmental benefits and reverse harms done before a project's implementation, as when paved space that was the province of motor vehicles is converted to pedestrian–bicyclist space or planted with trees, or when transportation energy consumption is reduced. This is very important since the sustainability agenda demands not just a cessation of damage to environments, but actual regeneration and repair of distressed places.

Social and cultural impacts

Any proposal for significant changes needs to be socially and culturally sensitive, while at the same time avoiding being culturally or socially bound to patterns that have very negative consequences for cities at large. Getting people out of cars can be made possible through attractive alternatives, which demonstrate mobility gains. Designs for higher-density housing as alternatives to sprawl can and should be sensitive to the ways different cultures interact with each other, varying attitudes towards private and public space, different internal layout requirements, and the need for attractive green spaces.

Timeliness and timelines

- Timetables establish a calendar or schedule indicating expectations of when certain tasks or goals are to be accomplished. Timeliness is of the essence so that all involved can see the 'horizon' of the project or change proposed.
- Benchmarks and benchmarking refer to the development of standards against which activities, such as the implementation of a plan, can be judged or measured. Cities can benchmark against each other and set goals based on achievements in cities that are looked to as models of ST factors.
- Milestones are significant points that define the progress that a plan is making.

The extent to which a plan meets these expectations should form part of a comprehensive and ongoing evaluation that provides feedback to the whole process where the trends in sustainability indicators can feature prominently.

Moving from planning and policy to regeneration, repair and renewal

The implications of implementing a new planning paradigm and mobility management are enormous. During the twenty-first century, which bears the cumulative debt of decades of many poor policies and practices in transportation and planning, it is no longer enough just to stop further damage. We must regenerate, repair and renew what is already degraded.

This can happen in three ways:

1   regeneration, repair and renewal of the physical environment;
2   regeneration, repair and renewal of the social and cultural environment;
3   regeneration, repair and renewal of governance and decision-making institutions and the economic assumptions underpinning them.

Regeneration, repair and renewal of the physical environment

This entails the physical transformation of all aspects of the human environment with which people are familiar. It includes all the movement and vehicle storage space that provide the mobility and accessibility needs of people and the greening of the environment in the broadest sense of the word. It also includes the restoration of public spaces, regeneration of transit systems and all their rights of way, stops and vehicles, the renewal of the private systems of transportation, the types of vehicles, the fuels they use and the emissions that they produce and their safety for those inside and outside vehicles.

Specific examples of physical regeneration, repair and renewal would include:

* car-free zones;
* traffic calming and street and highway reductions;
* complete streets;
* freeway removal;
* restoration of environments destroyed or seriously damaged by auto-based transportation;
* biophilic architecture for greening buildings and other manmade structures.

Car-free zones

The most radical way to regenerate or repair city environments from a transportation perspective is to simply exclude cars from them. The pedestrianization schemes in the central cities of Freiburg, Copenhagen, Munich, Barcelona (La Rambla) and countless other cities around the world, have transformed these centers into dynamic, beautiful and highly livable spaces. The success of such areas depends upon maintaining access by alternative modes and ensuring that there is the right mix and intensity of land uses to guarantee vitality for most hours of the day. Good transit systems, especially rail systems, often provide the alternative accessibility needed to support car-free centers, along with excellent access by foot and bicycle to ensure that all the land uses located in centers remain on the 'movement economy'.

Car-free zones can also apply to sub-centers around the city that have a sufficient critical mass of activity and alternative accessibility to support car-free operation. Excellent examples of these are the Bogenhausen District Center (or Arabella Park) in Munich. This center is home to about 10,000 residents and 18,000 jobs and is connected to the rest of

FIGURE 8.5A
Park, Pray or shop? The town square of St Valery-en-Caux in Normandy, France, serves as a pedestrianized farmers' market several days of the week, and as a church parking lot for automobiles on Sundays (1989)
Source: Preston L. Schiller

Munich by the U4 U-Bahn line and a variety of buses. The center also has excellent access for pedestrians and cyclists from surrounding areas. The new Messestadt-Riem Center in Munich, situated on the site of the old Munich airport and built on a U-Bahn extension, also has very extensive car-free zones around the main commercial center and extending right into surrounding medium-density housing areas. Sub-centers on Stockholm's metro system (Tunnelbana), such as Vällingby, also boast car-free zones at their heart and extending into the housing areas (Newman and Kenworthy 1999a). Also, see the example of the Vauban ecologically planned neighborhood in Freiburg, discussed in Chapters 9 and 10.

Car-free zones can also operate on a temporal basis, such as at weekends or after hours in certain quarters of cities, as with some main roads in central Tokyo at weekends, some streets in Istanbul that turn into outdoor dining areas in the evening, or areas in many cities that are regularly turned into farmers' markets. Obviously, such approaches do not provide permanent repair to areas, but do provide relief from traffic at certain times.

Traffic calming and street and highway reductions

The history of human environments since the automobile has been one of devoting more and more space to cars on streets. The original function of the street as both movement and social space has been lost. Traffic calming aims to rectify this situation by reclaiming space away from the car by fundamentally redesigning streets with the purpose of:

- reducing the severity and number of accidents in urban areas by reducing speed and calming drivers;
- reducing local air and noise pollution and vehicle fuel consumption by slowing and smoothing traffic flow;
- improving and greening the urban street environment for non-motorcar users by adding street furniture, widening sidewalks and planting gardens and trees;

FIGURE 8.5B
Lion stroll: The movement for pedestrianized zones led out of squares to the spread of long pedestrian streets in many cities, such as the linear pedestrian spine in Munich incorporating Marienplatz and Karlsplatz (and several S-Bahn and U-Bahn stations to deliver people to the center) (2008)
Source: Jeffrey R. Kenworthy

FIGURE 8.6
Leipzigerstrasse, a traffic calmed
street in Frankfurt, Germany
Source: Jeffrey R. Kenworthy

- reducing the automobile's dominance on roads by reclaiming road space for living space and the ability of people to meet and feel comfortable in streets;
- reducing the barrier effects of motor traffic on pedestrian and cycle movement; and
- enhancing local economic activity by creating a greener, better environment, which attracts and holds people for qualitative reasons compared to more auto-based environments (Newman and Kenworthy 1999a).

Traffic calming is not just a traffic management tool. The first traffic calming was the Dutch *woonerf*, or 'living yard', where the street became an extension of private living space and streets were redesigned to limit cars to walking pace. Traffic calming uses changes in the vertical and horizontal geometry of the road to slow traffic (chicanes, mid-block neck downs, street width reductions, entry statements, rumble strips and so on), and good traffic calming does this in the context of enhancing neighborhood design through beautification with trees and gardens and quality street furniture, such as new light poles, bollards, benches and bike racks. Where street closures occur, the closed blocks are turned into pocket parks with usable green space and even room for table tennis tables and other games. It enhances the desirability of whole neighborhoods: along with urban reforestation, it greens the city and adds carbon sinks; it can reduce the urban heat island effect; and it can enhance social interactions in neighborhoods. Traffic calming repairs neighborhoods and city environments hurt by traffic.

Traffic calming can be applied to residential streets, shopping and mixed-use streets, as well as larger arterial roads. In the case of arterial roads, traffic calming is a street and highway reduction strategy where sections of six-lane roads are reduced to four lanes or four-lane roads to two lanes. The reclaimed space is used for providing bicycle lanes on both sides of the road, widening sidewalks, providing streetcar alignments and making space for vegetation. One of the repair benefits is that the reclaimed surface is often a more permeable green or vegetative one, allowing better infiltration of rain into the ground. Traffic calming has entered the mainstream of the

FIGURE 8.7
'Woonerf' network: shared traffic-slowed and parking-limited streets can form a pedestrian corridor making it more pleasant and safer for walking (Groningen)
Source: Jeffrey R. Kenworthy

transportation planning world, especially at the city level. While traditional transportation departments may have resisted promoting this at all in the past, a simple web search on 'traffic calming' will reveal the huge number that are now embracing and implementing it.

Complete streets

Linked with the concept of traffic calming is the movement within the transportation and planning professions in the U.S. known variously as 'great streets', 'livable streets' and 'complete streets'. These efforts are focused on reconceptualizing the whole nature of streets from 'traffic sewers' to streets that are multi-purpose in nature. Kott (2011) describes how such streets are not only tasked to accommodate private motor vehicles, but also pedestrians, cyclists, transit and nature in the form of more trees and gardens or other green space. They are multi-modal transport links as well as places for social life and active living. The push for changing streets in this way can come from initiatives that experiment for a day with new street design, such as in Bellingham, Washington, where a 'Park-ing Day' turned many parking spaces along a main street into strips of green grass where people picnicked, played games and met in a community atmosphere reminiscent of the social vitality of pre-automobile streets. Complete streets restore the balance in the public environment in favor of non-auto users and the social function of city spaces.[12]

FIGURE 8.8A
Parking into parks: In 2008 Beth Beyers inaugurated a 'Park-ing Day' when she covered over a parking space in downtown Bellingham, Washington, with sod, placed a sign informing passers-by of the burden excessive parking space places on its central business district, and invited them to enjoy a bench, picnic or make music.
Source: Jack Weiss

The sign reads:

Park[ing]

In the Downtown core, 35% of developed land area is given over to surface parking lots. This does not include parking in the right of way (street parking)

	# of spaces
Off Street	
Customer Only	3635
Employee Only	1186
Resident Only	207
Monthly Permit	446
Daily Permit	458
Hourly Permit	265
Public	541
On Street	
Metered	1240
Unmetered	1361
TOTAL	9339

FIGURE 8.8B
Park-ing Day sign: since 2008 such days and installations have grown and some have become permanent facets of the downtown; sponsors of such parklets pay the city for their lost parking meter revenues.
Source: Jack Weiss

Freeway removal

A radical form of city repair and regeneration is to tear down whole sections of freeways. Traffic tends to expand to fill the space provided for it and likewise behaves more like a gas than a liquid when space is removed, shrinking so as not to 'overflow' its container. A high proportion of traffic simply disappears. Chapter 9 explains how this principle has been used to remove nearly 6 km of freeway in central Seoul to bring back to the surface a previously highly polluted river buried under the asphalt and to provide the city with a green linear heart, full of promenading pedestrians and playing children. Other cities have successfully removed freeways: Portland, in providing the Tom McCall Park downtown; the Embarcadero freeway in downtown San Francisco to regenerate the waterfront; and Milwaukee's removal of the 1.6 km-long Park East freeway. All such projects have had a positive effect on the city's land values, and new development nearby has occurred, while the physical and social environments of the city have improved.[13]

Restoration of environments destroyed or seriously damaged by auto-based transportation

There are many opportunities to regenerate and renew parts of cities or aspects of cities that have been damaged by auto-based transportation. These include:

- rehabilitation of the visual environment;
- converting shopping malls to more compact mixed-use TODs;
- redeveloping auto strip malls into Main Street-type environments;
- converting parking lots (including Park & Ride lots) and parking structures into parks, residences, natural areas and mixed-use developments;
- constructing new transit systems integrated with a more human- and ecologically-oriented public realm;
- shrinking and greening the city;
- new vehicle technology.

Rehabilitation of the visual environment

Much of the visual environment in cities today is geared towards the automobile (see 'Carchitecture' in Chapter 2). Signs are frequent, large and designed to be read at automobile speed, which Jan Gehl, the famous Danish urban designer, terms '100 km/h architecture'. The architecture of many buildings caters to the car, rather than appreciation by pedestrians. The visual environment is also dominated by the paraphernalia of traffic management systems, such as numerous signs and lights. These visual elements make it very hard to have attractive and consistent human-scale urban design qualities. In the Netherlands, traffic engineer Hans Monderman introduced a 'shared space' system into a few small cities: all traffic signs and traffic devices were removed, as well as the marked parking bays for cars, the idea being that the 'social world' of cities should have precedence over the 'traffic world' and people would have to just work things out for themselves and resolve conflicts. The small urban environments treated using this approach were surprisingly successful and had a palpable quality of peace that was not present in the frenetic traffic-oriented environments outside the treated areas (Engwicht 2005). Much, of course, can be done to regulate the use of oversized signs in cities to restore the visual environment, and planning can regulate the design of the built environment so that many of its lost visual qualities are restored. The concept of shared space, applied to date in only a handful of smaller cities, is considered controversial even among a fair number of supporters of sustainable transportation and will probably be explored and debated for many years.

Converting shopping malls to more compact mixed-use TODs

If urban environments are to be significantly renewed, then finding enough land that can be redeveloped into new forms with fundamentally different qualities is essential. One of the biggest land resources, certainly in the U.S. and significantly in other auto-based cultures, are the shopping malls with their vast car parks. Many of these malls are economically marginal[14] and there are now several examples of the conversion of these places into compact mixed-use centers. The aim is to create developments with more sustainable features, including sustainable water management, use of renewable energy and linking to the transit system. The basic planning principle is 'placemaking' where people feel they belong, and the environment is of a human scale. Their techniques include:

- adding stores that open to the outdoors;
- placing housing above some of the retail;
- replacing large surface parking lots with structured parking and more buildings;[15]
- creating street and pedestrian connections to nearby neighborhoods.

These efforts can knit these places back together and into surrounding communities, and result in travel patterns based on transit, walking and bicycling.

Redeveloping auto strip malls into 'Main Street'-type environments

Another type of land use in great supply in the U.S. and other auto-dominated societies is the 'strip mall' of endless businesses, offices and commercial developments set back along wide multilane streets and separated from streets by huge parking lots. The street environment is dominated by huge auto-oriented signs and architecture and usually has little housing and even less greenery. However, over time such damaged environments can also be turned into more sustainable ones with much lower car use. The Sierra Club has a series of step-by-step images showing how such places in California, Florida and Colorado can be gradually renewed.[16] The process is essentially one of constructing new higher-density, mixed-use buildings for businesses, shops and residential uses to the edge of the sidewalk to create active frontages and 'sleeving' (squeezing in) a reduced amount of parking behind the buildings. Sidewalks are widened, bicycle lanes are added, trees are planted and light rail transit lines are constructed in the center of the roads.

Converting parking lots (including Park & Ride lots) and parking structures into parks, residences, natural areas and mixed-use developments

In automobile cities, parking constitutes a high proportion of land. For the burden of urban parking and ways to reduce it, see Shoup 1997, 2011. The potential to repair cities by building out parking lots and structures with land uses that promote ST is quite large. Cities such as Portland, Oregon, have already demonstrated the improvements that can occur when this happens. Pioneer Courthouse Square, the main central city square, was constructed on a former parking lot. River Place, a large and attractive mixed-use, high-density development overlooking the river, also replaced parking areas in Portland. Portland has a rather unique approach to downtown parking lots by taking a continuous row of parking spaces around the perimeter to install a line of food trailers that add an active edge to the empty blocks, creating a much richer and more visually attractive pedestrian experience (Figure 8.9).

Park & Ride lots around transit stations in some cases may be a form of land banking in cities because they are usually owned by government agencies and can easily be consolidated and redeveloped for TOD at the opportune time. These can be built out in the future with attractive mixed-use, higher-density developments, perhaps with some Park & Ride bays retained under the developments (Figure 8.10). Such developments can include some soft surfaces to increase water infiltration. Very often though, Park & Ride lots and other parking facilities in cities are the biggest 'holes' in the urban fabric, creating visual blight and making the pedestrian experience less attractive. Parking build-out strategies are a key way, therefore, of helping to repair urban environments. While some Park & Rides have been partially converted, planners and policy-makers need to approach Park & Ride strategies—and investments—whether surface or the highly expensive parking structures, with considerable caution; once motorists get into the habit of 'drive-to transit', it may be hard to undertake conversions of these facilities to a better purpose (Schiller and Kenworthy 2011).

FIGURE 8.9
Parking lot in downtown Portland replaced a few parking stalls with various food vans to add an active frontage to an otherwise dead space and create more income for citizens and their city.
Source: Jeffrey R. Kenworthy

FIGURE 8.10
Fruitvale Station on the BART rail
system in San Francisco, California,
a former Park & Ride lot now an
attractive TOD (see also later section
on "Mending and renewing the social
fabric; overcoming transportation
inequities")
Source: Jeffrey R. Kenworthy

*Constructing new transit systems integrated with a more human- and
ecologically-oriented public realm*

All efforts towards fundamental change in transportation systems and patterns of use must
involve adding new transit systems and improving existing ones. Years of marginalization
of transit systems in automobile-oriented cities, and now in developing cities, means there
is a monumental legacy of neglect that must be overcome with significant investment in
new systems. Research has shown that fixed-track systems, especially rail systems, have the
biggest positive systemic effect on urban systems. When cities are classed and analyzed
in the framework of strong rail, weak rail and no rail cities, it has been demonstrated that
when the rail system is more significant, the use of the transit system service is higher, the
occurrence of walking and bicycling is greater, there is less parking in the city and the city
has lower energy use, transportation deaths, emissions, costs for transportation, etc.
(Kenworthy 2008; Litman 2015b).[17]

It is not just a matter of building the transit systems themselves. It is important that
these new systems have excellent waiting environments and that the vehicles be powered
as much as possible from renewable energy sources. The systems also need to be integrated
within environments that are greener, more human in scale and have attractive public spaces
that encourage a more public culture. The case of Portland, Oregon, discussed in Chapter 9,
shows how (concurrently with the implementation of the new LRT and streetcar system),
the whole central and inner suburban environments, as well as the more distant suburbs
near stations, were renewed into more sustainable and livable patterns. A similar process
is occurring around stations on the Washington Metro system.

Shrinking and greening the city

In the U.S., there are many cities that are no longer able to economically maintain the vast
areas of low density within the cities or in the surrounding suburban sprawl, which, due
to a variety of factors—including de-industrialization—now have very few people left living
in them. One solution put forward in the U.S. is to buy up and demolish vast tracts of
abandoned or near-abandoned areas, cluster residents in more compact neighborhood nodes

FIGURE 8.11A
Community gardens can be used to green urban spaces and improve social capital (Coquitlam, BC, Canada). Imagine turning some parking lots into urban gardens.
Source: Jeffrey R. Kenworthy

FIGURE 8.11B
Singapore has a comprehensive biophilic architecture program designed to green all available space in buildings, on top of buildings and at street level.
Source: Jeffrey R. Kenworthy

and return the empty spaces to meadows and forest or perhaps small-scale farming. This would mean more people having direct access to nature and local food, and the city would be a much better candidate for quality transit and could potentially be more suitable for walking and bicycling. This was seriously under discussion in Flint, Michigan—the original home of General Motors before it moved to Detroit—due to the problem of a drastically declining economic situation in the city. Because of the lead-polluted water crisis, created by its irresponsible right-wing governor and his administration, all of Flint's energies have been directed to responding to that immediate problem. This program could be examined for 50 declining cities, mainly in the Midwest and north-eastern 'rust belt', including Detroit, Philadelphia, Pittsburgh, Baltimore and Memphis. The analogy is made to pruning an overgrown tree so that it can bear fruit again.[18]

In Australia and other auto-oriented societies, the situation is not so bad, although there are some declining outer areas and even some middle suburbs that are in 'negative equity'[19] or increasingly less tenable as places to live.

There are less extreme ways of urban greening for cities not in crisis, including urban agriculture, community gardens and urban reforestation on areas of land that lend themselves to this kind of renewal. Community gardens are to be found already in many cities, large and small, worldwide, including central London on sites previously slated for office development (e.g. the Calthorpe Project and the Phoenix Community Garden). Denver also has numerous community gardens facilitated by a group called Denver Urban Gardens (Newman and Kenworthy 1999a). In European cities, and increasingly in the U.S., community allotments are a major part of the urban landscape, ensuring that much more green space is interwoven within the urban region than in automobile cities. Compact development intrinsically lends itself to having more land to express nature.

New vehicle technology

Some of the negative impact of the automobile can be attributed to the type of technology used—the internal combustion engine powered by liquid fossil fuels. Any city repair strategy needs to consider the introduction of alternative technologies for private vehicles. The most promising to date is perhaps the Vehicle to Grid (V2G) electric plug-in vehicle systems, which also act as storage systems for renewable energy generation. Such systems make the most sense in the context of much-reduced travel demand since the infrastructure requirements to support a vastly increased fleet of motor vehicles, even electrically powered, could create great environmental damages.

Biophilic architecture for greening buildings and other manmade structures

Denser more transit-oriented environments also need to be green. Biophilic architecture is the term given to the greening of buildings and other structures through techniques such as green roofs and green walls. Singapore is an exemplary city in this field, having many examples of biophilic architecture (Beatley 2010; Newman 2014; Newman and Kenworthy 2015).

Regeneration, repair and renewal of the social and cultural environment

This addresses some of the deep underlying assumptions and cultural norms upon which human society has been built over many decades. It portends a shift in collective consciousness on many levels. Specific examples of social and cultural regeneration, repair and renewal include:

- active transportation and healthy communities by design;
- car-free movements;
- car-sharing;
- mending and renewing the social fabric and overcoming transportation inequities.

Active transportation and healthy communities by design

Chapter 6 explained the importance of active transportation and healthy communities and how to facilitate that through urban design approaches. Understanding of the link between the design of communities, auto-dependence, sedentary lifestyles and negative health effects is growing rapidly.[20] Auto-based societies are all seeing increases in the rate of obesity in all age groups, but especially in children, who live increasingly chauffeured lifestyles. There is thus a strong alliance developing between urban planning, transportation planning and the health professions, which is working towards awareness of the need for more 'active transportation' and urban design that promotes walking, bicycling and walk-to (as opposed to 'drive-to') transit both for obligatory travel as well as recreation. The emphasis is simultaneously on improving individual health, creating healthy communities and healthy cities, and reducing the cost burden on the health system of obesity- and pollution-related diseases. The creation of more walkable communities is at the heart of these efforts. Physical health is not the only objective here. It is also to improve social and psychological health by creating communities where there are again connections between people and an informal network of support that operates because there is more contact between people in transit, on the street, across front fences and in local shops. This helps to repair both the physical and mental health of the individual and the community.

Car-free movements

There are several social movements around the world that are attempting to draw attention to the issues that are the subject of this book. They range in order of scale downwards from the now well-established, car-free cities movement, to car-free communities and car-free housing movements. In practice, they are all strongly networked and linked, especially through conferences and the internet, so the boundaries between these different levels of car-free activities are quite blurred.[21]

FIGURE 8.12
"Divide cities into two sections: Driving and non-driving'
Source: Andy Singer (www.andysinger.com)

The push for car-free cities is a worldwide movement that espouses the qualities of traditional walking cities, such as Sienna and Venice.[22] J. H. Crawford (2002, 2009) explains in detail the precedents for car-free cities, their benefits and how to design car-free cities based on walking, bicycling and transit, including a method for involving citizens in the process. There have been several car-free cities conferences dating back to 1997 in Lyon, France, and Timisoara, Romania (2000), attended by representatives of activist organizations around the world who share an interest in creating car-free cities. The car-busters organizations are involved in the conferences and other activism supporting the concept of car-free cities through their magazine.[23] Eric Britton has been a leader in providing valuable sources of information and numerous discussions about car-free cities and related matters at his website, www.newmobility.org. He has also charted the early history of car-free days beginning with the 1950s.[24]

As with car-free cities, there is a worldwide social movement that focuses on perhaps the more manageable and achievable task of creating car-free communities or car-free housing developments (e.g. the organization Carfree UK).[25] Such organizations try to promote car-free development by explaining why it is needed and how to go about achieving it. There is a larger umbrella organization called the World Carfree Network, which facilitates World Carfree Day every 22 September. On their website, they explain the following aims:

> By following ecological and socially inclusive principles, we can build exciting, beautiful and harmonious environments on a human scale. By creating pedestrian-oriented, bicycle-friendly human habitats, we can reintroduce routine physical activity into people's daily lives. We can make destinations easily accessible to children, the elderly, the poor and the physically handicapped. We can transform existing villages, towns and cities into more desirable places to live and work, with a healthy density and mix of homes, shops, businesses and cultural destinations. We can at the same time minimize our ecological footprint by dramatically reducing our contribution to oil dependence and climate change.[26]

Commonly cited car-free communities include Vauban in Freiburg (see Chapters 9 and 10); another is GWL Terrein—a development from 1998 near the center of Amsterdam,

FIGURE 8.13
Bike creep - When cycling has reached such a high level as to encroach upon pedestrian mobility, as it has in this photo of Amsterdam as well as some other parts of the Netherlands and Copenhagen, it is time to get some of or all those cars off the street, especially those parked there, and create a better situation for bicyclists and pedestrians (2015)
Source: Preston L. Schiller

which has 591 apartments but only 135 parking bays on one side of the development, with a surrounding controlled parking zone, with residents of GWL Terrein being ineligible for parking permits.[27] While there is considerable interest in car-free communities around the world, the unfortunate reality is, especially in the U.S., that it is extremely difficult to build significant car-free housing developments because of investor reluctance and obstacles posed in the municipal codes that regulate planning and development and require large streets and parking and 'zone-out' even moderate densification (Levine 2006). Scheurer (2001) provides a very detailed review of the performance of a selection of car-free housing areas.

Overall, the ever-increasing global movement involving conferences, web networking and other means to promote car-free development at various scales constitutes a significant change in the social and cultural underpinnings of urban and transportation planning development, and collectively this movement is constantly challenging, repairing and renewing, bit by bit, the norms that have shaped human settlements for the last 75 years or so. As the popularity of car-free days spreads across the globe, more and more cities are seeing them transform their centers for one day a year, or one day a month, or inspire more car-free zones. The ongoing effort of Paris is examined in 'From Pompidou to Paris Plages and Bike-Bus Lanes' in Chapter 2.

Car-sharing

In Europe, it is becoming increasingly popular not to own an automobile and to avoid all the associated expenses and problems of finding parking spaces and paying all the costs, but rather to join a car-sharing scheme, where one can gain access to a vehicle relatively easily and with a lot less administrative effort and expense. Car-sharing has spread all over the world, including a well-developed network in North America.[28] According to a 2014 report by Le Vine et al., there were worldwide 4.94 million members of car-sharing schemes, which involved some 92,200 vehicles, or about 54 members for every car. The research shows a dramatic growth in car-sharing, with only 350,000 car-sharing members in 2006 involving only 11,500 vehicles (or 30 persons per car-sharing vehicle), with some cities more advanced than others. Car-sharing is part of a process of social and cultural change towards how society manages the need for automobile transportation.

Mending and renewing the social fabric; overcoming transportation inequities

Many attempts at reducing automobile dependence focus on the physical aspects of producing an inherently less auto-dependent environment. It is less common to find examples that explicitly address issues to do with socioeconomic groups, age and race and the need to repair and renew these aspects in planning for lower auto-dependence. The Fruitvale TOD in Oakland (San Francisco Bay Area, California) on the BART system was built on a former surface Park & Ride lot and has developed into a very attractive, dense, mixed-use development, which caters very much to older people and people of lesser means.[29]

The development has a housing area for aged persons, as well as significant affordable housing for lower-income people and facilities for families, such as a daycare center. It is situated in a low-income area of mainly Hispanic composition and ongoing management of the development, including security issues, has been an important part of its continued success. The development ensures that many lower-income families have quality housing in a well-managed development, rich in shops and community facilities and close to transit. Further development of the site involves green buildings and energy saving systems, although a fair number of Park & Ride spaces have been retained on the surface and in a structure—which weakens the ability of the site to expand its density and activity.

Regeneration, repair and renewal of governance and decision-making institutions, and the economic assumptions underpinning them

This dimension of the '3 Rs' (regeneration, repair and renewal) involves the rolling-up of sleeves and the strenuous but often rewarding work of reforming important decision-making bodies, as well as moving policy deliberations in the direction of greater sustainability in transportation.

Up to this point, this chapter has attempted to advance the discussion of ST and develop a model of how it is structured. The next step is to develop a shorter list of priorities and agenda items for its realization based on the lessons learned from this and previous chapters. Some of the most pressing priorities include the regeneration, repair and renewal of governance, decision-making institutions and the economic assumptions underpinning them.

Fortunately, there are several exemplary efforts to redefine the relationship between citizens and governance and decision-making institutions that may be drawn upon. Often such efforts are led by citizens but may involve or attract the attention and participation of government officials and business leaders. Chapter 7 cites or discusses several examples of effective citizen participation that have made a difference. Four more innovative and low-cost ways in which citizens can empower themselves and help government and transportation agencies move towards sustainability are:

1   *Rescue Muni* and *SPUR*: examples of citizen-initiated efforts that have led to organizational, fiscal and service improvements at a major transit agency.
2   *City Repair*: a citizens' effort to traffic calm, and expand, beautify and celebrate the public realm in streets and parks.
3   *Transit Camp*: an innovative way for transit-enthusiastic computer and website experts to help their local transit agencies improve information services, planning and operations.
4   *Jane's Walk*: a grassroots movement honoring Jane Jacobs by organizing free urban walking tours that bring activists, experts, government officials and just plain folks together to learn and share thoughts about community.

Each of the four efforts encapsulated above brings different types of approaches and energies to the issues they are addressing. Three of the efforts, City Repair, Rescue Muni-SPUR (see Box 8.5) and Jane's Walk (see Box 8.8), are rooted in community and ongoing organizations' approaches to issues. Transit Camp (see Box 8.7) is more of the sort of shorter-term intense effort one finds in other parts of the virtual landscape. It will be very interesting to compare the admirable efforts of Transit Camp to influence well-established agency practices with those of the other 'more into it for the long haul' efforts.

FIGURE 8.14 People power - Joining hands after transforming an intersection into 'Share It Square', Portland, Oregon
Source: City Repair, Portland, Oregon

BOX 8.5 Rescue Muni and SPUR: Riders' and citizen's planners improve San Francisco's transit

Rescue Muni is a transit riders' organization for customers of Muni, San Francisco's Municipal Transportation Agency (SFMTA), which offers bus (conventional and electric trolleys), light rail streetcar and the famed cable car services. It was founded in 1996 by Muni riders to improve the system's reliability, service and safety. Muni had been plagued for years by uncertain and uneven year-to-year funding, organizational and operational issues and some areas of friction with its ridership base. From its outset, Rescue Muni has been oriented to placing Muni on a better financial footing, as well as working in a variety of ways to foster organizational, public participation, informational and service improvements. It advocates for walkable streets and other non-motorized improvements that benefit transit and the quality of urban life. The organization conducts an annual riders' survey, serves as a citizens' watchdog group for Muni and promotes expansion of transit service in San Francisco. Rescue Muni co-sponsored November 1999's Proposition E for Muni reform after circulating its own charter amendment earlier that year and participating in city hall negotiations. Rescue Muni is an independent non-partisan group that meets regularly in downtown San Francisco.[i]

The San Francisco Bay Area Planning and Urban Research Association (SPUR) is a large century-old citizen-led organization that engages in numerous activities around improving civic quality. One of the several areas in which it engages in policy-oriented research and analysis, education and citizen engagement is transportation. In 2007 SPUR and Rescue Muni were part of a broad citizens' effort to successfully pass Proposition A, to further reform and improve Muni. Proposition A, an amendment to the San Francisco City Charter—officially called the Emissions Reduction and Transit Reform Act—was intended to strengthen Proposition E from 1999, creating greater independence and more streamlined operations for Muni and providing more funding. It included reforms designed to improve labor management that were left out of Proposition E. It was passed by the voters and among its many 'firsts' were performance standards related to global warming emissions, establishing parking maximums and calling for a reduction in greenhouse gas emissions to 80% of 1990 levels.[ii]

Subsequently, SPUR has helped the agency's Muni Forward, an umbrella of numerous service improvements including transit priority and information resources—such as a simplified and user-friendly transit map.[iii] Both organizations continue their watch dog and citizen involvement efforts and continue to inform the broader sustainable transportation community as well (Bialick 2015).

[i] See: www.rescuemuni.org/ and www.sfmta.com/cms/home/sfmta.php (accessed 24 August 2016).
[ii] See: www.spur.org/publications/voter-guide/2007-11-01/proposition-muni-reform (accessed 24 August 2016).
[iii] See: www.sfmta.com/projects-planning/projects/muni-forward-0; www.sfmta.com/sites/default/files/projects/2015/Final_Map.pdf (accessed 24 August 2016).

Source: Preston L. Schiller

FIGURE 8.15
Celebrating 'Freda's Tree', another 'repaired' intersection, Portland, Oregon
Source: City Repair, Portland, Oregon

BOX 8.6 Portland's City Repair: intersection painting to slow traffic and build community

Part of the reason for Portland's success in developing sustainable transportation (ST) policies and projects has been the willingness of its city and regional governments and its transit agency to interact effectively with its citizenry, and often accommodate or incorporate citizen initiatives within its ongoing planning framework. The City of Portland has responded well to the 'bottom-up' example of City Repair, a neighborhood-based citizens' effort that began in the mid-1990s in a few neighborhoods and has since spread to many others, as well as to other jurisdictions. Its Intersection Repair program has been reclaiming and 'repairing' intersections in neighborhoods where traffic was degrading pedestrian conditions and neighborhood amenity. By decorating intersections and sidewalks and staging celebratory events, the variety of functions that streets can serve was demonstrated. The city's transportation department has co-operated with this effort and the city has changed or adapted policy to assist in these efforts.[i] Street and intersection painting has spread far beyond its Portland origins. Numerous cities are experiencing it in neighborhoods such as the 2013 and 2014 efforts in the Happy Valley and Lettered Streets neighborhoods of the small city of Bellingham, WA (Kahn 2013, Nolan 2014). By 2016 the community took to paint brushes again for 'touch-up'.[ii]

[i] Thanks to City Repair's Matt Phillips and Michael Cook for their helpful information and photos; for more, see: cityrepair.org/ (accessed 24 August 2016).
[ii] See the photos and video at happyvalleycommunitycrossroads.blogspot.com (accessed 24 August 2016).

Source: Preston L. Schiller

BOX 8.7 Transit Camp: cyber experts get on board to help providers

Transit Camp is an effort led by citizens in a few cities to upgrade the image and services offered by transit agencies. It originated in Toronto, Ontario. It has been inspired by the phenomenon of 'BarCamp', user-generated 'un-conferences' and participatory workshops that bring together persons in semi-formal and often playful problem-solving explorations. Transit Camp attracts many computer and website experts, as well as a range of talented citizens enthusiastic about improving transit. It offers a transit agency the opportunity to take advantage of the expertise, resources and creative energy of many people whose contributions are often overlooked in the everyday world of public transportation bureaucracies. Its format is generally that of an intense workshop, usually occurring over a weekend. Sometimes there are follow-up evening meetings and workshops. Transit Camps in Toronto, San Francisco's Bay Area, Vancouver and Calgary have focused on various issues, including website improvements, web-based trip planners, improving the image and marketing of transit, developing a 'transit culture', overcoming agency stodginess and inertia, and improving security around transit.[i] Transit Camp in Calgary appears to have lasted longer than the other efforts (https://transitcamp.ca/).

[i] See: Toronto, transitcamp.wik.is/; see also transitcamp.wik.is/2007_Transit_Camp/The_Story_of_TransitCamp; Bay Area Transit Camp, barcamp.org/TransitCampBayArea; Vancouver Transit Camp, justagwailo.com/2007/12/18/vancouver-transit-camp-recap, www.canada.com/vancouvercourier/news/story.html?id=9588 298d-6139-4b9e-ac4e-aed3bd7d0216 and skytrainunconference.ca/. Thanks to Karen Quinn Fung for sharing information about Vancouver's Transit Camp (all accessed 24 August 2016).

Source: Preston L. Schiller

BOX 8.8 **Jane's Walk**

Jane's Walk developed as a citizen-initiated commemoration of Jane Jacobs in Toronto in 2007. It has since been emulated in hundreds of cities, first across Canada and the U.S. and then spreading around the globe. Citizens volunteer to lead a neighborhood walk, which becomes a strolling conversation that can range from history and heritage to architecture and neighborhood problems and solutions. At its outset, many of the walks were led by people with special expertise or interest in urban design and historic neighborhoods, such as former Toronto Mayors David Crombie and David Miller, who have participated in walks.

Walks also reach out to more marginalized neighborhoods with large minority populations, often in suburbs or urban fringes. Local neighbors, including youths, are recruited to organize and lead walks, such as in the Dorset Park neighborhood of Scarborough, Toronto. At the time of writing, one problem that Jane's Walkers in Dorset Park, an area with many residents of Middle Eastern heritage, have identified and started to address is a narrow-fenced sidewalk extending several hundred meters through an industrial area between the junior public school and adjacent park and a dense residential development. The sidewalk and its chain-link fence have badly deteriorated. The fence is sagging, occasionally snaring children who brush against it. In winter the sidewalk is often not properly cleared, forcing residents and school-children to march single file, at times through deep snow. Neighborhood residents are now organizing to resolve this problem as their walking conversation evolves into community action.[i] Jane's Walks can now be undertaken in many cities: In 2016, over 1000 Jane's Walks took place in 212 cities in 36 countries across six continents.[ii] Another Jane's Walker, Shawn Micallef (2010), has written about what can be learned from observant walking about the city that Jane Jacobs inspired.

[i] See: janeswalk.org/ (accessed 24 August 2016); Micallef (2009).
[ii] See: janeswalk.org/information/cities/ (accessed 21 July 2016).

Source: Preston L. Schiller

FIGURE 8.16
Taking a Jane's Walk to discuss how to repair and improve a pedestrian pathway
Source: Jane Farrow, director, Jane's Walk

FIGURE 8.17
Jane Jacobs and other Stop Spadina veterans Jerry Englar (on bike) Alan Jacobs (rear) and Alan Powell (left), joined by author and harpsichord kit inventor Wolfgang Zuckermann (center) on the Toronto Islands at the 1991 Eco-City Conference and 20th-anniversary celebration of defeating the once-proposed but defeated Spadina Expressway.
Source: Preston L. Schiller

Sustainable transportation agenda and priorities

The examples above and the bulk of this chapter suggest some of the priorities for a ST agenda. Priorities would include:

- Strategic increases in density and mixed-land uses at critical nodes or sub-centers to develop a polycentric urban form.
- Prioritizing investment in transit, walking and cycling to overcome many decades of neglect and favoring of PMVs. First-rate transit systems must be built and land uses integrated around them (TOD) and new financing approaches to supplement scarce government funds need to be pursued.
- Transit systems to be given clear speed advantages over private traffic, especially through many more dedicated rights-of-way and much more traffic light priority.
- Reform of public transportation agencies that have for too long focused on maintaining their status quo and BAU, rather than becoming bold innovators and agents of change. Citizen-led efforts, such as Rescue Muni and Transit Camp, point to ways in which citizen energy can renew such agencies.
- Respecting, protecting and restoring the central importance of the public realm and its influence on non-motorized mobility and the social life of the city to ensure a livable, beautiful, connected city.
- Changing the ways in which citizens interact with governance and planning bodies. Examples of more productive forms of public participation have been presented in this chapter and Chapter 7. More will be presented in Chapter 9.

These are priorities that have been realized in some ways in several of the exemplary cities explored in the next chapter.

Agenda items for reforms that need to be accomplished but are difficult, especially at the city and metropolitan levels, because they require change at state–provincial, business, national and even some at international levels, include:

- Overcoming transportation inequities; cities may or may not be able to improve transit, walking and bicycling independent of national reforms or funding, but creating effective railway networks or reducing levels of air transport must be addressed at higher levels, as has been done very quickly by the Chinese government in building a vast high-speed rail network that only opened in 2007;

- Major economic and transportation pricing reforms; especially the de-subsidization of driving and other harmful dimensions of transportation.

The influence of a sustainable transportation 'prophet' is presented in Box 8.9.

BOX 8.9 Kenneth R. Schneider: fighting for change

Jeffrey R. Kenworthy

The writings of Kenneth R. Schneider in his books *Autokind vs Mankind: An analysis of tyranny – a proposal for rebellion, a plan for reconstruction* and *On the Nature of Cities: Towards enduring and creative human environments* remain today probably the most powerful and convincing dissections one can read about the excesses of automobile dependence and the irrationality of continuing down that path. Alas, in the early and even late 1970s in the USA, these were not the kind of analyses or exposés that most people in the transportation policy and decision-making community wanted to read, and even less respond to constructively. His writings at the time were truly voices crying in the wilderness, and yet for those of us beginning to see the lunacy of the transportation trajectories of that time his words were a great source of inspiration, a challenge and a call to action. Today, his words are part of an accepted wisdom about the need to tackle monocultural approaches to transportation systems.

As a young student, in 1979, I wrote to Ken after reading his second book praising its contents. He wrote back saying that my letter was the only one he had ever received—indeed the only positive thing anyone had ever said at the time about *On the Nature of Cities* or his other writings. He said he might just as well have written the book in Sanskrit. Ken became a good friend and I visited with him in Flagstaff, Arizona, where he lived at the time, and learned much from him about cities and their problems, and the foibles of modern auto-based planning, especially as it was practiced in the developing world (he was part of a UN Commission to help plan a new capital for Nigeria, an exercise that left him quite depressed because of the impregnable auto-orientation of all those around him). But Ken also provided wonderful insights into the desert and canyon country of Arizona and Utah, which he deeply loved, and the Hopi Indians with whom he worked as a teacher before turning his sights on the automobile.

Ken shared with me a still-unpublished manuscript called *The Community Spaceframe*, an impassioned 'built environment' response to the disconnected and inhuman ways he saw human settlements being built all around him. The community spaceframe in simple terms was a dense walking settlement, connected to high-quality transit, but it was above all a vision of a way of life where people again had human community, where they provided mutual support in an environment that did not build in isolation. He understood density; he understood that cities by their nature had to have certain threshold densities for their well-functioning. Low density, for him, was the disease of the automobile, which eliminated the very nature of what a city was all about. Of course, he was in good company here with Mumford and Jacobs.

Ken also confided that the book he still wanted to write about cities and transportation would be called *The City Fight Book*. This was not a wanton call to conflict. It was his clear thinking and experience that cities and their transportation systems can never change without a fight, whether that is a community-led rebellion against BAU or the headlong clash between different planning and transportation ideologies within the realm of government. Time has certainly proven him correct on this point.

Ken is no longer with us and he never got to write that book. Janette Sadik-Kahn, with co-author Seth Solomonow (2016), may have come closest to realizing Ken's dream with her *Street Fight* book (*Handbook for an Urban Revolution*). But he still stands as one of the great thinkers and dreamers about transportation and the cities they shape. He sounded among the clearest, most passionate and most articulate warnings and calls to action against the dominance of auto-based planning of any writer. Above all, he always had the 'common good' in cities foremost in his thoughts. He is sorely missed, but his writings helped shape a generation of thinkers and urban activists, and are still highly relevant as lucid reminders of where we have come from and the fights that remain to be won.

From the new paradigm to its embodiment

In the next chapter, we will explore several examples of cities that have engaged in the process of introducing sustainable transportation. What is clear from this chapter is that a truly significant task for any one city or country is to embrace all the potential factors that contribute to the success of ST. The clear message from exemplars seems to be that change begets change, so the first steps towards paradigm change in any of the areas discussed in this chapter can have a much bigger impact than the mere sum of the individual parts. They can be part of a multiplicative regeneration, repair and renewal process. Cities are eco-systems, and in ecosystems every factor and part is linked to every other factor and part.

In Chapter 9, it is shown how Seoul's removal of a central city freeway has restored and greened the physical environment, giving citizens a whole new space in which to walk and interact with other people. Its successful freeway removal has inspired more fundamental changes in the culture within planning organizations and the city's transportation planning orientation towards transit, walking and cycling. The Portland, Freiburg and Boulder exemplars also have elements of regeneration, repair and renewal of the physical, social, governance, decision-making and economic aspects of their cities. The examples of Mumbai, Shanghai, Beijing and Guangzhou give hope to giant cities that, given the right policies, they can effectively resist further motorization and indeed begin to claw back lost ground with strategies such new rail transit systems and car ownership controls. Certainly, these cities give much-needed hope to other cities grappling with the need to regenerate their urban environments.

Questions for discussion

- Identify at least one significant difference between business as usual (BAU)/predict and provide and mobility management/transportation demand management (TDM) approaches and orientations to urban transportation planning and provision.

- Discuss the differences between 'mobility' and 'accessibility' in terms of the differing approaches to planning and investment of each and some of their consequences for urban form, the economy and the environment.

- Compare a few of the differences between forecasting and the 'old paradigm' of business as usual (BAU) with backcasting and the 'new paradigm' of integrated planning, participation and policy-making in terms of likely outcomes.

- Why does it currently appear to be easier to advance a sustainable transportation program at the level of cities and regions than at the level of states/provinces or nations?

- What are the suite of options available for effectively limiting traffic in cities and controlling congestion? Why has no city in the world so far found a willingness and a way to implement citywide controls on congestion, as opposed only to disincentives on traffic entering central areas (as some cities such as London, Stockholm, Oslo and other cities practice)?

Notes

1   As it was then called; now it is known as 'transportation engineering'.
2   Norman Kennedy (1963) 'Evolving concept of transportation engineering', *Traffic Engineering and Control*, cited in Plowden (1972).
3   Newman and Kenworthy 1984, 1989, 1999a, 1999b; Newman et al. 1988; Goodwin et al. 1991; Kenworthy 2012
4   See Schwedler (2007); also see his endnote 1 and www.thepep.org/en/workplan/ia4pi/ia4pi. htm.

5   For more on this topic, see the excellent resources at the Victoria Transport Policy Institute (2008, 2009a, 2009b, 2009c).

6   See discussion of transit priority in Chapter 5, Box 5.1.

7   See a Europe-wide vision for such a system at www.rupprecht-consult.eu/uploads/tx_rupprecht/TRANSFORuM-RM-MIMP-Summary.pdf (accessed 24 August 2016).

8   see Kenworthy (2012) in this book and also Beimborn, E., Kennedy, R. and Schaefer, W. (1995, 2006) *Inside the Blackbox: Making Transportation Models Work for Livable Communities*. Environmental Defense Fund, New York, NY.

9   See: www.re-energy.ca/ridethewind/backgrounder.shtml.

10 'The *sparks effect* is a well proven phenomenon whereby passenger numbers significantly increase when a line is electrified.' See: citytransport.info/Electtrn.htm (accessed 21 July 2016).

11 For example, the new Entrepreneur Rail proposal taken up by the Federal Government in Australia—Newman et al. 2016.

12 See: www.completestreets.org/, www.tc.gc.ca/programs/environment/utsp/sidewalkCafes. htm, www.squirepark.org/project_pages/reclaiming-streets-for-the-people/ and www.bellingham herald.com/102/story/1076038.html (accessed 24 August 2016).

13 See: www.preservenet.com/freeways/FreewaysInducedReduced.html (accessed 24 August 2016).

14 For an extraordinary visual tour of defunct shopping malls in the U.S. and their stories, see: www.deadmalls.com (accessed 21 July 2016).

15 See: www.newurbannews.com/Mar08Malls.html (accessed 24 August 2016).

16 See: www.sierraclub.org/sprawl/community/transformations/ (accessed 24 August 2016).

17 For people's preferences for rail see also: usa.streetsblog.org/2012/06/21/explaining-the-psychological-appeal-of-rail-over-buses/ (accessed 24 August 2016).

18 See: www.telegraph.co.uk/finance/financetopics/financialcrisis/5516536/US-cities-may-haveto-be-bulldozed-in-order-to-survive.html (accessed 24 August 2016).

19 Carrying mortgages that are more than the house is now worth.

20 e.g. Besser and Dannenberg 2005; Frank et al. 2003; Jackson 2012; Lopez 2012.

21 Critical mass bike rides that are held in some 300 cities all around the world to draw attention to the bicycle as a legitimate means of transportations could be considered another manifestation of this worldwide car-free movement; see: en.wikipedia.org/wiki/Critical_Mass (accessed 24 August 2016).

22 See: www.carfree.com/ (accessed 24 August 2016).

23 See: carbusters.org (accessed 24 August 2016).

24 See: www.academia.edu/15248436/A_Short_History_of_Car_Free_Days_Origins_Timeline_Progress (accessed 24 August 2016).

25 See: www.carfree.org.uk/ (accessed 24 August 2016).

26 See: www.worldcarfree.net/about_us/global/charter.php (accessed 24 August 2016).

27 See: www.carfree.org.uk/043 (accessed 24 August 2016).

28 See: www.carsharing.net/ (accessed 24 August 2016).

29 See: www.unitycouncil.org/fruitvale/overview1.htm (accessed 24 August 2016).

CHAPTER NINE

Cities on the move: global exemplars of more sustainable transportation

Introduction

Most of the ideas underpinning the quest for more sustainable urban transportation systems are not 'rocket science'. Everyone knows that cities need to transfer more travel onto the green modes—transit, walking and cycling—and, to use one of the more recent terms, 'feral transportation': all those 'wild' and sometimes noisy or annoying modes including skateboards, dirt surfers, in-line skates, scooters etc. The most basic unifying element of sustainable transportation is to ensure that use of the high energy-consuming and space-demanding private automobile is minimized. It is not just about particular modes or technologies, but also those elements of land-use planning that facilitate the use of more sustainable modes such as transit-oriented development (TOD).

This chapter provides an overview of some cities around the world that are achieving significant gains towards more sustainable transportation and others in rapidly motorizing countries that are beginning to tame their traffic and see some positive trends. It highlights some of their most significant achievements, some ways in which they are doing this and some reasons for hope that cities in countries such as India and China may rather quickly curb their headlong pursuit of the automobile and not become automobile dependent.[1] Where possible, some recent and previously unpublished research results of trends in cities in transportation-related indicators are presented to highlight the success or otherwise of the world's cities towards becoming more sustainable in transportation.[2]

Not wishing to repeat the already copious information available about Curitiba's famous bus system and former Mayor Jaime Lerner or Bogotá's TransMilenio bus rapid transit system and its Mayor Enrique Peñalosa, this chapter leaves these excellent examples for readers to explore themselves or review elsewhere in this book. One point that is often unrecognized about Curitiba is that some of its most famous achievements were done in the military dictatorship period, when it was not unusual for elected officials to act precipitously in public matters.[3] Land use and transportation development are under the same regulatory control in Curitiba and dense development is easily directed at the structural axis of the city linked to the bus rapid transit system; a power most cities would like to be able to wield. Probably only Stockholm, among democratically responsive cities, has ever achieved such tight coordination of land-use and transportation development, as when it developed its Tunnelbana metro system and high-density satellite centres, commencing in the 1950s.[4]

This chapter has chosen as its primary focus cities from diverse urban cultural and socio-economic contexts that represent either more comprehensive achievements towards sustainable transportation or are presenting perhaps unexpected resistance to their motorization trend of recent years. Five of these are Vancouver (British Columbia), Portland (Oregon), Boulder (Colorado),[5] Freiburg im Breisgau (Germany) and Seoul (South Korea). It also examines some important data and trends in Mumbai, Beijing, Shanghai and Guangzhou, which suggest that there is no inevitable or inexorable trend toward motorization in dense, rapidly industrializing cities where the urban fabric has never been designed around the car. This sample of cities thus provides an instructive range of exemplars.

These are not the only case examples worthy of attention, but collectively they do touch on a significant number of the major issues of concern in promoting more sustainable transportation: public participation, increasing densities, promoting better transit, linking development better to transit (TOD), enhancing conditions for non-motorized modes, improving the public realm of cities, de-emphasizing roads such as through freeway removals, controlling car ownership. We provide an even greater sense of this global sea change in an appendix at the website accompanying this book comprised of resources about interesting and relevant initiatives from various other cities related to sustainable transportation, as well as some short biographies of some key figures and NGOs in sustainable transportation over the years.

Vancouver, British Columbia: Automobile city to a planner's pilgrimage

Vancouver is a metropolitan area of some 2.5 million people. Perhaps its most distinguishing feature in a North American context is that the City of Vancouver (627,000 people) at the core of the region[6] built no urban freeways apart from two very short viaducts, which were the opening salvos in the early 1970s for what was to become an extensive urban freeway system but which never eventuated. It has become to urban planners what Stockholm achieved in the 1950s when it built its Tunnelbana, or modern metro system, and proceeded to build whole communities of satellite towns around its stations, such as Vällingby and Kista. Stockholm became an official global pilgrimage site for planners to view the best in TOD, complete separation of cars from pedestrians and cyclists, and other excellent urban design features encouraging walking and cycling.

Vancouver's transformation from a typical auto-city with a relatively short urban history compared to its East Coast North American counterparts commenced during the early 1970s with the successful community-led fight to rid the city of all planned freeway construction within the City of Vancouver boundaries. This fight involved a then shop front lawyer named Michael Harcourt who helped the Chinatown community to remove the threat of a freeway. He later became a Vancouver city councilor, mayor of Vancouver and, finally, premier of British Columbia, a political career built significantly on fighting freeways and campaigning for more livable neighborhoods in their place.

Notwithstanding the reality of this community opposition, nor diminishing its importance in setting a future tone and course for the city, an alternative interpretation of why the City of Vancouver dodged the freeway bullet—while Montreal and Toronto largely did not, despite a lot of community unrest and opposition—is offered by Perl et al. (2015). In detailed case studies of expressway development in Montreal, Toronto and Vancouver, they found that expressway development is directly related to the timing and strength of global city aspirations and the particular local political conditions in the three cities at different times: Montreal in the freeway-oriented 1960s as a city of 'global status'; Toronto in the 1970s when funding was relatively plentiful; and Vancouver's case may have been due to the combination of community resistance and lessened availability of funding resources.[7]

FIGURE 9.1
View of False Creek South, Vancouver, British Columbia – an area that would have been lost to freeway infrastructure and is now a walkable neighborhood
Source: Jeffrey R. Kenworthy

TABLE 9.1 Vancouver key figures (Metro Vancouver or the former GVRD area)

Population (2014)	2,474,123
Population (2006)	2,116,581
Metropolitan GDP per capita	US$29,582
(US$ 1995; 2006 adjusted)	
Urban density (persons per hectare; 2006)	25.2
Road length per person (metres; 2006)	4.7
Car use per person (vehicle kilometres traveled, or VKT, per year; 2006)	6,971
Transit service (transit vehicle kilometres of service per person; 2012)	52
Transit service (transit vehicle kilometres of service per person; 2006)	55
Transit use (boardings per person; 2012)	150
Transit use (boardings per person; 2006)	134

*Source:*Jeffrey R. Kenworthy

Instead of large clover-leaf junctions punctuating the downtown area, Vancouver is home to perhaps one of the most dynamic and lively central and inner-city populations of any city in the auto-dependent world at places such as False Creek North and South, Yaletown, the city's West End, Coal Harbour Redevelopment, as well as many other sites. [8] The absence of high-speed road travel has meant that premium locations, near the heart of most amenities and speedy transit, have become the most popular places in which to live in order to maintain accessibility and acceptable daily travel times. The Vancouver region's average road traffic speed in 2006 was only 38.6 km/h, whereas metro areas in the U.S. and Australia average between 43 km/h and 52 km/h (Kenworthy 2009).

Vancouver comparisons

We can compare the Vancouver metropolitan area[9] with other Canadian and international metropolitan areas and examine the trends in some key factors primarily over the 1996 to 2006 period and earlier, with some selected data for 2012. In land-use terms, Vancouver had trends typical of North American cities between 1961 and 1981. Urban density declined from 24.9 persons per hectare in 1961 to 21.6 per hectare in 1971, to 18.4 per hectare in 1981. At the time that its strong re-urbanization policies began to cut in (discussed later), assisted significantly by the absence of high-speed private transportation options, it then started to increase in density. In 1991 it rose back to 20.8 persons per hectare; 1996 saw 21.6 persons per hectare; and in 2006 it exceeded its 1961 density and was sitting at 25.2 persons per hectare, a 17% increase in 10 years (Kenworthy and Laube 1999; Newman and Kenworthy 2015). Land-use change of this magnitude that is focused mainly in central and inner areas, but which generates a significant increase in density across an entire region of more than two million people, is hard to achieve, especially since some parts of the region are continuing to grow with lower suburban densities. One factor that has probably helped to raise the acceptability and success of high density in Vancouver is the large number of ex-Hong Kong residents who were courted by Vancouver prior to the return of Hong Kong to Chinese rule.

In terms of car use, per capita annual car kilometers in 1981 were 6,756 km, which rose to 8,361 km in 1991. By 1996, this was down to 6,746 km and in 2006 it had risen slightly (3.3%) to 6,971 km. But the net effect is that in the15 years between 1991 and 2006, car use per person in Metro Vancouver decreased by 17%. Part of the reason for this change is no doubt due to increases in density, which, in turn, have helped to increase transit usage. But density is not the only factor in increased transit use. Vancouver also commenced in 1986 to develop a rail backbone to its transit system in the form of its newly opened Skytrain system, which afforded much faster urban travel.

In 1981, transit use was 111 annual boardings per person, and this declined to 95 per person by 1991. In 1996 it rose to 118, in 2006 it stood at 134 boardings per person per annum and by 2012 it had reached 150.[10] This exceeds the 1961 figure of 138 trips per person, when car ownership in Vancouver was a mere 285 cars per 1,000 people. Now, with 9% more transit use as in 1961, the region has more than 500 cars per 1,000 people. Clearly, even in the context of high car ownership, transit is becoming more attractive and popular with Vancouverites due to a combination of better, speedier and more diversified services, and more attractive ticket offers, especially to students, but also because many more people are now living within walking distance to transit stops and feeder services to speedier rail, and bus services have improved greatly. Perhaps consequently, Vancouver's car ownership was even down by 3% in 2006 from the 1996 figure of 520 per 1,000. On the downside, transit—especially around Skytrain stations—has experienced increasing crime levels in the last few years, giving rise to many concerns in Vancouver.[11]

Part of this process of change is also reflected in central business district (CBD, downtown) parking per 1,000 jobs, which in 1971 stood at 341, rising to 342 in 1981 and then dramatically rising to 443 in 1991 and 444 in 1996. In 2006, CBD parking supply took a drop back to 389 spaces per 1,000 CBD jobs. For comparison, in 2005, U.S. cities averaged 509 spaces per 1,000 CBD jobs, or 31% more than in Vancouver. The low level of freeway provision in the region is also significant.[12] Freeway length per person fell from 0.077 m to 0.069 m between 1996 and 2006, while U.S. cities in 2005 stood at 0.159 m per person, some 130% more than in Vancouver. Other positive features of Vancouver's transportation trajectory are an increase in transit service per capita (vehicle kilometers per person), up by 13% from 1996 to 2012, and a fall in transportation-related deaths from 6.5 to 5.4 per 100,000 people.[13]

Better transit service

Compared to most American cities, Vancouver enjoys high levels of transit use; about triple that of the average for 20 medium-to-large U.S. metro areas of 51 boardings per person in 2010 (Kenworthy 2013). The New York–New Jersey–Connecticut (tri-state) metropolitan region is by far the most transit-oriented U.S. urban area and it had, in 2010, 192 boardings per person. Vancouver is also catching up to Montreal and Toronto, which have traditionally exceeded Vancouver's transit use by much larger margins. In 2012, the Montreal region had 210 transit boardings per person (up from 206 in 2006) and Toronto had 164 (up from 154 in 2006).

Vancouver's transit system consists of a comprehensive network of both diesel and elec-trified trolley buses; specialized bus services for people with disabilities; an advanced elevated and driverless light rail transit (LRT) system called Skytrain operating at less than two-minute intervals in the peak and three- to four-minute intervals in the off-peak; a commuter rail line called the West Coast Express, servicing distant suburban communities; and a ferry service called the Sea Bus. There is a new fully automated 18.5 km partially underground, partially elevated and partially at-grade rail line from the city to the airport and a branch into the Richmond suburbs, which opened in August 2009. It was expected to have an average weekday ridership of 100,000 per day by 2010,[14] but by June 2011 it had already reached 136,259.[15] On December 2, 2016, Vancouver opened an 11 km extension of the Skytrain system from Coquitlam City Centre through Port Moody town center and on to Lougheed Town Center.[16]

Within the City of Vancouver, which is built on a fine-grained traditional street grid, the bus system is relatively frequent, with buses operating north–south and east–west, providing good radial and cross-city travel opportunities, with speedier services called the B-Line in some areas. Overall, however, bus average speeds are mostly below 20 km/h due to frequent stops, many intersections,[17] low enactment of transit priority, a lack of transit-only lanes outside of the CBD, moderate traffic congestion and passenger loads that are often horrendously high, affording poor passenger comfort. The buses do, however, interconnect well with each other in many locations and transfers to Skytrain, the West Coast Express, the Sea Bus and the recently opened Canada Line are also well catered for, meaning that mobility in all directions across the whole region on transit is feasible without necessarily passing through the central area. The lack of freeways in the City of Vancouver means that although the bus system is often slow, travel speeds can still be competitive with the car, especially where a rail segment or B-line bus is involved.

The major challenges in Vancouver, due to its transit-conducive urban form and growing transit ridership, are to increase transit speed, frequency, capacity and comfort for riders, as well as to extend the rail system and bus rapid transit service options into other parts of the region.

Transit-oriented development (TOD)

A major success factor of transit development in Vancouver over the last 30 years has been the strong efforts to integrate high-density residential and mixed-use development in significant nodes around selected stations on the Skytrain, redevelopment of highly favored waterfront areas such as False Creek and Coal Harbour, and even, in some cases, the development of strong town centers around bus-only or bus plus commuter rail nodes such as Port Moody (now with a Skytrain service). Skytrain's development has gone together with planned TOD high-density development, from which it draws a lot of its patronage. Park & Ride around stations in the City of Vancouver, City of Burnaby and City of New Westminster have been expressly excluded in favor of high-density uses clustered close to station entrances. These developments exist at numerous stations such as major centers at Metrotown, New Westminster and smaller developments at other stations such as Joyce–Collingwood and Edmonds Stations and now on the Canada line.[18] South of the Fraser River in the Surrey suburbs, Park & Rides surround some stations such as Surrey Central, with development set back from the station. The resulting urban design outcomes are very poor compared to those north of the Fraser.

The larger nodes on Skytrain have mixed commercial, office, residential, retail and markets within a short walk of the station. The new housing consists of quality high-rise towers, three- to four-story condominium-style developments and townhouses. Some of the housing consists of individual housing co-operatives that have provided more affordable housing options.[19] The TOD at New Westminster is set along an attractive landscaped boardwalk on the Fraser River (between 10th Street and Rialto Court) that includes playgrounds for children and extensive gardens, trees and grassed areas (Figure 9.2). The family units have inner courtyards in which families and friends congregate. The farmers' market, where residents can do their shopping, is communally orientated with open eating areas and a more relaxed, less structured, less sterile atmosphere than a supermarket.

Some significant evidence for the preference of Vancouverites for such well-located, short-distance, non-auto travel option sites is the rapid increase in the population of the City of Vancouver, the core of the whole region, which grew from 431,147 in 1986 to 626,539 people in 2014, an increase of nearly 200,000 people, or 45%. The gross density of the City of Vancouver[20] has increased from 37.6 persons per ha to 52.5 persons per ha over this period. This density exceeds the 2005 urban density of cities such as Bern (42.8), Frankfurt (45.9) and Zurich (43.0) and now approximates the densities of Berlin (54.1) and London (58.4).

As well as the obvious nodes that have sprung up within the existing urbanized area around Skytrain in the years since its 1986 opening, the re-urbanization trend leading to the significant population increases just described has resulted in an enormous amount of other new development along the major diesel and trolley bus lines in the city, where a lot

FIGURE 9.2
TOD development along the Fraser River within walking distance of New Westminster Skytrain station, New Westminster, British Columbia
Source: Jeffrey R. Kenworthy

of mixed-use shopping and business activities already exist (e.g. the Arbutus Lands development). This development consists of medium- to high-density housing (sometimes shop-top housing) with special attention to the needs of families wishing to escape the car-dependent suburbs, though high prices are a problem to many. Specific design manuals are aimed at producing compact environments suitable for a whole range of household types.

Perhaps the most extensive and impressive of this redevelopment is the very high-density development at False Creek, located near to the downtown area and serviced by frequent trolley and diesel bus services and some Skytrain stations at points near its periphery.

Development at both False Creek South and North (Yaletown), as well as the new South-East False Creek, developed at even higher densities and as something of an 'ecological model', provide excellent examples of how to build high-density, transit-oriented urban villages in central locations with extensive and beautifully designed open spaces, together with mixed-land uses such as markets, schools, community areas, hotels, cultural activities, shops and restaurants (e.g. Granville Island). There is an enormous variety in housing forms and styles in these areas, including townhouses, terraced units, medium-rise and high-rise apartments, with many of the earlier ones being co-operative housing ventures. The extensive public spaces that knit all parts of False Creek together are traffic free, with smaller streets providing access to parking, which is mostly underground.

The public realm of the whole False Creek area consists of first-class, wide pedestrian- and bicycle-only facilities, gardens, squares and green spaces and it is this environment at ground level, below sometimes towering residential complexes, that gives people the option of sustainable transportation, as well as conviviality and convenience. Along this pedestrian system, there are local shops, community facilities, child-minding centers, professional suites for dentists and doctors, meeting areas, community playgrounds and sports areas, all integrated within walking or cycling distance of most residences. For a central city location, False Creek provides an exceptionally quiet area and, yet, a dynamic and varied urban location for residents and the many visitors who use the area for social and recreational purposes.

Developments discussed so far in Vancouver have helped to minimize growth in car use in inner areas by increasing transit use and making the use of non-motorized modes more feasible and attractive. The important point here is that Vancouver is trying to minimize outward sprawl and gradually reshaping itself into a more transit-oriented region.

FIGURE 9.3
Port Moody town center's attractive
public realm, suburban Vancouver
region
Source: Jeffrey R. Kenworthy

Apart from these waterfront areas, the Skytrain stations and high-density residential precincts in the inner city of Vancouver, the region has many areas of high-density development such as at Port Moody and North Vancouver. Within these centers pedestrians and cyclists are given attractive and comparatively safe conditions and there exists a civic life in the urban spaces that is atypical for most North American cities, where 'big-box' retail centers and office parks are more often the norm.

This process has been historically shaped by the Greater Vancouver's regional planning strategy (Livable Region), which effectively created a green belt for the region and limited the amount of suburban land that can be developed. This is on top of an already topographically constrained city due to mountainous terrain and the narrow Fraser River Valley. Metro Vancouver's new regional plan, *Metro Vancouver 2040: Shaping Our Future*, continues this process.[21] The region's efforts to manage growth also have been greatly aided by the New Democratic Party's 1973 Agricultural Land Reserve Act (ALR), which preserves forests, wetlands and farms.[22]

It has been public policy since the mid-1970s to try to concentrate much development in transit-rich locations. Public consultations with communities affected by Skytrain-linked redevelopments occurred as early as 1978, eight years ahead of the opening of the first Skytrain segment in 1986 for the Expo that occurred on the land now known as False Creek North, or Yaletown. This high density has occurred at stations in Vancouver as well as neighboring Burnaby and further down the line in New Westminster, at stations such as Joyce–Collingwood, Metrotown, Edmonds and New Westminster, and is now also happening around the Canada line and with significant proposed retrofits for Brentwood Mall and Lougheed Town Center. Such TODs are gradually reshaping the Vancouver region into a genuine polycentric 'transit metropolis' (Cervero 1998). An interesting article from 2016 with images captures the extent to which TOD is happening around rail stations in the Vancouver region.[23] Some key factors that have supported this land-use evolution have been:

- Part funding of rail by the British Columbia provincial government occurred and strong direction was made by the province to local authorities to actively support the transit investment through appropriate zoning of station precinct land.
- There was involvement of the provincial government in assembly and re-servicing of land for TOD. For example, at New Westminster, land for the very high density TOD

that has developed with superb public space centred on a boardwalk along the Fraser River was former logging industry land that needed rehabilitation and servicing with new infrastructure before land parcels could be released for high-density redevelopment.

- There was strong support for the idea of less car-oriented regional centers based on the Skytrain, with excellent conditions for pedestrians and cyclists. Most of the new centers on Skytrain pay special attention to the quality of urban design and to facilitating comfortable and convenient bicycle access from surrounding areas and within the center itself.

- Successful partnerships between BC Transit and private developers occurred: location and development of stations in the first stage of Skytrain was a joint exercise, including some joint financing of station costs.

- Early consultation and engagement with communities was a hallmark of TOD. Local area strategies were established for the 800 m radius of stations. Public meetings and local advisory committees were created to address citizen concerns, particularly in relation to crime and traffic.

- Land with highest densities was rezoned from derelict industrial uses; opposition was therefore minimal because it was a big improvement on existing conditions. Such sites were the 'low hanging fruit' in a wide range of redevelopment opportunities and gave government the opportunity to demonstrate the quality and livability that could be achieved at much higher densities on sites that presented the least problematic options in terms of community resistance. It was a smart strategy because much opposition to higher densities is based on fear of the unknown, so cities must go through a process of acceptance of such changes. Successful demonstration projects of compact, livable developments have created snowball effects in numerous cities (e.g. Perth, Western Australia).

- Despite huge criticism, BC Transit decided to not allow any Park & Ride at stations north of the Fraser River. Instead, strong bus feeders and improvements for pedestrians and cyclists leading to stations were implemented. The absence of this policy at stations south of the Fraser River, such as at Surrey Central, although there is a substantial bulk of new development (even architectural award-winning buildings), means that the difference in the public realm is tangible. At Surrey Central, buildings are set back from the station and large car parks hug the station environs (see online photo for this book), whereas at non-Park & Ride stations, high-density development and pedestrian environments are mostly connected directly or at least conveniently to station entries and exits.

- Apart from two small viaducts, the City of Vancouver abolished all freeway development within its borders during the early 1970s. This has meant that any higher-speed segregated rail service can offer a speed of service that is very often much higher than the equivalent car trip. For example, in 2012 the Skytrain operated at an average speed of 39.5 km/h, a little higher than average 24-hour car speed and significantly higher than peak period traffic speed. Likewise, the West Coast Express commuter rail service achieved in 2012 an average speed of 37.6 km/h, which again is higher than peak period road speeds in Vancouver and nearly the same as the 24-hour speed.

Importantly, Vancouver has conducted research that suggests a strong synergy between urban form, economic performance and liveability. The BC Sprawl Report 2004 (Alexander et al. 2004) used indicators of urban form, economic vitality and livability to compare neighbourhoods across the Vancouver region. It found a statistically significant positive link between higher densities and mixed uses, positive economic features and enhanced livability, which suggests a three-way winning scenario for policies that are aimed at creating less auto-dependent living and more walkable and sociable environments. More recently, another BC Sprawl Report shows that the walkability of communities in Vancouver has been linked to better health outcomes (Tomalty and Haider 2009).

Development of livable public places and increasing bike priority

Vancouver is not a city that has major pedestrian zones or extensive traffic calming of neighborhoods, as in many European cities. However, the City of Vancouver has become a highly livable place characterized by an exceptional amount of human activity along lively and interesting streets and in its public spaces. For example, one of the most interesting and livable public environments is Robson Street, the long avenue that connects the downtown with Stanley Park through the West End. The sidewalks are packed with pedestrians, notwithstanding the often bumper-to-bumper traffic and high-frequency trolley bus services that operate along the street. More recently, the street has been further humanized with some small reclamation of road space (see online photo for this book).

The West End of Vancouver is the second highest density residential area in North America outside Manhattan and enjoys thriving and diverse activities along its main roads, not only Robson, but also Denman and Davies Streets, while the grid-based, tree-lined residential streets that run across these major streets have numerous pocket parks created from selective street closures between blocks in the fine-grained street grid. The area also has the extensive Stanley Park and English Bay foreshore at its doorstep.

Recently two further steps forward have been taken in making Vancouver more livable and further reducing its car orientation. Although hotly debated by those whose fear traffic congestion and further upmarket redevelopment, a decision was made in October 2015 to tear down the Dunsmuir and Georgia Street viaducts to free up a large area of land for the North-East False Creek redevelopment (Figure 9.4), which will see a major auto-oriented swathe of urban wasteland turned into a new walkable community, including major new parkland, high-density mixed-use development and a boulevard-style street system.[24]

In the downtown area, road space is being reclaimed for the provision of protected bike lanes, which is giving this area a more people-oriented atmosphere.[25]

Punter (2003) describes this strong human dimension and Vancouver's detailed attention to urban design of the public realm as a hallmark of Vancouver's success as one of the world's most livable cities. This is in stark contrast to cities in the U.S., which all too frequently have very hostile street environments due to automobile-oriented development, particularly large freeways and interchanges.

FIGURE 9.4
Dunsmuir and Georgia Viaducts wasteland to be transformed into a walkable community and new parkland after the viaducts are demolished
Source: Jeffrey R. Kenworthy

Portland, Oregon: from 'a streetcar named expire' to an aspiring 'streetcar city'

Oregon has always been the leading U.S. state in terms of environmental initiatives. It was the first to introduce recycling and deposits on return of glass bottles and it was the first U.S. city to abandon plans for a giant freeway extension in favor of a surface light rail transit (LRT) system—which began in 1986. While San Diego had begun an LRT system in 1981, by 2010 the San Diego metropolitan region had only 31 boardings per capita on transit while the Portland metropolitan region had 54, a little higher than the average of 50 boardings per capita in 20 medium-to-large U.S. metropolitan areas in the same year. Most of the positive aspects of Portland discussed here are focused in the City of Portland, especially its central and inner area. Portland is still an auto-dependent metropolitan area.

Brief history and comparisons

The idea for an electric transit option, which culminated in the LRT called Metropolitan Area Express or MAX, was born in Portland in 1973 during the Arab oil embargo, and it was an idea championed by several visionaries in Portland at the time.[26] The campaign to get better transit in Portland was linked to a major campaign by Sensible Transportation Options for Portland (STOP), originally formed in 1972 to stop the Mount Hood Freeway (Carlson et al. 1995). The 13 years that followed up to the opening of the first light rail line eastwards to Gresham from the central city were not easy and were punctuated with fights (Edner and Arrington 1985). The local newspaper ran a competition to name the new trolley line and awarded first prize to 'A Streetcar Named Expire'.[27] The new transit line immediately proved itself, however, with very good levels of patronage. For some time, patronage was higher at weekends than on weekdays, affording people the easy opportunity of visiting the crowded downtown area for the Saturday market, later extended to Sundays due to immense popularity. Later a historical trolley car service was piggybacked onto part of the new LRT line. This synergy between LRT and the revitalized CBD, especially its high weekend ridership, is sometimes referred to as the 'MAX factor'.[28]

There are some key features that distinguish Portland from other U.S. cities. The most obvious physical manifestations of the difference are Portland's beautiful high-profile central city area and inner-city neighborhoods, which since 1986, with the opening of MAX, have become more and more anchored around this growing light rail system. Commencing with the first line east to Gresham of 24 km, it now has five lines of 97 km and the same number of stations. It also added the smaller Portland streetcar, an inner-city tram that opened with a 6.3 km line 2001. Its second line of 5.3 km opened in 2012. In addition,

TABLE 9.2 **Portland key figures**

Population (2010)	2,066,399
Population (2005)	1,918,188
Metropolitan GDP per capita (US$; 1995, 2005 adjusted)	US$37,342
Urban density (persons per hectare; 2005)	12.9
Road length per person (metres; 2005)	9.9
Car use per person (vehicle kilometres traveled, or VKT, per year; 2005)	10,753
Transit service (vehicle kilometres of service per person; 2010)	35
Transit service (vehicle kilometres of service per person; 2005)	34
Transit use (boardings per person; 2010)	54
Transit use (boardings per person; 2005)	58

Source: Jeffrey R. Kenworthy and Newman and Kenworthy (2015)

FIGURE 9.5
Pioneer Square Courthouse park,
Portland, Oregon - formerly a
parking lot, now a central meeting
place in the heart of the city,
Source: Jeffrey R. Kenworthy

Portland also has a small aerial tramway of 1 km, which opened in 2006 and carries around 1.2 million boardings a year.

Going in the direction of most U.S. cities during the 1960s and 1970s of a declining downtown with a rapid loss of retail opportunities to the suburbs, no rail-based or electric transit alternative and plans for many new freeways, Portland reversed this process and now has a downtown area like many cities in Europe today and a greater emphasis on transit system development than on freeways, notwithstanding the still strong auto credentials of the region. The key difference is that it started and continues a process of change. The rest of this brief case study explores the basis of Portland's success in more sustainable transportation.

The land use–transit connection

Any discussion of the distinction between transportation in Portland and other U.S. cities or, indeed, many cities in the world today inevitably involves land-use policy and the practical implementation measures that Portland has adopted, mainly in the last 30 years. However, Portland's planning pedigree predates the latest generation of activity, even back to the latter years of the Great Depression when Lewis Mumford, the great urban historian and spokesperson for 'cities for people, not cars', encouraged Portland to protect its downtown area of fine-grained street blocks and human scale, and to adopt a system of regional governance. Portland did both. It established Metro, which includes the Metropolitan Planning Organization (MPO) role for transportation planning and funding and it preserved and improved upon the human scale of its downtown.

But the roots of Portland's performance over the last 25 years or more in land-use and transportation development date back to the 1970s, when Governor Tom McCall spearheaded a statewide growth management strategy—in particular, the establishment and maintenance of urban growth boundaries (UGBs) in Oregon. Portland established such a boundary inside which all urban growth had to occur. This boundary has not only withstood numerous ballot and legal challenges, but has been linked to transportation through the 1991 Oregon Transportation Planning Rule, which applies a growth rule to limit increases in vehicle miles traveled (VMT), the most fundamental measure of car use. It is interesting, then, that the 2009 status report from Tri-Met and its various jurisdictional partners shows that between 1996 and 2006, daily VMT increased only 19% in the face of a 27% increase in population, while Tri-Met patronage rose 46% (Tri-Met 2009).

In a sample of 20 American metropolitan areas in 2010, the Portland region was above average in transit use per capita (Kenworthy 2013), but its 54 boardings per person is still low in an international context.[29] This shows how difficult it is to fundamentally change an entire auto-oriented metropolitan area, despite the positive things that have been done for transit and the changes in the central and inner areas of Portland.

The beginnings of Portland's comparatively strong transit success in a U.S. context can also be traced to the land use–transportation integration evident in Portland's 1973 Downtown Plan. A transit mall, which opened in 1978, was envisioned as the centerpiece of downtown revitalization and marked the beginnings of a trend to leverage broader community-building objectives through transit investment. Other achievements began to punctuate where Portland was going as a city:

- The creation of Pioneer Courthouse Square out of a parking lot, now a major community meeting point in downtown between the one-way pair of streets along which MAX operates. Pioneer Courthouse Square's success is due partly to the staging of regular formal events there and its amphitheater-like space fringed with food and drink outlets (see Figure 9.5).
- The tearing up of a freeway spur along the Willamette River downtown and conversion of it to Tom McCall Park, the site of Portland's annual Rose Festival, which attracted 1.2 million visitors in 2011[30] (see Figure 9.6).
- The River Place urban village redevelopment adjacent to the new park, itself built on a commuter parking lot, sprang up along the river, with a hotel, shops and cafes at ground level and several floors of apartments above (Figure 9.7).
- The City of Portland, independent of the regional transit agency, has been developing streetcar lines knitting together the CBD, Portland State University just south of the CBD, and adjacent residential and development areas such as the relatively newly created dense mixed-use neighborhood below the health sciences complex with an easy connection to its aerial tram (image in Chapter 4).

FIGURE 9.6
Tom McCall Park, Portland, Oregon - the site of a former freeway in downtown
Source: Jeffrey R. Kenworthy

301

FIGURE 9.7
The pedestrian link along the
Willamette River through the River
Place development, Portland,
Oregon—lively range of cafes and
people-oriented spaces
Source: Jeffrey R. Kenworthy

Further important steps in Portland's efforts to reinvent itself as a more sustainable and livable city came with the successful civil society opposition to the Western Bypass loop of the I-5 freeway through rural lands just outside the growth boundary. The initial opposition came from a revamped version of the community group STOP. The success of this opposition led to a study that was undertaken jointly with the U.S. Environmental Protection Agency (USEPA) and the growth management advocacy organization, 1000 Friends of Oregon, to develop a new approach to the problem, which culminated in a new planning model called land use, transportation, air quality (LUTRAQ). The solution to building the freeway was to cluster and moderately densify housing and mixed land uses together with transit provision and infrastructure for walking and cycling and traffic calming of streets. The freeway was scrapped and now transit-oriented development is evident on the Westside light rail line that opened in 1998, as well as at other places along the MAX system.[31] Metro, Portland's regional planning organization, is also strongly committed to TOD promotion.[32]

Planning in the 1990s for Portland's streetcar system was predicated on central city revitalization, especially in the Pearl District. Since opening in 2001, there has been over US$3.4 billion in new development and over 10,000 dwellings constructed along its route. Planning of the airport LRT extension was predicated on TOD and involved private-sector contributions to construction costs, and the interstate LRT line, opened in 2004, was located to achieve land development rather than speed. By 2009, Portland had 44 miles (71 km) of LRT and four miles (6.4 km) of streetcar tracks. By that time, over US$9 billion of development had occurred using transit-friendly land-use planning (Arrington 2009). David Taylor of the Congress for New Urbanism reports that properties in Portland within about 450 meters (1,500 feet) of a rail station have about 11% higher development value and that, with a public investment of $89 million, Portland's modest streetcar system has attracted $2.5 billion in private investment.[33] Portland has arguably the most aggressive approach of any U.S. city to TOD—which has evolved since the 1986 MAX line debut. Its 2040 Growth Management Strategy of 'build up, not out' is built around transit:

> ... (It) features a tight urban growth boundary, focusing growth in existing built-up areas and requiring local governments to limit parking and adopt zoning and comprehensive plan changes that are consistent with the growth management strategy.

FIGURE 9.8
Portland's streetcar running through
Portland's revitalized Pearl District
Source: Jeffrey R. Kenworthy

By 2040, two-thirds of jobs and 40 per cent of households are to be located in and around centers and corridors served by buses and light rail transit

(Arrington 2009, p. 4).

The toolbox used by planners to secure a very successful TOD program is at state, regional and local levels. At a state level, there is the UGB and the complementary Transportation Planning Rule. The 1993 Transportation and Growth Management Program also promotes and helps to fund high-quality community planning, the 1995 TOD Tax Exemption allows for up to a 10-year residential property tax exemption and the 2001 Vertical Housing Program encourages density and mixed-land use in community-designated areas, with up to an 80% property tax exemption over 10 years.

The 1994 Regional Growth Management plan, which is behind the 2040 vision, requires local government compliance through growth targets, parking maximums, density minimums and street connectivity standards to encourage walking and cycling and easy routing of buses. There is also the 1998 TOD Implementation Program, which has access to local and federal funds, mainly for supporting TOD construction through site acquisition and TOD easements.

Local tools include joint development (1997), where Tri-Met has written down the value of TOD project land to get the highest and best transit use, and the 1996 TOD Tax Exemption in the cities of Gresham and Portland.[34] Tax increment financing is used by the City of Portland in urban renewal districts for public investments, increasing densities and securing affordable housing. Finally, the Westside Station Area Planning (1993–97) helps local governments to prepare and adopt plans for 0.5 mile (800 m) radii around stations to ensure that density levels are adequate (a minimum density standard), parking spaces are minimized (through a maximum permitted parking supply), the right building orientation to transit and prohibition of automobile uses. Tri-Met, Metro and the Oregon Department of Transportation (DOT) help to fund the program.

Some large-scale results of this overall approach are that Portland area residents travel about 20% fewer miles every day and are twice as likely to use transit for the journey to work and seven times more likely to bicycle to work than the average metropolitan resident in the U.S. Interestingly, it is reported that 80% of Tri-Met's riders either have a car available for that trip or choose not to own a car. Consequently, Portlanders spend 15.1% of their household budget on transportation compared to 19.1% nationally (Arrington 2009).

In the early 2000s, Portland made a conscious policy and planning decision to improve upon its lackluster 1% mode share for bicycling to a 6% share by 2014 (very high for the U.S.) by improving the situation for cycling in several ways:

1   The most important was to improve the conditions on the several bridges connecting its CBD with adjacent communities—which dramatically increased riding in those corridors;
2   An accelerated program of bicycle lanes and boulevards, which have come to be known as neighborhood greenways;
3   Launching of a very successful bike-share program;
4   Cycling was promoted through several annual closures of some miles of streets to motor vehicle traffic and the creation of a festival atmosphere around these Sunday Parkways.[35]

Overall, Portland presents probably the best example of a coordinated and long-term effort to change a large, highly car-dependent U.S. metropolitan region into a more sustainable one. A 1990s perspective showed Portland neatly positioned between the more extreme auto-orientation of Seattle and the more transit-oriented Vancouver (Schiller and Kenworthy 1999). The mammoth nature of the task of turning around an auto-city cannot be underestimated, and while Portland represents a very concerted effort in a U.S. context it must be remembered that when the comparisons are drawn more widely it is still a car-dependent region. However, it is changing and will continue to change by building on past successes and developing new and stronger approaches to sustainable transportation, as it already has shown over many decades now.

Boulder, Colorado: small is beautiful and effective

Boulder is a small university town with a 2014 population of 105,112 people situated in the larger Boulder County area of 319,372 people in 2015.[36] Boulder County is part of the even larger and very highly automobile-dependent Denver metropolitan region of about three million people in 2015.[37] The City of Boulder was the first U.S. community to introduce a green belt to prevent both its own urban sprawl and the urban encroachment around it, and especially to protect the impressive landscape vista of the adjacent Rocky Mountain foothills. It did this through an innovative community organization called Plan Boulder, which still maintains an active involvement in Boulder's development.[38] Boulder has set itself apart in transportation terms from nearly all American communities of its size in numerous ways.

Up until about 1990 it had achieved some successes, such as the innovative Pearl Street pedestrian mall (Figure 9.9) in the city's center, dedicated in 1977 and extended several times since then.[39] It had improved pedestrian and cycling facilities but still maintained a traditional 'predict-and-provide' supply-side road-building approach to future transportation development. However, financial, political and physical realities intervened to make this approach unsustainable. In 1996, the Transportation Master Plan set a transportation demand management (TDM) goal to hold traffic levels to 1994 levels and to reduce single-occupant vehicle (SOV) mode share of Boulder residents to 25%, with 20% by 2035 being the goal in the 2014 Transportation Master Plan (TMP). In 2010, this mode share was 37%, with the trend line showing that by 2025 even a goal of 25% will not be reached unless more is done to reduce SOV travel. However, the headline objective of the 2003 TMP was 'no long term growth in vehicle travel', which has been met with the 1994 daily figure of 2.4 million VMT (3.9 million km) for the Boulder Valley remaining more or less constant until today.[40]

Strengthening the move away from the car continues to involve improving transit services through the Community Transit Network (CTN—see below), creating demand for transit trips, enhancing the bicycle and pedestrian system, building complete streets, marketing and providing good information about the new transportation choices, changing land use and urban design approaches such as the Transit Village Area Plan, tackling parking pricing, stopping large-scale road expansions in the region and establishing some dynamic relationships between the city and the University of Colorado (CU)—a 'town–gown' partnership (Toor and Havlick 2004; City of Boulder 2014). The new Transportation Master Plan of 2014, which involved extensive community consultation,[41] continues with this overall direction with many progressive and visionary planning goals.[42]

Comparisons and trends

Table 9.3 compiles some data on the city and compares it to the Denver metropolitan area in which it is located and Table 9.4 examines the current and prospective future modal share.

In terms of transit ridership, the trends are very revealing. Regional Transportation District (RTD) data from 1982 through to 2004 show that in Boulder (local services), where urban density is 31% higher than in the Denver metro area, there was a threefold increase in annual usage, from 2.12 million to 6.34 million, while in Denver all local services grew from 29.80 million to 40.23 million, or only a 1.3 times increase. From 2004 to 2012, local services in Boulder grew more modestly by only 15% to 7.3 million boardings under fiscal constraints (City of Boulder 2014). However, by 2012, local transit boardings per capita for the City of Boulder were 69 per capita, or 72% higher than the Denver metro area, with 40 per capita.

Table 9.3 also shows that the annual car use per capita of the City of Boulder in 2013 (984,855,676 km or 9,370 km per capita for residents, non-resident employees, students and visitors) was some 34% below that of the Denver metropolitan area and for residents and students only in the city (634,291,056 km), was 6,034 km per capita, or 57% below Denver (City of Boulder, p. 3–2). These data are despite the GDP per capita in the Boulder area being some 8% higher than the Denver area. Table 9.4 shows that Boulder's already low car modal share for city residents of 56% (certainly for an American city) should be

FIGURE 9.9
Residents and visitors listen to music at the Pearl Street pedestrian mall, Boulder, Colorado. A few decades ago the music would have been drowned out by the traffic of a once motorized main street
Source: Norman Koren (www.norman koren.com)

TABLE 9.3 Boulder/Denver key figures

Area	Boulder	Denver
Population (2014)	City: 105,112	3,011,536
Population (2015)	County: 319,372	–
Metropolitan GDP per capita (2014) in US$; 2009 Boulder and Denver MSAs[i])	$66,927	$61,903
Urban density (persons per hectare; 2005)	12.1 (County)	14.7
Urban density (persons per hectare; 2014)	19.3 (City)	–
Road length per person (metres; Boulder 2014; Denver 2005)	9.3 (County)	8.7
Car use per person (VKT per year; 2005)	9,370 (City)	14,176
Transit use (boardings per person; Denver 2010; Boulder 2012)	69	40

Source: Jeffrey R. Kenworthy[ii]
[i] MSA: Metropolitan Statistical Area
[ii] Other sources: For city population, www.city-data.com/city/Boulder-Colorado.html; for county population, www.census.gov/quickfacts/table/PST045215/08013; for Denver population, www.metrodenver.org/do-business/demographics/population/; for GDP data calculator, www.bea.gov, accessible at dtdapps.coloradodot.info/otis/Statistics; for Boulder VKT from TMP 2014, p. 3-2. Also note: VKT of residents and students only was 6,034 km per person; urban density of Boulder based on 24.7 square miles (6,397 ha), of which 85% is estimated from Google Earth to be urbanized land. Transit boardings per person are based on the TMP 2014 data (p. 2-4) of 20,000 local transit boardings per day (7,300,000 per year) which are attributed to the City of Boulder population. If one attributes all 32,000 daily transit boardings (11,680,000 per year) on local and regional services into and out of Boulder to the Boulder population, then per capita transit use is 111 transit trips per person, which is roughly the same as the Washington metro area figure in 2010 of 109 boardings per person (all accessed 25 June 2016).

further reduced to 35% for all daily trips by 2035. Plans to reduce the equivalent figure for non-residents is much more modest, from 90% to 86%.

Boulder is also amongst America's strongest communities for walking and cycling to work. The 2008–12 average percentage of commuters by foot and bicycle was 19%, just below Davis, California, with 22% and Ann Arbor, Michigan, with 20%. Additionally, almost 10% get to work by bus in Boulder compared to just over 4% in Denver and 5% nationally (City of Boulder, 2014, p. 2–2).

Boulder's success in sustainable transportation

The above data point to a significant and coordinated program of sustainable transportation. This sub-section briefly reviews the pillars of this success.

The bicycle and pedestrian program

Boulder has improved its cycling network through a program of new bicycle routes, bicycle paths and 374 miles (602 km) of bicycle lanes involving 75 bicycle underpasses.[43] It has introduced bicycle-actuated crossings at intersections and placed bicycle racks on all buses. These policy-driven changes, which commenced during the 1980s, were aimed at a fundamental change in transportation direction that stressed transportation demand management, walking, bicycling and transit.

One of the biggest successes has been on the campus of the University of Colorado (CU), where during the 1990s it was realized that building new parking structures to accommodate

TABLE 9.4 City of Boulder's current and prospective future modal share

	Current modal share for all daily trips		2020 targets for residents from 2008 TMP	New proposed 2035 modal share targets from 2014 TMP	
	Resident trips	Non-resident trips		Resident trips	Non-resident trips
Walk	20%	0%	24%	25%	0%
Bike	19%	1%	15%	30%	2%
Transit	5%	9%	7%	10%	12%
Cars	56%	90%	54%	35%	86%

Source: Modified from City of Boulder (2014), Figure 3–5, p. 3–7

auto commuting by staff and students was a mistake and the university cancelled them. Instead, the university worked with the city to foster a better transit system (see following sub-section) and to encourage greater walking and bicycling. Bicycle stations were set up to repair bicycles and provide information and there are now free CU bicycles that students can check out for their immediate travel needs. However, perhaps the biggest success has been the acceptance that it is simply much cheaper to provide for non-auto access on campus than it is to cater for car commuting. By examining the existing infrastructure costs per round-trip to the campus by faculty, staff and students and the costs of accommodating an additional new round trip, sustainable modes have achieved huge advantages. A report by Nelson/Nygaard Consulting Associates (2003) provides data[44] that show orders of magnitude differences in infrastructure costs for an existing and new trip to the campus by foot or bicycle compared to the same trips accommodated by car. Although it is not clear from the graph, the data presented in their report are annualized costs per trip.

In the light of growing obesity and environmental concerns, the 2014 TMP has a continued focus on bikes. With an average trip length in Boulder of four miles (6.4 km), a distance that is quite comfortable by bike, Boulder aims to produce an enhanced bicycle network that will be comfortable for all ages and levels of experience. Key developments (City of Boulder 2014, pp. 5–8 to 5–9) will be:

- An additional 95 miles, or 153 km, of bicycle lanes, routes and shoulders as well as new underpasses, overpasses and enhanced intersection treatments.
- A 'Living Lab' approach to all the whole community to test and evaluate temporary new bike installations and treatments to develop a set of Bicycle Facility Installation Guidelines for future works.
- A Low-Stress Bicycle Network whose aim is to attract a broader population of confident and comfortable bicyclists while developing a continuous bicycle network of safe cross-town corridors.
- Policies that stress coordination of government agencies, co-operation with property owners, developers and other key institutions, and education for and enforcement of safe and courteous use of facilities.
- Pedestrian improvements including: 'Walk Audits' and 'Walkabouts', with communities to identify where improvements are needed; a Neighborhood Access Tool to identify 15-minute walk or pedsheds that will gradually increase the number and variety of destinations that are safely available; continuous pedestrian networks that are safe, winter and summer, and the addition of 43 new underpasses, 27 enhanced pedestrian crossings, and nearly eight miles (13 km) of new pedestrian facilities.

The transit program

Probably the biggest and most successful innovation has been the Boulder Community Transit Network (CTN), a network of 10 differently branded types of routes that are part of the GO Boulder network, planned around minimum 10-minute peak frequencies to avoid the need for timetables and minimum 15-minute off-peak services. The goal is to double the current modal share of 5% of residents' trips by transit to 7% by 2020 and 10% by 2035. The CTN's expanding choice of routes are referred to as the Hop (1994), Skip (1997), Jump (2001), Bound (2001), Stampede (2003), Dash (2003) and Bolt (2005) buses. They are accordingly distinctly branded and utilize different size buses where feasible. More recently, GO Boulder has added a couple routes especially designed for CU students as well as a longer-distance commuter service connecting to several distant communities (https://bouldercolorado.gov/goboulder/bus). All these routes have achieved impressive ridership from their start.

The City of Boulder (2014, p. 2–4) shows that the current CTN avoids a minimum of over 91 million extra car miles (147 million km) per year. This does not consider the transit-leverage effect, which shows that one passenger mile on transit replaces *multiple* vehicle miles in cars, ranging on average from three to five (Newman and Kenworthy 2015), due to trip chaining by transit users to achieve multiple purposes, which would otherwise be done in multiple individual car trips. This, combined with greater walking and cycling, helps to explain the large difference between per capita car use in the Denver region compared to Boulder where transit boardings per capita are so much higher.

The CTN is, as the name implies, the product of a community consultation process. Boulder undertook its highly successful transit innovations[45] only after a year of extensive public involvement. A broad-based citizens' group of some 50 community leaders, working with several City of Boulder and transit agency staff, devoted a great deal of time and energy to this effort, with larger public meetings being held as well. Boulder did not adopt a business as usual approach, where an agency gets consultants to examine part of the transit 'problem' and then perhaps does a little tinkering to fine tune it. Significant changes to transit needed to be undertaken with the enlistment of public support to ensure usage and ownership of transit systems, and that is what Boulder did. They formed a new unit called GO Boulder as a way of going around the Public Works Department, which was operating on a business as usual approach. They also established the long-standing City of Boulder Transportation Committee, which ensured citizen interest in the issues.[46] But it took approximately 10 years to establish the CTN, and involved about one year of citizen-involved planning per route.

The CTN is now a well-supported, community-based design using buses that are family-friendly and bus drivers are employed as community ambassadors. The wider Regional Transportation District (RTD) owns and operates the CTN, while funding and planning services is a collaborative exercise between the RTD and the City. Strong transit use was developed through innovative pass programs described below, marketing and education, seamless interfaces between bus, bicycle and pedestrian facilities, good connections to regional services, and transit-supportive land use and urban design (Bruun 2004).

The development of the CTN has gone together with effective ways of generating new demand for transit through ticketing innovations. This was achieved through the EcoPass unlimited transit access program. EcoPasses with photo ID are only issued at a low-cost group rate to residents once enough households in a neighborhood have joined up.[47] Pricing is based on location, number of people or number of households and the level of transit service. Businesses generally get EcoPasses for employees through deals negotiated with the human resources manager. Pass programmes are also available to all downtown employees and all CU staff and students. In 2001, there were some 60,000 RTD EcoPasses and discount passes issued, 25,000 of which were for students, 6,500 were for CU staff, 22,200 were for businesses and 3,800 were for neighborhoods; an additional 2,500 were other passes. There were 70,000 annual EcoPasses in use in 2014 (City of Boulder 2014, p. 4–6), with plans to expand EcoPasses to the whole County of Boulder and proposals to expand the pass program to all city residents. CU students received the EcoPass in 1991, and annual ridership went from 300,000 to 1.5 million trips in the first five years.

The economic rationale for these improvements to transit for students and employees at the university is also evident in the same data from Nelson/Nygaard Consulting Associates (2003) outlined above for bicycles, which show that the annualized costs of existing and new trips to campus by faculty, staff and students on transit are dramatically below the costs of accommodating existing and new trips by car to the campus.

Boulder is continuing with its transit development plans. The current initiatives include:

- A variety of planned Bus Rapid Transit (BRT) services with coordinated traffic signals, superior-style buses with increased capacity and comfort and high-quality stops.
- A wide range of actions related to enhanced services and capital investment, among the most interesting being a hierarchy of transit stops, centers and hubs to encourage multi-modal connections. Each level of stop will have certain minimum facilities for shelter, seating, bicycle parking, universal access, transit information systems, lighting, pedestrian improvements within a 1/2 mile (800 meter) radius of each stop and other amenity enhancements. The mobility hubs and transit centers will aim generally for high standards (City of Boulder 2014: p. 5–14), which among other things will help overcome the 'last mile' problem of transit trips. BRT stops will have the highest amenity standards.

Overall, Boulder demonstrates what can be done in a smaller community with genuine rather than token public involvement and the positive effect of consistent and complementary public policies and political support for land-use planning, urban design and transportation strategies that have supported sustainability over a period approaching three decades. The 2014 TMP document ends with an inspiring statement stressing how Boulder's entire transportation and land-use planning approach is developed with the community and for the community with multiple lifelong benefits for all (City of Boulder 2014, p. 7–5).

Freiburg im Breisgau, Germany: a pin-up sustainable city

Freiburg im Breisgau is a university city of 224,191 people in 2010,[48] nestled in the Black Forest area of southern Germany and occupying 153 square kilometers, 66% of which is forest and farming land. It is situated within the Region Freiburg, an area of 2,211 square kilometers with 633,799 people in 2010 (Rikort et al. 2014). Within the region 86% of land is forest and farming. With the sunniest microclimate in Germany, it boasts one of the most comprehensive, coordinated and integrated approaches in the world to transit, walking and cycling, and land-use planning. Perhaps its most striking feature is its obvious attention to high-quality coherent urban design throughout the city. All development must pass through strict urban design guidelines before being implemented and there is strong citizen awareness of the need to protect the city's livability, especially from problems generated by reliance on private transportation.[49]

Freiburg has for many years been a 'pin-up' city for sustainable transportation and more generally for developing a much more sustainable city environment based on ecological building principles, renewable energy and prioritizing public transportation, walking and cycling, and all supported by superb urban design of the public realm (Buehler and Pucher 2011b). A critical event was probably the state government of Baden-Württemberg's decision in 1975 to build a nuclear reactor. Opposition to it was very intense and successful and spawned a civil society movement with heavy university involvement to ensure that Freiburg could then meet its future energy needs in a sustainable way. The 1980s was its

TABLE 9.5 Freiburg key figures

Population (Region; 2010)	633,799
Population (City; 2010)	219,345
Metropolitan GDP per capita (Region; 2010 in US$; 1995)	US$26,439
Urban density (persons per hectare; 2010)	46.1
Road length per person (metres; 2010)	2.3
Car use per person (VKT per year; 2010)	5,154
Transit use (boardings per person; 2005)	328

Source: Jeffrey R. Kenworthy

period of the energy supply concept: promoting renewable energies and doing everything possible to curb demand for energy, including focusing on transit, walking and cycling and creating a built form and public realm that favored these modes and minimized the need to travel (Peirce 2009). As early as 1989, it was referred to as the 'green planner's dream' (Roberts 1989). During the 1990s, Freiburg further responded to sustainability by basing its future development on a climate protection concept and from 2007 on a climate protection action plan that aims for a reduction of 40% of the current carbon dioxide (CO_2) level by 2030 through a focus on sustainable transportation and building and construction standards (Salomon 2009).

Freiburg's development for decades now has been strongly based on citizen action and participation. Citizens are shareholders in solar and wind power stations. There is direct participation in the spatial development plan and the municipal budget. Citizens act as technical experts on committees and there is much citizen-led environmental education and many campaigns. This citizen participation and commitment and the networks of stakeholders have helped to create a vision of integral sustainable development, which has formed a consensus across all political parties (Salomon 2009).

Freiburg comparisons

To appreciate the city of Freiburg in relation to other cities, it is useful to compare it to European, North American, Australian and Canadian cities (Newman and Kenworthy 2015). Table 9.6 depicts data for Freiburg against averages for these groups of cities, plus Graz, a similar-size city in Austria.

Freiburg is a typical German city, with a density of 46 persons per hectare,[50] which is approximately three times the density of typical auto-cities in the U.S. and Australia, but not quite double the density of cities in Canada. Its car ownership of 413 cars per 1,000 people in 2010 is relatively modest even in a European context (average 471). It appears that the city's long-standing commitment to more sustainable transportation has helped to suppress the need for car ownership. It is also partly to be explained by the nature of urban development in Freiburg, discussed later in the chapter, with its partial emphasis on car-free or car-reduced housing environments such as Vauban, Rieselfeld and Der Seepark. As a group, the auto-cities of North America and Australia average over 600 cars per 1,000 people.

In terms of motorcycle ownership, which has been increasing significantly everywhere in the world over the last 10 years, it is a typical European city, with 31 motorcycles per 1,000 people and is not quite double the typical level of ownership in the auto-cities.

In road supply, with 2.3 m per person, Freiburg is significantly below the European city average and that of Graz, with 3.1 m and 3.7 m per person respectively, and about one-third of the level to be found in the auto-cities in Table 9.6. In freeway provision, the city is below all other cities in the table.

TABLE 9.6 Some basic transportation-related data for Freiburg (2010) compared to other cities (2005–6)

Factor	Freiburg	Graz	20 European cities	10 American cities	4 Australian cities	5 Canadian cities
Population (averages)	224,191	247,248	1,783,827	6,425,359	2,840,875	2,655,793
Urban density (persons per ha)	46.1	35.9	47.9	15.4	14.0	25.8
Car ownership (cars per 1000)	413	471	463	640	647	522
Motorcycle ownership (motorcycles per 1000)	31	33	41	16	21	15
Road length per person (metres)	2.3	3.7	3.1	6.0	7.6	5.4
Freeway length per person (metres)	0.064	0.069	0.094	0.156	0.083	0.157
Per cent of total daily trips by NMM	50.0%	33.4%	34.5%	9.5%	14.2%	11.6%
Per cent of total daily trips by transit	18.0%	19.3%	22.4%	5.5%	7.5%	13.1%
Transport deaths per 100,000	4.46	2.83	3.40	9.51	6.21	6.26

Source: Newman and Kenworthy (2015); Freiburg: Rikort et al. (2014). Freiburg modal split data are from 1999 from the City of Freiburg.

TABLE 9.7 Freiburg modal split from 1982 to 1999 and projection for 2020

Mode	1982	1999	2020
Cars	38%	32%	28%
Transit	11%	18%	20%
Bicycles	15%	27%	28%
Walking	35%	23%	24%

Source: City of Freiburg[i]
[i] See: www.freiburg.de/pb/site/Freiburg/get/311570/Modal-Split.jpg (accessed 27 June 2016).

This lesser orientation to roads generally, and freeways specifically, helps to explain Freiburg's overall more sustainable patterns of transportation. What is most striking is the use of walking and cycling (NMM), which in 1999—the latest survey—was 50% of all daily trips, by far the highest in the table. When one adds in transit's contribution, 68% of all daily trips are met with green modes (projected as 72% by 2020), above the average for the 20 European cities (57%) and even higher than the similarly small Graz (53%). Freiburg is a city of short distances with a policy of decentralized but concentrated services and markets, focused on limiting urban sprawl and encouraging inner-city redevelopment, which is ideal for walking, cycling and transit. Table 9.7 shows the evolution of modal split in Freiburg from 1982 to 1999 and its goals for 2020 where car use continues to decline, while transit, walking and cycling modestly increase their share (perhaps plateauing).

Apart from progressive transportation policies themselves, Freiburg's success in transportation revolves around a series of other factors.

Better public transport

Freiburg's success in sustainable transportation was established relatively early. In 1969, it decided to keep and extend the older tram system, with new lines appearing in 1979. In 1973, it also began to restrict inner-city car traffic through large-scale pedestrianization of central city shopping streets, while still allowing access to trams and buses.

Light rail has become the backbone of Freiburg's public transit. In some places, LRT lines run along grassed track beds either on their own rights-of-way through parkland settings, or in the center of roads and some streets that are only for pedestrians and transit.

FIGURE 9.10
Bicycle- and pedestrian-friendly
Freiburg, Baden-Württemberg,
Germany
Source: Jeffrey R. Kenworthy

FIGURE 9.10
Bicycle- and pedestrian-friendly
Freiburg, Baden-Württemberg,
Germany
Source: Jeffrey R. Kenworthy

Buses have become primarily feeders to the light-rail system and mobility by transit improved greatly in the 1970s and 1980s (Pucher and Clorer 1992). The central city has benefited environmentally by having a clean, quiet mode of transport servicing it. Transit has been very cleverly and aggressively promoted through marketing campaigns to encourage people out of their cars and through attractive ticketing offers linked to environmental awareness. In 1984, Freiburg introduced the rainbow ticket, a monthly environmental travel card. This was initially resisted by the transit operator, but then strongly embraced in a much wider public transport zone when its success in attracting customers was evident (Bratzel 1999).

Along with the improvements to transit and its consequent upsurge in usage, the large increase in the use of bicycles has also been underpinned by many separated facilities for cyclists (and pedestrians), bicycle storage facilities around the city and superb attention to urban design. Some of the main segregated bicycle spines run parallel to the grassed light rail track beds and, in sections, run through small 'urban forests'.

Development of livable public places

A key part of Freiburg's strategy has been detailed attention to the quality of the city's public realm. The improvements in this area have been at least partly responsible for the big increase in the use of bicycles and a progressive enhancement in the quality of the pedestrian experience. Pedestrianization of almost the entire central area has played a large role in enhancing the livability of the city for people of all ages. The central area has many outdoor cafés and restaurants and an open-air marketplace. The pedestrianized streets have been resurfaced with a wide variety of cobbled surface designs. Trees have been introduced and many flower planters bring color to the city in warmer months. Creepers have been strategically planted to green many building surfaces. They have also been encouraged to grow across trellises to form bridges linking both sides of the street, as well as to form arched entry statements into traffic-calmed or pedestrianized streets.

A feature of the pedestrianized center and, indeed, the whole city is its water theme. The city celebrates water in its public areas. Its unusual system of gutters is termed '*Bächle*', once used to provide water for fire-fighting, to provide water for the city and to irrigate fields.

FIGURE 9.11
Part of Freiburg's central pedestrian zone showing greening efforts and an example of the Bächle on the right
Source: Jeffrey R. Kenworthy

Today the water theme continues, with freshwater running in small channels throughout the city and continuing into residential areas and new developments, such as those described below. Children, one of the most vulnerable and transport-disadvantaged groups in cities, are given great independence in Freiburg's streets and can be seen playing in the *Bächle*.

Freiburg's combined effect of the elements described above, plus street furniture and lighting, provide one of the most coherent and attractive urban environments in any city; one that is inclusive of all members of the population, regardless of age or ability. Many streets in many neighborhoods have been made safer and friendlier for bicycles and pedestrians through traffic-calming[51] treatments. These treatments include mid-block neck downs,[52] strong entry statements leading into residential areas such as those described above using creepers, canyons of trees to reduce perceptible width, changes in street surface to signal lower speed areas, strategic use of parked cars to increase separation between the sidewalk and road, and so on. Spaces such as parking areas have been reclaimed for civic uses and children's play areas as the city has become less car oriented. At least some surface parking areas in inner neighborhoods have been placed underground and the area above turned into open space.

Less auto-dependent urban development

There is a concerted effort to provide for Freiburg's population growth in planned urban communities linked to transit. Freiburg has several 'model neighborhoods' in this regard. Three are briefly described here, der Seepark, Rieselfeld and Vauban, in roughly chronological order.

Der Seepark

Der Seepark is a large urban village consisting of a variety of different types of multi-family dwellings. It is set adjacent to a light rail stop and its central feature is the large integrated lake and parkland on city property. The environment is mostly traffic free and internal circulation is all on foot and bicycle. Parking is underground or restricted to on-street bays along traffic-calmed peripheral streets. The public spaces were designed for a short-term

313

and long-term purpose—initially as the site of the state garden show in 1986 and then as a multi-purpose public park that melds with the surrounding housing as a seamless whole. The result is a very attractive, integrated and convenient living environment. People who reside there and people from other parts of Freiburg, of all ages, can be seen sharing the public spaces. Activities include: children's play areas; swimming in the central lake; cycling; strolling; in-line skating; eating in the on-site facilities; enjoying open-air concerts; using adjacent formal sports facilities; sunning in the 'meadows'; and resting in formal gardens. A very high proportion of the access to this neighborhood is by non-auto means and many people who are seen using the public realm of the neighborhood have arrived by transit, foot or bicycle.

Freiburg–Rieselfeld

The district of Freiburg–Rieselfeld was developed out of a need to provide for a very high demand for new housing during the late 1980s and early 1990s, and accommodates 11,000 people. Rieselfeld was only possible through an extension of Freiburg's excellent LRT system, along which there are several stops serving the new district. The LRT runs on a grass track bed through the new district, where there is a linear neighborhood center with a rich mix of shops, food stores, restaurants, professional suites and other uses, and sitting above those are several floors of housing. The whole of Rieselfeld is accessible by foot to the LRT stops, and both the main street and the residential streets connecting to it are very bicycle- and walking-friendly—indeed, children frequently ride bicycles, walk and play in the general street environment. Along this main LRT street are also civic functions, such as a library, churches and a large square where, during summer, children enjoy the computerized water fountains. Rieselfeld is an excellent example of TOD linked in a linear rather than nodal form to new urban development.[53] It also includes drainage swales and ponds that capture water on-site and serve as part of a green network and children's play areas. A survey conducted in 2010 found a high level of residents' satisfaction with the neighborhood and pointed again to the importance of civic engagement in ensuring success of city developments.[54]

FIGURE 9.12
Walkable, transit- and ecologically-oriented developments, Vauban
Note: Notice the mother and child easily crossing the LRT line (bottom).
Source: Jeffrey R. Kenworthy

Vauban

Vauban is a redevelopment area on a site of an old French military barracks on the edge of the city. It is linked to the rest of the city by an extension of the LRT system, again running along a green track bed at the site. Some of the old buildings have been retained and recycled into a kindergarten and other civic uses and newer ones focused on environmental technologies that have been built in the style of the energy saving 'passive haus' or 'energy plus' dwellings, which generate net energy to feed back into the grid. It has its own power plant burning waste organic material, mainly wood waste. Vauban is a mixed-use new neighborhood of 38 hectares with 5,000 people a density considerably greater than the rest of the city and rivalling many larger European cities. It is a 'car-free' neighborhood, meaning that if one wants to have a car one must store it in a solar parking structure on the fringe of the neighborhood. Vauban is strongly oriented towards transit, walking and cycling, and one of its most evident and endearing features is its family-friendly public realm. Throughout the development, men and women can be seen with children in prams, and children can be seen independently walking and riding bicycles around the area, simply because the street environments are comparatively safe with 30 km/h (19mph) residential zones. There are also many attractive parks that are intensively used by parents with children. Overall, Vauban is probably one of the most attractive sustainable transportation neighborhoods in the world, successfully blending high-density housing, mixed uses, green spaces, transit and walking facilities into a rich and highly livable, socially gregarious and safe public environment (also see the depiction of Vauban in Chapter 10, Box 10.7).

Three policies, which were used by Freiburg to 'tame the auto' and that are still being used, are:

- It has sharply restricted auto use in the city.
- It has provided affordable, convenient and safe alternatives to auto use.
- It has strictly regulated development to ensure a compact land-use pattern conducive to public transport, bicycling and walking (Pucher and Clorer 1992, p. 386).

FIGURE 9.13
Family and pedestrian-friendly streets in Vauban, Freiburg
Source: Jeffrey R. Kenworthy

TABLE 9.8 Car ownership trend in Freiburg, 1950–2010

Year	Cars per 1000 persons
1950	28
1960	113
1970	248
1980	361
1990	422
2000	420
2006	419
2010	413

Source: Buehler and Pucher (2009) for 1950 to 2006. Data for 2010 from Table 9.6, this book.

Table 9.8 shows how another culmination of Freiburg's progressive land use and transportation policies is declining car ownership, which appears to have started in the 1990s.

Seoul, South Korea: rivers of cars to rivers of water and people

Background and Seoul comparisons

The City of Seoul is a megacity with 10.4 million people in 2013. It lies at the heart of a metropolitan area of 25.6 million people (2013), including Inch'on and Kyonggi-do.[55] Seoul has a more sustainable transportation system than all the other metropolitan areas in this chapter by virtue of the region's very high density of 230 persons per hectare (Table 9.9), a very well-developed transit system (18 rail lines of different types adding to 332 km) with high usage, comparatively low car usage and relatively conducive conditions for walking and cycling—some 53% of daily trips were by these green modes and 47% by cars and motorcycles (Kenworthy and Laube 2001). The smaller City of Seoul (10.4 million or 41% of the metro population) had, in 2010, a moderate car ownership rate of 286 per 1,000 people but a 70% modal share for walking, cycling and transit with its 'Triple 30' vision aimed at 80% of all mobility needs by green modes. The Triple 30 Vision is to reduce car use by 30%, reduce average commute time on transit by 30% and increase the proportion of land area devoted to green modes by 30%, including median bus lanes, bike lanes and sidewalks.[56]

TABLE 9.9 Seoul Metropolitan Area key figures[i]

Population (2013)	25,640,000
Population (1995)	20,576,272
Metropolitan GDP per capita (US$, 1995)	10,305
Urban density (persons per hectare; 1995)	230.4
Road length per person (metres; 1995)	0.9
Car use per person (vehicle kilometres traveled, or VKT, per year; 1995)	2,564
Transit use (boardings per person; 1995)	359

Source: Jeffrey R. Kenworthy

[i] Seoul data here are for 1995 only due to the many complexities that make updating the city with these kind of data very difficult.

The Cheonggye Freeway demolition and Cheonggyecheon River restoration project

What makes Seoul an exemplar here is the boldest ever example of 'trip de-generation' ever undertaken. This involved the tearing down of 5.8km of the Cheonggye four-lane freeway and surface street below, which carried together 168,000 vehicles per day through the very heart of the city, to exhume the culturally significant Cheonggyecheon River.[57] The freeway alignment has been transformed into a linear green heart for the city, a place to promenade and enjoy. All of this occurred without any significant traffic disruption and furthermore changed the direction of transportation planning in the city towards prioritizing transit and non-motorized modes. The project was a large-scale example of the idea of traffic behaving more like a gas than a liquid. Traffic engineers and transportation planners are trained to think of traffic as a liquid that holds its volume and will flow over everything if blocked or allowed to grow beyond its current 'container'. However, traffic tends to shrink when road capacity is removed, as has been proven time and again when pedestrian zones have been created (Kenworthy 2012).

The full story of this project can be found in a 25-minute documentary called *Seoul: The Stream of Consciousness*.[58] The concept for the project started with two engineers turning over memories of the past and the idea of restoring the Cheonggyecheon River, which lay beneath, because the Cheonggye District had become one of the dirtiest and noisiest parts of the city and would continue this way so long as the freeway remained.

The district and river have a long history dating back to at least the early 1400s. Part of this history was the turning of the river into a sewage system and the development of squatter settlements of Korean War refugees along its banks. By the 1950s, the whole area had become a symbol of poverty and the legacy of 50 years of colonialism and war. The only way to remove the blight was to cover it over with a road, which occurred between 1955 and 1977, and at the time, like most freeway building enterprises, became a symbol of progress and modernization. However, Lee Myung-bak successfully ran for mayor in 2001, and he made his top political priority the tearing down of this freeway and surface road, converting it to a green river boulevard. He also happened to be, in a previous life, the chief executive officer (CEO) of the company that built the road in the first place and

FIGURE 9.14
High densities, intensely mixed uses, shared streets and transit, Seoul, South Korea – the result: a quite walkable and attractive human environment
Source: Jeffrey R. Kenworthy

was in the unique position of knowing in intimate detail the realities of getting rid of it. The demolition and river restoration were to revitalize the area economically, but also to set Seoul on a new path in attracting tourism and investment, giving the city green credentials internationally and emphasizing quality of life. This radical road deconstruction project set Lee Myung-bak on a successful political career and he was elected president of South Korea in December 2007.[59]

Project context and results

Prior to the removal of the roads between 2003 and 2005, Seoul had already embarked upon strategies to try to better manage private transportation in the city as a whole. In 1996, modest tolls of about US$2 were introduced on two major entry points into the CBD. Traffic fell by 14% and speeds improved by 38%. Traffic returned to pre-toll levels, but occupancy improved and average speeds remained higher. In 1997, regular fee increases were introduced for public parking, parking requirements were lowered for commercial buildings and a parking permit system was introduced for residential parking. In 2003, a voluntary No Driving Day was introduced, including financial inducements to participants.

The corridor in which the demolished roads were located is served by multiple subway lines; but importantly, the city overhauled the bus system. This included an expansion of a bus rapid transit system operating in exclusive median lanes, which had been introduced already in 1996. By 2005, there were four routes covering 22 miles (35 km); by 2007, there were seven routes covering 42 miles (68 km); and by 2014, there were 72 miles (115 km), with the objective being 211 km in the coming years. Average speeds of buses have improved 30%.[60] Curb-side bus-only lanes were also expanded, the fares and timetables were coordinated, including use of a smart card and intelligent transportation systems (ITS) technology, and services were integrated with the subway system and the various services color-coded for ease of use and identity. The Seoul Metropolitan Government provides an excellent report entitled *Seoul Public Transportation* on all the many recent and planned advances in Seoul's public transport system.[61] The changes were also widely publicized leading up to the roads coming down.

FIGURE 9.15A
Cheonggyecheon River restoration, Seoul, South Korea – a green, community-oriented corridor through the heart of the city
Source: Jeffrey R. Kenworthy

FIGURE 9.15B
The Cheonggyecheon River is now
a site for displays and community
events
Source: Jeffrey R. Kenworthy

The results were very good. Within months, transit user satisfaction had reached 90%, speeds for the BRT had improved by between 33% and 100% and accidents and injuries on all routes had fallen by one-third. But the litmus test of all of this was that in five months between January and May 2005, bus patronage rose by almost one million per day—or almost 25%—and the volume of private traffic through central Seoul dropped 9.1% and citywide traffic by 5.9%. The project planner Kee Yeon Hwang also said: 'as soon as we destroyed the road, the cars just disappeared and drivers changed their habits'. Other benefits of the project included:

- average 30% increases of adjacent land value;
- average speed of traffic in City of Seoul in the peak period *increased* from 21.7 km/h to 22.8 km/h after the freeway and road carrying nearly 170,000 vehicles per day were demolished;
- Car flow in and out of city reduced by 18.6% and subway ridership in central area increased 13.7%;[62]
- temperatures in the green corridor reduced from 36.3 to 32.7 Celsius in areas 0.25 miles (400 m) away;
- extra water, open space access and recreational opportunities with a jump in the quality of life of city center residents, workers and visitors;
- a re-branding of Seoul's image internationally to one of a more sustainability-focused city;
- long-term economic benefits of the project estimated by the Seoul Development Institute to be US$8.5 billion to $25 billion and 113,000 new jobs.[63]

Finally, the success of this project and the fact that it won a prestigious international sustainability award in Washington, DC, in 2006 has inspired a proliferation of further projects to focus even more on transit in Seoul and to enhance conditions for pedestrians and cyclists and to continue improvements to the public realm. Writing in *The Guardian* in 2014, Philippe Mesmer detailed how Seoul has been removing several expressways and promoting bus and bicycle lanes and the return of trams.[64] After the city began prioritizing the public realm of the city over freeways, it also began to formally introduce a much broader sharing culture (Johnson 2015),[65] which one expert expects should lay deeper foundations for thinking through, 'how we share the city's infrastructure and how we better work together to resolve issues that could be solved through sharing, such as parking, housing, and environmental issues'.[66]

Taming the traffic in non-motorized cities: positive perspectives on Mumbai, Beijing, Shanghai and Guangzhou

When the major impressions of what is happening to cities in India and China are drawn from popular reporting and visual impressions alone, it is difficult not to believe that cities such as Mumbai, Beijing, Shanghai and Guangzhou are simply drowning in traffic and slowly stewing in their own automotive emissions. While there is a lot of truth to such impressions, is it the whole story? A closer analysis of some key trends in these four cities suggests that there is far more involved than just these outward appearances of traffic chaos and pollution. This deeper, more analytical perspective offers an alternative interpretation of the evolution of these cities, and makes them worthy exemplars for cities in rapidly developing parts of the world.

To appreciate the approach to these exemplars, it is necessary to understand that cities globally can be classified into different archetypes based on their land use and transportation characteristics. This clustering of cities enables their key characteristics to be seen and their prospects for the future to be considered. Using the *Millennium Cities Database for Sustainable Transport* (Kenworthy and Laube 2001), containing data from the mid-1990s, a cluster analysis was performed on a large sample of cities from this global database. Priester et al. (2013) found six transportation archetypes into which all the cities could be placed. These were:

- Hybrid Cities
- Transit Cities
- Non-Motorized Cities
- Auto-Cities
- Traffic-Saturated Cities
- Paratransit Cities

The four cities in the non-motorized cluster were Mumbai, Beijing, Shanghai and Guangzhou, since the majority of their mobility at that time was by walking and mechanized, non-motorized modes (the latter, mainly some form of bike). Since 1995, a lot of changes have occurred in urban transportation, none perhaps more so than in Chinese and Indian cities, and none probably greater than the impacts on walking, cycling and other non-motorized modes (e.g. rickshaws) due to an onslaught of cars, motorcycles and trucks.

China has undergone extraordinary motorization, the story of which is captured in Gao et al. (2015). India, too, has become wealthier, with a significant increase in its vehicle population. All cities in India and China have traditionally been strongly oriented to non-motorized modes (NMM), due to their very dense and mixed-land uses, which led to short trip distances amenable to these modes. The NMM cities' average density was the highest of all clusters with 194 persons per ha in 1995 (Table 9.10).

In the study by Priester et al. (2013), NMM cities are likely to have experienced the largest changes in urban transportation conditions due to the sheer scale and rapidity of change in urban China and India. These four exemplars explore the evolution of traditional NMM cities using a recently assembled set of new data that demonstrate that such cities, although saturated with motorized vehicles, are far from becoming automobile dependent.

Data perspectives from 1995

To see which direction the four NMM cities may have moved over the last 20 years, we need to understand the characteristics of each city cluster type for the variables examined here. Table 9.10 presents this information.

Table 9.10 shows that there are significant and distinguishing differences between the various clusters on key land use, wealth and transportation characteristics. The NMM cities in 1995 were characterized by very low income, exceptionally high density, extremely low road supply and very meager freeway provision. Their level of car ownership was also tiny, though they had moderately high levels of motorcycle ownership. Transit use was high, second to the Transit Cities themselves. The use of walking and cycling for daily trips was radically higher than in any other group, transit as a proportion of total daily trips was also healthy (third highest of the six clusters). Finally, the NMM cities had the lowest use of private motorized modes of all city clusters.

In exploring how these four cities have moved over the last 20 years or so, some of these data will be compared to recent values of the variables for each city.

Mumbai

The Mumbai Metropolitan Region (MMR) is today a megalopolis of some 22 million people, up from 17 million in 1996. It is one of the largest and densest metropolitan regions in the world, with extensive areas of informal settlements, in both its inner area and more distant parts of the region. Despite high levels of congestion, less than 10% of its daily trips are by private motorized modes. Mumbai's severe congestion problems, long commuting times and poor amenities in its outer areas are placing huge development pressures on its inner areas, which are densifying rapidly. Similar processes are occurring in other dense megacities such as Karachi.[67] Table 9.11 summarizes the key data for the region, about which the following key points can be made.

Urban density

Despite having fallen in density from 337 per ha to 315 per ha in 15 years, the MMR remains as one of the world's densest cities of the modern era, as shown in Figure 9.16.[68] When

TABLE 9.10 Key characteristics of each of the six city clusters in 1995

Variable	NMM cities	Para-transit cities	Traffic-saturated cities	Transit cities	Hybrid cities	Auto cities
GDP per capita (USD 1995)	$2,003	$2,848	$5,197	$28,570	$26,236	$21,180
Urban density (persons per ha)	194	71	192	169	35	21
Length of road per person (m)	0.36	1.97	0.63	1.99	4.26	6.95
Length of freeway per person (m)	0.002	0.014	0.019	0.020	0.096	0.175
Passenger cars per 1000 persons	25	126	126	175	486	482
Motorcycles per 1000 persons	49	6	157	63	17	7
Car vehicle kilometres per person (VKT)	359	1,328	1,169	2,083	7,743	11,094
Public transit boardings per person	337	213	190	464	173	16
Daily trips by non-motorized modes (%)	61%	38%	31%	26%	20%	3%
Daily trips by public modes (%)	25%	30%	20%	35%	13%	1%
Daily trips by private modes (%)	14%	32%	49%	38%	67%	95%

Source: Priester et al. (2013)

FIGURE 9.16
Major parts of inner Mumbai are rapidly increasing in density due to development pressures caused by long travel times from amenity-poor distant areas
Source: Mezan Khaja

any city has such a high overall density, it is physically impossible due to road space constraints to accommodate high car dependence. So, despite the sheer visual, auditory and other sensory impact of motorized vehicles on Mumbai and on the life quality of its citizens and visitors, it is well to remember the city retains a density that lies unequivocally in the Walking City category of urban fabrics (see earlier chapters).

TABLE 9.11 Key variables for the Mumbai Metropolitan Region in 1996 and recently

Urban transportation indicators	1996	Recent	Year
Key transportation and land use variables			
GDP per capita (USD 1995)	$913	$4,194	2012
Urban density (persons per ha)	337.4	314.8	2011
Length of road per person (m)	0.35	0.40	2013
Passenger cars per 1000 persons	21.2	68.4	2014
Motorcycles per 1000 persons	32.2	122.5	2014
Total public transport boardings per person	224.6	232.4	2015
– Bus boardings per person	103.2	105.0	2015
– Rail boardings per person	121.4	127.4	2015
Modal split for total daily trips			
Daily trips by non-motorized modes	49.8%	63.6%	2006
Daily trips by motorized public modes	40.9%	31.9%	2006
Daily trips by motorized private modes	9.3%	4.5%	2006
Modal split for mechanized total daily trips			
Daily trips by mechanized, non-motorized modes	1.7%	11.0%	2006
Daily trips by motorized public modes	80.0%	78.0%	2006
Daily trips by motorized private modes	18.2%	11.0%	2006

Source: Kenworthy (2016)

Road supply

Such enormous density shapes mobility patterns in a profound way, as explained in similar case studies of São Paulo and Taipei in Newman and Kenworthy (2015) and much earlier by Thomson (1977). Put simply, the physical form of any city critically influences what is and is not possible in mobility terms. For example, if a city is very dense it inevitably means that its supply of road space will be severely constrained. Mumbai in 1996 had a meager 0.35 meters (35 cm) of road length per person, while the automobile-dependent megacities had 6.95 meters or just under 20 times more. By 2013 the road length per person in the MMR had only increased to 0.40 meters per person. If a city has such little road availability, it is physically impossible to accommodate a lot more flow of traffic in private vehicles. If the city is to remain functional, other modes simply must and do play a more profound role.

Cars and motorcycles

Since 1996, car ownership in the MMR increased from a miniscule 21 cars per 1,000 persons to only 68 in 2014. So, while the MMR has increased 3.2 times in car ownership in 18 years, it would still be one of the lowest rates of car ownership in the world.

In the face of growing wealth, rapid motorization and limited road supply, the next best alternative to a car is a motorcycle and Indian cities are renowned worldwide for their ubiquitous scooters. In 1996, motorcycles in the MMR stood at 32 per 1,000 persons, but by 2014 the ownership rate was 122, or 3.8 times higher. This is a natural response to limited road space (motorcycles enable users to maneuver in traffic and park in tight quarters), rising wealth and a poor transit system.

Wealth

Wealth is measured as GDP per person for each of the metro regions here, standardized to 1995 U.S. dollars. The MMR has significantly increased in wealth from only $913 in 1996 to $4,194 in 2012, a 4.6 times increase. Nevertheless, on a global scale this is still modest and such low and poorly distributed wealth makes the cheaper NMM and transit modes preferred by many people.

Public transit use

Mumbai's annual transit boardings per person of 232 were very modestly up from 225 in 1996. Globally, this level of transit use is modest for a city of Mumbai's size and density. The New York metropolitan region, with some 20 million people and a density of only 19 persons per ha (or only 6% of Mumbai density), had annual boardings per capita in 2005 of 168 per person.

Commonly circulated images of people hanging from trains and jammed into buses in Mumbai suggest a transit system that is operating way over its design capacity. The data suggest that transit is barely able to hold its own and that it is probably quite remarkable that the city has increased slightly in per capita use. Increases in transit use are limited in Mumbai by lack of capacity and quality of transit, which in turn relate to issues of finance, transportation capital spending priorities and governance in Indian cities generally.

Modal split for all daily trips

The latest modal split data is from the Mumbai Metropolitan Region Development Authority (2006) and show that the MMR had 63.6% of all trips by non-motorized modes, 31.9% by public transport and a tiny 4.5% by all private motorized modes (cars, motorcycles etc.). In 1996, the same figures were 49.8% NMM, 40.9% public transport and 9.3% private motorized modes. Ten years on from 1996, rather than weakening, NMM's contribution to daily trip-making had increased, while public and private transportation modal share has dropped. If one excludes walking trips from the equation and calculates the modal split only for mechanized modes of transport, then transit dominates with 78% of all non-walking trips, while bikes and private motorized modes share the rest equally (11% each). An additional piece of data from this latest mobility study is that *more than 40% of workers in the MMR walk to work*, a possibly unique achievement in the 2000s for a metropolis the size of Mumbai.

The great burden of serious health, environmental, socio-economic and resource use impacts created by the rapid growth of private motorized modes in India has been detailed by Badami (2009, p. 43), especially in regards to the loss of accessibility for pedestrians, which has created 'an urgent need for an integrated approach that addresses multiple impacts, caters to multiple modes and road users, and is sensitive to the needs, capabilities and constraints in the Indian context'.

Conclusions for Mumbai

The only conclusion possible for Mumbai from these data is that despite the overwhelming impact of motorized vehicles on every aspect of life, it can still be classed as an NMM city. Although cars and motorcycles have increased along with wealth and the situation on the roads has reached chaos levels due to limited road space, the density of the region is still huge. The transit system suffers dramatic capacity problems, just like the roads, so the only possibility—or indeed sensible avenue—for many trips is to walk or try to ride a bike, and indeed 40% of people do walk to work. Of course, the region is big and walking, cycling and rickshaws are only possible over relatively short distances. For a large proportion of daily needs by most people, NMM fortunately still work at a local level. The city obviously needs to dramatically improve and expand its rail-based transit modes and to protect and renew its overstretched bus systems. The private mobility alternative of trying to expand its road system is clearly not a viable proposition in such an extraordinarily dense urban region.

Shanghai

Shanghai is one of China's largest cities and most important commercial centers, and was the first city in China to introduce controls on car ownership. The key data to characterize the megacity of Shanghai are included in Table 9.12.

Urban density

In 1995, the population of the Shanghai metro region was 9,570,000, while in 2013 it was some 14,319,000. By 2009, under these growth pressures and expansion of the metropolitan area, the urban density of Shanghai had reduced from 196 to 170 persons per ha. By global standards, this is still an extremely high density, which in combination with the rapidly expanded metro system of 588 km and 364 stations in 2015 (up from 4.4 km in 1993) ensures the city is far from being automobile dependent.

Road supply

Shanghai in 1995 had only 0.31 meters of road per person, but by 2013 this had quadrupled to 1.22. In addition, the supply of freeways had grown from 0.003 meters per person to 0.057 per person (a 19-times increase). Shanghai has been very organized and well-

TABLE 9.12 Key variables for the Shanghai Metropolitan Region in 1995 and recently

Urban transportation indicators	1995	Recent	Year
Key transportation and land use variables			
GDP per capita (USD 1995)	$2,474	$7,530	2009
Urban density (persons per ha)	196.3	170.0	2009
Length of road per person (m)	0.31	1.22	2013
Length of freeway per person (m)	0.003	0.057	2013
Passenger cars per 1000 persons	15.2	144.7	2013
Motorcycles per 1000 persons	44.0	29.0	2013
Total public transit boardings per person	452.9	411.4	2014
– Bus boardings per person	452.9	197.5	2014
– Rail boardings person[i]	0.0	209.6	2014
– Ferry boardings per person	0.0	4.3	2014
Modal split for total daily trips			
Daily trips by non-motorized modes	77.9%	54.8%	2009
Daily trips by motorized public modes	15.1%	25.2%	2009
Daily trips by motorized private modes	7.0%	20.0%	2009
Modal split for mechanized total daily trips			
Daily trips by mechanized, non-motorized modes	67.1%	38.8%	2009
Daily trips by motorized public modes	22.5%	34.1%	2009
Daily trips by motorized private modes	10.4%	27.1%	2009

Source: Kenworthy (2016)

[i] Note that although for 1995, the Shanghai metro system was in operation, its annual boardings that year (on only 4.4 km for 4 months and 16.1 km of route length for 8 months) were only 230,000 or an unmeasurable 0.024 boardings per person and therefore not even figuring to one decimal point in the data. It was thus not included in the 1995 data.

resourced in developing all forms of transportation infrastructure, such that Shanghai is transforming itself into a fundamentally different metropolis than it was before the widespread adoption of private motorized modes.

Cars and motorcycles

In 1995, Shanghai had almost negligible car ownership of 15 cars per 1,000 persons. Under China's aggressively developed domestic automotive industry and growing links to foreign car firms, this had multiplied 9.5 times to 145 cars per 1,000 persons by 2013, although by international measures this is still very low urban car ownership (see Chapter 1).

Unlike Mumbai, Shanghai's 1995 ownership of motorcycles stood at 44 per 1,000 persons, but this had reduced to 29 per 1,000 persons by 2013. This is common to all three Chinese cities (see further), where motorcycles are playing less and less of a role in mobility, a trend that is uniquely counter to what is happening in most other world cities, where motorcycles are increasing (Newman and Kenworthy 2015).

Wealth

Shanghai's GDP per capita increased from $2,474 in 1995 to $7,530 in 2009 (USD 1995), though by comparison to wealthier cities around the world it is still very low (e.g. a large sample of European cities averaged $38,683 in 2005—Newman and Kenworthy 2015).

Public transit use

Shanghai's transit system consists of a very extensive metro network—now the longest in the world (588 km)—which all opened in the space of 22 years from 1993, plus a very extensive bus and trolley bus system and a very small ferry service. In 1995, Shanghai's bus system (the only mode available then) resulted in a very healthy 453 annual boardings per person, while in 2014 total transit boardings had fallen somewhat to 411 per person. With the rapid development of the metro system, buses have played a declining role (and likely would have without the metro because they cannot compete in speed terms with cars or motorcycles). So far, the metro system has almost compensated for the bus system losses, which is a considerable feat considering that car ownership has multiplied almost ten-fold over the same period. Notwithstanding competition from private motorized modes, the Shanghai metro system together with an improving and very extensive bus system are beginning to transform Shanghai into a modern transit metropolis, as the final data on modal split show.

Modal split for all daily trips

In 1995, Shanghai had an extraordinary 78% of all daily trips by foot or bike, another 15% by transit and a meager 7% by private motorized modes. By 2009, the latest data that are available on this comprehensive basis, NMM had lost a lot of ground, but still stood at an amazing 55% of all daily trips. This loss of NMM usage has, however, been picked up with a significant growth in transit's share of trips, up from 15% to 25% in 2009. Naturally, a big growth area has been private motorized modes, which in 2009 stood at 20%. While this represents almost a tripling from 1995, private modes are still very small in any global comparison, even though they have a radical effect on congestion, air pollution, the quality of public spaces and other environmental factors such as noise.

Conclusions for Shanghai

Comparing Tables 9.10 and 9.12, Shanghai has not become an Auto-City, a Hybrid City, a Paratransit City or even a Traffic-Saturated City. So, either it is still a NMM city or it

FIGURE 9.17
Shanghai's intensive pedestrian
environments
Source: Jeffrey R. Kenworthy

has evolved into a Transit City. With 55% of daily trips still by NMM, on this single factor it still has clear NMM credentials and is much better than the Transit Cities in 1995, which only had 26% NMM use. Shanghai's per capita use of transit today is significantly higher than in the NMM cities in 1995. The city's density has also dropped to be almost identical to the urban density for Transit Cities in 1995. Length of road and freeway per capita and car ownership are also not dissimilar to the Transit Cities in 1995. Shanghai's GDP per capita is, however, much lower today than the Transit Cities were in 1995.

In conclusion, we can say that Shanghai has become more like a Transit City, but has achieved this at a very much earlier stage in the economic development cycle, most likely due to the significant economic boom of China and its ability and willingness to invest vast sums of money in rail. But Shanghai is also a Transit City that maintains a very high level of NMM use, due partly at least to its very dense and mixed-use environment.

Beijing

Beijing has undergone major changes since 1995, not the least of which is its population growth from 8,164,000 people to 13,561,000 in 2012 (the latest year for corresponding land use data).[69] Table 9.13 captures some major changes in land use and transportation over this period of very significant growth.

TABLE 9.13 Key variables for the Beijing Metropolitan Region in 1995 and recently

Urban transportation indicators	1995	Recent	Year
Key transportation and land-use variables			
GDP per capita (USD 1995)	$1,829	$9,850	2012
Urban density (persons per ha)	123.1	102.0	2012
Length of road per person (m)	0.32	?	-
Length of freeway per person (m)	0.005	0.046	2012
Passenger cars per 1000 persons	42.9	230.9	2012
Motorcycles per 1000 persons	27.7	15.6	2012
Car vehicle kilometers per person (VKT)	785	3,017	2012
Total public transit boardings per person	456.7	408.6	2014
– Bus boardings per person	386.8	239.2	2014
– Rail boardings per person	68.4	169.4	2014
Modal split for total daily trips[i]			
Daily trips by non-motorized modes (%)	47.9%	21.8%	2012
Daily trips by motorized public modes (%)	27.8%	39.8%	2012
Daily trips by motorized private modes (%)	24.3%	38.3%	2012
Modal split for mechanized total daily trips			
Daily trips by mechanized, non-motorized modes (%)	42.6%	13.9%	2012
Daily trips by motorized public modes (%)	30.7%	44.0%	2012
Daily trips by motorized private modes (%)	26.7%	42.1%	2012

Source: Kenworthy (2016)

[i] Beijing strangely does not report the walking trips in its modal split anymore. However, in 1995 the walking trips only comprised 9% of the 47.9% split for non-motorized modes. Fully 39% of the trips were by bike and it is the bike mode that has been slashed. Based on the dramatic trend down in bikes and the apparent small use of walking modes in 1995, plus the other trends from 1995 to 2012 in all the other modes, a supportable estimate of the full modal split for 2012 including walking has been made. Thus the first set of modal split data in Table 9.13 for 2012 are estimates based on real data, while the second set are actual data.

Urban density

Beijing, like Shanghai, has reduced in density from 123 to 102 persons per ha under the outward forces of growth at lower densities, though this is still high density in a global perspective. This decrease in density, along with the other changes explained below, have pushed Beijing towards greater reliance on private motorized modes, though it is still very far from being an auto-dependent city.

Road supply

The overall data on the length of all road types in the Beijing region were not available, but freeway data show that Beijing's freeway length increased from a meager 42 km in 1995 to 922 km in 2012, a 22-fold increase in the space of 17 years. The per capita availability of freeway has multiplied by a little over nine times, from 0.005 to 0.046 meters per person. Both Shanghai and Beijing are similar in this regard. Freeways have been shown over decades since World War II to always encourage and facilitate greater motor vehicle traffic, so one can expect that this will have facilitated greater car use in Beijing.

Cars and motorcycles

Until about 2011, Beijing had an aggressive program promoting private vehicles—unlike Shanghai, which adopted early restraint of car ownership through an auction system like Singapore's Certificate of Entitlement. Shanghai's system started in 1986, but was only in full operation by 2000 (Suwei and Qiang 2013; Gao and Kenworthy 2016). Beijing has been forced to slow down its growth in motor vehicles due to congestion, globally publicized air pollution problems and sprawling, auto-oriented growth consuming too much food-producing land (*The Guardian* 2015). Effective January 2011, Beijing has a lottery system to limit the monthly number of new car registrations. However, the differences can be seen, with Beijing in 2012 having some 231 cars per 1,000 persons, compared to Shanghai with only 145 per 1,000. This growth in car numbers, more than any single factor, has been behind Beijing's increase in private mobility (see below).

Like Shanghai, the number of motorcycles per 1,000 persons has reduced in Beijing. In 2012, there were only 16 motorcycles per 1,000 persons compared to 28 per 1,000 in 1995. Electric motorcycles have been encouraged and conventional motorcycles discouraged, which may help explain the smaller numbers. The reducing number of motorcycles, which goes against global trends and the lower numbers of motorcycles than are typical for Asian cities, probably show the effect of the huge metro systems in Shanghai and Beijing; motorcycles are less needed because fast travel speeds are possible on transit.

Wealth

Beijing's GDP per capita has radically increased from $1,829 to $9,850 per capita, a 5.4 times increase. This also feeds into greater demand for private transportation, but where good transit systems are provided, it also improves the ability of people to pay for quality public modes such as new metro systems.

Public transit use

When Beijing opened its first metro line in 1969, it had a route length of 21 km. Today it is a system of 18 lines with 334 stations and a network length of 554 km, the second biggest in the world behind Shanghai, and most of it built since 2003. This has been critical in forging a transition from a NMM City to something that is more like a Transit City and very far from an Auto-City. It has helped to radically counter the freeway expansion.

Beijing in 1995 had 457 transit boardings per person, while in 2014 it was 409, a reduction over 17 years of about 10%. Rail boardings have grown a lot but the bus boardings have declined. Considering that Beijing's wealth and car ownership have multiplied some five times, its freeway system has expanded some 22 times and parking has burgeoned, this level of transit use is very commendable. European cities in 2005 averaged 386 transit boardings per person, while the two mature transit metropolises of Singapore and Hong Kong averaged 450 boardings per person (Chapter 1).

Beijing, notwithstanding its freeway expansion, is rapidly evolving into one of the world's major transit metropolises. The metro system is expected to be 1,000 km by 2020. This, combined with the lottery-based controls on car ownership growth that have been in place since 2011, Beijing's evolution to a Transit City seems assured.

Modal split for all daily trips

Beijing has lost a lot of mode share from non-motorized modes. The bicycle has declined from 63% of all trips (excluding walk trips) in the region in 1986 to just 14% in 2012. This has resulted in more than a halving of the modal split for NMM for all trips between 1995 and 2012 (48 to 22%).[70] On the positive side though, for all trips excluding those by foot, transit has increased from 31% to 44% of trips and in terms of all trips (including walking) transit stands at an estimated 40%. Private motorized modes (cars and motorcycles) are thus only accounting for 38% of all trips and 42% excluding walking.

Car use

Annual travel by cars has increased significantly from a tiny 785 km per person to just over 3,000 km, a 3.8-fold increase, though not as large as the increase in wealth or car ownership of 5.4 times. In a global perspective, Beijing's use of cars is still very low and is more in line with car usage levels in Transit Cities.

FIGURE 9.18A A walk on the wild side, Dalian, China – pedestrians forced to walk on the street
Source: Jeffrey R. Kenworthy

FIGURE 9.18B
"Tragedy of the commons", Dalian,
China – sidewalks formally allocated
to parking bays
Source: Jeffrey R. Kenworthy[71]

FIGURE 9.18B
"Tragedy of the commons", Dalian,
China – sidewalks formally allocated
to parking bays
Source: Jeffrey R. Kenworthy[71]

Conclusions for Beijing

Beijing is far from being an automobile-dependent region. It appears rather that Beijing is likely to have moved out of the NMM cluster and into the Transit City cluster or alternatively, like Shanghai, it might fit into a new cluster that could be called an *Emerging Transit City*. Its 2012 characteristics are more like a Transit City than any other cluster and with the continued aggressive development of Beijing's Metro and the relatively recent controls over car ownership, which will affect future growth in car use, one can only expect that Beijing will move further away from automobile dependence.

FIGURE 9.19
A modern tram in Dalian, China –
helps to traffic calm the city streets
Source: Jeffrey R. Kenworthy

Guangzhou

Guangzhou was the smallest of the three Chinese cities in 1995, with only 3,853,800 people. The whole region in 2012 had a population of 12,838,900.[72] However, it was also the wealthiest and the lowest density of the three Chinese cities. In 1995, it also had no rail system and no freeways. Table 9.14 captures key changes in Guangzhou from 1995 to recent years.

Urban density

Guangzhou's urban density in 1995 was 119 persons per ha. Since then, it has expanded outwards and population has grown by some nine million people. Guangzhou's density has fallen to 100 persons per ha (16% decline), comparable to the percentage fall in density in Shanghai and Beijing, but its density is still very high in any international comparison.

Road supply

Guangzhou's road availability grew from 0.47 meters per person in 1995 to 0.70 meters per person by 2014. This is extremely low road provision in an international perspective and is in keeping with Guangzhou's high density.

In contrast, it had no freeways at all in 1995; however, by 2014 it had built 852 km and freeway availability had risen to 0.065 meters per person. By 2014, Guangzhou had over three times the level of freeway provision per capita of Transit Cities in 1995 and the highest of all three Chinese cities today.

Cars and motorcycles

In 1995, Guangzhou had only 20 cars per 1,000 people, but by 2014 this had risen sharply to 147—a 7.3-times increase. Motorcycles had declined from a relatively high level of 94 per 1,000 persons in 1995 to only 20 per 1,000 persons in 2014. Motorcycle numbers peaked in 2003 at 1,120,000 and have systematically declined ever since to only 258,980 in 2014.

Wealth

Guangzhou's GDP per person has grown from $2,796 to $11,929 in 2012, 4.3-fold increase. As with the other two Chinese cities, this increase in wealth helps to facilitate private transportation, but can also help promote transit use where good systems are provided to meet growing demands and expectations.

Public transit use

Guangzhou's first metro line opened in 1997 and has increased to 268 km with nine lines and 167 stations, with many new lines and extensions currently under construction, approved or proposed. Guangzhou had only 215 transit boardings per person in 1995, but by 2012 it had radically increased this usage to 401. Unlike in the other two Chinese cities, bus usage has grown alongside the huge metro usage jump, from zero to 164 boardings per person. The three Chinese cities now have very similar total transit use per person (Guangzhou 401, Beijing 409 and Shanghai 411 boardings per capita). Guangzhou's transit performance is exemplary, when one considers the large increase in cars, wealth and freeways and its moderate decline in density.

Modal split for all daily trips

Non-motorized modes in Guangzhou have suffered a significant decline from 69% of all daily trips down to 42% in 2008. But this level of non-motorized mobility is still very big compared to many other cities and is still likely to be quite significant today. A culture of walking still exists in China and this is reflected in the strong street culture that still exists in many parts of Chinese cities. But the big success story in Guangzhou is transit. Transit boardings per person have taken a huge upturn and transit has radically improved from 14% of all trips to 34% in 2008, almost a 2.5-times increase (and this is 2008 data, when transit boardings in the city were much lower than in 2012). From 1995 to 2008, private motorized modes in Guangzhou had only increased from 16% to 23%, so that 77% of all daily needs in Guangzhou were still being met by NMM and transit.

Conclusions for Guangzhou

Guangzhou is very far indeed from being automobile dependent, even though its motorization characteristics have moved along apace over the 1995 to 2014 period. It still retains high NMM usage and has developed very high transit use through its rapidly expanding metro system. Transit growth has been one of the factors limiting expansion of private mobility.

Like Shanghai and Beijing, the only logical group into which the city may have moved is the Transit City cluster, or again, an *Emerging Transit City*. With its continued extensive plans for metro extensions and accompanying bus integration, as well as its car registration restriction scheme introduced in June 2012 (effective until July 2018) based on a monthly

TABLE 9.14 Key variables for the Guangzhou Metropolitan Region in 1995 and recently

Urban transportation indicators	1995	Recent	Year
Key transportation and land-use variables			
GDP per capita (USD 1995)	$2,796	$11,929	2012
Urban density (persons per ha)	119.0	100.2	2014
Length of road per person (m)	0.47	0.70	2014
Length of freeway per person (m)	0.000	0.065	2014
Passenger cars per 1000 persons	20.2	147.0	2014
Motorcycles per 1000 persons	93.7	19.8	2014
Car vehicle kilometers per person (VKT)	337	?	
Total public transit boardings per person	215.1	400.9	2012
– Bus boardings per person	196.7	234.7	2012
– Rail boardings per person	0.0	164.3	2012
– Ferry boardings per person	18.3	1.9	2012
Modal split for total daily trips			
Daily trips by non-motorized modes (%)	69.3%	42.2%	2008
Daily trips by motorized public modes (%)	14.2%	34.3%	2008
Daily trips by motorized private modes (%)	16.5%	23.5%	2008
Modal split for mechanized total daily trips			
Daily trips by mechanized, non-motorized modes (%)	52.8%	12.4%	2008
Daily trips by motorized public modes (%)	21.8%	52.0%	2008
Daily trips by motorized private modes (%)	25.3%	35.6%	2008

Source: Kenworthy (2016)

auction, but also partly on a lottery system (Suwei and Qiang 2013), it seems highly likely that Guangzhou will continue to strengthen its Transit City credentials.

Conclusions for Mumbai, Shanghai, Beijing and Guangzhou

Many cities in the rapidly industrializing world are experiencing overwhelming problems of air pollution, noise, traffic deaths, congestion, the destruction of civic space and even growing obesity rates due to the growth in private mobility. This is leading to a rethink and many cities are choosing to install extensive transit systems, limit car ownership and use and encourage walking and cycling for more trips. Some are also promoting dense, mixed land use around transit to lessen car dependence in the future.

In short, the glamour of the automobile in dense and space- and road-constrained cities has lost some of its shine. The Chinese cities—after an aggressive period of about 15 years of embracing the automobile—have, since around 2011, begun to moderate this stance, particularly in the larger cities. India too is making large efforts to build new transit systems (Newman et al. 2013).

In 1995 these four cities were all classified as Non-Motorized Cities. Mumbai, despite its traffic chaos, is still a NMM city. However, data for Shanghai, Beijing and Guangzhou indicate that they have all moved towards the Transit City category, or perhaps what could be called *Emerging Transit Cities*, in contrast to established or Mature Transit Cities such as Tokyo, Osaka or Hong Kong, which decades ago established themselves firmly in this category.

Based on trends in the Chinese cities, the main characteristics of an *Emerging Transit City* would be:

- Development of extensive rail systems early in the economic development cycle and over a relatively short period, i.e. they still have comparatively low, though rapidly growing, GDP per capita.
- Continued high-density land use patterns, exceeding 100 persons per ha.
- Implementation of controls on car ownership and use, as Singapore did from the 1970s.

- Significant and possibly growing levels of non-motorized mode use, notwithstanding early, often large reductions.
- High per capita transit use exceeding 400 annual boardings per person, and growing.
- Around 35% of total daily trips by transit, a figure likely to grow due to continued rapid expansion of metro systems.
- Comparatively low per capita use of cars (annual VKT per person).
- Private motorized modes less than transit and NMM combined, accounting for between 25% and 40% of total daily trips.
- Car ownership of generally less than 250 cars per 1,000 persons.

In terms of the future evolution of such cities, a likely prognosis based on current patterns would be:

- Continued per capita growth in transit use;
- Continued rapid development in wealth;
- Upturn or stabilization in the decline of NMM use;
- Slowing down in growth of cars and car use;
- Slowing down in growth of freeways;
- Stabilization in growth of modal split for private motorized modes;
- Longer-term trajectory towards a Mature Transit City with healthy NMM use.

Conclusions

This chapter has shown that it is possible to forge new directions in transportation in all kinds of cities, whether they are large or small, auto-oriented cities in North America, traditional European cities or less wealthy megacities in the Asian region. Good ideas abound in sustainable transportation; but if there is one single lesson binding these examples together, it is that without either strong leadership or effective civil society, or a dynamic combination of both, good ideas are not enough. In all the cities examined, political commitment, vision and financial investment to back it up, as well as in many cases strong civil society involvement, have been key factors in driving the achievements in each place. In other iconic examples not dealt with in this chapter, such as Bogotá and Curitiba, leadership and genuine respect for and engagement with the broader community, especially the poor and others generally without a strong voice, have been a hallmark of their success too.

Questions for discussion

- What are some common themes that run through the examples of success in sustainable transportation?

- What other cities have had success in sustainable transportation? What did they achieve and how?

- Why are major comprehensive successes in sustainable transportation relatively few and far between?

Notes

1 For example, engagement with urban communities. See also hopeful case studies of positive trends in São Paulo, Taipei and Prague in Newman and Kenworthy (2015).
2 Update of *The Millennium Cities Database for Sustainable Transportation* (Kenworthy and Laube 2001), some of which is published in Newman and Kenworthy (2015).

3 Based on personal communication with Klaus Frey.

4 Cervero 1995, 1998; Newman and Kenworthy 1999a.

5 Part of the Denver metropolitan area.

6 Circa 630,000 or more than 25% of the population.

7 Also see Christopher Leo (1977: 43)

8 Within this generally positive picture of Vancouver, it should be noted that there are nevertheless criticisms, such as housing affordability and general inequality in areas of high amenity. Housing throughout Vancouver is expensive and those areas that display the best of Vancouver's urban achievements are also the most expensive and largely unaffordable to those with modest incomes. There is therefore a need to increase the supply of more affordable housing in central and inner areas of the city as homelessness within the city increases. The City of Vancouver has been criticized for catering too much to the development industry as well as wealthy buyers and renters in its high-density redevelopment projects. This it is argued also increases housing demand in distant lower-density but more affordable suburbs, far from the amenities of the inner city. This has resulted in political ruptures such as the formation of a new local political party, OneCity which is attempting to address inequalities (e.g. rabble.ca/blogs/bloggers/michael-stewart/2014/05/new-left-wing-party-vancouver-joins-growing-chorus-criticisms). Some data on these aspects of the city can be found at vancouver.ca/files/cov/factsheet5-making-ends-meet.PDF and vancouver.ca/files/cov/factsheet2-home-for-everyone.PDF (all accessed 24 June 2016).

9 The metropolitan area of Vancouver was formerly known as the Greater Vancouver Regional District (GVRD) but is now called Metro Vancouver.

10 The data are for the whole transit region; ridership is likely to be significantly higher within the city limits.

11 See for example: www.vancouversun.com/news/transit-system-crime/most-violent.html (accessed 22 June 2016).

12 The freeway ban applied to the City of Vancouver only, so the region does have some freeways.

13 In contrast to U.S. cities at 9.5 deaths per 100,000 people in 2005, or 76% more than Vancouver, despite the U.S. cities themselves having also fallen by 25% over this period in transport deaths per 100,000 people.

14 The Canada Line: www.canadaline.ca (accessed 27 May 2009).

15 See www.translink.ca/en/About-Us/Media/2011/August/TransLink-reports-transit-ridership-heading-for-a-new-record.aspx (accessed 22 June 2016).

16 See www.evergreenline.gov.bc.ca (accessed 22 June 2016). The line opened ahead of time on 2 December 2016 and in early 2017 was already carrying 30,000 people per day.

17 Because of the fine-grained grid along which they operate.

18 See citiscope.org/story/2014/vancouvers-canada-line-model-transit-oriented-development-too (accessed 24 June 2016).

19 The housing co-operatives that were historically possible under a Canada Mortgage and Housing Corporation (CMHC) scheme are no longer available.

20 Total area is 114.97 square km and almost completely urban land.

21 See www.metrovancouver.org/services/regional-planning/metro-vancouver-2040/Pages/default.aspx (accessed 24 June 2016).

22 See www.alc.gov.bc.ca/alc/content/alr-maps

23 See michaelmortensenblog.com/2016/04/05/transit-oriented-development-room-for-smart-growth-in-greater-vancouver/ (accessed 24 June 2016).

24 See *Vancouver Sun*, 3 October 2015, p. H3 Kenworthy, J. Move to demolish viaducts praised, vancouver.ca/home-property-development/northeast-false-creek.aspx (accessed 24 June 2016).

25 See vancouver.ca/streets-transportation/protected-bicycle-lanes.aspx (accessed 24 June 2016).

26 Among the leaders was Neil Goldschmidt, the Governor of Oregon, who later became President Carter's Secretary for Transportation.

27 With no apologies to the theatrical play.

28 A pun on the name of a major cosmetics line.

29 Australian cities averaged 96 transit boardings per capita in 2006, Canadian cities 151 and European cities 386 (Newman and Kenworthy 2015).

30 See en.wikipedia.org/wiki/Portland_Rose_Festival#cite_note-gpas-1 (accessed 24 June 2016).

31 According to Arrington (2009), at the time of opening, 7,000 transit-supportive residential units were already under construction in station precincts.

32   For more see: www.oregonmetro.gov/tools-partners/grants-and-resources/transit-oriented-development-program (accessed 24 June 2016).

33   See www.aarp.org/content/dam/aarp/livable-communities/act/transportation/transit-oriented-development-aarp.pdf (accessed 24 June 2016).

34   Similar tool as at the state level.

35   www.portlandoregon.gov/transportation/article/156490; www.portlandoregon.gov/transportation/article/545858; www.cityclock.org/urban-cycling-mode-share/#.WCVfjygq8rg; http://bikeportland.org/ (all accessed November 11, 2016)

36   City population: www.city-data.com/city/Boulder-Colorado.html. County population: www.census.gov/quickfacts/table/PST045215/08013 (both accessed 24 June 2016).

37   See www.metrodenver.org/do-business/demographics/population/ (accessed 24 June 2016).

38   See www.planboulder.org/ (accessed 24 June 2016).

39   See www.boulderdowntown.com/discover/pearlstreethistory.html, accessed 29 June 2009.

40   See Havlick 2004, City of Boulder 2014, pp. 1–5.

41   Included advisory committees, Transportation Advisory Board Meetings, 2014 Walk Bike Summit, open houses, store front workshops, social media engagement. Community input stressed items such as the health effects of modal choice, deepening collaboration between Boulder institutions, bike corridors, strengthening the CTN, in particular real time travel information, better connections and school transit services, parking strategies, better connections to regional transportation planning, BRT, alignment of TMP with Climate Commitment goal including better integration of land use and transportation to support non-auto modes, providing more local work opportunities through better mixed use planning and planning for demographic change.

42   City of Boulder 2014, pp. 2–11.

43   See bouldercolorado.gov/goboulder/bike (accessed 26 June 2016).

44   In Figure 10.3 of their report.

45   Defining certain major corridors as high-frequency all-day, all-evening and weekend services.

46   For example, the former mayor, Will Toor, who started his civic involvement with this committee.

47   A minimum of US$5,000 from at least 100 households.

48   Comparative data in this exemplar are drawn primarily from Rikort, A, Markiewicz, M., Herrmann, M. and Kreisel, S. (2014) Comparative Urban Data Collection and Analysis Focussed on Freiburg im Breisgau: Transport and Land Use Sustainability in Cities. GEKO Master Project, Frankfurt University of Applied Sciences, Frankfurt am Main (supervised by Jeff Kenworthy).

49   Based on personal communication with Jürgen Dickmann, City of Freiburg, 1990.

50   The average for the German sample is 48 per hectare.

51   In the German, 'Verkehrsberuhigung'.

52   Room for only one vehicle at a time.

53   Although the new district itself is a 'node' within the city structure.

54   See www.freiburg.de/pb/site/Freiburg/get/params_E897417003/355169/Befragung_Rieselfeld_Englisch.pdf (p. 5, accessed 27 June 2016).

55   See worldpopulationreview.com/world-cities/seoul-population/ (accessed 24 June 2016).

56   See english.seoul.go.kr/wp-content/uploads/2014/06/Seoul-Public-Transportation-English.pdf (accessed 27 June 2016).

57   Seattle Urban Mobility Plan (2008): The Preservation Institute: www.preservenet.com/freeways/FreewaysCheonggye.html (accessed 27 June 2016).

58   See www.pbs.org/e2/transport.html, and watch full movie at www.youtube.com/watch?v=hOeJCcPAXmw (accessed 27 June 2016).

59   See www.seattle.gov/transportation/docs/ump/06%20SEATTLE%20Case%20studies%20in%20urban%20freeway%20removal.pdf (accessed 27 June 2016).

60   See english.seoul.go.kr/wp-content/uploads/2014/06/Seoul-Public-Transportation-English.pdf (accessed 27 June 2016).

61   See english.seoul.go.kr/wp-content/uploads/2014/06/Seoul-Public-Transportation-English.pdf (accessed 27 June 2016).

62   Lee, In-Keun (2006) Cheong Gye Cheon Restoration Project—a revolution in Seoul. ICLEI 2006. Available at de.slideshare.net/simrc/cheong-gye-cheon-restoration-project

63   See www.seattle.gov/transportation/docs/ump/06%20SEATTLE%20Case%20studies%20in %20urban%20freeway%20removal.pdf (accessed 27 June 2016).

64   See www.theguardian.com/world/2014/mar/13/seoul-south-korea-expressway-demolished (accessed 27 June 2016).

65   See www.shareable.net/blog/despite-slow-adoption-seoul-doubles-down-on-sharing-city-project (accessed 27 June 2016).

66   See english.sharehub.kr (accessed 27 June 2016).

67   See vimeo.com/79388544/ and www.urbandensity.org/houses-karachis-poor-want (accessed 28 June 2016).

68   See web.worldbank.org/WBSITE/EXTERNAL/TOPICS/EXTSDNET/EXTEOFD/0,,content MDK:23135639~pagePK:64168445~piPK:64168309~theSitePK:8426771,00.html (accessed 27 June 2016).

69   The populations here are for the 10 main central districts of the region. The whole metropolitan area of Beijing in 2012 had 20,132,000 people due to rapid expansion of this economic engine of China. The standardized data in Table 9.13 have been calculated to ensure the correct populations are used with each item.

70   Bearing in mind endnote 69.

71   The term 'Tragedy of the commons' is most commonly remembered through Garrett Hardin's classic article of the same name (Hardin 1968).

72   The equivalent metro area as it stood in 1995 had a 2012 population of 8,168,400. In 2014, the population for the whole region was 13,080,500, so it is a very rapidly growing metro area in China, due partly to its links and proximity to Hong Kong.

CHAPTER TEN

Conclusion: growing more exemplars

Necessities for growing more exemplars

The exemplary cities highlighted in Chapter 9 demonstrate that movement towards sustainable transportation can occur in diverse places under differing and often difficult circumstances. Chapter 8 presented a model for approaching sustainable transportation and an outline of what an agenda for accomplishing it might entail. In this concluding chapter, some of the ingredients and lessons learned from the two preceding chapters, in terms of themes or threads that run through successes in sustainable transportation, are distilled into a few of the critical and defining items necessary to 'grow' more exemplars involving various societal factors and heroic players: government officials who will lead, committed citizens, dedicated non-governmental organizations (NGOs) and visionary public intellectuals and academics. The chapter discusses some of the forces and factors that may equally work against the growth in sustainable transportation.

Political leadership

In many of the cases cited in Chapter 9 and elsewhere in the text, bold political leaders, especially mayors and other senior political figures, played a key role in working with citizens in developing and realizing a vision for change from business as usual (BAU) to sustainable transportation (ST). Very often, this required the politicians to go against the advice of their own bureaucracies and even to endure threats of legal action from business interests who felt threatened by the changes proposed. When one considers a wide range of the success stories in sustainable transportation, it is difficult to deny the importance of political leadership as a thread running through so many of the successes. Bold political leadership is needed at all levels of society and international arrangements. It will take leadership at national and international levels to promote effective passenger and freight rail systems and to reduce the excessive transporting of freight and individuals by the least sustainable modes, trucking and aviation, as well as reversing the destructive patterns of freight globalization.

Political leadership has demonstrated its capabilities effectively at the level of many cities and mayorships around the planet. In Europe during the 1960s and 1970s, mayors of many cities were behind the pedestrianization schemes in their central cities and were threatened with legal action from shop-owners who saw their businesses being ruined. The moves also went against the trajectories of growing motorization in European cities and the prescriptions of the transportation models and planners for more road infrastructure and parking. When the schemes were undertaken, the success of the pedestrianized areas was so strong that the mayors often had delegations of shop-owners from outside the pedestrianized zones asking that the schemes be extended to include their shops.

A similar thing happened in Curitiba, Brazil, with the first pedestrianized street being introduced over one weekend. It required determined political leadership to carry it through against very strong opposition. Three-time Mayor of Curitiba Jaime Lerner[1] provided this. Mayor Enrique Peñalosa of Bogotá, Colombia,[2] along with Lerner, have often been hailed as global leaders for the implementation of BRT systems in their respective cities, especially in less developed cities. This is notwithstanding the less well-known fact that the choice of BRT over rail in each city was highly contested and the decision-making subject to strong communities of interest in favor of buses, especially the powerful bus operators themselves (see later in chapter and Endnote 21). Without the support of Mayor Lee Myung-bak,[3] Seoul's demolition of the Cheonggye Freeway in South Korea, described in the previous chapter, would likely not have occurred.

In Toronto, starting around 1962, a huge controversy erupted over the proposed Spadina Expressway, which had the potential to wreck many Toronto neighborhoods—some quite affluent and influential, others neither affluent nor politically strong. Widespread and well-organized community opposition emerged, including involvement from author Jane Jacobs and some professors such as David Nowlan and Alan Powell. The complex and often bitter debate went on for around a decade involving provincial and local politics and an influential group called SSSOCCC (Stop Spadina Save Our City Coordinating Committee). Parts of the expressway were built between 1963 and 1969, but ultimately the expressway was terminated by Premier Bill Davis in 1971 in the face of massive community opposition, unsustainable costs and a looming provincial election when he made a now famous parliamentary speech in which he said:

> Cities were built for people and not cars. If we are building a transportation system to serve the automobile, the Spadina Expressway would be a good place to start. But if we are building a transportation system to serve people, the Spadina Expressway is a good place to stop.
>
> (Sewell 1993)

An important subway line was built instead and this led to a considerable change in transportation and land-use planning as many transit-oriented developments (TODs) began to spring up around its stations.

Former Mayor Ken Livingstone of London, U.K. (2000–08), is best known for the ground breaking central London congestion charge, which was a major success in reducing traffic and emissions, while also raising funds for more sustainable transportation. In Perth in Western Australia, Labor Party Minister for Transport Julian Grill (1983–86) was instrumental in the electrification of Perth's suburban rail system and the decision to build a 31 km line to the northern suburbs. This latter decision went against the advice of the transport bureaucracy and consultants at the time, which favored a busway. More recently, Alannah MacTiernan, Western Australia's minister for planning and infrastructure from 2000 to 2008, was instrumental in the complex fight to realize Perth's 70 km southern suburbs railway against considerable opposition from many quarters.

Strong and consistent political leadership on sustainable transportation in Boulder, Colorado, over a very extended period through local political figures such as Spenser Havlick and Will Toor has been instrumental in ensuring a consistent and clear message on the directions needed in the city to become more sustainable (see the Boulder section in the previous chapter).

Another example of politically inspired and politically led change of global significance is Singapore's Area Licensing Scheme (ALS) and other congestion control measures, whose origins trace back to the early 1970s when the city began charging motorists a fee for entering central Singapore. After this, the city introduced its now famous Certificate of Entitlement,[4] where people must bid for the right to purchase a car—the cost of which adds tens of thousands of extra dollars to the final price of putting a vehicle on the road.

The political vision behind Singapore's system is significantly attributable to the 30-year mostly autocratic rule of Lee Kuan Yew. Educated as a lawyer at Cambridge University and in the role of prime minister of Singapore from 1959 to 1990, he saw the necessity of limiting cars in the non-vehicle manufacturing, small island-state and the need to build a mass rapid transit system and not to rely only on buses. This conflicted with the views of the World Bank, and Singapore ultimately said 'no' to the World Bank's funding proposal for a bus-only system. Instead, it chose to fund its own metro system—around which it concentrated high-density, high-rise buildings, including much government-provided housing with mixed uses on ground level. This has resulted over the years in progressively more walkable and accessible environments with very good access to fast rail transit services.

A 'benevolent dictatorship' is not a favored way of achieving positive change in sustainable transportation, and the city-state's achievements are not without their political downsides (Townsend 2003). Singapore does, however, show how an entire metropolis can be gradually reshaped over many decades through both consistent political leadership and vision together with supportive actions and policies by governmental authorities. Singapore today has a well-functioning, orderly and livable urban environment, in contrast to many of its close neighbors in SE Asia, which suffer large congestion problems, inadequate transit and a very poor public realm.

Leadership in sustainable transportation is honored annually (and thus encouraged politically) in the Sustainable Transport Award, led by a committee comprised of many organizations, including the ITDP, the World Bank, ICLEI's Ecomobility and many more. Often the award has gone to political leaders, namely mayors. In 2013, it went to Mayor Marcelo Ebrard from Mexico City for multifaceted improvements such as enhanced public spaces, bike-sharing, parking reform, BRT and other initiatives. Previous winners have included Lee Myung-bak and Enrique Peñalosa, as well as the former mayor of New York City Michael Bloomberg, for initiatives improving walkability and biking in the city. Awards have also gone to San Francisco for better parking management, Paris for its bike-sharing scheme Vélib, London for its congestion pricing scheme and some cities in less developed

FIGURE 10.1
One of Singapore's new light rail lines showing high density housing and bus integration
Source: Jeffrey R. Kenworthy

countries, mainly for BRT. Although there seems to be an overemphasis in this award on choosing cities that embrace BRT, it is important to acknowledge the role of good political leadership in this field and such awards do highlight many worthwhile sustainable transportation initiatives.[5]

The list of politically driven changes towards more sustainable transportation could be greatly extended. In most cases, something deeper than self-interest alone lies behind this overtly political leadership. This is the more complex, private and personal desire and belief, which is inherent to an individual's character, upbringing and underlying ethics—a determination that it is important to make a positive difference in the world, to change things and to leave a good legacy that supports the 'common good'. Such individuals might be called 'legacy politicians' (Newman and Kenworthy 2015). This is a side to political figures that is rarely explored in the cut and thrust of politics, and hardly ever becomes a point of public discussion; however, without it, the political actions, courage and endurance to undertake projects that totally change the existing paradigm and status quo would most likely be lacking. It is perhaps the key difference that determines whether places are gifted with good political leadership, mediocre political leadership or worse.

Community or grassroots leadership

Many successful transformations of cities or aspects of them began as citizen efforts that ended in political and institutional changes. Often such efforts spawned activists who became accomplished experts and brought new perspectives and creative energy to their cities. One example is that of David Engwicht (1989, 1993, 2005), who emerged as a leader of a movement to block the building of a major road through the center of established inner residential areas in Brisbane, Australia. From a base of little or no knowledge of transportation, but with great creative energy and an ability to innovate, he embarked on a steep learning curve, producing extraordinarily valuable documents about traffic calming as a concept and a way to set a new direction in transportation thinking. His books have made large impacts in cities and towns around the world and his unique ways of engaging citizen participation have drawn attention to thorny transportation issues and to help find solutions.

Community-based citizens' organizations and non-governmental organizations (NGOs—discussed below in this chapter) are well positioned to watchdog and monitor changes once under way. Portland, Oregon's Meeky Blizzard reactivated an earlier freeway fighting organization (Sensible Transportation Options for People; STOP) to lead the 1990s effort to defeat a massive suburban highway expansion proposal and, working with the very dedicated 1000 Friends of Oregon, turned this sow's ear highway proposal into a silk planning purse that demonstrated the strength of urban development around improved transit, walking, bicycling and compact mixed-land uses. Before her retirement, Blizzard headed the Livable Communities effort for several years in the office of progressive Congressman Earl Blumenauer who, as a Portland city council member, played an important role in changing that city's transportation direction. The Center for Neighborhood Technology—a 'place-based' research and activist organization in Chicago under the leadership of Scott Bernstein and Jacky Grimshaw—has for decades, with considerable highly respected expertise, weighed in on numerous transportation, energy and urban planning issues locally and in national coalitions.[6]

As explained in Chapter 9, a key part of the Vancouver, British Columbia, success story is the role of Michael Harcourt, then a young shop-front lawyer, commissioned by residents of Chinatown in downtown Vancouver to help them fight destructive freeway plans. The proposed freeways and interchanges would now occupy the key sites that are today the hallmarks of Vancouver's success in building beautiful neighborhoods and a more sustainable city with more sustainable transportation. Harcourt went on to become a

FIGURE 10.2
The Trans Am Totem, Vancouver, BC: The Trans Am Totem by Marcus and Helene Bowcott, standing in an arterial median at Quebec Street and Pacific Boulevard in the False Creek neighborhood in inner Vancouver (BC), and juxtaposed against a Skytrain station and adjacent to the Dunsmuir and Georgia Viaducts slated for demolition (see Figure 9.4) (also see; http://marcusbowcott.com/?page_id=1070).
Source: Jeffrey R. Kenworthy

Vancouver city councilor, the mayor of Vancouver and, ultimately, premier of British Columbia—a political career built significantly on an agenda of preventing freeway development and, instead, the construction of world-class walkable neighborhoods. In practice, there were many others involved in the evolution of Vancouver in a positive direction and other factors were at work as well, as indicated in the Vancouver exemplar in the previous chapter. Vancouver today demonstrates, at least in part, the inherent power of grassroots community and political leadership. A recent symbol of such activism/engagement and the willingness of a community to be open enough to embrace it is the Trans Am Totem, pictured in Figure 10.2.[7] The transportation imagery is clear and engaging and the artist Martin Bowcott says: 'In a certain sense I'm saying, "Let's realize we're on the horns of a dilemma here" . . . We're fascinated by speed, we're fascinated by consumer objects, and this consumerism has an effect on our nature.'[8]

There are many unsung heroes of environmental stewardship and progressive transportation in cities the world over. These people work tirelessly without remuneration and over many years to achieve more sustainable objectives. To give due credit to this inestimably valuable work and to explore the achievements of such people would require an entire book. The following very small selection gives credit to a few sustainable transportation heroes to provide a flavor of the value and influence of such individuals and the organizations with whom they worked. Just as we examined several well-defined and long-standing exemplary cities in Chapter 9, we will explore several exemplary citizens, political leaders, public intellectuals and NGOs in this section and peppered elsewhere in other sections. Suffice it to say that without the leadership and skills of such people and organizations in so many cities around the world, there would be far fewer examples today to provide hope about what can be achieved in sustainable transportation. The 'confession' of Charles Marohn (Box 10.1), trained in the business as usual (BAU) canons of traffic engineering, gives us an example of an engineer who heroically broke with his training and early professional practice to learn from urban planning what would make for a sustainable community, both in land use and transportation. He has devoted the years since to creating and growing an NGO devoted to sustainability. His example has inspired many other young transportation engineers.

BOX 10.1 Confession of a recovering engineer[i]

Charles Marohn[ii]

After graduating from college with a civil engineering degree, I found myself working in my home town for a local engineering firm doing mostly municipal engineering (roads, sewer pipe, water pipe, stormwater). A fair percentage of my time was spent convincing people that, when it came to their road, I knew more than they did. . . . I had books and books of standards to follow.

. . . (W)hat business would I—let alone a property owner on a project I was working on—have in questioning the way things were done? Of course, the people who wrote the standards knew better than we did. That is why they wrote the standard.

When people would tell me that they did not want a wider street, I would tell them that they had to have it for safety reasons.

When they answered that a wider street would make people drive faster and that would seem to be less safe, especially in front of their house where their kids were playing, I would confidently tell them that the wider road was more safe, especially when combined with the other safety enhancements the standards called for.

When people objected to those other 'enhancements', like removing all of the trees near the road, I told them that for safety reasons we needed to improve the sight distances and ensure that the recovery zone was free of obstacles.

When they pointed out that the 'recovery zone' was also their 'yard' and that their kids played kickball and hopscotch there, I recommended that they put up a fence, so long as the fence was outside of the right-of-way.

When they objected to the cost of the wider, faster, treeless road that would turn their peaceful, front yard into the viewing area for a drag strip unless they built a concrete barricade along their front property line, I informed them that progress was sometimes expensive, but these standards have been shown to work across the state, the country and the world and I could not compromise with their safety.

In retrospect, I understand that this was utter insanity. Wider, faster, treeless roads not only ruin our public places, they kill people. Taking highway standards and applying them to urban and suburban streets, and even county roads, costs us thousands of lives every year. There is no earthly reason why an engineer would ever design a fourteen-foot lane for a city block, yet we do it continuously. Why?

The answer is utterly shameful: Because that is the standard.

In the engineering profession's version of defensive medicine, we can't recommend standards that are not in the manual. We can't use logic to vary from a standard that gives us 60 mph design speeds on roads with intersections every 200 feet. We can't question why two cars would need to travel at high speed in opposite directions on a city block, let alone why we would want them to. We can yield to public pressure and post a speed limit—itself a hazard—but we can't recommend a road section that is not in the highway manual.

When the public and politicians tell engineers that their top priorities are safety and then cost, the engineer's brain hears something completely different. The engineer hears, 'Once you set a design speed and handle the projected volume of traffic, safety is the top priority. Do what it takes to make the road safe, but do it as cheaply as you can.' This is why engineers return projects with asinine 'safety' features, like pedestrian bridges and tunnels that nobody will ever use, and costs that are astronomical.

An engineer designing a street or road prioritizes the world in this way, no matter how they are instructed:

1. Traffic speed
2. Traffic volume
3. Safety
4. Cost

The rest of the world generally would prioritize things differently, as follows:

1. Safety
2. Cost
3. Traffic volume
4. Traffic speed

continued

In other words, the engineer first assumes that all traffic must travel at speed. Given that speed, all roads and streets are then designed to handle a projected volume. Once those parameters are set, only then does an engineer look at mitigating for safety and, finally, how to reduce the overall cost (which at that point is nearly always ridiculously expensive).

In America, it is this thinking that has designed most of our built environment, and it is nonsensical. In many ways, it is professional malpractice. If we delivered what society asked us for, we would build our local roads and streets to be safe above all else. . . .

We go to enormous expense to save ourselves small increments of driving time.[ii] This would be delusional in and of itself if it were not also making our roads and streets much less safe. . . . [A] 2005 article from the APA Journal show[s] how narrower, slower streets dramatically reduce accidents, especially fatalities.[iv]

And it is that simple observation that all of those supposedly 'ignorant' property owners were trying to explain to me, the engineer with all the standards, so many years ago. When you can't let your kids play in the yard, let alone ride their bike to the store, because you know the street is dangerous, then the engineering profession is not providing society any real value. It's time to stand up and demand a change.

[i] Excerpted with permission from www.strongtowns.org/journal/2010/11/22/confessions-of-a-recovering-engineer.html (accessed 17 October 2016)

[ii] Professional Engineer (PE) licensed in the State of Minnesota and a member of the American Institute of Certified Planners (AICP); founder and president of Strong Towns; www.strongtowns.org

[iii] www.strongtowns.org/journal/2010/11/11/costs-and-benefits-part-5-finale.html; www.strongtowns.org/journal/2010/1/14/the-cost-of-40-seconds.html

[iv] www.naturewithin.info/Roadside/TransSafety_JAPA.pdf

Heroes and heroism in sustainable transportation

One of the best examples of what can transpire when visionary political leadership is linked with committed and energetic citizen involvement and responsive planners is that of Strasbourg, France, especially in the personage of elected official leader Andrée Buchmann and the NGO ASTUS, which she has worked with over the course of many years. This is described below in Box 10.2

Leadership and responsiveness within government

The best-laid plans of political and community leaders could easily 'go awry' without the enthusiastic support and technical skills of career government officials. By the same token, a hostile institutional environment can stymie and delay change, and sometimes government officials may be 'forced' to obey political dictates about transportation and planning matters that run against their personal beliefs or philosophies. In the worst cases, bureaucratic opposition leads to the undermining or even stoppage of often valuable politically led projects.

But there are also many leaders within government organizations who toil quietly behind the scenes and are often instrumental in changing the political climate through their influence on elected representatives. Because of the 'public service' nature of their employment, they do not necessarily receive the recognition due to them; however, they are an essential part of what ultimately unfolds. In significant projects and plans to change the paradigm in transportation, the interplay and dynamics between elected representatives and the government officials upon whom they rely determine the quality of the outcome. The timeframe of career government officials often extends beyond typical political terms, and

BOX 10.2 Strasbourg: synergy between political leadership, good planning and an exemplary NGO

Preston L. Schiller

I first encountered Andrée Buchmann, French environmental leader and prominent regional elected official, when she visited Seattle in 1995 as part of a German Marshall Fund educational program for political leaders. As one of the few environmental leaders in the area who spoke French, however poorly, I was tapped to be her guide. In early 2015, I traveled in Europe for three months assaying the progress of sustainable transportation in many cities in Scandinavia, and western and southern Europe. I wondered whether I should try to contact Andrée about my planned trip to Strasbourg—a city I had never visited. I delayed, wondering whether she would have time to meet with me, or even remember me. Finally, two weeks before I planned to visit, I sent a message to her wondering whether she might have any suggestions about whom I might meet with about sustainable transportation in Strasbourg. Much to my pleasant surprise, I received a quick response from her indicating that, not only did she remember well my guiding her in Seattle, she would set up several meetings for me with planning officials and citizen leaders.

The city of Strasbourg is an important regional capital in eastern France and the official seat of the European Parliament and the Council of Europe among other important European institutions. Because of the concentration of European institutions and its location, Strasbourg is a very cosmopolitan and politically aware city, believing itself to be the true 'capital of Europe'—or at least that it should share that title with Brussels. It is part of the region of Alsace, which has a long history of being contested between France, Germany and other historical imperial entities. French Alsace is part of a somewhat larger Alsatian cultural and, historically, linguistic region that spans the Rhine. Some of Strasbourg's transportation accomplishments can be understood in the context of its effort to maintain, if not invigorate, a broader regional identity and culture as well as to establish strong linkages across France and Europe.

Public transport in Strasbourg followed a familiar pattern after World War II: replacing tramways with buses; by 1960, they had completely abandoned the trams—which led to a dramatic decrease in ridership. By the late 1980s, a reversal of this trend galvanized around whether Strasbourg would build an expensive and somewhat limited automated grade-separated light rail system (VAL) or a less expensive but more easily expandable surface light rail transit (LRT) system. Socialist mayoral candidate Catherine Trautmann, assisted by Green Party representatives, campaigned for the LRT and prevailed. The first line opened in 1994.

Since then, an LRT network of six lines has been constructed, with more expansions and extensions planned or proposed. There is also a recently added bus rapid transit (BRT) line: Bus G. The LRT system has been closely linked with the regeneration and greening of Strasbourg's urban environment. Great strides in pedestrianization and passenger intermodalism have also been made as part of integrated transportation and land use planning. The entire Strasbourg region is being laced together by transit and pedestrian and bicycling improvements. The commercial sector, early doubters about using existing streets or placing any limits on motor vehicle space, has benefited considerably from these improvements. The LRT system and its extensions have also created easy and attractive access to the European District of governmental institutions on the city's edge, as well as to numerous other important destinations. In recognition of the superior quality of Strasbourg's integrated planning, the Princes Foundation for the Built Environment sent a study team there and published an extremely useful guide based on their experience (Isherwood et al. 2015)

Backing the forward-looking government officials who pushed along Strasbourg's emphasis on transit and other green modes were many committed citizens. Some of these formed the ASsociation des usagers des Transports Urbains de l'agglomération Strasbourgeoise (Association of urban transport users for the Strasbourg agglomeration; ASTUS)[i] in the same year that the first LRT line opened. ASTUS has been a highly effective force for public transportation improvements in the decades since. It has involved the public as well as working with government officials in planning and implementation issues around new lines and older existing services. It responds to and investigates rider concerns from the general to specific problems such as scheduling and maintenance issues. Its concerns go beyond the important arena of public transportation to the promotion of green modes and sustainable planning in general.

continued

Mme. Andrée Buchmann has been an outstanding political and environmental leader ever since her lycée days in the 1970s. Her activism and leadership include fighting against the placement of a nuclear generator in her region as well as working for forest protection; her work for sustainable transportation and protection of the atmosphere is especially prominent. She is also deeply interested in the historic and contemporary culture of Alsace and has been a long-time leader of the Green Party as well as collaborating with the Socialist Party at certain points. In 2011, she was awarded the highly prestigious national Legion of Honor award in recognition of her many contributions to Strasbourg, Alsace, France, Europe and the world's environment.

ASTUS and Andrée Buchmann have also actively supported the recent efforts to extend LRT to Kehl, just over the German border at the Rhine, as well as its redevelopment for affordable family housing. They have also supported the regional car co-op Citiz, which is designed to support the lessening of the need for private motor vehicle ownership[ii] as well as supporting the city's bike-share system, Vélhop.[iii] All Strasbourgeois and Alsatians on both sides of the border are justifiably proud of the Passerelle des Deux Rives (Foot-bridge of the two banks, which also accommodates bicycles) over the river Rhine. The Passerelle was the site of a major summit of Western leaders in 2009 when many heads-of-state—with Chancellor Merkel (at the head) and Presidents Obama and Sarkozy—led a crowd of officials in a walk from one bank to the other as a celebration of their unity and the recent rejoining of NATO by France.[iv]

Today the city of Strasbourg and the region of greater Alsace are being knit together by public transportation, walking and cycling—thanks in no small measure to the energy of citizen efforts such as that of ASTUS and visionary leaders such as Andrée Buchmann. But there are also forms of transportation expansions that are not being welcomed by them. Andrée Buchmann and ASTUS are in the forefront of a broad coalition of environmental, open space and agricultural interests; they are actively resisting plans for a regional highway bypass, which they believe will cause great environmental harm and not have the mobility issues it claims.[v] Figure 10.3 below shows Andrée Buchmann and ASTUS leaders addressing a large demonstration against the bypass. Similar actions are being taken by sustainable mobility and environmental groups against a bypass proposed for the Bordeaux region.

[i] See: astus67.fr/ (accessed 8 July 2016).
[ii] See: alsace.citiz.coop/ (accessed 8 July 2016).
[iii] See: www.velhop.strasbourg.eu/en/ (accessed 8 July 2016).
[iv] See: www.photo-alsace.com/photo-ref-n31779.html images of the Passarelle and www.state.gov/r/pa/ei/pix/eur/c29820.htm for images of the summit.
[v] See: gcononmerci.org/manifs/ (accessed 8 July 2016).

FIGURE 10.3
Drawing the line against the proposed Strasbourg highway bypass:
Andrée Buchmann and André Roth join other regional leaders and activists in drawing a line against the environmenally destructive proposed bypass.
Source: André Roth/ASTUS

so their leadership, consistency or ability to change their ideas and to innovate comprise an essential element in the story of sustainable transportation in most places.

The Livable Neighbourhoods Design Code in Perth, Western Australia, was led from within the planning agency by a graduate in sustainable urban design appointed as a senior planner in the 1980s. Perth up to this time had only one model of urban development: low-density, totally car-dependent suburbs with no mixed land use and road systems with too many culs-de-sac that were lacking in any real permeability for pedestrians, cyclists or transit vehicles. A process was started and led by this individual, in co-operation with other like-minded individuals both within and outside the bureaucracy, which proposed a whole new basis for suburban development based on walkability, grid-based road networks, not road hierarchies, narrower streets, better transit integration, neighborhood centers, higher density and so on (like the New Urbanism agenda described below). Urban design, as outlined in Chapter 6, became a critical part of the Western

Australian planning department's thinking and breathed new life into the whole planning enterprise, both strategic and statutory.

Through a very long and often difficult period of intra- and inter-departmental discussions, consultation and discussions with the development industry and local communities, a new statutory basis was established to guide the design of new suburban communities, one that would build in less dependence on automobiles. Reforming suburban development can never be achieved in one giant step, and the new code has been more successful in creating permeable road layouts and much more pedestrian-friendly and interactive local environments than it has at significantly raising densities and achieving greater mixed-land use (Falconer et al. 2010). But the process and the final changes in the code have been important in producing incrementally better suburbs and pioneering a much greater community-wide awareness that Perth's car dependence must be seriously reduced.

Academic and professional expertise, the 'long haul' and subverting the dominant paradigm

Another necessity is the joining of civic energies with the depth and expertise that comes from years of research and study. The academic and professional expertise that lies outside, and is independent of government, can be a very important part of the propagation and implementation of ideas in sustainable transportation. This is especially true when that expertise is combined with activism or government work for periods of time. There are many such academics, whose works are cited in the chapter references and endnotes, who have been very effective in combining the diverse worlds of academia, government and community activism. They have been notable actors in combating highway expansion and promoting visions involving better transit, bicycling, walking conditions and improved land-use planning because they have spent years researching these areas and applying results to real world situations. The critical attention of great thinkers outside of academe such as Lewis Mumford, Jane Jacobs and Ivan Illich, as well as academics such as Peter Hall and many others, has been, and still is, a necessary ingredient in the history of ideas that forge positive change.

An important aspect to acknowledge here is the influence of writers who were considerably ahead of their day. They gave voice to arguments that in their times had little support or popularity from within any sector of society and yet stood as beacons of hope, change and intellectual influence to a younger generation whose ideas were only just forming. One such writer was Kenneth R. Schneider (1972, 1979, Box 8.9), whose seminal books are among the earliest and best anatomies of the problem of the automobile and ideas for change. Where humanity is today in its thinking and evolution about more sustainable transportation is at least partially a tribute to the power of such 'voices in the wilderness', those who provided the first tentative steps in changing the seeming path dependence of automobile-based planning.

The influence of academics and other professionals and intellectuals—some of whom were autodidacts—whose ideas promote paradigm change is probably most effective when combined with some form of direct public contribution to political discourse and involvement in the direct support of community organizations and political parties or figures who are committed to change. The danger of this kind of high-profile position for the people concerned is that they can be labeled with having lost their 'academic objectivity' or 'perspective', and have become, rather, 'advocates'. As with politicians, this then boils down to the motivations and ideals of the individuals concerned and whether they feel compelled to change the course of transportation and planning or to take a more hands-off approach. In practice, it is possible for academics, writers and other professionals to successfully straddle both worlds, conducting sound new research while at the same time ensuring that it does not just gather dust on a shelf.

A major advantage on the part of academics, professionals and writers in the transportation field is that, like government officials, they are generally there for the 'long haul' and can transcend changing political agendas. But unlike government employees, they are not gagged from public comment on important issues. This enables them to continue working in the public sphere, bringing a consistent long-term message that challenges political policy positions when the winds of political change blow contrary to the aims of greater sustainability. They can also support, assist and give needed strength and credibility to progressive sustainability policy positions in transportation and planning when the political climate is amenable.

John Whitelegg has been a successful academic (e.g. Whitelegg 1993, 1996, 2016; Whitelegg and Haq 2003) and is founder and editor of the international journal *World Transport Policy and Practice*,[9] dedicated to more sustainable transportation. He has also acted as a Lancaster city councilor in NW England and been involved for decades in campaigning for more sustainable transportation through innumerable consulting studies, media appearances and other political activity, including through the U.K. Green Party.

A significant role, then, of academics, professionals and writers is persistence in keeping issues alive, telling the same story repeatedly and in different ways. These are among the people who are in the best position to be sturdy pioneers and to go out on a limb to forge change. New ideas are not accepted immediately; thus, it is important to have a strong voice with consistency and clarity over a long period, with mounting evidence. Eventually, and almost imperceptibly, ideas that once seemed radical and subversive become mainstream, and change then happens.[10]

Environmental and other non-governmental organizations (NGOs)

Well-organized and effective groups that fight for sustainability in the transportation and planning field are an important component in the mix of factors and forces that determine change. They can make the difference between political decisions against sustainable transportation succeeding or being defeated due to adverse publicity against such moves. On a smaller, more localized scale there are organizations such as:

- The Public Transport Users Association in Australia,[11] and similar groups the world over, which lobby and engage in political action that supports public transportation;
- The former Coalition of Tollway Action Groups in Sydney (later the Coalition of Transport Action Groups in both New South Wales and Victoria), who fought freeway development in the Sydney and Melbourne region over a number years;[12]
- Bicycle users and advocacy groups around the world; and
- Countless other community-based groups who provide skilled local action on a wide variety of topics such as traffic calming and other road space reclamation projects, better parking policies, urban greening and street enhancements that encourage more walking and cycling, 'complete streets',[13] more diverse housing choices for a wider range of incomes in compact, mixed-use settings and so on.

Such groups are important players in achieving sustainable transportation. Historically, we can see the mark of groups such as the Centre for Urban Research and Action (CURA), a Melbourne group that fought the planned freeway system there, which today has significant missing links dating back to their actions. Within hours, in the pre-internet and pre-mobile phone age of the 1960s and 1970s, this group could get hundreds of people together to protest imminent freeway construction activities. A former deputy prime minister of Australia was involved in CURA. In his later role as a senior political figure, he was also a key player in the Building Better Cities program, an Australian federal government initiative during the 1990s to provide funds to support innovations in urban development and transportation, and to promote greater equity in Australian cities.

Groups such as those above have quite targeted, local objectives such as stopping freeways or promoting bicycle travel, but they form part of a larger global coalition of like-minded organizations who often communicate and exchange information with each other. There are other affiliations of people whose activities range overtly from the national to the global level. For example, echoing the critical importance of urban design described in Chapter 6, Urbandesign.org campaigns for improvements in many areas of transportation and planning, such as Transit-Oriented Development, better public spaces, civic art, high-speed rail, higher density and more. Their website has a wealth of information, videos and visual material on projects from around the world that foster more sustainable transportation and greater livability, thereby offering a resource to innumerable other people and organizations worldwide.[14] In a similar vein, the now well-known new urbanism movement led by the Congress for the New Urbanism (cnu.org; Katz 1993; Calthorpe 2010) in North America, which also has a global reach, acts as a focal point for communities trying to develop less automobile-oriented urban development (see endnote 14 and Chapter 8, Box 8.3).

Within this vein, there are now many institutions worldwide that promote better practice in urban planning and transportation and act as conduits for bringing together and disseminating case studies or exemplars from around the world of places that are finding new ways of growing with much lower dependence on cars. For example, rudi.net provides best practice projects, including thousands of images, in areas such as sustainability, public space design, traffic calming, mixed use, pedestrian priority and more.[15]

There are eclectic umbrella organizations such as SLoCaT (Partnership on Sustainable Low Carbon Transport; www.slocat.net) established in 2009 and hosted by the United Nations Department of Economic and Social Affairs (UNDESA) to provide a global voice on Sustainable Transport. It has a hundred diverse global members covering the big global development banks, major private companies, research centers, international development aid organizations, large international associations in the transportation field, major United Nations organizations and many more. Although global in nature, the organization has a focus on transportation in developing countries, especially in regards to promoting green modes and sustainable development goals by providing access to or for goods and services by lower-income groups.[16]

More recently, in October 2016, emerging out of Habitat III in Quito, Ecuador we have the most recent and up to date United Nations statement about Sustainable Transport (UN Secretary-General's High Level Advisory Group on Sustainable Transport 2016) and how to achieve it to avoid the BAU projection of massive increases in GHGs.[17]

Jane Jacobs has provided the world with one of the most significant and enduring legacies of urban commentary and analysis, as well as direct activism. Her work is commemorated in Box 10.3. Another Jane, journalist and activist Jane Holtz Kay, had a long commitment to preserving what was good in cities, changing what was bad in architecture and urban design and promoting sustainable transportation. Her life and some of her contributions are remembered in Box 10.4.

Many environmental organizations in the U.S. and Canada are engaged in transportation issues at local, state and provincial, federal and even international levels. These include the Sierra Club(s), the Environmental Defense Fund (EDF), the Natural Resources Defense Council (NRDC), Friends of the Earth (FoE), the David Suzuki Foundation and Transport Action Canada. More examples, including international efforts, may be found in the resources toolboxes in the online appendices for this book. Some NGOs tend to focus on issues close at hand and are associated with sustainable transportation issues in specific locales. Boxes 10.5 and 10.6 present two NGOs who respectively focus on walking and cycling issues in their cities. The first is Walk Boston, a highly effective pedestrian advocacy group in Boston, MA, U.S.

The second walk or cycle NGO worthy of special mention and emulation elsewhere is Bordeaux's Vélo-Cité bicycle advocacy and education group (Box 10.6).

BOX 10.3 Jane Jacobs: an enduring legacy

Jeffrey R. Kenworthy

Writer and activist Jane Jacobs was almost prophetic of current urban agendas in her observations about the true nature of cities and what they require to function properly and fairly. *The Death and Life of Great American Cities* (Jacobs 1961), *The Economy of Cities* (Jacobs 1970) and *Cities and the Wealth of Nations: Principles of Economic Life* (Jacobs 1984), which identified cities rather than nations as the primary engines of economies, have left a legacy that is as relevant today as when she wrote them. Her work prefigures the invention of traffic calming and the current ascendancy of concepts such as 'complete streets', 'eyes on the street' and transit-oriented development (TOD). In *The Death and Life of Great American Cities* she states:

> Attrition of automobiles operates by making conditions *less* convenient for cars. Attrition as a steady, gradual process would steadily decrease the numbers of persons using private automobiles in a city . . . attrition of automobiles by cities is probably the only means by which absolute numbers of vehicles can be cut down . . . which give room to other necessary and desired city uses that happen to be in competition with automobile traffic needs. (p. 377)

Some of the important moves to create more sustainable transportation systems today—rebuilding strip malls by constructing buildings to the sidewalk and building over parking lots; widening sidewalks; providing cycle-ways and taking traffic lanes for light rail; building out of whole commuter parking lots to create public squares in the centers of cities such as Portland; taking parking lots for the creation of mixed-use urban villages with exemplary public space; and transforming shopping centers into mixed-use high-density centers—all demonstrate that uniquely simple idea from 1961: the 'attrition of automobiles by cities'.

The social critic and historian Christopher Lasch was a great admirer of her minute descriptions of neighborhoods and explications of how they work due to pedestrian traffic, social interactions, local shops and 'eyes on the street'.[i] Jane Jacobs's writings are so eloquent and yet so easily read and understood that they continually elucidate the true nature of cities to anyone prepared to read them. As is often the case, the truth of this kind of claim is perhaps best illustrated by a short story, in this case a personal one.

As a young student in the mid-1970s, quite serendipitously, the first thing I was required to read was the chapter in *Death and Life* where Jacobs describes how the North End of Boston operates as a community and how street security was maintained by the local Italian community. The writing was so clear and passionate, so richly human and so interesting that it stood out like a beacon of light amid often dull and convoluted academic discourse. It left an enduring impression and was central to a decision two-and-a-half years later to change the entire focus of my studies and research to cities.

Jane Jacobs's astute observations of the nature of cities and how to sustain them remain an enduring legacy of an extraordinarily perceptive thinker and writer, one who is essential to all students of transportation and other urban disciplines.

[i] See brief discussion in Chapter 1 and Lasch (1991).

FIGURE 10.4 Bike art critic Jane Jacobs. Ms Jacobs, who used to cycle to her job at *Fortune* magazine in 1950s Manhattan, inspects a functioning bicycle transformed into mobile artwork as part of the 'Bicycles as Art' competition presided over by Canada's New Democratic Party leader, the late Jack Layton, Toronto, Ontario (1991)
Source: Preston L. Schiller

Box 10.4 A remembrance and tribute to Jane Holtz Kay (d. 4 Nov. 2012)[i]

Preston L. Schiller

Jane Jacobs' name often comes up in discussions of the viability of modern urban life. Understandably so, since her *Death and Life of Great American Cities* probably has had more influence on urban planning debates than any other single work. But there was another Jane—Jane Holtz Kay—whose name comes up often in slightly smaller yet very influential circles. A Jane who worked tirelessly for decades in the trenches of architecture and urban design criticism, historic preservation and environmental journalism.

Perhaps it was her long admiration of Lewis Mumford, beginning with her 1960 Radcliffe senior thesis and first interview with him, that pushed her to range widely while paying close attention to the details of everyday life. She visited Mumford, physically and in her writing, several times over the decades. In her 1977 *American Institute of Architects Journal* interview, she takes us inside Mumford's work, legacy, household organization and daily life. She brings to life the breadth of his intellect, work habits and Amenia surrounds while also giving voice to Sophia—'wife, intellectual companion, life-support . . . breadwinning partner of his youth, the amanuensis of his old age.'[ii] But it was not a wholly blind devotion as this splendidly succinct paragraph from her 1982 *Christian Science Monitor* review of his autobiography reveals:

In his autobiography as in his life, Mumford's far-reaching intellectual aspirations and pessimistic moral outlook bring him both success and failure—failure because it is our Joshuas, not our Jeremiahs, who bring society's walls tumbling down; success because his reach for ethical suasion gave him access to the centuries.[iii]

Jane Holtz Kay published scores of articles—idea pieces, reviews, interviews, opinion, criticism and critique ranging from architecture, building crafts and 'car-burbs' to Olmsted, urban design and zoning, and many topics in between. Her publications alphabet ranged from *AIA, Alternet* and *Appalachia,* to *Sierra, Smithsonian, Technology* and *Urban Ecology* with contributions to the *Chronicle of Higher Education, Columbia Journalism Review, Harvard Business Review, Ms., Orion, Preservation, Progressive* and *Gristmagazine* among others. Her list of publications at *The New York Times* fills four web-pages. Ditto for *The Nation.* She was the author of *Lost Boston* (1980, 1999, 2006), a remarkable architectural and social history march through centuries of destroyed heritage, yet with hope about preservationist efforts. Its hundreds of evocative illustrations include a Park Street 'T' subway station political poster—a homage to her liberal father's 1950's failed Congressional bids; *Preserving New England* (1986), a tour of landscape and townscape; and her most influential work, *Asphalt Nation* (1997, 1998), exploring the transportation waterfront, from the environmental destruction of our overdependence on automobiles to the many promising reform efforts that were underway in the 1990s.

She walked the architecture beat for the *Boston Globe, Christian Science Monitor* and, of course, *The Nation*—where she reviewed buildings, plans, exhibits and many, many books, beginning in 1973. She was a frequent face and clear voice on the lecture, conference and interview circuits and an occasional academic. Her writing style was jaunty yet superbly polished with masterfully crafted paragraphs and pages playing off against clever sub-titles and catchy jargon.

In 1990, she helped Dorothea Hass launch WalkBoston and she remained close to it thereafter, part of her lifelong involvement in pedestrianism. A pioneer advocacy group, it became a model for the formation of many similar groups across the U.S. over the next two decades (see 'Walk Boston' Box 10.5).

So many damaging automobile and sprawl trends chronicled by Holtz Kay are still going in reverse; motor vehicle emissions increasing, a recent transportation act that guts many of the gains made under ISTEA and a Capitol still refusing to acknowledge or act upon climate change. Yet many of the promising movements that she praised and brought much-deserved attention to are bearing fruit: renewed interest in smart growth, transit revitalization—especially around rail—car-sharing, and a renaissance of urban cycling and walking.

I was fortunate to have been acquainted with the two Janes beginning in the early 1990s and I benefited greatly from talks and walks with each in their beloved neighborhoods. The two Janes met on at least one occasion and hit it off well, as Jacobs supplied a glowing blurb for the cover of *Asphalt Nation.* Perhaps they shared a sense of lonely sisterhood in a field heavily dominated by men only beginning to open to feminist

continued

viewpoints and participation. Of slight build but strong voice, Holtz Kay was anything but strident; a model of tact when negotiating the shoals of intellectual and political conflict. If she had a dog in the Mumford–Jacobs fracas over differing approaches to urban planning, alluded to obliquely in the 1977 Mumford interview, it was kept closely tethered and muzzled against barking.

Holtz Kay paid great attention to detail—especially human detail—but on occasion, a few of us 'transportation junkies' among her friends wished that she might have passed a few pages or an assertion by us before the presses rolled. Still, Martha Bianco, after criticizing a few of *Asphalt Nation's* 'academic shortcomings', wrote understandingly in a 1998 H-Net review:

> Her mission is to urge readers to action, to help light the fires of anti-auto activism. . . . voices such as hers need to be heard if we are to avoid lapsing into a complacency that got us so mired in the car-dependent culture in the first place. (Bianco, p. 3)

In our vast and expanding universe, where theoretical physicists assure us that anything and everything is possible, I imagine a car-free corner and a café table where Mumford and the two Janes are seated—Holtz Kay between the other two to maintain the peace. Passers-by slow to eavesdrop on a most spirited argument over the redesign of the sublime gated community where they are now resident (Schiller 2012).

[i] Originally published as 'Remembering Jane Holtz Kay', Preston L. Schiller, 11 December 2012, www.thenation.com/print/article/171705/remembering-jane-holtz-kay (accessed 10 July 2016).
[ii] Kay 1977, p. 41.
[iii] Kay 1982.

FIGURE 10.5A WalkBoston Tour includes the Downtown Crossing, heart of Boston's retail district, at its 2012 annual meeting.
Source: WalkBoston.org

FIGURE 10.5B WalkBoston at work. Staff member and co-founder Dorothea Hass leads Asian-American high school students doing an assessment of walking conditions as part of a summer training program sponsored by the Asian Community Development Corporation. The goal was to persuade the city to implement safety measures for walkers on Kneeland Street in Boston's Chinatown neighborhood.
Source: WalkBoston.org

Box 10.5 WalkBoston: changing a region one step at a time

Dorothea Hass[i]

WalkBoston was founded in 1990 and became the first American organization dedicated to bringing pedestrian concerns into transportation planning for cities and towns. The original focus was on funding pedestrian-focused design projects and then identifying the funds to build these projects. Almost immediately, WalkBoston was drawn into a major role in the 10-year planning process for the surface design of the Big Dig. WalkBoston's intervention resulted in narrower streets, shorter crosswalks, wider sidewalks and new riverside pathways integrated into the project.

Since that time, WalkBoston has expanded its realm of interests, moving toward the design of safe facilities throughout the state and using walking to improve community health. Beginning its first decade in the 1990s with the work of volunteers, WalkBoston has expanded to a staff of nine full- and part-time employees and interns in 2016, housed in a pedestrian-friendly Downtown Boston building. In parallel with its nurturing and housing of the national organization America Walks, WalkBoston has become a national leader of advocacy, with perhaps the largest professional staff of all pedestrian advocacy groups in the nation.

Although it began with a Boston orientation, WalkBoston expanded its work with the state legislature and additional communities and has, over 26 years, provided technical assistance or programs in 106 of the state's 351 municipalities. These include Boston and the 'Gateway Cities' of Worcester, Springfield, New Bedford, Fall River, Brockton and Lawrence. Statewide work includes the law requiring pedestrian/bike accommodations in all state road projects, the first Safe Routes to School programs in Massachusetts, the Governor's Bicycle/Pedestrian Advisory Committee and, most recently, a reduction in the prevailing speed limit that all communities are now free to adopt. WalkBoston has collaborated with Boston to establish goals and programs for a 'Vision Zero' plan that aims to eliminate pedestrian crashes.

WalkBoston created the 'Rural Walking Tool Kit' to help small communities serve pedestrians, and collaborated with Boston on Complete Streets Guidelines. WalkBoston trains new pedestrian advocates at walkability workshops, hosts periodic educational slide shows for a walk-in audience and continues to promote Good Walking is Good Business concepts with businesses statewide. Since the beginning of the organization, WalkBoston has led community walking events and has produced over 60 walking maps and a book, *WalkBoston: Walking Tours of Boston's Unique Neighborhoods*. WalkBoston also acts as a regional resource for planning for pedestrians, and demonstrates its reviewing strengths through close examinations of regional development projects for pedestrian benefits.

Partnering with other organizations has furthered pedestrian progress. WalkBoston worked with the Federal Transit Administration to publish *Improving Pedestrian Access to Transit* and to develop tools for public participation in transit planning. The organization works closely with the Massachusetts Departments of Transportation and Public Health to further joint goals for including improvements for walkers throughout the state. It has conducted safety trainings for elementary school children in numerous communities and for teens in Boston and Salem to advocate for walking improvements in underserved communities. For Massachusetts mayors, WalkBoston has conducted walkability audits of intersection and streets to outline detailed methods of improving pedestrian facilities. Partnering with six communities including Boston, Springfield. Northampton and Fall River, WalkBoston has installed nearly 500 wayfinding signs on routes designed to encourage walking.

[i] Dorothea Hass is a co-founder and senior project manager of WalkBoston, the country's first pedestrian advocacy organization. For more about her many activities and accomplishments see; http://walkboston.org/people/dorothea-hass

---

BOX 10.6 Bordeaux: bicycle NGO teaches newcomers how to ride

Preston L. Schiller

The city and metropolitan area of Bordeaux in southwest France offers an interesting comparison to similarly sized Strasbourg (see Box 10.2) in terms of its efforts to develop in the direction of sustainable transportation. Bordeaux has had considerable influence in the political life of France, with Jacques Chaban-Delmas and Alain Juppé alternating between times as mayor and times as prime minister. It is also a major transportation hub for roads, rail, aviation and shipping.

A beautifully historic city with an extensive and expansive promenade along the banks of the river Garonne, it also offers pedestrians an extensive network of pedestrianized streets and plazas, including the historically important commercial street of Rue Sainte Catherine. Its public policy stresses the promotion and expansion of transit—including extending the tramway to an expanding airport that employs thousands, optimization of boulevard space for transit, limiting the impact of automobiles and promoting cycling (Barthélémy 2016).

It began its tramway system a little later than Strasbourg but, like the Alsatian city, it used the development of the tram system to help its pedestrianization schemes. For aesthetic purposes, a special cable-tram was developed; in the historic areas, it gets its power through a sub-surface cable to which it attaches. Outside the historic areas it gets its power through conventional overhead catenaries.

Bordeaux has also made great efforts to promote and encourage bicycling through policy and infrastructure improvements. In these efforts, it has been greatly aided by an exemplary non-governmental organization (NGO): Vélo-Cité (City Bicycle) which is more than a cycling information and advocacy organization—although it does admirably well in those regards. Like Strasbourg's ASTUS, it sees itself as part of a broader effort to reverse overdependence on private motor vehicles (PMVs), combat pollution and humanize and green the urban environment. It participates in coalition with environmental efforts, mass rides and—like its counterparts in Strasbourg—protests against a large highway bypass proposed for its region.

One of its most interesting and important activities is the offering of a bicycling school (vélo-école) for adults who need to learn or re-learn how to cycle. For a modest fee, or a greatly reduced fee for persons of limited financial means, students will be supplied with helmets and bright reflective vests and be instructed by skilled volunteers. They will also be guided on rides along the spacious riverfront promenade and, when ready, taken onto streets to learn how to manage cycling in traffic. The program is especially popular with newcomers from cultures where bicycling was not encouraged—especially among women. Members also participate in making used bicycles available for sale as well as helping persons with repairs. Vélo-Cité offers a wealth of information about cycling at its website where its newsletter, covering cycling and much more of environmental and social interest, is accessible and archived.[i]

[i] See: velo-cite.org/ (accessed 13 October 2016).

FIGURE 10.6
Bordeaux's adult bicycling classes
Vélo-Cité (bicycle city) NGO offers cycling classes for adults, many of whom are recent immigrants who want to achieve the mobility that cycling affords.
Source: VéloCité (velo-cite.org)

The number of such action groups and NGOs, both big and small, around the world is impossible to count. But they can be collectively acknowledged as forming an important force, particularly where political leadership favoring sustainability is lacking and communities themselves need to try to shape changes in a more favorable direction. It is very clear that sustainable transportation has developed a global momentum and that the ideas, resources, expertise and motivation for sharing of best practices and exemplars are now much more organized and effective than perhaps ever before.

On a less positive note, it also has to be said, however, that some organizations can be very effective at stopping or manipulating change according their own more limited agendas, especially those that are referred to as NIMBY groups (Not in My Backyard).[18] For example, groups in Los Angeles and San Diego have in the past fought successfully to keep rail out of their communities for various reasons, especially those related to fear of crime being introduced. Others, such as the various Save Our Suburbs organizations[19] fight, with varying degrees of success, to keep denser development out of their neighborhoods. While such groups can raise legitimate concerns about the quality of more compact development, greenspace issues, parking, traffic and urban design, many arguments are driven by fear of change and emotively framed, such as a tendency to demonize high-rise buildings. Awareness and acknowledgment of the many good examples of compact development that improve walking and cycling possibilities and add amenity and convenience to neighborhoods are often lacking. There is also a tendency to deny the importance of higher density in generally improving urban sustainability and to simplistically cast higher density as synonymous with 'greedy developers' (Newman and Kenworthy 2015).

Still further, groups and affiliations may pressure for a variety of reasons, at least some related to an interplay between vested interests and local politics, to keep rail out of cities (Ardila Gómez 2004),[20] through well-funded campaigns for bus-based solutions such as BRT, the chief beneficiaries of which are powerful and profitable bus alliances in cities. Ross (2016) for example states:

> BRT now served many agendas. For powerful state highway agencies and their allies among construction contractors and carmakers, it remained an argument for pouring concrete instead of laying rail. Environmentalists, few of them familiar with the history, saw an affordable way to reduce car use. Economists had a use for their favored tool of cost–benefit analysis. The overlapping worlds of bureaucracy, philanthropy, and sponsored research seized on the much-desired technical fix, which, as in so many cases, promised to solve a recognized problem without challenging the power relationships that created it (in this case, by privileging highways over other forms of transportation).[21]

'NIMBY', however, may be an unfortunate and inappropriate term to apply as widely as it has come to be. It probably originated around 1980 by Walter Rodgers, a nuclear engineer frustrated by widespread local resistance to sites proposed for nuclear power generators in the 1970s. As the discussion above indicates, there are clearly some persons and groups that take advantage of public process to maintain certain privileges or practices (keeping 'undesirable' elements out of their neighborhood). There are, however, many instances where people perceive (often quite accurately and acutely) how a proposed project or change of procedure will have a negative impact on their lives (see for example Box 10.1).

The term was often used in the U.S. by real estate developers in the 1980s, and it appears to have then become standard parlance in many planning and policy circles for characterizing any critique or questioning of their proposals, even by highly responsible and thoughtful environmental groups. This is a convenient way for developers and bureaucrats to overlook the fact that much community rejection of planning and development proposals might be due to one or a combination of the following:

- Poor public involvement, especially late 'after-the-fact' presentations of plans or policies that have already progressed through formal channels for quite some time, heavily massaged by the interests proposing or planning to benefit from them.
- Poor preparation of public officials as to project benefits.
- Uncritical thinking on the part of public officials and planners about true benefits and disbenefits.[22]

Planning researcher Jonathan Levine (2006) has demonstrated that the zoning codes and protocols created decades ago by development and planning interests have taken on a life of their own in which much of the public has become so accustomed to large lot sizes and setbacks that there is a built-in inertia to the system and public perceptions about it. This has led to a scarcity of more compact alternatives from which persons seeking residences can choose and residents' reaction to poorly crafted densification proposals—which might, if badly realized, only bring more traffic but not more urban amenities to their neighborhood.

Private-sector leadership

Sustainable transportation requires the integration of government, the community and the private business sector to implement change. No single sector can do everything by itself. The private sector is driven by a profit motive and is inherently keyed to innovation and change to find new business opportunities, whereas government is often more geared towards stability, order and established ways of doing things (see Jacobs's 1994 discussion of the guardian and commercial moral syndromes).

Sometimes it is the private sector that can come knocking on the doors of government, seeking to pursue bold and unusual ventures that stretch existing planning and transportation frameworks and challenge existing communities and vested interests with their proposals. In Perth and Adelaide, there have in the past been private-sector proposals to the government to fully fund the development of urban rail systems in return for favorable land development opportunities close to railway stations. In both cases, the proposals were considered too bold for current thinking within government. The transportation bureaucracies found it too challenging and potentially complex to have funding of a major infrastructure project tied to the private sector instead of the simpler tried and tested way of getting capital funds through a state treasury borrowing for themselves to manage.

The disadvantage of this lack of government receptivity to potential innovation is that the rail projects were seen mainly as technical matters of engineering and construction, rather than being intimately concerned with integrated land-use development. The private-sector proposals inherently had the potential to involve greater land-use planning and to integrate high-density mixed-use developments, whereas the government-led projects focused more on the traditional P&R lots at rail stations.

In practice, however, if funding of transit systems either partially or fully through the private sector is to widely occur, leadership by government will be needed to establish new value capture frameworks, or 'value creation' as some are preferring to call it, in which the private sector can operate. Efforts in Australia are under way now to achieve this with the federal government embracing a new report entitled *Entrepreneur Rail Model: Tapping Private Investment for New Urban Rail* (Newman et al. 2016) and a new report in New South Wales entitled *Transit and Urban Renewal Value Creation* (LUTI Consulting 2016). Once the playing field is set by the government and is clear, this can then foster greater private-sector participation and leadership in this area (again showing the inextricable links between the different sectors in progressing more sustainable transportation and growing its exemplars).

Many examples of innovative ideas emanating from private-sector developers and architects are presented through efforts such as those of the Congress for the New Urbanism[23] and the Prince's Foundation for the Built Environment,[24] among many other efforts around the planet to overcome the weight of overly restrictive or archaic building codes and development practices.

Sometimes rethinking of the current business paradigm or a reassessment of its harmful effects emerges from within major corporations. Such was the case when Elmer Johnson, the former executive vice president and director of General Motors Corporation, led a study project of the American Academy of Arts and Sciences that produced a study highly critical of the impacts of unbridled automobility on urban areas (Johnson 1993). And many were surprised when the (then) California-based Bank of America (1995) joined with the Greenbelt Alliance, the California Resources Agency and the Low Income Housing Fund to produce a research paper highly critical of sprawl development.

The above examples of private-sector innovation relate mainly to improvements in the supply of new transit systems and related land-use development. Of course, the private sector plays an active role in other areas related to sustainable transportation, especially in the fields of new technologies and other engineering/technical matters. At present, three key areas of private sector technological innovation are pushing towards more private electric vehicles to replace the existing fleet of internal combustion engine vehicles (gasoline, diesel and gas powered), the development of autonomous vehicles—discussed in detail in Chapter 4—and the increasing use of smart technologies to create integrated multi-modal mobility management systems (see Box 8.4 on MaaS). Growing exemplars in these areas will be assisted by several other potentially important catalysts, modified below from Newman and Kenworthy (2015).

Whether such catalysts will work to provide new technologies and other technical advancements that are deployed in a way that advances more sustainable transportation or sets it back will remain to be seen. The previous discussion of autonomous vehicles certainly raises red flags about how new technologies, when backed by some of the factors listed below, can create a trajectory that is not necessarily rational, balanced or well-considered in its potential 'big picture' results. The success and value of these factors in shaping more sustainable transportation will thus depend critically on whether there is an overall vision that is based on a holistic understanding of what will create more sustainable transportation, or whether it is driven more by a belief that new technologies are panaceas and can be introduced successfully without consideration of rebound and feedback effects.

- Strong private-sector research and innovation, backed by bold venture capitalists to finance new ideas and potentially 'disruptive technologies/innovation' (Bower and Christensen 1995);
- Well-organized lobbying at high levels of government by private-sector interests selling their ideas;
- Ability of the private sector to read and influence public opinion about what motivates people and what people are concerned about, and then use that to develop and sell new ideas. The constantly changing attitudes within communities is critical here (e.g. the trend in many countries away from cars by younger generations—fewer driver's licenses, less driving and more transit use[25]);
- Strong public-sector research through universities, well-funded institutes and think tanks and other direct forms of public sector investment to support new technologies (e.g. investment in electric vehicle charging stations);
- Technically and politically competent, independent bureaucrats.

The important message is that, to implement sustainability, the private sector with its capital, skills and innovation is a key player in the push for greater sustainability. Its frequent aggressiveness needs, of course, to be always balanced against 'common good' interests; however, its role should not be underestimated or rejected simply on all too glibly handed-out stereotypes of the 'ugly, greedy entrepreneur', driven exclusively by a profit motive. People with vision and commitment to positive change, or even equality, do not just come from the government or the general community; they also exist in the business community. Where this does exist, it needs to be harnessed. Where it is in short supply, the government needs to act to protect the broader public interest, which means having a genuine desire and capacity to see the bigger picture and being able to build strong bulwarks against the lobbying and pure self-interest of the private sector when it is evident.

The creative class: breathing imagination into urban and transportation planning

Another source of energy that needs to be better used in the development of sustainable cities and transportation systems is that of creative people: musicians, artists, urban ecologists and a host of mostly younger individuals who are breathing life back into decaying neighborhoods, finding affordable housing in interesting communities, promoting community gardens and co-operatives, finding their niches and *modus vivendi* (which often involve alternative modes of getting around their communities), and, in the process, bringing fresh insight into addressing a range of urban and transportation issues.

In the USA, urban pioneers and 'millennials'[26] are moving into depressed cities such as Baltimore, Cleveland, St Louis and Detroit. Some of those returning to the hollowed cores of the formerly hallowed creative center of Detroit are neither pioneers nor millennials. They include Detroit native and artist Tyree Guyton, who never left, and founded the Heidelberg (Street) Project in 1986 (Figure 10.7).

Accomplished artist Nancy Mitchnick—who left the famed Cass Corridor Group of Detroit artists in the mid-1970s for a career of painting and teaching at Bard College, California Institute of the Arts and Harvard University—returned to undertake her own Detroit Project: the painting of numerous houses, beginning with those in the neighborhood in which she grew up, in a range of states of repair from good and tidy with hanging flower baskets and pink garages to completely dilapidated or burned out and abandoned by their owners in a city abandoned by the automobile industry.[27] Upon returning and starting the Detroit Project she has received awards and critical acclaim for her work (Stryker 2016).

Writing about one young woman who moved to a new job in a cyber security start-up in Baltimore, Hanes (2015) states how she:

> ... quickly realized that she had moved to a city that is full of other young professionals—and attracting more every month. There is a vibrant bar and restaurant scene, social sports leagues through which hundreds of young people get together to play

FIGURE 10.7
Detroit's Heidelberg (Street) Project. An example of the artistic energy and revival now apparent in parts of inner-city Detroit, fueled by a mix of young people, some new to the city, some life-long residents and some older returnees.
Source: Richard Register

kickball and other games, even a monthly bike ride—sponsored by a group working to make Baltimore less car dependent—in which participants dress up in costume and ride through the city.

Hanes also discusses how Millennials appear to be less attached to auto-dependent living:

> . . . the Millennial generation seems even more intent on urban living. Two-thirds of the country's 25- to 34-year-olds with a bachelor's degree live in the nation's 51 largest metropolitan areas. And many of those pick close-in urban neighborhoods, where they are able to walk or take public transportation to work and recreational activities. . . .

Then Hanes quotes urban economist Joe Cortright's 2014 report for the City Observatory: 'A lot of it has to do with the new urbanist bullet points. . . . People want dense, diverse, interesting places that are walkable, bikeable and transit-served.'

FIGURE 10.8A
Portland (OR) rail station creativity
While waiting for the new suburban Westside Diesel Multiple Unit (DMU), regional train riders can amuse themselves at this unique *Commedia dell'arte* 'talking heads' board game.
Source: Preston L. Schiller

FIGURE 10.8B
'For you to play.' A piano in the Gare Montparnasse railway station, Paris, offers an opportunity to practice a piece or meet fellow travelers or locals (2015). This is becoming a feature of many train stations.
Source: Preston L. Schiller

FIGURE 10.8C
Barcelona Busking Devil: creative street entertainment on La(s) Rambla(s) in central Barcelona.
Source: Jeffrey R. Kenworthy

Urban observer and analyst Richard Florida[28] has coined the term 'the creative class' (Florida 2002, 2005) in his effort to analyze why some U.S. cities were doing well in attracting talented and innovative younger persons, while others appeared to be declining, due in part to what he termed, borrowing from economist Mancur Olson, 'institutional sclerosis'.

It has taken creative imagination for planners to incorporate attractive and interactive activities into public transportation facilities, whether a clever game board at a suburban Portland (OR) commuter rail station (Figure 10.8a) or a piano 'for you to play' in the large confines of Paris's Gare Montparnasse railway station (Figure 10.8b). It also took creativity, entrepreneurial courage and civic commitment for environmental studies[29] graduate Ryan

FIGURE 10.9A
Congressional tricycle tour 2010 Pedicab and cargo bike entrepreneur Ryan Hashagen ("TAXI") and co-cabbie transport Cong. Peter DeFazio of Oregon (left) and the late Cong. James Oberstar of Minnesota (right; former chair of the U.S. House of Representatives Transportation and Infrastructure Committee) and staff on a guided tour of federally supported bicycle projects in Eugene, OR. Cong. Oberstar had also visited Muenster, the "bicycle capital of Germany" and drew inspiration from that city's experience.
Source: Lale Santelices, http://portlandpedals.com/

FIGURE 10.9B
Pedicab Panache. Lale Santelices transports visitors to one of Portland's Sunday Parkways (North Portland, 2012)
Source: Ryan Hashagen (http://portlandpedals.com/)

FIGURE 10.9C
Icicle Tricycle. Ryan Hashagen's ice cream cycles keep Portland Community Cycling Center campers happy in the summer (2012).
Source: Ryan Hashagen (http://portlandpedals.com/)

Hashagen to embark upon a career of creating pedicab services, including 'bicycle marriages' and manufacturing pedicabs and a variety of cargo bicycles, including 'icicle tricycles' based in Portland (OR) (Figures 10.9a, b, c). Ryan has also become a civic activist and leader giving generously of his time to the 'Better Block PDX' effort that brings together city officials, students in engineering and planning at Portland State University, citizens and activists to carefully and systematically demonstrate the ways in which existing motor vehicle infrastructure can be reclaimed for pedestrian and cycling mobility (Maus 2016).

It also took creative planning on the part of a transit agency to imagine how extra street rail space could be shared with a restaurant on wheels that allows tourists and locals alike to eat delicious food while savoring the beautiful sites of Zurich (online photo).

Artists such as Andy Singer (2001, andysinger.com), whose car-toons pepper several chapters of this book, capture the absurdities of BAU transportation and the playful energies that can be associated with bicycling, walking, community-building and even transit. David Byrne, creator of the Talking Heads band, has made bicycling a part of his daily life for over 30 years and derives much creative energy for his work from pedaling about New York and the cities where he tours. In conjunction with the release of his work, *Bicycle Diaries* (2009), Byrne organized an autumn 2009 tour, 'Cities, Bicycles and the Future of Getting Around', in which he shared the podium with local civic leaders, planning experts and bicycle advocates at numerous cities in the U.S. and Canada.[30] Byrne continues to incorporate bicycling into his personal as well as on-stage life. For his 2015 Meltdown Festival in London, he 'included his appreciation of cycling into the festival. Bike racks designed by Byrne and a valet service will be available to those ticket holders who have cycled to the gig.'[31] More energies like these need to be harnessed to advance sustainable cities and sustainable transportation.

Success builds success: the power of demonstration projects

This discussion has set out some of the key factors or themes in achieving successes in sustainable transportation. In the end, it is the power of the projects themselves, what they demonstrate and how they can lead to more change that matter. It is always possible to criticize and snipe at new ideas and proposals or be fearful of them before they are realized, but what is often most needed is to build something new that shows in concrete terms the power of such transformations. It is often the only way to silence critics and opposition and create a new direction. To draw an analogy, in chemistry there is a term called the 'rate-limiting', 'rate-determining' or 'rate-setting step' in a chemical reaction. It is the slowest step in the reaction, which, once transcended, leads to an accelerated reaction. The absence of any projects that demonstrate the desired direction in sustainable transportation and planning frequently constitutes the 'rate-limiting step'. It took creativity and courage for the City of Kirkland, WA in the Seattle area to convert a redundant and lake-encroaching roadway into a mile-long promenade for pedestrians, cyclists and nature lovers of many generations (Figure 10.10).

FIGURE 10.10
From road to sanctuary. Kirkland is a suburb of Seattle known for its pedestrian-friendly downtown and waterfront and encouragement of walking. It rerouted a lakefront road and converted the original one to a mile-long promenade for bicyclists and pedestrians; many generations can now pedal, stroll, watch birds and enjoy the restored shoreline.
Source: https://maps.google.com/

Portland's light rail transit (LRT) system, the Metropolitan Area Express (MAX), was roundly and relentlessly criticized by the press during its planning and construction, as were new rail developments in Perth. After opening, the success of the systems built a new direction. In the case of Portland, the arguments were no longer over the wisdom of building more new rail transit lines, but over which community should get the next extension. The City of Portland also went on to build a streetcar system on its own when it was not a high funding priority for the regional transit agency.

As already touched upon, pedestrianization of city centers or traffic calming schemes and the economic success of businesses located in them have led to a desire for further extensions and sometimes offers to help pay for extensions by businesses not covered in the initial scheme. This is in stark contrast to the threats of lawsuits that have been brought on cities all over the world when the initial proposals were made. People need to see and experience for themselves before they can appreciate what changes can do.

It is frequently argued that people are wedded to their cars and low-density forms of living, but this is often due to a paucity of choices. Once such choices become available, such as the high-density transit-oriented developments in Vancouver, it begins to break the stereotype of a city of only suburban house dwellers and car owners by showing people that high-quality alternatives are available that offer a different but also very livable, more sustainable way of life. The success of such new offers in the marketplace gives the private sector confidence to break out of some of their 'cookie cutter' approaches that have proven successful and to diversify their lifestyle offers.

Perth's first Transit-Oriented Development around the inner suburban Subiaco railway station, planned and implemented by a state government redevelopment authority, has helped gain traction for TOD in the city and expand the idea to other stations on Perth's rail network (Figure 10.11).

For so many decades after the destruction of its extensive rail system (Klein and Olsen 1996), Los Angeles has been one of the world's pin-up cities for unsustainable transportation. However, since 1990, when LA opened its first new light rail line since the early decades of the twentieth century (Blue Line from Downtown to Long Beach), it has developed a light rail and metro rail system with a combined length of some 178 km. Perhaps as importantly, it has also been focusing new development around stations on both systems

FIGURE 10.11
Subi-Centro, Perth high density, walkable and green TOD station area
Source: Jeffrey R. Kenworthy

FIGURE 10.12A
Hollywood/Highland station on the
Red Metro Line in Los Angeles
Source: Tanya Babaeff

FIGURE 10.12B
Hollywood/Vine station on the Red
Metro Line in Los Angeles
Source: Tanya Babaeff

(Figures 10.12a and b). Many people and businesses are now demonstrating a desire to locate near quality transit, an impossible dream in LA without the initial breakthrough Blue LRT line and Red Metro line (1993), which helped create a cascade effect. The real estate market there is now responding to the increased accessibility afforded by Los Angeles's 104 rail stations with major new residential and commercial/retail development, especially since chronic freeway congestion makes life almost intolerable for so many Los Angelenos.

The fine example of environmentally and sustainable transportation oriented planning in Freiburg im Breisgau, Germany, was examined in Chapter 9. It is appropriate in the context of exploring how such leading examples can be learned from and applied in efforts in different places that an in-depth look at the ecologically planned community Vauban in Freiburg is now presented in Box 10.7.

BOX 10.7 Life in the Vauban ecologically planned community: growing free-range kids

Preston L. Schiller

I was intrigued by Jeffrey Kenworthy's depiction of Freiburg, especially its Vauban ecologically planned community, in our 2010 edition of this book. I resolved to visit, and in February 2015 I spent two weeks living in the heart of the Vauban as well as daily exploring Freiburg on foot and by tram. The following is an account of what I learned from that time and why I feel that the example of the Vauban merits wide attention and deserves imitation, within the limits of cross-cultural application, in many other cities–especially in the overly car-oriented urban environments of the U.S. and Canada.

Sébastien Le Prestre de Vauban (1633–1707), who earned the titles of Marquis de Vauban and Maréchal de France, was an important military engineer and strategist who designed many fortifications for France as well as directing several assaults and sieges during his lifetime. He directed the design and construction of a large fortification in French-controlled Freiburg (c.1680). For the next several decades the French occupied or retreated from Freiburg depending on the vagaries of wars and treaties. In 1745, on their way out of town after their final occupation, the French destroyed their fortifications. This area has come to be known as Schlossberg, with a large observation tower with magnificent views of Freiburg and the surrounding Black Forest.

An area at the southwestern edge of Freiburg became the site of a 1936 Nazi military installation. The French military again occupied Freiburg and that military site in the aftermath of WWII. No doubt historically minded, they named their base Vauban after the esteemed engineer. In 1992, the French found that it was no longer necessary to occupy Freiburg—or Germany—and its substantial space was given back to the City of Freiburg without being demolished by the French military on their way out of town.

A period of several years of contested proposals and partial installations ensued before a final plan to divide the site between several preserved barracks for university students and affordable housing and social activists associated with SUSI (self-organized independent settlement initiative). The former building that housed the French military's offices and mess hall has been preserved and made into offices and the mess hall has become a popular bistro. The other barracks were cleared for new co-operative eco-housing that pioneered the extremely energy-efficient passive house design, which also allowed the original residents to configure their units horizontally (on the same floor) or vertically (more than one-story units) within the same building envelope.[i] The whole site benefited from preserving and expanding upon existing green space. The former military stables and adjacent pasturage were preserved for use by the community for outdoor experiential learning: youngsters to learn and practice horsemanship and to engage in a community summer farm and garden school.

There are many things that can be learned from the Vauban experience. Its greatest development and realization successes stemmed from the combination of strong public and NGO participation and deliberation with co-operation among government officials and construction and financing interests. A high level of planning went into both the siting and construction of model energy-efficient multi-story buildings[ii] with usable green-spaces, maximizing pedestrianization and non-motorized access while minimizing motorized access. Planning and policy established many easily accessible amenities including several grocery, bakery and restaurant options as well as child care, which are clustered around a commercial area and elementary school at the edge of the Vauban. An organic food co-op and café are closer to the community's center.

One of the most important aspects of the Vauban's design is to maintain residential areas protected from private motor vehicles (PMVs) while still allowing some PMV circulation on a couple of streets around its edges. Some of the paths that tie the Vauban together can be used by PMVs on a temporary basis when proximity to a residence is needed for either heavy loads or service work. The unnecessary use of PMVs is discouraged in this way, as is the Vauban's parking policy and the amount of parking provided. No long-term parking by residents is allowed on any street in the Vauban. The original plan worked out with the City called for three large parking garages, and a very high fee (around $40,000) for each stall. One parking garage was built next to the commercial area along a major street; it is shared with the commercial uses and the floors reserved

continued

for Vaubanites are greatly underutilized (perhaps at only 15%–25%) and probably will allow for some conversion to commercial use in the future if needed. The other parking garage, located closer to many residences, is more utilized but still not at maximum capacity. A third parking structure was never built due to lack of demand and its site has become de facto greenspace.

The great environmental achievements of the Vauban come into clear relief when compared to another well-planned and compact Freiburg community of roughly the same vintage: Rieselfeld. Both planned communities benefited from similar planning considerations; affordability, good bus connections, eventually replaced by LRT, extended to their core as they were under development; excellent non-motorized infrastructure and connections and collaboration between potential residents, the City and the designers and builders. Both were built to greater densities than average for Freiburg. Rieselfeld was built on a completely vacant site, which had been part of a very large leaching area where sewage was carted in the period before a municipal sewer system existed. Part of the larger area not developed adjacent to Rieselfeld was made into a large nature preserve.

Rieselfeld is also a well-planned and attractive community in many regards. Its design is compact while still allowing for green spaces and the many communal courtyards also serve as play spaces; several shopping and service opportunities are close-by, which include conveniently located day care and a gymnasium whose sod-covered arc roof makes for a great play space; a church shared by Protestants and Catholics; purchasing and financing options promoting affordability; and a centrally situated elementary school and library.

It is in the domains of sustainable transportation design and neighborhood circulation that the differences between Rieselfeld and Vauban, each roughly the same distance from the city center, become sharpest, as Table 10.1 indicates. Rieselfeld began a few years earlier than Vauban, and while all its streets are traffic calmed with 30 km/h speed limits, the sounds and sights of motorized movement are still noticeable. The numerous communal courtyards, many entryways away from streets, and the expansive town square offer opportunities for interaction or personal quiet away from even the very light traffic, but the presence of even light traffic gives Rieselfeld a different feel than Vauban. As with much else in urban life, it all comes down to parking—or lack thereof. Rieselfeld was built with the provision of one parking space per residence, often below residential buildings, and a generous amount of on-street parking.

Before my two weeks in the Vauban were up, I came to realize that it was children who were the greatest benefactors of its design and realization. In the U.S., the debate over whether children should be hovered over by 'helicopter parents' or allowed to be 'free-range kids' rages on, with government authorities even going so far as to level charges of neglect against the parents of children encouraged (and prepared) to walk around their neighborhoods without adult supervision. While both developments have many young ones, and playing children are present throughout Rieselfeld, their presence seems to dominate the Vauban: playing solo or with friends, walking and cycling about, impromptu sports. The density and design of the Vauban affords a wide choice of playmates and opportunities readily at hand, with the community's 'eyes on the street' (or path) ever present.

One Sunday morning, I took the LRT from Vauban to the Freiburg train station en route to a day in Karlsruhe. On the Vauban station platform was a youngster, no older than eight years in my estimate, waiting. She boarded the tram and took a solo seat. She was not truly alone; her doll accompanied. She rode all the way into the center of the city and, without prompting from the operator, deboarded—ostensibly to meet a relative or family friend. In Silver Springs, MD, that might have occasioned someone fearfully calling the police. In Freiburg, it was not a remarkable event (see Chapter 6, Box 6.2 for more about 'free-range kids').

If all cities, or at least all cities in Europe and the Americas, were to transform themselves along the lines of Rieselfeld, we would have phenomenally improved urban environments and much-lowered energy, both in structures and mobility and dramatically less urban space consumption. If all the same cities were to transform themselves along the lines of the Vauban, well, we'd be in heaven and maybe our own children would even know how to navigate through their own cities and beyond.

[i] (Also see the discussion and photos of Freiburg and the Vauban in Chapter 9)

[ii] See: www.energy-cities.eu/db/freiburg2_579_en.pdf

TABLE 10.1 Comparison of Vauban and Rieselfeld neighborhoods with the City of Freiburg

	Vauban	Rieselfeld	Freiburg
Area (ha)	41	70	15,280
Residents (Vauban 2013†; Rieselfeld 2009>; Freiburg 2014)	5,500	9,000	222,000
Density (persons/ha)	134*	129> (derived)	48*
Jobs per resident	0.12**	0.09**	NA (a)
Households	2,500†	3,400 (2009)>	114,000*
Households with children (%)	38*	48*	17*
Residents under age 18 (%)	28*	32*	16*
Residents ages 18–60 (%)	68*	61*	64*
Residents over 60 (%)	3*	7*	21*
PMVs/1000 people	169*	292*	408*
Parking/residence	<0.5**	1.2**	NA
Car-free households (registered)	422	NA	NA
Mode share all trips			
Drive (%) total	16**	30**	32*
Drive (%) car free	2*		
Drive (%) own car	28*		
Transit (%)	19**	25**	18*
Bicycle (%) car free	50*	29*	27††
Bicycle (%) own car	40*		
Walk (%) car free	34*	16*	23††
Walk (%) own car	27*		
Total non-motorized (%)	64**	45**	50††

Sources: *Broaddus (2010); **Field (2014); > Siegl (2009); † Green City Freiburg (2013); †† Buehler and Pucher (2011)
(a) Probably considerably higher than Vauban or Rieselfeld; greatly concentrated in city center due to universities, hospitals, government offices and related professional employment.

FIGURE 10.13A
Vauban partial panorama PassivHaus and solar roof design; medium rise but considerable density with good outdoors and solar exposure; the structure undergoing renovation (far left) is a former barracks undergoing an energy efficiency upgrade.
Source: Preston L. Schiller

FIGURE 10.13B
Convivial Vauban residents gather in
the late afternoon and early evening
to socialize
Source: Preston L. Schiller

FIGURE 10.13C
Unattended "free-range" child waits
after school, doesn't mind the rain:
The Vauban elementary school
(left) was built into the fabric of the
community adjacent to a commercial
center, a transit center and
residences. The school's
playgrounds and fields are located
behind the school away from the
street
Source: Preston L. Schiller

Conclusion

In the end, people must experience and feel the difference between unsustainable transportation and sustainable transportation-based ways of life, and the kind of overall
environments and 'lifestyle packages' that this can create. It must bring to them personal
benefits, not just accrue benefits to society. Every place needs a successful project, something
that can be experienced, felt and enjoyed. With successful projects to prove the worthiness
of sustainable transportation, all the efforts of politicians, bureaucrats, academics, writers
and community groups will gather momentum and gain direction, creating a 'virtuous circle'
of change.

FIGURE 10.13D
Traffic-calmed shared street near the Vauban. The example of the Vauban has influenced an adjacent neighborhood to make one of its streets into a shared and traffic-calmed play street.
Source: Preston L. Schiller

FIGURE 10.13E
"Free-range" child alone on transit from Vauban to Freiburg Center: An unaccompanied "free-range" girl (left) and her doll ride the LRT line from the Vauban to the center of Freiburg on a Sunday morning in February, 2015. The young musician on the right is going to a rehearsal, and the skis (right) and their owner (not in photo) are going to the train station for a regional train to the nearby mountains.
Source: Preston L. Schiller

David Brower, an environmental 'archdruid', would engage audiences when the issue of transportation arose in discussion with: 'All in favor of sustainable transportation, raise your right foot!' (Schiller 2002b).

Are you raising your right foot? Now, how about your left? That's it: keep on walking or pedaling or ambling to the transit stop.

Questions for discussion

- Discuss the different types of leadership that are needed to make a community 'exemplary'.

- Using Jane Jacobs as an example, what are some of the issues around being a researcher or urban analyst *and* a community activist?

- How can your university and community become exemplars?

- Discuss some of the forces and factors that can work against growing more exemplars of sustainable transportation.

- Find a city of your own and describe why it is a good exemplar of sustainable transportation and the main factors that have enabled it to reach its achievements.

- What are some of the (several) ways in which the parking situation at the Vauban encourages car-freedom, walking, cycling and transit use?

Notes

1 1971–74, 1979–83, 1989–92; later governor of Paraná Province in Brazil.
2 1998–2001 and incumbent again since 2016.
3 Mayor 2002–06, president of South Korea 2008–13.
4 For information about the working of the scheme, see: www.lta.gov.sg/content/ltaweb/en/roads-and-motoring/owning-a-vehicle/vehicle-quota-system/certificate-of-entitlement-coe.html (accessed 18 July 2016).
5 Since the award was established in 2005, no city has been cited for progressing rail initiatives, not even Shanghai or Beijing or any other Chinese city for their exemplary investment in some of the world's largest metro systems. Guangzhou did win it in 2011 for its BRT, apparently ignoring its important metro system, 193 km of which existed at the time of the award, after opening the first line only in 1997 (in 2015 the metro had daily usage of about 6.6 million passengers).
6 cnt.org
7 See: www.vancouversun.com/trans+totem+playful+monument+motion+rises+vancouver/10935861/story.html and www.insidevancouver.ca/2015/04/04/giant-totem-pole-made-of-stacked-cars-goes-up-in-vancouver/ (accessed 8 July 2016).
8 Quote from: www.insidevancouver.ca/2015/04/04/giant-totem-pole-made-of-stacked-cars-goes-up-in-vancouver/ (accessed 8 July 2016).
9 See: worldtransportjournal.com/ (accessed 8 July 2016).
10 For a discussion of the subversiveness of such ideas and paradigm changes, see Bradbury (1998).
11 Public Transport Users Association (PTUA) www.ptua.org.au/ (accessed 10 July 2016).
12 See for example: www.greenleft.org.au/node/9143, www.ycat.org.au/october-18-coalition-of-transport-action-groups-ctag-community-protest-rally-picnic-media-release/, news.google.com/newspapers?nid=1301&dat=19890427&id=3TRWAAAAIBAJ&sjid=0ecDAAAAIBAJ&pg=3659,5662759&hl=en (accessed 14 July 2016).
13 See: www.smartgrowthamerica.org/complete-streets (accessed 13 July 2016).
14 See: www.urbandesign.org; *also*, see the Congress for the New Urbanism, www.cnu.org (accessed 14 July 2016).
15 See: www.rudi.net/pages/95 and www.rudi.net/information_zone/case_studies_good_practice (accessed 14 July 2016).
16 See: www.slocat.net/slocatpartnership (accessed 10 July 2016).
17 See: www.un.org/climatechange/summit/2014/09/commitment-sustainable-transport-mobilized-un-climate-summit/ (accessed 10 July 2016).
18 The NIMBY term has morphed into dozens of other derogatory terms such NIMTOO (Not In My Term Of Office) See: yuriartibise.com/25-nimby-spinoffs/ (accessed 13 July 2016).
19 See: www.saveoursuburbs.org.au; www.sos.org.au; www.saveoursuburbs.org (accessed 11 July 2016).

20   In explaining the detailed politics and events surrounding the decision to build the TransMilenio BRT in Bogotá and the strong opposition to the Metro, despite consulting studies supporting its feasibility, Ardila Gómez (2004) explains some of the dynamics of what happened—essentially the planners introduced delays in the metro planning, assembled a coalition against it and tried to get studies to say the metro was not feasible (p. 315). In relation to Curitiba, a globally lauded example of successful bus-based transit, Ardila Gómez (2004) also points out that decisions to support BRT over LRT were politicized, even against the findings of a major study recommending LRT over long saturated BRT lines (p. 192, 201–2). Finally, he concludes that the coalition between planners, politicians and bus operators had grown still stronger, at least up to 2004 (p. 206).

21   Providing buses with their own rights-of-way free of traffic congestion will significantly enhance bus reliability, speed and attraction of riders. Buses are essential in every city as they are the only mid-level load mode available and much more should be done to enhance their competitiveness with the car (e.g. see Bradley and Kenworthy (2012) for a detailed case to improve bus services by better controlling congestion). The main problem arises if the argument for BRT is presented as BRT being equivalent to rail in every sense and where rail is cast as being an inferior and a too costly solution in every circumstance, especially in less wealthy cities ('cities never need rail'). Such approaches are motivated by vested interests acting not in the best interests of the city, but in their own narrow self-interest and the results that flow from that will ultimately need to be rectified (such as BRT lines needing to be replaced by rail due to capacity problems).

22   Also, see Burningham et al. (2006) for further discussion of these issues.

23   See: www.cnu.org (accessed 11 July 2016).

24   See: www.princes-foundation.org (accessed 11 July 2016).

25   For example, see: www.csmonitor.com/USA/USA-Update/2016/0120/Why-are-Millennials-forgoing-driving (accessed 12 July 2016).

26   Millennials or Generation Y (Gen Y) are imprecisely defined but are generally considered to begin with people who were born between the early 1980s and the mid-1990s to early 2000s. Some definitions are more prescriptive citing 1982 to 2004; see: www.urbandictionary.com/define.php?term=Millennial; another definition is people aged 18–34 in 2015; see www.pewresearch.org/fact-tank/2016/04/25/millennials-overtake-baby-boomers/ (accessed 12 July 2016).

27   www.nancymmitchnick.com/detroit-project-2/; also see: www.kresgeartsindetroit.org/portfolio-posts/nancy-m-mitchnick

28   See: www.creativeclass.com/richard_florida/ (accessed 12 July 2016).

29   Huxley College of the Environment, Western Washington University, Bellingham.

30   See: www.davidbyrne.com/art/books/bicycle_diaries/index.php#events (accessed 12 July 2016).

31   Vincent, A. (2015).

Glossary

Readers are also referred to the index for specific locations and definition usages in this volume or to a search of the electronic version.

Analytic hierarchy process (AHP) A technique for the weighting of incommensurable inputs and then comparing a variety of alternative projects with the intent of selecting the best one.

Automobile The major type of personal motor vehicle (PMV), which includes light trucks and sports utility vehicles (SUVs).

Backcasting Working backwards from a vision of a preferred future to its planning and enactment (distinct from the use of historic data to evaluate a project, used in other contexts).

Bus rapid transit (BRT) Service designed to emulate most of the features of light rail transit (LRT), including use of right of way B, longer station spacings than regular bus services, transit signal priority, and other intelligent transportation systems (ITS) features and passenger amenities.

Car-share(ing) A co-operatively or privately available vehicle service where persons can rent personal vehicles for brief time periods.

Charrette Planning exercise; community representatives and experts create, comment upon or change proposed project alternatives, often involving visual renderings or computer simulations.

Ciclovía Spanish for bicycle-way; also a celebration of walking and bicycling.

Community Transit Network (CTN) Boulder, Colorado, transit system.

Fordism Pattern of mechanized mass industrial production initiated by Henry Ford's automobile assembly line.

Hybrid (vehicles) Combining more than one power source.

Intelligent Transportation Systems (ITS) Hardware and software specifically designed for improving transportation operations, information to the public and service planning.

Intermodal Travel involving connections between modes.

Light Rail Transit (LRT) Streetcars, trolleys, trams, light rail.

Metropolitan Area Express (MAX) Portland area LRT transit system.

Metropolitan Planning Organization (MPO) Governmental body conducting transportation forecasting, planning and funds distribution for a metro region (U.S.; similar forms elsewhere).

Mode The way in which travel occurs; walking, bicycling, types of public transit (bus, rail), ships and ferries, aviation.

Multi-modal Involves the use or availability of more than one transportation mode.

Opportunity cost The forgone possibilities when resources are committed to a particular project alternative.

Paradigm A framework within which a complex phenomenon operates and defines activities such as planning, financing, attitudes etc.

Passenger kilometers traveled/passenger miles traveled (pkt/pmt) Measure of passenger travel.

Peak (demand, hour) Time and/or direction of greatest road traffic volume.

Public–Private Partnership (PPP) A method of project development in which responsibilities and finances are divided among various parties in recognition of the benefits that each can receive.

Regional Transportation District (RTD) Denver, Colorado, area regional transit system.

Right of way A (RoW A) A right of way with full physical separation from all other paths, providing the highest operating speeds and most reliable travel times.

Right of way B (RoW B) A right of way where transit vehicles have lateral separation from other traffic, but still share intersections with cross-traffic.

Right of way C (RoW C) A right of way where transit vehicles operate in mixed traffic, providing the slowest operating speeds and least reliable travel times.

Sloanism The marketing strategy initiated by General Motor's Alfred P. Sloan that modified Fordism (see above) to include offering new automobile makes and models annually. Often the changes involved appearances and only very minor modifications of previous products.

Tax increment financing (TIF) A method based on assessing a charge on properties close to new transit services that assumes that property owners benefit from the new public investment.

Teu 20 foot equivalent unit; measure of cargo container equivalence.

Time–area A resource consumption measure multiplying the space required by a vehicle and the time for which it occupies it; computed for both parked vehicles and vehicles in the traffic stream.

Tonne kilometer (tkm) Measure of distance that freight travels (1 tonne travels 1 km = 1 tkm). The measure can also be expressed in miles (tmi).

Trackage refers either to a railway's tracks or arrangements for their shared or rented use.

Trip Travel between two points, often between an origin and a destination, but sometimes meaningless (not to be confused with drug-induced states, where origin/destination does not matter).

Trip degeneration Opposite of trip generation; elimination of trips, especially by PMVs.

Trip generation The factors that lead to PMV travel; also the first step in the four-step sequential model where trips are created based on the type and size of activity occurring at a given location.

Vehicle kilometers traveled/vehicle miles traveled (vkt/vmt) Measure of vehicle travel.

Verkehrsberuhigung German term for traffic calming.

References

350.org (2016) *350.org Annual Report 2015*, 350.org, accessed 12 July 2016.

A.W. (2015) 'Frequent flyers: The sad, sick life of the business traveler', *The Economist*, 17 August, www.economist.com/node/21661208/print, accessed 13 June 2016.

Aarsæther, N., Nyseth, T. and Røiseland, A. (2002) 'Neighbourhood councils – municipal instruments or grass-roots movement? Some reflections on results from two Norwegian surveys', in P. McLaverty (ed.) *Public Participation and Innovations in Community Governance*, Ashgate, Aldershot, UK.

Abers, R. N. (1998) 'Learning democratic practice: Distributing government resources through popular participation in Porto Alegre, Brazil', in M. Douglass and J. Friedmann (eds), *Cities for Citizens: Planning and Rise of Civil Society in a Global Age*, Wiley and Sons, New York, NY.

Abers, R. N. (2000) *Inventing Local Democracy: Grassroots Politics in Brazil*, Lynne Rienner, Boulder, CO.

Abrams, R. (2016) 'Walmart Looks to Drones to Speed Distribution', *The New York Times*, 2 June, http://nyti.ms/1X1fAud, accessed 13 November 2016.

Adams, J. (1985) *Risk and Freedom: The Record of Road Safety Regulation*, Brefi Press, Birmingham, UK.

Adams, J. (1999) 'The social implications of hypermobility', in *OECD, Project on Sustainable Transportation (EST): The Economic and Social Implications of Sustainable Transportation*, Proceedings of the Ottawa Workshop, 20–21 October 1998, OECD Publications, Paris, pp. 95–134.

Adams, J. (2000) 'Hypermobility', *Prospect*, 27–31 March, www.prospectmagazine.co.uk/2000/03/hypermobility/, accessed 1 September 2009.

Adams, J. (2009) 'Risk management in a hypermobile world', *OMEGA Centre Seminar Series 2009*, www.youtube.com/watch?v=BoenT86BQFA, accessed 25 March 2016 (82 minutes).

Airport World (2014) 'Scottish spaceports to launch tourists into space by 2018?' *Airport World Magazine*, 14 July, www.airport-world.com/news/general-news/4185-scottish-spaceports-to-launch-tourists-into-space-by-2018.html, accessed 20 August 2016.

Akaha, T. (ed.) (1990) *International Handbook of Transportation Policy*, Greenwood, Westport, CT.

Alexander, D., Tomalty, R. and Anielski, M. (2004) *BC Sprawl Report: Economic Vitality and Livable Communities*, Smart Growth BC, Vancouver, Canada.

Alexander, E. R. (2002) 'The public interest in planning: From legitimation to substantive plan evaluation', *Planning Theory*, vol 1, no 3, 226–249, plt.sagepub.com/content/1/3/226.full.pdf+html, accessed 24 August 2016.

Alexander, I. (1980) 'Office dispersal in metropolitan areas II: Case study results and conclusions', *Geoforum*, vol 11, 249–275.

Alexander, I. (1981) 'Employment dispersal in metropolitan areas: Equitable and energy saving?', *Proceedings of 51st ANZAAS Conference, Architecture and Planning Section*, May.

All For Outdoor (2016) www.all-for-outdoor.com/254573/electric-scooters/freego-f-3-2-wheel-self-balancing-electric-personal-mobility-vehicle-pt.html, accessed 1 August 2016.

Allam, S., Hertrich, V., Kostic, N., Kostyuchenko, N., Meyer, M., Seidner, G. and Seubert, J. (2016) *Developing sustainable sub-centers in cities: A comparison of Neu-Isenburg and Langen in the Rhein-Main-Region*, Master Project GEKO, University of Applied Sciences, Frankfurt am Main, Germany.

Alonso, W. (1964) *Location and Land Use: Toward a General Theory of Land Rent*, Harvard University Press, Cambridge, MA.

Alqhatani, M, Setunge, S. and Moridpour, S. (2014) 'Accessibility development by shifting from monocentric structure to polycentric structure: A comparison of Riyadh, Saudi Arabia and Melbourne, Australia', *Journal of Traffic and Logistics Engineering*, vol 2, no 3, 218–223.

Amato, J. (2004) *On Foot: A History of Walking*, New York University Press, New York, NY.

American Academy of Pediatrics (AAP, Committee on Public Education) (1999) 'Media education', *Pediatrics*, vol 104, no 2, 341–343.

American Academy of Pediatrics (AAP) (2006) 'Active healthy living: Prevention of childhood obesity through increased physical activity', *Pediatrics*, vol 117, no 5, 1834–1842.

Anderson, J. E. (2000) *Public Policymaking: An Introduction*, Houghton Mifflin, Boston, MA.

Anonymous (1895) 'Bicycles and bicycle riders', *Public Opinion*, pp. 342–343.

Anonymous (1897) 'Against bloomers and bicycles', *The New York Times*.

APEC (2015) *Follow-up Peer Review on Energy Efficiency in Thailand Final Report Bangkok, Thailand, Final Report for the APEC Energy Working Group*, December, Tokyo.

Appleyard, D., Gerson, M. and Lintell, M. (1981) *Livable Streets*, University of California Press, Berkeley, CA.

APTA; American Public Transportation Association (2016) 'The hidden transportation safety solution: Public transportation', September, www.apta.com/resources/reportsandpublications/Documents/APTA-Hidden-Traffic-Safety-Solution-Public-Transportation.pdf, accessed 14 November 2016.

Ardila Gómez, A. (2004) *Transit Planning in Curitiba and Bogotá: Roles in Interaction, Risk, and Change*, Doctoral Dissertation, MIT Press, Cambridge, MA, dspace.mit.edu/handle/1721.1/28791, accessed 24 August 2016.

Arieff A. (2016) 'Can a 700 M.P.H. Train in a Tube Be for Real?' *The New York Times*. 19 May. http://nyti.ms/1rVDg6G (accessed 25 July 2017)

Armstrong, D. and J. Guidera (2002) 'Rolling along: Lobbying campaign could determine fate of a hyped scooter – It is illegal on most sidewalks, but maker has influence; Will the Segway sell? – Wowing the U.S. engineer', *Wall Street Journal*, 1 March, retrieved from proquest.com 1 August 2016.

Arnstein, S. R. (1969) 'A ladder of citizen participation', *Journal of the American Institute of Planners*, vol 35, no 4, 216–224.

Arnstein, S. R. and Metcalf, E. I. (1976) *Effective Participation in Transportation Planning, Volume II, A Catalog of Techniques*, USDOT, Washington, DC.

Arrington, G. B. (2009) 'Portland's TOD evolution: From planning to lifestyle', in C. Curtis, J. L. Renne and L. Bertolini (eds) *Transit Oriented Development: Making It Happen*, Ashgate, Surrey, UK.

Arrufat, E. (2013) 'Elon Musk's "Hyperloop" ultra-fast travel system to be unveiled', *Digital Journal*, 12 August, www.digitaljournal.com/article/356346, accessed 17 January 2014.

Ashurst, J. and Wagner, B. (2015) 'Injuries following Segway personal transporter accidents: Case report and review of the literature', *Western Journal of Emergency Medicine*, vol XVI, no 5, 693–695.

Association for Safe International Road Travel (ASIRT) (undated) 'Annual global road crash statistics', asirt.org/initiatives/informing-road-users/road-safety-facts/road-crash-statistics, accessed 25 March 2016.

Atkinson, C. (2014) 'Uber hooks up with Blade choppers for Hamptons trips', *New York Post*, 30 June, nypost.com/2014/06/30/uber-car-service-hooks-up-with-blade-choppers-for-hamptons-trips/, accessed 20 August 2016.

Austen, B. (2011) 'The megabus effect', *Bloomberg Businessweek*, 7 April, www.bloomberg.com/news/articles/2011-04-07/the-megabus-effect, accessed 20 August 2016.

Automotive Digest (2009) 'World automobile population 2005–2020', *Automotive Digest*, www.automotivedigest.com/content/displayArticle.aspx?a=55782, accessed 14 September 2009.

Autostadt, https://en.wikipedia.org/wiki/Autostadt, accessed 18 July 2016.

Badami, M. G. (2009) 'Urban transport policy as if people and the environment mattered: Pedestrian accessibility the first step'. *Economic and Political Weekly*, vol XLIV, no 33, 43–51.

Badstuber, N. and Smales, C. (2013) 'London overground – A success story: Transforming neglected urban railway infrastructure to meet capacity and connectivity demands', ro.uow.edu.au/cgi/viewcontent.cgi?article=1004&context=isngi2013, accessed 18 August 2016.

Bagaeen, S. and Uduku, O. (2012) *Gated Communities: Social Sustainability in Contemporary and Historical Gated Developments*. Routledge, Oxford.

Baillieu Knight Frank (1991) 'The wasting of the CBD: A paper on infrastructure use and employment in Melbourne', *BKF Research*, Melbourne, Australia.

Baker, K. (2014) '21st century limited: The lost glory of America's railroads', *Harpers Magazine*, July, harpers.org/archive/2014/07/21st-century-limited/, accessed 26 July 2016.

Banister, D. (2000) 'Sustainable urban development and transport: A Eurovision for 2020', *Transport Reviews*, vol 20, no 1, 113–130.

Banister, D. (2008) 'The sustainable mobility paradigm', *Transport Policy*, vol 15, 73–80.

Banister, D. (2010) 'The trilogy of distance, speed and time', *Journal of Transport Geography*, vol 19, no 2011, 950–959.

Banjo, S. (2013) 'Rampant Returns Plague E-Retailers', *Wall Street Journal*, 22 December, www.wsj.com/articles/SB10001424052702304773104579270260683155216, accessed 13 November 2016.

Bank of America, Greenbelt Alliance, the California Resources Agency and the Low Income Housing Fund (1995) *Beyond Sprawl: New Patterns of Growth to Fit the New California*, Bank of America (Environmental Division), San Francisco, CA.

Barber, B. R. (1984) *Strong Democracy: Participatory Politics for a New Age*, University of California Press, Berkeley, CA.

Barber, J. (1995) 'Mending our lovely metros', *The Globe and Mail*, Focus Section D, 9 September.

Barker, T. and Gerhold, D. (1995) *The Rise and Rise of Road Transport, 1700–1990*, Cambridge University Press, Cambridge, UK.

Barnes & Noble (2016) 'Car and vehicle racing – teen fiction', www.barnesandnoble.com/b/books/sports-teen-fiction/car-and-vehicle-racing-teen-fiction/_/N-29Z8q8Z1a38, accessed 17 July 2016.

Barnes, R. (2010) 'NASCAR: From back alleys to big bucks', May 20, www.investopedia.com/financial-edge/0510/nascar-from-back-alleys-to-big-bucks.aspx, accessed 18 July 2016.

Barter, P. A. (1999) *An International Comparative Perspective on Urban Transport and Urban Form in Pacific Asia: Responses to the Challenge of Motorisation in Dense Cities*, PhD thesis, Murdoch University, Perth, Australia.

Barter, P. A. (2000) 'Urban transport in Asia: Problems and prospects for high-density cities', *Asia–Pacific Development Monitor*, vol 2, no 1, 33–66.

Barthélémy, S. (2016) 'Bordeaux Métropole esquisse ses transports pour 2026', *Rue89 Bordeaux*, 23 January, rue89bordeaux.com/2016/01/bordeaux-metropole-esquisse-ses-transports-pour-2026/, accessed 16 September 2016.

Bassett, D., Pucher, J., Buehler, R., Thompson, D. and Crouter, S. (2008) 'Walking, cycling, and obesity rates in Europe, North America and Australia', *Journal of Physical Activity and Health*, vol 5, no 6, 795–814.

Bassett, D., Pucher, J., Buehler, R., Thompson, D. and Crouter, S. (2011) 'Active transportation and obesity in Europe, North America, and Australia', *ITE Journal*, vol 81, no 8, 24–28.

Batty, M., Chapman D., Evans, S., Haklay, M., Kueppers, S., Shiode, N., Smith, A. and Torrens, P. (2000) 'Visualizing the city: Communicating urban design to planners and decision-makers', *CASA Working Papers*, vol 26, Centre for Advanced Spatial Analysis, London, www.casa.ucl.ac.uk/publications/workingPaperDetail.asp?ID=26, accessed 15 June 2009.

Beatley, T. (2010) *Biophilic Cities: Integrating Nature into Urban Design and Nature*, Island Press, Washington, DC.

Beimborn, E. (2006) 'Transit technology alternatives', www4.uwm.edu/cuts/utp/techno.pdf, accessed 15 September 2009.

Beimborn, E., Kennedy, R. and Schaefer, W. (1995, 2006) *Inside the Blackbox: Making Transportation Models Work for Livable Communities. Environmental Defense Fund*, New York, NY.

Belasco, W. (1983) 'Motivatin' with Chuck Berry and Frederick Jackson Turner', in D. L. Lewis and L. Goldstein (eds) *The Automobile and American Culture*, University of Michigan Press, Ann Arbor, MI.

Bellis, M. (undated) 'The history of streetcars–cable cars: Streetcars and the first cable cars', http://inventors.about.com/library/inventors/blstreetcars.htm, accessed 14 July 2009.

Benfield, F. K. and Replogle, M. (2002) 'The roads more traveled: Sustainable transportation in America', *Environmental Law Review*, vol 32, 10633.

Benfield, K. (2012) 'Just how bad is noise pollution for our health?', www.citylab.com/design/2012/05/just-how-bad-noise-pollution-our-health/2008/, accessed 20 July 2016.

Bentley, I., Alcock, A., Murrain, P., McGlynn, S., and G. Smith (1985) *Responsive Environments: A Manual for Designers*, Architectural Press, London.

Berger, M. L. (2001) *The Automobile in American History and Culture: A Reference Guide*, Greenwood Press, Westport, CN.

Bertaud, A. (2003) 'The spatial organization of cities: Deliberate outcome or unforeseen consequence?', *World Development Report 2003: Dynamic Development in a Sustainable World*, World Bank, Washington, DC.

Berton, P. (1972) *The Great Railway* (Illustrated), McClleland and Stewart, Toronto, Canada.

Besser, L. M. and Dannenberg, A. L. (2005) 'Walking to public transit: Steps to help meet physical activity recommendations', *American Journal of Preventive Medicine*, vol 29, no 4, 273–280.

Betsey, C. L. (2014) 'Black-White differences in consumption: An update and some policy implications', *Revue of Black Political Economy*, vol 41, 259–270.

Bever, L. (2014) '"Text neck" is becoming an "epidemic"' and could wreck your spine", *Washington Post*, 20 November, www.washingtonpost.com/news/morning-mix/wp/2014/11/20/text-neck-is-becoming-an-epidemic-and-could-wreck-your-spine/, accessed 11 October 2016.

Bialick, A. (2015) 'Will Muni's largest service increase in decades have staying power?', 8 April, sf.streetsblog.org/2015/04/08/will-munis-largest-service-increase-in-decades-have-staying-power/, accessed 1 September 2016.

Bianco, M. J. (1998) 'Review of Kay, Jane Holtz, Asphalt Nation: How the automobile took over America and how we can take it back', *H-Urban, H-Net Reviews*, March, www.h-net.org/reviews/showrev.php?id=1826, accessed 16 September 2016.

Billington CyberSecurity (2016) 'Global automotive cybersecurity summit, 22 July 2016 Cobo Center, Detroit, MI', www.billingtoncybersecurity.com/global-automotive-cybersecurity-summit/, accessed 20 July 2016.

Birkland, T. A. (2005) *An Introduction to the Policy Process: Theories, Concepts, and Models of Public Policy Making*, ME Sharpe, Armonk, NY.

Blakely, E. J. and Snyder, M. G. (1999) *Fortress America: Gated Communities in the United States*. Brookings Institution Press, Washington, DC.

Blanchard, A. (ed.) (1919) *American Highway Engineer's Handbook*, J. Wiley, New York, NY.

Bly, P.H. and F.V. Webster, eds. (1980) *The Demand for Public Transport: Report of the International Collaborative Study of the Factors Affecting Public Transport Patronage*. Transport and Road Research Laboratory. Crowthorne, U.K.

Boisson de Chazournes, L. (undated) 'The Kyoto Protocol to the United Nations Framework Convention on Climate Change: Kyoto, 11 December 1997', https://unfccc.int/resource/docs/convkp/kpeng.pdf, accessed 16 June 2009.

Bonsor, K. (undated) 'How flying cars will work', auto.howstuffworks.com/flying-car1.htm, accessed 25 July 2016.

Bottles, S. (1987) *Los Angeles and the Automobile: The Making of the Modern City*, University of California Press, Berkeley, CA.

Boudette, N. E. (2016) 'For driverless cars, Citylike test sites offer the unpredictable', *The New York Times*, 4 June, nyti.ms/1ssx6Lr, accessed 5 June 2016.

Bower, J. L. and Christensen, C. M. (1995) 'Disruptive technologies: Catching the wave', *Harvard Business Review*, vol 73, no 1 (January–February), 43–53.

Bradbury, R. (1966) *The Pedestrian: A Fantasy in One Act*, Samuel French, New York, NY.

Bradbury, R. H. (1998) 'Sustainable development as a subversive issue', *Nature & Resources*, (UNESCO), www.tjurunga.com/thinking/papers/sustain.html, accessed 15 September 2009.

Bradbury, R. (2001) 'The pedestrian', in R. Bradbury (ed.) *A Medicine for Melancholy*, Perennial–HarperCollins, New York, NY (originally published in 7 August 1951 edition of *The Reporter*).

Bradley, M. and Kenworthy, J. (2012) 'Congestion offsets: Transforming cities by letting buses compete', *World Transport Policy and Practice*, vol 18, no 4, 46–69.

Brainerd, H. B. (1931) 'Airport-docks for New York', *Everyday Science and Mechanics*, November, blog.modernmechanix.com/airport-docks-for-new-york/, accessed 20 July 2016.

Brand, P and Dávila, J. D. (2011) 'Mobility innovation at the urban margins', *City*, vol 15, no 6, December, accessed 12 November 2016.

Bratzel, S. (1999) 'Conditions of success in sustainable urban transport policy – Policy change in relatively successful European cities', *Transport Reviews*, vol 19, no 2, 177–190.

Britton, E. (2009) 'The new mobility agenda', www.newmobility.org, accessed 1 October 2009.

Broaddus, A. (2010). 'Tale of two ecosuburbs in Freiburg, Germany: Encouraging transit and bicycle use by restricting parking provision. *Transportation Research Record: Journal of the Transportation Research Board*, vol 2187, 114–122.

Brög, W. and Erl, E. (2003) '(Auto) mobility in the conurbation: Is mobility dominated by the car?', *Socialdata*, www.socialdata.de/info/(Auto)%20Mobility%20in%20the%20Conurbation.pdf, accessed 15 September 2009.

Brown, J. R. and Thompson, G. L. (2008) 'Service orientation, bus–rail service integration, and transit performance examination of 45 U.S. metropolitan areas', *Transportation Research Record: Journal of the Transportation Research Board*, vol 2042, 82–89.

Brown, L. R. (2008) *Plan B 3.0: Mobilizing to Save Civilization* (Substantially Revised), W. W. Norton and Company, New York, NY.

Brown, S. F. (2010). Revolutionary RAIL. *Scientific American*, 302(5), 54–59.

Brown, W. (2004) '1950s Cadillac dreams involved more than cars', *Washington Post,* 12 November, pG02, www.washingtonpost.com/wp-dyn/articles/A46149-2004Nov12.html?nav=rss_business/columns/autos/carculture.

Bruch, C. (ed.) (2002) *The New 'Public': The Globalization of Public Participation*, Environmental Law Institute, Washington, DC, www.eli.org/sites/default/files/eli-pubs/d1205.pdf, accessed 13 June 2009.

Brustein, J. (2016) 'Uber and Lyft want to replace public buses', www.bloomberg.com/news/articles/2016-08-15/uber-and-lyft-want-to-replace-public-buses, accessed 16 August 2016.

Bruun, E. (2004) *Community Oriented Transit Best Practices*, Working Paper 1, Independent Assessment Study of District 2 Transit Services, Alameda–Contra Costa Transit District, Transit Resource Center, Oviedo, FL.

Bruun, E. (2007) 'The role of intelligent transportation systems', Chapter 4, *Better Public Transit Systems: Analyzing Investments and Performance,* APA Press, Chicago, IL.

Bruun, E. (2014) *Better Public Transit Systems: Analyzing Investments and Performance*, Routledge, London and New York.

Bruun, E. and M. Givoni (2015) 'Sustainable mobility: Six research routes to steer transport policy', *Nature*, vol 523, no 2 (July), 29–31.

Bruun, E. C. (2013) *Better Public Transit Systems: Analyzing Investments and Performance* 2nd edn, Routledge, New York, NY.

BTS (Bureau of Transportation Statistics) (2006) 'National Transportation Statistics 2006', U.S. Department of Transportation, Research and Innovative Technology Administration, Washington, DC, www.rita.dot.gov/bts/sites/rita.dot.gov.bts/files/publications/national_transportation_statistics/2006/pdf/entire.pdf, accessed 14 September 2009.

BTS (Bureau of Transportation Statistics), RITA (Research and Innovative Technology Administration) and U.S. Government (2002) 'Table 1–1: System mileage within the United States (statute miles)', www.bts.gov/publications/national_transportation_statistics/2002/html/table_01_01.html, accessed 15 July 2009.

Buchanan, C. (Head of Working Group) (1963) *Traffic in Towns: A Study of the Long Term Problems of Traffic in Urban Areas*, The Buchanan Report, Reports of the Steering Group and Working Group appointed by the Minister of Transport, HMSO, London.

Buehler, R. and Hamre, A. (2016) 'An examination of recent trends in multimodal travel behavior among American motorists', *International Journal of Sustainable Transportation*, vol 10, no 4, 354–364.

Buehler, R. and Pucher, J. (2009) 'Sustainable Transport that works: Lessons from Germany'. *World Transport Policy and Practice* vol 15, no 1, 13–46.

Buehler, R. and Pucher, J. (2011a) 'Making public transport financially sustainable', *Transport Policy*, vol 18, no 1, 126–138.

Buehler, R. and Pucher, J. (2011b) 'Sustainable transport in Freiburg: Lessons from Germany's environmental capital', *International Journal of Sustainable Transportation*, vol 5, no 1, 43–70.

Buehler, R., Pucher, J., Gerike, R. and Götschi, T. (2016) 'Reducing car dependence in the heart of Europe: Lessons from Germany, Austria, and Switzerland', *Transport Reviews*, dx.doi.org/10.1080/01441647.2016.1177799, accessed 24 August 2016.

Bullard, R. D. (2003) 'Addressing urban transportation equity in the United States', *Fordham Urban Law Journal*, vol 31, no 5, art 2.

Bullard, R. D. and Johnson, G. S. (eds), (1997) *Just Transportation: Dismantling Race and Class Barriers to Mobility*, New Society, Gabriola Island., Canada.

Bullard, R. D, Johnson, G. S. and Torres, A. O. (eds), (2004) *Highway Robbery: Transportation Racism and New Routes to Equity*, South End Press, Cambridge, MA.

Bürer, M.J., Goldstein, D. B. and Holtzclaw, J. (2004) 'Location efficiency as the missing piece of the energy puzzle: How smart growth can unlock trillion dollar consumer cost savings', *ACEEE Summer Study on Energy Efficiency in Buildings*, August, Asilomar, CA, citeseerx.ist. psu.edu/viewdoc/download?doi=10.1.1.579.8548&rep=rep1&type=pdf, accessed 20 July 2016.

Burningham, K., Barnett, J. and Thrush, D. (2006) 'The limitations of the NIMBY concept for understanding public engagement with renewable energy technologies: A literature review', School of Environment and Development, University of Manchester, geography.exeter.ac.uk/ beyond_nimbyism/deliverables/bn_wp1_3.pdf, accessed 17 September 2016.

Busbee, J. (2009) 'Wreck-filled Talladega ends in spectacular, terrifying fashion', sports. yahoo.com/nascar/blog/from_the_marbles/post/Wreck-filled-Talladega-ends-in-spectacular-terr?urn=nascar,159022 26 April, accessed 18 July 2016.

Bush, E. (2016) 'Uber, Lyft get OK to fetch passengers at airport', *The Seattle Times*, 30 March, www.seattletimes.com/seattle-news/transportation/uber-gets-ok-to-fetch-passengers-at-airport-starting-thursday/, accessed 16 August 2016.

Button, K. J. and Hensher, D. A. (eds) (2005) *Handbook of Transport Strategy, Policy and Institutions*, Elsevier, Oxford, UK.

Byrne, D. (2009) *Bicycle Diaries*, Viking, New York, NY.

Cairns, S., Hass-Klau, C. and Goodwin, P. (1998) *Traffic Impact of Highway Capacity Reductions: Assessment of the Evidence*, Landor, London.

Calthorpe, P. (1993) *The Next American Metropolis: Ecology and Urban Form*, Princeton Architectural Press, Princeton, NJ.

Calthorpe, P. (2010) *Urbanism in the Age of Climate Change*, Island Press, Washington, DC.

Campbell, H. and Marshall, R. (2000) 'Public involvement and planning: Looking beyond the one to the many', *International Planning Studies*, vol 5, no 3, 321–344.

Cappiello, D. (2014) 'Study: Fuels from corn waste not better than gas', *Associated Press*, 20 April.

Carlson, D. Wormser, L. and Ulberg, C. (1995) *At Road's End: Transportation and Land-Use Choices for Communities*, Island Press, Washington, DC.

Caro, R. (1975) *The Power Broker: Robert Moses and the Fall of New York*, Vintage, New York, NY.

Carriere, K. (2015) 'Best and worst automotive product placement', autoTrader.ca, 2 June, www.autotrader.ca/newsfeatures/20150602/best-and-worst-automotive-product-placement/ #XoDq6srJ2GIGpW5C.97, accessed 18 July 2016.

Cars 2. Dirs. Lasseter, John and Lewis, Brad. Walt Disney Pictures, Pixar Animation Studios, (2011). Animated Film.

CDC (Centers for Disease Control) (2006) U.S. Public Health Service (undated) stateofobesity.org/ rates/, nccd.cdc.gov/NPAO_DTM/IndicatorSummary.aspx?category=28&indicator=64&year= 2013&yearId=17, accessed 1 March 2016.

CDC (Centers for Disease Control) (2009) 'Recommended community strategies and measurements to prevent obesity in the United States', in *MMWR Recommendations and Reports*, 24 July, 58(RR07), www.cdc.gov/mmwr/preview/mmwrhtml/rr5807a1.htm, accessed 1 September 2009.

Center for Neighborhood Technology (CNT) (undated) 'Location efficiency hub', www.cnt.org/ projects/location-efficiency-hub, accessed 5 August 2016.

Cervero, R. (1986) *Suburban gridlock*, Rutgers Center for Urban Policy Research, New Brunswick, NJ.

Cervero, R. (1995) 'Sustainable new towns: Stockholm's rail served satellites', *Cities*, vol 12, no 1, 41–51.

Cervero, R. (1998) *The Transit Metropolis: A Global Inquiry*, Island Press, Washington, DC.

Cervero, R. and Landis, J. (1992) 'Suburbanization of jobs and the journey to work: A submarket analysis of commuting in the San Francisco Bay area', *Journal of Advanced Transportation*, vol 26, no 3, 275–297.

Chafe, Z. (2007) 'Transportation and communication', *Worldwatch Institute*, November, www.worldwatch.org/taxonomy/term/517, accessed 14 September 2009.

Chalodhorn, R., Grimes, D., Grochow, K., and Rao, R. (2010) 'Learning to walk by imitation in low-dimensional subspaces', *Advanced Robotics*, vol 24, no 1-2, 207–232.

Chesterton, G., Perris, G. and Garnett, E. (eds) (1903) *Leo Tolstoy*, Hodder and Stoughton, London.

Choi, S., Hansson, F., Kaas, H-W. and Newman, J. (2016) 'Capturing the advanced driver-assistance opportunity', *McKinsey and Company*, January, www.mckinsey.com/industries/automotive-and-assembly/our-insights/capturing-the-advanced-driver-assistance-systems-opportunity, accessed 20 July 2016.

Christensen, J. (2013) 'The hyperloop and the annihilation of space and time', *The New Yorker*, 20 August, www.newyorker.com/tech/elements/the-hyperloop-and-the-annihilation-of-space-and-time, accessed 21 May 2016.

Citizen Science Alliance (2016) 'What is the Citizen Science Alliance?', www.citizenscience alliance.org/, accessed 27 August 2016.

City of Boulder (2014) *TMP 2014: Transportation Master Plan*, City of Boulder, Boulder, CO.

Clark, N. (2015) 'Low U.S. rail spending leads to poor safety, experts say', *The New York Times*, May 20, nyti.ms/1KjiSmk, accessed 7 December 2015.

Clark, R. (2015) 'Elon Musk's hyperloop may be nothing more than a pipe dream', *Multibriefs*, August 24, exclusive.multibriefs.com/content/elon-musks-hyperloop-may-be-nothing-more-than-a-pipe-dream/transportation-technology-automotive, accessed 27 August 2015.

Clear Channel Outdoor, en.wikipedia.org/wiki/Clear_Channel_Outdoor, accessed 7 July 2016.

CNU (Congress for the New Urbanism) (undated) *Urban Thoroughfares Manual*, www.cnu.org/streets, accessed 11 July 2009.

Cochran, C. L. and Malone, E. F. (1999) *Public Policy: Perspectives and Choices*, McGraw–Hill, New York, NY.

Cohen, D. (2016) 'The deal that could hurt D.C. for 50 years', www.huffingtonpost.com/donald-cohen/the-deal-that-could-hurt_b_12030766.html, accessed 23 October 2016.

Cohen, J. (2008) 'Calming traffic on Bogotá's killing streets', *Science*, vol 319, no 5864, 742–743.

Cohen, S. A. and Gössling, S. (2015) 'A darker side of hypermobility', *Environment and Planning A*, vol 47, 1661–1679.

Collie, S. (2016) 'Production e-Go aircraft lands with first buyer', *GizMag*, 15 June, www.gizmag.com/e-go-aircraft/43858/, accessed 15 June 2016.

Conan Doyle, A. (1903/1920) 'The adventure of the solitary cyclist', in *The Complete Sherlock Holmes (Volume 2)*, Doubleday, Garden City, NY.

Condliffe, J. (2012) 'Folding city car is finally a reality', 26 January, http://gizmodo.com/5879489/mits-folding-city-car-is-finally-a-reality, accessed 3 November 2016.

Coogan, M. A., MarketSense Consulting LLC and Jacobs Consultancy (2008) 'Ground access to major airports by public transportation', Airport Cooperative Research Program (ACRP), Transportation Research Board (TRB), Washington, DC, onlinepubs.trb.org/onlinepubs/acrp/acrp_rpt_004.pdf, accessed 15 August 2016.

Cornish, A. (2014) 'To get their cars in films, automakers turn to a movie motor wrangler', *NPR*, 26 June, www.npr.org/templates/transcript/transcript.php?storyId=325909309, accessed 8 May 2016.

Corporations and Health (2015) 'Advertising Happy Meals to children—An interview with Jim Sargent', 12 March, corporationsandhealth.org/2015/03/12/advertising-happy-meals-to-children-an-interview-with-jim-sargent/, accessed 15 July 2016.

Cowan, R. (1993) 'The new urban design agenda', introduction and summary of the symposium of The Working Group on Urban Design, www.rudi.net/books/11737, accessed 14 May 2016.

Crawford J. H. (2002) *Carfree Cities*, International Books, Utrecht, The Netherlands.

Crawford J. H. (2009) *Carfree Design Manual*, International Books, Utrecht, The Netherlands.

Creutzig, F. (2016) 'Evolving narratives of low-carbon futures in transportation', *Transport Reviews*, vol 36, no 3, 341–360.

CST (Centre for Sustainable Transportation) (1998) *Sustainable Transportation Monitor*, no 1, Toronto, Ontario

Curtis, F. (undated) 'Climate change in the context of peak oil', www.e3network.org/Curtis_9.pdf, accessed 15 June 2009.

Dantz, C. (2015) 'Living in New Hampshire is easy to love: Why one woman calls the Granite State home', 12 June, www.howmoneywalks.com/living-in-new-hampshire-is-easy-to-love-why-one-woman-calls-the-granite-state-home/, accessed 1 August 2016.

Davidson, J. and Sweeney, M. (2003), *On the Move: Transportation and the American Story*, National Geographic, Washington, DC.

Davies, H. and Davies M.-H. (1982) *Holy Days and Holidays: The Medieval Pilgrimage to Compostela*, Bucknell University Press, Lewisburg, PA.

Davies, R. (1975) *The Age of Asphalt: The Automobile, the Freeway, and the Condition of Metropolitan America*, Lippincott, Philadelphia, PA.

Dávila, J. D. (2013) *Urban Mobility and Poverty: Lessons from Medellín and Soacha*, Development Planning Unit, UCL and Faculty of Architecture, Universidad Nacional de Colombia (Medellín campus), www.bartlett.ucl.ac.uk/dpu/metrocables/book, accessed 12 November 2016.

Davis, B., Dutzik, T. and Baxandall, P. (2012) *Transportation and the New Generation: Why Young People Are Driving Less and What it Means for Transportation Policy*, www.uspirg.org/sites/pirg/files/reports/Transportation%20%26%20the%20New%20Generation%20vUS_0.pdf, accessed 30 May 2016.

Davis, C., Wilburn, K. and Robinson, R. (eds) (1991) *Railway Imperialism*, Greenwood, Westport, CT.

Davis, M. (1990) *City of Quartz: Excavating the Future in Los Angeles*, Vintage, London.

Day, D. (1997) 'Citizen participation in the planning process: An essentially contested concept?', *Journal of Planning Literature*, vol 11, no 3, 412–434.

DB (Deutsche Bahn) (2016) 'Mobility-apps of Deutschen Bahn', www.bahn.de/p_en/view/booking/tickets-and-seats/mobile/mobility-apps.shtml, accessed 20 August 2016.

De Decker, K. (2013) 'High speed trains are killing the European railway network', *Low-tech Magazine*, December, www.lowtechmagazine.com/2013/12/high-speed-trains-are-killing-the-european-railway-network.html, accessed 24 December 2013.

Demerjian, D. (2008) 'UN wants us to fly less, teleconference more', *Wired*, www.wired.com/autopia/2008/07/un-wants-us-to/, accessed 6 July 2009.

Department for Planning and Infrastructure (2002a) *Sustainable Urban Design: Practical Fieldwork Project*, Government of Western Australia: Department for Planning and Infrastructure (in association with ISTP, Murdoch University and Mirvac Fini), Perth, Australia.

Department for Planning and Infrastructure (2002b) *Which suburbs work? A comparison between traditionally planned suburbs and conventional suburban development*, lecture given by Malcolm McKay, Urban Design and Major Places Unit, Department for Planning and Infrastructure, Perth, Australia.

Derry, T. and Williams, T. (1993) *A Short History of Technology: From the Earliest Times to A.D. 1900*, Dover, New York, NY.

Dery, M. (1995) 'Downsizing the future: Beyond blade runner, an interview with Mike Davis', *Future Noir 21-C*, no 3, 43–47, www.otthollo.de/JONA/.../Davis%20Downsizing%20the%20Future.pdf, accessed 15 September 2009.

DeSantis, N. (1939) 'Skyscraper airport for city of tomorrow', *Popular Science*, November, 70–71, blog.modernmechanix.com/skyscraper-airport-for-city-of-tomorrow/1/#mmGal, accessed 20 July 2016.

Dewey, J. (1920/1950) *Reconstruction in Philosophy*, New American Library, New York, NY.

Didik, F. (undated) 'History and directory of electric cars from 1834–1987', www.didik.com/ev_hist.htm, accessed 6 July 2009.

Dietz, T. and Stern, P. C. (eds) (2008) *Public Participation in Environmental Assessment and Decision Making: Panel on Public Participation in Environmental Assessment and Decision Making*, National Academies Press, Washington, DC, www.nap.edu/catalog.php?record_id=12434, accessed 17 June 2009.

Dilger, R. J. (2015) 'Federalism issues in surface transportation policy: A historical perspective', *Congressional Research Service 7-5700*, www.crs.gov, 8 December, www.fas.org/sgp/crs/misc/R40431.pdf, accessed 22 August 2016.

Dimitriou, H. (2013) *Urban Transport Planning: A Developmental Approach*, Routledge Revivals, London (originally published 1992).

Dobb, K. (undated) 'An alternative form of long distance cycling: The British Roads Records Association', www.randonneurs.bc.ca/history/an-alternative-form-of-long-distance-cycling_part-4.html, accessed 10 July 2009.

Dobruszkes, F., Dehon, C. and Givoni, M. (2014) 'Does European high-speed rail affect the current level of air services? An EU-wide analysis', *Transportation Research Part A*, vol 69, 461–475.

Dodson, J. and Sipe, N. (2006) 'Shocking the suburbs: Urban location, housing and oil vulnerability in the Australian city', Griffith University, Urban Research Program, Research Paper 8, www.98.griffith.edu.au/.../Dodson2006ShockingTheSuburbs_ATRF.pdf, accessed 14 September 2009.

Dodson, J and Sipe, N. (2014) 'Oil vulnerability scenarios and regional visioning in Australia: The South-East Queensland regional plan', in L. Bazzanella, L. Caneparo, F. Corsico, G. Roccasalva (eds), *The Future of Cities and Regions: Simulation, Scenario and Visioning, Governance and Scale*, Springer, London & New York, pp. 205–222.

Dougherty, C. (2015) 'California D.M.V. stops short of fully embracing driverless cars', *The New York Times*, December 16, nyti.ms/1k3xWcR, accessed 17 December 2016.

Dow Chemical Company (undated) 'Highway Hearing' (video) www.youtube.com/watch?v=XBEgxp69WLc

Doyle, A. (2007) 'Surging transport threatens EU Kyoto goals report', www.reuters.com/article/environmentNews/idUSL2669609620070227, accessed 16 June 2009.

Dryzek, J. S. (1990) *Discursive Democracy: Politics, Policy, and Political Science*, Cambridge University Press, Cambridge, UK.

Duane, C. (2010) 'Weston & pedestrian era walking contest rules', *Walking: The World On Foot & Online*, http://walkapedia.org/walking/reading/research/136-weston-a-pedestrian-era-walking-contest-rules.html, accessed 11 October 2016.

Dunham-Jones, E. and Williamson, J. (2011) *Retrofitting Suburbia: Urban Design Solutions for Redesigning Suburbs*, Wiley, Hoboken, NJ.

Dunn, R. (1989) *The Adventures of Ibn Battuta: A Muslim Traveler of the 14th Century*, University of California Press, Berkeley and Los Angeles, CA.

Durning, A. (2006–2010) 'The year of living car-lessly experiment', (series) *Sightline Institute*, www.sightline.org/series/the-year-of-living-car-lessly-experiment/, accessed 18 August 2016.

Ebiri, B. (2015) 'The 29 greatest car movies ever', www.vulture.com/2015/04/29-greatest-car-movies-ever.html, accessed 16 July 2016.

Economy-point.org (2006) 'Karl Drais', www.economy-point.org/k/karl-drais.html, accessed 9 July 2009.

Edner, S. M. and Arrington, G. B. (1985) *Urban Decision Making for Transportation Investment: Portland's Light Rail Transit Line*, U.S. Department of Transportation, Technology Sharing Program, Report No DOT-I-85-03, U.S. Government Printing office, Washington, DC.

Ellis, C. (2005) 'Lewis Mumford and Norman Bel Geddes: The highway, the city and the future', *Planning Perspectives*, vol 20, no1, 51–68.

Engler, G. (2009) 'A critical mess? Yes it is. If we lock up all those responsible for current traffic problems, the traffic jams would be gone', *Vancouver Sun*, 15 August.

Engwicht, D. (1993) *Reclaiming Our Cities & Towns: Better Living with Less Traffic*, New Society, Gabriola Island, Canada.

Engwicht, D. (ed.) (1989) *Traffic Calming: The Solution to Urban Traffic and a New Vision for Neighborhood Livability*, CART (Citizens Advocating Responsible Transportation), Ashgrove, Australia, reprinted (1993) STOP (Sensible Transportation Options for People), Tigard, OR.

Engwicht, D. (2005) *Mental Speed Bumps*, Envirobooks, Sydney, Australia.

Eno Transportation Foundation (undated) 'William Phelps Eno', www.enotrans.com/index.asp?Type=B_EV&SEC={59B58976-4BBF-43AF-9CC0-14664D065FD5}, accessed 11 July 2009.

EPRS: European Parliament Research Service (2016) 'Briefing', January, www.europarl.europa.eu/RegData/etudes/BRIE/2016/573902/EPRS_BRI(2016)573902_EN.pdf, accessed 20 July 2016.

Epstein, P. R., et al. (2011) 'Full cost accounting for the life cycle of coal', in R. Costanza, K. Limburg, and I. Kubiszewski (eds), *Ecological Economics Reviews*, Annals of the New York Academy of Sciences, 1219, 73–98. http://onlinelibrary.wiley.com/doi/10.1111/j.1749-6632.2010.05890.x/full, accessed 13 November 2016.

Erik (2011) 'Top 40 product placements of all time: 10-1', *Brands & Films*, 13 Jan, brandsandfilms.com/2011/01/top-40-product-placements-of-all-time-10-1/, accessed 18 July 2016.

Eriksen, L. (2015) 'The innovative delivery system transforming Gothenburg's roads', *The Guardian*, 18 November, www.theguardian.com/cities/2015/nov/18/innovative-delivery-system-transforming-gothenburg-roads, accessed 3 November 2016.

Erlichman, H. (2006) Camino del Norte: How a Series of Watering Holes, Fords, and Dirt Trails Evolved into Interstate 35 in Texas, Texas A&M Press, College Station, TX.

Evans, A. W. (1991) 'Are urban bus services natural monopolies?', *Transportation,* vol 18, no 2, 131–150.

Ewing, J. (2016) 'Volkswagen not alone in flouting pollution limits' (International Edition), *The New York Times,* 9 June, nyti.ms/1XIXMVG, accessed 20 July 2016.

Ewing, R., Brownson, R. C., and Berrigan, D. (2006) 'Relationship between urban sprawl and weight of United States youth', *American Journal of Preventive Medicine,* vol 3, no 6, 464–474, doi.org/10.1016/j.amepre.2006.08.020, accessed 20 July 2016.

Ewing, R., Meakins, G., Hamidi, S. and Nelson, A. C. (2014) 'Relationship between urban sprawl and physical activity, obesity, and morbidity – update and refinement', *Health & Place,* vol 26, 118–126, www.sciencedirect.com/science/article/pii/S135382921300172X, accessed 1 March 2016.

Face the Facts USA, www.facethefactsusa.org/facts/93-percent-of-us-transport-remains-reliant-on-oil (accessed 22 July 2017)

Fagnant, D.J. and K. Kockelman (2015) 'Preparing a nation for autonomous vehicles: opportunities, barriers and policy recommendations', *Transportation Research Part A,* vol 77, 167–181.

Falconer, R., Newman, P. and Giles-Corti, B. (2010) 'Is practice aligned with the principles? Implementing new urbanism in Perth, Western Australia', *Transport Policy,* vol 17, no 5, 287–294.

Fallows, J. (2001) Freedom of the Skies. *The Atlantic,* vol 287, no 6, 37–49.

Falola, T. and Warnock, A. (2007) *Encyclopedia of the Middle Passage,* Greenwood, Westport, CT.

Farr, D. (2013) *Mustang: Fifty Years: Celebrating America's Only True Pony Car* (foreword by Edsel B. Ford), Motorbooks, Minneapolis, MN.

Felau, G. (2006) *The Recumbent Bicycle,* Out Your Backdoor Press, Williamston, MI.

FHWA (Federal Highway Administration) (2006) 'Revised Apportionment of Fiscal Year (FY) 2006 Surface Transportation Program Funds', U.S. Department of Transportation, www.fhwa.dot.gov/, accessed 1 September 2009.

FHWA (Federal Highway Administration) and USDOT (U.S. Department of Transportation) (undated) 'Teleconferencing', www.fhwa.dot.gov/REPORTS/PITTD/teleconf.htm, accessed 4 July 2009.

Field, S. (2014) 'Case study: Vauban Freiburg, Germany', in *Europe's Vibrant New Low Car(bon) Communities,* Institute for Transportation and Development Policy (ITDP), New York, pp95–106, www.itdp.org/wp-content/uploads/2014/07/26.-092211_ITDP_NED_Vauban.pdf, accessed 18 September 2016.

Fischer, F. (1990) *Technocracy and the Politics of Expertise,* Sage Publications, Newbury Park, CA.

Fletcher, K. (2008) 'The pre-history of the motor car, 1550–1850', an exhibition at the ABA antiquarian book fair, The Assembly Rooms, George Street, Edinburgh, www.aba.org.uk/edinexhib.pdf (14/15 March 2008 description) and www.aba.org.uk/edinexhibcat1.pdf (full exhibit description), accessed 11 July 2009.

Flightless Travel (undated) *Cargo Ship Travel,* www.flightlesstravel.com/plan/cargo-ships/

Flink, J. J. (1975) *The Car Culture,* MIT Press, Cambridge, MA.

Flink, J. J. (1988) *The Automobile Age,* MIT Press, Cambridge, MA.

Flint, J. (2014) 'TV networks load up on commercials', *Los Angeles Times,* 12 May, http://touch.latimes.com/#section/-1/article/p2p-80166285/, accessed 7 December 2016.

Flores, A. (2002) 'Tlalpan neighbourhood committees: A true participatory option', in P. McLaverty (ed.) *Public Participation and Innovations in Community Governance,* Ashgate, Aldershot, UK.

Florida, R. (2002) 'The rise of the creative class: Why cities without gays and rock bands are losing the economic development race', *Washington Monthly,* www.washingtonmonthly.com/features/2001/0205.florida.html, accessed 15 September 2009.

Florida, R. (2005) *Cities and the Creative Class,* Routledge, New York, NY.

FlyerTalk Forums (2010) 'Ford MyKey deactivation', www.flyertalk.com/forum/national-emerald-club/1143383-ford-mykey-deactivation-2.html, accessed 18 July 2016.

Forester, J. (1989) *Planning in the Face of Power,* University of California Press, Berkeley, CA.

Fountain, H. (2016) 'A slow ride toward the future of public transportation', *The New York Times,* November 4, http://nyti.ms/2elCA3t, accessed 11 November 2016.

Fraade, J. (2015) 'Driverless cars won't save Los Angeles', 12 December, america.aljazeera.com/opinions/2015/12/driverless-cars-wont-save-los-angeles.html, accessed 12 December 2015.

Francois, C. (2014) 'Self-driving cars will turn surveillance woes into a mainstream worry', *WIRED.com*, 30 May, www.wired.com/2014/05/self-driving-cars-will-turn-surveillance-woes-into-a-mainstream-issue/, accessed 27 June 2016.

Frank L., Engelke P. and Schmid T. (2003) *Health and Community Design: The Impact of the Built Environment on Physical Activity*, Island Press, Washington, DC.

Frayer, L. and Cater, F. (2015) 'How a folding electric vehicle went from car of the future to "obsolete"', November 5, www.npr.org/sections/alltechconsidered/2015/11/05/454693583/how-a-folding-electric-vehicle-went-from-car-of-the-future-to-obsolete, accessed 3 November 2016.

Freemark, Y. (2009) 'Despite extraordinary ridership, Vancouver's New Canada line is suffering', www.thetransportpolitic.com/2009/11/17/despite-extraordinary-ridership-vancouvers-new-canada-line-is-suffering/, accessed 5 September 2016.

Freund, P. and Martin, G. (1993) *The Ecology of the Automobile*, Black Rose Books, Montreal, Quebec, Canada.

Friedman, D., Bratvold, D., Mirsky, S., Kaiser, G., Schaudies, P., Bolz, E., Castor, R. and Latham, F. (2006) *A Guide to Transportation's Role in Public Health Disasters*, NCHRP Report 525, Transportation Research Board, Washington, DC, www.trb.org/publications/nchrp/nchrp_rpt_525v10.pdf, accessed 15 July 2009.

Friedman, T. (2007) 'No, no, no, don't follow us', *The New York Times*, 4 November, nyti.ms/1LpiuEX, accessed 23 July 2016.

Fruin, J. J. (1971) *Pedestrian Planning and Design*, Metropolitan Association of Urban Designers and Environmental Planners, New York, NY.

Gakenheimer, R. (ed.) (1978) *The Automobile and the Environment: An International Perspective*, MIT Press, Cambridge, MA.

Gambino, M. (2009) 'A salute to the wheel', June 17, www.smithsonianmag.com/science-nature/a-salute-to-the-wheel-31805121/?no-ist, accessed 17 July 2016.

Gao, Y. and Kenworthy, J. (2016) 'China' In: D. Pojani and D. Stead (eds), *The Urban Transport Crisis in Emerging Economies*, pp. 33–58, Springer, Cham, Switzerland.

Gao, Y., Kenworthy, J. and Newman, P. (2015) 'Growth of a giant: A historical and current perspective on the Chinese automobile industry', *World Transport Policy and Practice* vol 21, no 2, 40–55.

Garreau, J. (1991) *Edge City: Life on the New Frontier,* Doubleday, New York, NY.

Gehl, J. (1987) *Life Between Buildings: Using Public Space*, Island Press, Washington, DC.

Gehl, J. (2010) *Cities for People*, Island Press, Washington, DC.

Gehl, J. and Gemzøe, L. (2000) *New City Spaces*, Danish Architectural Press, Copenhagen, Denmark.

Gehl, J. and Gemzøe, L. (2004) *Public Spaces, Public life*, Danish Architectural Press, Copenhagen, Denmark.

Gehl, J., Modin, A. Wittenmark, J. Grassow, L. Matan, A. Hagströmer, E. Bernado, L. and Enhörning, J. (2009) *Perth 2009: Public Spaces and Public Life: Study Report*, City of Perth/Gehl Architects, Perth, Australia and Copenhagen, Denmark.

Gehl, J., Mortensen, H., Ducourtial, P., Duckett, I. S., Nielsen, L. H., Nielsen, J. M. R., Adams, R., Rymer, R., Rayment, J., Moore, R. and Campbell, A. (2004) *Places for People: Study Report*, City of Melbourne/Gehl Architects, Melbourne, Australia and Copenhagen, Denmark.

Geisel, T. S. (a.k.a. Dr Seuss) (1971) *The Lorax*, Random House, New York, NY.

Gerston, L. N. (1997) *Public Policy Making: Process and Principles*, M. E. Sharpe, Armonk, NY.

Gifford, J. (2003) *Flexible Urban Transportation*, Elsevier, Oxford, UK.

Gil, A., Calado, H. and Bentz, J. (2011) 'Public participation in municipal transport planning processes – the case of the sustainable mobility plan of Ponta Delgada, Azores, Portugal', *Journal of Transport Geography*, vol 19, no 6, 1309–1319, citeseerx.ist.psu.edu/viewdoc/download?doi=10.1.1.473.8032&rep=rep1&type=pdf, accessed 26 August 2016.

Gilbert, R. and Perl, A. (2008 and 2010) *Transport Revolutions: Moving People and Freight without Oil*, Earthscan, London.

Gilbert, R. and Wiederkehr, P. (eds) (2002) *Policy Instruments for Achieving Environmentally Sustainable Transport*, Organisation for Economic Co-operation and Development, Paris.

Giles-Corti, B., Ryan, K. and Foster, S. (2012) *Increasing Density in Australia - Maximizing the Health Benefits and Minimizing Harm: Report*, National Heart Foundation, Canberra, Australia.

Giuliano, G. and Small, K. A. (1993) 'Is the journey to work explained by urban structure?', *Urban Studies,* vol 30, no 9, 1485–1500.

Givoni, M. and Banister, D. (2010) *Integrated Transport: From Policy to Practice,* Routledge, Taylor and Francis, London and New York, NY.

Glazebrook, G.P. de T. (1964) *A History of Transportation in Canada, Volumes 1 & 2,* Carleton University Press, Ottawa, Canada.

GMC (1940) *Futurama,* GM Corporation, U.S., acquired through InterLibrary Loan: OCLC Number 4920548, Wesleyan University, lender, catalogue number 607.34 G286f.

Goddard, S. (1996) *Getting There: The Epic Struggle between Road and Rail in the American Century,* University of Chicago Press, Chicago, IL.

Goddard, S. (2000) *Colonel Albert Pope and his American Dream Machine: The Life and Times of a Bicycle Tycoon Turned Automotive Pioneer,* McFarland, Jefferson, NC.

GoEuro (undated) '14 European flights that are actually faster by train', www.goeuro.co.uk/travel/europe-travel-planner, accessed 25 July 2016.

Goldstein, L. (1998) 'The automobile and American poetry', in D. L. Lewis and L. Goldstein (eds) *The Automobile and American Culture,* University of Michigan Press, Ann Arbor, MI.

Gollagher, M. and Hartz-Karp, J. (2013) 'The role of deliberative collaborative governance in achieving sustainable cities'. *Sustainability* vol 5, 2343–2326.

Gompertz, L. (1851) *Mechanical Inventions and Suggestions on Land and Water Locomotion, Tooth Machinery, and Various Other Branches of Theoretical and Practical Mechanics,* 2nd edn, W. Horsell, London (Original from the University of Michigan, digitized 8 September 2006), http://books.google.com/books?id=fJQPAAAAMAAJ, accessed 24 May 2009.

Goodwin, P. E., Hallett, S., Kenny, F. and Stokes, G. (1991) *Transport: The New Realism,* Transport Studies Unit, Oxford University Press, Oxford, UK.

Gordon, P., Kumar, A. and Richardson, H. W. (1989) 'The influence of metropolitan spatial structure on commuting time', *Journal of Urban Economics,* vol 26, no 2, 138–151.

Gordon, P., Richardson, H. W. and Jun, M-J. (1991) 'The commuting paradox evidence from the top twenty', *Journal of the American Planning Association,* vol 57, no 4, 416–420.

Gorz, A. (1973) 'The social ideology of the motorcar', *Le Sauvage,* September–October, rts.gn.apc.org/socid.htm, accessed 1 September 2009.

Gössling, S., Schröder, M., Späth, P. and Freytag, T. (2016) Urban Space Distribution and Sustainable Transport. *Transport Reviews* vol 36, no 5, 659–679.

GPS.gov (2016) 'How to report residential truck traffic due to improper route suggestions', www.gps.gov/support/user/mapfix/truck-traffic/, accessed 23 July 2016.

Graham, S. and Marvin S. (2001) *Splintering Urbanism: Networked Infrastructures, Technological Mobilities and the Urban Condition.* Routledge, Oxford, UK.

Grava, S. (2003) *Urban Transportation Systems: Choices for Communities,* McGraw Hill, New York, NY.

Green Car Congress (2015) 'Largest ultra-fast EV charging station goes live in Beijing: Supporting electric buses out of Xiaoying Terminal', 7 December, www.greencarcongress.com/2015/12/20151207-xiaoying.html, accessed 23 July 2016.

Green City Freiburg (2013) 'Quartier Vauban', www.freiburg.de/pb/site/Freiburg/get/params_E-1604864046/647919/Infotafeln_Vauban_en.pdf, accessed 18 September 2016.

Grescoe, Taras (2016) 'The dirty truth about "clean diesel"', *The New York Times,* 2 January, nyti.ms/1ZGzedT, accessed 23 July 2016.

Grush, B. and J. Niles (2016) 'Manifesto for the end of driving', endofdriving.org/manifesto-for-the-end-of-driving/, in progress, accessed 20 July 2016.

GTZ (2003) *Sustainable Transportation: A Sourcebook for Policy-Makers in Developing Countries,* Sustainable Urban Transport Project, www.sutp.org, accessed 15 September 2009.

Guerrero, A. (2015) 'National plutocrat radio: Corporate one-percenters dominate NPR affiliates' boards', *Fairness & Accuracy in Reporting (FAIR),* 2 July, fair.org/home/national-plutocrat-radio/, accessed 15 July 2016.

Gunderson, A. G. (1995) *The Environmental Promise of Democratic Deliberation,* University of Wisconsin Press, Madison, WI.

Gutfreund, O. (2004) *Twentieth-Century Sprawl: Highways and the Reshaping of the American Landscape,* Oxford University Press, New York, NY

Haines, A. (2006) 'Sustainable communities: Lessons from Wisconsin and Sweden', *Land Use Tracker,* vol 6, no 2, Center for Land Use Education, www.sustaindane.org/Pages/ecomunicipality_where.htm, accessed 13 June 2009.

Hairulsyah (2013) 'The influence of public participation on sustainable transportation and regional development in Medan', *Indonesian Journal of Geography*, vol 45, no 1, (June) 62–79, jurnal.ugm.ac.id/ijg/article/view/2407, accessed 26 August 2016.

Hall, D. (2008) 'Transport, tourism and leisure', in R. Knowles, J. Shaw and I. Docherty (eds) *Transport Geographies: Mobilities, Flows and Spaces*, Blackwell, Oxford, UK.

Hall, P. (1988) *Cities of Tomorrow: An Intellectual History of Urban Planning and Design in the Twentieth Century*, Basil Blackwell, Oxford, UK.

Hall, P. (1998) *Cities in Civilization*, Pantheon, New York, NY.

Halpern, S. (2016) 'Our driverless future', *The New York Review of Books*, 24 November, www.nybooks.com/articles/2016/11/24/driverless-intelligent-cars-road-ahead/, accessed 11 November 2016.

Hamer, M. (1987) *Wheels Within Wheels: A Study of the Road Lobby*, Routledge and Kegan Paul, London.

Hamilton-Wentworth Regional Municipality (1997) 'Summary report, VISION 2020 sustainable community initiative', March, www2.hamilton.ca/NR/rdonlyres/EC58DE3E-AF99-4F9B-8877-76E480FE5D3E/0/VISION2020Overview97.pdf, accessed 27 August 2016.

Hanes, S. (2015) 'The new "cool" cities for millennials', *The Christian Science Monitor*, 1 February, www.csmonitor.com/USA/Society/2015/0201/The-new-cool-cities-for-Millennials, accessed 15 September 2016.

Hanson, S. and Giuliano, G. (eds) (2004) *The Geography of Urban Transportation*, 3rd edn, Guilford Press, New York, NY.

Hardin, G. (1968) 'The Tragedy of the Commons'. *Science*, vol 162, no 3859, 1243–1248.

Haskins, C. H. (1971) *The Renaissance of the Twelfth Century*, Harvard University Press, Cambridge, MA.

Hass-Klau, C., Crampton, G., Biereth, C. and Deutsch, V. (2003) *Bus or Light Rail: Making the Right Choice – A Financial, Operational and Demand Comparison of Light Rail, Guided Buses, Busways and Bus Lanes*, Environmental and Transport Planning, Brighton, UK.

Havlick, S. (2004) *TDM in Boulder: A Town–Gown Partnership*, Powerpoint presentation, The University of Colorado, Boulder, CO.

Hawkins, A.J. (2016) 'How to build a Hyperloop'. The Verge. www.theverge.com/2016/2/3/10904424/hyperloop-design-competition-report-texas-elon-musk (accessed 25 July 2017)

Healey, J. R. (2009) 'Obama's auto faux pas leads to history lesson', *USA TODAY*, 24 February, www.usatoday.com/money/autos/2009-02-25-obama-claim-daimler-differs_N.htm, accessed 8 May 2009.

Health Canada (2006) *It's Your Health – Obesity*, www.hc-sc.gc.ca/hl-vs/iyh-vsv/life-vie/obes-eng.php, accessed 1 September 2009.

Health Canada (2016) *Eat Well and Be Active Educational Toolkit(s)*, www.hc-sc.gc.ca/fn-an/food-guide-aliment/educ-comm/toolkit-trousse/plan-5-eng.php, accessed 8 May 2016.

Heikkilä S. (2014) 'Mobility as a service – a proposal for action for the public administration: Case Helsinki', Thesis, Aalto University, MS, aaltodoc.aalto.fi/bitstream/handle/123456789/13133/master_Heikkilä_Sonja_2014.pdf?sequence=1, accessed 28 October 2015.

Herlihy, D. V. (1992) 'The bicycle story', *Invention and Technology*, vol 7, no 4, 48–59.

Herlihy, D. V. (2004) *Bicycle: The History*, Yale University Press, New Haven, CT, and London.

Hey, K. (1983) 'Cars and films in American culture, 1929–1959', in D. L. Lewis and L. Goldstein (eds) *The Automobile and American Culture*, University of Michigan Press, Ann Arbor, MI.

High Rise Facilities (2013) 'High-rise car elevators allow residents to have an attached private garage', *High Rise Facilities,* April 22, highrisefacilities.com/high-rise-car-elevators-allow-residents-to-have-an-attached-private-garage/, accessed 18 July 2016.

Hillegas, J. V. (2004) ' "Pushing forward with the determination of the machine age": Planning and building Interstate 5 Bellingham, WA, 1945–1966', *Journal of the Whatcom County Historical Society,* Special Edition Bellingham Centennial, Bellingham, WA.

Hillman, M., Adams, J. and Whitelegg, J. (1990) *One False Move: A Study of Children's Independent Mobility,* Policy Studies Institute (PSI), London.

Hiltzik, M. (2014) 'How PBS sold its soul to a billionaire donor', *Los Angeles Times,* articles.latimes.com/print/2014/feb/17/business/la-fi-mh-how-pbs-soldr-20140217, accessed 18 July 2016.

Hindley, G. (1971) *A History of Roads*, Peter Davies, London.

Hoag, J. (2012) 'Hack your ride: Cheat codes and workarounds for your car's tech annoyances', 14 March, lifehacker.com/5893227/hack-your-ride-cheat-codes-and-workarounds-for-your-cars-tech-annoyances, accessed 18 July 2016.

Hodge, G. and Gordon, D. L. A. (2014) *Planning Canadian Communities*, 6th edn, Nelson Education, Toronto, Canada.

Holtzclaw, J. (1994) 'Using residential patterns and transit to decrease auto dependence and costs', *Natural Resources Defense Council*, www.nrdc.org/sites/default/files/sma_09121401a.pdf, accessed 10 August 2016.

Holtzclaw, J., Clear, R., Dittmar, H. Goldstein, D. and Haas, P. (2002) 'Location efficiency: Neighborhood and socio-economic characteristics determine auto ownership and use – studies in Chicago, Los Angeles and San Francisco', *Transportation Planning and Technology*, vol 25, no 1, 1–27.

Hook, W. (2005) *Training Course on Non-Motorized Transport*, GTZ, Eschborn, Germany.

Hotten, R. (2015) 'Volkswagen: The scandal explained', *BBC News*, 10 December, www.bbc.com/news/business-34324772, accessed 25 March 2016.

Hoyle, B. and Knowles, R. (eds) (1998) *Modern Transport Geography*, 2nd edn, John Wiley and Sons, Chichester, UK.

Hudda, N. and Fruin, S. (2016) 'International airport impacts to air quality: Size and related properties of large increases in ultrafine particle number concentrations', *Environmental Science & Technology*, vol 50, no 7, 3362–3370.

Hudda, N. Gould, T., Hartin, K., Larson, T., and Fruin, S. (2014) 'Emissions from an international airport increase particle number concentrations 4-fold at 10 km downwind', *Environmental Science & Technology*, vol 48, no 12, 6628–6635.

Hudson, S., Hudson, D. and J. Peloza (2008) 'Meet the parents: A parents' perspective on product placement in children's films', *Journal of Business Ethics*, vol 80, no 2, 289–304.

Huffman, J.P. and M. Magrath (2013) 'The 100 greatest movie and TV cars of all time: Hollywood's real superstars', 29 July, www.edmunds.com/car-reviews/features/the-100-greatest-movie-and-tv-cars-of-all-time.html, accessed 18 July 2016.

Hughes, P. (1974) 'The sacred rac," in J. C. Millar (ed.) *Focusing on Global Poverty and Development*, Overseas Development Council, Washington, DC, pp. §357–358.

Hughes, R. (2011) *Rome: A Cultural, Visual, and Personal History*, Alfred A. Knopf, New York, NY.

Hume, B. (webmaster) (undated) ' "The invention of the modern automobile": Chronology of the history of science', campus.udayton.edu/~hume/Automobile/auto.htm, accessed 6 July 2009.

Hummel, T., et al. (2011) 'Advanced driver assistance systems: An investigation of their potential safety benefits based on an analysis of insurance claims in German', *GDV-UDV*, German Insurance Association Insurers Accident Research, udv.de/sites/default/files/tx_udvpublications/RR_12__fas.pdf, accessed 20 July 2016.

Hunter, M. (2011) 'Shake it, baby, shake it: Consumption and the new gender relation in hip-hop', *Sociological Perspectives*, vol 54, no 1, 15–36.

Huttman, G. (ed.) (2006) 'Karl Drais – the new biography', www.karl-drais.de/en_biography.pdf, accessed 24 May 2009.

Huurdeman, A. (2003) *The Worldwide History of Telecommunications*, Wiley Blackwell, New York, NY.

Hyatt, J. (2005) 'Post-event narrative: Towards car-free cities VI – Bogotá, Columbia', http://carfreeBogotá.blogspot.com/2006/10/post-event-narrative.html, accessed 23 June 2009.

Hyslop, J. (1984) *The Inka Road System*, Academic Press, Orlando, FL.

iHeartMedia, en.wikipedia.org/wiki/IHeartMedia, accessed 7 July 2016.

Illich, I. (1973) *Tools for Conviviality*, Calder and Boyars, London.

Illich, I. (1976) *Energy and Equity*, Marion Boyars, London.

IMCDB (Internet Movie Cars Database), www.imcdb.org/makes.php, accessed 16 July 2016. *Who Framed Roger Rabbit?* Dir. Zemeckis, Robert. Touchstone Pictures (1988).

Indiantelevision.com (2008) 'GM to launch new TVC for Chevy: Announces "cashless ownership"', www.indiantelevision.com/mam/headlines/y2k8/mar/marmam52.php, accessed 15 August 2009.

Infrastructure Australia, Major Cities Unit (2010) 'Liveability of Australian cities', in *State of Australian Cities 2010*, infrastructure.gov.au/infrastructure/pab/soac/2010.aspx, accessed 20 July 2016.

Innes, J. (1995) 'Planning theory's emerging paradigm: Communicative action and interactive practice', *Journal of Planning Education and Research*, vol 14, no 3, 183–189

Ipsos MORI (2016) 'The future of driving: Five ways connected cars will changeyour life', 14 June, www.ipsos-mori.com/newsevents/ca/1776/The-future-of-driving-Five-ways-connected-cars-will-change-your-life.aspx, accessed 7 July 2016.

Iron Gate Motor Condos, www.irongatemotorcondos.com, accessed 15 July 2016.

Irwin, A. (1995) *Citizen Science: A Study of People, Expertise, and Sustainable Development*, Routledge, London.

Isaac, L. (2016) 'Driving towards driverless: A guide for government agencies', WSP-Parsons Brinckerhoff, New York, NY, www.wsp-pb.com/Globaln/USA/Transportation%20and%20Infrastructure/driving-towards-driverless-WBP-Fellow-monograph-lauren-isaac-feb-24-2016.pdf, accessed 20 October 2016.

ISC (International Speedway Corporation) (2009) *Industry Overview*, ir.iscmotorsports.com/phoenix.zhtml?c=113983&p=irol-industryoverview, accessed 15 September 2009.

Isherwood, N., Pinzon, L. and Colburn, J. (2015) 'Strasbourg: Regaining the public realm', Princes Foundation for the Built Environment, London, hankdittmar.com/wp-content/uploads/2015/09/StrasbourgReport_revi.pdf, accessed 15 September 2016.

ITE (Institute of Transportation Engineers) (2006) Context Sensitive Solutions in Designing Major Urban Thoroughfares for Walkable Communities: An ITE Proposed Recommended Practice, ITE, Washington, DC.

IVCA (International Veteran Cycle Association) (undated) ivca-online.org/, accessed 15 July 2009.

Jackson, C. (2016) 'Storage units, now with space to cook, relax and entertain', *The Wall Street Journal*, 3 March, www.wsj.com/articles/storage-units-now-with-space-to-cook-relax-and-entertain-1457026958, accessed 15 July 2016.

Jackson, K. (1985) Crabgrass Frontier: The Suburbanization of the United States, Oxford University Press, New York, NY.

Jackson, R.J. (with S. Sinclair) (2012) *Designing Healthy Communities*, Jossey-Bass, San Francisco, CA.

Jacobs, J. (1961) *The Death and Life of Great American Cities*, Penguin Books, Harmondsworth, UK.

Jacobs, J. (1970) *The Economy of Cities*, Vintage, New York, NY.

Jacobs, J. (1984) *Cities and the Wealth of Nations: Principles of Economic Life*, Random House, New York, NY.

Jacobs, J. (1994) *Systems of Survival: A Dialogue on the Moral Foundations of Commerce and Politics*, Vintage, London.

Jam Handy (film organization) (1940) 'To new horizons (1940) GM Futurama', www.youtube.com/watch?v=aIu6DTbYnog, accessed 18 July 2016.

James, S. (1998) 'Rick Prelinger, Our Secret Century: Archival Films from the Darker Side of the American Dream', *Material History Review*, vol 47 (Spring) I Revue d'histoire de la culture matérielle 47 (printemps 1998), journals.lib.unb.ca/index.php/MCR/article/view/17748/22206, accessed 17 July 2016.

Jane's Walk (2009) www.janeswalk.net, accessed 24 August 2016.

Jawetz, P. (2009) 'The Kyoto Protocol, signed in 1997, was widely viewed as badly flawed; President Obama will place the United States at the forefront of the international climate effort raising hopes that an effective international accord is possible', www.sustainabilitank.info/2009/03/02/the-kyoto-protocol-signed-in-1997-was-widely-viewed-as-badly-flawed-president-obama-will-place-the-united-states-at-the-forefront-of-the-international-climate-effort-raising-hopes-that-an-effective/, accessed 10 June 2009.

John, P. (2012) *Analyzing Public Policy*, 2nd edn, Routledge textbooks in policy studies, Taylor & Francis, New York.

Johnson, E. W. (1993) *Avoiding the Collision of Cities and Cars: Urban Transportation Policy for the Twenty-First Century*, American Academy of Arts and Sciences, Chicago, IL.

Johnson, J. (2015) 'Cars are so yesterday for young people', March 21, www.vancouverobserver.com/news/cars-are-so-yesterday-young-people-they-use-transit-here-come-facts, accessed 30 May 2016.

Johnson, J. H. (1949) 'Why negroes buy Cadillacs' (Photo-Editorial), in *Ebony Magazine*, vol 4, no 11, 34–35.

Johnson, J. M. (2008) 'Gardens in the round: In Seattle, traffic circles have become bonus open space', *Planning*, www.entrepreneur.com/tradejournals/article/176651969.html, accessed 10 June 2009.

Judt, T. (2011) 'Bring back the rails!', *The New York Review of Books*, 13 January, www.nybooks.com/articles/2011/01/13/bring-back-rails/?printpage=true, accessed 14 July, 2016.

Juri, C and Frassinelli, M. (2011) 'Jitney minibuses offer a cheaper option for N.J. passengers, but ride can be risky', *The Star-Ledger*, 20 January, blog.nj.com/ledgerupdates_impact/print.html?entry=/2010/07/jitney_minibuses_provide_a_che.html, accessed 16 August 2016.

Kahn, D. (2013) 'Happy Valley residents hope to turn intersection into gathering spot', *The Bellingham Herald*, 29 June.

Kang, C. (2016) 'Amazon leans on government in its quest to be a delivery powerhouse', *The New York Times*, 20 March, http://nyti.ms/1UuYzra, accessed 13 November 2016.

Kanter, J. (2009) 'Europe expected to outperform Kyoto goals', *The New York Times*, greeninc.blogs.nytimes.com/2009/05/29/dimas-europe-will-outperform-kyoto-goals/, accessed 17 June 2009.

Kasarda, J. D. and Lindsay, G. (2011) *Aerotropolis: The Way We'll Live Next*, Farrar, Strauss and Giroux, New York, NY.

Katz, P. (1993) *The New Urbanism: Toward an Architecture of Community*, McGraw-Hill Education, Columbus, OH.

Katz, P. (1994) *The New Urbanism: Toward an Architecture of Community*, McGraw Hill, New York, NY.

Kaufman, J. D., Adar, S. D., Barr, R. G. et al. (2016) 'Association between air pollution and coronary artery calcification within six metropolitan areas in the USA (the multi-ethnic study of atherosclerosis and air pollution): A longitudinal cohort study', *Lancet*, vol 388, no 10045, accessed 25 June 2016.

Kay, J. H. (1977) 'A conversation with Mumford: "The human things are ignored"', *AIA Journal*, vol LXVI (June), 38–41.

Kay, J. H. (1982) 'Lewis Mumford; An autobiography', *The Christian Science Monitor*, 18 June, www.csmonitor.com/1982/0618/061865.html.

Kay, J. H. (1997, 1998). *Asphalt Nation: How the Automobile Took Over America, and How We Can Take It Back*, Crown Publishers, New York, NY; University of California Press, Berkeley, CA.

Kay, J. H. (2002) 'A runway to sprawl: The consequences of a way out yonder lifestyle', Michigan Land Use Institute, 22 May, www.mlui.org/mlui/news-views/articles-from-1995-to-2012.html?archive_id=85#.V5ZzsSgq8rg, accessed 25 July 2016.

Kay, J. H. and Harrell, P. C. (1980, 1999, 2006) *Lost Boston* (expanded and updated edn), University of Massachusetts Press, Amherst, MA.

Kay, J. H., and Harrell, P. C. (1986) *Preserving New England: Connecticut, Rhode Island, Massachusetts, Vermont, New Hampshire, Maine* (1st ed.) Pantheon Books, New York. Pantheon Books.

Kelley, P. (2016) 'Cars vs. health: UW's Moudon, Dannenberg contribute to Lancet series on urban planning, public health', *University of Washington*, www.washington.edu/news/2016/10/12/cars-vs-health-uws-moudon-dannenberg-contribute-to-lancet-series-on-urban-planning-public-health/ accessed 16 October 2016.

Kenworthy, J. R. (1991a) 'The land use/transit connection in Toronto: Some lessons for Australian cities', *Australian Planner*, vol 29, no 3, 149–154.

Kenworthy, J. R. (1991b) From urban consolidation to urban villages *Urban Policy and Research*, vol 9, no 1, 96–100.

Kenworthy, J. R. (1997) 'Automobile dependence in Bangkok: An international comparison with implications for planning policies and air pollution', in T. Fletcher and A. J. Michael (eds), *Health at the Crossroads: Transport Policy and Urban Health*, John Wiley and Sons, Chichester, UK. Chapter 19, pp. 215–233.

Kenworthy, J. R. (2000) 'Building more livable cities by overcoming automobile dependence: An international comparative reviews', in R. Lawrence (ed.), *Sustaining Human Settlement: A Challenge for the New Millennium*, Urban International Press, Newcastle-upon-Tyne, UK, pp. 271–314.

Kenworthy, J. R. (2006) 'The eco-city: Ten key transport and planning dimensions for sustainable city development', *Environment and Urbanization*, vol 18, no 1, 67–85.

Kenworthy, J. (2008) 'An international review of the significance of rail in developing more sustainable urban transport systems in higher income cities', *World Transport Policy and Practice*, vol 14, no 2, 21–37

Kenworthy, J. R. (2010a) 'Making eco-cities a reality: Some key dimensions for eco city development with best practice examples', in Z. Tang (ed.), *Eco-City and Green Community: The Evolution of Planning Theory and Practice*, NOVA Science Publishers, Hauppauge, NY, pp. 39–58.

Kenworthy, J. (2010b) 'An international comparative perspective on fast rising motorisation and automobile dependence in developing cities', in H. Dimitriou and R. Gackenheimer (eds), *Transport Policy Making and Planning for Cities of the Developing World*, Edward Elgar, London, pp. 74–112.

Kenworthy, J. (2012) 'Don't shoot me I'm only the transport planner (apologies to Sir Elton John)', *World Transport Policy and Practice*, vol 18, no 4, 6–26.

Kenworthy, J. (2013) 'Deteriorating or improving? Transport sustainability trends in global metropolitan areas', in J. Renne and W. M. Fields (eds), *Transport Beyond Oil: Policy Choices for a Multi-Modal Future*, Island Press, Washington DC.

Kenworthy, J. (2016) *Non-Motorized Mode Cities in a Global Cities Cluster Analysis: A Study of Trends in Mumbai, Shanghai, Beijing and Guangzhou Since 1995*, Report for Hosoya Schaefer Architects AG, Zurich, Switzerland.

Kenworthy, J. R. and Hu, G. (2002) 'Transport and urban form in Chinese cities: An international and comparative policy perspective with implications for sustainable urban transport in China', *DISP*, vol 151, 4–14.

Kenworthy, J. R. and Laube, F. B. (1999) *An International Sourcebook of Automobile Dependence in Cities, 1960–1990* University Press of Colorado, Niwot, Boulder, CO.

Kenworthy, J. and Laube, F. (2001) *The Millennium Cities Database for Sustainable Transport. (CDROM Database)*, International Union (Association) of Public Transport, (UITP), Brussels and Institute for Sustainability and Technology Policy (ISTP), Perth, Australia.

Kenworthy, J. R., Newman, P. W. G., Barter, P. and Poboon, C. (1995) 'Is increasing automobile dependence inevitable in booming economies? Asian cities in an international context', *IATSS Research*, vol 19, no 2, 58–67.

Kenworthy, J. R. and Townsend, C. (2002) 'An international comparative perspective on motorisation in urban China: Problems and prospects', *IATSS Research*, vol 26, no 2, 99–109.

Ker, I. and Ginn, S. (2003) 'Myths and realities in walkable catchments: The case of walking and transit,' *Road and Transport Research*, vol 12, no 2, 69–80.

Kessler, A.M. (2015) 'Hands-free cars take wheel, and law isn't stopping them', *The New York Times*, May 2, nyti.ms/1DLptNS, accessed 10 May 2015.

Kihlstedt, F. (1983) 'The automobile and the transformation of the American house, 1910–35', in D. L. Lewis and L. Goldstein (eds), *The Automobile and American Culture*, University of Michigan Press, Ann Arbor, MI.

King, M. (2010) 'Imataa Manistsi: Blackfoot dog travois', web.prm.ox.ac.uk/blackfootshirts/attachments/028_Imataa%20Manistsi-%20Blackfoot%20Dog%20Travois.pdf, accessed 17 July 2016.

Kirsch, D. (2000) *The Electric Vehicle and the Burden of History*, Rutgers University Press, New Brunswick, NJ.

Klaus, P. (2004) 'Carjacking, 1993–2002', *Bureau of Justice Statistics Crime Data Brief*, U.S. Department of Justice, July, www.bjs.gov/content/pub/pdf/c02.pdf, accessed 18 August 2016.

Klein, J. and Olson, M. (1996) *Taken for a Ride*, New Day Films, www.newday.com/films/Taken_for_a_Ride.html, accessed 15 September 2009 and ww.pbs.org/pov/takenforaride/, accessed 12 July 2016.

Klein, N. (2002) *No Logo*, Picador, New York, NY.

Klinger, T., Kenworthy, J. and Lanzendorf, M. (2013) 'Dimensions of urban mobility cultures – a comparison of German cities', *Journal of Transport Geography*, vol 31, 18–29.

Knowles, R., Shaw, J. and Docherty, I. (eds), (2008) *Transport Geographies: Mobilities, Flows and Spaces*, Blackwell, Oxford, UK.

Komanoff, C. (1994) 'Pollution taxes for roadway transportation', *Pace Environmental Law Review*, vol 12, no 1, 121–184.

Koppenjan, J. (undated) 'Involving politicians in interactive policy making processes: Theoretical considerations and practical experiences', in *Papers for the International Conference on Democratic Network Governance*, Copenhagen, Denmark, 21–22 October 2004, www.ruc.dk/demnetgov_en/Conferences_and_Seminars/int_conf/papers/, accessed 12 June 2009.

Kostof, S. (1991) *The City Shaped: Urban Patterns and Meaning Through History*, Bulfinch Press, Little, Brown and Company, New York, NY.

Kott, J. (2011) *Streets of Clay: Design and Assessment of Sustainable Urban and Suburban Streets*, PhD Thesis, Curtin University, Perth, Australia.

Kramer, F. (2012) 'NPR Planet Money host Adam Davidson under fire from rogue media ethicists [updated]', *Observer*, 8 September, observer.com/2012/08/adam-davidson-planet-money-media-ethics-08092012/, accessed 1 May 2016.

Kunstler, J. H. (1993) *The Geography of Nowhere*, Simon & Schuster, Touchstone, New York, NY.

Kunstler, J. H. (1996) *Home from Nowhere: Remaking Our Everyday World for the 21st Century*, Simon & Schuster, New York, NY.

Kunstler, J. H. (2005) 'They lied to us', www.democraticunderground.com/discuss/duboard.php?az=view_all&address=103x169504, 31 October, accessed 10 April 2016.

Kunstler, J. H. (2006) *The Long Emergency: Surviving the End of Oil, Climate Change, and Other Converging Catastrophes of the Twenty-First Century*, Grove Press, New York, NY.

Ladd, B. (2008) *Autophobia: Love and Hate in the Automotive Age*, University of Chicago Press, Chicago, IL.

Laing, R., Tait, E. and Gray, D. (2012) 'Public engagement and participation in sustainable transport issues', in *Proceedings of RICS COBRA, Las Vegas*, September 11–13, archive.northsearegion.eu/files/repository/20130812123945_COBRA.pdf, accessed 26 August 2016.

Lasch, C. (1991) 'Liberalism and civic virtue', *Telos*, vol 88, 57–68.

LAW (League of American Wheelmen, now League of American Bicyclists) (undated) www.bike-league.org/about/history.php, accessed 15 July 2009.

Lawrence, A. T., Weber, J. and Post, J. E. (2005) 'Influencing the political environment', in A. T. Lawrence, J. W. Weber, and J. E. Post (eds), *Business and Society: Stakeholders, Ethics, Public Policy*, 11th edn, McGraw-Hill College, New York, NY, pp. 166–187.

Lay, M. (1992) *Ways of the World: A History of the World's Roads and of the Vehicles That Used Them*, Rutgers University Press, New Brunswick, NJ.

Le Vine, S. Zolfaghari, A. and Polak, J. (2014) *Car Sharing: Evolution, Challenges and Opportunities*, ACEA, Scientific Advisory Group Report, Imperial College, London, www.acea.be/uploads/publications/SAG_Report_-_Car_Sharing.pdf, accessed 24 August 2016.

Lee, D. S., Fahey, D. W., Forster, P. M., et al. (2009) 'Aviation and global climate change in the 21st century', *Atmospheric Environment*, vol 43, no 22, 3520–3537.

Lee, K. (1993) *Compass and Gyroscope: Integrating Science and Politics for the Environment*, Island Press, Washington, DC.

Leo, C. (1977) *The Politics of Urban Development: Canadian Urban Expressway Disputes*. Institute of Public Administration, Toronto

Leon, J. K. (2014) 'What Broadacre City can teach us', *Metropolis*, 2 July, www.metropolismag.com/Point-of-View/July-2014/What-Broadacre-City-Can-Teach-Us/, accessed 1 August 2016.

LePla, J. (2002) 'Give your company a personality test', www.workz.com/content/view_content.html?section_id=469&content_id=5212), accessed 16 August 2009.

Levi, J., Segal L. M., Rayburn, J. and Martin, A. (2015) *The State of Obesity: Better Policies for a Healthier America*, stateofobesity.org/files/stateofobesity2015.pdf, accessed 1 March 2016.

Levine, J. (2006) *Zoned Out: Regulation, Markets, and Choices in Transportation and Metropolitan Land-Use*, Resources for the Future, Washington, DC.

Levy, R. M. (2006) 'Urban design and computer visualization: Applications in community planning', in S. Tsenkova (ed.), *People and Places: Planning New Communities*, www.ucalgary.ca/cities/files/cities/PlanningNewCommunities.pdf, accessed 17 June 2009.

Lewis, D. and Goldstein, L. (eds), (1983) *The Automobile and American Culture*, University of Michigan Press, Ann Arbor, MI.

Lewis, D. L. (1983) 'Sex and the automobile: From rumble seats to rockin' vans', in D. L. Lewis and L. Goldstein (eds), *The Automobile and American Culture*, University of Michigan Press, Ann Arbor, MI, pp. 123–133.

Lewis, T. (1997) *Divided Highways: Building the Interstate Highways, Transforming American Life*, Penguin Putnam, New York, NY.

Lewyn, M. and Rosenman, J. S. (2015) 'No parking anytime: The legality and wisdom of maximum parking and minimum density requirements', *Washburn Law Journal*. vol 54, no 2, *Touro Law Center Legal Studies Research Paper Series*, no 16-07, *University of Pittsburgh Legal Studies Research Paper*, no 2016-04, ssrn.com/abstract=2681147, accessed 24 August 2016.

Library of Congress (date or original uncertain) Reproduction Number: LC-DIG-ds-07962; digital file from original item, http://cdn.loc.gov/service/pnp/ds/07900/07962v.jpg, accessed 9 October 2016.

Lin, D., Allan, A., Cui, J. and McLaughlin, R. (2012) 'The effects of polycentric development on commuting patterns in metropolitan areas', *Regional Studies Association Global Conference*, Beijing, China.

Linn, S. (2004) *Consuming Kids: The Hostile Takeover of Childhood*, New Press, New York, NY.

Litman, T. (2003) 'Reinventing transportation: Exploring the paradigm shift needed for sustainable transportation', *Victoria Transport Policy Institute*, www.vtpi.org/reinvent.pdf, accessed 15 September 2009.

Litman, T. (2010) 'Generated traffic and induced travel: Implications for transport planning', *Victoria Transport Policy Institute*, www.vtpi.org/gentraf.pdf, accessed 5 December 2010.

Litman, T. (2015a) 'Evaluating public transit benefits and costs: Best practices guidebook', *Victoria Transport Policy Institute*, www.vtpi.org/tranben.pdf, accessed 10 August 2015.

Litman, T. (2015b) Rail transit in America: A comprehensive evaluation of benefits, Victoria Transport Policy Institute, www.vtpi.org/railben.pdf, accessed 21 July 2016.

Litman, T. (2016) 'Safer than you think! Revising the transit safety narrative', August, *Victoria Transport Policy Institute*, www.vtpi.org/safer.pdf, accessed 18 August 2016.

Lopez, R. P. (2012) *The Built Environment and Public Health*, Jossey-Bass, San Francisco, CA.

Lovins, A. (1977) *Soft energy paths: Toward a durable peace*, Friends of the Earth International, San Francisco, CA.

Low, N. and Gleeson, B. (2003) *Making Urban Transport Sustainable*, Palgrave Macmillan, New York, NY.

LUTI Consulting (2016) *Transit and Urban Renewal Value Creation*, LUTI Consulting, Hobart, www.luticonsulting.com.au/projects/hedonic-price-modelling-assessment-of-sydneys-key-transit/, accessed 15 September 2016.

Lynch, K. (1960) *The Image of the City*, MIT Press, Cambridge, MA.

Lynch, K. (ed.) (1977) *Growing Up in Cities: Studies of the Spatial Environment of Adolescence in Cracow, Melbourne, Mexico City, Salta, Toluca and Warszawa*, MIT Press, Cambridge, MA, and UNESCO, Paris.

McAlinder, S. P., Hill, K. and Swiedic, B. (2003) *Economic Contribution of the Automotive Industry to the U.S. Economy – An Update*, Center for Automotive Research, Ann Arbor, MI.

McCarthy, R. J. (2016) 'Bus stop uncertain at new Walmart, raising echoes of Cynthia Wiggins tragedy', *The Buffalo News*, www.buffalonews.com/city-region/cheektowaga/bus-stop-uncertain-at-new-walmart-raising-echoes-of-cynthia-wiggins-tragedy-20160308, accessed 5 August 2016.

McCartney, K. (2016) 'Cargo bike-sharing programs in Europe', *Shareable*, 4 January, www.shareable.net/blog/8-cargo-bike-sharing-programs-in-europe? accessed 3 November 2016.

Mcglade, C. and Ekins, P. (2014) 'Un-burnable oil: An examination of oil resource utilisation in a decarbonised energy system', *Energy Policy*, vol 64, 102–112.

McHarry, J. (1994) 'Stress and the environment: The impact of the motor vehicle', in J. Rose (ed.) *Human Stress and the Environment*, Gordon and Breach, Yverdon, 209–224.

McHugh, M. (2015) 'Tesla's cars now drive themselves, kinda', *Wired*, 14 October, www.wired.com/2015/10/tesla-self-driving-over-air-update-live/, accessed 16 October 2016.

McIntosh, J., Trubka, R., Kenworthy, J. and Newman, P. (2014) 'The role of urban form and transit in city car dependence: Analysis of 26 global cities from 1960 – 2000', *Transportation Research D*, vol 33, 95–110.

Mackay, H. (1993) *Reinventing Australia: The Mind and Mood of Australia in the '90s*, Angus and Robertson, Sydney, Australia.

Mackay, H. (1994) 'The future stops here', in *The Weekend Australian: The Weekend Review*, 3–4 September, p. 16.

MacKechnie, C. (2016) 'How much do rail transit projects cost to build and operate?', *ThoughtCo.* www.publictransport.about.com/od/Transit_Projects/a/How-Much-Do-Rail-Transit-Projects-Cost-To-Build-And-Operate.htm, accessed 20 July 2016.

McKnight, C. E., Levinson, H., Ozbay, K., Kamga, K. C. and Paaswell, R. E. (2003) 'Impact of congestion on bus operations and costs', U.S. Department of Transportation, Federal Highway Administration, report FHWA-NJ-2003-008, ntl.bts.gov/lib/24000/24200/24208/24208.pdf_, accessed 10 August 2016.

McManus, R. (2006) 'Imagine a city with 30 percent fewer cars: Low-tech transit is the fastest route to a great city, says a Brazilian architect', www.sierraclub.org/sierra/200601/interview.asp, accessed 10 June 2009.

McShane, C. (1994) *Down the Asphalt Path: The Automobile and the American City*, Columbia University Press, New York, NY.

Manchester, K. (ed.) (2007) *The Silk Road and Beyond: Travel, Trade, and Transformation*, Art Institute of Chicago, Yale University Press, New Haven, CT.

Manjoo, F. (2016a) 'Car-pooling helps Uber go the extra mile', *The New York Times*, 30 March, nyti.ms/1qiwDuc, accessed 30 March 2016.

Manjoo, F. (2016b) 'The Uber model, it turns out, doesn't translate', *The New York Times*, 23 March, nyti.ms/25lD8fY, accessed 24 March 2016.

Manjoo, F. (2016c) 'Think Amazon's drone delivery idea is a gimmick? Think again', *The New York Times*, 10 August, http://nyti.ms/2b5FoUt, accessed 16 November 2016.

Mann, B. (2011) 'Here's why the right wing dominates talk radio today', *The Huffington Post*, www.huffingtonpost.com/bill-mann/heres-why-the-right-wing_b_206444.html, accessed 18 July 2016.

Manners, E. (2002) *The Role of Participatory Democracy in Achieving Environmental Sustainability*, MA thesis, Griffith University, South East Queensland, Australia.

Mapes, J. (2009) Pedaling Revolution: How Cyclists Are Changing American Cities, Oregon State University Press, Eugene, OR.

Marchetti, C. (1994) 'Anthropological invariants in travel behaviour', *Technical Forecasting and Social Change*, vol 47, no 1, 75–78.

Margolis, M. (1992) 'A third world city that works', *World Monitor*, vol 5, no 3 (March), 42–50.

Marinova, D, McGrath, N. and Newman, P. (2004) 'Dialogue with the city: An era of participatory planning for provision of more sustainable infrastructure in Perth?', *Proceedings of International Summer Academy on Technology Studies*, Deutschlandsberg, Austria, 195–210.

MarketingCharts staff (2016) 'Do commuters listen to AM/FM radio ads in the car?', 18 April, www.marketingcharts.com/traditional/do-commuters-listen-to-amfm-radio-ads-in-the-car-66883/, accessed 15 July 2016.

Markoff, J. (2016) 'Want to buy a self-driving car? Big-rig trucks may come first', *The New York Times*, 17 May, nyti.ms/1rQAM9E, accessed 17 May 2016.

Marx, K. (1857–1861) *Gundrisse: Foundations of the Critique of Political Economy (Rough draft)*, translated by M. Nicolaus, www.marxists.org/archive/marx/works/1857/grundrisse/ch10.htm, accessed 17 July 2016.

Massachusetts Institute of Technology (MIT) (2012) 'Commercial version of the MIT Media Lab CityCar unveiled at European Union commission headquarters', *MIT Media Lab*, www.media.mit.edu/news/citycar, accessed 3 November 2016.

Matthews, K. D. Jr. (1960) 'The embattled driver in Ancient Rome', *Expedition Magazine*, vol 2, no 3, 22–27, www.penn.museum/sites/expedition/?p=135, accessed 17 July 2016.

Matyszczyk, C. (2015) 'Man shoots down drone hovering over house', *CNet*, www.cnet.com/news/man-shoots-down-drone-hovering-over-house/, accessed 13 November 2016.

Maus, J. (2011) 'Auto industry archives', (several postings about GM's anti-bike/anti-pedestrian advertising campaign), *Bike* Portland, BikePortland.org, accessed 15 July 2016.

Maus, J. (2016) 'Better Block PDX', *Bike Portland*, http://bikeportland.org/tag/better-block-pdx, accessed 1 November 2016.

Mayer, J. (2013) 'A word from our sponsor: Public television's attempts to placate David Koch', *The New Yorker*, 27 May, www.newyorker.com/magazine/2013/05/27/a-word-from-our-sponsor, accessed 5 May 2016.

Meek, S., Ison, S., and Enoch, M. (2008) 'Role of bus_based park and ride in the UK: A temporal and evaluative review', *Transport Reviews*, vol 28, no 6, 781–803.

Mees, P. (2010) *Transport for Suburbia: Beyond the Automobile Age*, Earthscan, London and Sterling, VA.

Melczer, W. (1993) *The Pilgrim's Guide to Santiago de Compostela: First English Translation*, with Introduction, Commentaries, and Notes, Italica Press, New York, NY.

Mercer (2017) *Quality of Living Survey 2017*. Mercer Canada, 14 March 2017, www.mercer.ca/en/newsroom/mercer-2017-retirement-quality-of-living-rankings.html

Merington, M. (1895) 'Woman and the bicycle', *Scribner's Magazine*, vol 17, 703.

Micallef, S. (2009) 'The (sub)urban village', *Spacing*, summer–fall, pp. 60–63.

Micallef, S. (author) and Zuber, M. (illustrator) (2010) *Stroll: Psychogeographic Walking Tours of Toronto*, Coach House Books, Toronto, Canada.

Milbrath, L. W. (1989) *Envisioning a Sustainable Society: Learning our Way Out*, State University of New York Press, Albany, NY.

Millage, K. (2008) 'Teen gets a crash course at the fair: Ferndale High grad builds demolition derby car as senior project', *Bellingham Herald*, 12 August, www.bellinghamherald.com/255/story/493659, accessed 2 October 2016.

Miller, L. (2007) 'After 7-Eleven, Simpsons Move to eBay,' *The New York Times*, 20 August.

Mingardo, G. (2013) 'Transport and environmental effects of rail-based park and ride: Evidence from the Netherlands, *Journal of Transport Geography*, vol 30, 7–16.

Mitchell, K. (2014) 'I'm fighting to save night trains – the ticket to my daughter's future', *The Guardian*, 18 September, www.theguardian.com/commentisfree/2014/sep/18/save-night-trains-ticket-daughter-rail-greenest-travel-europe-sleeper-services, accessed 20 August 2016.

Mitchell, R. B., and Rapkin, C. (1954). *Urban Traffic: A Function of Land Use*, Columbia University Press, New York, NY.

Mohan, D. (2015) 'Autonomous vehicles and their future in low and middle-income countries', *Conference on Driverless Technology and its Urban Impact, Institute of Urban Management*, New York, May 28-29, www.marroninstitute.nyu.edu/content/working-papers/autonomous-vehicles-and-their-future-in-low-and-middle-income-countries, accessed 10 November 2015.

Mohr, R. (1991) *Time, Space and Equity*, discussion paper prepared for the Australian Council of Social Service (ACOSS), Sydney, Australia.

Mokhtarian, P. (2003) 'Telecommunications and travel: The case for complementarity', *Journal of Industrial Ecology*, vol 6, no 2, 43–57, www.its.ucdavis.edu/telecom/, accessed 6 July 2009.

Monheim, R. (1988) 'Pedestrian zones in West Germany - The dynamic development of an effective instrument to enliven the city centre', in C. Hass-Klau (ed.), *New Life for City Centres: Planning Transport and Conservation in British and German Cities*, Anglo-German Foundation, London, pp107–130.

Mooradian, D. (2000) 'NASCAR attendance doubles during past decade', *All Business*, www.allbusiness.com/services/amusement-recreation-services/4557259-1.html, accessed 15 September 2009.

Moore, F. (2005) 'Product placements infiltrate TV shows', *Associated Press*, 19 July, www.commercialalert.org/news/featured-in/2005/07/product-placements-infiltrate-tv-shows, accessed 18 July 2016.

Moore, R. (2006) 'A drive for more biking and walking options: 2006 Oberstar Forum addresses the role of non-motorized modes of transportation', *University of Minnesota News*, 11 April, www1.umn.edu/umnnews/Feature_Stories/A_drive_for_more_biking_and_walking_options.html, accessed 24 August 2016.

Morlok, E. (2005) 'First permanent railroad in the U.S. and its connection to the University of Pennsylvania', *Penn Engineering*, www.seas.upenn.edu/~morlok/morlokpage/transp_data.html, accessed 6 July 2009.

Morris, A. E. J. (2013) *History of Urban Form Before the Industrial Revolution*, Routledge, London and New York, NY.

Morris, J. (1981) 'Urban public transport', in P. N. Troy (ed.) *Equity in the City*, George Allen and Unwin, Sydney, Australia.

Moudon, A. V. (ed.) (1987) *Public Streets for Public Use*, Van Nostrand Reinhold, New York, NY.

Mumbai Metropolitan Region Development Authority (2006) *Report 4: Field Survey (Household Interview Survey and Other Surveys, vol 1)*, MMRDA, Mumbai, India.

Mumford, L. (1938) *The Culture of Cities*, Harcourt Brace and Company, New York, NY.

Mumford, L. (1961) *The City in History: Its Origins, Its Transformations, and Its Prospects*, Harcourt Brace, San Diego, CA.

Musk, E. (2013) 'Hyperloop Alpha'. www.spacex.com/sites/spacex/files/hyperloop_alpha-20130812.pdf (accessed 25 July 2017).

Naess, P. (1993a) 'Energy use for transport in 22 Nordic towns', *NIBR Report No 2*, Norwegian Institute for Urban and Regional Research, Oslo.

Naess, P. (1993b) 'Transportation energy in Swedish towns and regions', *Scandinavian Housing and Planning Research*, vol 10, 187–206.

Naess, P. (1995) *Urban form and energy use for transport: A Nordic experience*, PhD. thesis, Norwegian Institute of Technology.

Nasar, J. L., and D. Troyer (2013) 'Pedestrian injuries due to mobile phone use in public places'. *Accident Analysis & Prevention*, 57: 91–95; http://facweb.knowlton.ohio-state.edu/jnasar/crpinfo/research/AAP3092Accidents_Final2013.pdf, accessed 11 October 2016.

National Complete Streets Coalition (2009) 'Frequently asked questions', www.completestreets.org/complete-streets-fundamentals/complete-streets-faq/, accessed 15 September 2009.

National Transit Database (2015) 'National transit summary and trends', Federal Transit Administration U.S. Department of Transportation, Office of Budget and Policy, February.

Native Languages of the Americas (2016) 'American Indian travois', www.native-languages.org/travois.htm, accessed 17 July 2016.

NCSL (National Conference of State Legislatures) (2015) 'Non-emergency medical transportation: A vital lifeline for a healthy community', 7 January, www.ncsl.org/research/transportation/non-emergency-medical-transportation-a-vital-lifeline-for-a-healthy-community.aspx, accessed 16 August 2016.

Nelson/Nygaard Consulting Associates (2003) *Parking and Transportation Micro-Master Transportation Plan: Existing Conditions*, University of Colorado at Boulder, Boulder, CO.

Newcomb, D. (2016) 'Bloomberg initiative will help cities prepare for self-driving cars', www.forbes.com/ 26 October, accessed 11 November 2016.

Newman, F. and Holzman, L. (1993) *Lev Vygotsky: Revolutionary Scientist*, Routledge, London.

Newman, O. (1973) *Defensible Space: Crime Prevention Through Urban Design*, Macmillan Publishing, New York.

Newman, P. (2014) 'Biophilic urbanism: A case study of Singapore', *Australian Planner*, vol 51, no 1, 47–65.

Newman, P., Jones, E., Green, J. and Davies-Slate, S. (2016) 'Entrepreneur Rail Model: Tapping private investment for new urban rail', Discussion Paper, Curtin University, Perth, Australia.

Newman, P. W. G. and Kenworthy, J. R. (1984) 'The use and abuse of driving cycle research: Clarifying the relationship between traffic congestion, energy and emissions', *Transportation Quarterly*, vol 38, 615–635.

Newman, P. W. G. and Kenworthy, J. R. (1989) *Cities and Automobile Dependence: A Sourcebook*, Gower Technical, Aldershot, UK, and Brookfield, VT.

Newman, P. and Kenworthy, J. (1992) 'Transit-oriented urban villages: Design model for the 90s', *Urban Futures*, vol 2, no 1, 50–58.

Newman, P.W.G. and Kenworthy, J.R. (1996) 'The land use–transport connection: An overview', *Land Use Policy*, vol 13, no 1, 1–22.

Newman, P. W. G. and Kenworthy, J. R. (1999a) *Sustainability and Cities: Overcoming Automobile Dependence*, Island Press, Washington, DC.

Newman, P. and Kenworthy, J. (1999b) '"Relative speed" not "time savings": A new indicator for sustainable transport', Papers of the 23rd Australasian Transport Research Forum, Perth Western Australia, 29 September—1 October, 23(1), pp. 425–440.

Newman, P. and Kenworthy, J. (2006) 'Urban design to reduce automobile dependence: How much development will make urban centers viable?', *Opolis*, vol 2, no 1, 35–52.

Newman, P. and Kenworthy, J. (2015) *The End of Automobile Dependence: How Cities Are Moving Away from Car-Based Planning*, Island Press, Washington, DC.

Newman, P. Kenworthy, J. and Glazebrook, G. (2013) 'Peak car and the rise and rise of global rail: Why this is happening and what it means for large and small cities', *Journal of Transportation Technologies*, vol 3, 272–287.

Newman, P. W. G., Kenworthy, J. R. and Lyons, T. J. (1988) 'Does free-flowing traffic save energy and lower emissions in cities?, *Search*, vol 19, no 5/6, 267–272.

Newman, P. W. G., Kenworthy, J. R. and Lyons, T. J. (1990) *Transport Energy Conservation Policies for Australian Cities: Strategies for Reducing Automobile Dependence, Institute for Science and Technology Policy*, Murdoch University, Perth, Western Australia.

Newman, P. W. G., Kenworthy, J. and Vintila, P. (1992) 'Housing, transport and urban form', Background Paper 15 + Appendices for the National Housing Strategy, Commonwealth of Australia, Canberra.

Newman, P., Kosonen, L. and Kenworthy, J. (2016) 'Theory of urban fabrics: Planning the walking, transit/public transport and automobile/motor car cities for reduced car dependency', *Town Planning Review*, vol 87, no 4, 429–458.

NIEHS (National Institutes of Health, Department of Health & Human Services) (undated) 'Daisy bell (a bicycle built for two)', http://kids.niehs.nih.gov/lyrics/daisy.htm, accessed 15 July 2009.

Nielsen Media Research (2007) 'Nielsen Monitor-Plus Report: U.S. advertising spending rose 4.6 per cent in 2006', www.nielsenmedia.com, accessed 1 September 2009.

Niles, J. (2009) 'Global telematics', www.globaltelematics.com/mediachoice/index.htm, accessed 7 July 2009.

NIOSH; National Institute for Occupational Safety and Health (2012) 'Health concerns for flight attendants', www.cdc.gov/niosh/pgms/worknotify/pdfs/FA_Notification_FINAL.pdf, accessed 13 June 2016.

Nolan, M. (2014) 'Bellingham neighbors decorate Walnut Street with lengthy mural', *The Bellingham Herald*, 27 June.

Noland, R. B. (2001) 'Relationships between highway capacity and induced vehicle travel', *Transportation Research Part A*, vol 35, 47–72.

Nordahl, D. (2012) *Making Transit Fun! How to Entice Motorists from Their Cars (and Onto Their Feet, a Bike, or Bus)*, Island Press E-ssentials.

Norton, P. D. (2007) 'Street rivals: Jaywalking and the invention of the motor age street', *Technology and Culture*, vol 48, 331–359.

Norton, P. D. (2008) *Fighting Traffic: The Dawn of the Motor Age in the American City*, MIT Press, Cambridge, MA.

Nowakowski, C., Shadover, S. E., Chan, C-Y, and H-S Tan (2014) 'Development of California regulations to govern testing and operation of automated driving systems', *TRR*, vol 2489, 137–144.

Nowlan, D. and Nowlan, N. (1970) *The Bad Trip: The Untold Story of the Spadina Expressway*, New Press, House of Anansi, Toronto, Ontario.

Nowlan, D. M. and Stewart, G. (1991) 'Downtown population growth and commuting trips: Recent Toronto experience', *Journal of the American Planning Association*, vol 57, no 2, 165–182.

NTIA (2014) 'Exploring the Digital Nation: Embracing the Mobile Internet,' National Telecommunications and Information Administration (NTIA), U.S. Department of Commerce, Washington, D.C.

O'Connell, O. (2015) 'Pimp my penthouse! Inside the $20 million New York apartment boasting its own CAR ELEVATOR', Daily Mail, 19 March, www.dailymail.co.uk/news/article-3001606/Pimp-penthouse-Inside-20-million-New-York-apartment-boasting-CAR-ELEVATOR.html, accessed 18 July 2016.

O'Hagan, A. (2009) 'A car of one's own', *London Review of Books*, vol 31, no 11, www.lrb.co.uk/v31/n11/ohag01_.html, accessed 1 September 2009.

OECD (Organisation for Economic Co-operation and Development) (2015) 'A new paradigm for urban mobility how fleets of shared vehicles can end the car dependency of cities', www.itf-oecd.org/sites/default/files/docs/cop-pdf-03.pdf_, accessed 19 August 2016.

OECD-ITF; Organisation for Economic Co-operation and Development—International Transport Forum (2013) '2013 statistics brief: trends in the transport sector', December, www.itf-oecd.org/sites/default/files/docs/2013-12-trends-perspective.pdf, accessed 20 October 2016.

Okubo, D. (2000) *The community visioning and strategic planning handbook*, National Civic League Press, Denver, CO, third edition, www.ncl.org/publications/online/VSPHandbook.pdf, accessed 20 August 2009.

Onkst, D. (undated) 'Barnstormers', U.S. Centennial of Flight Commission, www.centennialofflight.gov/essay/Explorers_Record_Setters_and_Daredevils/barnstormers/EX12.htm, accessed 11 July 2009.

Packer, J. (2008) *Mobility without Mayhem: Safety, Cars and Citizenship*, Duke University Press, Durham and London.

Page, S. (1998) 'Transport for recreation and tourism', in B. Hoyle and R. Knowles (eds), *Modern Transport Geography* (2nd edn), John Wiley and Sons, Chichester, UK.

Palmer, V. (2005) 'Private-sector portion of RAV risk isn't so private, after all', *The Vancouver Sun*, 10 August, A3.

Parasram, V. (2003) 'Efficient transportation for successful urban planning in Curitiba', www.solutions-site.org/artman/publish/printer_62.shtml, accessed 16 January 2008.

Parchesky, J. (2006) 'Women in the driver's seat: The auto-erotics of early women's films', *Film History: An International Journal*, vol 18, no 2, 174–184.

Pardo, C. F. (2008) 'Bogotá's time machine', list.jca.apc.org/public/sustran-discuss/2008-April/006120.html, accessed 23 June 2009.

Park, R. (2012) 'Contesting the norm: Women and professional sports in late nineteenth-century America', *The International Journal of the History of Sport*, vol 29, no 5, 730–749.

Parkhurst, G. (2000) Influence of bus-based park and ride facilities on users' car traffic. *Transport Policy*, vol 7, no 2, 159–172.

Pathak, P. (2010) 'Tata Towers come to rescue for congestion on roads', www.cartrade.com/car-bike-news/tata-towers-come-to-rescue-for-congestion-on-roads-113120.html, accessed 23 July 2016.

Pedwell, T. (2016) 'Driverless cars would mean "a lot more sex" behind the wheel: Expert', thewhig.com, www.thewhig.com/2016/04/30/driverless-cars-would-mean-a-lot-more-sex-behind-the-wheel-expert, accessed 2 May 2016.

Peirce, N. (2009) 'German city emerges as a world class energy saver', Washington Post Writers Group, http://citiwire.net/post/973/, accessed 30 July 2009.

Peñalosa, E. (2003) 'Sustainable transportation: A sourcebook for policy-makers in developing countries', Sustainable Urban Transport Project, www.sutp.org, www.vtpi.org/gtz_module.pdf, accessed 15 September 2009.

Peñalosa , E. (2005) 'The role of transport in urban development policy', Sustainable Transport: A Sourcebook for Policy-Makers in Developing Cities, Module 1a, Deutsche Gessellschaft für Technische Zusammenarbeit (GTZ), Eschborn, Germany, www.gtz.de, accessed 12 June 2009.

Penny, D. and Singarimbun, M. (1973) *Population and Poverty in Rural Java: Some Economic Arithmetic from Sriharjo*. Department of Agricultural Economics, New York State College of Agriculture and Life Sciences, Ithaca, NY.

Perez-Pena, R. (2016) 'A toddler, a loose gun in a car, and a mother dies', *The New York Times*, 27 April, nyti.ms/1VD21Rt, accessed 16 July 2016.

Perl, A. and J.A. Dunn, Jr. (2007) 'Reframing automobile fuel economy policy in North America: The politics of punctuating a policy equilibrium', *Transport Reviews*, vol 27, no 1, 1–35.

Perl, A., Hern, M. and Kenworthy, J. (2015) 'Streets paved with gold: Urban expressway building and global city formation in Montreal, Toronto and Vancouver', *Canadian Journal of Urban Research*, vol 24, no 2, 91–116.

Perlroth, N. (2015) 'Security researchers find a way to hack cars', *The New York Times*, 21 July, nyti.ms/1VqrtYr, accessed 29 July 2016.

Perry, F. et al. (2016) 'A good wander unveils the wonder of a city: Readers on urban walking', *The Guardian*, Aug. 6, www.theguardian.com/cities/2016/aug/06/a-good-wander-unveils-the-wonder-of-a-city-readers-on-urban-walking, accessed 9 August 2016.

Perry, L. (2013) 'The emergence of the airport city in the United States', focus, LeighFisher (consulting), October, www.leighfisher.com, accessed 20 July 2016.

Pilgrim, D. (2012) 'Who was Jim Crow', Jim Crow Museum of Racist Memorabilia, www.ferris.edu/jimcrow/who.htm, accessed 20 July 2016.

Pilgrim, P. (1991) *Peace Pilgrim: Her Life and Work in Her Own Words*, Ocean Tree, Santa Fe, NM.

Plowden, S. (1972) *Towns Against Traffic*, Deutsch, London.

Plowden, S. (1980) *Taming Traffic*, Deutsch, London.

Poboon, C. (1997) *Anatomy of a traffic disaster: Towards a sustainable solution to Bangkok's traffic problems*, PhD thesis, Murdoch University at Perth, Australia.

Polo, M. (1958) *The Travels of Marco Polo* (translator unknown), Orion Press, New York, NY.

Port of Bellingham (undated) 'Waterfront redevelopment', www.portofbellingham.com/content/ArchivesItem_147_1163_v, accessed 14 June 2009.

POS (Port of Seattle) (2010) '2010 Seattle-Tacoma International Airport activity report', Aviation Planning Department, Seattle, WA, www.portseattle.org/About/Publications/Statistics/Documents/2010activity.pdf, accessed 15 August 2016.

Pow, C.P. (2009) *Gated Communities in China: Class, Privilege and the Moral Politics of the Good Life*. Routledge, Oxford.

Powell, M. (2011) 'City of the future: An airport?', *The New York Times*, 4 March, www.nytimes.com/2011/03/06/books/review/Powell-t.html?_r=0, accessed 8 June 2016.

PPN (Product Placement News) (2009) 'Ford branded products for teenage girls', www.productplacement.biz/200904173051/News/Branded-Entertainment/ford-branded-products-for-teenage-girls.html, accessed 16 August 2009.

PPP Canada (2016) www.p3canada.ca/en/, accessed 20 August 2016.

Prelinger Library, www.archive.org/movies/index.html.

Preston, J. (2010) 'Measuring the costs and benefits of integrated transport policies and schemes', in M. Givoni and D. Banister (eds), *Integrated Transport: From Policy to Practice*, Routledge, Taylor and Francis, London and New York, pp. 207–222.

Priester, R. Kenworthy, J and Wulfhorst, G. (2013) 'The diversity of megacities worldwide: Challenges for the future of mobility', in Institute for Mobility Research (ed.), *Megacity Mobility Culture: How Cities Move on in a Diverse World (Lecture Notes in Mobility)*, Springer, Munich, pp. 23–54.

Pritchard, J. (2013) 'Elon Musk unveils "hyperloop" transport concept', AP, 12 August, news.yahoo.com/elon-musk-unveils-hyperloop-transport-concept-224638943.html, accessed 17 January 2014.

PSRC (Puget Sound Regional Council) (2005) 'Regional airport ground access plan', www.psrc.org/assets/219/groundaccess.pdf, accessed 20 August 2016.

Pucher, J. (1997) 'Bicycling boom in Germany: A revival engineered by public policy', *Transportation Quarterly*, vol 51, no 4, 31–46.

Pucher, J. (2004) 'Public transportation', in S. Hanson and G. Giuliano (eds), *The Geography of Urban Transportation* (3rd edn), Guilford Press, New York, NY.

Pucher, J. and Buehler, R. (2007) 'At the frontiers of cycling: Policy innovations in the Netherlands, Denmark and Germany', *World Transport Policy and Practice*, vol 13, no 3, 8–56.

Pucher, J. and Buehler, R. (2008) 'Making cycling irresistible: Lessons from the Netherlands, Denmark and Germany', *Transport Reviews*, vol 28, no 4, 495–528, http://dx.doi.org/10.1080/01441640701806612, accessed 17 June 2009.

Pucher, J. and Buehler, R. (2009) 'Sustainable transport that works: Lessons from Germany', *World Transport Policy and Practice*, vol 15, no 1, 13–46, www.eco-logica.co.uk/pdf/wtpp15.1.pdf, accessed 17 June 2009.

Pucher, J. and Buehler, R. (2010) 'Walking and cycling for healthy cities', *Built Environment*, vol 36, no 4, 391–414.

Pucher, J., Buehler, R., Bassett, D. and Dannenberg, A. (2010) 'Walking and cycling to health: Recent evidence from city, state, and international comparisons', *American Journal of Public Health*, vol 100, no 10, 1986–1992.

Pucher, J. and Clorer, S. (1992) 'Taming the automobile in Germany', *Transportation Quarterly*, vol 46, no 3, 383–395.

Pucher, J. and Lefevre, C. (1996) *The Urban Transport Crisis in Europe and North America*, Macmillan, Basingstoke, UK.

Punter, J. (2003) *The Vancouver Achievement: Urban Planning and Design*, UBC Press, Vancouver, BC.

Putnam, R. (2001) *Bowling Alone: The Collapse and Revival of American Community*. Touchstone Books, Simon and Schuster, New York.

Pyle, K. (2014) 'Google's potential end game: Transport and organize the world's people, not just information', Viodi, 2 June, viodi.com/2014/06/02/googles-potential-end-game-transport-and-organize-the-worlds-people-not-just-information/, accessed 20 July 2016.

Quain, J. (2016) 'Skeptics of self-driving cars span generations', *The New York Times*, 16 June, nyti.ms/1rslxTi, accessed 16 June 2016.

Quill, E., (2011) 'Ancient Rome forbade downtown traffic in day', *Science News*, vol 180, no 8, 32.

Rae, J. B. (1965) *The American Automobile: A Brief History*, University of Chicago Press, Chicago, IL.

Railteam (2009) 'Welcome to railteam: Seamless high speed travel across Europe', www.railteam. co.uk, accessed 15 August 2009.

Railway Gazette (2016) 'Chinese high speed network to double in latest master plan', 21 July, www.railwaygazette.com/news/infrastructure/single-view/view/chinese-high-speed-network-to-double-in-latest-master-plan.html, accessed 25 July 2016.

Raimond, T. and Milthorpe, F. (2010) 'Why are young people driving less? Trends in licence-holding and travel behavior', Australasian Transport Research Forum 2010 Proceedings, 29 September–1 October 2010, Canberra, Australia Publication, www.patrec.org/atrf.aspx.

Rainie, L. and J. Poushter (2014) 'Emerging nations catching up to U.S. on technology adoption, especially mobile and social media use', Pew Research Center, www.pewresearch.org, accessed 17 July 2016.

Ran Kim, S. and Horn, A. (1999) 'Regulation policies concerning natural monopolies in developing and transition economies', United Nations Department of Economic and Social Affairs (DESA), March 1999, www.un.org/esa/esa99dp8.pdf, accessed 18 August 2016.

Rawls, J. (1971) *A Theory of Justice*, Belknap Press, Cambridge, MA.

Region of Hamilton–Wentworth (1999) *Summary of the Sustainable Community Planning Process, 1990 to 1999*, Region of Hamilton–Wentworth, Hamilton, Ontario, Canada.

Region of Hamilton–Wentworth (circa 1996) 'Creating a sustainable community: Hamilton–Wentworth's VISION 2020—Canada', www.vcn.bc.ca/citizenshandbook/unesco/most/usa4.html, accessed 13 August 2009.

remix.com (accessed 23 July 2017).

Rescue Muni (undated) 'A transit riders' association for San Francisco', www.rescuemuni.org/, accessed 15 September 2009.

Richards, B. (1976) *Moving in Cities*, Westview, Boulder, CO.

Richland, J., Lee, J. and Butto, E. D. (2016) 'Steering autonomous vehicle policy: The role of public health', Altarum Institute, Ann Arbor, http://altarum.org/sites/default/files/uploaded-related-files/Autonomous%20Vehicles%20Report_final031816.pdf, accessed 20 October 2016.

Rikort, A, Markiewicz, M., Herrmann, M. and Kreisel, S. (2014) *Comparative Urban Data Collection and Analysis Focussed on Freiburg im Breisgau: Transport and Land Use Sustainability in Cities*, GEKO Master Project, Frankfurt University of Applied Sciences, Frankfurt am Main.

Riley, E.A., Gould, T., Hartin, K., Fruin, S.A., Simpson, C.D., Yost, M.G. and Larson, T. (2016) 'Ultrafine particle size as a tracer for aircraft turbine emissions'. *Atmospheric Environment*, vol 139, 20–29.

Rittel, H. and Webber, M. (1973) 'Dilemmas in a general theory of planning', *Policy Sciences*, vol 4, no 2, 155–169.

Road Safety Foundation (undated) 'Too many children die on our roads', www.roadsafetyfoundation. co.za/RoadSafety/tabid/56/Default.aspx, accessed 5 September 2009.

Roberts, J. (1989) *Quality Streets: How Traditional Urban Centers Benefit from Traffic-Calming, Transport and Environment Studies*, TEST report no 75, London.

Roberts, J. (1992) *Trip Degeneration*, TEST, London.

Roberts, N. (2004) 'Public deliberation in an age of direct citizen participation', *American Review of Public Administration*, vol 34, no 4, 315–353.

Robson, D. (2014) 'We are primed to see faces in every corner of the visual world', BBC, Neuroscience Report, 30 July, www.bbc.com/future/story/20140730-why-do-we-see-faces-in-objects, accessed 1 May 2016.

Rogers, K. (2016) 'Snapchat at 107 MPH? Lawsuit blames teenager (and Snapchat)', *The New York Times*, 3 May, nyti.ms/1SZgkiJ, accessed 15 July 2016.

Rogge, M., Wollny, S. and Sauer, D.U. (2015) 'Fast charging battery buses for the electrification of urban public transport: A feasibility study focusing on charging infrastructure and energy storage requirements', *Energies*, vol 8, 4587–4606, www.mdpi.com/1996-1073/8/5/4587/pdf, accessed 24 July 2016.

Roider, D., Busch, C., Spitaler, R. and Hertz, H. (2016) 'Segway® related injuries in Vienna: Report from the Lorenz Böhler Trauma Centre', *European Journal of Trauma and Emergency Surgery*, vol 42, 203–205.

Rose, M. H. (1979) *Interstate: Express Highway Politics, 1941–1956*, The Regents Press of Kansas, Lawrence, KS.

Ross, B. (2016) 'Big philanthropy takes the bus', *Dissent Magazine*, www.dissentmagazine.org/article/brt-bus-rapid-transit-big-philanthropy-oil-lobby, accessed 10 July 2016.

Roth, G. (2010) 'Federal highway funding', Cato Institute, www.downsizinggovernment.org/transportation/federal-highway-funding, accessed 15 August 2016.

Rothschild, E. (1973) *Paradise Lost: The Decline of the Auto-Industrial Age*, Random House, New York, NY.

Rothschild, E. (2009) 'Can we transform the auto-industrial society?', *The New York Review of Books*, vol 56, no 3, www.nybooks.com/articles/22333, accessed 3 July 2009.

Rucker, P. (2012) 'Mitt Romney's dog-on-the-car-roof story still proves to be his critics' best friend', *The Washington Post*, 12 Mar, www.washingtonpost.com/politics/mitt-romneys-dog-on-the-car-roof-story-still-proves-to-be-his-critics-best-friend/2012/03/14/gIQAp2LxCS_story.html, accessed 18 July 2016.

Rudolph, S. (2016) 'E-commerce Product Return Statistics and Trends [Infographic]', www.business2community.com/infographics/e-commerce-product-return-statistics-trends-infographic-01505394#v4JpT81tz4SL1izg.97, accessed 13 November 2016.

Ruhl, T., and Trnavskis, B. (1998) 'Airport trip generation', Institute of Transportation Engineers, *ITE Journal*, vol 68, no 5, 24–29.

SAAQ, Société de l'assurance automobile du Québec (2012) 'Report on automobile advertising: Guidelines', saaq.gouv.qc.ca/fileadmin/documents/publications/report-automobile-advertising-guidelines.pdf, accessed 2 May 2016.

Sachs, W. (1983) 'Are energy intensive life-images fading? The cultural meaning of the automobile in transition', *Journal of Economic Psychology*, vol 3, 347–365.

Sachs, W. (1992) *For Love of the Automobile: Looking Back into the History of Our Desires*, University of California Press, Berkeley, CA.

SACTRA (1994) *Trunk roads and the generation of traffic*, Department of Transport, Standing Advisory Committee on Trunk Road Assessment, London.

Sadik-Kahn, J. and S. Solomonow (2016) *Street Fight: Handbook for an Urban Revolution*. Viking, New York.

Safire, W. (2008) *Safire's Political Dictionary*, Oxford University Press, New York, NY.

Salomon, D. (2009) 'Freiburg Green City: Approaches to sustainability. Presentation to European Green Capital Award, 1 December 2009', http://ec.europa.eu/environment/europeangreencapital/docs/cities/2010–2011/freiburg_presentation.pdf, accessed 30 July 2009.

Samilton, T. (2011) 'Minivans fight 'Loser Cruiser' stereotype with new sex appeal', Michigan Radio, 29 March, michiganradio.org/post/minivans-fight-loser-cruiser-stereotype-new-sex-appeal#stream/0, accessed 15 July 2016.

Sandercock, L. (1998) *Towards Cosmopolis: Planning for Multicultural Cities*, John Wiley and Sons, Chichester, UK.

Sandy, B. (2002) 'Jam Handy', *Oakland University Journal*, Spring 2002, no 4, 82–92, www2.oakland.edu/oujournal/files/4_sandy.pdf, accessed 17 July 2016.

Saul, J.R. (1999) *The Unconscious Civilization*. Free Press, New York.

Schaefer, S. (director) (2006) *Contested Streets: Breaking New York City Gridlock*, Streetfilms, Cicala Filmworks, www.streetfilms.org.

Schaeffer, K. and Sclar, E. (1975) *Access for All: Transportation and Urban Growth*, Penguin, Baltimore, MD.

Scharf, V. (1991) *Taking the Wheel: Women and the Coming of the Motor Age*, Free Press, New York, NY.

Scheurer, J. (2001) 'Urban ecology, innovations in housing policy and the future of cities: Towards sustainability in neighbourhood communities', PhD thesis, Murdoch University at Perth, Australia.

Schiller, P. L. (1992) 'Turn off the traffic rap', *Eastside Week*, Seattle, WA, 13 May, p. 2.

Schiller, P. L. (1997a) 'Fighting airport expansion: Turning planes into trains,' *Planet*, Sierra Club, April, San Francisco, CA.

Schiller, P. (1997b) *Parking—A Primer: How to Improve Communities while Promoting Alternatives to Driving*, ALT-TRANS, Washington Coalition for Transportation Alternatives, Seattle, WA.

Schiller, P. L. (1998) 'High occupancy vehicle (HOV) lanes: Highway expansions in search of meaning', *World Transport Policy and Practice*, vol 4, no 2, 32–38, www.eco-logica.co.uk/WTPPdownloads.html (then select <wtpp04.2.pdf>), accessed 14 November 2016.

Schiller, P. L. (2002a) 'Taking the high road', Trust for Public Land, Washington, DC, www.tpl.org/tier3_cd.cfm?content_item_id=10863&folder_id=188, accessed 15 August 2009.

Schiller, P. L. (2002b) 'Lift your right foot, now!', *The Every Other Weekly*, Bellingham, WA, 7–20 March, p. 8.

Schiller, P. L. (2008) 'Connections within the western U.S.–Canada border region: Toward more sustainable transportation practices', in J. Loucky, D. K. Alper and J. C. Day (eds), *Transboundary Policy Challenges in the Pacific Border Regions of North America*, University of Calgary Press, Calgary, Alberta, Chapter 5.

Schiller, P. L. (2012) 'Remembering Jane Holtz Kay', thenation.com, 11 December, www.thenation.com/print/article/171705/remembering-jane-holtz-kay, accessed 17 September 2016.

Schiller, P. L. (2014) 'Transportation', in D. Rowe (ed.) *Achieving Sustainability: Visions, Principles and Practices* (Gale virtual reference library). Macmillan Reference USA, Cengage Learning, Detroit.

Schiller, P. L. (2016) 'Automated and connected vehicles: High tech hope or hype?', *World Transport Policy and Practice*, vol 22.3, Oct., 28–44, http://worldtransportjournal.com/wp-content/uploads/2016/10/4th-Oct-opt.pdf, accessed 20 October 2016.

Schiller, P. L. (in press) 'History of sustainable transportation', in J. Caradonna (ed.) *Routledge Handbook of the History of Sustainability*, Routledge, London and New York

Schiller, P. L., Bruun, E. C. and Kenworthy, J. (2010) *An Introduction to Sustainable Transportation: Policy, Planning and Implementation.* Earthscan, London.

Schiller, P. L. and DeLille, B. (1997) *Green Streets*, STTP, Washington, DC.

Schiller, P. and Kenworthy, J. R. (1999) 'Prospects for sustainable transportation in the Pacific Northwest: A comparison of Vancouver, Seattle and Portland', *World Transport Policy and Practice*, vol 5, no 1, 30–38.

Schiller, P. and Kenworthy, J. R. (2003) 'Prospects for sustainable transportation in the Pacific Northwest', in J. Whitelegg and G. Haq (eds), *The Earthscan Reader on World Transport Policy & Practice*, Earthscan, London.

Schiller, P. and Kenworthy, J. (2011) 'Walk-to transit or drive-to transit?', Proceedings (Charter Papers) Walk21, Vancouver, BC, www.academia.edu/12341874/Walk_to_transit_or_drive_to_transit, accessed 24 August 2016.

Schivelbusch, W. (1986) *The Railway Journey*, University of California Press, Berkeley, CA.

Schivelbusch, W. (2007) *Three New Deals: Reflections on Roosevelt's America, Mussolini's Italy, and Hitler's Germany, 1933–1939*, Picador, New York, NY.

Schively, C. (2007) 'Enhancing transportation: The effects of public involvement in planning and design processes', Humphrey Institute of Public Affairs, University of Minnesota, FHWA Report No CTS 07–10, Minneapolis, www.cts.umn.edu/Publications/ResearchReports/pdfdownload.pl?id=824, accessed 18 June 2009.

Schley, F. (2001) 'Urban transport strategy review: Experiences from Germany and Zurich', Deutsche Gesellschaft für Technische Zusammenarbeit (GTZ) GmbH, Division 44, Environmental Management, Water, Energy, Transport, Postfach 5180, 65726 Eschborn, Federal Republic of Germany.

Schmitt, A. (2011) 'John Kasich's sad war on transit (and cities)', 15 April, StreetsBlog.org, usa.streetsblog.org/2011/04/15/john-kasichs-sad-war-on-transit-and-cities/, accessed 31 July 2011.

Schneider, J. (undated) 'Personal Rapid Transit (PRT), Personal Automated Transport (PAT), PodCar, IPM and ATN Quicklinks', faculty.washington.edu/jbs/itrans/prtquick.htm, accessed 28 July 2016.

Schneider, K. (1972) *Autokind vs Mankind: An Analysis of Tyranny, a Proposal for Rebellion, a Plan for Reconstruction*, Schocken, New York, NY.

Schneider, K. (1979) *On the Nature of Cities: Towards Creative and Enduring Human Environments*, Jossey-Bass, San Francisco.

Schoettle, B. and M. Sivak (2015) 'A preliminary analysis of real-world crashes involving self-driving vehicles', University of Michigan Transportation Research Institute (UMTRI-2015–34), www.umich.edu/~umtriswt/PDF/UMTRI-2015-34.pdf, accessed 10 July 2016.

Schommer, J. (2003) 'A charrette is the center of the urban design process', www.charrettecenter.net/charrettecenter.asp?a=spf&pfk=7&gk=261, accessed 18 June 2009.

Schreiber, R. (2013) 'Automotive wayback machine: The Jam Handy Organization archive', www.thetruthaboutcars.com/2013/12/automotive-wayback-machine-the-jam-handy-organization-archive/?print=1, accessed 16 July 2016.

Schwedler, H.-U. (2007) 'Supportive institutional conditions for policy integration of transport, environment and health', European Academy of the Urban Environment, Berlin, www.eaue.de/PUBS.HTM, accessed 17 June 2009.

Scientific American (2016) 'Citizen science: Help make science happen by volunteering for a real research project', www.scientificamerican.com/citizen-science/, accessed 27 August 2016.

Sclar, E. (2000) *You Don't Always Get What You Pay for: The Economics of Privatization*, Century Foundation Book, Cornell University Press, Ithaca, NY.

Seattle Urban Mobility Plan (2008) 'Case studies in urban freeway removal', Chapter 6, www.cityofseattle.net/Transportation/docs/ump/06%20SEATTLE%20Case%20studies%20in%20urban%20freeway%20removal.pdf, accessed 10 August 2009.

Segway (2016) 'Become familiar with the regulations in your state', www.segway.com/support/regulatory-information, accessed 1 August 2016.

Seiler, C. (2009) *Republic of Driver: A Cultural History of Automobility in America*, University of Chicago Press, Chicago, IL.

Sewell, J. (1993) *The Shape of the City: Toronto Struggles with Modern Planning*, University of Toronto Press, Toronto.

Shaver-Crandell, A., Gerson, P. and Stones, A. (1995) *The Pilgrim's Guide to Santiago de Compostela: A Gazetteer*, Harvey Miller, London.

Sheller, M. and Urry, J. (2000) 'The city and the car', *International Journal of Urban and Regional Research*, vol 24, no 4, 737–757.

Sheller, M, and Urry, J. (eds) (2004) *Tourism mobilities. Places to play, places in play*, Routledge, London.

Shin, Y., Vuchic, V., and Bruun, E. (2009) 'Land consumption impacts of a transportation system on a city: An analysis', *Transportation Research Record: Journal of the Transportation Research Board*, vol 2110, 69–77.

Shoup, D. (1997) 'Cashing Out Employer-Paid Parking', NTIS Report Number FTA-CA-11-0035-92-1.

Shoup, D. (2011) *The High Cost of Free Parking* (updated edn), APA Planners Press, pp. 262–266.

Siegl, K. (2009) 'The new district of Freiburg-Rieselfeld: A case study of successful, sustainable urban development', Rieselfeld Projekt Group, Stadt Freiburg im Bresgau, www.energy-cities.eu/IMG/pdf/0902_19_Rieselfeld_engl.pdf, see end for attribution, Rieselfeld Projekt Group, accessed 17 September 2016.

Siemiatycki, M. (2006) 'Implications of private-public partnerships on the development of urban public transit infrastructure: The case of Vancouver, Canada', *Journal of Planning Education and Research*, vol 26, 137–151.

Singer, A. (2001) *CARtoons*, Car Busters, Prague, www.andysinger.com, accessed 15 September 2016.

Sisario, B. (2014) 'Clear Channel renames itself iHeartMedia in nod to digital', *The New York Times*, 16 September, nyti.ms/1tYw205, accessed 16 July 2016.

Sivak, M. and Schoettle, B. (2015) 'Motion sickness in self-driving vehicles', The University of Michigan Transportation Research Institute (UMTRI), April, deepblue.lib.umich.edu/bitstream/handle/2027.42/111747/103189.pdf, accessed 29 July 2016.

Sivak, M. and Schoettle, B. (2016) 'Would self-driving vehicles increase occupant productivity?', Sustainable Worldwide Transportation, The University of Michigan, Ann Arbor, http://umich.edu/~umtriswt/PDF/SWT-2016–11_Abstract_English.pdf, accessed 20 October 2016.

Slater, R. E. and Linton, G. J. (eds) (2003) 'A guide to metropolitan transportation planning under ISTEA—how the pieces fit together', http://ntl.bts.gov/DOCS/424MTP.html, accessed 10 June 2009.

Smart Growth America (2013) *Complete Streets: Local Policy Workbook*, Smart Growth America and National Complete Streets Coalition, Washington, DC.

Smith, G. and Wales, C. (2000) 'Citizens' juries and deliberative democracy', *Political Studies*, vol 48, no 1, 51–65.

Smith, J. (1983) 'Runaway match: The automobile in the American film, 1900–1920', in D. L. Lewis and L. Goldstein (eds), *The Automobile and American Culture*, University of Michigan Press, Ann Arbor, MI.

Smith, M.S. (1996) 'Crime prevention through environmental design in parking facilities', National Institute of Justice: Research in Brief, April, www.ncjrs.gov/pdffiles/cptedpkg.pdf, accessed 18 August 2016.

Smith, R. S. (2008) 'Obesity crisis: Get paid to lose weight', *The Telegraph*, 24 January, www.telegraph.co.uk/news/uknews/1576430/Obesity-crisis-get-paid-to-lose-weight.html, accessed 25 March 2016.

Smoak, S. (2007) 'Framing the automobile in twentieth century American literature: A spatial approach', PhD thesis, University of North Carolina at Greensboro, NC.

SNCF (2009) 'TGV reservations', www.tgv.com/EN/index_HD.html, accessed 15 September 2009.

Socialdata (undated) socialdata.us/links.php, www.socialdata.de, accessed 24 August 2016.

Socialdata America (undated) socialdata.us/index.php, accessed 10 September 2009.

Solnit, R. (2000) *Wanderlust: A History of Walking*, Penguin, New York, NY.

Solnit, R. (2015) 'Power in Paris', *Harper's Magazine*, December, pp. 5–7.

Speck, J. (2012) *Walkable City: How Downtown Can Save America, One Step at a Time*, Farrar, Straus and Giroux, New York.

Starky, S. (2005) 'The Obesity Epidemic in Canada' (PRB 05–11E), Economics Division, Parliamentary Information and Research Service (PIRS), Library of Parliament—Bibliotheque du Parlement, Ottawa, ON, www.parl.gc.ca/information/library/prbpubs/prb0511-e.htm, accessed 1 September 2009.

STARS (Shock Trauma Air Rescue Service) (2016) www.stars.ca, accessed 16 August 2016.

Statista.com, www.statista.com/statistics/258075/us-motor-vehicle-and-parts-manufacturing-gross-output/, accessed 2 May 2016.

STATTAUTO (undated) www.eaue.de/winuwd/86.htm, accessed 15 August 2009.

Steadman, I. (2013) 'High Speed 2 could have been a maglev, but isn't, and that's OK'. *New Statesman*, 19 November. http://www.newstatesman.com/print/node/137219

Steg, L. (2005) 'Car use: lust and must. Instrumental, symbolic and affective motives for car use', *Transportation Research Part A*, vol 39, 147–162.

Steinbeck, J. (1939) *The Grapes of Wrath*, Viking Compass, New York, NY.

Steinbeck, J. (1962) *Travels with Charley*, Viking, New York.

Stenquist, P. (2012) 'Amphibious car is still waiting to catch a wave', 12 October, *The New York Times*, nyti.ms/RSgVAR, accessed 25 July 2016.

Stevens, H. (2004) *Transport Policy in the European Union*, Palgrave Macmillan, Basingstoke, UK.

Stewart, J. and A. Bertaud (2015) 'Self-driving vehicles conference 2015 (Marron Institute)', marroninstitute.nyu.edu/content/blog/self-driving-vehicles-conference-2015, accessed 24 June 2016.

Stone, B. (2012) *The City and the Coming Climate: Climate Change in the Places We Live*. Cambridge University Press, Cambridge

Stone, T. (1971) *Beyond the Automobile: Reshaping the Transportation Environment*, Prentice-Hall, Englewood Cliffs, NJ.

Strathman, J. G. and Dueker, K. J. (1996) 'Transit service, parking charges, and mode choice for the journey to work: An analysis of the 1990 NPTS', *Journal of Public Transportation*, vol 1, 13–38.

Strickland, J. (2009) 'Energy efficiency of different modes of transportation', adl.stanford.edu/aa260/lecture_notes_files/transport_fuel_consumption.pdf, accessed 31 July 2016.

Strickler, J. (2011) 'Garage to your dream home—minus the house', *Star-Tribune*, www.startribune.com/garage-to-your-dream-home-minus-the-house/128359633/, accessed 16 July 2016.

Stringer, P. and Wenzel, H. (1976) *Transportation Planning for a Better Environment*, Plenum Press, New York, NY.

Stromberg, J. (2015) ' "Bicycle face": A 19th-century health problem made up to scare women away from biking', 24 March, www.vox.com/2014/7/8/5880931/the-19th-century-health-scare-that-told-women-to-worry-about-bicycle, accessed 14 July 2016.

Stryker, M. (2016) 'Detroit painter Nancy Mitchnick goes her own way', *Detroit Free Press*, 13 June, www.freep.com/story/entertainment/arts/2016/06/13/nancy-mitchnick-mocad-exhibition/84338932/, accessed 31 October 2016.

Sucher, D. (2003) *City Comforts: How to Build an Urban Village*. City Comforts Inc., Seattle.

Sugrue, T. J. (2012) 'Driving while black: The car and race relations in modern America', Automobile in American Life and Society 2004–2010, University of Michigan-Dearborn, Web 1, www.autolife.umd.umich.edu/Race/R_Casestudy/R_Casestudy.htm, accessed 16 July 2016.

Sumption, J. (1975) *Pilgrimage: An Image of Mediaeval Religion*, Rowman and Littlefield, Totowa, NJ.

Suwei, F. and Qiang, L. (2013) 'Car ownership control in Chinese cities: Shanghai, Beijing and Guangzhou', *Journeys*, September, 40–49, www.lta.gov.sg/ltaacademy/doc/13Sep040-Feng_CarOwnershipControl.pdf, accessed 15 July 2016.

Swift, P. (undated) 'New urbanism: Clustered, mixed-use, multi-modal neighborhood design', www.vtpi.org/tdm/tdm24.htm, accessed 15 September 2009.

Szyliowicz, J. (2003) 'Decision-making, intermodal transportation, and sustainable mobility: Towards a new paradigm', *International Social Science Journal*, vol 55, no 176, 185–197.

T4A (Transportation for America) (2011) 'Transportation 101: An introduction to federal transportation policy', t4america.org/maps-tools/transportation101/, accessed 26 August 2016.

T4A (Transportation for America) (2015) 'Think FAST—the good, the bad and the ugly in Congress' new five-year transportation bill', t4america.org/2015/12/02/think-fast-the-good-the-bad-and-the-ugly-in-congress-new-five-year-transportation-bill/, accessed 22 August 2016.

T4America (Transportation for America) (2012) 'Thinking outside the farebox: Creative approaches to financing transit projects', t4america.org/wp-content/.../T4-Financing-Transit-Guidebook.pdf_, accessed 19 August 2016.

Taso, H. S. J. and Botha, J. L. (2003) 'Definition and evaluation of bus and truck automation operations concepts: Final report', California Partners for Advanced Transportation Technology, UC Berkeley, escholarship.org/uc/item/9pz7n1gr, accessed 27 June 2016.

Taylor, D. (2013) 'Porsche design tower elevator deposits car and driver inside their luxury apartment', 3 June, www.gizmag.com/porsche-design-tower-car-elevator/27764/, accessed 18 July 2016.

Taylor, I. and Sloman, L. (2012) 'Rebuilding rail: Final report', Transport for Quality of Life Ltd, June, www.transportforqualityoflife.com/u/files/120630_Rebuilding_Rail_Final_Report_print_version.pdf, accessed 18 August 2016.

Thanawala, S. (2007) 'Embedded advertising: A new revenue model for cinema', FICCI (Federation of Indian Chambers of Commerce) Frames 2007, www.exchange4media.com/FICCI/2007/ficci_fullstory07.asp?news_id=25457, accessed 15 August 2009.

The Bravern (2016) thebravern.com/, vimeo.com/84234780, accessed 25 July 2016.

The Guardian (2015) 'Smog envelops Beijing: Before and after pictures as city goes on red alert', *The Guardian*, 7 December, www.theguardian.com/cities/gallery/2015/dec/08/beijing-air-pollution-red-alert-smog-before-after-pictures, accessed 25 March 2016.

The Transport Politic (2014) 'Openings and construction starts planned for 2014', www.thetransportpolitic.com/2014/01/05/openings-and-construction-starts-planned-for-2014/, accessed 25 July 2016.

Thompson, G. L., and Matoff, T. G. (2003) 'Keeping up with the Joneses: Planning for transit in decentralizing regions', *Journal of the American Planning Association*, vol 69, no 3, 296–312.

Thomson, J. M. (1977) *Great Cities and Their Traffic*, Penguin Books, Middlesex.

Ticoll, D. (2015) 'Driving changes: Automated vehicles in Toronto', Discussion paper: City of Toronto Transportation Services Division and University of Toronto Transportation Research Institute (UTTRI), 15 October.

Tohline, A.M. (2009) ' "Around the corner": How Jam Handy's films reflected and shaped the 1930s and beyond', MA Thesis, School of Film, Ohio University, etd.ohiolink.edu/rws_etd/document/get/ohiou1248295030/inline, accessed 17 July 2016.

Tolley, R. (ed.) (1990) *The Greening of Urban Transport: Planning for Walking and Cycling in Western Cities*, Belhaven Press, London.

Tomalty, R. and Haider, M. (2009) *BC Sprawl Report 2009: Walkability and Health 2009*, Smart Growth British Columbia, Vancouver, BC.

Tomer, A. and Puentes, R. (2009) 'Expect delays: An analysis of air travel trends in the United States', Brookings Institution, Washington, DC, www.brookings.edu/.../expect-delays-an-analysis-of-air-travel-trends-in-the-united-states/_, accessed 15 August 2016.

Toor, W. and Havlick, S. (2004) *Transportation and Sustainable Campus Communities: Issues, Examples, Solutions*, Island Press, Washington, DC.

Toronto (City) 'Did Toronto have toll gates?', www.toronto.ca/archives/toronto_history_faqs.htm#tollgates, accessed 10 July 2009.

Townsend, C. (2003) *In whose interest? A critical approach to Southeast Asia's urban transport dynamics*, PhD Thesis, Murdoch University, Perth, Australia.

Transit Camp (San Francisco Bay Area) (2009) barcamp.org/TransitCampBayArea, accessed 15 September 2009.

Transit Camp (Toronto) (2009) transitcamp.wik.is/, accessed 15 September 2009.

Transport and Environment (2016a) 'Biodiesel increasing EU transport emissions by 4% instead of cutting CO_2', Bulletin 246, May, www.transportenvironment.org.

Transport and Environment (2016b) 'Carmakers' abominable April crushes consumers' trust in them', Bulletin 246, May, www.transportenvironment.org.

Transport WA (1999) *TravelSmart 2010: A 10 Year Plan*, Transport WA, Perth, Australia.

Transportation Research Board (TRB), Transit Cooperative Research Program (TCRP), www.trb.org/TCRP/TCRP.aspx

Transportation Research Board (2002) 'Going public: Involving communities in transportation decisions', *TR News*, no 220, May–June 2002, http://trb.org/publications/trnews/trnews220toc.pdf, accessed 20 August 2009.

Tri-Met (2009) Status Report, Spring, Tri-Met, Portland, Oregon.

Trimble, T. E., Bishop, R. Morgan, J. F. and Blanco, M. (2014) 'Human factors evaluation of Level 2 and Level 3 automated driving concepts: Past research, state of automation technology, and emerging system concepts', National Highway Traffic Safety Administration (NHTSA), Report No DOT HS 812 043.

Troyat, H. (2001) *Tolstoy*, translated by N. Amphoux, Grove Press, New York, NY.

Trubka, R., Newman, P. and Bilsborough, D. (2012) *Assessing the Costs of Alternative Development Paths in Australian Cities*, Curtin University Sustainability Policy Institute and Parsons Brinckerhoff, Perth.

Truong, L.C. and Marshall, W.E. 2014) 'Are park-and-rides saving the environment or just saving parking costs? Case study of Denver, Colorado, Light Rail system', *Transportation Research Record*, no 2419, 109–117.

ttbook.org: (2016) To the best of our knowledge. *Walking*, 5 November, www.ttbook.org/book/walking, accessed 5 November 2016.

Ultra Global prt (undated) www.ultraglobalprt.com/wheres-it-used/where-can-it-be-used/, accessed 28 July 2016.

UMTRI; University of Michigan Transportation Research Institute (2014) 'Connected vehicles 101: Learning through experience', *UMTRI Research Review*, July–Sept., 1–2, http://triweb02.miserver.it.umich.edu/content/rr_45_3.pdf, accessed 20 October 2016.

UN Aarhus Convention on access to Information (1998) 'Public participation in decision-making and access to justice in environmental matters', www.unece.org/env/pp/, accessed 12 June 2009.

UN Secretary-General's High Level Advisory Group on Sustainable Transport (2016) *Mobilizing Sustainable Transport for Development: Analysis and Policy Recommendations*. United Nations, New York.

Underwood, S. E., Marshall, S. and Niles, J. (2014) 'Automated, connected, and electric vehicles: An assessment of emerging transportation technologies and a policy roadmap for more sustainable transportation', Graham Environmental Sustainability Institute, University of Michigan, Ann Arbor, http://graham.umich.edu/media/files/LC-IA-Final-Underwood.pdf, accessed 20 October 2016.

UNESCO (undated) 'Creating a sustainable community: Hamilton-Wentworth's VISION 2020 (Canada)', www.unesco.org/most/usa4.htm, accessed 27 August 2016.

United Nations (1992) 'Rio Declaration on Environment and Development', in Report of the United Nations Conference on the Human Environment, www.unep.org/Documents.Multilingual/Default.asp?documentid=78&articleid=1163, 5–16 July, accessed 17 June 2009.

United Nations Economic Commission for Europe (UNECE) (2011) 'Transport for sustainable development', 19th session of the United Nations Commission on Sustainable Development, www.unece.org/trans/side-events/transport-for-sustainable-development.html, accessed 25 March 2016.

United Nations Economic Commission for Europe (UNECE) (undated) 'Millenium development goals', www.unece.org/es/sustainable-development/millennium-development-goals/millennium-development-goals.html, accessed 25 March 2016.

United Nations Economic Commission for Europe (UNECE) (undated) 'Sustainable development', www.unece.org/sustainable-development/sustainable-development/home.html, accessed 25 March 2016.

Untermann, R. (1984) *Accommodating the Pedestrian: Adapting Towns and Neighborhoods for Walking and Biking*, Van Nostrand Reinhold Company, New York, NY.

Urban Design Group (undated) 'What is urban design?', www.udg.org.uk/about/what-is-urban-design, accessed 14 May 2016.

Urban Research Program, Griffith University (2008) 'Vulnerability assessment for mortgage, petrol and inflation risks and expenditure: 2006 census data analysis of Melbourne', The Age, www.theage.com.au/ed_docs/Vulnerability.pdf, accessed 25 March 2016.

Urry, J. (2002) 'Mobility and proximity', *Sociology*, vol 36, no 2, 255–274.

Urry, J. (2004) 'The "system" of automobility', *Theory, Culture & Society*, vol 21, no 4/5, 25–39.

Urry, J. (2006) 'Inhabiting the car', *Sociological Review*, vol 54, 17–31.

Urry, J. (2010) 'Consuming the planet to excess', *Theory, Culture and Society*, vol 27, no 2–3, 191–212.

U.S. Bureau of Transportation Statistics (2006) 'National transportation statistics 2006', U.S. Department of Transportation, Research and Innovative Technology Administration, Washington, DC, www.bts. gov/.../national_transportation_statistics/2006/pdf/entire.pdf, accessed 14 September 2009.

U.S. Census Bureau (2008) 'FT 920 U.S. merchandise trade selected highlights', www.census.gov/foreign-trade/balance/c5700.html#2009, accessed 5 August 2009.

U.S. Conference of Mayors (2008) Protecting and Developing the Urban Tree Canopy: A 135-City Survey. US Conference of Mayors. www.mayors.org/trees/treefinalreport2008.pdf

USDOT (United States Department of Transportation) (2006) 'Transportation's role in climate change: Transportation and greenhouse gas emissions', http://climate.dot.gov/about/transportations-role/overview.html, accessed 20 October 2016.

USEIA (United States Energy Information Administration) (2016) 'What is U.S. electricity generation by energy source?', www.eia.gov/tools/faqs/faq.cfm?id=427&t=3, 1 April, climate.dot.gov/about/transportations-role/overview.html, accessed 2 June 2016.

Vance, A. and Stone, B. (2016) 'Welcome to Larry Page's secret flying-car factories: With Zee.Aero and Kitty Hawk, the Google co-founder looks to the skies', *Bloomberg Businessweek*, 9 June, www.bloomberg.com/news/articles/2016–06–09/welcome-to-larry-page-s-secret-flying-car-factories, accessed 10 June 2016.

VandeHei, J. (2003) 'Lobbying to put the Segway on profit path', *The Washington Post*, 24 February, www.washingtonpost.com/archive/politics/2003/02/24/lobbying-to-put-the-segway-on-profit-path/6a87b91b-e3b3–45eb-8c80–3b4347d55710/, accessed 1 August 2016.

Vanderbilt. T. (2008) *Traffic: Why We Drive the Way We Do (And What It Says About Us)*, Alfred A. Knopf, New York, NY.

Vanek, F. M., Angenent, L. T., Banks, J. H., Daziano, R. A. and Turnquist, M. A. (2014) *Sustainable Transportation Engineering Systems*, McGraw-Hill Education, New York.

van Vliet, W. (1983) 'Children's travel behaviour', *Ekistics*, vol 298, 61–65.

Vasconcellos, E. (2001) *Urban Transport, Environment and Equity: The Case for Developing Countries*, Earthscan, London.

Victoria Transport Policy Institute (2008) 'Road pricing', Victoria Transport Policy Institute, www.vtpi.org/tdm/tdm35.htm, accessed 15 September 2009.

Victoria Transport Policy Institute (2009a) 'Transportation management programs', Victoria Transport Policy Institute, www.vtpi.org/tdm/tdm42.htm, accessed 15 September 2009.

Victoria Transport Policy Institute (2009b) 'Online TDM encyclopedia', Victoria Transport Policy Institute, www.vtpi.org/tdm, accessed 15 September 2009.

Victoria Transport Policy Institute (2009c) 'Incentives to use alternative modes and reduce driving', www.vtpi.org/tdm/index.php#incentives, accessed 15 September 2009.

Vincent, A. (2015) 'David Byrne's meltdown: Books, bikes and Brian Eno', 16 June, www.telegraph.co.uk/culture/music/music-news/11678389/David-Byrnes-Meltdown-books-bikes-and-Brian-Eno.html, accessed 12 October 2016.

Vuchic, V. R. (2007) 'Urban passenger transport modes', in V. R. Vuchic (ed.) *Urban Transit: Systems and Technology*, John Wiley and Sons, Somerset, NJ.

Vuchic, V., & Casello, J. (2002) An evaluation of maglev technology and its comparison with high speed rail. *Transportation Quarterly*, vol 56, no 2, 33-49.

Wackernagel, M. and Rees, W. (1996) *Our Ecological Footprint: Reducing Human Impact on the Earth*, New Society, Gabriola Island, BC.

Wadud, Z., MacKenzie, D., and Leiby, P. (2016) 'Help or hindrance? The travel, energy and carbon impacts of highly automated vehicles', *Transportation Research Part A*, vol 86, 1–18.

Walker, J. (2012) 'Portland: The grid is 30 years old ... thank a planner!', humantransit.org/2012/08/portland-the-grid-is-30-thank-a-planner.html, accessed 16 August 2016.

Waller, P. (1983) *Town, City, and Nation: England 1850–1914*, Oxford University Press, Oxford, UK.

Wang, Y. (2013) 'High-speed rail is at the foundation of China's growth strategy', *Quartz*, 22 August, qz.com/116190/high-speed-rail-is-at-the-foundation-of-chinas-growth-strategy/, accessed 25 July 2016.

Warburton, D., Wilson, R. and Rainbow, E. (undated) 'Making a difference: A guide to evaluating public participation in central government', www.involve.org.uk/making_a_difference/, accessed 15 June 2009.

Warner, P. (undated) 'Organising the study circle process: A brief introduction', Worker Education Association in Sweden, www.adulteduc.gr/001/pdfs/Oganising_the_study_circle_process.pdf, accessed 15 June 2009.

Wassenhoven, L. (2008) 'Territorial governance, participation, cooperation and partnership: A matter of national culture?', *Boletin de la A.G.E.*, no 46, 53–76.

WCED (World Commission on Environment and Development) (1987) *Our common future*, Brundtland Commission, www.unece.org/oes/nutshell/2004–2005/focus_sustainable_development.htm, accessed 22 February 2008.

Webber, M. (1963) 'Order in diversity: Community without propinquity', In L. Wingo (ed.), *Cities and Space: The Future Use of Urban Land*, John Hopkins University Press, Baltimore.

Webber, M. (1964) 'The urban place and the non-place urban realm', In M. Webber (ed.), *Explorations in urban structures*, University of Pennsylvania Press, Philadelphia.

Webber, M. (1968) 'The post city age', *Daedalus*, vol 97, no 4, 1093–1099.

Weigel, D. (2011) 'Off the rails: Why do conservatives hate trains so much?', slate.com, 8 March, www.slate.com/articles/news_and_politics/politics/2011/03/off_the_rails.html, accessed 31 July 2016.

Westneat, D. (2016) 'With a billionaire ally, Tim Eyman's just biding his time', *The Seattle Times*, 3 June, www.seattletimes.com/seattle-news/with-a-billionaire-ally-tim-eymans-just-biding-his-time/, accessed 27 August 2016.

White, T. (1992) 'Return of the Scorcher', www.youtube.com/watch?v=gsFgWJwYMP8

Whitelegg, J. (1993) *Transport for a Sustainable Future: The Case for Europe*, Belhaven Press, London.

Whitelegg, J. (1997) *Critical Mass: Transport Environment and Society in the Twenty-First Century*, Pluto Press, London.

Whitelegg, J. (2000) 'AVIATION: The social, economic and environmental impact of flying', Ashden Trust, London, areco.org/air10.pdf, accessed 16 August 2016.

Whitelegg, J. (2016) Mobility: *A New Urban Design and Transport Planning Philosophy for a Sustainable Future*, Straw Barnes Press (Amazon Digital Services LLC), Church Stretton, UK.

Whitelegg, J. and Cambridge, H. (2004) 'Aviation and sustainability: A policy paper', Stockholm Environment Institute, Stockholm.

Whitelegg, J. and Haq, G. (eds) (2003) *The Earthscan Reader on World Transport Policy and Practice*, Earthscan, London.

Whitfield, S. (1999) *Life Along the Silk Road*, University of California Press, Berkeley and Los Angeles, CA.

WHO (2004a) 'World report on road traffic injury prevention', http://whqlibdoc.who.int/publications/2004/9241562609.pdf, accessed 30 May 2009.

WHO (2004b) 'WHO warns of mounting death toll on Asian roads', www.wpro.who.int/media_centre/press_releases/pr_20040405.htm, accessed 30 May 2009.

WHO (2016) 'Road traffic injuries', www.who.int/mediacentre/factsheets/fs358/en/, accessed 31 March 2016.

Wiederkehr, P., Gilbert, R., Crist, P. and Caïd, N. (2004) 'Environmentally sustainable transport (EST): Concept, goal, and strategy—the OECD's EST project', richardgilbert.ca/Files/2004/EST,%20Concept,%20Goal,%20and%20Strategy.pdf, accessed 29 February 2016.

Wikipedia (undated) 'Funicular', https://en.wikipedia.org/wiki/Funicular (accessed 22 July 2017)

Wikipedia (undated) 'Velocipede', http://en.wikipedia.org/wiki/Velocipede, accessed 9 July 2009.

Wild, O. (1992) 'The Silk Road', www.ess.uci.edu/~oliver/silk3.html, accessed 25 June 2009.

Wilford, J. (1993) 'New finds suggest even earlier trade on fabled Silk Road', www.nytimes.com/1993/03/16/science/new-finds-suggest-even-earlier-trade-on-fabled-silk-road.html, accessed 25 June 2009.

Williams, J. A. (2010) ' "You never been on a ride like this befo": Los Angeles, automotive listening, and Dr. Dre's "G-Funk" ', *Popular Music History*, vol 4, no 2, 160–176.

Williams, V. and Noland, R. (2005) 'Variability of contrail formation conditions and the implications for policies to reduce the climate impacts of aviation', *Transportation Research Part D*, vol 10, no 4, 269–280.

Williams, V., Noland, R., Majumdar, A., et al. (2007) 'Reducing environmental impacts of aviation with innovative air traffic management technologies', *The Aeronautical Journal*, vol 111, no 1125, 741–749.

Williamson, L. (2013) 'Tomorrow's cities: Just how smart is Songdo?', BBC News, Seoul, 2 September, www.bbc.com/news/technology-23757738, accessed 1 July 2016.

Wilson, D., Papadopoulos, J. and Whitt, F. R. (2004) *Bicycling Science*, MIT Press, Cambridge, MA.

Winkelman, Steve (2009) 'Transportation's role in climate change and reducing greenhouse gases', Senate Committee on Environment and Public Works, 14 July, www.epw.senate.gov/public/_cache/files/8a92a671-848a-4eef-b75d-79b150d3e944/winkelmanepwtestimony71409.pdf, accessed 29 July 2016.

Wohlwill, J. F. (1985) 'Residential density as a variable in child development research', in J. F. Wohlwill and W. van Vliet (eds), *Habitats for Children: The Impacts of Density*, Lawrence Erlbaum Associates, Publishers, Hillsdale, NJ.

Wood, F. (2002) *The Silk Road: Two Thousand Years in the Heart of Asia*, University of California Press, Berkeley and Los Angeles, CA.

Woolf, A. (Dir.) (2010) *Beyond the motor city*, Blueprint America, PBS, Film, 8 Feb, www.pbs.org/wnet/blueprintamerica/featured/beyond-the-motor-city-preview/861/, accessed 15 July 2016.

World Air Quality (undated) 'Beijing air pollution: Real-time air quality index (AQI)', aqicn.org/city/beijing/, accessed 25 March 2016.

World Bank (2006) 'World Development Indicators', World Bank, Washington, DC, http://devdata.worldbank.org/wdi2006/contents/cover.htm, accessed 13 September 2009.

World Bank Group (2016) 'About public-private partnerships', ppp.worldbank.org/public-private-partnership/node/335/, accessed 18 August 2016.

Wright, D., Frost, M., Dunn, T. and Effron, L. (2015) 'Crash queens: Demolition derby moms smash cars with the best of them', ABC News, 23 Jul, abcnews.go.com/Lifestyle/crash-queens-demolition-derby-moms-smash-cars-best/story?id=32505174, accessed 18 July 2016.

Wuslich, J. (2012) 'Carjacking', *Violent Crimes* (U.S. Dept. of Justice), January, vol 60, no 1, 46–51, www.justice.gov/sites/default/files/usao/legacy/2012/01/26/usab6001.pdf, accessed 18 August 2016.

Wyatt, D. A. (2016) 'Rimouski, Québec' in 'all-time list of Canadian transit systems Québec communities (L—R)', home.cc.umanitoba.ca/~wyatt/alltime/l2r-qc.html, accessed 16 August 2016.

Wynne, G. (ed.) (1980) *Traffic Restraints in Residential Neighborhoods*, Transaction Books, New Brunswick, NJ.

Yago, G. (1983) 'The sociology of transportation', *Annual Review of Sociology*, vol 9, 171–190.

Yago, G. (1984) *The Decline of Transit: Urban Transportation in German and U.S. Cities, 1900–1970*, Cambridge University Press, Cambridge, UK.

Young, A. (2015) 'Global electric car market: About 43% of all electric passenger cars were bought in 2014, say German clean energy researchers', 24 March, www.ibtimes.com/global-electric-car-market-about-43-all-electric-passenger-cars-were-bought-2014-say-1857670, accessed 29 July 2016.

Zhao J., Chen T., Block-Schachter D. and Wang S. (2014) 'Superficial fairness of Beijing's vehicle license lottery policy', Proceedings of the 93rd Annual Meeting of the Transportation Research Board, Washington, DC, 12–16 January.

Zolfagharifard, E. (2015) 'When Tesla's autopilot goes wrong', *Dailymail.com*, 20 October, www.dailymail.co.uk/sciencetech/article-3281562/Tesla-autopilot-fail-videos-emerge-Terrifying-footage-shows-happens-autonomous-driving-goes-wrong.html, accessed 27 June 2016.

Zuckermann, W. (1991) *End of the Road: The World Car Crisis and How We Can Solve It*, Lutterworth Press, Cambridge, MA, and Chelsea Green Publishing Company, Post Mills, VT.

Index